Ancient religions, modern politics

Ancient religions, modern politics

THE ISLAMIC CASE IN COMPARATIVE PERSPECTIVE

Michael Cook

PRINCETON UNIVERSITY PRESS
PRINCETON AND OXFORD

Published by Princeton University Press, 41 William Street, Princeton, New Jersey 08540
In the United Kingdom: Princeton University Press, 6 Oxford Street, Woodstock, Oxfordshire OX20 1TR

press.princeton.edu

Cover art: Yahya ben Mahmud al-Wasiti. *Départ d'une caravane de pèlerins pour la Mecque,* 1237. RC-A-23269, ARABE 5847. Courtesy of Bibliothèque nationale de France

Second printing, first paperback printing, 2017

Paperback ISBN: 978-0-691-17334-4

The Library of Congress has cataloged the cloth edition of this book as follows:

Cook, Michael, 1940–
Ancient religions, modern politics : the Islamic case in comparative perspective / Michael Cook.
pages cm
Includes bibliographical references and index.
ISBN-13: 978-0-691-14490-0 (hardback)
ISBN-10: 0-691-14490-7 (cloth)
1. Islam and politics. 2. Christianity and politics. 3. Hinduism and politics. 4. Islamic fundamentalism—Political aspects. 5. Religious fundamentalism—Political aspects. I. Title.
BP173.7.C665 2014
297.2'72—dc23

2013039833

British Library Cataloging-in-Publication Data is available

This book has been composed in Charis SIL

Printed on acid-free paper. ∞

Printed in the United States of America

3 5 7 9 10 8 6 4 2

This book is for Jackie,

who rashly promised to read it

Contents

Part Two: Values

Part Three: Fundamentalism

Preface

ANYONE WHO LIVES IN THE early twenty-first century and follows the news will have noticed that ancient religions play a significant part in modern politics. These religions are not, however, by any means interchangeable in their political roles. Most obviously, it is hard to miss the fact that Islam today has a higher political profile than any of its competitors. But why should that be so? Is there something about the formal or substantive character of the Islamic tradition that makes its invocation an attractive option for Muslim individuals and groups that are politically active in a modern context—something that is not found in other religious traditions? Is there a reason why one can understand the contemporary politics of India and Latin America perfectly well without having heard of such medieval luminaries as Mādhava and Aquinas, whereas one cannot hope to understand the politics of the contemporary Islamic world without having heard of Ibn Taymiyya? This is a major question about the world we live in, but my sense is that much of the literature on the politics of the Islamic world tends either not to attend to the issue or to deal with it rather crudely. In this book I attempt to respond to the question with at least a partial answer.

To do this I have approached the Islamic case in a comparative setting. I thus seek to compare the role of Islam in modern politics with the parts played by Hinduism and Christianity—the latter mainly in the Latin American context. That I picked this particular pair is in some measure accidental, but there is also a certain logic to it: I wanted heritages to which large Third-World populations owe allegiance. This does not prevent me from referring occasionally to such faiths as Judaism and Sikhism, but I make no attempt to include them in a systematic way. The methods I employ throughout are those of a historian, since these are just about the only ones I know how to use. I would hope, however, that my disciplinary readership will not be limited to historians. Thus, political scientists may find some of the book of interest, though it will not attempt to emulate the methodological rigors of their discipline. So also may those engaged in the academic study of religion, though they may find my treatment rather philistine—my subject, after all, is religion in politics, not religion in itself. But I would also hope that the book will be accessible, and have some illumination to offer, to reasonably determined readers coming to it with nothing more than an interest in one or another of the relevant aspects of world affairs.

The answer I offer to the question I pose is partial not just for the obvious reason that my treatment is uneven and incomplete—what I know being nothing compared to what I don't know. It is also partial because my primary focus is on the differences between the three traditions, even if I have a lot to say about the differences between the political contexts in which they are invoked or ignored. My main argument is that the three traditions offer significantly different combinations of assets and liabilities for those engaged in modern politics and that this makes them variously attractive or unattractive to such actors as political resources.[1] In this connection I have sometimes been tempted to think of a religious heritage as a set of circuits that the politically inclined may or may not choose to switch on or as a menu from which they may or may not choose to make a selection; that is to say, an ancient religion, like a menu, provides its modern adherents with a set of options that do not determine their choices but do constrain them.[2] There are, of course, very different ways to think about the relationship between ancient heritages and political action in the modern world—for example, one could see them as mascons exercising a subterranean pull on the political trajectories of their adherents; but such a conception is not central to my argument. In the same way there are many good questions other than mine to be asked about the role of religion in contemporary politics, but answering them is not at the core of the task I have set myself.

As a glance at the table of contents will show, the book, like Gaul, is divided into three parts, each devoted to a major comparative theme.

Part One is about the role of the three religious traditions in modern political identity. Its core argument is that Islam provides a political identity that, for all its limitations, is not adequately matched by Hinduism, let alone Christianity. Chapter 1 seeks to establish the balance between the ethnic and religious forms of political identity in the tra-

[1] This is, of course, complicated by the fact that what is an asset for one actor in one context may be a liability for another actor in another context, and also by the tendency of assets and liabilities to come packaged together.

[2] As pointed out to me by Qasim Zaman, even this may exaggerate the degree of freedom of choice. Often one should perhaps think rather of a menu dispensed by a waiter anxious to sell the house specials.

ditional Islamic world, Arab and non-Arab, and to gauge the strength of Muslim political identity in pre-modern times. It then goes on to ask what has become of the old balance, and more particularly of Muslim political identity, under modern conditions. Chapter 2 is about the limited extent to which the Hindu tradition provides a counterpart to Muslim political identity, and the mixture of success and failure that has attended the attempts of the Hindu nationalists to render this identity operational in recent Indian politics. Chapter 3 completes the argument by showing that in the context of Latin American Christianity a political identity of this kind is even more elusive than in the Hindu case.

Part Two is about the contribution of the three heritages to broadly political values in a modern setting.[3] The organization is different from that of Part One: here each chapter is devoted to a theme, and provides coverage of all three religions. Chapter 4 is concerned with social values and inquires whether the values embodied in each heritage are likely to be assets or liabilities in modern politics; in each case it identifies one particular feature of the religion in question as particularly relevant, though the features differ greatly from each other. Chapter 5 moves on to attitudes to warfare; its primary focus is on the Islamic value of jihad, its political costs and benefits in the contemporary world, and the extent to which parallel phenomena can or cannot be found in Hinduism and Christianity. Chapter 6 is about the ways in which the three religions relate to various forms of culture. It tries to tease out differences in the extent to which these traditions claim sovereignty over particular cultural domains, and the degree to which they, or their adherents, are committed to maintaining that sovereignty. The contrasts that emerge are perhaps most striking in the legal domain. Chapter 7 takes up conceptions of the polity. On the one hand it shows that the three religions shared a pattern of close relations with kingship for most of their history; but on the other hand it brings out the distinctiveness of the early caliphate and its latter-day appeal. In different ways each of these chapters throws the Islamic case into relief.

Part Three is about fundamentalism, by which I mean the choice to return to the original foundations of one's faith and take one's religion

[3]For purposes of exposition, I use the term "values" in a sense that excludes identity. This is arbitrary but convenient; one could perfectly well treat identity as a value, and even if one does not, identities and values are manifestly linked.

from its earliest sources. Here I revert to the organization of Part One: I give each religion a separate chapter. The primary questions are how far each religion lends itself to fundamentalization, how far those invoking its heritage in modern politics are in fact fundamentalists, and—to the extent that they are—what their fundamentalism does for them (I take it for granted that people do not adopt fundamentalisms that do nothing for them). For the second and third questions in particular, the answers differ widely for the three religions. These chapters too bring out the ways in which the Islamic case is distinctive.

Each of the three parts of the book begins and ends with a short essay relevant to its theme; some of these excursions are broad and general, but others—notably those preceding and following Part Two—serve as an excuse to deal with specific matters not attended to in the main chapters of the book. For summaries of the wider argument, the reader should look rather to the conclusions of the individual chapters and to the afterword. Like most authors, I have written the book on the assumption that the reader will begin at the beginning, but anyone who prefers to jump in at some other point will get assistance from the cross-references. Indeed, some of the chapters of Part Two may be easier reading than those of Part One.

I should add some cautions about what the book does not do. First, though it has a lot to say about the pre-modern world, it does not provide an account of that world for its own sake, and anyone who read the book as if it did would be likely to come away with a seriously distorted picture. This is perhaps particularly so in the Islamic case—and for two reasons. One is that, to put it bluntly, Islamic civilization died quite some time ago, unlike Islam which is very much alive; we will thus be concerned with the wider civilization only when it is relevant to features of the enduring religious heritage. The other reason is that a major component—perhaps *the* major component—of pre-modern Islam was Ṣūfism. Today Ṣūfism is by no means dead, but it is not at the cutting edge of the developments that concern us; instead its role is mainly that of a target for movements that see themselves as propagating pure Islam. Second, my primary concern in this book is with "great traditions," not with "little traditions" and their increasingly eroded autonomy. But even here my focus is not usually on the minutiae of doctrine; in the end what matters for my purposes is rather what can fire the political imagination. Third, I am not in the business of anticipating the Last Judgment. In particular, comparing the values of ancient heritages with those prevalent in the world today sometimes has the effect of making those heritages look good and sometimes of making them look bad. This is pretty much inevitable, since current values happen to be the ones we believe in, but it is irrelevant to my purpose which, like Bīrūnī's in his study of India, is descriptive and analytical. Fourth, while I make occasional reference to Shīʿism, the main focus of this book is on Sunnī Islam.

It may be useful to say something here about the presuppositions of the book. Obviously I take it for granted that it does make a difference whether your religious heritage is Islamic, Hindu, or Christian. Though this assumption strikes me as common sense, not everyone will agree with it; those who disagree may still find some of the book useful in incidental ways.

It follows that I have no great sympathy with the idea that religious traditions are putty in the hands of exegetes—as if a heritage could successfully be interpreted to mean whatever one wanted and all interpretations were equally plausible to one's fellow believers. Heritages do change under exegetical and other pressures, but they do so gradually and against considerable inertia—a force whose role in human affairs is by no means to be thought of as limited to physical objects. In the meantime, to borrow an insight from the history of early modern England, "what it is possible to do in politics is generally limited by what it is possible to legitimise. What you can hope to legitimise, however, depends on what courses of action you can plausibly range under existing normative principles."[4]

Something analogous is perhaps worth saying about collective identities, particularly those that really matter to people—so much so that they may be willing to die for them. Identities of this kind, like values, can and do change, but they are not, as academic rhetoric would sometimes have it, in constant flux.[5] The reason is simple: like shared currencies, shared identities are the basis of claims that people can make on each other, and without a degree of stability such an identity would be as useless as a hyperinflating currency. So it is not surprising that in the real world collective identities, though not immutable, often prove

[4] Skinner, *Liberty before liberalism*, 105; see further his "Principles and practice," especially 127–28.

[5] People can, of course, have multiple identities in the sense that they can be members of a variety of groups. But which of their identities comes to the fore on a given occasion is likely to depend more on objective context than on subjective choice.

robust and recalcitrant, at times disconcertingly so. As the authors of a study of the politics of Ulster point out, "there is a major difference between thinking that identities are durable and maintaining that they are immutably primordial."[6]

My approach likewise diverges from the view that there is no such thing as Islam, just many local Islams. This view is perfectly coherent in principle, and some fragments of reality do indeed help us to imagine what it would be like to live in a world in which it was true. A plausible example of the ever-increasing religious entropy that would characterize such a world may be found among the Muslim Chams of Indo-China, particularly those of Annam, as described by French observers in the late nineteenth and early twentieth centuries. Their pantheon overlapped with that of their neighbors, the Hindu Chams, and included a mother goddess.[7] They had a manuscript of the Bible that told of the creation of the sun god and moon goddess,[8] and a central role in one of their rituals was played by a priestess.[9] This is not to say that they had lost touch with other forms of Islam altogether. They still knew about Allāh; indeed such was their respect for him that they abstained from sex on Mondays, the day of his birth.[10] They still recited texts that bore some relationship to the Koran, and while the laity observed only a three-day Ramaḍān, the priests fasted for the full month.[11] Yet it does not take a card-carrying Wahhābī to feel an element of shock at this picture. We have here an example of a religion that has drifted so far from its origins as to be within sight of exemplifying a teasing idea developed by a philosopher of intellectual history: a tradition that has gradually changed over time to the point that no single element present at the start is still there at the end.[12] But to think of the Muslim world as nothing but a mosaic of religious traditions like that of the Chams would be very misleading. In the world in which we actually live, such unchecked drift is unlikely to continue indefinitely.

[6] McGarry and O'Leary, *Northern Ireland conflict*, 32.

[7] Baudesson, *Indo-China*, 275–77.

[8] Ibid., 318.

[9] Ibid., 305-8.

[10] Ibid., 257.

[11] Ibid., 267. Similar information may be found in other French accounts; thus for polytheism among the Muslim Chams, see also Aymonier, *Les Tchames*, 79, 89, 91, 95; Cabaton, *Nouvelles recherches*, 17; Durand, "Les Chams Bani," 54–55, 60, 62; Leuba, *Les Chams d'autrefois*, 99–100.

[12] Bevir, *History of ideas*, 202, 204; this book was brought to my attention by Qasim Zaman.

A few centuries ago Islam was undoubtedly more polylithic than it is today, but it has never been a heap of rubble[13]—the centrifugal forces of time and distance are countered by the pull of homogenization.[14] Such homogenizing forces were already at work in pre-modern times; more metropolitan forms of Islam have always had the potential to trump local differentiation. Modern conditions have rendered the effect even stronger. The Chams are again a case in point: a French source of 1891 mentions that some years previously three Muslim villages had abruptly abandoned the worship of their Cham gods; this was after a foreign Muslim who had made the pilgrimage to Mecca was passing through and condemned such practices.[15] The pilgrim from Mecca had clearly put the Chams on the spot. But in a world in which there really was no such thing as Islam, just many local Islams, there would have been no spot for him to put them on.

There is a wider point about religious commitment that arises from the Cham experience and is of some importance for the thinking of this book. If I adhere to a simple local cult that does not even have a priesthood, it may well be the case that there is nothing anyone can tell me about my religion that I don't already know. But if I am, say, an Anglican Christian, the chances are that there is a great deal about my religion that I don't know. Suppose, for example, that, being of a generous disposition, I tend to think that good people of all religions may be saved. I mention this to you as a fellow Anglican. But instead of assenting to my harmless platitude, you respond sharply by citing the eighteenth of the Thirty-Nine Articles adopted by the Anglican Church in 1562 "for the avoiding of diversities of opinions"—a text of whose existence I was perhaps vaguely aware but not one that I had ever gone so far as to read. The eighteenth article does indeed state that one is accursed if one presumes to say that "every man shall be saved by the Law or Sect which he professeth, so that he be diligent to frame his life

[13]For an intriguing indication that the Islamic world may be culturally more homogeneous than might be expected, see Inglehart and Welzel, *Modernization, cultural change*, 63, figure 2.4. This diagram, entitled "Cultural map of the world about 2000," shows where a considerable number of the world's nations fall on two axes: one represents the continuum from "traditional values" to "secular-rational values" and the other that from "survival values" to "self-expression values." Nine of the eleven Muslim countries shown cluster closely together, the outliers being Azerbaijan and Albania in respect of the first axis. The data derive from the World Values Survey. But in this book I neither assume nor set out to confirm such cultural findings.

[14]For this point see Robinson, "Islam and Muslim society," especially 50, 56, 57.

[15]Aymonier, *Les Tchames*, 79; and cf. Robinson, "Islam and Muslim society," 53.

according to that Law, and the light of Nature."[16] How might I respond to your rebuke? One response would be "personally I don't bother with that stuff." Another might be "wait a minute—do we really *know* that God in his infinite mercy would never choose to save a virtuous Buddhist?"[17] Yet another could be "thank you for telling me, I didn't know, and now I do." But however I respond, you have put me on the spot by invoking not a specific Anglican belief that I actually hold but rather the general commitment to Anglican beliefs that arises from my membership of the Anglican church, irrespective of whether I actually hold those beliefs or am even aware of them. In the Anglican case the dilution of ecclesiastical authority in this day and age is such that the most likely response might well be the first—I brush you off. But the third response—accepting that one stands corrected—is exactly how the Muslims of the three Cham villages reacted to their critical visitor. That even members of a religious tradition that had drifted so far from anything recognizable to us as Islam should respond in this way is telling—they at least, one might have thought, would have shrugged their shoulders and said, "What's that to us? This is what we do here." That in turn suggests that more mainstream Muslims could easily be put on the spot with regard to disparities between what they currently believe and do and what their general commitment to Islam could be held to imply that they should believe and do.[18]

Something needs to be said about conventions. I use the terms "Islamism" and "Islamic fundamentalism" in distinct senses.[19] By "Islamism" I mean "Islam as a modern ideology and a political program,"[20] and I use the term synonymously with "political Islam." By "Islamic fundamentalism" I mean, as indicated above, the choice to return to the original foundations of Islam. It is a contingent fact about the world we live in, and an important one, that many Islamists have a marked fundamentalist bent and that many with such a bent are also Islamists. But there is no lack of exceptions. An Islamist like Fethullah Gülen, who

[16] Church of England, *Book of common prayer*, 619; for the reference to "diversities of opinions," see 607.

[17] This and other conundrums that could encourage diversities of opinions are discussed in the learned and judicious commentary of Gilbert Burnet (d. 1715), bishop of Salisbury (see Gilbert Bishop of Sarum, *Thirty-nine articles*, 171–74).

[18] It is this potentially open-ended commitment that is swept under the carpet by the adage of well-intentioned Western scholars that "Islam is what Muslims do."

[19] For these terms and their history, see Kramer, "Coming to terms."

[20] Ibid., 71b.

takes much of his inspiration from Ṣūfism, is not a fundamentalist;[21] apolitical Salafis are fundamentalists in many of their beliefs and practices, but they are not Islamists. Moreover Islamists are, as I see it, a reasonably well-defined group; fundamentalists, at least in the Islamic context, are not.

Turning from terminology to transcription, a book that ranges as widely as this one comes up against a variety of languages and scripts. Anglicized forms apart, where a language is written in the Latin script, as with Spanish or modern Turkish, I simply adopt its standard orthography. Where a language is written in some other script, as with Arabic or Sanskrit, I use the form of scholarly transcription standard for that language, including the appropriate diacritics. The major problem I have encountered is that for obvious historical reasons scholars working on India tend to recognize a much wider range of Anglicized forms than scholars working on the Middle East. For the sake of consistency I have thus tended to use transcribed forms more extensively than a South Asianist would do.[22] A minor problem concerns the use of the underdot: for Arabic it marks emphatic consonants, whereas for Indian languages it marks retroflex consonants.

Finally, where I cite a passage in both the original language and a translation, I link the two references with an equals sign.

The idea of this book came to me several years ago in the course of my undergraduate teaching. At the time I had no prospect of finding the leisure to do the requisite research and thinking, and I therefore reluctantly added the project to a long list of those that I planned to take up, if at all, in my next life. I owe the unexpected opportunity to bring the idea forward to my present life entirely to the Andrew W. Mellon Foundation, whose generous three-year award of 2002 transformed my situation beyond recognition.

I am deeply indebted to those who read and commented on drafts of the book, discussed aspects of it with me, or—in the case of undergraduate students—contributed their thinking to the courses in which I developed my ideas. My colleagues Bernard Haykel and Qasim Zaman read the whole typescript and gave me numerous insights, cautions, corrections, and suggestions. So did Christophe Jaffrelot, Martin Marty, and Andrew March, who read the typescript for the Press; their comments

[21] See Sarıtoprak, "Fethullah Gülen," 160–69.

[22] But I have not always tried to be consistent, let alone succeeded, as in my rendering of *anusvāra*.

have led me to make a large number of changes. Robert Wright read Part One in an early draft and helped me to sharpen the argument considerably. Patricia Crone read not one but two drafts of the entire book; the second draft was the result of her unwelcome but irrefutable judgment that the first needed drastic recasting. Brigitta van Rheinberg at the Press read my first draft, made numerous comments on it, and showed extraordinary patience as I revised it. I have also benefited greatly over the years from conversations with Shivaji Sondhi on Indian and other matters. In addition, numerous people have helped me on particular points, and my debts to them are acknowledged in their proper places. None of those thanked here bear any responsibility for the deficiencies of the book, but the reader can be assured that without their input it would have been a much worse one than it is. While writing the book I have never been in any doubt that I was trying to do something worthwhile, but I have often had misgivings about whether I was going about it in the right way.

A note of the form "See 73" (as opposed to "See ibid., 73") is a cross-reference.

Part One

Identity

Introduction to Part One

The preferred form of political identity in the modern world is belonging to a nation. In this conception, the world is made up of nations, just as the organization that brings them together is the "United Nations." Each nation is entitled to its state, so that the basic building block of the international order is the nation state. This international order represents an extension to the world at large of a pattern that developed in Europe over a long period. France, for example, has been a nation state in some sense since the Middle Ages, Spain since the sixteenth century, Germany only since the nineteenth century. But however recent some of the current political geography of Europe may be, the existence of nations was already a basic feature of its political landscape in late medieval times, and these nations in turn had roots going back into the early Middle Ages. Just how real the continuity was, and how inevitable the shaping of the political geography of Europe as a community of nations, are not questions we need concern ourselves with. It is enough that this European pattern of nation states gradually emerged and was exported in modern times to the non-European world. Or more precisely, the new Westernized elites of non-European societies were at pains to import it—and for good reason: it enabled them to claim independence from Europe in the name of a European value. This did not mean that in real life every country became a nation state; but some did, and those that did not were under pressure to fake it.

A crucial feature of the concept of the nation is the centrality of ethnicity to it.[1] Europe had come to see itself as a community of nations

[1] I use the term ethnicity in contradistinction to religious affiliation. Ethnicity in this conception is what makes a Breton a Breton and a Basque a Basque, and a key part of what makes a Frenchman French and a Spaniard Spanish; but it is not what makes a Buddhist a Buddhist.

sharing a civilization, and to an extent a religion, but divided by ethnicity, and this was the nationalist paradigm that was then widely adopted in the non-European world. Nations were peoples—like the French, the Poles, and the Danes, who were differentiated most obviously by the fact that they spoke French, Polish, and Danish respectively. By the same token nations were not religiously defined groups: Catholics and Protestants, or Lutherans and Calvinists, are not peoples in the European sense, and so do not qualify as nations. It is in this respect that the nations of Europe were always a secular phenomenon. The doctrine of secularism is, of course, a modern development, and in pre-modern times the religious tradition of Europe had political pretensions that no secularist could have accepted. But those pretensions had always coexisted with non-religious, ethnically defined political identities. This coexistence could naturally take more than one form. There could be intimate symbiosis, as in the case of Protestantism and English nationalism after the Reformation; or religion might be pushed aside, as in French nationalism since the Revolution. This second pattern, in which religion is seen as irrelevant or even pernicious, has been far more widespread in the modern than in the pre-modern world. But the key point is that whatever their relationship to religion, nations as such were identified in ethnic, not religious terms: English and French, not Protestant and Catholic. It was ethnicity, not religion, that was constitutive of nations, and the religious tradition of Europe was always one that left space for ethnic identities.

This European way of looking at things was by no means idiosyncratic, but neither was it universal. Other parts of the world had their own ethnic and religious traditions, and the relationship of these to political identity could be very different. Thus, exporting the European conception of political identity to such regions was bound to produce some distinctly un-European outcomes. We begin with the Islamic world.

CHAPTER 1

Islam and identity

1. Introduction

What would be the outcome were the European conception of the nation state to encounter a tradition in which political identity had long been vested in religion rather than ethnicity? The traditional Islamic world did not lack for ethnic identities, and they certainly mattered in the political history of the region; but as will become clear in the course of an examination of several centuries of Islamic history, prevailing attitudes did not accord them the same normative status as they did to religious identity. In this setting the advent of the concept of the nation amounted to a decisive shift in a long-standing indigenous balance between religion and ethnicity. Given that ethnic identity was associated with modernity and religious identity with Islam, what would we expect to be the outcome of the encounter? And what has it been in historical fact? These are the questions this chapter is intended to answer. But we need to start by getting a sense of the roles of ethnic and religious identity in the pre-modern Muslim world.

2. Pre-modern ethnic identity: Turks and Trojans

In an account of a pilgrimage to the Holy Land in 1506, a chaplain from England made the following incidental comment: "And all the countre of Troya is the Turkes owne countre by inherytance, and that countre is properly called nowe Turkey, and none other. Neuerthelasse he hath lately vsurped Grece, with many other countreys, and calleth theym all Turkey."[1] In other words, the Turks had a valid claim to the land of Troy based on their descent from the ancient Trojans, an idea well known at the time; but they had no business extending their dominion any farther. This is one of many Western European reactions to the

[1] Ellis, *Pylgrymage of Sir Richard Guylforde*, 13, cited in Spencer, "Turks and Trojans," 332.

shift of power from Byzantines to Ottomans that marked the later Middle Ages; most reactions, as might be expected, were more hostile.[2] A characteristic feature of these reactions was that they could be couched in either religious or ethnic terms: in religious terms, unbelievers were making war on believers, while in ethnic terms, Turks were making war on Greeks. Neither perspective fully determined one's view of the rights and wrongs of the conflict. On the religious side, one could not, of course, side with the unbelievers; but if one lacked sympathy for the Byzantine victims of the conflict, one could brand them as heretics who were getting what they deserved. On the ethnic side, in addition to seeing the latter-day Greeks as either noble or ignoble descendants of their celebrated ancestors,[3] one could argue about the ancestry of the Turks. If one took the view that they were of Scythian descent,[4] then by implication they had no title to the lands they had recently conquered. But if they were of Trojan descent, it could be maintained that they had every right to reclaim their ancient homeland. That a Christian chaplain on pilgrimage should express this view, and see the ethnic identity of the Turks as a valid title to territory, is particularly notable. So also is the fact that in these centuries the common Trojan descent of the Turks and Italians could be advanced as a reason why the two peoples should not make war on each other.[5] In other words, ethnic identity as a basis of moral claims was not just some local copper coinage; it met the gold standard of the day. Against the wider background of European history, this is in no way unexpected. But to anyone more familiar with the Ottoman way of seeing things, it is arresting.

From an Ottoman viewpoint, the European religious perspective looks immediately familiar: all we have to do is flip believers and unbelievers and we have a central component of the Ottoman worldview. The ethnic perspective, by contrast, looks outlandish. It is true that the Trojan theme seems to have meant something to Mehmed II (ruled

[2] That scholars have tended to exaggerate the extent of belief in the Trojan origins of the Turks, and the use of this belief in ways favorable to them, is the central argument of Meserve, *Empires of Islam*, chap. 1. She does not, of course, deny the existence of either phenomenon altogether (see, for example, 23, 25, 42), and it is the conceptual interest of the Trojan theme, not its historical importance, that concerns us here.

[3] See Spencer, "Turks and Trojans," 330.

[4] For the Scythian, as opposed to Trojan, descent of the Turks, see Meserve, *Empires of Islam*, chap. 2, especially 99.

[5] This argument appears in a letter pretending to have been written by a Turkish ruler and clearly intended to diminish ardor for a crusade against the Turks (for a mid-fourteenth century Latin version, see Gay, *Le pape Clément VI*, 173; for a mid-fifteenth-century French version, see Spencer, "Turks and Trojans," 331).

1451–1481)[6] but not as part of his public persona as a Muslim ruler. The point is not that ethnicity signified nothing to the Ottomans but rather that it was not a currency in which legitimate claims could be made to something as important as territory.[7] In other words, the moral reach of ethnic identity was significantly less in the Ottoman context than it was in Western Europe. Why should that be so?

Whatever the answer, it was not a historic weakness of ethnic identity among the Turks. One of the earliest extended texts in which a Turk speaks to us in his own language is the memorial inscription erected in 732 by the pagan ruler Bilgä Qaghan for his brother, located in what is now Mongolia. The text is pervaded by a strong sense of Turkish identity. Thus, the ruler introduces himself at the beginning of the inscription as "the Heaven-like and Heaven-born Turkish Bilgä Kagan," addresses himself to the "Turkish people" or to the "Turkish lords and people," speaks about the "Turkish people," the "Turkish lords," the "Turkish common people," and refers to "the Turkish god above and the Turkish holy earth and water."[8] Moreover, he sets great store by the Turkish people having its own state; he has the Turkish common people lament that "we used to be a people who had an (independent) state (*illig bodun*). Where is our own state now? . . . We used to be a people who had its own kagan. Where is our own kagan now?"[9] A modern nationalist in search of a medieval charter of national identity could hardly ask for more.

If we move on a quarter of a millennium to the time when Turks—Oghuz Turks in particular—were first entering the Islamic world in large numbers, we encounter a work written by a Turkish author, Maḥmūd al-Kāshgharī, in 1072–1074. He explains that since the Turks now exercise political power, people need access to them; his response to this need is to compile in Arabic a lexicon of the Turkish language.[10] In his entry on the word "Türk," he makes the following observation: "You say 'Kim sän?,' meaning 'Who are you?,' and he'll say 'Türk män,' meaning 'I'm a Turk.' "[11] In the same entry he naturally has good things

[6] See Raby, "Mehmed."

[7] Contrast the inherent legitimacy in Ottoman eyes of the acquisition of infidel territory through jihad (see Imber, "Ottoman dynastic myth," 12, and cf. 13, 22).

[8] Tekin, *Orkhon Turkic*, 261-62, 264-65.

[9] Ibid., 264-65 (for the original Turkish, see 233 E9). Cf. also 263 on "the state and institutions of the Turkish people," and 264 on how "the Turkish people caused their state which they had established to go to ruin."

[10] Kāshgharī, *Dīwān*, 1: 2.7.

[11] Ibid., 1:294.14; Dankoff, "Kāšγarī," 28.

to say about the Turks. Quoting a Prophetic tradition we will come to,[12] he boasts that they are superior to any other people in that God himself undertook to name them, settled them in the most elevated place with the best climate in the world, and called them his army; add to that their good looks, good breeding, respect for elders, fidelity to their promises, avoidance of bragging, and the like.[13]

Two circumstances conspired to sustain this sense of Turkish ethnicity in the northern Middle East in one form or another over the following centuries: the fact that many Turks continued to live a nomadic life there and the fact that nomads drove the political metabolism of the region—doing so down to the nineteenth century in Iran and down to the fourteenth century in Anatolia. As one fifteenth-century Turkish ruler advised his sons: "Do not become sedentary, for sovereignty resides in those who practice the nomadic Turkmen way of life."[14]

The Ottomans began their long imperial history as one among many such Turcoman dynasties in early fourteenth-century Anatolia. A Byzantine historian describes them in 1329 as "still under tents in the valleys, as the spring was in its middle, in the month of May," and adds that "the barbarians were about to move from the lowlands to higher altitudes, avoiding the heat of the summer; for this was their custom, as they were nomads."[15] Likewise, the oldest account of Ottoman history we possess, written in the early fifteenth century, speaks of the presence of many Oghuz among the followers of the first Ottoman ruler,[16] and the dynasty itself seems to have acquired its claim to descent from an Oghuz clan in the first half of that century.[17]

[12] See 16.

[13] Kāshgharī, *Dīwān*, 1: 294.4.

[14] Woods, *Aqquyunlu*, 17 and 237n50; and cf. 56. A Türkmen or Turcoman is a Turkish nomad. Compare the instructions of Timur (ruled 1370–1405) to a subordinate in western Iran regarding the treatment of two rulers: "Aḥmad Jalāyir has acquired the temperament of a Tājīk, so there is no need to worry about him. But keep a close watch on Qarā Yūsuf the Turcoman" (Sümer, *Kara Koyunlular*, 67n187). The first ruler was of Mongol descent, the second a member of a Turkish dynasty, and a Tājīk is a sedentary Iranian.

[15] Arnakis, "Gregory Palamas," 113. Compare Ibn Khaldūn's account of the reign of the Ottoman sultan Orkhān (ruled 1324–1360), also cited by Arnakis: "When Mongol authority faded away in Anatolia . . . these Turcomans overran the land beyond the passes as far as the Gulf of Constantinople. Their king settled in the city of Bursa in that region . . . and adopted it as their capital city. But he did not abandon tents for palaces, and would camp in his tents in the open country around it" (Ibn Khaldūn, *ʿIbar*, 5: 562.22).

[16] See the transcription of the relevant part of Aḥmedī's *İskendernāme* in Banarlı, "Ahmedî," 113 line 34 (*Oğuzdan çok kişi*); the passage is noted in Imber, "Ottoman dynastic myth," 16–17.

[17] Imber, "Ottoman dynastic myth," 16–20.

Yet this sense of the Turkish ethnicity of the Ottomans, though well preserved in the western Arab world,[18] faded out among the Ottomans themselves, to return only under the impact of Western modernity in the nineteenth century.[19] In fact, the process had already begun among the cultured Muslims of the cities of Anatolia even before they came under Ottoman rule. For them the Turks were the wild tribes of the Anatolian steppes, uncultured savages dedicated until the Resurrection to the remorseless destruction of civilization.[20] In the meantime we find the Ottomans—whom the Europeans never stopped calling Turks—now referring to themselves as Rūmīs, a term more geographical than ethnic in origin. Thus, in the late sixteenth century the Ottoman writer Muṣṭafā ʿĀlī uses the term in referring to people that we would unhesitatingly call Turks.[21] He tells us that Rūmīs (*merdüm-i Rūmī*) are best—better than Arabs or Persians; indeed today they are a hundred times better than Persians, for to them belongs a glory (*ʿizzet*) that the Persians no longer possess.[22] Yet, at the same time, he speaks pejoratively of Turks (*Etrāk*) in contexts in which it is clear that he has in mind a population of Anatolian peasant stock.[23] Such usage points to a significant

[18] A Moroccan chronicler who died in the 1740s regularly speaks of the Ottomans as Turks (Ifrānī, *Nuzhat al-ḥādī*, 45.13, 51.23, 71.13, 73.7, 82.10, 83.3, 93.6, etc.). A Morisco writing in 1637 speaks of "the Ottoman Turkish Sultans" (*al-salāṭīn . . . al-ʿUthmāniyyūn al-Turkiyyūn*, see Ḥajarī, *Nāṣir al-dīn*, 126.16 = 183). The Ottomans were likewise referred to as Turks in the Mahdist state in the Sudan (see Holt, *Mahdist state*, 14, 42, 59, 82, 110, 149, 152, 160).

[19] Thus Aḥmed Jevdet Pasha (d. 1895) describes the Ottoman Empire as in reality "a Turkish state," the real strength of which "lies with the Turks" (Deringil, *Well-protected domains*, 169–70). See further Kushner, *Rise of Turkish nationalism*, 28, and B. Lewis, *Emergence of modern Turkey*, 2–3, 326–27, 337.

[20] Küçükhüseyin, *Selbst- und Fremdwahrnehmung*, 411–18, especially the passage quoted at 418, for which see also Kafadar, "Rome of one's own," 11.

[21] Tietze, *Muṣṭafā ʿĀlī's description*, 92.12 = 26 (and n5 to the translation), 106.22 = 35 (where the term *Rūmīlük* is used in the sense of "Turkishness"), and futher references given in the index to the translation; see also Fleischer, *Bureaucrat and intellectual*, 254. Fleischer further cites a document of 1585 in which the governor of Baghdad is instructed that fiefs are to be given only to Rūmī warriors (156). For the use of the term in the Arab lands and elsewhere to refer to the Anatolian Turks, see *Encyclopaedia of Islam*, 2nd ed. (hereafter *EI*²), art. "Rūmī" (H. İnalcık). I am grateful to Şükrü Hanioğlu for several of these references.

[22] Özbaran, *Bir Osmanlı kimliği*, 96. For the survival of this ethnic term in modern Kurdish and its application to Turks, see 92–93 and Chyet, *Kurdish-English dictionary*, 522b. Note that the language of Rūmīs is nevertheless Turkish (Türkī): "Speak Turkish to us because we are Rūmīs," as a sixteenth-century poet has it (Özbaran, *Bir Osmanlı kimliği*, 117).

[23] He derides an upstart Ottoman functionary from a western Anatolian village as "a foreign Turk" (*ecnebī bir Türk*, Tietze, *Muṣṭafā ʿĀlī's description*, 146.31 = 63; "foreign"

downgrading of ethnicity in the Ottoman context. Being a Turk no longer cut any ice in the state apparatus; being a Rūmī did, but it was not a currency in which claims were made to territory or statehood.[24] Several events are likely to have contributed to this downgrading: the rise of a non-Turkish military elite through the Ottoman practice of enslavement in the Balkans, the fragmentation of the Turkish world of the northern Middle East through the espousal of Shīʿism by the Ṣafawid dynasty in Iran, and the extension of Ottoman rule to the Arab lands, including the Ḥijāz.[25] But a deeper factor may also have been at work: the increasing salience of the mainstream Islamic tradition in the public values of the Ottoman Empire as it transformed itself from a peripheral Turcoman principality into a metropolitan Islamic state.

3. Pre-modern ethnic identity: the Islamic factor

Islam is a world religion, and it could not be one if it did not possess resources for rising above ethnicity. Muḥammad is thus reputed to have addressed his followers in terms that precluded any ethnic or racial inequality among them: "O people! Truly your God is one, and you are all descended from the same ancestor! Truly the Arab has no superiority over the non-Arab, nor the non-Arab over the Arab, nor the black over the white, not the white over the black, except in piety."[26] So Islam is manifestly a playing field on which members of diverse ethnic groups can join in. But is it a level playing field? We come here to a fundamental contrast between the early histories of Islam and Christianity. The Jews gave birth to Christianity and within a few decades went on to endure one of the worst ethnic traumas of their history; so there was room for a Christian category of "verus Israel"—the "true Israel," as opposed to the Jews—and it was now up for grabs among the nations. The Arabs, by contrast, gave birth to Islam and within a few decades achieved one of the greatest ethnic successes of all time.

---

implies that he has no business being employed by the state); and he makes a proposal to tax the large number of low-class Turks (*Etrāk-i ʿavāmm*) who have moved from their villages to Istanbul, Bursa, and Edirne to take up a variety of trades (Tietze, *Muṣṭafā ʿĀlī's Counsel*, 1: 150.15 = 57, and cf. 151.26 = 58). Both passages are cited in Haarmann, "Ideology and history," 177 and 191nn15–16.

[24] Note also the comment of Kafadar that "no land survey, tax register, or court document would use it as an operational category" (Kadafar, "Rome of one's own," 12a).

[25] B. Lewis, *Emergence of modern Turkey*, 326.

[26] Qurṭubī, *Jāmiʿ*, 16: 342.2.

Hence there was no room here for a category of "verus Ishmael" that excluded and expropriated the Arabs: they were and remained the core ethnicity of the religion.[27] The implications of this fact would obviously be different for Arabs and non-Arabs. Let us take the Arabs first.

In Muḥammad's day the Arabs were still for the most part confined to the Arabian peninsula and the Syrian desert. Despite the absence of any tradition of political unity before the rise of Islam, it seems clear that they identified themselves as a distinct people[28] and were so identified by others. This was not just an empty label: they were in fact speakers of a single language, despite variations of dialect, and they had significant elements of their culture in common.[29] For example, the Arabic genealogical tradition shows the name al-Ḥārith to have been current in all the major tribal groupings of Arabian society.[30]

Islam then proceeded to adopt the ethnic identity of the Arabs and make it special. Muḥammad was an Arab prophet who brought the Arabs a scripture in their own language, an "Arabic Koran" (e.g., Q42:7); as one tradition has him say, "I am an Arab, the Koran is Arabic, and the language of the people of Paradise is Arabic."[31] Another tradition gives these as the three reasons why one should love the Arabs.[32] Moreover, Muḥammad confirmed the holiness of an Arabian sanctuary, the Meccan Kaʿba; and he tied these ideas into the older monotheist tradition by elaborating on a belief that was common knowledge at the time, namely that the Arabs were the descendants of Ishmael, the elder son of the patriarch Abraham.[33] The effect was to establish the Arabs as the ethnic heirs of an Abrahamic monotheism of their own.

In the conditions of early Islamic times there was more to this special status of the Arabs than mere sentiment. The empire that emerged from the rise of Islam was conquered and ruled by Arabs. "We Arabs were

[27] For this contrast between Christianity and Islam, see Crone, *Nativist prophets*, 173–77.

[28] It is noteworthy that in the early Islamic period, when being an Arab was a title to participation in an enterprise that generated unprecedented wealth and power, there were no major disputes between the tribes over the question who was to count as an Arab. Even in the case of the Ḥimyarites, with their distinct South Arabian ethnic past, there seems to have been no attempt to define them out of the political community on ethnic grounds.

[29] See the discussion of "Arabhood and Arabisation" in Hoyland, *Arabia and the Arabs*, chap. 9. For the importance of the emergence of Arabic poetry in this context, see 242–43.

[30] See Caskel, *Ǧamharat an-nasab*, 2: 300b–315b, and compare the list of tribal groupings, 1: 132.

[31] Ṭabarānī, *al-Muʿjam al-awsaṭ*, 9: 69 no. 9147.

[32] Irāqī, *Qurab*, 4.9.

[33] For a brief account of these matters, see, for example, M. Cook, *Muhammad*, 35–40.

underdogs (*innā maʿshar al-ʿArab kunnā adhilla*), people walked all over us while we didn't do the same to them; then God sent a prophet from among us," as an Arab emissary informed the Persians in the heart of their country; "he told us things that we found to be just as he said, and among the things he promised us was that we would take possession of all this and prevail over it."[34] The resulting structure of power was neatly reflected in the way in which non-Arabs converted to Islam. The key institution here was clientage (*walāʾ*).[35] Individual non-Arabs who had either voluntarily left their native societies to join the conquerors, or been involuntarily removed from them by enslavement in the course of the conquests, became the clients (*mawālī*) of individual Arabs and converted to Islam at their hands. The result was to create a social structure through which individual non-Arabs were incorporated into the Muslim community while remaining what we would call second-class citizens—and exposed to no small amount of Arab chauvinism. We are told, for example, that Arabs did not walk side by side with clients, that clients present at a meal were left standing while Arabs sat and ate, and that a client would not be allowed to undertake the prayer at a funeral if an Arab were present.[36] In other words, in this early period non-Arab *people* could convert to Islam, but non-Arab *peoples* could not; in that sense the community remained effectively monoethnic. The linguistic aspect of this is caught in a remark of an early Shīʿite: to establish the fact that people recognize the superiority of Arabic over Persian, he observes that "no Persian who converts to this religion fails to give up the language of his people and adopt the language of the Arabs."[37]

The changes that marked later centuries had the effect of making this early Arab identity both less salient and less sharply defined.

One key change was that from the ninth century onwards Arab power was in steep decline. Being an Arab no longer constituted an effective title to participate in ruling the world. This change provoked its share of laments. Thus the great Arab poet Mutanabbī (d. 965) ob-

[34] Abū Yūsuf, *Kharāj*, 82.15, cited in Rodinson, *Mohammed*, 295.

[35] *EI*², art. "Mawlā" (P. Crone), especially 875–76.

[36] B. Lewis, *Islam from Muhammad*, 2: 204, translating a passage from Ibn ʿAbd Rabbih, *ʿIqd*, 3: 413.5. We have here the rudiments of a caste system; it is by no means obvious why such attitudes, which were current at a time when Islamic law was taking shape, had so little influence on the legal tradition. Part of the reason is no doubt the number of non-Arabs among early Islamic scholars (see Nawas, "Profile of *mawālī ʿulamāʾ*," , 456 fig. 1).

[37] Zayd ibn ʿAlī, *Ṣafwa*, 23.9. Since the text refers to *lisān al-ʿAjam* in the singular, I take it to refer to Persian. The word *qabāʾil* in line 10 seems to be superfluous.

serves that Arabs ruled by non-Arabs do not prosper; a scholiast writing in the next century explains that this is because of mutual distance and ill will, and the difference of natures and language that separates the two groups.[38] Likewise the Egyptian scholar Maqrīzī (d. 1442) complains of the malign role of the Caliph al-Muʿtaṣim (ruled 833–842) in the dispossession of the Arabs: "He removed from the pay-registers the Arabs, the Messenger of God's people, the race through whose agency God had established the religion of Islam. . . . With al-Mu'tasim, and through his deliberate agency, the rule of the Arabs came to an end; henceforth, during his reign and under his political régime, the Turks, upon whom the Messenger of God had vowed to make war, assumed power."[39] Any Arab claims to territory and statehood were now relegated to the periphery. Thus the leader of a thirteenth-century Arab revolt in Upper Egypt proclaimed that "we are the owners of the country" and "more entitled to kingship than the Mamlūks"; but his rebellion went nowhere.[40]

Another and far less visible change was the rise of non-Arab conversion *in situ*: instead of individuals coming or being brought to join the conquerors, substantial numbers of people were now converting without leaving their traditional abodes. It is this change that lies behind the fact that the Muslim population of the world today consists mostly of non-Arab peoples. Only where Islam was spread by Arab conquest was there any serious prospect of the native populations being Arabized on a large scale. And even here the Persians and other Iranian peoples retained their non-Arab ethnic identities and languages despite their conversion to Islam; the same was true of the Berber populations of North Africa for many centuries and remains so to a diminished extent even today. Outside the region conquered by the Arabs in early Islamic times, the chances of Arabization were much more limited. Major new conquests were not the work of the Arabs; thus in Anatolia and India, it was mostly the Turks who enlarged the frontiers of the Islamic world, assimilating much of the population of Anatolia, though not that of India. In regions like Southeast Asia, where Islam was not spread by conquest from outside, Arabization of the indigenous population was just as unlikely.

[38] Mutanabbī, *Dīwān,* 148.24. The poet goes on to complain of the rule of slaves (149.4); the scholiast explains that this refers to the Turkish slaves of the caliphs. The passage is cited in Goldziher, *Muslim studies,* 1: 142.

[39] Maqrīzī, *Contention and strife,* 101 §138.

[40] Maqrīzī, *Sulūk,* 1: 386.15, cited in Ḥasan, *Arabs and Sudan,* 100.

The Arabization of many of the peoples originally conquered by the Arabs was nevertheless a process of great historical importance,[41] despite a certain blurring of ethnic identity that accompanied it. In Iraq, Syria, Egypt, and eventually as far west as Morocco, the mass of the population not only converted to Islam but also adopted Arabic, thereby losing its pre-Islamic ethnic identities and languages along with its former religions.[42] This is why we do not have Muslim populations speaking Syriac or Coptic comparable to those that retain Persian or Berber. The blurring consisted in the fact that in common parlance this Arabization did not necessarily confer on the assimilated populations a straightforwardly Arab ethnic identity—at least not until modern times. Thus we find people belonging to the non-tribal Arabic-speaking population of these regions being referred to as "sons of the Arabs" (*abnāʾ al-ʿArab*) and the like, rather than as Arabs *tout court.*[43] For example, a fifteenth-century Egyptian author writing in praise of the Turks describes the people among whom Muḥammad was given his mission as "the pure Arabs" (*al-ʿArab al-khullaṣ*), but when he speaks of the group to which he himself belonged, he uses the phrase "we scholars from among the sons of the Arabs (*min abnāʾ al-ʿArab*)."[44] Yet usage was by no means consistent. Thus an Iraqi work of the mid-nineteenth century gives an account of a conversation between a scholar of Baghdad and a prominent Ṣūfī—both of whom died in the 1820s—in which

[41] Its extent was recognized by the Syrian scholar Ibn Taymiyya (d. 1328) when he observed that most people in his day were of unknown origin, and did not know whether they were descended from Arabs or non-Arabs (Ibn Taymiyya, *Iqtiḍāʾ*, 167.11).

[42] Perhaps significantly, the geographical limits of this phenomenon roughly match those of the environment suitable for Arab pastoral nomads; conquest alone seems not to have been enough.

[43] Contrast the usage of ninth-century Umayyad Spain, where a population of this kind was referred to as *muwalladūn*, with the clear implication that they were not Arabs; indeed the sources describe them as virulently anti-Arab (see Fierro, "*Mawālī* and *muwalladūn*," 220, 223, 228, 235). One feature of the environment that this phenomenon surely reflects is the continuing political dominance of Arabs in Muslim Spain at a time when they had lost out elsewhere.

[44] Abū Ḥāmid al-Qudsī, *Duwal al-Islām*, 102.10, 108.13, and see 107.12. Some occurrences of the term *evlād-i ʿArab* ("sons of the Arabs") in Ottoman documents relating to Palestine a century or so later look like examples of the same usage (Heyd, *Ottoman documents on Palestine*, 48–49 and n2, 55n6, 153 and n5). See further Baer, *Egyptian guilds*, 14 and n60, 15n63; Raymond, *Artisans et commerçants*, 739–40 (*awlād al-ʿArab min al-Miṣriyyīn waʾl-Shāmiyyīn*); Winter, *Egyptian society*, 31, 46, 55, 159 (where the *awlād al-ʿArab* in question are scholars), 236–37; El-Rouayheb, *Before homosexuality*, 163n6 (citing examples from Jabartī); Rafeq, *Province of Damascus*, 7n1, 88–89; and cf. Ṭabbākh, *Iʿlām*, 6: 529.6, cited in Marcus, *Eve of modernity*, 21 (a passage in which *abnāʾ al-ʿArab* are thrice opposed to *Atrāk*).

the argument turns on a contrast between the Kurdish and Arab scholars (*ʿulamāʾ al-Akrād, ʿulamāʾ al-ʿArab*) of their time;[45] this text does not find it necessary to speak of "sons of the Arabs." In a similar way the Ottomans used the term ʿArabistān to refer not to Arabia but rather to the Arabic-speaking lands of the Fertile Crescent.[46] More significantly, at least one scholar held the view that these Arabized populations were quite simply Arab. In a late seventeenth-century polemic directed against a Rūmī (i.e., Turkish) scholar, the Damascene Ṣūfī ʿAbd al-Ghanī al-Nābulusī (d. 1731) writes that "what is meant by an Arab (*al-murād min al-ʿArabī*) in our age and others, past and future, is someone who speaks the Arabic language (*al-lugha al-ʿarabiyya*) naturally and fluently."[47] Without this historic process of Arabization there would at the present day be no such thing as an Arab world.

Moreover the sense that Arab identity resonated with Islam did not disappear. Thus the tenth-century philosopher Abū ʾl-Ḥasan al-ʿĀmirī, in a work in praise of Islam, emphasized that thanks to their ethnic tie (*al-nisba al-jinsiyya*) to the Prophet even those Arabs—the majority of them—who had remained in their homeland at the time of the conquests had been honored by the fact that Islam could be called "the religion of the Arabs" (*dīn al-ʿArab*) and the resulting state their kingdom (*mulk al-ʿArab*).[48] In the fourteenth century an author who was born in Kurdistan but spent much of his life in Egypt wrote a pamphlet collecting traditions in which Muḥammad said good things about the Arabs. This author begins by praising God who bestowed excellence on the Arabs by sending Muḥammad as their prophet, who revealed the best of books—the Arabic Koran—in their language, and who made Arabic

[45] Ālūsī, *Gharāʾib*, 91.5, cited in El-Rouayheb, "Myth," 215–16. Note also that in the continuation of the passage cited in Baer, *Egyptian guilds*, 15n63, the *abnāʾ al-ʿArab* are referred to simply as *al-ʿArab*.

[46] For this and similar terms, see Heyd, *Ottoman documents on Palestine*, 42, 48n2, 66 and n6, 115, 123, 155. One document describes Jerusalem and Hebron as located on the frontier of ʿArabistān, where rebellious Beduin disturb the peace (76); I am not sure why Heyd felt it necessary to make an exception here and translate the term as "Arabia."

[47] The passage is paraphrased in Winter, "Polemical treatise," 96; for the original, see ʿAbd al-Ghanī, *al-Qawl al-sadīd*, f. 212a.24. The idea that whoever speaks Arabic is an Arab appears already in the mouth of the Prophet (Goldziher, *Muslim studies*, 1: 111–12). As noted by Winter, ʿAbd al-Ghanī immediately goes on to make it clear that speaking colloquial (as opposed to literary) Arabic is no bar to being an Arab (*lā yaḍurruhu ʾl-laḥn fī-mā ʾʿtādat bihi lughat qawmihi*; also f. 212b.2, referring to *al-ʿawāmm min al-ʿArab fī hādhā ʾl-zamān wa-ghayrihi*). The passage and Winter's article were drawn to my attention by Khaled El-Rouayheb, who also kindly supplied me with a copy of the text.

[48] Āmirī, *Iʿlām*, 173.20.

the language of the inhabitants of Paradise.[49] He then quotes such sayings of Muḥammad as this: "To love the Arabs is faith, and to hate them is unbelief. Whoever loves the Arabs loves me, and whoever hates them hates me."[50] A seventeenth-century Syrian scholar made use of such traditions and much else in a demonstration of the superiority of the Arabs over the non-Arabs,[51] and the same ʿAbd al-Ghanī al-Nābulusī averred that the Arabs are the lords of the Persians and Byzantines and that it was well known that the Arabs are more excellent than others.[52] A Syrian scholar of the next generation, Muṣṭafā ibn Kamāl al-Dīn al-Bakrī al-Ṣiddīqī (d. 1749)—a descendant of the first caliph—wrote a book on the difference between Arabs and non-Arabs;[53] the opening passage speaks of the great honor that God has bestowed on the Arabs, their role in the manifestation of Islam, the fact that Muḥammad was an Arab who received his revelation in the language of his people, and the like.[54]

Such ideas were not confined to the Arabic-speaking parts of the Islamic world. In the eighteenth century the lingering prestige of the Arabs is evident in the attitudes of the great Indian scholar Shāh Walī Allāh Dihlawī (d. 1762), who claimed descent from the second caliph.[55] Thus, in a testament he left for his children and friends, he stated: "We are Arab people (*mardum-i ʿArabī*) whose ancestors fell into exile

[49] Irāqī, *Qurab*, 2.2. In saying this, he is paraphrasing the tradition in which Muḥammad gives three reasons why one should love the Arabs: "because I am an Arab, because the Koran is Arabic, and because the language of the inhabitants of Paradise is Arabic" (4.10).

[50] Ibid., 4.4. Compare the bilingual (Arabic and Turkish) teaching of Maḥmūd al-Anṭākī (d. 1748) in Aleppo: he would urge the Turks to love the *abnāʾ al-ʿArab*, citing among other things the Prophetic tradition about the three reasons on account of which one should love the Arabs (Ṭabbākh, *Iʿlām*, 6: 529.9, cited in Marcus, *Eve of modernity*, 21). Note incidentally the implication that the *abnāʾ al-ʿArab* are Arabs.

[51] See Winter, "Polemical treatise," 94–95, summarizing a long quotation from a work of Najm al-Dīn al-Ghazzī (d. 1651) found in ʿAbd al-Ghanī, *al-Qawl al-sadīd*, ff. 210a.4-212a.23. Unlike ʿAbd al-Ghanī, Ghazzī here makes no explicit reference to the Arabs of his own time.

[52] Winter, "Polemical treatise," 94; ʿAbd al-Ghanī, *al-Qawl al-sadīd*, f. 209b.20 (*al-ʿArab sādāt al-ʿAjam waʾl-Rūm*), f. 209b.28 (*wa-maʿlūm anna ʾl-ʿArab afḍal min ghayrihim*).

[53] Bakrī, *Faraq* (for this manuscript, see Arberry, *Chester Beatty Library*, 6: 82–83). I owe my knowledge of this work to Khaled El-Rouayheb.

[54] Bakrī, *Faraq*, 1.2 (I use the pagination found at the top of each page). Bakrī implicitly describes himself as an Arab (*al-muntamī li-fakhr wuld ʿAdnān*, 2.20). He too cites the Prophetic tradition that whoever speaks Arabic is an Arab (129.21) and holds that colloquial Arabic is still Arabic (135.5); he goes on to provide a brief ranking of the colloquial dialects of the Arab lands (135.20).

[55] See Baljon, *Religion and thought*, 1–2, for this claim, and for more on his pride in his Arab descent.

in the land of Hindūstān. The Arabness of our descent and language (*ʿArabīyat-i nasab wa ʿArabīyat-i lisān*) are alike sources of pride for us." The ground he gave for this pride in Arab identity was that it rendered the family close to Muḥammad; in gratitude for this great blessing, he urged that "so far as possible we should not give up the manners and customs of the ancient Arabs (*ʿArab-i awwal*) from whom the Prophet sprang, and that we should not allow among us the manners of the Persians and the customs of the Hindus."[56]

What then of non-Arab ethnic identities within the Islamic community? There was a strain in Islamic thought that rejected the very idea that there could be an Islamic language other than Arabic—and by implication, a non-Arab but authentically Muslim ethnic identity. In early Islamic times there were those who disapproved of speaking Persian; one of them overheard some people conversing in that language and made the tart observation, "Why Magianism after Islam?"[57] A distinguished representative of such views in a later period was Ibn Taymiyya (d. 1328).[58] He pointed out that "the Arabic language is the symbol of Islam and the Muslims (*shiʿār al-Islām wa-ahlihi*)"; he set great store by language, since "languages are among the most powerful symbols of nations (*umam*), which are distinguished from one another by them."[59] He accordingly held that it was undesirable for people to get into the habit of speaking a language other than Arabic in everyday life, as this amounted to imitating non-Arabs. At the time of the conquests, he claimed, the Muslims had made a point of accustoming the natives to speak Arabic—though regretably they eventually failed in Khurāsān, where Persian continued to be spoken. The proper course is for people to get used to speaking Arabic so that children learn it in their homes and schools and the symbol of Islam and the Muslims prevails.[60] Yet such extreme views did not win out. Thus, the jurist Shāfiʿī (d. 820) held that everyone who could do so had a duty to learn Arabic as the language chosen by God but that this did not mean that it was forbidden to speak a non-Arabic language.[61] Sooner or later non-Arabic languages, and by

[56] Walī Allāh, *Tafhīmāt*, 2: 296.4 (for the audience, see 288.9); the passage is quoted in Schimmel, *Islam*, 157.

[57] Ibn Abī Shayba, *Muṣannaf*, 5: 299 no. 26,282.

[58] Ibn Taymiyya, *Iqtiḍāʾ*, 206.13 = Memon, *Ibn Taymīya's struggle*, 206.

[59] Ibn Taymiyya, *Iqtiḍāʾ*, 203.7 = Memon, *Ibn Taymīya's struggle*, 205.

[60] He has in mind the spoken Arabic dialects of his day, as is clear from his earlier reference to the incorrect Arabic of Syria and other regions (*mā dakhala ʿalā lisān al-ʿArab min al-laḥn*, Ibn Taymiyya, *Iqtiḍāʾ*, 166.12).

[61] Ibn Taymiyya, *Iqtiḍāʾ*, 204.21.

implication non-Arab ethnic identities, were accepted as an inescapable reality.[62] There was even a possible Koranic justification for ethnic diversity, though it depended on one's precise understanding of the verse: "O mankind, We have created you male and female, and made you peoples (*shuʿūb*) and tribes that you may know one another" (Q49:13).[63]

Islam nevertheless constituted a somewhat inhospitable environment for the robust assertion of the ethnic identities of non-Arab peoples. A telling sign of the gradient they faced was the tendency for such peoples to lay claim to Arab descent.[64] Another revealing strategy of accommodation was to claim to have played a part in the rise of Islam from the start. The Persians were well placed to do this thanks to the fact that the Prophet's close Companion Salmān al-Fārisī was one of them. A sixteenth-century Persian biographer of the Prophet tells the story of Salmān's suggestion at the consultation prior to the battle of the Khandaq in 627 that the Muslims should dig a trench (*khandaq*) to secure the northern periphery of Medina against attack by enemy cavalry. He goes on to speak of Salmān's outstanding contribution to the hard labor this involved and the recognition this won him from the Prophet and his followers alike; the biographer comments that the high standing of Salmān on that day is something that all Persian-speakers (*Fārsī-zabānān*) can glory in till the day of the resurrection.[65] Somewhat similar is the way in which Maḥmūd al-Kāshgharī leans heavily on traditions ascribed to the Prophet in which the Turks are mentioned. Thus his assertion that they have a superiority over any other people in that God himself named them and called them his army derives from a tradition in which the Prophet quotes God as saying: "I have an army which I have called 'the Turks' and placed in the east; when I am angry with a people, I give them into their power."[66] It is not an obviously philo-Turkish tradition, but it is as good as he can find.

[62] We can see a kind of compromise in the widespread practice of writing non-Arabic languages spoken by Muslims in the Arabic script.

[63] For the views of the exegetes on the meaning of the key term *shuʿūb*, see Mottahedeh, "Shuʿûbîyah controversy," 166–70 (and 172 for the sense of the Persian term *shahr* in this context). The issue was whether the word referred to larger tribal units such as were found among the Arabs or to non-tribal units such as were found among the non-Arabs (cf. my tendentious rendering "peoples"). Mottahedeh shows that the second view found more favor among Iranian commentators.

[64] Goldziher gives the examples of the Kurds, the Berbers, and the Fula (*Muslim studies*, 1: 134–35; and see 147).

[65] Astarābādī, *Āthār-i Aḥmadī*, 200.9, 201.8. Note how a linguistic category here functions as an ethnic identity.

[66] Kāshgharī, *Dīwān*, 1: 294.1.

A full-blooded assertion of a non-Arab ethnic identity outside the framework of deference to Islam and its partiality for the Arabs is harder to mount and sustain. It can be done, the most impressive case being Iran. Here a conspicuous feature of the story is the articulation of the royal heritage of pre-Islamic Iran in the *Shāhnāma* ("Book of kings") of the poet Firdawsī; this was completed in 1010 and became enmeshed in the life of Muslim Iranians. And yet this book was a celebration of what from a strictly Islamic point of view could only be reckoned an evil empire. The problem, as tradition would have it, went back to the time of the Prophet. We are told that when he tried to warn his fellow Meccans by describing the fates of the disobedient communities of the past, he faced unwelcome competition from a rival who would regale them with stories about Rustam, Isfandiyār, and the kings of Persia.[67] But this was not the end of it. In 1089 a poet composed a long epic about the wars of ʿAlī in the meter used by Firdawsī.[68] He did not deny the aesthetic appeal of the *Shāhnāma* but disparaged it as lies (*durūgh*);[69] at one point he spoke of it as a "Book of Magi" (*Mughnāma*).[70] Likewise an Imāmī Shīʿite scholar of the second half of the twelfth century states it as the consensus of the community of Muḥammad that singing the praises of Magians is a pernicious innovation;[71] in his view the storytellers whose stock-in-trade was narratives about the famous figures of ancient Iran owed their existence to a Sunnī plot to divert attention from those who sang the praises of ʿAlī.[72] An Imāmī Shīʿite poet writing in the early fourteenth century describes the "Book of Kings" (*Shahnāma*) as a "book of sins" (*gunahnāma*).[73] Ḍiyāʾ al-Dīn Baranī, a fourteenth-century Sunnī courtier writing in Persian in northern India, sought to justify the adoption of this royal heritage by Muslim rulers; but he did so by arguing that such adoption was allowable in the same

[67] Ibn Hishām, *Sīra*, 1–2: 300.8, 358.2 = *Life of Muhammad*, 136, 162; and see *EI*[2], art. "al-Naḍr b. al-Ḥārith" (C. Pellat). The anecdote is regularly quoted in Koranic exegesis to Q31:6, see for example Ṭabrisī, *Majmaʿ al-bayān*, 4: 313.17; Zamakhsharī, *Kashshāf*, 5: 6.8.

[68] Rabīʿ, *ʿAlī-nāma*. Basic information about the work is conveniently summarized in Omidsalar's English introduction, 5-8. The poet borrows more than the meter from the *Shāhnāma*; he echoes verses from it and makes many references to Rustam (see 40–41 of Shafīʿī's Persian introduction).

[69] Rabīʿ, *ʿAlī-nāma*, 5.18, and see Shafīʿī's introduction, 15.

[70] Rabīʿ, *ʿAlī-nāma*, 162.1, and see Shafīʿī's introduction, 12.

[71] Qazwīnī, *Naqḍ*, 34.24 (*madḥ-i gabrakān khwāndan bidʿat va-ḍalālat ast*).

[72] Ibid., 34.19.

[73] Ḥasan Kāshī, "Maʿrifatnāma," 159.24 (the text is corrupt, but the equation of *Shahnāma* and *gunahnāma* is clear). He too condemns poems about Magians (*Gabrān*, 160.2). Cf. also 153.11, and 29–31 of the editor's introduction; for the dating, see 32.

way that one is permitted to eat carrion under conditions of dire necessity.[74] A seventeenth-century Imāmī Shīʿite scholar warns that some authorities have pronounced vain and frivolous Magian tales such as the *Shāhnāma* to be forbidden even if true.[75] But despite these cavils the poem never lost its prominence in Persian culture.

4. Eighteenth-century identity politics

We can end this survey of the status of ethnic identity in the pre-modern Islamic world with a story about identity politics set in Istanbul in the late 1730s.[76] The milieu to which the story relates is the community of religious scholars in the city. As might be expected, these scholars came from a variety of ethnic backgrounds, and they included Arabs. But the Arab jurists (*fuqahāʾ al-ʿArab*) had a grievance: the non-Arabs kept the top jobs for themselves and left the Arabs at the bottom of the pile. So the Arabs submitted a petition in protest against this ethnic discrimination, presenting their complaint in a grand historical framework. They distinguished two phases of Islamic history. The first was the good old days when the Arabs dominated the Islamic polity, and displayed extraordinary enlightenment and unselfishness in their treatment of non-Arab Muslims, to the extent of practicing reverse discrimination in the distribution of political and religious offices. The second phase, continuing into their own time, was characterised by the domination of the non-Arabs, who signally failed to return the favor. To this petition the non-Arab scholars responded in measured terms. They began by conceding that the Arab account of ethnic relations in early Islamic times was entirely correct. But they went on to point out that in later centuries the Arabs had gone to the dogs.[77] In fact they showed themselves so grossly unfit to rule—allowing the Crusaders to occupy Syria, for example—that Islam itself was in danger. It was at that point that non-Arab rulers—Kurds, Seljūqs, Chorasmians, Ottomans—came to the rescue and put things to rights. By analogy, promoting contemporary

[74] Baranī, *Fatāwā*, 140.14; Habib and Khan, *Political theory*, 39–40; Bary et al., *Sources of Indian tradition*, 472–73.

[75] Majlisī, *ʿAyn al-ḥayāt*, 1136.11 (in a work written in Persian for the laity, cf. 204.3). I am indebted to Hossein Modarressi for guiding me to most of my references in this paragraph, and for generous assistance with them.

[76] Zayyānī, *al-Turjumāna al-kubrā*, 360.16–362.20.

[77] For this theme of Arab moral decline, compare Haarmann, "*Rather the injustice*," 70, and Abū Ḥāmid al-Qudsī, *Duwal al-Islām*, especially 101.13, 103.5.

Arabs to high religious office would invite disaster; the Arabs should leave such offices to the non-Arabs and be content with what they had.

This story is interesting from a number of points of view. First, there is an asymmetry about the identity politics described here. The Arabs put forward a claim on the basis of Arab ethnicity, but the non-Arabs do not impute to themselves any particular ethnic identity or make any claim on that basis, and their rejection of the Arab claim is expressed in terms of the wider public interest, just as it was Islam at large that the non-Arab rulers of earlier centuries had saved. Thus even in an empire ruled by non-Arabs, Arab ethnic identity seems to mean more than that of the rulers. Secondly, the claim of the Arabs is about jobs; jobs matter, but they are not in the same league as territory and statehood. Third, the story is nevertheless likely to strike us as out of place in eighteenth-century Istanbul, and it is indeed a good question whether anything like it really happened. Our authority for it is Abū ʾl-Qāsim al-Zayyānī (d. 1833), a Moroccan scholar and diplomat who spent several years in Istanbul in the late eighteenth century and described his time there in a book he completed in 1818. He in turn writes that a friend of Tunisian origin whom he met in Istanbul had found the petition in the office of the Shaykh al-Islām, the highest religious official of the empire. In short, it is hard to discern whether the imagination behind the story came out of Istanbul, Tunis, or Fez. All we can say with confidence is that we have here a story about the politics of ethnic identity that made sense to an author, and presumably some of his readers, in an Islamic world that had not yet been penetrated by modern Western ideas of nationalism.

There is, however, one scrap of evidence that tends to confirm this picture of Arab aspiration to a larger share in the Ottoman enterprise. Bakrī, in his work on the differences between Arabs and non-Arabs, recounts a dream of one of his teachers, Muḥammad al-Khalīlī (d. 1734–1735).[78] In this dream Khalīlī saw the Ottoman sultan Aḥmed III (ruled 1703–1730), who complained to him about the loss of territory to the unbelievers and the misconduct of evildoers. In response, Khalīlī advised the sultan to seek the help of the Arabs, for no others would help him.[79] This is not a nationalist dream, but it is undoubtedly an ethnic and a political one. It too helps to establish a baseline for the role of ethnicity in the Muslim world on the eve of the Western impact.

[78] Bakrī, *Faraq*, 77.11.

[79] Ibid., 77.15 (*ʿalayka biʾl-ʿArab fa-innahu lā yanjuduka ghayruhum*).

5. Pre-modern Muslim identity: formation and decay

So far we have been looking at what Islam means for ethnic identity. We now need to look at it as an identity in its own right. Our starting point is a familiar feature of the early history of the religion: for the last ten years of the lifetime of the founder, from Muḥammad's arrival in Medina in 622 to his death in 632, his followers constituted not just a religious but also a political community. It is not hard to imagine what this would mean for the formation of a Muslim identity. When adherence to a religion is linked to membership of a polity, solidarity among coreligionists immediately acquires a political as well as a religious dimension. This in itself was likely to render commitment to the religion more salient, as was the initially small and highly participatory character of Muḥammad's polity. Given that the religion was very much a work in progress at this time, the role of these circumstances in shaping its future was also likely to be a profound one.

All this sounds plausible enough, but does anything in the early sources bear out such expectations? One value worth attention here is Muslim brotherhood. "The believers indeed are brothers (*ikhwa*)," as the Koran tells us (Q49:10). Moreover the context of this observation is inherently political: the passage lays down that in the event that two groups of believers are fighting each other, it is one's duty to try to put things right between them, if necessary by fighting the delinquent party till it comes round (Q49:9f).[80] Another verse says of the polytheists that if they repent, pray, and pay alms, they then become "your brothers in religion" (*ikhwānukum fī ʾl-dīn*, Q9:11);[81] here we see that religious brotherhood has something like a fiscal aspect. Broadly similar statements are to be found among Muḥammad's sayings. "Every Muslim is brother to a Muslim, and the Muslims are brothers (*ikhwa*)," he tells his followers on the occasion of his last pilgrimage to Mecca; this time the emphasis is on the implication that no Muslim man may shed the blood of his brother Muslim or take his property against his will.[82] In these texts and others God and his Prophet put strong emphasis on the need

[80] Compare the verse that tells the believers that they have become brothers, though formerly enemies (Q3:103).

[81] This phrase recurs in a verse condemning the practice of adoption: you should call your adopted sons after their fathers, and if you don't know who their fathers are, then they (sc. the adopted sons) are "your brothers in religion" (Q33:5).

[82] Wāqidī, *Maghāzī*, 1113.4; slightly differently Ibn Hishām, *Sīra*, 3–4: 604.16 = 651.

for solidarity among the believers.[83] As might be expected, they also suggest the existence of identities that could undermine this solidarity, but they do not tell us much about them.

A more revealing text in this respect, and a manifestly political one, is the document that has come to be known as the "Constitution of Medina."[84] This document presents itself as an agreement devised by Muḥammad between the "believers and Muslims"[85] of Quraysh (referring to his Meccan followers) and Yathrib (referring to his Medinese followers), together with those who follow them, join them, and wage jihad with them (referring to Jews who were members of the polity in its earliest years).[86] Though the document does not use the metaphor of brotherhood, its opening stipulation is that the parties to the agreement constitute a "single people" (*umma wāḥida*) to the exclusion of others.[87] Yet it immediately becomes clear that we are not to think in terms of an undifferentiated mass of adherents who had renounced all earlier identities at the point at which they entered the community. On the contrary, a succession of tribal groups is now named, and of each of them we are told that it retains responsibility for such matters as blood money and the ransoming of captives. Moreover, it seems that in doing so these groups still act according to their former customs (*ʿalā ribāʿatihim*),[88] while at the same time observing what is customary and equitable among the believers.[89] The document thus recognizes the continuing existence of old tribal identities and practices within the "single people." But it goes on to specify ways in which the new Muslim identity takes precedence over the old tribal loyalties. For example, a believer is not to kill another believer in retaliation for an unbeliever nor to aid an unbeliever against a believer;[90] the believers

[83] For further examples among the sayings of Muḥammad, see Wensinck, *Early Muhammadan tradition*, 70b, 173b–174a, in the entries "Faithful" and "Muslim(s)."

[84] Ibn Hishām, *Sīra*, 1–2: 501–4 = 231–33. For the latest edition, translation, and discussion see Lecker, *Constitution of Medina*. The document is often obscure and partly for that reason widely accepted as authentic.

[85] For our purposes, here and elsewhere, we can treat these two terms as synonymous.

[86] In fact a large part of the document is concerned with relations with these Jews; since for our purposes this early inclusiveness does not matter, I have left these relations aside.

[87] Ibn Hishām, *Sīra*, 1–2: 501.23 = 232; see Lecker, *Constitution of Medina*, 88–92.

[88] Lecker translates this phrase as "keep to their tribal organization and leadership" (*Constitution of Medina*, 98–103).

[89] I follow Lecker's translation (ibid., 105–6).

[90] Ibn Hishām, *Sīra*, 1–2: 502.19 = 232; see Lecker, *Constitution of Medina*, 113–12.

are each others' allies (*mawālī*) to the exclusion of other people;[91] the peace (*silm*) of the believers is indivisible, so that one believer may not make peace to the exclusion of another while fighting in the way of God, except on a basis of mutual fairness.[92] Here in each case it is implicit that when the two orders conflict, the new religious bond is to trump the old tribal ones.

This early bond within a small, concentrated community is only our starting point. What would become of it as Islam expanded, first in Arabia in the last years of Muḥammad's life and then far outside it under his successors? In the short run the phenomenal political and military success of the new religion must have worked to strengthen the bond as participation in the Muslim enterprise became more and more rewarding. We get a sense of the tight bonding of the community from an anecdote about an emissary to Rustam, the Persian general in Iraq at the time of the Muslim conquest. When he was asked whether he had the authority to agree to a brief truce on behalf of the Muslims, the envoy replied that though he was not their chief, "the Muslims are like a body, parts of a whole," and consequently the lowliest among them could extend protection on behalf of the highest.[93] This was also the time when Islam was most closely identified with the Arabs. Thus, at the moment of their most dazzling imperial success, the believers were indeed brothers—religiously, ethnically, and politically. But the very magnitude of this success—leading to the establishment of an empire extending from Spain and Morocco in the west to Central Asia and Sindh in the east—set in motion a slow but relentless process of decay.

Most obviously, the problem was the sheer extent of the Islamic world. This meant that in the long run the chances of holding it together under the power of a single ruler were minimal. It is remarkable enough that most of the lands inhabited by Muslims remained within the borders of a single state well into the ninth century. Thereafter the rule of the caliphs gave way to the bewildering assortment of some two hundred regional dynasties that characterizes most of Islamic history into modern times.[94] Moreover, in the course of the centuries following

[91] Ibn Hishām, *Sīra*, 1–2: 502.20 = 232; see Lecker, *Constitution of Medina*, 117–18.

[92] Ibn Hishām, *Sīra*, 1–2: 503.2 = 232; and see Lecker, *Constitution of Medina*, 120–21.

[93] Ṭabarī, *Taʾrīkh*, Series 1, 2272.10 = *History of al-Ṭabarī*, 12: 68. This language echoes that of the Constitution of Medina (see below, 321–22). For the various stories of the emissaries sent to Rustam and their historical significance, see Kennedy, *Great Arab conquests*, 111–15; I return to them several times below (169–70, 185, 321).

[94] The standard guide to the dynasties of the Islamic world recognizes 186 of them; the first three include all the caliphs who ruled the Islamic lands as a whole down to

its political disintegration, the Islamic world still continued on balance to expand, sometimes dramatically. This ongoing geographical success rendered the restoration of political unity yet more unlikely. Even a state the size of the Ottoman Empire at its sixteenth-century zenith never came close to ruling the Islamic world as a whole. Under such conditions Muslims could no longer be political brothers in any sense that involved being members of the same polity.

But the dissolution of political unity was not the only factor making for the decay of Muslim identity. For one thing, Islam spread not just outwards but also downwards. No longer just the religion of an ethnically homogeneous political and military elite, it was now being adopted by ethnically diverse populations at all levels of society. Thus, even Muslims unaffected by the emergence of sectarian splits within Islam no longer had as much in common as they did in early Islamic times. For another thing, the absence of a Muslim counterpart to the Christian church meant the lack of an organization charged with strengthening the religious bonds between different parts of the Muslim world. There was indeed the Ḥajj, the annual pilgrimage that brought Muslims to Mecca from all parts of the Muslim world, but there were no councils in the manner of early Buddhism or late antique Christianity,[95] let alone a Pope. If all that was left was a diffuse brotherhood in religion, it might seem that Muslims would be even more weakly bonded than Buddhists and Christians.

6. The Residue of Muslim Identity on the Eve of Modern Times

Just what was left of Muslim identity on the eve of modern times is not in fact an easy question to answer. What we really want to know is whether Muslim brotherhood still possessed a character and strength apt to provide a foundation for political identity in the modern world, and we would like to establish this without the distortions of hindsight.

---

the ninth century, while the other 183 are regional dynasties (see the table of contents of Bosworth, *New Islamic dynasties*). The coverage of minor regional dynasties does not claim to be complete (xvii).

[95] In the twentieth century Muslims readily adopted the idea of holding pan-Islamic congresses (for the results, see the summary in Kramer, *Islam assembled*, 166–69). As we will see, the Viśva Hindu Pariṣad (VHP) later did the same for Hinduism (see 112–13).

All I will attempt here is to sketch a couple of indirect approaches to the issue.

One relates to what might be called the apostasy threshold of Islam. A broad but sound observation about the history of the Muslim world would be that once people convert to Islam, they do not usually leave it. Here it is the period down to the eighteenth century that concerns us. We can begin by noting that no pre-modern Muslim population of any size is known to have abandoned Islam for another religion without having first been conquered by unbelievers. That may not in itself serve to set Islam apart from Christianity, the obvious benchmark for comparison, but we can usefully ask what happens when Muslims and Christians conquer each other. The pre-modern record of Muslim expansion at the expense of Christian societies is extensive: we have the Arab conquest of Syria, Egypt, North Africa, and southern Spain, plus the Turkish conquest of Anatolia and the Balkans. The outcome was that Christians survived well in the Ottoman Balkans but elsewhere were reduced to minorities or disappeared altogether. This implies that Christians converted to Islam on a large scale. Such conversion was undoubtedly helped by a measure of ill treatment, but it was not the product of systematic persecution. The record of Christian conquest of comparable Muslim societies is much more limited in pre-modern times, but if we leave aside Mediterranean islands as too small to count, two examples stand out: Spain after the completion of the Reconquista in 1492[96] and Tatarstan after the Russian conquest of Kazan in 1552.[97] From a Christian point of view, the results look dispiriting.

Despite their geographical separation, the two cases have significant features in common. One is the stripping away of the indigenous aristocracy, whether through dispossession or assimilation[98]—processes already familiar to Christian populations under Muslim rule. Another feature, far less typical of Muslim rule over Christians, is forced conversion[99] and more generally a pattern of unsteady but sometimes heavy persecution,[100] issuing in the telltale phenomenon of nominal Chris-

[96] Harvey, *Muslims in Spain*. For a survey of the earlier record of conversion from Islam to Christianity under Christian rule in the Mediterranean world, see Kedar, *Crusade and mission*, chap. 2, with a summary at 83–84.

[97] Lemercier-Quelquejay, "Missions orthodoxes."

[98] Harvey, *Muslims in Spain*, 35, 37, 250–51; Lemercier-Quelquejay, "Missions orthodoxes," 378–79, 380.

[99] Harvey, *Muslims in Spain*, 14; Lemercier-Quelquejay, "Missions orthodoxes," 389.

[100] For persecution over and above forced conversion, see, for example, Harvey, *Muslims in Spain*, 71–72, 211, and Lemercier-Quelquejay, "Missions orthodoxes," 372, 379,

tians who were Muslims in secret.[101] In the Spanish case the entire Muslim population was forcibly converted in the early sixteenth century,[102] but by the beginning of the seventeenth century it was the consensus that by and large the conversion had not taken, and in 1609–1614 this "Morisco" population was expelled from the country.[103] In the Tatar case the early conversions did take,[104] but the forced baptisms of the eighteenth century did not: many of the converts later apostatized,[105] and most Tatars remained unconverted even in name.[106] Certainly in the Tatar case, and very likely in the Spanish case, hard-line policies did enjoy some measure of success.[107] But in each instance the overall failure was far more conspicuous. The Tatar Muslims went on to play their part in the modern history of Islam. The Moriscos did not, but as late as 1690–1691 a Moroccan ambassador in Madrid was visited repeatedly by Christians whose ancestors had been Muslims and who felt close to him for that reason. "We are of Muslim stock," as one of them told him, in an intimation of a Muslim solidarity that still meant something even without Islam.[108] Small wonder that both Moriscos and Tatars were known to the respective Christian authorities for their obstinacy.[109] Thus the author of a document apparently written close to the time of the expulsion of the Moriscos complains that "as those who have been engaged in the conversion have discovered, it is not just

---

380, 388, 389, 392, 397, 398–99, 400–401; for its unsteadiness, see Harvey, *Muslims in Spain*, 109, 212, 242–43, 254, and Lemercier-Quelquejay, "Missions orthodoxes," 371, 381, 382, 386–87, 392.

[101] Harvey, *Muslims in Spain*, 60–63, 71, 101; Lemercier-Quelquejay, "Missions orthodoxes," 383, 385, 388, 390–91, 397.

[102] Harvey, *Muslims in Spain*, 31, 56–58, 94.

[103] Ibid., chap. 9.

[104] Lemercier-Quelquejay, "Missions orthodoxes," 378, 379, 397–98; but note the apostasy of the early 1580s (379). Unlike the later converts, some of the early ones brought with them elements of a pagan heritage, suggesting that their Islam did not go very deep (373 and n3).

[105] Lemercier-Quelquejay, "Missions orthodoxes," 385, 392–93, 397, 401.

[106] Figures for 1828–1829 show a Tatar population that was 80 percent Muslim and 20 percent Christian; the second figure was made up of 10 percent who were genuine Christians and another 10 percent who were ready to apostatize (Lemercier-Quelquejay, "Missions orthodoxes," 398, my arithmetic; for the low level of success in converting the Tatars, see also 389–91, 400).

[107] For the question of assimilation in the Spanish case, see Harvey, *Muslims in Spain*, 250–52.

[108] Ghassānī, *Riḥla*, 53.14 (*naḥnu min jins al-Muslimīn*). They asked a lot about Islam (54.5). See also Harvey, *Muslims in Spain*, 252.

[109] For the Tatars, see Lemercier-Quelquejay, "Missions orthodoxes," 385 and n3, 389, and cf. 399.

that nothing has been achieved, but that every time some effort has been made, their stubbornness and ill will has only increased, without a single one of them ever being converted, in spite of all the hopes."[110] It is, of course, quite possible that over a timescale of a millennium the Muslims of Spain and Tatarstan would have become good Christians, just as most Christians in the regions conquered by the Arabs became good Muslims. But over the timescale that history has given us, Muslim resistance to conversion was formidable. Even persecution did not seem to help much in turning Muslims into Christians.

Another way in which Muslim brotherhood should manifest itself is by inhibiting Muslims from doing to each other unpleasant things that they might do to others, such as fighting or enslaving them. Other things being equal, for Muslims to fight Muslims was wrong and a source of embarrassment, particularly when it involved alliances with unbelievers,[111] whereas fighting unbelievers was right and a source of pride, since it was jihad in the way of God.[112] Yet historically it is not obvious that Muslim solidarity had any discernible effect in reducing the amount of warfare between Muslims. Such fighting already appears in the Koran as a potential problem (Q49:9). It happened on a large scale in two seventh-century civil wars, in the first of which the rival armies were led by Muḥammad's own Companions. Thereafter it was a recurrent feature of Muslim history in all centuries and all parts of the Muslim world. Against this background it would take some statistical sophistication to show that Muslims had a greater propensity to fight unbelievers than fellow believers. To the naked eye at least, Muslims look no different in this respect from Christians, Buddhists, or Hindus.[113]

Enslavement is another matter. In Islamic law a slave could be a Muslim, but the rule from early on was that a free Muslim could not become a slave.[114] Not even rebels could be enslaved, though heretics

[110] Harvey, *Muslims in Spain*, 307.

[111] For a fifteenth-century Muslim ruler in India who obtained a *fatwā* from the scholars to justify his alliance with a Hindu ruler against a Muslim one, see Schimmel, *Islam*, 39. For the disagreement among the nineteenth-century Wahhābī scholars over the question whether a Saudi ruler could ally with the polytheistic Ottomans against a challenger, see Wagemakers, "Enduring legacy," 96, and cf. 95.

[112] On the idea of jihad, see Crone, *Medieval Islamic political thought*, 362–85.

[113] A good question to ask would be whether Muslim brotherhood had any effect in rendering warfare among Muslims less atrocious than warfare against unbelievers. To my knowledge, no one has attempted a systematic answer to this question.

[114] "Slavery can originate only through birth or through captivity, i.e. if a non-Muslim who is protected neither by treaty nor by a safe-conduct falls into the hands of the Muslims" (Schacht, *Introduction to Islamic law*, 127). There is evidence of somewhat more

could be if deemed non-Muslims.[115] Leaving aside slight later hesitations that we will come to,[116] the real question is whether this rule was observed in practice. Unquestionably it was not always observed, as the jurists were well aware. One example comes from Umayyad Spain, where the conditions brought about by the prolonged rebellion of Ibn Ḥafṣūn (d. 918) obliged them to reckon with the fact that many free people were being sold into slavery.[117] Another example comes from Africa several centuries later: here Aḥmad Bābā (d. 1627), a scholar of Timbuktu, was consulted on the enslavement of free Muslims in the course of intra-Muslim warfare in the sub-Saharan region.[118] The phenomenon is also well attested in the heartlands of the Ottoman Empire.[119] Nevertheless, one historian of slavery in the Muslim world has written that "by and large, and certainly in the central lands of Islam, under regimes of high civilization, the rule was honored," with the result that slaves had either to be imported from outside the Muslim world or to be born into slavery within it.[120] This is probably the general impression of modern scholars—and were it not the case, it would be hard to account for the persistence of the large-scale import of slaves into the Muslim world across punishing geographical barriers.[121] No one has attempted a systematic collection of the evidence for or against this impression, but a recent study tends to confirm it: there are numerous instances of the violation of the rule, but they fall mainly in the less economically favored regions of the Islamic world, or are the work of people recently arrived from such regions.[122] A mid-sixteenth-century European observer, by contrast, noted that the Turks abstained

permissive views on the enslavement of free Muslims in the early history of Islamic law (see I. Schneider, *Kinderverkauf*, 351–54, where the author conveniently summarizes her findings).

[115] For the case of rebels, see Abou El Fadl, *Rebellion and violence*, for example 145, 161, 173, 221, 314.

[116] See 29–30.

[117] See Vidal Castro, "Sobre la compraventa ," 1: 428 = 427, drawn to my attention by Maribel Fierro.

[118] Aḥmad Bābā, *Miʿrāj al-ṣuʿūd*, 43.6 = 13, 53.1 = 23, 79.11 = 41, 90.5 = 50; and see 95.4 = 11, 95.17 = 12 for a somewhat earlier discussion describing the problem as epidemic in the region.

[119] See Zilfi, *Women and slavery*, 206–13.

[120] B. Lewis, *Race and slavery*, 6, 9–10.

[121] For estimates of the scale of the slave trade across the world's largest desert, see J. Wright, *Trans-Saharan slave trade*, 167–68.

[122] Clarence-Smith, *Abolition of slavery*, 43–45, 74–78 (the author does not remark on the geographical distribution of his data). Note the increasing insistence on the rule in Southeast Asia as Islam spread and deepened there (44).

from "exercising the rights of war over men of their own religion," allowing them to "retain the status of freemen unimpaired."[123]

In comparative terms the existence of a rule barring enslavement within a given community is not in itself exceptional. For example, there is indirect but convincing evidence that the sale of free people was against the law in China under the Western Han dynasty.[124] More selectively, an ancient Indian jurist stressed that a Brahmin could not be made a slave even to another Brahmin—the wider, and very Hindu, principle behind this being that one can only be a slave to a master whose class (*varṇa*) is above one's own.[125] Likewise Roman law forbad the sale or acquisition of Roman citizens.[126] Restrictions of this kind were not universal—for centuries it was legal to sell oneself into slavery in Russia[127]—but they were common enough. The real question, again, is not whether such rules existed, but how far they were kept.

Here famine can serve as an acid test.[128] "Famine and slavery in China are cause and effect," as one scholar has written, noting the recurrent sale of children during famines from Han times to the early twentieth century and adding that extensive warfare almost always leads to famine.[129] For India we lack a historical record contemporary with the ancient jurists,[130] but famine and the sale of children were associated from at least the sixteenth century over large parts of the subcontinent.[131] Thus we encounter the practice in western India under

[123] Forster and Blackburne Daniell, *Ogier Ghiselin de Busbecq*, 1: 211. This abstention apart, he describes slave-hunting as "the chief source of profit to the Turkish soldier."

[124] Wilbur, *Slavery in China*, 88–90.

[125] Kane, *History of Dharmaśāstra*, 2: 185–86 (my copy of this work is made up of reprints of various dates). For the more restrictive view that an Aryan cannot be enslaved, see 183.

[126] For the law in question, see Crook, *Law and life*, 60.

[127] Blum, *Lord and peasant*, 51, 113–14, and cf. 273; Hellie, *Slavery in Russia*, 48, and cf. 376. Self-sale was likewise legal in Visigothic law (Verlinden, *Esclavage*, 78).

[128] Not *the* acid test, since another would be enslavement in the course of warfare within the Muslim world, specifically between rival Sunnī rulers.

[129] See Wilbur, *Slavery in China*, 85–88, for these remarks and supporting evidence from the Western Han period. For a man who sold his wife in the face of starvation in 1655, but then died of grief, see Li, *Fighting famine*, 35.

[130] For references to enslavement during famines in the ancient juristic literature, see Kane, *History of Dharmaśāstra*, 2: 184–85.

[131] See Moreland, *India*, 266 (the Coromandel coast and Gujarat); Moreland, *Akbar to Aurangzeb*, 207 (Vijayanagar), 212 (Gujarat); Habib, *Agrarian system*, 101 (Gujarat), 102 (Kashmir), 103 (presumably Gujarat), 105 and n35 (Punjab), 107 (Patna), 108 (Rajasthan), 109 (Deccan), 110 and n76; Chattopadhyay, *Slavery*, 12, 14–16 (Bengal); Banaji, *Slavery in British India*, 44–52 (including Calcutta and Madras). Chattopadhyay quotes a

Hindu rule around 1800,[132] and in the early nineteenth century we hear of thousands being sold in a great famine in southwestern Rajasthan.[133] Further west, Basil of Caesarea (d. 379) anticipated the sale of children as an inevitable consequence of an impending famine in 369, vividly describing the agony of a father deciding which of his children to sell first.[134] Turning to Europe, we read that during a famine in Italy in 450 large numbers of people sold their children and relatives.[135] Likewise in eleventh-century England a woman decided to manumit a group of people "whose heads she took in exchange for food in those evil days."[136]

How often did such things happen in the Muslim world? Again, they were not unheard of. The early jurists knew such practices as self-sale and the sale of children.[137] In later centuries the sale of women and children was known in Morocco in times of famine, and there was even a minority view that Islamic law permitted it.[138] It is reported that during a famine of 1867 in Tripolitania, some inhabitants of the border areas sold themselves into slavery.[139] A dispatch from Aleppo describing a famine in 1757 mentions refugees from Mosul, Diyārbekir, and Urfa who were selling their children, especially the girls,[140] and in 1841 Muslim parents were selling their children in the Mosul area "on account of their extreme poverty."[141] In India we hear a good deal about Muslims selling their children and even themselves in time of famine.[142] As in Morocco there was a view that such sales

deed of sale in which a mother named Sāvitrī—the name is obviously Hindu—sells her six-year-old daughter for three rupees for want of food (*Slavery*, 15–16).

[132] S. Guha, "Slavery, society," 167–68.

[133] R. Sreenivasan, "Drudges, dancing girls," 140.

[134] Harper, *Slavery*, 410–11.

[135] A.H.M. Jones, *Later Roman Empire*, 853–54. For instances from North Africa in Roman and Vandal times, see Mitteis, *Reichsrecht und Volksrecht*, 362, cited in I. Schneider, *Kinderverkauf*, 314.

[136] Pelteret, *Slavery*, 162 (I owe this reference to William C. Jordan).

[137] I. Schneider, *Kinderverkauf*, 383 (self-sale); 385, 386–87 (sale of children). See also Crone, *Medieval Islamic political thought*, 352n92.

[138] Bazzāz, *Tārīkh al-awbiʾa*, 359.

[139] Toledano, *Ottoman slave trade*, 19.

[140] Marseilles, Archives de la Chambre de Commerce de Marseille, File J 914, consular report from Aleppo dated September 1, 1757. This report was drawn to my attention by Yaron Ayalon, who kindly supplied me with a copy.

[141] Erdem, *Slavery*, 48 and 197n26, cited in Clarence-Smith, *Abolition of slavery*, 75.

[142] Clarence-Smith, *Abolition of slavery*, 75.

were permitted by Islamic law,[143] but in real life the prominence of the practice among Muslims is likely to have derived from the Hindu environment. The Indian case apart, the data seem compatible with the idea that the practice was rare in the more prosperous areas of the Islamic world.[144] For example, the famines of medieval Egypt have received serious attention from scholars (both medieval and modern), and here enslavement does not appear to be part of the syndrome.[145] If that is an accurate observation, and more widely applicable, it may be as good an indication as we can hope to get that Muslim solidarity meant something on the ground.[146]

There is a related point worth considering in this context: the relationship between concubinage and slavery. The effect of the bar on the enslavement of Muslims was that a free Muslim woman could not become a concubine. This meant that elite males had no legal access to lower-class females unless they were willing to marry them. The situation was somewhat different among the Imāmī Shīʿites since there the acceptance of the institution of "temporary marriage" (*mutʿa*) made possible the recognition of an arrangement that, though legally a form of marriage, could be considered tantamount to free concubinage.[147] Islamicists tend to think of the Sunnī rejection of temporary marriage as the norm and the Imāmī stance as a deviation from it. But on a broader comparative canvas, the question may rather be why the institution was classed as a form of marriage at all, and why even then the Sunnīs

[143] Ibid., 75–76, and cf. 77; Macnaghten, *Principles and precedents*, xxxiii, in the footnote.

[144] For further instances from recent centuries, see I. Schneider, *Kinderverkauf*, 357n3. The most economically advanced region to which she refers is Egypt in the 1830s, where her source suggests that the practice of selling children existed but was not common (Lane, *Manners and customs*, 205–6).

[145] For a modern study, see Sabra, *Poverty and charity*, 138–64 (with case studies of ten food shortages or famines in the period covered); note that Sabra's sources are not too squeamish to mention cannibalism (141, 142, 143, 153). For a medieval collection of data on famines in Egypt, see Maqrīzī, *Ighātha* = Allouche, *Mamluk economics*; here again cannibalism is freely mentioned (see, for example, 29.8 = 41), but the only reference to enslavement—specifically people selling their children to buy food—comes in an aside on Yemen (34.14 = 44–45). However, an Egyptian source mentions the sale of children during a famine in 1296 (see Chapoutot-Remadi, "Une grande crise," 235).

[146] Contrast Harper's observations on the persistence of enslavement within the Roman empire in late antiquity (Harper, *Slavery*, 78–83). He describes internal sources as "a major input to the Roman slave supply" (79); one significant source that would seem to have disappeared in Islamic times was child exposure (81–83, 393).

[147] See *EI*², art. "Mutʿa" (W. Heffening). Some early Sunnī authorities likewise considered *mutʿa* to be legal.

rejected it.[148] The upshot is that it is only by marriage that a Muslim gains sexual access to the daughter of a free fellow Muslim.

In sum, it does not seem fanciful to see evidence of Muslim solidarity in the strength of the Muslim record of resistance to conversion on the one hand and a degree of abstention from the enslavement of fellow Muslims on the other.[149] Altogether, the political solidarity of the early Muslim community, itself imperfect, had come to be spread so thin as to be residual; but the residue seems to have been one that could still make a difference. Even in the eighteenth century people still did things "for the sake of the unity of Islam" (*jihet-i vaḥdet-i Islām ichün*).[150] Or at least they talked that way. When the ruler of Bukhara wrote to the Ottomans in 1722 to propose military cooperation against the Russian and Kalmuk unbelievers, he averred that "we are brothers in religion."[151] Likewise when the Ottoman sultan drafted a letter to the ruler of Bukhara in 1787, he invoked "religious brotherhood" (*ukhuvvet-i dīniyye*) and "Islamic bonds of unity" (*revābiṭ-i ittiḥād-i Islāmiyye*) against the infidel enemies of the Islamic community.[152]

[148] Thus for the ease with which free women from lower-class families could become concubines of upper-class males in Sung China, see Ebrey, *Inner quarters*, chap. 12, especially 222–24 and 233; for a more limited version of the same phenomenon in medieval Europe, see Strayer, *Dictionary of Middle Ages*, art. "Concubinage, Western" (R. H. Helmholz).

[149] Another question worth investigating here would be the extent to which widely separated Muslim populations—those beyond the range of economic or geopolitical interaction under pre-modern conditions—show interest in news about each other. For example, a Morisco writer of the first half of the seventeenth century rejoices that most of the inhabited world belongs to the Muslims (Ḥajarī, *Nāṣir al-dīn*, 126.3 = 182) and gives a survey of it extending as far as India, regarding which he reports some information he obtained from an Indian whom he met in Cairo (123.15 = 180). He also takes pride in the spread of Islam in the East Indies (*al-Hunūd al-Mashriqiyya*), but he knows of this development only through European Christian sources, oral and written (124.11, 125.12 = 181–82). The question poses itself whether he would have seen the Islamic world in the way he did but for his European horizons.

[150] See B. Lewis, *Muslim discovery*, 46–47, translating an Ottoman account mentioning the role of the sultan of Morocco in the release of some Algerians held captive in Spain. Lewis aptly renders the phrase as "inspired by Muslim solidarity" (for the original, see Jevdet, *Tārīkh*, 4: 358.9).

[151] Saray, *Münasebetler*, 15 (*Biz din karundaşıyız*), cited in Özcan, *Pan-Islamism*, 25 (where the date of the letter is given as 1719). Cf. also Saray, *Münasebetler*, 13 (paraphrasing a letter of 1707), 15 (paraphrasing one of 1736).

[152] Saray, *Münasebetler*, 121.9, cited in Özcan, *Pan-Islamism*, 25 (where the date of this draft letter is given as 1786); cf. also Saray, *Münasebetler*, 120.29, in the same letter. In a letter written to the ruler of Bukhara at the end of 1789 or the beginning of 1790, the sultan again invoked "religious brotherhood" (*ukhuvvet-i dīniyye*) and Islamic unity (*yekjihetī-yi Islāmiyye*, 130.20; for the reading, see the reproduction, 133.9, and for the date, 27n77).

7. Modern ethnic and Muslim identity: expectations

The modern Islamic world thus inherited from its past a combination of a set of regional ethnic identities and an overarching, albeit distended and somewhat fractured religious identity. How then were the tensions between them likely to play out? We could imagine a universe in which ethnicity came to be everything and Islam no longer had implications for political identity, and we could equally imagine one in which Islamic solidarity swept all before it.[153] The first would be the ideal universe of a secularist, the second of an Islamist. We would, however, expect reality to be somewhere in between; the question is just where. But before we come to what actually happened, let us look at two factors that could be expected to influence the outcome one way or the other.

What favored the secularist outcome was the salience of Western values in the world brought into being by the European expansion. As we have already noted, European nations were defined by ethnicity,[154] and this was the nationalist paradigm that came to be widely adopted by the increasingly Europeanized elites of the non-Western world. In this perspective religious affiliation appeared as secondary or irrelevant. To champion Muslim brotherhood as a political identity in such a world was thus to swim against the tide of Western modernity.

What favored the Islamist outcome was the stubborn survival of the pre-modern sense of Muslim identity despite the tide. Above we used the relative rarity of apostasy and enslavement as indications of the strength of that identity; enslavement becomes more or less irrelevant in the modern world, but we can still learn something from the incidence of Muslim apostasy.[155] As in pre-modern times it is not that Muslims never convert. Small numbers living in isolation among non-Muslim populations may end up abandoning Islam. Thus Muslims in

[153] In the modern period the term "Islamic solidarity" (*al-taḍāmun al-Islāmī*) is adopted into Muslim usage (see Landau, *Politics of Pan-Islam*, 261–62, 266), though references to Muslim brotherhood naturally continue (see, for example, 189, 191).

[154] See 1–2.

[155] Another modern phenomenon that could be construed as an indication of Muslim solidarity is the difference in murder rates between Muslim and non-Muslim countries, with the Muslim rate being about a third of the non-Muslim rate (see Fish, *Are Muslims distinctive?*, 119–31). As Fish remarks, the differences are dramatic (120); he observes that in cross-national studies "something like what might be called cultural integration emerges as a leading explanation" (127), and he concludes that the evidence seems to point to the possibility that Durkheimian "anomie" may be lower in Muslim societies (131).

the town of Ross in North Dakota began building themselves a mosque in 1920 but gave it up because many of their number converted to Christianity.[156] Individuals can likewise be impelled to break with a group for idiosyncratic personal reasons: one very human motive for Muslim women to apostatize in British India was to get out of unhappy marriages.[157] These, however, are extreme situations. Under normal conditions the rewards of missionary work among Muslims have been meagre in modern times, just as they had been earlier. Thus in Algeria, the French governor tartly observed in 1885: "Les Indigènes sont imperméables à la foi chrétienne."[158] Against that background it makes sense that the only significant success of Catholic proselytism in Algeria in this period involved children shaken loose from their parents by the famine of 1867–1868.[159] Likewise the attempts of Christian missionaries to convert Egyptian Muslims made little headway: a recent study gives the number of living converts in 1953 as around 200[160] and stresses the cataclysmic "familial and communal rupture" that accompanied conversion.[161] In the Middle East in general, such success as the missionaries achieved was mainly among the indigenous Christian minorities of the region, not the Muslims. Conditions in British India were more favorable, since in most of the subcontinent Muslims lacked demographic dominance and the population was under the direct or indirect rule of more or less observant Christians. Yet even here the success of missionaries in converting Muslims was very limited,[162] and the missionary expectation that "at a time when the Muslims had lost courage and fortitude due to their political downfall, propagation of Christianity and condemnation of Islam would result in their conversion"[163] turned out to be a mirage. As in Algeria we hear of the conversion of

[156] J. I. Smith, *Islam in America*, 56.

[157] Zaman, *Ulama*, 29. The numbers involved are unclear (see Zaman, *Ashraf 'Ali Thanawi*, 62).

[158] Ageron, *Algériens musulmans*, 304–5.

[159] Ibid., 302–3.

[160] Sharkey, *American evangelicals*, 1, 219. For the trickle of converts at earlier dates, see 63–64; cf. also the photograph of the Converts' Society in 1923 (70).

[161] Ibid., 69, 77, and note her references to "Muslim social solidarity," "the violent rage of families" (66), and "social death" (68); she likewise quotes a missionary on the complete "severance from the community" that followed conversion (220). The best candidates for conversion were thus those who lacked families: orphans and ex-slaves (77–78).

[162] See, for example, Powell, *Muslims and missionaries*, 95–96, 110–16, 213–14, 288; R. B. Sharma, *Christian missions*, 178, 179.

[163] Quoted in Sharma, *Christian missions*, 177.

minors during famines as a partial exception.[164] In eastern Java the conversion of Muslims to Christianity did lead to the emergence of a Christian minority, but the circumstances of this development were highly unusual, reflecting as they did the earlier formation and survival into modern times of a distinctive synthesis combining Islam with the Indic traditions of pre-Islamic Java.[165]

This impermeability stands in stark contrast to the reception accorded to Christianity in many parts of the non-Muslim world in the same period. Perhaps the most remarkable case is South Korea, where over a quarter of the population is now Christian, mostly as a result of conversion since the 1960s.[166] This process does not seem to have been accompanied by any deep sense of social rupture on the part of either the converts or the population at large. There does exist a nationalist right that decries Evangelicalism as an alien influence, but it does not seem to have significant public support.[167] Indeed, any sense that to be a Christian in South Korea might be a political liability is belied by the fact that of the two presidents who held office between 1993 and 2003, the first was a Presbyterian elder and the second a devout Catholic.[168] Nor do the divisions within South Korean Christianity—between Catholics and Protestants and within Protestantism[169]—translate into a fractured polity. The whole phenomenon of South Korean Christianity reflects attitudes to religion quite different from those prevailing in the Islamic world and which are in some measure typical of East Asia in general. It is significant in this context that half the population of South Korea claims no religious affiliation at all[170] and that all the major denominations—Buddhists, Catholics, and Protestants—suffer from high dropout rates; indeed that of the Protestants is so high that there are more former Protestants than current ones.[171] By contrast, "once a Muslim always a Muslim" remains reliable as a rule of thumb, and it encourages us to look for a continuing political role of Muslim

[164] Ibid., 180; cf. also Powell, *Muslims and missionaries*, 160, 162.

[165] See Hefner, "Faith and commitment," especially 107–9 (drawn to my attention by Heather Sharkey). This Christian minority is estimated at about 4 percent of the ethnic Javanese population (100).

[166] For the figures see D. Baker, "Sibling rivalry," 283–84.

[167] Lee, "Beleaguered success," 344–45.

[168] Ibid., 337.

[169] For the distance between Catholics and Protestants, see Baker, "Sibling rivalry," 304, and for the fragmentation of the Protestant community, 297.

[170] Ibid., 285.

[171] Ibid., 303.

identity in the modern world, albeit one in competition with a variety of ethnic identities.

8. Modern ethnic and Muslim identity: realizations

So much for expectations. Let us turn now to the actual record of the interaction between Muslim identity and the ethnic identities of the modern Islamic world.

An obvious question to start with is whether Muslim identity has shown the power to override ethnic divisions within a Muslim country. Clearly it can underwrite a religious rhetoric that rises above such quarrels in a way that nationalism cannot. For example, Turkish Islamists have been able to take a less hostile view of Kurdish ethnic sentiment than Turkish secularists.[172] Likewise the Pakistanis saw merit in Islamism as a prescription for Afghanistan because it had some potential to transcend the ethnic irredentism that threatened to detach the Pashtūns of Pakistan and reunite them with their kinsmen in Afghanistan.[173] But overall, there is no evidence that Islamic solidarity can provide innoculation against ethnic conflict. Thus, there is a Berber problem in Algeria and a Kurdish problem in several Middle Eastern countries, just as there is a Basque problem in Spain and a Breton problem in France. In Afghanistan Islamism has shown no power to contain conflict between the Pashtūns of the south and the Tājīks and other ethnic groups of the north, as is demonstrated by the ethnic splintering of the religious resistance to the Soviet occupation and the largely ethnic character of the prolonged civil war that followed the Soviet withdrawal.[174] Indeed, so far as identity is concerned, were it not for the

[172] Reynolds, *Echoes of empire*, 8–10, 16–18.

[173] Rubin, *Fragmentation of Afghanistan*, xii, 199, and cf. 88. The limits of the service Islamism could render to the Pakistani state are shown by the fact that the Ṭālibān regime—Pakistani clients and Islamists, but Pashtūns nonetheless—refused to recognize the relevant stretch of the border or to abandon irredentist claims on Pakistani territory (Rashid, *Taliban*, 187).

[174] The parallel trajectories of the Communists and Islamists are instructive. The principal Communist organization split into two factions, Khalq and Parcham, in 1967 (Rubin, *Fragmentation of Afghanistan*, 82), and the Islamist organization split into Ḥikmatyār's Ḥizb-i Islāmī and Rabbānī's Jamʿīyat-i Islāmī in 1975 (83). Pashto—the language of the Pashtūns—was the main language within Khalq and the Ḥizb, as was Persian—the language of the northerners—within Parcham and the Jamʿīyat (93). Thus the Ḥizb was about three-quarters Pashtūn (215), whereas the Jamʿīyat was predominantly Tājīk and the main voice of non-Pashtūns (218; see also 213, 219, 234). Significantly, some anti-

peculiarly septic quality of relations between the Shīʿite Hazāras and the Pashtūn Ṭālibān—and the role of Wahhābī Arabs in the massacre of Hazāras[175]—we might be tempted to think of Islam as but a ripple on the surface of the ethnic politics of the country. Likewise ethnic tension between Bengalis and Punjabis led to the secession of the eastern wing of the original Pakistan, and tensions between Punjabis and other ethnic groups have seriously disrupted the politics of what had been the western wing; Pakistan is a particularly telling case inasmuch as the point of the creation of the country was to provide a haven for Muslim political identity. Of course, in any given case we can doubtless find other factors working toward the same outcome. In the Afghan case, for example, it is clearly relevant that a united resistance to the Soviets would not have suited the Pakistanis,[176] while in the Bengali case the continuation of the *status quo* would not have suited the Indians. But to dwell on such factors in every case would amount to special pleading. Even the global jihadi camaraderie of al-Qāʿida is undermined by ethnic tensions. A Sudanese defector describing conditions in Peshawar in somewhat ungrammatical English had this to say: "We have people from Nigeria, from Tunisia, from Siberia, why is Egyptian people got more chance than other people run everything?"[177]

Yet, in a nasty world our failure to find Muslim solidarity playing an effective unifying role in the face of ethnic divisions should not discourage us from considering the reverse effect: the power of Muslim identity in religiously divided countries to disrupt what might otherwise be reasonably cohesive ethnic communities. Ethnic groups divided between Muslims and non-Muslims have shown a marked tendency to splinter under pressure. Obvious examples are the partition of the Punjab and Bengal as the British were leaving India and the eruption of civil war in Lebanon. Another case in point is that of the Bosnians. This is a population with a secularized, European middle class for whom an Islamist

---

Pashtūn Tājīk leftists ("Maoists") joined the Jamʿīyat (219; and cf. 82, 101). After the Soviet Union broke up in 1991, Khalqī units joined Ḥikmatyār and became the backbone of his military forces (265). In 1992, as the northerners closed in on Kābul, Khalqīs cooperated with the Ḥizb, and not for the first time (271; cf. also 149, 151, 152). Thus the feud between Khalq and Parcham, and that between the Ḥizb and the Jamʿīyat, came together and took on the character of a battle between Pashtūns and non-Pashtūns for control of Afghanistan (272).

175 Rashid, *Taliban*, 58–59, 62–63, 64, 73–76, 83, 139.

176 Rubin, *Fragmentation of Afghanistan*, 181, 198–99.

177 Gerges, *Far enemy*, 104; see also 64, 141. For ethnic tensions between Arab and other jihadis in Afghanistan, see V. Brown et al., *Cracks*, 8.

attempt to suppress Father Christmas was ludicrous,[178] a population that preferred helpful Iranian Shīʿites to cantankerous Arab militants belonging to its own Sunnī confession.[179] Yet the Muslim identity of the Bosnians has rendered them as distinct from Serbs and Croats as the latter are from each other—for all that they speak the same language and share many vernacular traditions and however much the middle-class population of Sarajevo might have preferred otherwise.[180] In the Palestinian context the increasing salience of Muslim identity carries the implication that Palestinian Christians do not belong to the political community, and the Ḥamās charter seems to agree: it promises Islamic toleration to non-Muslims who are not hostile to the movement,[181] but it provides no place for specifically Palestinian Christians within it.[182] In such contexts as these Islamic identity clearly does make a significant difference in the real world, and one has the definite impression across the globe that it makes more difference than adherence to Christianity or Buddhism. But this is not an iron law: there are exceptions, Albania being a particularly striking case.[183]

[178] Kepel, *Jihad*, 253.

[179] Ibid., 239, 247, 249–51.

[180] Ibid., 245.

[181] Articles 31 and 36, in Mishal and Sela, *Palestinian Hamas*, 195, 199.

[182] For a less authoritative Ḥamās document categorizing the Christians of Palestine as "an inseparable part of the Palestinian people," see Hroub, *Hamas*, 135–36, and for the view of some Ḥamās leaders that there is no reason in principle why Christians should not join the movement, see 139. But Hroub stresses "the inability of Hamas to get beyond a certain point in Christian-Muslim relations in practice."

[183] The population of Albania is about 70 percent Muslim and about 30 percent Christian; historically the Muslims were divided between Sunnīs and Bektāshīs, and the Christians remain divided between Catholics and Orthodox. Given the disastrous condition of Albania when Communist rule came to an end in the early 1990s, the weakness of the state, and the toxic mix of Muslim and Christian missionaries who proceeded to descend on the country, no one would have been surprised if religious differences had become a major axis of political turmoil. As of this writing, this has yet to happen; the pyramid banking crisis of 1997 posed a far more serious threat to the body politic than religious tension has done. Two authors of a study of Albania published in the later 1990s devoted a chapter to the revival of religion (Vickers and Pettifer, *Albania*, chap. 6). But when they published a new study a decade later, they did not bother with such a chapter, remarking that "to date religion has been a moderate and sensible aspect of Albanian and Kosovar life and has not entered the political arena as a determinant factor" (Pettifer and Vickers, *Albanian question*, xxii). Similarly the author of a recent study of the origins of Albanian nationalism says of the present: "le discours dominant du nationalisme albanais, ou des nationalismes albanais, reste a-confessionnel" (Clayer, *Aux origines*, 721). A noteworthy and perhaps significant detail is that when the revival of religion began, Muslims and Christians helped each other to restore mosques and churches (Vickers and Pettifer, *Albania*, 99–100, and cf. 109–10 on the Papal visit of 1993). The roots of the robust sense

A similar power to disrupt ethnic communities attaches to sectarian divisions within Islam since these represent latent or manifest breaks in Muslim solidarity. The most obvious example is the tense relations that often obtain between Imāmī Shīʿite and Sunnī communities. Thus there is a Shīʿite problem in Pakistan[184] and in several Arab countries[185]—except that in the context of the Arab population of Iraq since the American invasion, we should perhaps speak rather of a Sunnī problem, and a highly septic one. In itself, of course, this is no more an exclusively Islamic phenomenon than ethnic conflict: a contemporary European example involving a Christian sectarian division would be the antagonism between Catholics and Protestants in Northern Ireland. But in the world today the phenomenon is disproportionately Islamic. Sectarian divisions that are more or less politically quiescent do exist in the Islamic world, as in the case of Ibāḍīs and Sunnīs in Oman. But such political quiescence is far more common outside the Islamic world, as for example between Śaivas and Vaiṣṇavas in India and between Catholics and Protestants in Latin America. In this context nationalism is clearly a more benign form of political identity than Islam: at least in principle sectarian divisions should not matter in a national context, whereas they can hardly fail to matter in a religious one.

So far we have considered populations of two kinds: those who are brothers in religion but not in ethnicity and those who are brothers in ethnicity but not in religion. This leaves us to consider those who are brothers in both or neither, though we will find such cases less illuminating. A good example of a country whose citizens are overwhelmingly brothers in both is Tunisia, where the minority Ibāḍī and Berber populations are very small. In such a society we might expect Muslim

---

of Albanian ethnicity go back at least to the involvement of the different religious communities in the emergence of Albanian nationalism in the later nineteenth century (see, for example, Clayer, *Aux origines*, 272), but we should probably also give some credit to the Communist dictator Enver Hoxha for his decision to abolish religion in 1967. All in all, the optimistic judgment of E. A. Freeman in 1877 remains valid: "If Albania is among the most backward parts of the peninsula, still it is, by all accounts, the part where there is most hope of men of different religions joining together against the common enemy" ("Race and language," 216).

[184] See Zaman, *Ulama*, chap. 5. Pakistan is not, of course, an ethnically homogeneous society, but there is no clear ethnic dimension to this sectarian conflict (I am indebted to Qasim Zaman for clarifying this point). I leave aside the Hazāras of central Afghanistan precisely because they are distinguished from the traditionally dominant Pashtūns by their ethnic identity as well as their Shīʿism.

[185] See Nakash, *Reaching for power*, for the cases of Lebanon, Iraq, Saudi Arabia, and Bahrain.

solidarity to play a benign role in holding the country together, and the record of recent Tunisian history is certainly compatible with this expectation. But the strength of the effect is hard to gauge, and there is always the case of Somalia. Turning to countries whose citizens are brothers in neither, cases where religious and ethnic divisions coincide are legion, and here we would expect Muslim solidarity to enhance the disruptive force of the ethnic factor. There is indeed evidence that this is so, but it mostly turns on overall quantitative effects that cannot adequately be reviewed here. The discussion goes back to the incidental but much-criticized remark of a political scientist in 1993 that "Islam has bloody borders."[186] Three years later he came back with quantitative evidence in support of his observation,[187] and more elaborate quantitative studies that reject his wider thinking nevertheless afford him a degree of corroboration on this particular issue.[188] At the same time some of his particular instances are arresting: thus he points out that the ethnic

[186] Huntington, "Clash of civilizations," 35; for the criticism that this led to, see Huntington, *Clash of civilizations*, 258, in the footnote. One has, of course, to allow for the fact that the Islamic world has particularly long borders by virtue of its geographical location; as Huntington remarks, "Muslim and non-Muslim expansion by land . . . resulted in Muslims and non-Muslims living in close physical proximity throughout Eurasia" (263); he could have added much of Africa.

[187] Huntington, *Clash*, 255–58. The evidence relates only to the years 1992–1994, but so far as it goes it is quite telling.

[188] One such study is Fox, "Is Islam more conflict prone?" By "ethnoreligious conflict" Fox means "conflict between two ethnic groups who happen to be of different religions" (17). His conclusion is that "the actual level of conflict, as measured by rebellion, protest and mobilization for rebellion and protest, does not vary greatly between types of ethnoreligious minorities" (15), so that the evidence does not support the view that "Islamic ethnoreligious groups are particularly violent" (16). However, he finds that Islamic minorities engage in more violence than Christian minorities and remarks that closer examination of the data shows that "Islamic groups appear disproportionately at the highest levels of both protest and rebellion" (16). He also finds that "religion tends to be a more important issue in conflicts involving Islamic groups"; thus "the more Islamic groups are involved in an ethnoreligious conflict the more important religion is to that conflict, and the more Christian groups are involved the less important religion is" (15). It fits with this that "Islamic majority groups engage in more than double the average level of religious discrimination as non-Islamic groups and nearly five times the average level of Christian majority groups" (11). Another such study by the same author is Fox, "Two civilizations." Here he finds that, in the period 1990–1998, there was a Muslim party in two-thirds of those ethnic conflicts within states that on Huntington's criteria would rate as civilizational (464 Table 1; for what counts as a civilizational conflict, see 462–63). He observes: "That the majority of civilizational ethnic conflicts involve Islamic groups, and the majority of ethnic conflicts involving Islamic groups are civilizational, lends support to Huntington's thesis that Islam is one of the greatest participants in civilizational conflicts" (463). Fox is by and large a critic of Huntington's thesis of the clash of civilizations.

Chinese presence has not been problematic in Buddhist Thailand or the Catholic Philippines but has led to violence in Muslim Indonesia and Malaysia.[189]

In sum, our findings with regard to the interaction between religious and ethnic identity suggest that Muslim solidarity cannot override ethnic division, but that it can easily disrupt ethnic unity (as can sectarian divisions within Islam) and that it tends to reinforce ethnic conflicts where it is aligned with them. The negative effects of this are often remarked on in impressionistic ways. Thus the political scientist quoted above observes that "Confucians, Buddhists, Hindus, Western Christians, and Orthodox Christians have less difficulty adapting to and living with each other than any one of them has in adapting to and living with Muslims."[190] He also quotes an anonymous statesman remarking, with reference to the mixed population of his own country, on the "indigestibility" of Muslims.[191] In a more polemical vein a Hindu nationalist ascetic and propagandist complains that Muslims tend to be like a lemon in the milk rather than to live with Hindus like milk and sugar.[192] Whatever one's taste in simile, and whatever the degree of exaggeration in these observations, they are backhanded compliments to a Muslim solidarity that has remained real enough to matter.

What did this mean for the prospects of nationalism in the Islamic world? Given the wide adoption of the nationalist paradigm outside the West from the later nineteenth century onwards, we might have expected the Islamic world to conform to the standard global pattern. And to a considerable extent it did, at least until the last third of the twentieth century. Turkey developed a nationalism that appealed to the pre-Islamic past of the Turks—though adopting the Hittites rather than the Trojans as their preferred local ancestors. Iran followed suit. Both sidelined Islam, though neither, of course, went so far as to abandon it.[193] Arab nationalism, for reasons analyzed above, had a less discordant relationship with Islam,[194] but it was still emphatically a form of nationalism—quite apart from the fact that it achieved its first political success by collaborating with the Christian British against the Muslim

[189] Huntington, *Clash,* 264.

[190] Ibid.

[191] Ibid.

[192] Kakar, *Colors of violence,* 159.

[193] For the rare example of those Javanese who decided that their loyalty to traditional Javanese culture outweighed their allegiance to Islam, see Hefner, "Faith and commitment" 108–9.

[194] See 9–10.

Ottomans in the First World War. The major exception to this pattern was the Muslim population of British India, among whom a separatism based on religious affiliation was to lead in 1947 to the partition of the subcontinent on religious, not ethnic lines. But this unusual development had a great deal to do with the minority predicament of Indian Muslims, a predicament that already in the later nineteenth century was articulated through a degree of sympathy and support for the Ottoman Empire in its travails that was unique in the Muslim world.[195] And even in India it was only quite late in the day that religious separatism swept the board. Thus leaving the Indian exception aside, it might have been possible in this period to dismiss Muslim political identity as an archaic residue of an earlier epoch, a lingering sentiment without a future. And yet it would have been less than perceptive to leave the Indian exception aside. If we ask why the Indian Muslims were the kind of religious minority that would seek a state of their own, we come up against the fact that Muslim separatism, however belated its triumph, had deep roots, and not just local ones.[196] Jinnah would seem to have been pretty much correct in his claim that "it is a dream that the Hindus and Muslims can ever evolve a common nationality."[197] Moreover, the fact that Indian Muslims were a minority could be said to have made manifest something that was in fact present but obscured elsewhere in the Muslim world. At an elite level the Turkish war of independence of 1919–1922 and the Algerian war of independence of 1954–1962 tended to be seen as nationalist movements that delivered the Turkish and Algerian nations from their ethnically foreign enemies. But it was no secret that at a more popular level both were perceived as conflicts pitting Muslims against unbelievers—indeed in the Turkish

[195] For the response of Indian Muslims to the Ottoman-Russian war of 1877-1878, see Özcan, *Pan-Islamism*, 64–78, especially 76–77. No less strong were their reactions to the Italian invasion of Libya in 1911, the Balkan wars of 1912–1913, and above all the threat to the Ottoman caliphate following the defeat of the empire in the First World War (138–45, 147–50, 189–91). As one speaker put it in 1911, according to the Koran "all Muslims are brethren," and therefore "Muslims should unite and help Turkey in every possible way" (140). The limits of this response are, however, shown by the lack of a strong reaction among Indian Muslims to the First World War itself, despite their unhappiness with it (179–83).

[196] Francis Robinson has argued rather convincingly that Muslim separatism had such roots in the Islamic tradition and in the character assumed by this tradition in India, implying that an unfractured Indian nationalism was an inherently unlikely outcome irrespective of the actions of the British and the Hindus (see Robinson, "Islam and Muslim separatism").

[197] Robinson, "Congress and Muslims," 212.

case Muṣṭafā Kemāl Pasha himself initially worked hard to appeal to this perception through an exaggeratedly Islamic choreography.[198] One could thus argue that what made the Indian case different was simply the fact that the Muslim elite of the subcontinent had adopted a perspective that was elsewhere the popular way of seeing things. Yet, even if all this is so, it would still have made little sense before the later twentieth century to see Muslim solidarity as a force that could challenge the credentials of nationalism across the Islamic world.

Since then the balance of ideological plausibility has shifted. It is not that the forces that made the nation state seem like the natural order of things have simply gone away. But in the Muslim context the Islamic revival has wrong-footed them. To a significant extent appeals to Muslim brotherhood can now be used to trump nationalism, and Islam can be marketed as a political identity sufficient in itself. The pioneer Islamist thinkers of the mid-twentieth century already took strong stands against the new nationalisms of their day.[199] Thus the Indian—later Pakistani—Abū ʾl-Aʿlā Mawdūdī (d. 1979) lamented that the Muslims had adopted "the non-believers' cult of nationalism" and had torn to pieces their "precious mantle of international brotherhood."[200] For him the rise among Muslims of a sense of Turkish, Indian, Afghan, or Arab nationalism (*qawmiyya*) could only lead to the death of the sense of "Islamic nationalism" (*al-qawmiyya al-Islāmiyya*).[201] It is, of course, an eloquent testimony to the tide he was swimming against at the time that he should appropriate rather than reject the Western term "nationalism."[202] Meanwhile the Egyptian Sayyid Quṭb (d. 1966),

[198] For this phase see Hanioğlu, *Atatürk*, 102–5.

[199] For brief surveys, see Sivan, *Radical Islam*, 38–40, and Kepel, *Jihad*, 24–26.

[200] Maududi, *Unity*, 26, and more generally 24–28. For this work see Ahmad and Ansari, *Mawlānā Mawdūdī*, 36 no. 62. Ahmad and Ansari provide a useful numbered list of Mawdūdī's many works, often with dates of first publication (33–40); where I have been able to identify a work in their list, I normally give its number and the date of the original publication if provided by them. Since most of these works were orginally written in Urdu, which I do not read, I am usually dependant on English or Arabic translations (or both). Note that in citing Mawdūdī's works I give his name as it appears on the title page of the work in question.

[201] Mawdūdī, *Bayn al-daʿwa al-qawmiyya*, 72.6, and see also 68.2. In the same way he warned that if "the religious spirit" were to cool down, it would be impossible to stop the growth of Bengali nationalism in East Pakistan and something similar would happen in West Pakistan (Maudūdī, "Problem of electorate," 331; this was in 1955, see 323). He likewise emphasizes that the Prophet was not an Arab nationalist (Mawdūdī, *Minhāj al-inqilāb al-Islāmī*, 64.7; this is a talk given in 1940, see 5.2).

[202] Mawdūdī took the view that it was the Prophet himself who brought Islamic nationalism into being (*Bayn al-daʿwa al-qawmiyya*, 38.14).

who was initially quite sympathetic to Arab national sentiment within a wider Islamic framework,[203] came to insist that a Muslim has no fatherland but that in which God's law is implemented, just as he has no nationality (*jinsiyya*) other than his creed, by virtue of which he is a member of the Muslim community (*al-umma al-Muslima*);[204] he warns against the hidden polytheism of devotion to a land, a nation (*jins*), or a people (*qawm*).[205] He too thinks in terms of Islamic "nationality" (*jinsiyya*).[206] Likewise the Syrian Saʿīd Ḥawwā (d. 1989), in a purple passage lamenting the retreat of Islam from life, bemoans the fact that the concept of the Muslim community (*al-umma*) has given way to that of nationalism (*qawmiyya*).[207] Meanwhile the Indian Abū ʾl-Ḥasan Nadwī (d. 1999) fears that Arab nationalism (*al-qawmiyya al-ʿArabiyya*) is becoming a religion in itself and a rival of Islam;[208] as one

[203] For this sympathy—and his later abandonment of it—see Sivan, *Radical Islam*, 30–32 (the philo-Arab passage translated by Sivan may also be found in Quṭb, *Dirāsāt Islāmiyya*, 166.10; this volume is a collection of previously published articles); see further Carré, *Mysticism and politics*, 155–56. This way of thinking is close to that of Ḥasan al-Bannā (d. 1949) (see, for example, *Majmūʿat rasāʾil*, 280.18, 281.11, 281.21, 283.17, 284.6, and the discussion in Mitchell, *Society of Muslim Brothers*, 264–69). In a work apparently dating from the 1960s, Quṭb still assigns to Islam the credit for the survival of the Arabs as a people down the centuries, with the clear implication that this survival was a good thing (Quṭb, *Mustaqbal*, 110.16 = Sayyid Qutb, *Islam: religion of the future*, 81–82). For the date of this work, see Moussalli, *Radical Islamic fundamentalism*, 49 no. 22; Moussalli gives a list of Quṭb's religious works (46–55, with descriptions of twenty-four works, including the date of first publication where known).

[204] Quṭb, *Maʿālim*, 138.9 = Kutb, *Milestones*, 118–19; and see 144.14 = 124, 145.16 = 125. Sivan translates parts of this discussion in his *Radical Islam*, 31, attributing to Quṭb the aphorism "Islam is the only identity worthy of man"; Quṭb does not exactly say this (cf. *Maʿālim*, 145.17 = 125), but it catches his drift.

[205] Quṭb, *Maʿālim*, 146.25 = 126; similarly Quṭb, *Fiqh al-daʿwa*, 49.16 (where even Arab nationalism is condemned as an idol), and cf. 52.6. For Quṭb's negative view of nationalism cf. also Quṭb, *ʿAdāla*, 90.23 = Shepard, *Sayyid Qutb*, 107 (I identify the Arabic text I am using as the first edition, that of 1949, since its readings at 26.22, 26.23, and 27.21 fit the information about that edition given by Shepard in the footnotes to his translation, 31nn67–68 and 32n73); Quṭb, *al-Salām al-ʿālamī*, 133.6 = Sayyid Qutb, *Islam and universal peace*, 73.

[206] Quṭb, *Hādhā ʾl-dīn*, 85.9 = Qutb, *Islam—true religion*, 86; this work was first published in 1962 (Moussalli, *Radical Islamic fundamentalism*, 49 no. 21).

[207] Ḥawwā, *Jund Allāh thaqāfatan*, 12.3, translated in Sivan, *Radical Islam*, 45; for Ḥawwā's disparaging references to nationalism, see also *Jund Allāh thaqāfatan*, 16.6, 230.10, 249.13. Compare the Islamist complaint that school textbooks speak of "Arabs" not "Muslims," blame the Turks, and ignore Ottoman achievements (Sivan, *Radical Islam*, 8–9).

[208] Nadwī, *al-ʿArab waʾl-Islām*, 10.9, 11.9, 15.1 (blaming the Christian Arabs), and cf. 13.3 (speaking of "the echo of irreligious Western nationalism"); see further Zaman, *Ulama*, 162–65, where the whole passage is discussed.

scholar puts it, Nadwī regards it as ultimately a Western plot to divide Muslims and blunt the force of their Islamic consciousness.[209] It is noteworthy that such Islamists are prepared to condemn Arab nationalism, whose central historical myth is nothing else than the rise of Islam, in the same breath as they dismiss the un-Islamic national myths of non-Arab peoples like the Turks. This kind of thinking remains very much alive in Islamist circles; as a Turkish Islamist put it in 2002, "people who belong to the same religion should not form two different nations, just as people who become a nation should not belong to different religions."[210] At the same time it has wider resonance among Muslim populations at large. Over a large part of the Third World today, nationalism may be somewhat the worse for wear, and it has undoubtedly been battered by the forces of globalization; but only in the Islamic world has it been pushed into an ideological corner.[211]

This is not to say that Muslim solidarity has achieved wide success in displacing nationalism in the various countries of the Muslim world—or is likely to. One reason for this is simply that nationalism still fits better with the modern world because most Islamist causes play out in particular national contexts. Consider the stance taken by the Palestinian Ḥamās, an off-shoot of the Muslim Brothers, in its quarrel with the PLO, whose old-fashioned Palestinian nationalism has a focus on the immediate predicament of the Palestinians that an undifferentiated allegiance to the Islamic community would lack. In rhetorical terms what Ḥamās accordingly does is not to disown this nationalism but to transcend it. According to its charter, other nationalisms—which we can take to include that of the PLO—appeal to material, human, or territorial considerations; that of Ḥamās includes all of these but goes on to add "the more important divine factors." What makes Ḥamās different is thus the fact that its nationalism is "part and parcel of its reli-

[209] Zaman, *Ulama*, 162.

[210] Karasipahi, *Muslims in modern Turkey*, 102. I owe my knowledge of this study to İren Özgür.

[211] One of the rare exceptions to this development in the Sunnī world is Kurdish nationalism, which so far has faced relatively little challenge from Islamists (for Islamist organizations in Iraqi Kurdistan, see Stansfield, "Governing Kurdistan," 196, 212, and cf. 199). Iran, of course, is different, thanks to the fact that its Shīʿite and Iranian heritages adventitiously combine in setting it off from the Islamic world at large (for the often conspicuous ways in which Iranian nationalism continues to inform the thought of the Islamic Republic, see Ansari, *Politics of nationalism*, 203–4, 218–22, 228–30, 232–33, 249, 255–56, 259–60, 269–70, 278–82, and cf. 193).

gious creed."[212] Here the movement has gone well beyond Mawdūdī's appropriation of the term "nationalism" to refer to Islamic solidarity; the political engagement of Ḥamās has led it to adopt a specifically Palestinian nationalism, something Muslims with a more global perspective look askance at.[213] Yet in adapting to the local context in this way, Ḥamās is not out of line with the wider movement it stems from. The Muslim Brothers represent a loose transnational organization made up of largely independent national branches,[214] and a willingness to accommodate an Egyptian or Arab nationalism that was not religiously subversive goes back to the first decades of the movement.[215]

Another reason for the persistence of nationalism has to do with incumbency. The mid-twentieth century was the period when the largest number of Muslim societies achieved independence from Western imperial rule, and at that time the heirs of the departing Europeans were almost inevitably nationalists of one kind or another. By the time the Islamists were in a position to seek the leadership of such struggles, with their rich potential for generating political legitimacy, it was for the most part too late. Thus in Algeria the opportunity of the war of independence fell to the nationalists, whereas the Islamists of the 1990s were left with only a civil war to wage—an activity that corrodes legitimacy rather than creating it. Muslim populations still awaiting liberation in the later twentieth century tended in one way or another to be hard if not hopeless cases, as with those of Palestine, Chechnya, or the southern Philippines. To these the intrusions of the superpowers added a couple of badly fragmented societies that came under non-Muslim occupation in the later twentieth or early twenty-first centuries: Afghanistan and Iraq. Such conflicts could achieve an iconic status as Muslim causes and draw jihadis from distant parts of the Islamic world to fight

[212] See Article 12 of the Ḥamās charter, translated in Mishal and Sela, *Palestinian Hamas*, 182. Note also the reference to "the Palestinian people" in Article 13 (183), the statement that "the Palestinian cause is a religious one" in Article 15 (185), the profession of respect and promise of support to other nationalist movements working for the liberation of Palestine in Article 25 (191–92), the explicit extension of this respect to the PLO in Article 27 (192–93), and above all the eclectic affirmation that there are three circles—Palestinian, Arab, and Islamic—to which the liberation of Palestine is bound in Article 14 (184). The charter reflected the determination of Ḥamās to compete with the PLO (43).

[213] For the hostility of al-Qāʿida to the nationalism of Ḥamās, see Paz, "Jihadists and nationalist Islamists," 207, 210, 216–17.

[214] For this characterization, see M. Lynch, "Islam divided," 167.

[215] See Mitchell, *Society of Muslim Brothers*, 264–69.

for populations whose ethnic identities they did not share and whose languages they did not understand—as dramatic a display of Muslim solidarity as one could ask for.[216] Moreover, several of these regions offered wild tribal environments—"areas of chaos," as one jihadi strategist put it—that lent themselves to insurrectionary activity.[217] But none of them provided a venue for a straightforward triumph of Islamism that could convincingly have superseded nationalism; as in the Algerian case, many of them sooner or later became entangled in debilitating civil war.

In sum, Muslim solidarity has not displaced nationalism, but it has established itself as an alternative to it. It has done remarkably well in shifting the moral terms of trade in favor of Islam as a political identity and against the various nationalisms of the Muslim world, thereby putting them on the defensive.[218] It can also have a special appeal within one small but articulate group of Muslims, those who live as a diaspora outside the Islamic world. These qualitative observations find some support from a survey of 2005 that asked Muslims in six mainly Muslim countries whether they saw themselves as citizens of their countries first or as Muslims first. In all but Lebanon more respondents identified primarily as Muslims than as national citizens; those identifying primarily as Muslims were an absolute majority in Pakistan (79 percent), Morocco (70 percent), and Jordan (63 percent).[219] A further survey of 2006 added more Muslim countries and posed comparable questions to some non-Muslim populations. The majority of Muslims identified as such in Egypt (59 percent) and Nigeria (71 percent); the same was true of the Muslim diaspora in Europe except in France, though even here a plurality (46 percent) conformed to the wider Muslim pattern.

[216] A leading expert on the phenomenon writes: "Since 1980 between 10,000 and 30,000 such fighters have inserted themselves into conflicts from Bosnia in the west to the Philippines in the east" (Hegghammer, "Muslim foreign fighters," 53). These fighters have been predominantly but not exclusively Arabs (60). Note the contrast with the much more limited response to the Algerian war of independence (59) and the rarity of analogous non-Muslim phenomena (90). Hegghammer's central argument is that it was the institutionalization of pan-Islamic activism in the Ḥijāz in the 1970s that lay behind the scale of the phenomenon.

[217] For Abū Muṣʿab al-Sūrī's remarks on this subject, see Lia, *Architect of global jihad*, 461, 465.

[218] A report on the resistance to the Asad regime in northwestern Syria in July 2012 mentions homegrown Syrian groups with names like "Free Men of Syria" and "Hawks of Syria" but quotes the leader of such a group who was expanding his council to include jihadis as saying of the latter: "They consider the entire world the Muslim homeland, so they refused any national, Syrian name" (MacFarquhar and Saad, "Jihadists").

[219] See Pew Global Attitudes Project, *Islamic extremism*, 21.

By contrast, in all the five European countries covered, majorities of Christians identified as citizens of their countries first rather than as Christians. This was not the case in the United States, but even here a plurality did so: 48 percent identified as citizens of the country first, and 42 percent as Christians first.[220] It is clear, then, that Muslim identity is politically more salient than Christian identity.

9. Muslim identity and geopolitics

So far we have looked at the ways in which Muslim identity has interacted with ethnicity and nationalism in particular countries; to round off this picture, we should now consider its implications at the international level. To anyone who sees geopolitics in terms of the religious allegiances of the players, the Muslim geopolitical predicament in the modern world is not a very eligible one. Two circumstances combine to make this so. In the first place, though a few Muslim states are rich, most are not, and none has the status of a First-World country. In the second place, there are no Muslim states deriving power from sheer size, no Muslim Russia, China, India, America, or Brazil.[221] In other words, there is no actual or potential great power in today's Islamic world,[222] which thus has a geopolitical configuration very different

[220] See Pew Global Attitudes Project, *Muslims in Europe*, 3–4, 10–11, 27 (my thanks to Juliana Menasce Horowitz for directing me to this survey). Where countries were covered in both 2005 and 2006, the figures for the two years are sometimes different enough to suggest some real instability in attitudes; thus in Pakistan the number identifying as Muslim first rose from 79 percent to 87 percent. But such changes do not affect the overall picture.

[221] Huntington propounds the thesis that each of the civilizations into which he divides the world typically contains a "core state," in other words a large and powerful state around which other countries belonging to the civilization group themselves (*Clash*, 135–36 and chap. 7). Islam, he points out, has lacked such a state since the demise of the Ottoman Empire (135, 155, 177, 264–65).

[222] Iran may well succeed in increasing its power, but it has little chance of achieving great-power status in any foreseeable future. If it acquires nuclear weapons, this will increase its ability to threaten the interests of all outside powers that are dependent on the Persian Gulf for oil and to cause grief to the United States with respect to the security of Israel. But thanks to the simple facts of geography, Iran already has the military capacity to disrupt oil exports from the Persian Gulf, and delivering on nuclear threats would be an act of desperation unlikely to advance its interests. At the same time Iran's limited population (not to mention its poor economic performance) precludes it from developing the conventional military capacity required of a great power; Pakistan possesses nuclear weapons and a population twice the size of Iran's but is unable to deploy effective military power even within its own borders. In the improbable event that Iran

from what it enjoyed in the heyday of ʿAbbāsid or Ottoman rule; even in 1872 it still made a certain sense for the Young Ottoman intellectual Nāmıq Kemāl (d. 1888) to call for some kind of Islamic unity under Ottoman leadership in order to spread civilization in the Muslim world and thereby create a counterweight to Europe.[223] A loose transnational institution like the Organization of the Islamic Conference (OIC), chartered in 1972 and backed by the Saudis, is clearly no substitute for the existence of such a power.[224] Muslim solidarity is thus unlikely to have a transforming impact on the current structures of the international order—certainly nothing remotely comparable to the anticipated geopolitical consequences of the rise of China.

This has not, however, discouraged Islamists from thinking about Muslim solidarity in geopolitical terms. Thus a disciple of Mawdūdī's laments that Muslims "have no effective voice in the world affairs," and have become "passive camp-followers of others"; they suffer in Palestine, Kashmir, Cyprus, Eritrea, Nigeria, and Somalia, but "all these voices of agony and anguish fall on deaf ears."[225] Mawdūdī himself reminds us that the Muslims "command a vast part of the globe, stretching from Indonesia to Morocco and endowed with great man-power and enormous resources"; if this whole bloc were to unite under the banner of Islam and adopt the Islamic way of life, no power would be able to "stand in its way and stop its march on the road to progress."[226] It must, after all, be "squarely stated" that Islam is the only ideology that can "serve as a basis for a world state."[227] In the meantime the Muslims should "join their hands to strengthen their defence" and "try to pool their resources to develop armament industry."[228] Ḥasan al-Bannā

were able to expand its territory to include large new populations, these would mostly be neither Persian-speaking nor Shīʿite, and the likely outcome would be debilitating internal conflict. In demographic terms Indonesia is the largest Muslim country, but its maritime character undermines its capacity to project military power on any scale, should it wish to do so.

[223] B. Lewis, *Emergence of modern Turkey*, 138–39, 335.

[224] For the establishment of the OIC, see Landau, *Politics of Pan-Islam*, 287–89. As Huntington notes, the OIC is unique: outside the Muslim world, there are no interstate organizations with memberships based on religion (*Clash*, 176).

[225] Khurshid Ahmad in his foreword to Maududi, *Unity*, v–vi.

[226] Mawdudi, *Islam today*, 43; for this work see Ahmad and Ansari, *Mawlānā Mawdūdī*, 35 no. 37. For a Pakistani proponent of such a state at the middle of the twentieth century, see W. C. Smith, *Islam in modern history*, 88n69; for an earlier Ottoman pamphlet with the same idea, see Landau, *Politics of Pan-Islam*, 79–80 (Landau dates the pamphlet around 1911, but a more recent author dates it to 1873, see Özcan, *Pan-Islamism*, 37).

[227] Maududi, *Unity*, 16.

[228] Ibid., 39.

(d. 1949), the founder of the Muslim Brothers, identifies two fundamental goals: to liberate the "Islamic fatherland" (*al-waṭan al-Islāmī*) from all foreign domination and to establish a free Islamic state in this free fatherland.[229] This state would presumably be a caliphate, since this institution is the symbol of Islamic unity (*ramz al-waḥda al-Islāmiyya*).[230] Quṭb follows Bannā in speaking of the "Islamic fatherland";[231] he seeks the restoration of its unity and the recovery of its strength.[232] He would like to see the emergence of an Islamic block (*kutla Islāmiyya*) to save the Islamic fatherland from Western imperialism.[233] He extols "Muslim brotherhood" (*al-ukhuwwa al-Islāmiyya*),[234] avers that Islam is a creed that unites the hearts of Muslims all over the world,[235] and shows his concern for persecuted Muslims in Ethiopia, Yugoslavia, Russia, China, and India.[236] Saʿīd Ḥawwā, whom we met above as an antinationalist, starts from the premise that the Muslims have the duty of making the whole world submit to the authority (*sulṭān*) of God. Hence all the prerequisites for bringing this about are obligatory for them—measures such as the unification of the Muslim world, the restoration of the caliphate, and the development of industrial and other resources so that the strength of the Muslim community matches that of the rest of the world.[237] More specifically, he sees it as one of the goals of the "Party of God" (*Ḥizb Allāh*) to unify the Islamic countries (*al-aqṭār al-Islāmiyya*) into a single state (*dawla wāḥida*). As usual there is geopolitical aspiration at work here alongside Muslim pride and nostalgia for the early caliphate: the Muslim community (*al-umma al-Islāmiyya*) is to become "the greatest political, economic, and military power (*quwwa*) in the world."[238] The Ḥizb al-Taḥrīr, in its proposed constitution of 1979 for an Islamic state ruled by a caliph, says of the existing states of the Islamic world that they are considered as if they "all lie within a single

[229] Bannā, *Majmūʿat rasāʾil*, 225.13 = Wendell (trans.), *Five tracts*, 31.

[230] Bannā, *Majmūʿat rasāʾil*, 284.12.

[231] See, for example, Quṭb, *Naḥw mujtamaʿ Islāmī*, 5.2, 131.10 (this book is a collection of articles that were originally published in 1951, see Moussalli, *Radical Islamic fundamentalism*, 53 no. 27).

[232] Quṭb, *Dirāsāt Islāmiyya*, 192.7.

[233] Ibid., 192.3, and see 174.15.

[234] Quṭb, *Naḥw mujtamaʿ Islāmī*, 99.11.

[235] Quṭb, *Dirāsāt Islāmiyya*, 201.13.

[236] Ibid., 221.3.

[237] Ḥawwā, *Jund Allāh thaqāfatan*, 481.12.

[238] Ibid., 48.2, and see 14.13, 43.14. For a similar view advanced by a leader of the militant Sipāh-i Ṣaḥāba in Pakistan, see Zaman, "South Asian Islam," 77.

country" and adds, "Every effort must be made to unite them all in a single state."[239]

Bin Laden was an heir to this worldview. He speaks of "the brotherhood of faith that joins Muslims everywhere from east to west";[240] currently, he laments, the "enormous powers" of the Muslim community are fettered, but he insists that it has been promised victory[241] and that it is "the greatest human power"—or would be if only religion were properly established.[242] What distinguishes him and his followers from his predecessors is that he has taken the vision to the point of violent action. Of course, even within the jihadi movement the number who devote themselves to this truly global level of jihad is small, and because they are so unusual they are a historically contingent phenomenon. Thus we can reasonably see al-Qāʿida as a by-product of the proxy war in which the Americans joined with the Saudis and Pakistanis to make life difficult for the Soviet Union in Afghanistan in the 1980s.[243] But the phenomenon can still tell us something about the contemporary Islamic world. The United States, after all, supported proxy wars in the non-Muslim world that had no such outcome; the Contras, for example, did not come back to haunt those who armed and financed them.[244] Likewise anti-Americanism has been epidemic since at least the end of the Cold War, but it is only in the Islamic world that it has brought into existence what is perhaps the first genuinely international terrorist movement.

Predictably, neither pan-Islamist ideas nor the actions of al-Qāʿida have had any discernible success in reshaping the international order. This does not, of course, render them politically unimportant. For example, the jihadi Abū Muḥammad al-Maqdisī and others could create considerable discomfort for the Saudi regime by condemning it for its alliance with the infidel Americans against fellow Muslims.[245] One factor, moreover, has done something to increase the potential for world-

[239] Taji-Farouki, *Fundamental quest*, 214 Article 185(i). The original version of the article, dating from 1953, includes the qualification that Muslims living in the Domain of Unbelief are aliens (218).

[240] Lawrence, *Messages*, 202.

[241] Ibid., 190.

[242] Ibid., 191. For the geopolitical vision of Ayman al-Ẓawāhirī, see below, 233, 361–62.

[243] The states involved in the conflict did not themselves arm the foreign fighters; see Hegghammer, "Muslim foreign fighters," 62.

[244] Cf. Mamdani, *Good Muslim*, 233–35.

[245] What made this polemic particularly effective in Saudi Arabia was the fact that its authors were able to invoke the views of authoritative Wahhābī scholars of the nineteenth century (see Wagemakers, "Enduring legacy," 99–104; cf. above, 26n111).

wide Muslim solidarity: the development of global communications of a kind that readily transcend particular national contexts and reduce the isolation from the Islamic world of Muslims in the diaspora. Explaining the decision of thousands of young Muslims to enlist in jihad to defend their fellow believers in other parts of the world, one scholar writes that, as never before, "the new media, particularly Arab satellite television stations . . . made Muslims aware of the suffering of one another."[246] The widespread Muslim reaction to the Danish cartoons of Muḥammad published in 2005 is another case in point.[247] But such responses would not have taken place but for an Islamic conductivity that was already there many centuries ago. Modern communications are, after all, at least as widespread in the Buddhist as in the Islamic world, and yet the international outrage provoked by the destruction of the giant Buddhas of Bāmiyān at the hands of the Ṭālibān in 2001 owed more to Western art lovers than to Asian Buddhists. No angry Buddhists poured into the streets to riot, to attack local Muslims, to sack the Pakistani embassy, or to sign up to go and fight against the Ṭālibān.[248]

10. Conclusion

Ethnic identities are, and have always been, political realities in the Islamic world. The rise of Islam itself accentuated one particular ethnic identity, that of the Arabs: Islam was initially their religion, just as

[246] Gerges, *Far enemy*, 299n36, and see 60. This is noteworthy inasmuch as the new media were Arab rather than Islamist (see M. Lynch, *Voices*, 30–36, 83–88).

[247] For a summary of the events, see Cram, "Danish cartoons," 311–13. Note, however, that the globalization of the controversy may not have been inevitable: initially it was largely confined to Denmark, and it can be argued that this changed only as a result of actions taken by Danish Muslim leaders who subsequently had reason to regret this choice and did not repeat it when the cartoons were republished in 2008 (Lindekilde, "Soft repression," 451–52, 459–60, 465).

[248] Reports available on the web indicate that Buddhists in Japan and Thailand responded verbally (see "All we are breaking"), and that a replica of one of the desecrated Buddhas was later carved out of a mountain in Sri Lanka ("Sri Lanka marks anniversary"). But the tone of these reactions was mild in comparison to that of an Indian *Muslim*, Syed Shahabuddin, who denounced the attack on the Buddhas as "an act of cultural genocide against humanity" ("Muslim leaders condemn"; for his earlier role in Muslim efforts to prevent the destruction of the Bābrī Masjid, see Jaffrelot, *Hindu nationalist movement*, 372–73). Likewise it was Muslims, not Buddhists, who had dispatched a delegation to Afghanistan in an attempt to avert the destruction (see R. W. Baker, *Islam without fear*, 78–80, with a summary of the account of a leading Egyptian Islamist journalist who found the Afghan scholars he encountered deplorably backward).

the caliphate was initially their empire, and they never entirely lost their sense of religious and cultural centrality. But the decline of Arab power from the ninth century onwards, and the eventual spread of Islam beyond what had been the frontiers of Arab rule, opened up space for non-Arab ethnic identities within the Islamic fold. Yet such non-Arab identities were likely to find themselves more in tension with Islam than that of the Arabs; even in Iran the *Shāhnāma*, as we have seen, had its enemies, and in the Ottoman context the sense of Turkish ethnicity came to be blurred. There was nevertheless enough ethnic sentiment, Arab and non-Arab, to fuel an emergence of nationalism in the modern Islamic world—an emergence that at first fully conformed to the global pattern. Alongside these ethnic identities, however, there was also a Muslim political identity. It had emerged in a strong form from the crucible of seventh-century state-formation, and its inevitable decay in later centuries did not mean its disappearance; it still made a palpable difference on the eve of modernity. Under modern conditions, despite being wrong-footed by the nationalist paradigm, Muslim identity has proved sufficiently resilient to benefit dramatically from the rapid development of communications, and this enhancement of an old Islamic conductivity has made possible some notable episodes of transnational mobilization. Overall, the result could be described as a standoff between ethnic and religious identity. Ethnic identities still matter, sometimes a lot. Thus Muslim identity has not been able to displace or override them, or to erase national borders, and any pan-Islamic reconstruction of the international order remains a dream; at the same the more moderate trend of Islamist thought is willing to accommodate nationalist sentiments provided they do not take an anti-Islamic turn. But even in this modern guise of nationalism, ethnic identities have not been able to retain the moral high ground—witness the majorities of Muslims identifying first and foremost as Muslims rather than as citizens of their countries.[249] How then does this outcome compare to the Hindu and Latin American cases?

[249] See 46, and cf. also 120.

CHAPTER 2

Hinduism and identity

1. Introduction

Who lives in South Asia? Of the present population of the region, between a quarter and a third are Muslims. They are, of course, very unevenly distributed: while Pakistan is as much as 97 percent Muslim and Bangladesh 83 percent, the census of 2001 showed the Muslims of India as only 13.4 percent.[1] Most of the rest of the population can be described as in some sense Hindu, with the obvious implication that it is mainly to be found in India. In this chapter it is the Hindus, not the Muslims, that are at the center of our attention, and specifically the Hindus of India. But we will not be able to pursue this interest very far without encountering the Muslims of the subcontinent, and together with those of the world at large they will also provide us with a series of contrasts in both the pre-modern and modern settings. In fact a contrast already lurks in my presentation of the current demographic situation. The figures for the proportion of Muslims in the various countries may not be entirely accurate, but they are notably precise, and this reflects the fact that there is not much doubt about who is and is not a Muslim. By contrast, the vagueness of my remarks about the Hindu population has to do with the fact that it is often an open question who is or is not a Hindu, and the ramifications of this fact will occupy us extensively in the course of this chapter.

None of this says anything about ethnicity, where the regional variation is much greater. In the words of a fourteenth-century Sanskrit inscription from Āndhra, the subcontinent is marked by "diversity in language and customs" (*bhāṣā-samācāra-bhidā*) and by division into many distinct "lands" (*deśas*).[2] If we leave aside customs to concentrate on language, we can add that since ancient times India has been divided into two major linguistic zones: the larger north where Indo-Aryan languages

[1] See 94n266.

[2] So the Vilasa Grant of around 1330 (Venkataramanayya and Somasekhara Sarma, "Vilasa grant," 241, 260 lines 10–11; for the dating, see 256). The passage is cited in Chattopadhyaya, *Representing the Other*, 58.

prevail and the smaller south where the Dravidian languages hold sway. The major language of the north, and by far the most widespread in India today, is Hindi, spoken by over 40 percent of the Indian population; in its various forms it extends across the northern plains to form the "Hindi belt," but without reaching the sea on either side. No other language is spoken by as much as 10 percent of Indians; thus Tamil, the Dravidian language spoken by the Tamils in the south east, is spoken by a little less than 6 percent.[3] Just how far such linguistic differences are markers of ethnic differences is a question we can leave open; that they are so to at least some extent is clear.

2. The weakness of pre-modern ethnic and Hindu identity

As in the Islamic case, we begin by looking at Indian ethnic and religious identities in pre-modern times, that is to say, before the colonial period.

As far as ethnic identity is concerned, we can best begin with an exception. Among the peoples speaking Dravidian languages, it is the Tamils who preserve the most ancient literary heritage; it includes an epic that may date from the fifth century and was the object of a medieval commentarial tradition.[4] This epic provides a vivid articulation of an ethnic pride directed against the Aryans of the north, and there is even a passing mention, not pursued, of the idea of "imposing Tamil rule over the entire world."[5] But the quarrel with the north is very clearly ethnic, not civilizational. Thus the Aryans and their kings are not demonized, just soundly thrashed by the Tamil king and his brave Tamil warriors, whose valor the northerners had been foolish enough to doubt;[6] those who "had hurled insults at the Tamil kings, now bit the dust" and the army of the "northern Āryas" was routed.[7] Likewise it is northern power, not northern culture that is rejected: on his triumphal expedition to the north, the Tamil king promises his support to "all

[3] Data from the census of 2001, http://censusindia.gov.in/Census_Data_2001/Census_Data_Online/Language/Statement6.htm.

[4] Parthasarathy, *Cilappatikāram*; see Zvelebil, *Tamil literature*, 114. The poem survives in at least twenty-five manuscripts.

[5] Parthasarathy, *Cilappatikāram*, 225.

[6] Ibid., 225, 233–36, 238, 253–54, 258.

[7] Ibid., 207, 236.

those in the northern country who honor the Vedas."[8] We thus find ourselves in a familiar setting, quite comparable to the ethnic rivalries that existed to a greater or lesser extent among both Muslim and Christian populations in pre-modern times.

This epic, however, is highly exceptional. It is not typical of Tamil literature, and it seems to be without parallel in the vernacular literatures of the other peoples of traditional India, whether in the south or the north. As the author of a recent study of the emergence of vernacular literatures in medieval India puts it, nowhere in the pre-modern vernacular texts that modern scholars have read to date is it "possible to point to a discourse that links language, identity, and polity; in other words, nowhere does ethnicity . . . find even faint expression."[9] He goes on to draw an explicit contrast with medieval Europe: "narratives of ethnicity and histories of ethnic origins of the sort that obsessed late-medieval Europe did not exist in any form in South Asia before the modern period."[10] The contrast with the medieval Islamic world would be less drastic but still real. Why traditional Indian ethnic identities should have been so weak is a good question. Just as in the Islamic case, we have to do with a religious tradition associated with a core ethnicity, in this case that of the Aryans; as we saw, in the Tamil epic the Aryans appear as the ethnic group against whom the Tamils do battle. Yet the resulting tensions in the Indian case manifest themselves as social rather than ethnic—a point that will occupy us at some length in this chapter. As this may suggest, a large part of the explanation for the weakness of Indian ethnic identities is very likely to be found in the strength of the caste system;[11] but fortunately we need not pursue the question further.

We turn then to religious identity, which will require a more extensive treatment than its ethnic counterpart. But to anticipate, our main finding will be that Hindu identity too is in significant ways weak. Let us start with words; they are not everything, but they can sometimes be very revealing.

[8] Ibid., 237.

[9] Pollock, *Language of gods*, 475.

[10] Ibid., 476, and more generally 468–77, of the section on "European particularism and Indian difference." He notes the contrast between the way things were seen in India and the epigram of a tenth-century Christian poet that "a language makes a people" (474)—an epigram that, as we have seen, would definitely have meant something to Ibn Taymiyya (see above, 15).

[11] Cf. ibid., 475–76: "No doubt social forces such as caste endogamy . . . worked against integrative ethnicity."

The terms "Hindu" and "Hinduism" are a case in point. Unlike "Muslim" and "Islam," they are foreign, not native words. The people we call "Hindus" did not begin to apply the term to themselves until they learned the usage from others, specifically from Muslims.[12] Thus we find "Hindu" as a self-appelation in vernacular texts composed by Hindus of the sixteenth to eighteenth centuries in Rajasthan,[13] Bengal,[14] and Maharashtra;[15] and these texts also refer occasionally to *Hindudharm*, "Hindu religion," or as we would say Hinduism.[16] Further south, a Hindu ruler had adopted the title "Sultan among Hindu kings" (*hindurāya suratrāṇa*) as early as 1352; his successors were still using the title in 1551.[17] The wholesale adoption of the terms "Hindu" and "Hinduism" in English as written and spoken under British rule was thus to be expected and need not point to dependence on Muslim informants. That the usage was foreign might not have meant much if the imported terms had merely taken the place of native ones serving the same function; but in fact this was not the case, for the foreign terms represented foreign concepts. Such borrowings can, of course, become fully domesticated, given time and the right conditions; it would be foolish to infer

[12] For evidence that this process was already well advanced by the time the British arrived in India, see Lorenzen, "Who invented Hinduism?," 648–53.

[13] The word appears several times in various spellings in the hagiographical poem *Kabīr parcaī* of the Rāmānandī ascetic Anantadās (fl. around 1588). See Lorenzen, *Kabir legends*, 166 (7.2 = 107), 167 (7.5 = 107), 170 (7.14 = 109), 171 (7.15 = 109), 205 (13.3 = 125). For occurrences of the term in the earliest manuscript (dating from 1636), see 230 (80), 231 (85), 233 (92), 251 (182). See also Callewaert, *Hagiographies of Anantadās*, 73 (7.1), 74 (7.4), 76 (7.14), 93 (13.3). For the date, affiliation, and location of Anantadās, see 1, 31–32; for the manuscript of 1636, see 23. Cf. Vaudeville, *Weaver named Kabir*, 152, 154, 227, 233, 240, for the term "Hindu" in translations of the poetry of Kabīr himself. See also Lorenzen, "Who invented Hinduism?," 649–51, for the use of the term "Hindu" by both poets.

[14] O'Connell, "Word 'Hindu'," 340–44, cited in Jaffrelot, *Hindu nationalist movement*, 4.

[15] Wagle, "Hindu-Muslim interactions," 139–41 (quoting from a sixteenth-century Hindu text from Maharashtra describing a Hindu-Muslim debate, for which see also Lorenzen, "Who invented Hinduism?," 648–49); Wagle and Kulkarni, *Vallabha's Paraśarāma Caritra*, 2.49 (33 = 155–56), 3.10 (60 = 40), 4.34 (46 = 73), 4.45 (47 = 74–75; this work dates from the late eighteenth century, see 2). Cf. also Raeside, *Decade of Panipat*, 39, 53, 72, 95, 98 (translating a chronicle probably dating from the late eighteenth century, see xi), 125 (translating a letter of 1757); Gordon, "Maratha patronage," 334 ("Hindu" in a Marāṭhā documentary context, 1760).

[16] O'Connell, "The word 'Hindu,'" 342b, 344a; Wagle and Kulkarni, *Vallabha's Paraśarāma Caritra*, 3.26 (41 = 63); also Laine, *Shivaji*, 51; and cf. Raeside, *Decade of Panipat*, 53, 72, 98.

[17] Wagoner, "Sultan among Hindu Kings," 861–63 (drawn to my attention by Sanjay Subrahmanyam).

from etymology that there can be no authentic Hindu identity in India today. Likewise alien etymology has not prevented the Hindu nationalists from coining the term *Hindutva*, combining the borrowed term with an ancient Sanskrit suffix to convey the sense of "Hindu-ness,"[18] or Hindu identity. As might be expected, the Hindu nationalists are not nationalist enough to renounce the loanword in which their identity is vested.

It is nevertheless worth noting here that the foreign origin of the term "Hindu" was to give rise to some discomfort in modern India. One response was to deny this origin: V. D. Sāvarkar (d. 1966), in a classic text of Hindu nationalism, felt obliged to argue on specious philological grounds that the term was not a loanword at all.[19] A more radical response was to reject the term altogether: in 1873 Dayānand Sarasvatī (d. 1883), a radical religious reformer whose name will recur in this study, told his audience in Calcutta that they should discard the label "Hindu" imposed on them by foreigners, and instead call themselves "Aryans."[20] Likewise in 1877 he inspired the establishment in Lahore of the reformist Ārya Samāj, the "Aryan Association"[21]—and not, as one might have expected, the "Hindu Samāj." For unlike "Hindu," "Aryan" is incontrovertibly native, an authentic ethnic and religious term inherited from high antiquity. Yet as early as 1902, Lajpat Rāi (Rāy) (d. 1928), a member of the Ārya Samāj of twenty years standing, was seeking to reinstate the use of the term "Hindu" rather than "Aryan,"[22] and in 1911 the members of the Samāj declared themselves as Hindus to the census takers in the Punjab.[23] If this was the attitude of the Ārya Samāj, the chances of "Aryan" being adopted more widely to articulate a Hindu identity in modern times were slim. What, then, was wrong with the term?

One point that is relevant here is precisely the antiquity of the term "Aryan." It was no longer in current use as an ethnic category, and other things being equal we would expect that in a matter as intimate as identity people would prefer continuity to revival. But the record

[18] "Had not linguistic usage stood in our way then 'Hinduness' would have certainly been a better word than Hinduism as a near parallel to Hindutva" (Savarkar, *Hindutva*, 4; this book was first published in 1923).

[19] Ibid., *Hindutva*, 6–10, and cf. 70–71.

[20] Jordens, *Dayānanda Sarasvatī*, 90. For a Maharashtrian parallel from the same period, see Dalmia, *Nationalization of Hindu traditions*, 35n17.

[21] K. W. Jones, *Arya Dharm*, 37–38.

[22] Ibid., 251; for a short biography, see 332–33.

[23] Jaffrelot, *Hindu nationalist movement*, 18.

does show that when other things are not equal, revived identities can stick. The people we know as Greeks mostly called themselves "Romans" for over a thousand years, yet they abandoned this usage on entering the modern world and instead took to calling themselves by the ancient term "Hellenes."[24] There must have been a time when this neologism (or rather paleologism) struck Greek speakers as formal and affected, but today it is as authentic a part of the language as the number system. If the Greeks could successfully adopt a revived identity on emerging from centuries of foreign rule, then why not the Hindus? Part of the answer is that, as we will see in a later chapter, Dayānand's revival of Aryan identity was part and parcel of a peculiar fundamentalist doctrine that never had more than a marginal impact on modern India at large;[25] the return to antiquity was far more central to the cultural evolution of modern Greece than it was to that of modern India.

A more significant disadvantage of the term "Aryan" was its linkage to a theme that will figure prominently in this study: the caste (*jāti*) system.[26] In its classical articulation the backbone of traditional Indian society consisted of four classes (*varṇas*). Of these, the top three were "twice-born" (*dvija*), namely the Brahmins (typically priests), the Kṣatriyas (typically rulers or soldiers), and the Vaiśyas (typically merchants); by contrast, the Śūdras, who made up the lowest class of the four, were servile. The social system as it actually evolved was far more complex and at the same time varied from region to region. The number of castes was far greater than the number of classes, with each caste being assigned (with or without contestation) to an appropriate class; and beneath the Śūdras emerged the "Untouchables," a large population divided into castes of their own. The total number of castes in India today is reckoned to be a few thousand. The relevant point here is that, according to the standard doctrine of the four classes, only the twice-born were Aryans; thus an ancient legal source uses the term

[24] For these competing identities see Herzfeld, *Ours once more*, 124.

[25] See 404–9.

[26] The nature and history of caste in India have been the subject of much research and controversy. For a survey of both, see S. Bayly, *Caste, society and politics*. Like Bayly, I take it for granted that caste is real (see, for example, 6, 345, 366), and that it is ancient (see, for example, 13, 25, 366). She also argues throughout the book that in recent centuries caste has become much more salient and widespread in Indian society, and she dates the beginning of this change to the late pre-colonial period (see, for example, 25, 196, 368–69). Though this view may be correct, and is to an extent historically plausible, the book does not present evidence that would unambiguously support it.

anārya, "non-Aryan," in the sense of Śūdra.[27] This meant that much of the population—in all likelihood most of it at most times and places—was traditionally precluded from assuming an Aryan identity.[28]

Like the foreign origin of the term "Hindu," this caste-bound character of the term "Aryan" was to be a cause of some embarrassment in modern India. It would not have bothered Śraddhā Rām (d. 1881), a conservative *paṇḍit* of the Punjab who felt comfortable speaking of Hinduism as the "religion of the twice-born" (*dvijadharma*).[29] But his contemporary Dayānand seems to have thought very differently. The Aryans, he said, had already divided themselves into the *four* classes in the Tibetan homeland of mankind and then migrated to northern India, where there was no pre-Aryan population;[30] that implies that Śūdras are as Aryan as the twice-born.[31] However, this more inclusive conception does not seem to have carried much conviction. Thus among the twentieth-century Yādavs, a Śūdra caste significantly influenced by the Ārya Samāj, the claim to be Aryan was closely linked with pretensions to Kṣatriya status.[32] As a rallying point for the Hindu masses, "Aryan" was an unpromising identity.

Yet even the borrowed term "Hindu" could lose its apparent inclusiveness when adopted in the native social context: though it was readily used to embrace Śūdras, there was a tendency to exclude Untouchables from its scope. Until it became politically desirable for Hindus to maximize the size of their population, this exclusion was a problem for British census officials. As one of them noted in 1881, "Many of the more bigoted high caste Hindoos employed as census enumerators or supervisors objected to record such low persons as of the Hindoo religion."[33] Moreover, the Untouchables themselves have shown a tendency to reserve the term "Hindu" for the castes above them.[34] In 1962 an Untouchable politician belonging to the Camār caste, which

[27] Kane, *History of Dharmaśāstra*, 2:35.

[28] Contrast the situation among a religious community that preserved a comparably ancient ethnic identity: all Jews are Israelites.

[29] K. W. Jones, "Two *sanātan dharma* leaders," 231.

[30] Jordens, *Dayānanda Sarasvatī*, 254.

[31] For a second-generation member of the Ārya Samāj who likewise considered Śūdras to be Aryans, see Jaffrelot, *Hindu nationalism*, 52.

[32] Jaffrelot, *India's silent revolution*, 187–89, 192–96.

[33] Mendelsohn and Vicziany, *Untouchables*, 27–28.

[34] U. Sharma, *Caste*, 51, citing Searle-Chatterjee, "Caste, religion," 161; also Searle-Chatterjee, "Urban 'untouchables,' " 17 (the fieldwork relates to Benares, see 14).

had taken to calling itself Jātav, campaigned in the ʿAlīgaṛh district of Uttar Pradesh with the slogan "Jātavs and Muslims are brothers, where do the Hindu people (*Hindu qaum*) come from?"[35] The Camārs, then, were no more Hindus than the Muslims. As we will see, some of them, including the politician in question, had recently converted to Buddhism;[36] but Camār use of the phrase "Hindu people" to refer to higher-caste Hindus went back at least to the 1920s.[37]

The corollary of this lack of a traditional native concept doing the work of the borrowed term "Hindu" is the absence of a clear-cut concept of the non-Hindu. In place of a dichotomy we find something more graded. Roughly speaking, the Brahmins are on the inside track, followed by the Kṣatriyas, followed by the Vaiśyas, followed by the non-Aryan Śūdras, followed by the Untouchable and tribal populations, followed perhaps by the barbarians (*mlecchas*), who in later times typically came from outside India altogether. Again, just where are we to draw the line, if a single line is to be drawn? Or more importantly, where are *they* to draw it? There is nothing here to compare with the relative sharpness of the Muslim partition of humanity into believers and unbelievers. Of course, Muslims argue about who exactly is an unbeliever and make distinctions within the category of non-Muslims; but Hindus lack such a category altogether. In the light of this it hardly seems out of place that the Hindus should owe to the Muslims their very concept of the Hindu.

In short, this glance at the traditional vocabulary available for the construction of a Hindu political identity has revealed two problematic features. One was the choice between a foreign term in current use and an ancient term in need of revival. The other was the lack of a sharp binary distinction between those who belong and those who do not. And thanks to their entanglement with the caste system, these features were linked to substantive issues that affected a significant part of the Indian population.

A rather different problem was the lack of a well-defined set of beliefs and rituals constituting the core of Hinduism. In this respect Hinduism is very different from Islam, with its two-part confession of faith and its five pillars. The ascetic Nārāyaṇa Guru (d. 1928), the leader of a low-caste religious movement in Kerala, was not without justi-

[35] Jaffrelot, *India's silent revolution*, 109 (for the Camārs as Jātavs, see 207–8, 457).
[36] See 77.
[37] See J. Leslie, *Authority and meaning*, 56, for an instance from 1927.

fication in taking the extreme nominalist view that "there is no such religion as Hinduism," just a plethora of distinct religions.[38] Likewise a Western scholar has argued cogently that, if we were to use our terms consistently, we would have to choose between referring to Hinduism as a plurality of religions and referring to Judaism, Christianity, and Islam as sects of a single religion.[39] Bāḷ Gangādhar Ṭiḷak (d. 1920), a Citpāvan Brahmin from Maharashtra and an early Indian nationalist, thus had a point when he averred in 1895 that for the Hindus of even one province to unite to worship the same god for ten days in every year was an event of no mean significance (he was referring to the Gaṇapati festival in Maharashtra).[40] Diversity of beliefs and rituals may not be an absolute bar to solidarity, but it certainly does not help—as Ṭiḷak was keenly aware.

3. Aspects of Hindu coherence

Yet there are countervailing aspects of the Hindu tradition. They are not common to all forms of Hinduism, but they are sufficiently widespread to give it a certain coherence. Three examples of such themes, and their continuity into modern times, should be enough to convey this; each of the themes introduced here will reengage us later in this study.[41]

A first example is the widespread, though by no means universal, recognition accorded to the Vedas, the texts whose transmission is central to the role of the Brahmins. To give just one example of the standing of the Vedas in pre-modern times, a purple passage on Muslim depredations in a southern text of the later fourteenth century laments that "the chant of the Vedas" has deserted the villages and that "the Veda is forgotten."[42] Yet, if we look at the attitudes of the devotional cults that have been so prominent in Hinduism for the last thousand years and more, we see great variation. At one extreme, the Tamil adherents of mainstream Śaivism regarded the Vedas as part of

[38] K. Sreenivasan, *Sree Narayana Guru*, 133, quoted in A. Sharma, *Modern Hindu thought*, 226–27.

[39] Stietencron, "Hinduism," 40–41, 46–47.

[40] Jaffrelot, "Politics of processions," 63n2.

[41] For the Vedas, see 400–2; for cow-killing, see 296, 421–22; for the Rām cult, see 422–24.

[42] Nilakanta Sastri, *Pāṇḍyan kingdom*, 242–43, whence Chattopadhyaya, *Representing the Other*, 57.

Śiva's revelation.[43] At the other extreme, sects like the Vīraśaivas or Lingāyats—a Śaiva sect in the region of Hyderabad and Mysore founded in the twelfth century—tended to reject the Vedas outright;[44] while in northern India Kabīr, a low-caste Vaiṣṇava or Ṣūfī who may have lived in the early fifteenth century and was a devotee of Rām, declared the Veda and Koran equally worthless.[45] The case of Kabīr is telling: if we consider him as a Ṣūfī, his attitude to the Koran seems very much an Indian one and sharply at variance with Ṣūfī views elsewhere in the Islamic world. Altogether, the Vedas do not have the same core status in Hinduism as the Koran does in Islam. And yet the fact that the Vedas were the obvious target for anyone in the business of rejecting ancient textual authority is in itself a testimony to their overall recognition.

This pattern continued into modern times. Thus the early liturgy of the Brāhma Samāj, a reformist movement founded by Rām Mohan Roy (Rāy, d. 1833) in Bengal in 1828, included the chanting of the Vedas, at first in a side room to which only Brahmins were admitted, but later for the whole congregation;[46] yet this was emphatically not a religiously conservative sect. Śraddhā Rām in the Punjab held uncompromisingly that anyone who "thinks that the Vedas, and Dharm Shastras are the products only of the Brahmans" cannot be "a true Hindu"[47] (the *śāstras* or *dharmaśāstras* are the Hindu law books). Vivekānanda (d. 1902), who did more than anyone else to render elite Hinduism a prestige export to the West, rather tendentiously told an Indian audience that the only point on which "all our sects" perhaps agree is that "we all believe in the scriptures," namely the Vedas[48] (though he had views of his own regarding the extent of Vedic authority).[49] A more recent and less cosmopolitan figure, a Śankarācārya of the Śṛngerī monastery (an office we will come to shortly),[50] gave this advice: "Accept the teach-

[43] Hudson, "Arumuga Navalar," 28 (on the Śaiva Siddhānta of the thirteenth to eighteenth centuries).

[44] Renou, *Le destin du Véda*, 3–4, 6–8 (with further sectarian examples); contrast Rao, *Śiva's warriors*, 7 (on the thirteenth-century Vīraśaiva Somanātha, who rejects the Brahmins but not the Vedas).

[45] Vaudeville, *Weaver named Kabir*, 154, and cf. 149, 151, 216, 221, 234, 246, 262 (but 228 is kinder).

[46] Damen, *Crisis and religious renewal*, 25, 33.

[47] K. W. Jones, *Arya Dharm*, 27.

[48] Rambachan, *Limits of scripture*, 57.

[49] See 401.

[50] See 67.

ing of the Vedas. Then one can worship any particular deity."[51] But again, while most people recognized the high standing of these venerable texts, others backhandedly acknowledged their prominence in the Hindu tradition by making a point of trashing them. Thus Jotirāo Phule (d. 1890), who developed an innovative low-caste ideology in Maharashtra, attributed the origin of the Vedas to Brahmā, here depicted as the cunning leader of the Aryan invaders; he "collected together some magical incantations and false fables that he knew off by heart."[52]

A second example of a feature that is widespread but not universal in Hinduism is revulsion at the killing of cows. This is a recurrent theme in friction between Hindus and Muslims.[53] What may be the earliest reference to Muslims in an Indian text correctly ascribes to them the view that there is no sin in eating animals such as cattle.[54] A late twelfth-century poet in the north gives a fanciful explanation of the ugly physical features of a Muslim ambassador in terms of "the vast number of cows he had slain."[55] A southern poetess describing Muslim maraudings in the second half of the fourteenth century speaks of a river "flowing red with the blood of slaughtered cows."[56] A Marāṭhī ballad that may date from the seventeenth century tells of a Muslim general who desecrated a Hindu idol and built a mosque in its place: "After the mosque was built," the ballad continues, "a cow was slaughtered."[57] Another early ballad describes a particularly obnoxious Muslim—a Rājpūt convert and a voracious cow-eater—who went so far as to order the sacrifice of a pregnant cow.[58] Muslim sources complement this picture. For example, Shaykh Aḥmad Sirhindī (d. 1624) saw

[51] Cenkner, *Tradition of teachers*, 136. This Śankarācārya, I think, held the office from 1954 to 1989 (see ibid., 122, and Jaffrelot, *Hindu nationalist movement*, 470).

[52] O'Hanlon, *Caste, conflict*, 145; and cf. his repeated references to the spurious scriptures of the Brahmins (Phule, *Collected works*, 2: 11, 31, 32, 77, 83).

[53] For references to the cow as a point of friction between Hindus and Muslims in pre-modern times further to those that follow, see Haider, "Holi riot," 131, 133, 143n37.

[54] Kuijp, "Earliest Indian reference," 200 (drawn to my attention by Shahab Ahmed).

[55] Pollock, "Rāmāyaṇa and political imagination," 276–77 (with further examples from the same poem); for the dating, see 274.

[56] Nilakanta Sastri, *Pāṇḍyan kingdom*, 242, whence Chattopadhyaya, *Representing the Other*, 57. The Vilasa grant of around 1330 identifies the three characteristic vices of the invaders as drinking wine, eating the meat of cows (*gopiśita*), and slaying the twice-born (Venkataramanayya and Somasekhara Sarma, "Vilasa grant," 241, 261 line 36, cited in Chattopadhyaya, *Representing the Other*, 59).

[57] Laine, "Śivājī as epic hero," 6–7.

[58] Laine, *Shivaji*, 29, and cf. 24, 49, 59.

the sacrifice of the cow as "one of the most important rites" of Islam in India,[59] precisely because of its offensiveness to Hindus[60]—though wise or weak Muslim rulers would from time to time forbid the practice for just that reason.[61] This old theme gained new vigor with the development of mass politics in modern India. An early example is Dayānand's cow protection campaign of 1881.[62] Another dates from the time of the annual Muslim sacrifice in 1917, when "snowball" letters were circulating in the district of Shāhābād (now in Bihar).[63] One of them insisted on the need for "all of us Hindus to unite so that Mother Cow (*gau mātā*) may be protected."[64] Another urged that "if you are a Hindu, you must liberate the cow" and spelled out the corollary: "That is why, you are instructed that wherever you catch a Musulman, you must kill him and loot his village."[65]

Here again, we are dealing with a feature of Hinduism that is widespread rather than universal. As an orthodox Tamil Brahmin declared in the mid-twentieth century, veneration of the cow could not be regarded as an essential feature of Hinduism; he pointed out that the "horror of cow-killing grew with time."[66] Indeed the whole tradition is deeply conflicted. Thus the Ṛg Veda has the god Indra remark that "they cook for me fifteen plus twenty oxen" and refers to the slaughter of a cow for a marriage.[67] Yet in over forty passages the Vedas refer to the cow with an epithet meaning "not to be slain" (*aghnyā*).[68] Since Vedic times the tradition has shifted against the cow killers, but not all the way. Thus, juristic literature of the last millennium and a half generally disapproves of cow killing in the present age;[69] but the best-known commentator on the law book of Manu states that cow killing

[59] Friedmann, *Shaykh Aḥmad Sirhindī*, 33 (*min ajall shaʿāʾir al-Islām fī ʾl-Hind*).

[60] See Rizvi, *Muslim revivalist movements*, 249, and cf. 309.

[61] Sirhindī was lamenting that the tyrannical ruler of his day had done so. For another instance, see Laine, *Shivaji*, 61.

[62] See Jordens, *Dayānanda Sarasvatī*, 220–23, and cf. 290 for the anti-Muslim animus of the campaign.

[63] Pandey, *Construction of communalism*, 262–66; for the background, see 167–74. The sacrifice is that of the ʿĪd al-Aḍḥā, on which any of a variety of animals may be sacrificed; but it is known in north India as Baqr-Id, sc. the festival at which cows (Arabic *baqar*) are sacrificed.

[64] Ibid., 264 no. 5.

[65] Ibid., 265 no. 6.

[66] Rangaswami Aiyangar, *Hindu view of life*, 19.

[67] D. N. Jha, *Holy cow*, 29, 33; and see Kane, *History of Dharmaśāstra*, 2: 772.

[68] D. N. Jha, *Holy cow*, 37; and see Kane, *History of Dharmaśāstra*, 2: 772.

[69] D. N. Jha, *Holy cow*, 113–15, 119.

is proper on certain ritual occasions.[70] Even Dayānand's views on the cow were more utilitarian than spiritual: "One cow can feed 100,000 people, but its meat can feed scarcely eighty."[71]

A third and final example is the cult of the god Rām, and in particular of his birthplace in Ayodhyā. This cult has, of course, become the subject of considerable obfuscation thanks to the destruction of the Bābrī Masjid, the mosque built for the Mughal emperor Bābur (ruled 1526–1530) in 1528–1529 and alleged to occupy the exact site of the birthplace of Rām. But for our purposes the outlines of the history of the cult are clear enough. It was an old one in the Ayodhyā region but not prominent until around the twelfth century.[72] The relevant vernacular version of the *Rāmāyaṇa*, the epic devoted to the life of Rām, was that composed by the poet Tulsīdās (d. 1623). It was in Avadhī, the form of Hindi prevalent in the region around Ayodhyā,[73] and the poet began its composition when he was in Ayodhyā on the occasion of Rām's birthday in 1574.[74] This was very much a living tradition: a peasant revolt that broke out in Awadh in 1920 was imbued with it, and the leading spokesman of the rebels was an itinerant reciter of the Tulsīdās *Rāmāyaṇa*.[75] There was likewise nothing inauthentic about the belief that Rām was born in Ayodhyā, where he came down to earth as a man "for the sake of Brāmans and cows and gods and saints."[76] It is a good question where, if anywhere, Ayodhyā was located in ancient times, but the medieval Ayodhyā was undoubtedly where it is now,[77] and pilgrims have been visiting Rām's birthplace there for centuries. A traditional pilgrim guide to Ayodhyā exists in several recensions, approximately datable between the thirteenth and the seventeenth centuries.[78] All describe Rām's birthplace (the Janmabhūmi or

[70] Ibid., 93, citing the commentary of Medhātithi, for which see G. Jha, *Manusmṛti*, 5: 39, 40, 52.

[71] Jordens, *Dayānanda Sarasvatī*, 125, and see 219, 220–21. His cow-protection campaign thus smacks of political opportunism.

[72] Bakker, *Ayodhyā*, 1: 66 (summarizing a detailed discussion of the rise of the Rām cult).

[73] Masica, *Indo-Aryan languages*, 57, 422.

[74] Bakker, *Ayodhyā*, 1: 124; Hill, *Holy lake*, x.

[75] Lutgendorf, "Interpreting Rāmrāj, 269f, based on Pandey, "Peasant revolt," 258–61. Pandey's authorities include Nehru (*Autobiography*, 53).

[76] Hill, *Holy lake*, 87–89 (Tulsīdās here refers to Ayodhyā with the vernacular form "Avadh"). The belief is ancient (Vālmīki, *Rāmāyaṇa*, 159, and cf. 134).

[77] Bakker, *Ayodhyā*, 1: 12.

[78] Bakker gives a summary presentation of his datings of the versions of the *Ayodhyāmāhātmya* in a table (ibid., 1: 153). For an English rendering of the guide, see Rám Náráyan, "Ayodhyá Máhátmya."

Janmasthān).[79] Thus, the oldest version assures the pilgrim that a man who has seen the birthplace will not have to undergo a further rebirth and will attain the same merit as someone who makes an offering of a thousand red cows a day.[80] What we do not know is the age of the tradition that locates the birthplace precisely where the mosque was built for Bābur[81] and whether a Hindu temple marking the spot was in fact destroyed to build it. In the second half of the nineteenth century the Hindus were making their offerings on a platform outside the mosque.[82] But in 1949 Hindu idols appeared inside the mosque,[83] and thereafter the microgeography of the conflict was unambiguous.

At the same time the Rām cult extended far beyond Ayodhyā and its environs. Its presence was not uniform: one scholar describes the god's popularity today as concentrated in the Hindi-speaking north,[84] and this pattern doubtless antedates the twentieth century. Yet versions of the *Rāmāyaṇa* existed in most of the major vernacular languages of India, and the story also found its way into the literatures of the Jains and Buddhists.[85] Significantly, the legend of Rām was already being invoked in the context of resistance against Muslims in pre-modern times; the *Rāmāyaṇa*, unlike the *Mahābhārata*, has the advantage of demonizing the enemy.[86] Thus a court poet of the Hindu ruler Śivājī (ruled 1674–1680) dubs his patron's Muslim enemy a "second Rāvaṇa" (Rāvaṇa being the leading villain of the epic), and puts these words into Śivājī's mouth:

> The Muslims are demons incarnate
> Arisen to flood the earth with their own religion.
> Therefore, I will destroy these demons
> Who have taken the form of Muslims
> And I will spread the way of *dharma* fearlessly![87]

[79] Baker, *Ayodhyā*, 2: 143, 149.

[80] Ibid., 1: 128.

[81] Cf. ibid., 2: 146.

[82] Ibid., 2: 147–48.

[83] Jaffrelot, *Hindu nationalist movement*, 92–96.

[84] Fuller, *Camphor flame*, 270. Fuller links the popularity of Rām to two characteristics of the region: the role of the Tulsīdās *Rāmāyaṇa* as a favorite devotional text and the observance of the Rām Līlā festival (see 121–23).

[85] For a survey of these versions, see Brockington, *Righteous Rāma*, 260–62, 266–86.

[86] Pollock, "Rāmāyaṇa and political imagination" (see especially 283, 287); more summarily Lutgendorf, "Interpreting Rāmrāj," 258–59.

[87] Laine, "Śivājī as epic hero," 10–11. See also Laine, *Shivaji*, 23.

In the Tamil country an indigenist revaluation going back to the late nineteenth century turned the tables and denounced Rām as an Aryan villain;[88] later the Tamil separatist Periyār (d. 1973) was the author of a notoriously blasphemous pamphlet about the *Rāmāyaṇa*.[89] But this was modern innovation.

To these themes that give Hinduism a certain coherence we should add that the tradition possesses a remarkably sharp territorial sense. The Hindus may owe to the Muslims the idea of the Hindu, but their traditional idea of India is very much their own.[90]

Let us start with a set of Vedāntist monasteries (*maṭhas*) whose foundation was attributed to the Vedāntist sage Śankara. Like so many of the major religious figures of the Indian past, Śankara is resistant to precise dating; current scholarship tends to place him around 700.[91] We know him above all as the author of a set of works that made him the classic exponent of a particular tradition of religious philosophy, Advaita Vedānta. What concerns us here, however, is the action he took, or was later believed to have taken, to institutionalize it. According to the medieval biographical tradition, much of it already legendary in character, he traveled all over India, founding a number of major monasteries (*maṭhāmnāyas*) where his teachings were preserved and propagated. There was general agreement that one of them was located at Śṛngerī, in what is now Karnataka, and that others were placed at Dvārkā on the coast of Gujarat, at Purī on the coast of Orissa, and at Badrīnāth in the Himalayas; the status of a further such institution at Kāñcī near Madras has been more contentious.[92] These monasteries are spread out over India at large distances from each other, with no sign of regional clustering; all remain within the borders of India at the present day. Each one of these major monasteries was—and is—headed by a Śankarācārya. The individual monasteries typically preserve lists of their successive heads; this tradition seems to date from the later middle ages and cannot take us much further back with any confidence.[93] But there is a geographical vision here, and while we cannot

[88] Irschick, *Politics and social conflict*, 283–84, 294, 339.

[89] On Periyār (as his admirers called him) and his pamphlet, see Richman, "Ramasami's reading."

[90] Khilnani, *Idea of India*, 154–57.

[91] Thus Pande, *Life of Śaṅkarācārya*, 52 (arguing for the second half of the seventh century).

[92] Ibid., 338, 357, 363, and cf. 337 on his travels.

[93] Ibid., 43, 360–61.

say for sure that it goes back to Śankara himself, it is clear that it had been realized on the ground by late medieval times if not before.

This vision invites comparison with the geographical terms enshrined in the tradition. Āryāvarta, the land within which Aryans may dwell, is defined by Manu as extending from the Himalayas in the north to the Vindhyas of central India in the south and from the sea in the west to the sea in the east.[94] In this connection Badrīnāth, Dvārkā, and Purī have a clear geographical significance as marking the northern, western, and eastern limits of Āryāvarta. Only in the south do the monasteries depart from this pattern: they are located too far south to mark the southern border of Āryāvarta but too far north to fit the later concept of Bhāratavarṣa, which extends all the way south to Cape Comorin (Kanyā Kumārī).[95]

These monasteries represent a Śaiva vision of religious geography, but a comparable if less dramatic sense of India as a sacred space emerges from the record of Vaiṣṇava pilgrimages. Vallabhācārya, a Vaiṣṇava sect-founder who died—or ascended to heaven—in 1531, went on pilgrimages that had a geographical reach comparable to Śankara's travels; the locations of significant events in his life are commemorated by eighty-four widely dispersed shrines.[96] A Vaiṣṇava saint in the late eighteenth century visited Badrīnāth, Purī, Kāñcī, Rāmeśvaram, and Dvārkā;[97] Rāmeśvaram is located on an island between India and Ceylon. The practices of Vaiṣṇava ascetics in the twentieth century are also relevant here—and likely to be old. The Rāmānandī ascetics traditionally sent new recruits to circumambulate India, visiting Badrīnāth, Purī, Rāmeśvaram, and Dvārkā.[98] One Rāmānandī was told by his guru to go to the source of the Ganges, fill a copper pot with its sacred water, and pour it out at Rāmeśvaram—an act of devotion considered extremely auspicious; he also visited Badrīnāth, Purī, and Dvārkā.[99]

Śaivas and Vaiṣṇavas thus shared a Hindu idea of India as a domain of religious activity distinct from the rest of the world. As we have seen, this idea was linked to the old notion of Āryāvarta, later extended as Bhāratavarṣa to include the south. Though these conceptions may

[94] Manu, *Laws*, 19 (2.21–22). Other early texts have different views, particularly on the east-west axis (Kane, *History of Dharmaśāstra*, 2: 13–15).

[95] Kane, *History of Dharmaśāstra*, 2: 17.

[96] Barz, *Bhakti sect*, 27–28.

[97] R. B. Williams, *New face of Hinduism*, 10 (for the chronology, see 9, 11).

[98] Gross, "Hindu asceticism," 172.

[99] Ibid., 604–8 (and see also 188, cited in Jaffrelot, *Hindu nationalist movement*, 361n97).

have meant little or nothing to most of the inhabitants of the peninsula, they were not confined to the scholastic culture of the religious elite. We find both terms used in the context of military hostilities against Muslims.[100] A Maharashtrian chronicle of the late eighteenth century, written in the Marāṭhī vernacular of the region, devotes a passage to sketching this idea of India as a domain of religious actions (*karmabhūmī*). This domain is encircled by the sea on the east, west, and south and bounded on the north by the Himalayas. It is characterized by abundant temples, study of the Vedas and *śāstras*, places of pilgrimage that bring instant rewards, abodes of gods, families of Brahmins, and the like. Our author concludes his sketch with the remark that "this auspicious land, where the good *karma* ripens, is limited to fifty-six regions (*deśas*)."[101] Hinduism was thus endowed with a conception of its territory that was both clear and, once the south had been incorporated, stable. Islam too has a clear sense of its territory, the "abode of Islam" (*dār al-Islām*), but the borders of this abode are not intended to be stable; it is only the original core territory of Islam, the Arabian peninsula (*arḍ al-ʿArab, Jazīrat al-ʿArab*), or still more narrowly the Ḥijāz, that remains fixed.[102]

The role of pilgrimage in maintaining the territorial cohesion of India was not limited to marking its borders. Long-distance pilgrimages involving large numbers of people could do something to integrate a religious community in another way, by enabling its members to make contact with each other and disseminate ideas. The most impressive example of this anywhere in the world is, of course, the Muslim Ḥajj, a pilgrimage that brings together people from all parts of the Islamic world at the same place and time each lunar year.[103] Hinduism has nothing quite like this, any more than do Buddhism and Christianity. But it does have a set of large-scale pilgrimages each of which takes place every twelve years.[104] Of these the most important is the Kumbh

[100] Pollock, "Rāmāyaṇa and political imagination," 278 (Āryāvarta); Venkataramanayya and Somasekhara Sarma, "Vilasa grant," 241, 260 line 10, cited in Chattopadhyaya, *Representing the Other*, 58 (Bhāratavarṣa).

[101] Wagle and Kulkarni, *Vallabha's Paraśarāma Caritra*, 2.12–14 (24 = 152). For the term *karmabhūmi*, see Kane, *History of Dharmaśāstra*, 2: 17; for the fifty-six regions, see 3: 136.

[102] For traditions requiring that only Muslims live in the core area, see Friedmann, *Tolerance and coercion*, 85–86, 90–93.

[103] Note that Muslim pilgrims patrol the sacred core of the Islamic world, but not its borders.

[104] Cf. Bhardwaj, *Hindu places of pilgrimage*, 117–19, 212.

Melā at Hardvār, near Badrīnāth, in the region where the Ganges descends from the Himalayas onto the plains. Though not ancient, this pilgrimage seems to be old, and Hardvār is already mentioned as a place of pilgrimage in a medieval Purāṇic text.[105] We lack evidence of the geographical provenance of the pilgrims before modern times, but data from 1968 show pilgrims coming to Badrīnāth from all over India though, as might be expected, some regions were poorly represented and pilgrims tended to associate with fellow pilgrims from their own region.[106] It is significant that the Kumbh Melā figures prominently in the life of Dayānand, despite the fact that he did not believe in it. He was present three times: in 1855, when he was too taken up with yoga to participate; in 1867, when he distributed thousands of copies of a reformist pamphlet to little effect, railing against such evils as idolatry and sacred rivers; and in 1879, when he distributed a manifesto but came down with acute dysentery (ideas are not the only entities that can spread at mass pilgrimages).[107] For comparison, in 1968 the Indian authorities were making similar use of the pilgrimage for their own purposes, setting up a temporary family-planning exhibition with a clinic.[108]

To sum up, we have seen that both ethnic and religious identity were considerably weaker in the traditional Hindu world than in the traditional Islamic world. The weakness of the Hindu identity in particular comes across in the problematic character of the terms associated with it, the ambiguity as to who is in and who is out, and the lack of a common core of beliefs and rituals. But there were countervailing elements that gave the religion a degree of coherence, notably the widespread recognition of the Vedas, the hostility to cow killing, and the veneration of Rām; to these we can add the existence of a territorial idea of India reinforced by monasteries and pilgrimages. In all this two things are worth highlighting. One is the role of caste in the fraying of Hindu identity as one moves down the social pyramid (and perhaps also in the weakness of ethnic identity). The other is the part played by Muslims not just in giving the Hindus a name for themselves but also in serving as their historic enemy for the last thousand years.

[105] Ibid., 62, map (Haridvāra, from the *Garuḍa Purāṇa*).

[106] Ibid., 125–27, and see 119, 222 (on Hardvār).

[107] Jordens, *Dayānanda Sarasvatī*, 23–24, 46–47, 185, 207–8.

[108] Bhardwaj, *Hindu places of pilgrimage*, 215 (and see the photographic section following 96).

4. Modern ethnic and Hindu identity

We now turn to the role played by these identities in the context of modern politics, that is to say, in forms of politics heavily influenced by Western institutions and values. One of these values is, of course, nationalism, and its reception in the region might lead us to expect ethnic identities to acquire a higher political profile than religious identities. But this has not in fact been the case. Religious identity has continued to play a very prominent role in making the subcontinent what it is. It lay behind the Muslim separatism that led to the partition of India in 1947 and has since been central to the politics of Indian Kashmir. For some years it inspired a militant Sikh separatism in the Indian Punjab. It has also given us the Hindu nationalist movement, in association with no small amount of communal violence. Ethnic identity can compete with this record only in two contexts, neither of which is central to our concerns. One is the northeastern fringe of India, where separatist insurrection has been rampant among populations that were to a large extent outside the traditional Hindu world. The other is Pakistan, where the hegemony of the Punjabis was a major factor behind the secession of Bangladesh and has given rise to violent tensions in the rest of the country. But within India since independence, outside the northeast, the role of ethnic identities has been much quieter. That this should be so was by no means obvious a priori. The early years of independence saw strong pressure for the creation of linguistic states within the federal structure, and the rulers of India gave way to this pressure with great reluctance, fearing that it would lead to the disintegration of the country. But since the major linguistic states were established in the decade 1956–1966,[109] the problem has more or less gone away. This undoubtedly reflects the weakness of India's ethnic identities in pre-modern times. Today even the Tamils, the only one of these linguistic groups to take their particularism to the point of separatism, seem satisfied. Thus, there is little more that needs to be said here about ethnic identity, though we will return to it briefly in connection with its role as an obstacle to Hindu nationalism, and it will resurface in the course of our discussion of caste.[110]

[109] For this process see Brass, *Politics of India*, 169–74; R. Guha, *India after Gandhi*, chap. 9. Contrast the lack of such accommodation of ethnic groups in Pakistan.

[110] See 73, 75–76. In a very Indian fashion caste played a hidden but significant role in the formation of the linguistic states (see Jaffrelot, "From Indian territory," 201–2).

Our main concern from this point on is with Hindu identity. In the politics of modern India as a whole this identity is very much the property of the Hindu nationalist movement, a close-knit set of political organizations; and since the names of these organizations will recur in what follows, it may be useful to list them here. The Rāṣṭriya Svayamsevak Sangh (RSS) is the oldest member of the "family" of Hindu nationalist organizations (the Sangh Parivār), and its continuing core—or at least its conscience. It was founded in the city of Nāgpūr in 1925.[111] In 1951 the movement established a political party, the Jana Sangh;[112] its heir is the Bhāratīya Janatā Party (BJP), formed in 1980.[113] Meanwhile in 1964 the movement had also created the Viśva Hindu Pariṣad (VHP), or World Hindu Council as it is known in English, a body established for the defense of Hinduism.[114] The other member of the family we should note is Sevā Bhārtī, an agency for social work set up in 1979.[115] Also worth mentioning here is the Shiv Sena, the violent populist movement that dominates the politics of Bombay; though it is entirely independent of the Hindu nationalist family and has a quite distinct local origin, it has come to share some of the attitudes of the Hindu nationalists. The Shiv Sena apart, this ramification of institutions represents a division of labor within a movement that has so far proved remarkably free of schism; the contrast with Islamist movements is noteworthy. There has nevertheless been persisting tension within the family, and it relates to the terms on which the movement is to participate in the wider field of Indian politics.[116] On one side are the RSS activists, who tend to remain loyal to the basic values of the movement through thick and thin; on the other side are the BJP politicians, whose pragmatism reflects their awareness of the compromises they have to make if the party is to enjoy the fruits of power through electoral competition.[117] These remarks are intended only as a prelimi-

[111] Jaffrelot, *Hindu nationalist movement,* 33.

[112] Ibid., 118–19.

[113] Ibid., 315.

[114] Ibid., 193.

[115] Ibid., 530.

[116] See, for example, ibid., 10, 222, 230, 315, 368.

[117] The pragmatism has also been in evidence in foreign policy. On a visit to Lahore in 1999, Vajpayee visited one of Pakistan's key symbolic sites, the Mīnār-i Pākistān, where the "Lahore Resolution" of 1940 was passed by the Muslim League (Jaffrelot, *History of Pakistan,* 118; and cf. Jaffrelot, *Hindu nationalist movement,* 285, for his visit to Islamabad in 1978). In Karachi in 2005, Advani put in an appearance at Jinnah's mausoleum, where he praised Jinnah in terms that caused great distress to the RSS (Iyer, "Jinnah favoured a secular Pakistan").

nary orientation; we will take up the question of the broader nature of Hindu nationalism toward the end of this chapter.[118] In the meantime I will trace the political fortunes of Hindu identity on three fronts: ethnic, social, and religious—though in practice they are hard to separate.

As indicated, the ethnic front will not occupy us long. It is a well-known fact that Hindu nationalism finds much more support in the north of the country than it does in the south.[119] One reason for this is historical: the Hindu nationalists originally wanted to see the adoption of Hindi as the national language.[120] This was a recipe for alienating the Dravidian south, now divided into four linguistic states, each with its own language. However, the Hindu nationalists were wise enough to abandon their Hindi chauvinism,[121] so it hardly explains the fact that their support has continued to trail in the south. As we will soon see, this may have as much to do with caste as ethnicity—though there are contexts in which the two become blurred.

This brings us to the social front, which needs more elaborate treatment. Our concern here is with the caste system. Traditionally its central feature was a set of exclusions that grew ever more drastic as one descended the caste hierarchy: no intermarriage, no interdining, and the like. Since we have already encountered the Vedas and will meet them again, let us use them to illustrate the symbolic aspect of these exclusions. In traditional Hindu society, the Brahmins can teach and hear the Vedas; the other twice-born castes can hear but not teach them; the Śūdras can do neither, still less the Untouchables.[122] Thus an ancient source prescribes that if a Śūdra listens to the Veda with a view to memorizing it, he gets molten lead in his ears, while if he utters it, his tongue may be cut off, and if he has mastered it, he should

[118] See 103–20.

[119] Jaffrelot, *Hindu nationalist movement*, 439–41. Of the four southern states, Karnataka is the only one in which the BJP has made serious headway; in the general election of 2004, it won 18 of its 138 seats in this state and received 35 percent of the vote there. This is a significant modification of the party's geographical base and may be one reason for its diminishing interest in issues such as Ayodhyā (Jaffrelot, "BJP," 240–41, and the table, 242; in the general election of 2009, the party won 19 of the 28 seats in Karnataka and received 42 percent of the vote, while winning no seats in the other three states; see the Wikipedia article "Indian general election, 2009,"). In this connection it may be worth noting the weakness of political bonding around Kannaḍa, the language of the state (see Manor, "Language, religion," especially 171–75).

[120] Jaffrelot, *Hindu nationalist movement*, 160.

[121] Ibid., 439.

[122] For the exclusion of the Śūdras, see Kane, *History of Dharmaśāstra*, 2: 154–55. There is an isolated view implying the contrary (36, 156–57).

be hacked to pieces.[123] This denial of access to the text also meant exclusion from Vedic ritual. Śūdras could not use Vedic mantras—Vedic verses possessing religious efficacy—in their worship.[124] In this connection the "mother of the Veda" (*Vedamātā*)[125]—we might be tempted to say the mother of all mantras—is the Gāyatrī mantra. This Vedic verse is an invocation of the sun god: "Let us think on the lovely splendour of the god Savitṛ, that he may inspire our minds."[126] It was to be taught to the twice-born boy following his initiation.[127] Thereafter multiple repetitions of the Gāyatrī were to play a key role in the ritual prayer (*sandhyā*) performed three times a day.[128] Over the course of a lifetime, one should repeat the verse twenty-four hundred thousand times, if need be getting others to help out; we hear of a ceremony held in the early twentieth century at which seventy Brahmins each repeated the Gāyatrī four thousand times a day for thirteen days.[129] Like the Vedas at large, the verse is closely associated with Brahmins; there is even a view in the ancient sources that it is for Brahmins alone, to the exclusion of the other twice-born classes.[130] In any case the Śūdras were excluded—and so by implication were the Untouchables.

This symbolic example doubtless makes caste sound like an archaism that would not survive the onset of modernity. In fact, as we will see, caste has often been fostered as much as eroded by modern conditions. What then are its implications for identity? Here two things seem obvious a priori. The first is that such a system was likely to give rise to enormous resentment in its lower reaches, particularly under modern conditions. The second is that the resentful would be strongly tempted to opt out of the Hindu hierarchy. Examples of both effects are not hard to find.

We have already met Jotirāo Phule, who in the mid-nineteenth century launched a non-Brahmin movement in the region of Poona in Maharashtra.[131] His social program was designed to bring education—and

[123] Ibid., 2: 155.

[124] Ibid., 2: 158, 159.

[125] Ibid., 2: 303, 304.

[126] This is Basham's translation of Ṛg Veda 3.62.10 (Basham, *Wonder that was India*, 162, with the original).

[127] Kane, *History of Dharmaśāstra*, 2: 300.

[128] Stevenson, *Rites of the Twice-born*, 210–25, especially 218–19, 221–23.

[129] Ibid., 348–50. For a recitation of the Gāyatrī by 125 Brahmins in 1890, see K. W. Jones, *Socio-religious reform movements*, 79.

[130] Kane, *History of Dharmaśāstra*, 2: 302–3.

[131] O'Hanlon, *Caste, conflict* (a monographic study); Jaffrelot, *India's silent revolution*, 153–57. Jaffrelot notes that Phule found inspiration in the emancipation of the black slave population of the United States (153).

hence power—to the non-Brahmins, his primary constituency being the Marāṭhās and associated castes, traditionally classed as Śūdras.[132] The identity he offered them involved a dramatic reshaping of their history.[133] They were, he told them, the native population of the region. Originally they were Kṣatriyas who lived in peace and happiness (he supplied them with a new and appropriate etymology of the term "Kṣatriya" that associated it with the word for "field," *kṣetra*, rather than with warfare). This golden age continued until disaster struck in the shape of the Aryan invasions; he owed this notion of the Aryans as alien intruders—as originally they almost certainly were—to European scholarship.[134] These invasions, he explained, brought Brahmin domination, and with it the reduction of the indigenous population to the status of Śūdras and worse. Eventually, he taught, the Creator in his mercy sent first the Muslims and then the English to liberate the natives from the Aryan yoke; the Muslims showed themselves to be utterly corrupt, but the English fortunately did not.[135] Meanwhile the Brahmins had elaborated their false religion as part of their conspiracy to subjugate and exploit the native population; we have already encountered Phule's unflattering account of the compilation of the Vedas.[136] Two things are particularly striking about his vision. The first is his transposition of caste difference into ethnic difference. The second is his rejection, not just of the Brahmins but of the core of the religious tradition associated with them, from the Vedas to Śankara.[137] We hear less of what he wanted to see in its place, though he made much of Khaṇḍobā, a prominent deity of the castes to whom he was making his main appeal.[138]

Phule's exclusion of the Brahmins from the community was echoed by other dissidents over the following century. By far the most conspicuous instance of such notions was the indigenist movement that was to lead to Tamil separatism.[139] The Tamils, of course, were particularly well placed to play the indigenist card: unlike the speakers of Marāṭhī, they

[132] O'Hanlon, *Caste, conflict*, 129, 140.

[133] Ibid., 136, 137, 141–42; cf. 72–73.

[134] As might be expected, the idea that the Aryans were invaders has not found favor with the Hindu nationalists (Jaffrelot, *Hindu nationalism*, 278, and cf. 366).

[135] Phule, *Collected works*, 2: 10–11, quoted in A. Sharma, *Modern Hindu thought*, 145; see also O'Hanlon, *Caste, conflict*, 129.

[136] See 63.

[137] For the latter, see O'Hanlon, *Caste, conflict*, 204.

[138] Ibid., 152–53.

[139] Jaffrelot, *India's silent revolution*, 168–72, 244–45.

were one of the four major southern peoples set off from the northerners by the fact that they spoke and wrote Dravidian languages, and of these peoples they possessed by far the most ancient and distinctive literary heritage. Yet even in the north, caste divisions could be construed as ethnic divisions by those determined to do so. Thus Svāmī Achūtānand (d. 1933), an Untouchable leader in United Provinces and a Camār, in 1917 set out his views about the "Ādi-Hindus" or proto-Hindus, a category in which he included Śūdras, Untouchables, and Tribals—in contrast to the twice-born Brahmins, whom he considered "as foreign to India as are the British" (indeed he clearly considered the British an improvement on the Brahmins).[140] The Ādi-Hindu religion was, he said, "the oldest religion," a religion of hundreds of saints, one in which all are equal before God, in contrast to the ways of the Brahmins; "we do not need any other religion."[141]

To return to Maharashtra, what Phule did for the lower castes in the nineteenth century, Bhim Rāo Āmbeḍkar (d. 1956) did for the smaller but more downtrodden Untouchable population in the twentieth and with a much greater impact on people of the same status in India at large.[142] It was he who coined the term "Dalits,"[143] which has come to be used more or less with the sense of "Untouchables with attitude." Again, he rewrote history to recover an allegedly lost identity for his constituency. This was primarily his own Mahār caste, the largest Untouchable caste in Maharashtra; its members traditionally provided their villages with a variety of services, including the removal of dead animals.[144] In this case, however, the lost identity was a religious, not an ethnic one: Dalits, Āmbeḍkar explained, were former Buddhists who had been reduced to their current abject condition through the medieval resurgence of Hinduism.[145] Considerable numbers of Untouchables in Maharashtra, mainly members of the Mahār caste, accordingly opted out of Hindu society by "returning" to Buddhism in a ceremony

[140] Ibid., 200–205. For such ideas see also 157 (an Untouchable from Nāgpūr in 1909), 223 (a dissenting member of the first Backward Classes Commission, that appointed in 1953), 390–91, 394 (Kānśī Rām, who founded the Bahujan Samāj Party in 1984); J. Leslie, *Authority and meaning*, 55–57 (the Ādi-dharm movement in the Punjab in the later 1920s); Schaller, "Sanskritization, 111–13, and Juergensmeyer, *Religion as social vision*, 45–46, 112, 261 (also on the Ādi-dharm movement).

[141] Jaffrelot, *India's silent revolution*, 203–4.

[142] Ibid., 19–23.

[143] Ibid., 22.

[144] Gokhale, *From concessions to confrontation*, 29–34.

[145] Jaffrelot, *India's silent revolution*, 22–23.

orchestrated by Āmbeḍkar in the year of his death.[146] Thus Buddhism, a religion doctrinally indifferent to caste, was adopted as a badge of opposition to it.

As with Phule's ideas, subsequent decades have shown that Āmbeḍkar's interest in Buddhism was not just a passing idiosyncrasy. A few months after he died—foully murdered, it was said, by Congress "giving him poisonous injections through a Brahman"[147]—the energetic Camār politician active in the ʿAlīgaṛh district converted to Buddhism and went on to infuriate the upper castes by organizing a huge conversion meeting at which, he claimed, a hundred thousand Camārs adopted Buddhism, with Hindu temples becoming Buddhist ones.[148] Kānśī Rām (d. 2006), who seems likewise to have been a Camār[149] and had learned about Āmbeḍkar's ideas from a Mahār Buddhist, was not in favor of conversion to Buddhism unless all Dalits were to convert at once.[150] But Māyawatī, a Camār woman with unlimited attitude, whom he had recruited to the cause, made use of Buddhist symbolism during her brief spells of power in Uttar Pradesh in 1995 and 1997, naming a district for the Buddha's mother and referring to Āmbeḍkar as a Bodhisattva in a dedicatory inscription;[151] during her third spell as chief minister in 2002–2003, she threatened to follow Āmbeḍkar and convert to Buddhism together with Kānśī Rām and several hundred thousand members of the Bahujan Samāj Party,[152] and in 2006 she gave him a Buddhist funeral.[153] In Āmbeḍkar's thinking the rupture between the Untouchables and the higher castes was religious, not ethnic; indeed it is a significant feature of the Buddhist option that Buddhism is incontrovertibly Indian—one reason he did no more than flirt with the Muslim option.[154] But we also find cases, several of them antedating Āmbeḍkar, where indigenist and Buddhist notions came

[146] Gokhale, *From concessions to confrontation*, 180–81. The Mahārs were seriously considering a conversion as early as 1935 (164), but in those days Sikhism seemed a more likely choice (169–70). For Buddhist activity in India in the decades prior to the Mahār conversion, see Coward, "Revival of Buddhism," 277–84.

[147] For this belief see Duncan, "Levels," 287, citing an election pamphlet from ʿAlīgaṛh.

[148] Jaffrelot, *India's silent revolution*, 109. For Camār Buddhism, see also 457.

[149] Mendelsohn and Vicziany, *Untouchables*, 219; Jaffrelot, *India's silent revolution*, 388.

[150] Jaffrelot, *India's silent revolution*, 390, 423.

[151] Ibid., 414–15, 419n78. For Āmbeḍkar as a Bodhisattva, see Gokhale, *From concessions to confrontation*, 126, 182, 186.

[152] "Maya threatens to embrace Buddhism."

[153] See, for example, "Mayawati justifies lighting Kanshi Ram's funeral pyre." I owe this information to Christophe Jaffrelot.

[154] See Gokhale, *From concessions to confrontation*, 168–70.

together;[155] thus, one indigenist from the Āndhra region celebrated the Buddha's birthday in 1913.[156]

Not every religious option open to those at the bottom of the pile could be presented as Indian. With the advent of Muslim and later Christian rule, it became relatively easy to leave the Indian religious tradition altogether, adopting instead a faith of foreign origin that was at least in principle caste blind: if you were not admitted to the Hindu temple, you could turn to the mosque or the church. The result was a hemorrhage of lower-caste and Untouchable Hindus through conversion,[157] and this hemorrhage did not stop when Muslim and Christian rule eventually came to an end. In 1981 Indian public opinion was badly shaken when some thousand Untouchables converted to Islam in a village in the Tamil south under the auspices of the leaders of the Muslim League; this was followed by thousands of conversions in the region. These events engendered reports of a grand Muslim conspiracy using Arab oil money to entice large numbers of Hindus to turn Muslim, and a majority of Indians—especially in the northern cities—wanted government action to end such conversions.[158]

There was, of course, a potentially more harmonious alternative to the processes we have been looking at. The excluded could be included. Such a change might be initiated either from below or from above. Initiation from below tends to take the form of "Sanskritization."[159] Here the caste hierarchy appears as a ladder, and an aspiring caste may seek to climb it—rather than walk away from it—by adopting the manners and customs of the higher castes. Vivekānanda was strongly in favor of this course: "I tell you men who belong to the lower castes, the only way to raise your condition is to study Sanskrit, and this fighting and writing and frothing against the higher castes is in vain"; "use all your energies in acquiring the culture which the Brâhman has, and the thing is done."[160] We have already met one typical example of a caste seek-

[155] Jaffrelot, *India's silent revolution*, 168, 170, 203–4, 208.

[156] See Omvedt, *Dalits*, 121–24.

[157] See, for example, K. W. Jones, *Arya Dharm*, 5, 10–12, 144, and, for a conspicuous example of conversion to Christianity among an Untouchable caste of the far south, K. W. Jones, *Socio-religious reform movements*, 156–60.

[158] Jaffrelot, *Hindu nationalist movement*, 340–42.

[159] The term was coined by the anthropologist M. N. Srinivas in 1947 to label a process by which a caste stakes a claim to a higher position in the hierarchy by adopting "the customs and way of life of a higher caste" (Srinivas, "Note on Sanskritization," 200, 202; for the date, see further his article "Cohesive role of Sanskritization," 235n1).

[160] Vivekānanda, *Complete works*, 3: 291, 298 (partly quoted in Dixit, "Political and social dimensions," 304–5; this article is thoroughly hostile to Vivekānanda but rich in

ing to climb the ladder: the claims of the Yādavs to Kṣatriya status.[161] In taking to calling themselves Yādavs rather than Ahīrs, they were identifying themselves with an ancient tribe and a medieval dynasty.[162] They were helped by the fact that they were traditionally herdsmen, which linked them to the sacred cow.[163] An earlier example of the same phenomenon would be the contentious claims of the Marāṭhā elite to Kṣatriya status in the mid-nineteenth century, at a time when the end of the rule of the Brahmin Peśvās and the indifference of the new British overlords to matters of caste discipline had made it harder to keep people in their places.[164] These claims were endorsed by the outcome of a formal debate held in 1830,[165] though as late as 1865 it was still being argued that no Marāṭhā could claim to be anything but a Śūdra.[166] Those whose attempts to climb the ladder were blocked from above could sometimes get results by threatening to walk away from it. Lower-caste Hindus seeking to pry open the temples of Kerala backed up their demonstrations with an implicit threat to convert to other religions if their demands were not met; the Maharaja of Travancore stepped in and opened the temples of his principality in 1936.[167] Yet such attempts to climb the social ladder were at the same time endorsements of the ladder itself.[168] One of the most outspoken protagonists on the Marāṭhā side in nineteenth-century Maharashtra was just as vehement in denouncing people lower down on the ladder who aspired to enter his own caste.[169]

There were also pressures for inclusion coming from above. Modern politics, particularly electoral politics, put a premium on large constituencies. Hence the tendency of the excluded to opt out of Hindu society could not leave high-caste Hindus indifferent, and considerable efforts

---

quotations). Vivekānanda himself was a Kāyasth and thus a member of a literate caste of ambiguous status; he claimed vociferously to be a Kṣatriya rather than a Śūdra (305–6; Vivekānanda, *Complete works*, 3: 211; and cf. Kane, *History of Dharmaśāstra*, 2: 75–77).

[161] See 59.

[162] For these, see Basham, *Wonder that was India*, 41, 75, 134, 304.

[163] Jaffrelot, *India's silent revolution*, 187–88.

[164] For these claims and their ramifications, see O'Hanlon, *Caste, conflict*, 24–27, 32–45.

[165] Ibid., 33–34.

[166] Ibid., 41–42.

[167] Deliège, *Untouchables of India*, 156–57. Cf. also Jaffrelot, *Hindu nationalist movement*, 21.

[168] Compare Āmbeḍkar's analysis of "graded inequality" (Jaffrelot, *India's silent revolution*, 20–21).

[169] O'Hanlon, *Caste, conflict*, 38–39.

were made by Hindu reformers to eliminate or at least mitigate the traditional exclusions of Hinduism. Yet in real life concessions were not made easily or quickly. We may return here to the case of the Gāyatrī mantra, denounced by Phule as an incantation that the Aryan invaders had strict instructions not to reveal to the natives.[170] It long remained a contentious issue in Maharashtra whether Śivājī had been permitted to recite it at his coronation;[171] he might have been a celebrated champion of Hinduism, but he was no more than a Śūdra with recently concocted claims to Kṣatriya descent. Dayānand himself initially took for granted the exclusion of Śūdras from the Veda,[172] but later he passionately supported their right to study it—had not God made it to shine for all?[173] In a part of the Punjab where his arrival was greeted by Hindu mobs hurling stones and bricks, he had the audacity to discuss the Gāyatrī in front of a mixed audience of Hindus and Muslims;[174] and if he thought it in order for Muslims to hear it, he can hardly have withheld it from Śūdras. But it was not all plain sailing. In 1924 the Hindu Mahāsabhā, an offshoot of Congress that did not want Untouchables converting to Islam, recommended a number of reforms to give them a better deal, including allowing them entry to temples; but it was still not prepared to countenance teaching them the Vedas.[175]

The effort of reform from above that most concerns us is that of the Hindu nationalists. One of the problems of the early RSS in its Maharashtrian homeland was that it was not broadly representative of the local population, since the core of its membership was Brahmin.[176] Though the number of low-caste members in the movement has increased since then, they are still far from numerous and have tended not to rise very high in the organization.[177] This does not mean that the RSS represented a narrow projection of the interests of the upper castes—the Hindu nationalists were as aware as anyone of the danger of losing the Hindu masses to conversion,[178] and they were inspired by a nationalist vision of Hindu society as "one single homogenous

[170] Ibid., 147.

[171] Ibid., 20n12, 147n19.

[172] Jordens, *Dayānanda Sarasvatī*, 96, 104 (with a qualification).

[173] Ibid., 262. He included even Untouchables (*ati-śūdras*), not to mention girls.

[174] K. W. Jones, *Arya Dharm*, 40; cf. also Jordens, *Dayānanda Sarasvatī*, 51, 52.

[175] Jaffrelot, *India's silent revolution*, 16.

[176] Jaffrelot, *Hindu nationalist movement*, 45–47.

[177] Ibid., 49.

[178] See, for example, ibid., 358–59, on the reconversion efforts of the VHP in 1981–1982.

family."[179] Statements made by the RSS and its leaders rejected the traditional Hindu class (*varṇa*) system and called for the abolition of caste, including Untouchability;[180] as far as Sāvarkar was concerned, the more everyone intermarried the better it would be for the Hindu people.[181] This was rhetoric, but it was not mere rhetoric. Already in the early years of the movement, we hear of meals eaten in common with low-caste Hindus and of high-caste members living side by side with Untouchables.[182] In the same spirit the VHP, when organizing the massive pilgrimages of 1983, included Untouchables among those assigned the task of carrying holy water.[183]

The process of assimilation was nevertheless an asymmetric one. The culture of the movement was "Sanskritized," a culture of Brahmins;[184] one Untouchable member accordingly made a point of learning Sanskrit and displaying his knowledge of it.[185] At a month-long Hindu nationalist course held annually in a village near Śṛngerī, Vedic coaching would be given to boys from "all sects and castes," including a number of Untouchables; it was noted that "some of the best Vedic chanters turned out from such camps are from the backward sections."[186] The Vedic theme recurs in the activities of Sevā Bhārtī, the RSS organization established in 1979 and devoted to something the Hindu nationalists have been good at, namely social work; thus Sevā Bhārtī runs schools for Untouchables in the slums of Āgrā.[187] As in all the schools operated by the organization, the day begins with the pupils—who here come

[179] Ibid., 349.

[180] Ibid,, 61, 235n19, 349, and cf. 347 (on the VHP). For a rousing statement by Sāvarkar to the same effect, see Lederle, *Philosophical trends*, 290; and cf. Savarkar, *Hindutva*, 39.

[181] Savarkar, *Hindutva*, 138–39.

[182] Jaffrelot, *Hindu nationalist movement*, 45.

[183] Ibid., 361, and cf. 403.

[184] Ibid., 47.

[185] Ibid., 49; Jaffrelot, *India's silent revolution*, 477; and cf. Jaffrelot, *Hindu nationalist movement*, 509, on low-caste members of the BJP.

[186] Seshadri, *RSS*, 125, in a section headed "Vedas for All" ("backward" is a euphemism for "low-caste"). The book is a compilation of good news sent in by members of the RSS and edited by Seshadri.

[187] For the work of Sevā Bhārtī in the slums of Āgrā, see Jaffrelot, *India's silent revolution*, 456–62; for Sevā Bhārtī in general, see 454–56. The Hindu nationalists likewise went to work among the unemployed rural immigrants of Bhopāl (Jaffrelot, *Hindu nationalist movement*, 511), and responded to natural disasters (ibid., 284n11; Hansen, "BJP," 144). At the time of the partition of India, they did much to aid Hindu refugees from West Pakistan, especially in Delhi (Jaffrelot, *Hindu nationalist movement*, 75–76); this city, with its large refugee population, thus became a Hindu nationalist stronghold (ibid., 226n170).

disproportionately from the lowest of the Untouchable castes—reciting the Gāyatrī.[188] Untouchables are likewise encouraged to participate in Hindu festivals from which they have previously been excluded.[189] All this is a program of uplift, intended to help "our underprivileged brothers" to "gain self-confidence."[190] In an earlier epoch the message would have been expressed more bluntly, as in an address by the secretary of the Mangalore Depressed Classes Mission to an Untouchable audience in 1908: "If higher caste people ever beat you, that is because you become abusive when drunk. Behave properly, be humble and polite but at the same time try to improve your condition."[191] In our day the tone is somewhat subtler: "Social justice can be rendered to the weaker sections of society only when the entire society is imbued with the spirit of oneness and internal harmony," as a leading member of the RSS admonished in 1993. "It is only with the goodwill and cooperation of the entire society that they can get the necessary opportunities to raise themselves up."[192] This patronizing tone is one reason why members of the largest Untouchable caste of Āgrā, the Camārs, have no use for Sevā Bhārtī, which they regard as condescending.[193] In the same way, as one observer puts it, this RSS strategy has found "few takers" on its home ground in Maharashtra, where the prevailing culture is antithetical to social hierarchy.[194] Even within the Hindu nationalist movement lower-caste resentment can occasionally be heard. In the 1990s Umā Bhārtī, whose powers of religious oratory already gave her a certain importance in the BJP of Madhya Pradesh despite her lower-caste origin, had not achieved full acceptance by the party chiefs there, and complained that the lower-caste cadres of the party "have an upper caste mentality."[195]

To complete this picture of the way in which caste politics pose an obstacle to the marketing of Hindu identity by the Hindu nationalists, we need to extend it to include the contentious matter of reservations.

[188] Jaffrelot, *India's silent revolution*, 458; and see Jaffrelot, "Hindu nationalism," 208, on a village school in Madhya Pradesh.

[189] Jaffrelot, *India's silent revolution*, 459.

[190] Ibid., 455.

[191] S. Bayly, *Caste, society and politics*, 184.

[192] Jaffrelot, *India's silent revolution*, 454 and n4; Jaffrelot, *Hindu nationalist movement*, 535 and n4.

[193] Jaffrelot, *India's silent revolution*, 461–62.

[194] Hansen, "BJP," 124–25.

[195] Jaffrelot, *India's silent revolution*, 477, 478; Jaffrelot, *Hindu nationalist movement*, 388, 509. She is a Lodhī, and thus stems from the "Other Backward Classes" (OBCs), not from the Untouchables.

This institution is the prime example of the fact that caste politics are not just about symbols and sentiments; they relate to the real interests of the parties in very concrete ways. Reservations are quotas imposed by the state in favor of the less advantaged castes. They invite comparison with what Americans call affirmative action, though such policies have given rise to far more dissension in India than in the United States. Whereas white students in America mount legal challenges to affirmative action, their high-caste counterparts in India may burn buses, derail trains, sack government buildings, and immolate themselves.[196]

The institution of reservations has a history going back over a century. Because the Brahmins were traditionally the educated elite of Indian society, both British and native rulers tended to give them a disproportionate share of the administrative positions open to Indians. The question then arose whether this tendency should be countered by reserving some proportion of appointments (or of other good things dispensed by the state) for members of less privileged castes. An early move in this direction was made in 1902 by the Marāṭhā ruler of Kolhāpūr in what is now Maharashtra. He was on bad terms with his Brahmins, partly as a result of a dispute over the terms on which they were prepared to accept his claims to Kṣatriya status, and to spite them he decided to reserve half the future vacancies in his administration for non-Brahmins, primarily fellow-Marāṭhās.[197] Elsewhere reservations first made headway in the south,[198] but in due course they were extended all over India.[199] At independence the system was inherited by the new Indian rulers from the outgoing British.

Over time, it came to be marked by two significant asymmetries. The first was that, thanks to continuing initiatives taken by state governments in the south after independence, it was much broader and more effective there than in the north.[200] As a result, the politics of the south had undergone a sea change by 1980, whereas in the north the higher castes remained dominant, with the positions set aside for the disadvantaged often left unfilled and their leaders regularly co-opted by their social superiors.[201] The second asymmetry was within the north. Here

[196] Jaffrelot, *India's silent revolution*, 316, 326, 347.
[197] Cashman, *Myth of the Lokamanya*, 115–17.
[198] Jaffrelot, *India's silent revolution*, 172–75, 238–41.
[199] Ibid., 185.
[200] Ibid., 237–46, 324–25.
[201] Ibid., 90–92, 102.

reservations in favor of Untouchables were an established feature of the system; for this purpose Untouchables had come to be known in official parlance as the "Scheduled Castes," a term brought into use by the British in 1935.[202] But little had been done in the north about reservations in favor of the castes in the middle of the pile, which came to be known in the same parlance as "Other Backward Classes" (OBCs) thanks to Nehru's use of this phrase in a resolution of 1946.[203] Two commissions were set up to report on the OBC question at the national level, one in 1953 and the other—the Maṇḍal Commission—in 1978.[204] They differed in a significant respect: the first was led by a Brahmin, the second by a Yādav[205]—the Yādavs being a leading example of the OBC category. Yet nothing came of their reports until 1990, when prime minister V. P. Singh announced the implementation of the Maṇḍal report.[206] This time it was for real, and the resulting "Maṇḍalization" played a major role in the "silent revolution" that, for all its incompleteness and unevenness, has upended the caste hierarchies of large parts of the north over the last generation.[207]

The implementation of the Maṇḍal report provides a good example of the problematic character of reservations for the Hindu nationalists. On the one hand they could not afford to alienate the party faithful, who stemmed disproportionately from the higher castes, but on the other hand they needed lower-caste votes to get elected. In this context the increased political consciousness of the OBCs was a crucial force working against the BJP.[208] While the ideologically zealous RSS felt free to attack the Maṇḍal Report head-on,[209] the vote-conscious BJP was inevitably under pressure to come to terms with the new social order (or disorder). Its attempts to do so have been a vital, if rather indeterminate, chapter in the history of the party, with considerable variation over space and time; the party organization in Maharashtra, for example, stood out for its clear-cut support for the Maṇḍal

[202] Ibid., 214; Galanter, *Competing equalities*, 34n46, and cf. 130.

[203] For the background of this term, see Jaffrelot, *India's silent revolution*, 214–15; Galanter, *Competing equalities*, 159.

[204] Jaffrelot, *India's silent revolution*, 221–29, 320–24.

[205] Ibid., 221, 268.

[206] Ibid., 338.

[207] For a summary statement, see ibid., 9–10. For the unevenness of this transformation, see, for example, 362–63 on the contrast between Bihar and Rajasthan.

[208] Jaffrelot, *Hindu nationalist movement*, 493.

[209] Ibid., 414–15; Jaffrelot, *India's silent revolution*, 453.

Report.[210] To a significant extent the party is resigned to "Maṇḍalizing" itself,[211] though the results have been mixed and more in evidence at the bottom of the party than at the top.[212] Despite the elective affinity of Hindutva for the higher castes, and their historically dominant role in the movement, it is not inconceivable that the caste character of the party could eventually undergo more drastic change. The Shiv Sena, after all, represents a politically successful appropriation of Hindu nationalism by a party with no pretensions to high-caste status. But whether, or how fast, the BJP can evolve in such a direction remains to be seen.

One thing that this and other stories about reservations tell us is that the robustness of caste politics in India is not just a matter of social inertia. The fact that the state, even while disapproving of caste as a relic of an earlier epoch, was prepared to make it the basis of a set of policies shaping the distribution of good things to its subjects gave the institution a political salience it would not otherwise have enjoyed. There is a marked contrast here with the societies of Pakistan and Sri Lanka, where public policy does not engage with caste, partly at least because the dominant religious values are either hostile or indifferent to it.[213] The result is that in these countries caste, though socially real, is far less politically salient;[214] instead the conflict over who gets what is more ethnic and regional. But even in India the policies of the state were not formulated at the level of actual caste communities. Instead, they spoke of "Scheduled Castes" and "Other Backward Classes." Neither sounds like an identity worth dying for. As noted, the Scheduled Castes are the Untouchables, itself a term of convenience that has no equivalent in the vernacular languages of India;[215] there is no Untouchable community, just a large number of castes for which it is useful to have this generic label. The same goes for the OBCs.

[210] Hansen, "BJP," 134.

[211] Jaffrelot, *India's silent revolution*, 426.

[212] Ibid., 463, 473–74, 478–80, 484–90, 490–91.

[213] Compare also the role of Marxism as a caste-blind ideology in West Bengal under Communist rule (ibid., 255), for all that the Party has tended to be dominated by the kind of Communists that Āmbeḍkar referred to as "a bunch of Brahman boys" (Mendelsohn and Vicziany, *Untouchables*, 211).

[214] For the social reality of caste in Pakistan, see Jaffrelot, *History of Pakistan*, chap. 9; for the contrast with India, "a country where the castes are willing to speak their names," see ibid., 216.

[215] Deliège, *Untouchables of India*, 12.

Since the redistributive policies of the state do give these large-scale groupings of castes some interests in common, they can form political coalitions while the sense of common interest lasts. There was accordingly a significant coalition of OBCs in the early 1990s thanks to the implementation of the Maṇḍal report, but it faded in the later years of the decade.[216]

This is where social inertia—the survival of traditional caste identities —is crucial.[217] Embedded within the categories created by the state are real caste communities, and the relative solidarity of a limited number of large communities is the bedrock of caste politics.[218] We have already encountered two instances of such castes, and it is worth reviewing them here.

The first is the Camārs, the Untouchable caste of the Hindi belt that gave the world Svāmī Achūtānand, formed an alliance with Muslims, played with Buddhism, and had no use for Hindu nationalist social work. They are the major Untouchable caste of the region, indeed the largest in India; traditionally they had been leatherworkers, though in practice most of them are agricultural laborers.[219] Already in the first half of the nineteenth century the Camārs of central India had given rise to the Satnāmī movement, which articulated their resentment against the upper castes, partly by encouraging them to walk away from the ladder (since all men are equal), and partly by urging them to climb it (as by wearing the sacred thread of the twice-born).[220] In India today the Bahujan Samāj Party, founded by Kānśī Rām and named after a phrase of Phule's,[221] is a Camār party; other Untouchable castes tend to vote for different parties, including the BJP.[222] When Māyawatī wanted to highlight the turmoil that would ensue were she assassinated, her threat was that the members of the Camār community

[216] Jaffrelot, *India's silent revolution*, 349, 363, 384.

[217] The extent of this survival is evident from the "matrimonials" section of the *Sunday Times* of New Delhi for December 23, 2012. Many advertisements for brides and grooms appear under the relevant caste names; though some announce that caste is no bar, they are a minority. Muslims play the game alongside Hindus: one "Ansari boy" generously states that subcaste is no bar, another that his preference is for a girl from the same caste. I owe my copy of this item and my understanding of its significance to Bernard Haykel.

[218] Jaffrelot, *India's silent revolution*, 384 (on the OBC castes). Compare the role of the Mahārs as the solid core of Āmbeḍkar's movement.

[219] Mukerji, *Chamars of Uttar Pradesh*, 19, 21, 26; Mendelsohn and Vicziany, *Untouchables*, 48, 219.

[220] K. W. Jones, *Socio-religious reform movements*, 128–31.

[221] Jaffrelot, *India's silent revolution*, 153.

[222] Ibid., 424, 462.

would "create a havoc";[223] in this emotive context she did not speak of Untouchables, Scheduled Castes, or even Dalits.

The second example is the Yādavs, the caste that came under the influence of the Ārya Samāj, aspired to Kṣatriya status, and supplied the politician who gave his name to the Maṇḍal Commission. Though traditionally herdsmen, they are in fact mostly cultivators, and form one of the largest castes of Uttar Pradesh and Bihar.[224] Unlike the Camārs, they have no claim not to be Hindus, but they are uninterested in the politics of Hindu identity.[225] Two Yādav politicians were prominent in state politics in the 1990s and beyond. One was Mulāyam Singh Yādav leading his Samājvādī (i.e., Socialist) Party in Uttar Pradesh. The other was the leader of the Janatā Dal in Bihar, who made a point of horrifying the elite by speaking in the local Bhojpurī dialect, or in English with a thick Bhojpurī accent; as so often in lower-caste politics, it is essential to be seen to "diss" the twice-born.[226] But the gratifications that go with this political prominence are not just symbolic. In general, the benefits of the "silent revolution" went mainly to a small number of castes, rather than to the OBCs as a whole;[227] and it is no surprise that the Yādavs are the prime example of this.[228] They were accordingly resented by other OBC castes,[229] who might show their dislike by voting for the BJP.[230] Altogether, the Camārs and Yādavs constitute large lumps in the electorate that the BJP and its Hindu nationalist ideology has had no chance of digesting.

It is not that all castes matter in politics; probably most do not, either because they are too small and localized or because they have too little sense of community. But there are enough large castes enjoying the rooted loyalties of their members to have a serious impact on the political environment. For such castes old-fashioned caste consciousness

[223] Ibid., 424n94.

[224] Ibid., 187–88.

[225] Note, however, the emergence of Kṛṣṇa as the patron deity of the Yādavs (Fuller, *Camphor flame*, 275–76); the claim that "Krishna was a Yadav" could thus facilitate a convergence with Hindu nationalism in the event that the Yādavs' conception of their caste interests were to change.

[226] Jaffrelot, *India's silent revolution*, 379. Compare the comment of a contemporary on the Buddhist politician in ʿAlīgaṛh: "it is Maurya's abuse of Brahmans and Thakurs that earned him the adoration of his caste" (Duncan, "Levels," 274–75). The Ṭhākurs are Kṣatriyas.

[227] Jaffrelot, *India's silent revolution*, 352.

[228] Ibid., 364, 377–78, 383–84.

[229] Cf. ibid., 234–35 (an earlier case of such resentment).

[230] Ibid., 376–77.

has been far more of a given than any newfangled leftist class consciousness; the class identities so laboriously constructed by twentieth-century Communists look jerry-built by comparison. The past is not necessarily the future, but it does have inertia on its side.

In this context of vivid caste loyalties, at once inherited from the past and stimulated by modern politics, it was electorally disastrous for the BJP to be perceived as a party of the twice-born. As a prominent member of the party in Maharashtra lamented, "We are branded as a Brahmin party"; he saw this as a "major obstacle" in the way of the party's success.[231] All in all, the politics of caste in modern India have shown a potential to erode the clientelistic hierarchies that had previously maintained the dominance of the higher castes,[232] and have immunized large sectors of the electorate to the appeal of Hindu nationalism. This is a politics of attitude but also a politics of interest. "Do not take the candy of reservations and divide yourselves into castes," implored Ritambarā, a Hindu nationalist female ascetic (*sādhvī*), giving a speech in Hyderabad in 1991;[233] but to those who never had it before, candy tastes uncommonly good. Caste is the Achilles heel of Hindu identity.

What is so remarkable in comparative terms is that our long discussion of the travails of Hindu identity on the social front had no parallel in the Islamic case, where our attention was concentrated instead on ethnic tensions. Many Muslim countries contain non-Muslim or sectarian minorities, such as Christians and Shīʿites. But we encountered no populations that were excluded from the Muslim community, or felt themselves not to belong to it, for reasons related to social stratification. Thus Pakistan, like India, inherited the institution of caste at independence, and despite a hostile religious environment it remains a fact of life; and yet those at the bottom of the pile do not respond by rejecting a Muslim identity, nor are they immune to the blandishments of Islamists.[234] Islamists can face many problems in mobilizing Muslim populations, but a tendency for the underprivileged to opt out of Islam is not one of them. A scholar who has paid attention to the social ap-

[231] Hansen, "BJP," 126; cf. the derogatory identification of the party as the new Peśvās (130) and "the murderers of Gandhiji" (132–33). The RSS has been tactless enough to hold an annual meeting at the former Peśvā palace (Hansen, *Saffron wave*, 117).

[232] Jaffrelot, *India's silent revolution*, 385.

[233] Kakar, *Colors of violence*, 158.

[234] If there is such immunity anywhere in the Islamic world, it is ethnic—as with Kurds and Kabyles.

peal of Islamism across the Islamic world stresses the "two-pronged" character of the movement from the outset: it was able to mobilize the devout middle class and the slum dwellers alike.[235] Its problem was rather to hold together two constituencies with such divergent interests—witness the recent split in the Islamist vote in Egypt between the Muslim Brothers and the Salafīs and the analogous division in Tunisia. All this is in a way so obvious that it hardly needs saying. But it helps to dramatize a very basic contrast between Muslim and Hindu identity: socially speaking, Muslim identity is potentially integrative, whereas Hindu identity is almost inevitably divisive.

What would it be like if Islam did provide doctrinal support for a caste system? The question is not entirely hypothetical. Even in the Arab core of the Islamic world there exist, or existed until recently, a few Muslim societies with social groups that could aptly be described as castes. Two cases in point are Upper Egypt and Ḥaḍramawt (not to mention Yemen at large). In each case society is or was divided into three broad castes: an aristocracy of descendants of the Prophet (Ashrāf or Sāda); a tribal population disproportionately endowed with the means of violence (referred to in Upper Egypt as Arabs);[236] and an underclass of peasants, artisans, servants, or the like.[237] The descendants of the Prophet enjoy a certain prestige in many Muslim societies, but only in exceptional cases like these have they constituted a religious aristocracy comparable to the Brahmins. In such societies it is obviously the members of the underclass that have the least stake in the system and are most likely to feel themselves to be the victims of discrimination; notably, they are precluded from marrying women of higher castes.[238] On the Indian analogy one might accordingly expect that they would be tempted to convert to other religions. In fact, of course, nothing of the kind has happened. This is hardly puzzling in the case of Upper Egypt, where the process of labor migration that in

[235] Kepel, *Jihad*, 6. This is perhaps the central theme of the book.

[236] For this usage, see Fandy, "Egypt's Islamic Group," 612–13. Here, as with "Aryan," an ethnic term has been incorporated into a caste system. Contrast the unrestricted application of the term "Arab" to all who speak the language by ʿAbd al-Ghanī al-Nābulusī and Bakrī (see above, 13, 14n54).

[237] For Upper Egypt, see Fandy, "Egypt's Islamic Group," 612–13; for Ḥaḍramawt, see Bujra, *Politics of stratification*, 13–15 (a summary statement expanded in the rest of the chapter); also Freitag, *Indian Ocean migrants*, 39–42. As might be expected, there is some academic mileage to be gained from stressing diversity within the stratificatory patterns of Ḥaḍramawt (see Camelin, "Reflections").

[238] Bujra, *Politics of stratification*, 95.

recent decades has opened the underclass to external influences took its members to the solidly Muslim—and Muslim-ruled—societies of the Persian Gulf.[239] It is perhaps a little more arresting in the Ḥaḍramī case, where much of the corresponding migration took place earlier and was directed to regions under European rule whose populations were less uniformly Muslim.[240] Yet in both cases the discontent of the underclass was expressed in properly Islamic terms, by appealing to the wider Islamic tradition against the socially inegalitarian forms of it that had hitherto prevailed locally.[241] Thus in each case the socially disadvantaged rejected the aristocratic pretensions of the descendants of the Prophet; but in each case they did this by invoking the message of the Prophet himself—something that they could do because the mainstream tradition is not a socially exclusive one.[242] Thus Phule had no counterpart in Upper Egypt or Ḥaḍramawt, and Bin Laden—whose family is reputed to stem from the Ḥaḍramī underclass—was destined to become an Islamist rather than an apostate. One reason for this contrast is that the religious discrimination to which members of the Muslim underclass were exposed was less marked than that experienced by their Indian counterparts: they were not excluded from mosques, and in Upper Egypt they were in fact conspicuous for their attendance.[243] The other reason is, again, that Muslim identity and Hindu identity are different. The result is that the defection to other religions so common in the Hindu case is not just unparalleled but also unnecessary and indeed unthinkable in the Islamic case.

In a traditional agrarian society, where the majority of the population was effectively outside the political community, an identity that did not reach significantly beyond the elite was not a serious problem. Perhaps in a modern society under strongly authoritarian rule it might still be viable, though probably not indefinitely; under such conditions the twice-born might function as some kind of local equivalent of the

[239] Fandy, "Egypt's Islamic Group," 617–18.

[240] Bujra, *Politics of stratification*, 4–5, 77–81; Freitag, *Indian Ocean migrants*, 50–59.

[241] In the Egyptian case, the discontent came to a head in the late twentieth century and was articulated by radical Islamism (Fandy, "Egypt's Islamic Group," 611, 613–14, and cf. 615n29). In the Ḥaḍramī case the dissidence began early in the twentieth century and was articulated by an Islamic reformist movement known as Irshādism (Bujra, *Politics of stratification*, 94, 130–33; Freitag, *Indian Ocean migrants*, 245–58).

[242] For the Islamic terms of the argument in Upper Egypt, see Fandy, "Egypt's Islamic Group," 613–14; for the Ḥaḍramī case, see Bujra, *Politics of stratification*, 94, 131; Freitag, *Indian Ocean migrants*, 245–46; Mobini-Kesheh, "Islamic modernism," 241.

[243] Fandy, "Egypt's Islamic Group," 614.

Communist Party in contemporary China. But given the robust electoral politics of India since independence, and the disruption of traditional hierarchies, the old dominance of the upper castes was unsustainable—and has not been sustained. Marketing a Hindu political identity under these conditions has not been easy.

5. Rallying Hindus against Muslims

Given all this, one might begin to wonder how Hindu identity could ever have stood a chance in the politics of modern India. Yet the political movement formed around it eventually achieved sufficient electoral success to serve more than once as the core of a governing coalition. There are no doubt many reasons for this success but only one that is so central both to the rise of the BJP and to our concerns in this study as to merit discussion at some length. This is the repeated efforts of the Hindu nationalists, with varying success, to rally Hindus against Muslims.

Before we come to these efforts, a glance at the Shiv Sena may be instructive. This organization is well acquainted with the importance of choosing one's enemy wisely. When it was formed in 1966, the first enemy it chose for itself was the immigrant south Indian population of Bombay; but the southerners showed themselves to be bad enemies by learning to speak fluent Marāṭhī and putting up busts of the Marāṭhā hero Śivājī in their restaurants.[244] The movement was then in some trouble until it discovered the Muslims in the 1980s, as the RSS had done long before, and borrowed the RSS rhetoric of Hindutva; however shallow and opportunistic its commitment to Hindutva may appear to members of the RSS,[245] from then on Shiv Sena did not look back.[246] To make do for now with a trivial example, on one occasion when its leader was concerned to make political noise, he demanded that two women in a film who develop a lesbian relationship be given Muslim names.[247] Without question the change of tack has paid political dividends, and the moral is that Muslims make better enemies than southerners.

There are several reasons why Muslims make good enemies in the Indian context. One is that Muslims, whether they like it or not, are

[244] Eckert, *Charisma of direct action*, 88–89.
[245] Hansen, "BJP," 131.
[246] Eckert, *Charisma of direct action*, 90–91, 103–4.
[247] Ibid., 257.

historically identified with the invaders who did most to destroy Hindu culture. Of course, not all the Muslim elite in India espoused this program assiduously, and many did not pursue it at all or indeed did the opposite. But there was enough rhetoric of destruction, and enough actual destruction, to lend support to a deep sense of Hindu grievance. For example, we have seen how Muslim cow killing had given rise to a centuries-old tradition of insult and injury;[248] and whether or not the Muslims demolished a temple at the site of the Rām's birthplace, they had unquestionably destroyed many others, for example, that of Somnāth.[249] As to rhetoric, Sirhindī, who, as we saw, laid such emphasis on sacrificing cows to offend Hindus, tells us that the coexistence of Islam and unbelief is unthinkable and that one of them can only get ahead at the expense of the other. Within this zero-sum relationship, "to honour the one amounts to insulting the other." The honor of Islam thus lies in insulting unbelievers, and anyone who respects them dishonors the Muslims.[250] In mining the resulting vein of Hindu resentment, the Hindu nationalists were not particularly scrupulous; it would, for example, be hard to cite chapter and verse for the seventy-seven battles that according to the VHP had been fought by Hindus against Muslims at Ayodhyā to prevent the destruction of the temple and completion of the mosque.[251] But even if their scholarly standards had been higher, the Hindu nationalists would not have needed to be very selective.

A second reason is that since Partition the Muslims of India, again whether they like it or not, have been associated with Pakistan, the Muslim separatist state that broke the unity of undivided India, treats India with studied hostility, and has a track record of supporting its insurgent movements. The loyalty of India's Muslims is accordingly easy to call in question. As a Shiv Sena politician put it in 1992: "India and Pakistan play a cricket game. The Indian team loses and Pakistan wins. Fire crackers go off in Bhendi Bazaar. Bhendi Bazaar [is a] Muslim area. That means what? Their loyalty is not for India but

[248] See 63–64.

[249] For the modern resonances of this destruction, see R. Guha, *India after Gandhi*, 141–42. For a list of eighty historically attested Muslim temple desecrations in India over the period 1192–1760, see Eaton, "Temple desecration," preceding 275. Eaton argues that, despite the religious rhetoric accompanying such desecrations, the motivation was political (see for example 260, 268).

[250] Rizvi, *Muslim revivalist movements*, 248.

[251] Jaffrelot, *Hindu nationalist movement*, 402, 423.

for Pakistan."[252] At the same time Partition encourages the sense that if India's unity has been broken and the massive Muslim populations of the western Punjab and eastern Bengal have seceded, then at least what remains should be Hindustan, the land of the Hindus. As the ascetic Ritambarā puts it, "The Muslims got their Pakistan"; "Hindustan is ours!"[253] The Shiv Sena politician followed his account of the cricket match by telling his interviewer that "this country is Hindustan. It is Hindustan of the Hindus. What is wrong with calling it Hindustan? Like Pakistan, which is a Muslim country. This is a country which belongs to Hindus. Communal riots will increase in the future."[254] From this perspective secularism appears as "a euphemism for the policy of Muslim appeasement."[255] This does not leave much room for Muslims in India, and according to one slogan shouted by demonstrators, Muslims belong either in Pakistan or in the cemetery (*qabristān*).[256]

A third reason is the existence of a sufficient number of Muslims with enough attitude to provide an inviting target—Muslims who do not behave in the manner of the Shiv Sena's ill-chosen southern enemies, and who accordingly, in a favorite phrase of the Hindu nationalists, need to be taught a lesson.[257] In 1987 the Muslim countermovement that developed during the struggle to defend the Bābrī Masjid obliged the Hindu nationalists by calling for a boycott of India's Republic Day ceremonies.[258] A couple of years earlier the "Shāh Bāno affair" of 1985, a legal fracas to which we will come in a later chapter, may have involved the largest mobilization of Indian Muslims since the partition of the subcontinent.[259] External factors also helped, notably the global Islamic revival and the wealth accruing to Indian Muslims thanks to labor migration to the Persian Gulf.[260] Even among the Tamil Muslims, a population traditionally at ease with the wider culture of

[252] Interview quoted in Banerjee, *Warriors in politics*, 150; for more such denunciation of the disloyalty of the inhabitants of this Muslim quarter in Bombay, see Eckert, *Charisma of direct action*, 91. Cricket matches between India and Pakistan have been described as "war minus the shooting" for most viewers (R. Guha, *India after Gandhi*, 725).

[253] Kakar, *Colors of violence*, 161, 165.

[254] Banerjee, *Warriors in politics*, 150. The politician gives these views on the authority of his "political guru," the leader of the Shiv Sena.

[255] Graham, *Hindu nationalism*, 50.

[256] Jaffrelot, *Hindu nationalist movement*, 459.

[257] Jaffrelot, "Politics of processions," 86; and cf. Eckert, *Charisma of direct action*, 119.

[258] Brass, *Politics of India*, 247.

[259] Jaffrelot, *Hindu nationalist movement*, 334–35. For this affair, see below, 288–89.

[260] Cf. ibid., 338–40, 362n103. Hansen reports that in private a fair number of Muslims who had worked in the Persian Gulf would confide that their experiences with Arab

their homeland,[261] two recent songs include the tactless claim to have "ruled India for eight hundred years."[262]

By way of illustration, one observer has given us a fine portrait of a Muslim with attitude in the southern city of Hyderabad, where the Muslim community is unusually large.[263] This Akbar, a wrestler from a family of wrestlers, is the proud and violent champion of his community. Muslims, he tells his interviewer, are tougher than Hindus; in Hyderabad, at least, more Hindus than Muslims get killed in riots. Likewise Muslims are united, whereas Hindus are divided. Moreover Muslims have larger families than Hindus, and lower-caste Hindus convert to Islam. So the future, he declares, is on the side of the Muslims: "There won't be many Hindus left."[264] Interestingly, the same observer also gives us long extracts from the speech given in Hyderabad in 1991 by the Hindu nationalist ascetic Ritambarā, who echoes the same themes from the other side.[265] Hindus are tolerant—maybe too tolerant; the devotees of Gandhi are wimps, our current rulers are hermaphrodites. Muslims breed like mosquitoes and flies and have no use for family planning. There is a conspiracy to make Hindus a minority in their own country.[266] The enemy in this rhetoric is not the Muslims as such: "Wherever I go, I say 'Muslims, live and prosper among us. Live like milk and sugar.' " The enemy is the Muslim with attitude: "Is it our fault if he seems bent upon being a lemon in the milk?"[267] In all this there is no disagreement between Akbar and Ritambarā over the facts. It is just that Akbar's dream is Ritambarā's nightmare—and both are projections of communal hatred.

---

employers had destroyed their faith in Muslim solidarity, but in India they could not say this in public (*Saffron wave*, 256n24).

[261] See Narayanan, "Religious vocabulary," 74–76. The text to which the article is devoted is a seventeenth-century Tamil life of the Prophet Muḥammad whose title combines two literary terms, the Muslim *sīra* and the Hindu *purāṇa* (79).

[262] Ibid., 93–94.

[263] Kakar, *Colors of violence*, 59–69.

[264] Ibid., 62, 64.

[265] Ibid., 153–66.

[266] This Hindu demographic paranoia was a product of the decennial census instituted by the British in 1871. Thus in 1909 one Hindu commentator was warning that Hindus would disappear within 420 years (Jaffrelot, *Hindu nationalist movement*, 24). For a Hindu nationalist account of the continuing demographic peril in a publication of 1999, see Jaffrelot, *Hindu nationalism*, 244–50. The fear does not come out of thin air: the decennial censuses show the proportion of Muslims in the Indian population rising from 10.7 percent to 13.4 percent between 1961 and 2001 and the proportion of Hindus falling from 83.5 percent to 80.5 percent (Pew Forum, *Spirit and power*, 81).

[267] Kakar, *Colors of violence*, 159–64.

Of course many Muslims are not militant, even in the face of strong provocation. A few years after the massive anti-Muslim riots in Bombay in the winter of 1992–1993, a Muslim businessman remarked: "The moment the Shiv Sena is out of power, Muslims are in danger. So we have to just try and keep them in power."[268] At the same time Muslim leaders adopted a policy of developing closer relations with the police, since, as one of them put it, "Now I realize that working with the police is the way to prevent another riot here"; leading police officials were invited to Muslim festivals, and small constructions were erected at street corners to provide shade for police constables.[269] Muslims in Karnataka did not appreciate it when the Congress Party leadership sought their votes by laying on broadcasts from Bangalore in Urdu, thereby provoking anti-Muslim rioting in 1994.[270] In 1979 Muslims in an industrial center in Bihar agreed to allow a Hindu procession to pass through the Muslim quarters, thereby temporarily upsetting the plans of the RSS—though in the event the organization succeeded in starting its riot all the same.[271] Muslim leaders in Bhopāl undertook to organize and pay for the repair of a Hindu temple damaged in the riots following the demolition of the mosque at Ayodhyā.[272] And one Muslim cleric argued against any attempt to secure the restoration of the Bābrī Masjid itself on the ground that this would only exacerbate hostility against Muslims.[273] But from the Hindu nationalist point of view that still leaves enough Muslims asking to be taught a lesson.

A final reason why the Muslims made good enemies was that they were, in a way, just the kind of community the Hindu nationalists wanted to create. The Hindus, or so a Hindu nationalist lamented in 1923, are divided into numerous "water-tight compartments" that rarely think it worth their while to come to each other's aid; the Muslims, by contrast, form "one organic community," any part of which feels an injury done to another part.[274] Muslim identity thus provided an image of what Hindu identity ought to be.

The Muslims were accordingly the obvious domestic enemy of the Hindu nationalists. They did not belong in the country. As M. S. Goḷwalkar

[268] Eckert, *Charisma of direct action*, 204.

[269] Hansen, *Wages of violence*, 153–54.

[270] Manor, "Southern discomfort," 190–91.

[271] Jaffrelot, "Politics of processions," 74–75.

[272] Jaffrelot, *Hindu nationalist movement*, 463n62.

[273] Zaman, *Ulama*, 183–84 (on Mawlānā Waḥīd al-Dīn Khān).

[274] Jaffrelot, *Hindu nationalist movement*, 20. Jaffrelot labels the effect seen here as "stigmatisation and emulation."

(d. 1973), leader of the RSS from 1940, put it in a book of 1939, "The Hindus alone are the Nation," while Muslims, "if not actually antinational are at least outside the body of the Nation."[275] They were welcome to "merge themselves in the national race and adopt its culture," but if they did not wish to avail themselves of this offer, their only option was "to live at its mercy so long as the national race may allow them to do so and to quit the country at the sweet will of the national race."[276] Since then the tone of the Hindu nationalists has mellowed somewhat.[277] Vajpayee in 1961 observed that the Indian Muslims were the descendants of Hindus and that "by changing religion one does not change one's nationality or culture";[278] we will see more of such thinking later in this chapter.[279] But a strong vein of hostility to Muslims has remained an endemic feature of Hindu nationalism. This brings us to a notorious aspect of urban politics in India: the communal riot.

These riots are typically the "orchestration of spontaneity."[280] Spontaneity matters, since even the most accomplished arsonist is doomed to fail if he has nothing inflammable to set a light to. Hence a robust heritage of communal mistrust, fear, and hatred greatly increases the chances of a violent outbreak; it would be a thankless task to try to foment a riot against Episcopalians in Princeton, New Jersey. In recent Western academic writing on Indian politics, as might be expected, there has been a tendency to downplay this role of the communal heritage.[281] Such a tendency is also widely shared, as an acute observer has pointed out, by "men of goodwill" in riot-prone towns and cities of India.[282] But it proves hard to adhere consistently and convincingly to such a position,[283] particularly in the light of evidence that the phe-

[275] Golwalkar, *We or our nationhood*, 53 n.

[276] Ibid., 47 (another such passage is quoted in Jaffrelot, *Hindu nationalist movement*, 56). For Goḷwalkar, concessions to minorities courted the "disastrous fate of the unfortunate Czechoslovakia" (49–50).

[277] For a possible softening in Goḷwalkar's own later views, see Gold, "Organized Hinduisms," 566.

[278] Graham, *Hindu nationalism*, 96.

[279] See 110–11.

[280] Eckert, *Charisma of direct action*, 126; similarly Jaffrelot, "Politics of processions," 84.

[281] For an outstanding study that follows this line of analysis, see Brass, *Hindu-Muslim violence*.

[282] Kakar, *Colors of violence*, 150–51. His comments on the whole debate seem eminently sensible (149–53).

[283] Brass states that his analysis "relegates all spontaneity theories of the causes of riots to the realm of blame displacement" (*Hindu-Muslim violence*, 16). But he later observes that there is "little spontaneous about Hindu-Muslim riots" (377–78—he does not

nomenon of communal riots antedates the coming of modern politics to India.[284] What is, of course, true is that the communal heritage is not the same everywhere. Thus there has been a marked contrast between the north and south of India, with more hatred in the north.[285] In December 1992 a poll showed 53 percent approving the demolition of the Bābrī Masjid in the north, but only 17 percent in the south.[286] In the following year BJP representatives in the southern states were demanding that the national leadership talk about issues other than Ayodhyā because a communalist message "would not sell in the South."[287]

What concerns us here, however, is the orchestration.[288] It can be a fairly simple matter to start a communal riot. Hindu religious processions are a very convenient way to trigger them,[289] as the founder of the RSS knew well from events that took place in Nāgpūr in 1923.[290] For this purpose a procession needs to take a route through a Muslim quarter,[291] preferably timing its movements so that it passes by a major mosque during the Friday prayer (if there is a risk of arriving at the mosque too early, the procession can always slow down).[292] Such a procession is, of course, accompanied by musicians. In the good old days,

say "nothing spontaneous"); he speaks of "elements both of spontaneity and planning" that contribute to them, of "prejudices" that interact with purposive action (358), and of "latent hostilities" that are deliberately mobilized (378). Perhaps most strikingly, he remarks that "there exists in India a discourse of Hindu-Muslim communalism that has corrupted history, penetrated memory, and contributes in the present to the production and perpetuation of communal violence in the country" (34). The only question that leaves is how long this discourse has been in existence.

[284]For a riot "between the communities of Hindus and Muslims" in Gujarat in 1714, as described in sources written by contemporaries, see Haider, "Holi riot," 128–32. For one in Calcutta in 1789, see C. A. Bayly, "Pre-history of 'communalism,' " 199.

[285]For the case of Karnataka, see Manor, "Karnataka," 322; Manor, "Southern discomfort," 182. For an explanation of the Tamil case in terms of the early development of caste-based politics in the south, see Wilkinson, *Votes and violence*, 194–96. But for adverse trends in the south, see Jaffrelot, "Politics of processions," 87.

[286]Jaffrelot, *Hindu nationalist movement*, 473, and cf. 467. But see also 425–26, 476, on more irenic attitudes in the rural north; communal riots are an urban, not a rural phenomenon (Varshney, *Ethnic conflict*, 6, 95–97).

[287]Manor, "Southern discomfort," 189. There is also a marked contrast between the west (where Gujarat became a disaster area) and the east (where Orissa has never been one); see Varshney, *Ethnic conflict*, 97–101.

[288]For orchestration at the micro-political level, note one observer's account of the role of meetings of "strong men" representing different localities in deciding where "the wind (*havā*) is to be spread" in the course of a riot (Kakar, *Colors of violence*, 80).

[289]Jaffrelot, "Politics of processions," with numerous examples.

[290]Jaffrelot, *Hindu nationalist movement*, 34; Jaffrelot, "Politics of processions," 66.

[291]As in Poona in 1982 (Jaffrelot, "Politics of processions," 76).

[292]As in Madras in 1995 (ibid., 87).

when Hindus and Muslims participated in each others' processions, the musicians would have been Muslims and would respectfully have fallen silent while passing the mosque;[293] but these days they are Hindus and make a point of maintaining the decibel level.[294] The Muslims can be expected to respond angrily to this provocation. They stream out of the mosque, or they may already be praying in the street because the mosque is overflowing with worshippers; they attack the procession, and a riot has begun. Processions were already being used, albeit on a more modest scale, to mobilize Hindus in the late nineteenth century. But there are, of course, other routes to the same result. In Bombay a ritual known as the Mahā Ārtī was developed into a stationary challenge to Muslim congregational prayers;[295] since no procession was involved, the problem of timing was eased. Nationally, the agitation over the birthplace of Rām in Ayodhyā was associated with massive processions all over India, and at the same time it elevated the hated Bābrī Masjid and the projected temple of Rām into a source of synchronized communal tension for the entire country. When the news of the destruction of the mosque spread in December 1992, some of the ensuing riots were started by Hindu victory processions, while others arose from reactions to the demolition on the part of angry Muslims.[296]

The political advantage to be gained by Hindu politicians from a successful communal riot is clear enough.[297] The point is to get people to identify first and foremost as Hindus and vote accordingly—for the BJP or, in the case of riots in Bombay, for the Shiv Sena. There is no doubt that Hindu nationalist politicians believe that communal riots can get out the Hindu vote for them, and students of Indian politics have noted many instances where the outcome suggests that they were

[293] As in Allāhābād before 1924 (ibid., 68–69).

[294] As already in Nāgpūr in the 1920s (ibid., 66).

[295] Ibid., 86; Eckert, *Charisma of direct action*, 115–16.

[296] Jaffrelot, *Hindu nationalist movement*, 458–63; for the case of Bombay, see also Eckert, *Charisma of direct action*, 114–17.

[297] Muslim politicians, by contrast, do not stand to benefit. The fact that Muslims are a minority means that they are likely to be on the losing side in a communal riot and that solidifying the Muslim vote does not help to get Muslims elected. But Muslims do start riots. This was the case in Calcutta in 1996, where it was a Muslim procession that insisted on making its way through a Hindu quarter (Jaffrelot, "Politics of processions," 88), and on some accounts in Gujarat in 2002 (for the Gujarat riots, see Brass, *Hindu-Muslim violence*, 387–91); for the disputed events that triggered the riots, see also Jaffrelot, "2002 pogrom," 174–75.

correct.[298] Thus in Gujarat, where there is a strong history of Hindu-Muslim riots, those of the early 1990s helped to bring the BJP to power for the first time in 1995.[299] However, the government soon fell, owing to caste divisions within the party.[300] Fresh riots in 2002 then gave the BJP a much stronger grip on power in the state.[301] So, under the right conditions the communal riot is a winning strategy. But, of course, conditions are not always right;[302] if they were, the BJP would by now have engrossed enough of the Indian vote to be able to rule the country without the need to accommodate difficult and demanding coalition partners.[303] Nevertheless, conditions have been favorable in enough places for enough of the time to make the orchestration of communal riots a familiar implement in the Hindu nationalist toolbox.[304]

[298] For the link between riots and elections, see Jaffrelot, *Hindu nationalist movement*, 395, 448, 513; Jaffrelot, "Politics of processions," 68–71, 73, 78–81; Shah, "BJP's riddle," 248, 249; Eckert, *Charisma of direct action*, 127–28; Brass, *Hindu-Muslim violence*, 33–34; Wilkinson, *Votes and violence*, 49–51. There is also a scatter of southern examples (Manor, "Southern discomfort," 167, 172, 173, 174).

[299] Shah, "BJP's riddle," 249.

[300] Ibid., 261–65.

[301] Jaffrelot, "2002 pogrom," 182.

[302] Two recent studies probe these conditions. One compares cities that are riot prone with cities that are not and concludes that intercommunal civic engagement is a major factor in reducing the probability of riots (Varshney, *Ethnic conflict*, 281). Another makes the case that the key factor is the electoral interests of state governments, since they control the police and thereby decide whether an incipient riot is to continue or not (Wilkinson, *Votes and violence*, 4, 16–17; for his explanation of the Gujarat riots of 2002 in these terms, see 7–8, 59–62, 154–60). Cf. the view of a senior police officer in 1995 that no communal riot can continue for more than twenty-four hours unless the state government wants it to (Jaffrelot, "Politics of processions," 90).

[303] The ambivalence of the BJP response at the national level to the Gujarat riots of 2002 is instructive. Prime minister Vajpayee denounced the riots on television, but the state government was not dismissed for its failure to maintain law and order; he visited Gujarat, but only after a considerable delay, and he took Umā Bhārtī with him; a firm, even-handed police chief with a track record for handling communal violence effectively was dispatched to Gujarat, where he was less than welcome to the state leader, but he was not given the force he asked for (Brass, *Hindu-Muslim violence*, 390–91). Presumably one factor here was the need to appease coalition partners; another may have been the emergence among the BJP's constituencies of a middle class that wants to see India governed by a strong, disciplined, no-nonsense nationalist party—not a party of chaos and disorder (see Jaffrelot, *Hindu nationalist movement*, 432–35, 448, 449–50, 451, 458, 528, and Manor, "In part, a myth," 66; and cf. Jaffrelot, "Politics of processions," 86–87 on rural voters, and Manor, "Southern discomfort," 189–90 and n73 on both middle-class and rural voters in Karnataka).

[304] This is not to say that the technique was monopolized by the Hindu nationalists: for the role of Congress politicians in fomenting riots against Sikhs following the assassination of Indira Gandhi in 1984, see R. Guha, *India after Gandhi*, 565–66.

In their efforts to bring about the triumph of a Hindu identity, the Hindu nationalists fight on two fronts, the caste front and the Muslim front. Their underlying strategy could be summed up as recouping on the Muslim front their losses on the caste front. In this context it is worth noting that the agitation over the Bābrī Masjid, the most aggressive anti-Muslim campaign ever launched by the Hindu nationalists, was at the same time an attempt to change the subject by diverting attention from the implementation of the Maṇḍal report.[305] The strategy can work well, as when Untouchables join in attacks on Muslims, as they did during the Bombay riots of 1992–1993, despite their antipathy toward the Shiv Sena.[306] But it can also work badly, especially when the caste enemies of the Hindu nationalists join their Muslim enemies.[307] At the Untouchable level we have already met a slogan proclaiming a Camār-Muslim alignment against the upper castes: "Jātavs and Muslims are brothers, where do the Hindu people come from?"[308] Ironically, this invites comparison with Gandhi's nightmare of 1932 during his fast-unto-death against a separate electorate for Untouchables: " 'Untouchable' hooligans will make common cause with Muslim hooligans and kill caste-Hindus."[309] The same alignment was reasserted when the Camār politician Māyawatī extended reservations to low-caste Muslims in Uttar Pradesh in 1995 and reserved 8 percent of police officers' posts for them; Muslims also appreciated her refusal to allow the VHP to target a mosque said to occupy the birthplace of Kṛṣṇa

[305] Jaffrelot, *Hindu nationalist movement*, 415–16.

[306] Eckert, *Charisma of direct action*, 221, and cf. Hansen, "BJP," 158–59; also Jaffrelot, *Hindu nationalist movement*, 448, and Brass, *Hindu-Muslim violence*, 184–85.

[307] See, for example, Manor, "Karnataka," 354 (the coalition of the disadvantaged put together by an enterprising politician in the 1970s); Jaffrelot, *India's silent revolution*, 248 (Gujarat in the late 1970s), 391, 394, 402 (Kānśī Rām's parties from the 1970s to the 1990s), 371–72 (a Yādav-led socialist party of the 1990s), 381–83 (a Yādav-led party in Bihar in the same period). The availability of allies gives the Muslims a leverage in Indian politics that they would not have outside the framework of electoral democracy. Thus the autonomy of the Muslim University in ʿAlīgaṛh was curtailed in 1951 but expanded in 1981, and their protests over the Shāh Bāno affair won them a law resolving the issue in their favor (for both examples, see Brass, *Politics of India*, 233–34).

[308] Jaffrelot, *India's silent revolution*, 109 (the slogan was used in the campaign of a Camār Buddhist politician in Uttar Pradesh in the context of an alliance with Muslims in 1962, see above, 59–60). Compare a document of the Ādi-dharm movement in the Punjab which opposes independence for India in the immediate future as prejudicial to "India's weak minorities—especially Ad Dharmis and the Mohammedan people" (Juergensmeyer, *Religion as social vision*, 125).

[309] Desai, *Diary*, 301; Jaffrelot, *India's silent revolution*, 24. For an example from 1926 in which the Brahmin leader of the RSS was physically attacked by Muslim and low-caste Hindu activists at a public meeting, see Bacchetta, "Hindu nationalist women," 128.

in Mathurā.[310] At the OBC level Caraṇ Singh (d. 1987), the leading proponent of "peasant (*kisān*) politics,"[311] in 1979 demanded the expulsion of the Hindu nationalists from the Janatā Party (an amalgamation of opposition parties formed in 1977) on the ground that they would cost it support among Muslims.[312] In 1994, following the Bombay riots, the Samājvādī Party moved into the city through alliances with prominent Muslim businessmen; its leader, Mulāyam Singh Yādav, generously promised a large crowd in Bombay that he would guarantee the safety of Muslims in India.[313] He had some standing to do this, thanks to his role during the agitation over Ayodhyā: it was under his government in Uttar Pradesh in 1990 that large numbers of Hindu nationalists were arrested and a smaller number of them shot, earning him the nickname "Mullā Yādav."[314] Allying with the group that Hindu nationalists saw as the internal enemy cannot have cost these politicians the support of their own constituencies or they would not have done it.[315]

The importance of both fronts is indicated by the fact that each involves what by the standards of a Western democracy is a high level of violence. As we have seen, the characteristic form taken by communal violence is the riot; its counterpart in caste politics is the atrocity.[316] Caste atrocities are counted in thousands. Thus, in Maharashtra in 1994 the number of cases filed was over four thousand, involving rape, murder, and arson;[317] in Uttar Pradesh in 1995 it reached almost fifteen thousand.[318] In Bihar caste militias have been involved.[319] Usually it is the upper castes who take it out on the lower castes, but the contrary is not unheard of. After the assassination of Gandhi in 1948, there were lynchings of Brahmins in Maharashtra and riots that rendered thousands of them homeless.[320] It would be of some interest to know how the number of fatalities in the sudden cloudbursts of communal rioting compares with those attributable to the steady drizzle of caste atrocities. And yet all this violence should not obscure the contribution

[310] Jaffrelot, *India's silent revolution*, 416 and n66.

[311] Ibid., 279–89.

[312] Jaffrelot, *Hindu nationalist movement*, 308.

[313] Hansen, *Wages of violence*, 181, 182.

[314] Jaffrelot, *Hindu nationalist movement*, 420–22.

[315] Note also that Muslim votes are relatively cheap: Muslims are looking for security, not the candy of reservations (Wilkinson, *Votes and violence*, 17, 144–45).

[316] Mendelsohn and Vicziany, *Untouchables*, chap. 2.

[317] Eckert, *Charisma of direct action*, 218–19.

[318] Jaffrelot, *India's silent revolution*, 411, table 11.10; and cf. 405, 445.

[319] Mendelsohn and Vicziany, *Untouchables*, 57.

[320] Jaffrelot, *Hindu nationalist movement*, 86–87; Hansen, "BJP," 122–23.

of communal and caste tensions to a key structural fact about Indian politics: over time, as one observer has put it, the plurality of identities in play "prevents conflict from being concentrated along one particular fault line in Indian society"[321]—including the fault line along which the Hindu nationalists would most like to concentrate it.

Another testimony to the significance of the two fronts is the power of the emotional symbols used to rally the contenders, whether in "just and urgent defence" or to give "wanton offence" to their enemies.[322] In communal politics no symbolic issue was more potent than the scheme to demolish the mosque at Ayodhyā and erect a Hindu temple in its stead—though as an Untouchable villager in Uttar Pradesh told a reporter in 1991, "We can't even enter the temple in the village, so what does the Ram Mandir in Ayodhya mean to us?"[323] Of course, there were more overt ways to hit back at Rām: Māyawatī was delighted to convene a meeting in Lucknow in 1995 to honor the legacy of Periyār, the Tamil separatist author of the blasphemous pamphlet denouncing Rām as a villain[324]—a man who had also championed the conversion of Untouchables to Islam and the formation of Pakistan.[325] He was to have had a huge statue in the new Revolution Square in Lucknow alongside Phule and Āmbeḍkar.[326] The nearest equivalent to Ayodhyā in caste politics might be putting up and pulling down statues of Āmbeḍkar;[327] Māyawatī erected fifteen thousand of them while in office in 1997.[328] The parallels between caste alienation and communal alienation can go quite far. Āmbeḍkar had ideas of a Dalit homeland, though he did not take his dream as far as Jinnah was to take his.[329] Likewise the slogans shouted by demonstrators may give Muslims the choice of Pakistan or

[321] Manor, "Regional parties," 121 (with a contrast to Canada and Sri Lanka); see also 118–19, 122.

[322] The phrases are Sāvarkar's (*Hindutva*, 140). The salience of such symbolic politics in India marks a strong contrast with China since the Cultural Revolution.

[323] Fuller, *Camphor flame*, 261.

[324] Jaffrelot, *India's silent revolution*, 415, and see above, 67. Imagine a conference to celebrate the life and work of Salman Rushdie being held in Lahore.

[325] See More, *Muslim identity*, 148–50, 153, 160. I owe my knowledge of this study to Mahmood Kooria.

[326] Mendelsohn and Vicziany, *Untouchables*, 230.

[327] Jaffrelot, *India's silent revolution*, 412, 415, 419; cf. Trivedy, "Breaking the status quo," 53–54 (on the vandalization of Āmbeḍkar statues by "upper caste goondas" in villages near Lucknow), and Eckert, *Charisma of direct action*, 220n15, 221 (on riots following the desecration of an Āmbeḍkar statue in Bombay).

[328] Jaffrelot, *India's silent revolution*, 419.

[329] Ibid., 105 and n49. A Camār leader of the same period flirted with the idea of a homeland for Untouchables (Achūtistān, see J. Leslie, *Authority and meaning*, 60).

the cemetery,[330] or they may call for the Brahmin bastards (*Brāhmaṇ sālā*) to leave the land.[331] It all depends.

6. What are the Hindu nationalists?

So far in this chapter we have encountered the Hindu nationalists repeatedly without asking what they are. Calling them "Hindu nationalists," of course, implies that they are a species of nationalist and thus comparable to nationalists in the Islamic world and elsewhere; religion, in other words, is secondary. But they are also sometimes seen as the counterpart of the Islamists, which is presumably what those who refer to them as "Hindu fundamentalists" have in mind.[332] Which is correct? A full answer to this question cannot be given at this point because it turns on the relationship of the movement to Hindu values, as opposed to Hindu identity. But certain points are already worth making here.

At first sight the role of Hindu religious figures in and around the movement might suggest that we are dealing with a religious rather than a nationalist phenomenon. Of these the most august are the Śankarācāryas, the heads of the major monasteries that act as custodians of the teachings of Śankara. In the twentieth century they came to form something of an all-Indian religious leadership, though by no means a well-coordinated one. It helped that they were above sectarian squabbles: one Śankarācārya of Dvārkā held the balance by installing 1331 phallic symbols (*lingas*) of Śiva on the one hand and 1220 black stones (*śālagrāmas*) with images representing Viṣṇu on the other.[333] It also helped that their origins were not always local. One Śankarācārya of Purī was from Gujarat, one Śankarācārya of Dvārkā was from Karnataka.[334] They were often good speakers in several languages and traveled widely throughout India; one Śankarācārya of Kāñcī did 1500 miles on foot.[335] At the same time modern communications helped to put them in closer contact with each other. Admittedly, one result of this was a vocal dispute over the claim of the Kāñcī monastery to be an authentic foundation of Śankara's; Śṛngerī and Kāñcī have been at

[330] See 93.
[331] Jaffrelot, *India's silent revolution*, 347.
[332] For this usage, see 399.
[333] Cenkner, *Tradition of teachers*, 116, and see 143–44.
[334] Ibid., 125.
[335] Ibid., 103, 122, 123, 124, 125, 126, 130–31.

loggerheads over this since about the middle of the nineteenth century, and the other Śankarācāryas have been drawn into the conflict.[336] But increased contact has also meant increased cooperation, as meetings of the Śankarācāryas became more frequent in the second half of the twentieth century.[337] Moreover, these leaders have come to terms with at least some aspects of the modern world. The Śankarācārya of Śṛngerī in the first half of the twentieth century was against modern education and Westernization,[338] but the Śankarācārya of Dvārkā in 1960 established an Indological research institute affilated with a major university.[339]

The Śankarācāryas were thus well placed to advance the Hindu nationalist cause, and to an extent they did so—but only to an extent. In 1966 the Śankarācārya of Purī fasted for seventy-three days in the course of a massive agitation for cow protection mounted by the Hindu nationalists—and was jailed for his pains.[340] The Śankarācāryas of Purī were in fact precociously political,[341] and of the major Śankarācāryas they were perhaps the least unreliable as allies of the Hindu nationalists.[342] But even they could be loose cannons: in 1969 the same Śankarācārya of Purī angered the Maharashtrian Buddhists by asserting on a visit to Poona that untouchability was an integral part of Hinduism.[343] The general unreliability of the Śankarācāryas was particularly apparent in 1993, when four of them held a meeting at Śṛngerī and agreed on a compromise proposal to resolve the issue of the Bābrī Masjid, thereby undermining the position of the VHP.[344] Admittedly the relationship had its moments: in an emotive scene played out in 1990, a minor local Śankarācārya joined the VHP at a mass meeting in Bhopāl and handed out medals to volunteers (*karsevaks*) returning

[336] Pande, *Life of Śaṅkarācārya*, 35; Cenkner, *Tradition of teachers*, 114–15.

[337] Cenkner, *Tradition of teachers*, 114–15; Jaffrelot, *Hindu nationalist movement*, 470.

[338] Cenkner, *Tradition of teachers*, 104. There are two splendid photographs of this Śankarācārya in Glasenapp, *Heilige Stätten Indiens*, plates 126–27.

[339] Cenkner, *Tradition of teachers*, 119.

[340] Ibid., 125, 132; Jaffrelot, *Hindu nationalist movement*, 204–8.

[341] Lütt, "Śankarācārya of Puri," 414–19; Cenkner, *Tradition of teachers*, 131–32. But see also Jaffrelot, *Hindu nationalist movement*, 23–24, on a minor Maharashtrian Śankarācārya.

[342] See Jaffrelot, *Hindu nationalist movement*, 198, 356–57, 362, 372, 413, 470, 488.

[343] Cenkner, *Tradition of teachers*, 143; his predecessor had opposed Gandhi on this issue (132).

[344] Jaffrelot, *Hindu nationalist movement*, 470–71.

from the agitation in Ayodhyā.[345] But this was untypical of a complicated and mutually rather unsatisfactory relationship.

Less prestigious religious figures—ascetics (*sādhus*) and others—have also played their part and in much larger numbers.[346] They too have not been very dependable allies[347] nor altogether welcome when they have displayed too direct an interest in getting into politics.[348] Their support can nevertheless extend the reach of the movement on the ground and perhaps help to confer a measure of religious legitimacy on it—though one should not overestimate this latter effect, since Indian public opinion takes almost as dim a view of religious leaders as it does of politicians.[349] In any event, it is noteworthy that these saffron-clad religious figures, like the Śankarācāryas, have mostly remained on the periphery of the movement. Umā Bhārtī, who owes part of her prestige to her familiarity with the *Rāmāyaṇa* of Tulsīdās,[350] wears saffron, and she is not the only BJP politician to do so.[351] But the activists of the RSS and even the VHP wear white, not saffron.[352] In short, the role played by religious figures is not evidence that the fundamental character of the movement is religious; the men in saffron are not the counterparts of the Iranian clergy.

At the same time the presence of non-Hindus in the movement provides positive evidence that it is not religious in a way that would make it comparable to Islamism. Thus Jains play a minor but persistent role.[353] Of the twelve volunteers who received medals at the mass

[345] Ibid., 423–24. Such volunteers are typically unemployed urban youths; their involvement in the movement gives them a measure of self-respect and an opportunity to model themselves on the "stereotypical heroes of Hindi popular cinema" (428f). The Shiv Sena has a similar appeal to the young and unemployed male who longs "to be the hero of a Bombay film in which violence leads to justice" (429; cf. Banerjee, *Warriors in politics*, 71–72).

[346] See, for example, Jaffrelot, *Hindu nationalist movement*, 194–96, 198–200, 206–7, 338, 350–55, 362, 363, 373.

[347] Ibid., 210, 348–49, 488.

[348] Ibid., 479–80, 483–84.

[349] Ibid., 480, reporting a poll conducted in five metropolitan cities in 1993.

[350] Ibid., 388.

[351] Ibid., 479.

[352] Cf. ibid., 357–58. There is perhaps more spillover of color in the case of the Shiv Sena: members paint their buildings in saffron (Eckert, *Charisma of direct action*, 16, 211), and wear it on occasion (211).

[353] I have not seen a study devoted to this theme. Presumably it is because relations between the Hindu nationalists and the Jains are not a problem for either side that nobody seems to be interested in the topic—which is a pity.

meeting staged by the VHP in Bhopāl in 1990, two were Jains.[354] We find Jains holding office not just in the RSS[355] but also in the VHP.[356] The BJP nominates Jain candidates,[357] rich Jains may contribute to its funds,[358] and Jain holy men may support it.[359] There were Jains among those carrying holy water during the "pilgrimage" (*yātrā*) organized by the VHP in 1983,[360] and Jain Studios played a role in broadcasting Hindu nationalist propaganda.[361] Just as noteworthy is the lack of any reference to tension in this regard—even hidden tension of the kind that has affected the participation of Christian Arabs in Arab nationalist movements.[362] Jainism, after all, is a religion that broke with the Hindu mainstream some twenty-five centuries ago, rejecting the Vedas and the rituals associated with them. Indeed Dayānand, for whom such things mattered, saw the Jains as alien intruders who could be blamed for corrupting Indian religion by introducing idolatry[363]—and this despite the fact that he came from a region in which Hindus and Jains lived in a peculiarly intimate symbiosis.[364] But the Hindu nationalists do not think in this way. Sāvarkar, for example, appealed to the example of the Jains to prove his point that "a man can be as truly a Hindu as any without believing even in the Vedas as an independent religious authority,"[365] and he listed Mahāvīra, the founder of Jainism, as a paradigmatic Hindu.[366] It is as if the Muslim Brothers were to see no problem in recruiting the local Christians, Jews, and Samaritans. What this suggests, of course, is that for the Hindu nationalists—in marked contrast to the Muslim Brothers—religion is a culture rather than a creed; for despite its credal incompatibility with Hinduism, Jainism is unmistakably a product of the same Indian cultural milieu. Even Dayānand

[354] Jaffrelot, *Hindu nationalist movement*, 430.

[355] Ibid., 140–41 (also mentioning a Jain active in the Ārya Samāj).

[356] Ibid., 353, 354.

[357] Ibid., 509, and cf. 38n114.

[358] Laidlaw, *Riches and renunciation*, 104.

[359] Shah, "BJP's riddle ," 258.

[360] Jaffrelot, *Hindu nationalist movement*, 361.

[361] Ibid., 425, 486–87, 531.

[362] For a letter written by the Arab nationalist Khalīl al-Sakākīnī (d. 1953), a Palestinian Christian, to his son, in which he complains that in Muslim eyes "as long as I am not a Moslem I am naught," see Kedourie, "Religion and politics," 339–40; for Sakākīnī's career, see 318–19.

[363] Jordens, *Dayānanda Sarasvatī*, 111. For some reason he thought the Jains came from the region of China.

[364] For this, see Jordens, *Dayānanda Sarasvatī*, 12–13.

[365] Savarkar, *Hindutva*, 81.

[366] Ibid., 38.

must have shared this attitude at some level: a couple of years before his death he was investing members of the higher castes in Rajasthan with the sacred thread, and half of them were Jains.[367]

The underlying attitude of the Hindu nationalists to Buddhists and Sikhs seems no different, though surface features tend to overlay it. In the Buddhist case the survival of the religion down the centuries was associated with regions outside India; when Untouchables reintroduced it in the twentieth century, this marked a deliberate break with the very community that the Hindu nationalists stand for. In other words, the trouble with Buddhism is not that it split off from Hinduism almost as long ago as Jainism but rather that its modern Indian reincarnation took place in a divisive caste context. Thus the Shiv Sena sides with those Untouchables who are "proud to be Hindu," in contrast to the Buddhists among them.[368] The Buddha is nevertheless a revered figure in the Hindu nationalist pantheon. In his book of 1939, Goḷwalkar referred to him as "the Great Master," and spoke of "the spiritual awakening under Lord Buddha."[369] A later Hindu nationalist author tells us that Lord Buddha came at a time when "addiction to religious practices and blind adherence to tradition brought society to a state of stagnation"; he accordingly "battled with the distortions that had crept into Hindu religion."[370] The RSS "morning meditation" (*prātaḥsmaraṇam*) invokes him in a long list of Indian worthies.[371] Ritambarā, the Hindu nationalist ascetic, begins a flight of oratory by hailing the Buddha among others, though we hear no more of him once she shifts her saintly attention to the Muslims.[372] And it was the Dalai Lama who opened the conference held by the VHP in Allāhābād in 1979,[373] for all that he is neither an Indian nor a Hindu. One Hindu nationalist author describes how the distinguished visitor was met at the railway station with Vedic chanting and later reciprocated by declaring that Buddhism was "truly a product of this soil."[374]

In the Sikh case the complicating circumstance was again historical rather than doctrinal. Unlike common or garden Hindu sects, the

[367] Jordens, *Dayānanda Sarasvatī*, 229.

[368] Eckert, *Charisma of direct action*, 220.

[369] Golwalkar, *We or our nationhood*, 10, 66.

[370] Mishra, *RSS*, 96. He also includes in this mission "Lord Mahavira," the founder of Jainism.

[371] Malkani, *RSS story*, 205.

[372] Kakar, *Colors of violence*, 155–56 (the Jains and Sikhs are likewise represented). For a sample of her anti-Muslim venom, see 165.

[373] Jaffrelot, *Hindu nationalist movement*, 347.

[374] Seshadri, *RSS*, 137–38.

Sikhs had acquired a military base among the caste of peasant warriors known as the Jāṭs, and in the late eighteenth century they had used it to establish a state. Hence no doubt their tendency—already apparent in the late nineteenth century—to see themselves as a non-Hindu community,[375] culminating in the separatist terrorism that afflicted the Punjab in the 1980s. Dayānand, of course, insisted on doctrine: he regarded the Sikhs as in effect idolaters,[376] and Ārya polemics against Sikhism soon put an end to the early presence of Sikhs in the Ārya Samāj.[377] But again, the Hindu nationalists do not seem to have been bothered by considerations of creed. For Sāvarkar, "Sikhs are Hindus in the sense of our definition of Hindutva and not in any religious sense whatever."[378] Instead, they were accorded an iconic status thanks to their historical record of fighting Muslims. Goḷwalkar had nothing but praise for "that band of unconquerable Hindu heroes, the Sikhs, headed by their immortal Gurus."[379] Hence the Hindu nationalist reaction to Sikh terrorism in the Punjab—which included the slaughter of considerable numbers of RSS activists and the ethnic cleansing of Hindus—was marked more by sorrow than by anger.[380] Sikh devotees of the movement were sent to reason with the terrorists,[381] and the RSS took pride in the role played by its members in sheltering Sikhs during the disturbances that followed the assassination of Indira Gandhi in 1984.[382] In earlier, happier days there had been Sikh representatives present at the founding congress of the VHP held in 1964.[383] Even in 1983 Sikhs shared with Jains the task of carrying holy water in a pilgrimage organized by the VHP.[384] In short, the Hindu nationalists share the wider indifference of Indian society to credal differences between culturally Indian religions.

If credal differences do not matter, it becomes an interesting question whether the movement can in principle accommodate Muslims. This is a delicate issue. There are in fact Muslims in the movement, even in the core membership, though as one might expect they are

[375] K. W. Jones, *Arya Dharm*, 205–7.

[376] Ibid., 135–36.

[377] Ibid., 136–39. The star role in this outcome was played by the zealous Paṇḍit Guru Datta (d. 1890).

[378] Savarkar, *Hindutva*, 125; see also 126.

[379] Golwalkar, *We or our nationhood*, 10, and see also 58, 66.

[380] Jaffrelot, *Hindu nationalist movement*, 343, 345.

[381] Frykenberg, "Hindu fundamentalism," 245.

[382] Seshadri, *RSS*, 105–7; Gold, "Organized Hinduisms," 575 and 590n200.

[383] Jaffrelot, *Hindu nationalist movement*, 198.

[384] Ibid., 361.

not numerous. One Muslim, Sikander Bakht, has risen high in the BJP, though not through the RSS,[385] and the party sometimes nominates Muslim candidates in elections.[386] Of the twelve volunteers recognized in Bhopāl in 1990, one was a Muslim—and received the warmest applause.[387] The author of a good-news book on the activities of the RSS published in 1988 remarked with satisfaction that instances of Muslim boys and youths attending meetings at RSS branches were "though not very common, not rare," and gave a couple of examples. One was an apparently troubled Muslim youth who joined the movement while his father was absent in Dubai; when his father heard this alarming news, his wife was able to reassure him that, thanks to the care of the local RSS leader, "Aziz has improved a lot."[388] But as might be expected, many in the movement were not keen to include Muslims. When an elderly Gandhian idealist invited the RSS to open itself to Muslims and Christians in a speech of 1977, the response was tepid.[389] In 1982 there was disapproval in the ranks of the RSS when BJP politicians sought to cultivate Muslims by participating in their prayer rituals.[390] And in 1993 local activists sabotaged the electoral campaign of a Muslim candidate.[391] But we are concerned here mainly with principle, and at this level too there has been a significant divergence of views.

One view, which we have already met in Goḷwalkar's book of 1939, categorically excluded Muslims from the nation and a fortiori from the movement.[392] The general question Goḷwalkar was addressing was "what is to be the fate of all those, who, today, happen to live upon the land, though not belonging to the Hindu Race, Religion and culture?"—a category in which the Muslims clearly predominated. His answer was that such people "can have no place in the national life, unless they abandon their differences, adopt the religion, culture and language of the Nation and completely merge themselves in the National Race."[393] Sāvarkar had already considered the question in his book of 1923. His first line of argument was that the exclusion of Muslims was not a matter of "any religious beliefs that we as a race may hold in

[385] Ibid., 315–16, 325. Cf. also 326 on ʿĀrif Beg.
[386] Ibid., 325, 509.
[387] Ibid., 423, 430.
[388] Seshadri, *RSS*, 141–42.
[389] Jaffrelot, *Hindu nationalist movement*, 303–4.
[390] Ibid., 327.
[391] Ibid., 503.
[392] See 95–96.
[393] Golwalkar, *We or our nationhood*, 45.

common" but was rather due to the fact that they do not share "our Hindu culture."[394] But what if they did share Hindu culture? Here he went on to introduce a specifically religious criterion: a Hindu was someone for whom the country was not just a fatherland but also a holy land (*puṇyabhūmi*). Thus the reason why even Muslims sharing a fatherland and most of their culture with Hindus could not belong was that their holy land was "far off in Arabia"—"their love is divided."[395] They were, of course, more than welcome to return to the Hindu fold.[396]

Against this background Sāvarkar's polite nod to the idea that Hindus, Muslims, and the rest might come to feel "as Indians first and every other thing afterwards" seems unconvincing.[397] But such a view has certainly existed in the movement—the view, that is to say, that there can be such a thing as a good Muslim. A good Muslim shares Hindu culture and reveres the heroes of the Hindu epics as national symbols, just as Sikander Bakht does.[398] One high official of the RSS in 1993 held up the Javanese Muslims as an appropriate model: "Islam did not prevent Indonesian Muslims to proclaim Mahabharat and Ramayan as their cultural epics and Ram and Krishna as their forefathers."[399] A VHP convention organized in Hardvār in 1988 is said to have demanded a little more: if Indians regard Rām and Kṛṣṇa as "national heroes," and touch India's sacred ground three times in prostration while saying, "Hail, Mother India!," then they may belong to "any religion"[400]—a view that invites comparison with the attitude of imperial Rome toward its Christian minority. In 2011 a Hindu nationalist politician was happy to include in the nation Muslims who "acknowledge with pride that though they may be Muslims, their ancestors were Hindus."[401] A simi-

[394] Savarkar, *Hindutva*, 91–92, 99, 100–101.

[395] Ibid., 111, 113, and cf. 102. As Muḥammad Iqbāl (d. 1938) had written some years earlier, "In as much as the average man demands a material centre of nationality, the Muslim looks for it in the holy town of Mecca" (quoted in Shaikh, "*Millat* and *mazhab*," 386).

[396] Savarkar, *Hindutva*, 114–15.

[397] Ibid., 139.

[398] Jaffrelot, *Hindu nationalist movement*, 325. Incidentally, the idea that an Indian Muslim could be proud of the Hindu cultural heritage received a measure of endorsement from no less an authority than Jamāl al-Dīn al-Afghānī (d. 1897), see Keddie, *Islamic response*, 58–59; Keddie, *Sayyid Jamāl ad-Dīn "al-Afghānī,"* 159–60.

[399] Jaffrelot, *Hindu nationalist movement*, 57.

[400] McKean, "Bhārat Mātā," 259–60.

[401] Subramanian Swamy, "How to wipe out Islamic terror." This politician would like to see the imposition of a uniform civil code, the compulsory study of Sanskrit, the renaming of the country as "Hindustan," and a law prohibiting conversion from Hinduism to any other religion. I owe my knowledge of his views to Bernard Haykel.

lar benevolence toward good Muslims is found among the Shiv Sena.[402] One follower of the movement strongly approves of the Muslims of the Konkaṇ as "Maharashtrians in their heart" who "speak Marathi" and "even dress like Hindus"; he contrasts them with other Muslim groups who "keep to themselves" so that one never knows "where their loyalties lie."[403] In this way the Shiv Sena too is opposed only to "anti-national" Muslims; indeed one of its Muslim adherents has been minister of labor,[404] a position that one might expect to confer considerable patronage resources. Of course, many, perhaps most, Muslims are not by Hindu nationalist standards good Muslims, but that is not the point.

In short, despite the hard line taken by the patriarchs of the movement, if someone has the right cultural loyalties, then religion as such is not of overwhelming importance to the Hindu nationalists. It is in this sense that the BJP's rhetoric of "unity in diversity" has in principle a potential to include even Muslims.[405] Indeed what finer icon of cultural diversity could there be than the projected Sanskrit translation of the Koran, announced by the Minorities Cell of the BJP in 1995 as a way of building "a bridge to the Muslim masses"?[406] (Presumably it will not include the verses that Umā Bhārtī assures us instruct Muslims to skin idolaters alive and "stuff them in animal skins.")[407] And even in his categorical excision of Muslims from the nation, Sāvarkar introduced only the bare minimum of religious belief needed to exclude them. In all this what we see is the logic of cultural nationalism, not the logic of religious fanaticism.

So far we have looked at the role played in the movement by religious figures on the one hand and non-Hindus on the other. But these phenomena, though instructive, are somewhat peripheral, and we should now turn to the movement at large. Its members are certainly not alienated from religion. From the start the RSS had significant

[402] Cf. the Shiv Sena website in 2000: "It is Shiv Sena's belief that whatever may be our religion, whatever may be our form of worship, our culture is Hindu" (quoted in Eckert, *Charisma of direct action*, 93; and cf. Katzenstein et al., "Rebirth of Shiv Sena," 378).

[403] Eckert, *Charisma of direct action*, 185.

[404] Ibid., 92; and see Katzenstein et al., "Rebirth of Shiv Sena," 378.

[405] Jaffrelot, *Hindu nationalist movement*, 317, quoting a statement from a BJP manifesto of 1984; the phrase already appears in a Jana Sangh manifesto of 1951 (Graham, *Hindu nationalism*, 50).

[406] Hansen, *Saffron wave*, 225. Compare the presence of "important Dharma Sutras from all the religions of India," including Islam, in the Bhārat Mātā Mandir at Hardvār (McKean, "Bhārat Mātā," 275).

[407] Hansen, *Saffron wave*, 180.

features in common with Hindu sects,[408] and it possessed a ritual calendar mixing traditional Hindu festivals with nationalist elements relating to the figure of Śivājī.[409] Yet, as one commentator has aptly observed, the literature of the RSS has remarkably little to say about religious beliefs and does not waste much time on deploying proof-texts or asserting the authority of a scriptural canon; moreover he reports that "in private conversations its members frequently emphasize that they are not religious."[410] This was a movement that in its early days owed much to European nationalism, Italian and German,[411] while the Sunday parade of its original devotees was marked by the use of English martial music and drill commands.[412] Perhaps the symbol that best captures what these devotees were about is the Śivājī cult: their day began with a salute to the Bhagvā Dhvaj,[413] the saffron flag particularly associated with Śivājī, an emblem that "brings before our eyes the living image of our ancient, sacred and integrated national life in all its pristine purity."[414] The members of Shiv Sena likewise sport the saffron flag.[415] As their leader explains the "Shiv" in "Shiv Sena": "In politics it's Shivaji, in religion it's Shiva."[416] And indeed they honor Śiva by equipping themselves with the trident (*triśūl*), his traditional weapon.[417] Yet despite such elements of religiosity, it would be hard to mistake either the RSS or the Shiv Sena for a religious movement.

If there is a specifically religious organization among the Hindu nationalists, it is the VHP.[418] It has indeed concerned itself with properly religious questions, and as we will see it has sought to reshape Hinduism in significant ways, both by organizing it and by seeking to identify elements of the religion that everyone can agree on.[419] At this point we need remark only that the religiosity of the VHP does not seem to be out of line with that of the Hindu nationalist movement in general. A

[408] Jaffrelot, *Hindu nationalist movement*, 40–45.

[409] Ibid., 39.

[410] Embree, "Rashtriya Swayamsevak Sangh," 629–30.

[411] Jaffrelot, *Hindu nationalist movement*, 26, 51–54.

[412] Ibid., 37. The music has changed since India became independent (Seshadri, *RSS*, 260–61).

[413] Jaffrelot, *Hindu nationalist movement*, 39.

[414] Ibid., 41n128 (quoting Goḷwalkar).

[415] Eckert, *Charisma of direct action*, 16, 211; Banerjee, *Warriors in politics*, 152.

[416] Banerjee, *Warriors in politics*, 119. "Śiv Senā" means "Army of Śiva."

[417] Ibid., 1, 119, 152–53; cf. Graham, *Hindu nationalism*, 152; Jaffrelot, *Hindu nationalist movement*, 417n22.

[418] For a brief description of the VHP, see Jaffrelot, "Vishva Hindu Parishad."

[419] See 297, 428.

telling example is the initiative of the VHP in summoning assemblies to deliberate on the state of Hinduism in 1966 and 1979.[420] Both times it held them at Allāhābād in Uttar Pradesh.[421] There was an explicit historical reference here.[422] Allāhābād is the ancient Prayāg, a Hindu holy place at the confluence of the Ganges and the Jumna, and it was there that Harṣa, the last native ruler of an imperial state in northern India, held his quinquennial assemblies in the first half of the seventh century.[423] But quinquennial assemblies were a Buddhist, not a Hindu tradition, for all that Brahmins were also present at Harṣa's convocations.[424] As this indicates, the VHP's project is primarily a nationalist one;[425] it is in line with the tradition of the early nationalist Ṭiḷak, who wanted "to consolidate all the different sects into a mighty Hindu nation"—not a sublime Hindu religion.[426]

One final point of contrast between Hindu nationalists and Islamists concerns the transnational dimension of the identity they champion—or the lack of it. For Islamists the worldwide Muslim community is a primary focus of loyalty irrespective of political boundaries. Hindus lack a wider community on this scale; in contrasting the situation of the Muslims and Hindus of India, an early member of the Ārya Samāj observed that "Mohammadans have Constantinople behind their back," whereas the Hindus "are circumscribed within the four walls of Hindustan and have no outside assistance to influence the attitude of their rulers."[427] There are, however, significant Hindu populations outside India in several countries of South Asia, namely Pakistan, Nepal, Bangladesh, and Sri Lanka, and there is a considerable Hindu diaspora in other parts of the world. We could thus imagine a Hindu movement aiming to unite Hindus wherever they may be found, stirring up the Hindu populations of the smaller South Asian countries and feeding on tensions between the Hindu diaspora and its host societies. But such a movement does not exist. The VHP is very interested in the Hindu diaspora, particularly

[420]The idea of such an assembly went back to the nineteenth century, making its first appearance with Dayānand's teacher Virjānand (Jordens, *Dayānanda Sarasvatī*, 37, and cf. 155–56).

[421]Jaffrelot, *Hindu nationalist movement*, 198, 346, and cf. 373.

[422]Ibid., 201.

[423]Devahuti, *Harsha*, 180–81.

[424]Ibid., 181n1; Lamotte, *History of Indian Buddhism*, 60, 292.

[425]Veer, "Hindu nationalism," 666. A curious exception is the VHP's dislike of the use of Hindu names by Christians (A. Sharma, *Modern Hindu thought*, 247n21); a Hindu nationalist should surely welcome this practice as a sign of assimilation of Hindu culture.

[426]Wolpert, *Tilak and Gokhale*, 179, in a speech of 1906.

[427]Jaffrelot, *Hindu nationalism*, 40–41; and see K. W. Jones, *Arya Dharm*, 285–86.

the part of it that resides in the First World—and for good reason: it needs to raise money.[428] But we do not hear persistent complaints about Hindu nationalists making political trouble among the Hindu populations of Nepal, Sri Lanka, Fiji, or Surinam, let alone Bali; Nepal in particular, during the decades when it was the world's only surviving Hindu monarchy, seems to have functioned more as an icon and a ceremonial stage than as a place to engage in serious political work.[429] In any case, the political horizons of the Hindu nationalists do not reach beyond the boundaries of India as defined by Śankara's monasteries.[430] And even in the case of the territories lost to India through Partition, there has been a notable lack of irredentism—hardly what one would expect, given the strength of the movement's original commitment to an undivided India.[431] In sum, the aspiration behind the Hindu nationalist invocation of religion is to redefine the nation within the current borders of India, not to transcend it; this is religion in the service of nationalism, not religion sweeping nationalism away.

How then should we characterize the conception of Hindu identity prevalent among the Hindu nationalists? Obviously they are not secular nationalists in the style of Nehru, but neither are they true believers in the manner of Dayānand. One way to describe them, and an adequate one, is to call them "cultural nationalists," meaning nationalists for whom the nation is made up of the bearers of a particular cultural tradition.[432] It was not just wishful thinking when an RSS activist from an Untouchable background averred that there was "no caste and no religion" in the RSS, the only religion being Mother India[433]—where Mother India (Bhārat Mātā) is a modern nationalist addition to the Hindu pantheon.[434] This was also how the patriarchs of the move-

[428] For brief surveys of Hindu nationalist activity in the diaspora, see Jaffrelot, *Hindu nationalism*, 361–64, and Therwath, "Far and wide." Therwath suggests that a decision was taken in the 1990s to "emulate Muslim transnationalism" (417); if so, the emulation has not been very successful.

[429] Thus one of the component processions of the Ekātmatā Yātrā set out from Nepal (Jaffrelot, *Hindu nationalist movement*, 360). See also Seshadri, *RSS*, 36–37; Gellner et al., *Nationalism and ethnicity*, 80, 166 and 183n8, 504–5.

[430] For the Hindu nationalist conception of territory, see Jaffrelot, "From Indian territory," 207–13.

[431] Literally "unbroken India" (*akhaṇḍ Bhārat*).

[432] The term "cultural nationalism" is applied to Hindu nationalism by Lal ("Economic impact," 416); cf. also Keddie, "New Religious Politics," 710.

[433] Jaffrelot, *Hindu nationalist movement*, 49n166.

[434] On the cult of Bhārat Mātā, see Kinsley, *Hindu goddesses*, 181–84; McKean, "Bhārat Mātā," 250–65.

ment saw things. Thus Sāvarkar, who had a seminal influence on the RSS, minimized the religious component of Hindutva in his book of 1923, putting most of his emphasis on a shared fatherland, blood, and culture;[435] "Hinduism," he wrote, "is only a derivative, a fraction, a part of Hindutva."[436] He did not eliminate religion altogether: as we have seen, he made recognition of India as a holy land a litmus test, and in that respect Hinduism had a key role to play in his idea of Hindutva.[437] But he was consistent in emptying the notion of any credal content: "Some of us are monists, some, pantheists; some theists and some atheists. But monotheists or atheists—we are all Hindus and own a common blood."[438] It is hard to imagine an Islamist saying anything like this. Goḷwalkar in 1939 sounded more like an Islamist. "With us," he wrote, "every action in life, individual, social or political, is a command of Religion."[439] But unlike an Islamist, he had no problem with the "variety" comprehended within the "organic whole" of his religion;[440] and most tellingly, the reason he gave for not giving up "religion in our National life" was that "it would mean that we have turned faithless to our Race-Spirit."[441] Like Sāvarkar, he showed no interest in the question whether traditional Hindu beliefs are *true*.

What then was the point of adopting a cultural nationalism in the Indian context? Here the key contrast is with the secular nationalism of Congress, not with Islamism. The Indian nationalist movement that developed under the rule of the British and came to power on their departure was a secular one. This feature had its origin in the nationalist package imported from Europe, but in the Indian environment it proved adaptive to the extent that it made possible an appeal to all Indians irrespective of their religious affiliations: "We are Indians first," went a statement of the message dating from 1905 "and Hindus, Mahomedans, Parsees or Christians afterwards."[442] But unlike the secular nationalisms of Europe, this inclusive Indian nationalism was not grounded in a strong sense of ethnic community; the subcontinent was

[435] See, for example, Savarkar, *Hindutva*, 91–92; also Jaffrelot, *Hindu nationalist movement*, 26–27.

[436] Savarkar, *Hindutva*, 3.

[437] See 110.

[438] Savarkar, *Hindutva*, 89, and see 4.

[439] Golwalkar, *We or our nationhood*, 22.

[440] Ibid., 40–41.

[441] Ibid., 24. See also Jaffrelot, *Hindu nationalist movement*, 54–55.

[442] G. K. Gokhale (d. 1915) in Parvate, *Gopal Krishna Gokhale*, 192, quoted in A. Sharma, *Modern Hindu thought*, 188.

marked by an ethnic diversity more reminiscent of Europe as a whole than of any single European country. Secular nationalism in the Indian context was thus characterized by a certain emotional threadbareness, largely based as it was on a combination of the geographical unity of the subcontinent and the shared exposure of its inhabitants to British rule.[443] "The Congress," as it said about itself in 1886, "is a community of temporal interests and not of spiritual convictions."[444] This pragmatic conception of the nation led Goḷwalkar to complain that Congress was turning India into one big hotel: "Indeed they have made our country a veritable serai!"[445] The eventual departure of the British may have been a triumph for the secular nationalists, but it could only exacerbate the problem of threadbareness.

An alternative was to cultivate a nationalism that foregrounded a religious heritage as a national culture. The pull of such a cultural nationalism was already evident in the last decades of British rule and not just among the Hindu nationalists and their precursors; perhaps more significant at the time was the presence of such attitudes within Congress itself. Though relatively inhibited at the center, they were widespread at the local level. Thus, a study of the politics of the United Provinces in the last decades of British rule shows how persistently Congress politicians made use of the Holī festival, the *Rāmāyaṇa*, and cow protection for the purpose of mobilization.[446] It would have been politically irrational for them to forego the use of these resources, but even with the best intentions (and intentions were not always the best), such a repertoire tended to suggest that Muslims were not part of the nation. The contrast between the central and local manifestations of Congress helps to explain how the members of the same party could appear as self-hating Hindus to the Hindu nationalists and as Hindu chauvinists to many Muslims. Independence and its aftermath then benefited the Hindu nationalist cause in two practical ways. First, the secession of the two main Muslim-majority regions of the subcontinent—what we can call the hard partition of India—considerably reduced the need

[443] The unsuccessful Telengana movement of 1969–1971, which expressed the resentment of the Telugu-speaking districts of the former state of Hyderabad at having been merged into Andhra Pradesh in 1956 and thereby exposed to Āndhra domination, faced an analogous problem on a smaller scale: its mostly Hindu leaders could hardly claim a separate identity on the basis of having previously been ruled and influenced by Muslims (Bernstorff, "Region and nation," 139–43).

[444] D. E. Smith, *India*, 88.

[445] Golwalkar, *We or our nationhood*, 59–60; and see 63 on "the serai theory."

[446] Gould, *Hindu nationalism*, 58–63, 71–73, 76–84; also the summary at 265–74.

for a nationalist doctrine that sidelined religion. As we have seen, once the Muslims had their Pakistan, India came to look a lot more like Hindustan, thereby increasing the plausibility of Goḷwalkar's insistence in 1939 that "in Hindusthan, the land of the Hindus, lives and should live the Hindu Nation."[447] Second, the restructuring of India as a federation of linguistic states—the soft partition—averted the danger of political disintegration under the impact of competing ethnic nationalisms, though at the cost of dimming the prospects of Hindi as an indigenous national language.[448] Thus, Hindu nationalism figured as the only credible alternative to secular nationalism if India was not to dispense with nationalism altogether. It is this recycling of a religious heritage as cultural nationalism that has won for the Hindu nationalists their current role in Indian politics. On the one hand it has enabled them to achieve a centrality that eluded true believers like Dayānand, and on the other hand it has allowed them to take full advantage of the inhibitions of Congress in relation to the Hindu heritage. What it has not given them is dominance of the political system: too many Indians have reason to feel more comfortable with Indian nationalism that with Hindu nationalism.

Before we leave South Asia, it is worth pausing to identify the counterparts of the Hindu nationalists across the border in Pakistan. It should be clear from what precedes that they are not the Islamists. They are, in fact, the politicians of the Muslim League, those who brought Pakistan into existence and ruled it off and on thereafter.[449] Like the Hindu nationalists, the members of this elite were not particularly religious, but they were strongly identified with the cultural and political fortunes of a religiously demarcated community. At first they also resembled the Hindu nationalists in another significant respect: exacerbating the tensions between Muslims and Hindus with cries that Islam was in danger could serve to divert the Muslim vote from their competitors.[450] There was even a minor Muslim League analog of Ayodhyā at Sukkur

[447] Golwalkar, *We or our nationhood,* 44. "Hindusthān" is a Sanskritization of the Persian form "Hindustān."

[448] The abandonment of the axiom of linguistic nationalism that Hindus should speak Hindi, just as Germans speak German, also reflects the continuing demand for English in the educational marketplace, even among Hindi speakers; thus brochures about a Hindu nationalist boarding school in Madhya Pradesh emphasized the teaching of English as a selling point (Jaffrelot, "Hindu nationalism," 206–7; and see Kumar, "Hindu revivalism," 550, on English as a medium of instruction in the schools of the Ārya Samāj). The RSS also sponsors the teaching of spoken Sanskrit (Seshadri, *RSS,* 125, 234–36) but without any apparent ambition to see it displace the vernacular languages.

[449] As noted by Varshney (*Ethnic conflict,* 71).

[450] Jaffrelot, *History of Pakistan,* 13–16.

in Sindh. Here a domed building, the Manzilgāh, had been claimed by the local Muslims to be a mosque since 1920 (the Hindus had no claim to it themselves but wanted the Muslims kept out). In 1939 the cause was taken up by the Muslim League in order to undermine the position of the communally mixed government then in power in Sindh. The agitation involved Muslim volunteers congregating in Sukkur, the seizure of the building by Muslim demonstrators despite a police presence, and several days of communal rioting following the eventual expulsion of the demonstrators; the Hindus appear to have started this outbreak by jeering at the Muslims when they were expelled, but the loss of life was mainly on the Hindu side.[451] After independence, however, such strategies tended to lose their effectiveness in Pakistan.[452] One reason for the divergence between the two countries may have been demographic, namely the absence of a politically significant Hindu minority in West Pakistan; by 2000, there were fewer than three million Hindus in Pakistan, though many more in Bangladesh. Another reason was the weakening of electoral democracy. Unlike India, Pakistan was dominated by an ethnic core that was unwilling to accommodate other ethnic groups through an Indian-style federal system. Moreover, the bottom line of the Punjabi hegemony was the army, which unlike the Indian armed forces, has intervened three times in politics to establish long-lasting military regimes. Only during the Emergency of 1975–1977 did the politics of India look at all like those of Pakistan, and even then the reaction of the Indian politicians was to anticipate the resumption of politics as usual. For both these reasons, playing the old communal card came to be far less advantageous in Pakistan than in India.

This was not, however, the only way in which the cultural nationalists of Pakistan found themselves in a very different political environment from their Indian counterparts. For one thing, the secular, territorial conception of nationalism that was dominant in Nehru's India could have no viable equivalent in Pakistan. There had, of course, been Indian Muslims who thought like Nehru, such as Sir Sayyid Aḥmad Khān (d. 1898), for whom "the words Hindu and Mahomedan are only meant for religious distinction," so that all inhabitants of the country should be regarded as "belonging to one and the same nation."[453] Even

[451] Talbot, *Pakistan*, 78, based on the detailed account in A. K. Jones, "Muslim politics," 184–200.

[452] For attacks on Hindus after independence, see Jaffrelot, *History of Pakistan*, 37–38, 56; Jaffrelot, *Hindu nationalist movement*, 96.

[453] W. C. Smith, *Modern Islām in India*, 25.

Jinnah could sound like this on occasion: in a speech of 1947 to the Constituent Assembly of Pakistan, he looked forward to a time when, in a political as opposed to a religious sense, Hindus would cease to be Hindus and Muslims to be Muslims; both alike would be citizens of the state.[454] But this kind of thinking did not make much sense in Pakistan, a country created for a community whose "bedrock and sheet-anchor" was Islam.[455] For another thing, the rulers of Pakistan had to share their country with Islamists, for whom the political claims of Islam went far beyond the creation of a mere Muslim state, in the sense of a national state for the benefit of Indian Muslims; as we have seen, the Islamists and their Islamic state had no Hindu counterparts.[456] In short, Jinnah and his successors differed from the Hindu nationalists in having no Nehru to their left and Mawdūdī to their right.

In each country we can accordingly think of the cultural nationalists as clinging to a slippery slope—but with the slopes facing in opposite directions. To hold power, Hindu nationalist politicians are obliged to do deals with people of more secularist inclinations than their own.[457] Hence such projects as the construction of the temple of Rām in Ayodhyā get shelved, as happened in the coalition building of 1998.[458] To quote a comment made at that point by the leading academic expert on the Hindu nationalists: "In some ways, the BJP appeared to have adopted the role of the post-independence Congress Party by providing a relatively neutral pivot around which other groups could arrange themselves"[459]—an outcome that, taken on its own, would place the BJP well on the way to the bottom of the slope. Pakistani politicians, by contrast, are obliged to co-opt or placate people more religious than themselves, resulting in a persistent drift toward Islamization. One result of this has been increasing deference to Islamic law, another the rising level of sectarian conflict among Muslims. Whereas in 1953 the politicians held the fort in the face of religious agitation against the Aḥmadīs, they

[454] Jinnah, *Speeches and writings*, 2: 404, drawn to my attention by Qasim Zaman.

[455] So Jinnah in a speech of 1944 (ibid., 2: 24).

[456] The "Hindu state" (*Hindu Rāṣṭra*) of the RSS (Jaffrelot, *Hindu nationalist movement*, 44, 50, 114, 115) is a state that exists for Hindus, not an embodiment of the political values enshrined in the Hindu heritage.

[457] Compare the politics of the Hindu Tamils of Sri Lanka: the Tamil Tigers never had to face the danger of being outflanked by a religious rival. In Palestinian terms there was no Tamil Ḥamās to challenge the secular nationalists.

[458] Jaffrelot, *Hindu nationalist movement*, 551–52.

[459] Ibid., 552. A telling detail is reported from an election in Karnataka in 1991: the BJP activists were hoping for fair weather on election day, and it was their competitors who wanted rain to discourage less determined voters (Manor, "Southern discomfort," 181).

were unable or unwilling to do so in 1973–1974;[460] and since the late 1970s, for reasons partly domestic and partly foreign, sectarian conflict has extended to relations between Sunnīs and Shīʿites.[461] One might contrast this with the absence of any revival of traditional tensions between Śaivas and Vaiṣṇavas in the politics of India.[462] No commentator on modern Indian politics ever emphasizes the importance of not alienating the Śaiva vote or speculates about which of the two sects might be more likely to form an alliance with the Muslims against its rival.[463] All in all, it is hard to say which slope is more slippery, and in neither country have the cultural nationalists yet reached the bottom. We tend to have a greater awareness of the Pakistani case, where the results look malign, than of the Indian case, where the results, if we notice them, look benign. The net effect is that in each country the cultural nationalists are in recurrent danger of being outflanked, but on different sides. The findings of a survey carried out in 2006 shed an interesting light on this. In Pakistan 87 percent of Muslims identified as Muslims first, rather than citizens of their country; in India only 10 percent of Hindus identified in this way.[464]

7. Conclusion

In the course of the millennia of its history, India had acquired a certain diffuse unity. It was not an ethnic unity, though its ethnic divisions were at least relatively shallow. Nor was it a religious unity: there

[460] Jaffrelot, *History of Pakistan*, 230, 242–43, 245, and cf. 37, 231, 241.

[461] Ibid., 231–34, 259–60.

[462] To go back no further than the nineteenth century, see the vivid account of a Śaiva persecution of the Vaiṣṇava sects in one of the native states of Rajasthan in the 1860s given in Clémentin-Ojha, *Le trident sur le palais*, 95–107 (353 in the English summary). Dayānand and others saw sectarian division as a major aspect of Hindu degeneration (Jordens, *Dayānanda Sarasvatī*, 37–38, 51, 69, 129).

[463] Ritambarā in the preamble to her speech in Hyderabad has a string of invocations related to Viṣnu (Sītā, Hanumān, Rām, Kṛṣṇa, Vālmīki) but only one related to Śiva, namely Lord Viśvanāth of Kāśī (Kakar, *Colors of violence*, 155–56). Yet this may reflect no more than the fact that the current agitation was about the Rām cult in Ayodhyā (Kṛṣṇa, the only invocation related to Viṣṇu that does not tie into the Rām cult, is doubtless there for Mathurā, site of another mosque slated for destruction, and the reference to Kāśī has a similar thrust, see Jaffrelot, *Hindu nationalist movement*, 547–48).

[464] See Pew Global Attitudes Project, *Muslims in Europe*, 3, 11, 27. The wording used is "in India fully 90% of the public self-identifies as Indian rather than Hindu" (11), leaving a mere 10 percent identifying primarily as Hindu. I take it that "the public" in this context refers only to Hindus, but this is not quite clear. See also Kull, *Feeling betrayed*, 34.

was no sharp sense of who was and was not a Hindu, and indeed the very idea of a Hindu was of foreign origin. Nevertheless, a number of religious themes—such as the veneration of the Vedas and the Rām cult—were widespread in the subcontinent, and there were elements of the religious tradition that staked out a clear territorial definition of the country. Yet this was far less than would have been needed to make India a plausible European-style nation. Here the Hindu nationalists offered a way to bridge the plausibility gap in the form of a cultural nationalism that highlighted a religious heritage. In this respect they had something to offer that Congress with its commitment to secularism could not provide—or at least not overtly. The major problem the Hindu nationalists faced in marketing their conception of Hindu political identity was the way the caste system worked against them. The tactless manner in which the Hindu tradition articulated its vision of the subjection and exclusion of the lower castes was in itself an incitement to its victims to defect under modern conditions, to walk away from the caste ladder rather than try to climb it. Such defection could be articulated in either ethnic or religious terms. Moreover, the increasingly extensive system of reservations exacerbated the situation: the more the underprivileged castes stood to benefit from horizontal solidarity, the less they were attracted to vertical ties with upper-caste patrons. This meant that the lowest castes—the Untouchables—had little reason to revisit their traditional sense of exclusion from Hindu society, and those immediately above them—the OBCs—lacked motivation to behave as political Hindus and so forego the candy of reservations. It was thus an ambitious program for the Hindu nationalists to seek to create a single homogeneous family. The solution to their caste problem, insofar as there was one, was to rally Hindus against their historic Muslim enemy, orchestrating the spontaneity of communal tensions to win elections. Sometimes they have used this strategy with success, but at other times they have seen their caste enemies—be they Camārs or Yādavs—ally with the Muslims against them. All this meant letting religion flood into politics. But at least in the field of identity—which is all that we have looked at so far—this did not mean the development of a Hindu emulation of Islamism. As we have seen, the Hindu nationalists had no problem with welcoming into their movement non-Hindus with the right cultural credentials, be they Jains, Buddhists, or Sikhs—perhaps even good Muslims, though this was rare and contested. Had the Hindu nationalists been Muslim politicians in Pakistan, they would have had just as little trouble including Shīʿites and Aḥmadīs. In other words, they were the counterparts of the Muslim League, not of the Islamists, and unlike the Islamists, they adhered to the broad global consensus that modern political identity has to be national. Their problem was that large numbers of Indians—not just Muslims—still found their particular brand of nationalism unappealing.

CHAPTER 3

Catholicism and identity in Latin America

1. Introduction

To get a sense that Catholicism might matter for political identity in Latin America, we need look no further than the Virgin of Guadalupe, and she will indeed be the first item on our agenda. But what if we do in fact persist in looking further? One can certainly muster some reasons to expect that Catholicism and political identity would interact strongly, but the actual record will show that by and large they do not. Our main task will then be to understand why this is so.

2. The Virgin of Guadalupe

One of the most dazzling contributions of religion to the articulation of national identity anywhere in the world is the cult of the Virgin of Guadalupe, the queen of Mexico and the mother of its people.[1] In the late nineteenth century a Mexican journalist aptly described the cult as "the national idolatry."[2] A century later one observer commented that over half the women of Mexico have "Guadalupe" as one of their names and that her image is the commonest tattoo on male bodies.[3] The Virgin of Guadalupe is thus the Bhārat Mātā of Mexico—but unlike the parvenue Bhārat Mātā, she has deep roots in Mexican religiosity.

Her cult is centered on her basilica at Tepeyac close to Mexico City. According to the tradition it was established there in 1531; it is historically attested from the 1550s and well documented from the late 1640s. By the second half of the seventeenth century, the cult was widespread in the Mexican highlands.[4] In the next century the rise of

[1] Cf. the use of the terms "Queen of the Mexican People" and "Mother of the Mexicans" in the context of the coronation of the image in 1895 (Brading, *Mexican phoenix*, 302, 304).

[2] Ibid., 256.

[3] H. L. Johnson, "Virgin of Guadalupe," 190.

[4] Poole, *Our Lady of Guadalupe*, 2, listing six provincial locations. This book gives a helpful presentation of the early testimonies to the existence of the cult; for the attestation of 1555, see 51.

the Virgin of Guadalupe continued. She achieved the status of patron of Mexico City in 1737; this role was rapidly extended to the rest of New Spain and confirmed by the pope in 1754.[5] These promotions made it only natural for her to become the patron saint of newly independent Mexico early in the nineteenth century.

A key aspect of her eligibility for this role was her relationship to a feature of colonial society in Latin America that we will come to later, the caste system.[6] At the top she came to be fully acceptable to the Spanish ecclesiastical hierarchy; indeed her cult seems to have had roots in medieval Spain.[7] Yet at the same time she had links to the native population of Mexico. There is credible testimony from the sixteenth century to the effect that she had taken over the role of an indigenous goddess previously worshipped at the same site.[8] The traditional account of the origins of the cult is known to us from the middle of the seventeenth century, not just in Spanish but also in Nahuatl, the major Amerindian language of the Mexican highlands.[9] Moreover, this account identifies the man to whom the Virgin made her appearance as "an Indian,"[10] emphasizing that this favor shown to the natives was "in order to make very clear that it was precisely for them that she came searching, that she came lovingly desiring that they take her for their queen."[11] In addition, the Virgin as she appears in her image is swarthy (*morena*)[12] and so plausibly indigenous. She thus appealed to native and Spaniard alike;[13] she was everybody's Virgin.

In the nineteenth century she showed a comparable ability to transcend deep ideological rifts and secure the loyalties of all parties. In

[5] Ibid., 175-7.

[6] See 128.

[7] It can hardly be an accident that Guadalupe in Extremadura had been the site of a major cult of the Virgin since the early fourteenth century (Brading, *Mexican phoenix*, 36–37), but the exact nature of the connection is obscure (77).

[8] Poole, *Our Lady of Guadalupe*, 78.

[9] Sousa et al., *Story of Guadalupe* (with an introduction and a facing-page translation).

[10] So the Spanish version (see the translation ibid., 131). The Nahuatl version identifies him as a "humble commoner" (61); for the ethnic force of this term, see 37, and note that the language of "humble commoners" is Nahuatl (55).

[11] Ibid., 121.

[12] "Sois hermosa, aunque morena," as a late sixteenth-century "Canción a Nuestra Señora" begins (Torre, *En torno al Guadalupanismo*, 76). The Nahuatl version of the traditional account describes the color of the Virgin of Guadalupe as "somewhat dark," the Spanish version as "light brunette" (Sousa et al., *Story of Guadalupe*, 89, 139).

[13] So the eighteenth-century hymn translated in Torre, *En torno al Guadalupanismo*, 103; and see Poole, *Our Lady of Guadalupe*, 202, for the participation of both Spaniards and Amerindians in the cult in the eighteenth century.

the war of independence it was the rebels who were most successful in recruiting her for their cause, while the loyalists vainly denounced the impudent hypocrisy of the rebel claim;[14] hence the liberal Simón Bolívar (d. 1830) wrote admiringly in 1815 that the leaders of the Mexican independence movement had "profited from fanaticism with the greatest skill, proclaiming the famous Virgin of Guadalupe as queen of the patriots."[15] But as the Mexican journalist quoted above pointed out, she had the allegiance of both sides in the Mexican civil wars of the nineteenth century.[16] Even Benito Juárez, the despoiler of the Mexican church, is said to have made a point of returning the property of the Virgin of Guadalupe.[17] In the same way she survived the upheavals and anticlericalism of the Mexican revolution in the twentieth century. As could be expected, she was particularly dear to the hearts of the pious Cristero rebels of western Mexico in the late 1920s;[18] but despite a bomb that went off in her basilica in 1921,[19] her cult was at no time interrupted during the years of the revolution, and its four-hundredth anniversary was duly celebrated in 1931.[20] By contrast, when followers of the virulently anticlerical governor of Michoacán dared to desecrate an image of the Virgin of Guadalupe in 1921, some ten thousand people turned out in protest.[21] Her worship is not universal among the Mexican population today; a journalist's report on the cult of "Saint Death" (Santa Muerte) among the low life of Mexico City cites a statement by one devotee of this underclass saint to the effect that the Virgin of Guadalupe takes care of well-off people with college degrees and nice clothes.[22] But her status as a national symbol and the wide dissemination

[14] For such denunciation see Torre, *En torno al Guadalupanismo*, 119–20. The belief that only the rebels followed the Virgin of Guadalupe, while the loyalists adhered to another Virgin, is refuted in García Gutiérrez, "La Virgen insurgente"; see also Brading, *Mexican phoenix*, 230.

[15] Simón Bolívar, *Obras completas*, 1: 174 (in a letter of September 6, 1815), as translated in Brading, *Origins of Mexican nationalism*, 49.

[16] See Torre, *En torno al Guadalupanismo*, 140.

[17] Ibid., 137–38.

[18] For a passage of Cristero rhetoric invoking her, see J. A. Meyer, *La cristiada*, 3: 280. See also J. A. Meyer, *Cristero rebellion*, 186, 188, and Brading, *Mexican phoenix*, 315 (a Cristero flag centered on an image of the Virgin of Guadalupe). I understand the Cristeros as the champions of a cause, rather than an identity, and thus will have more to say about them in later chapters (see 202–3, 245–46; contrast the reference to the Catholic identity of the Cristeros in Purnell, *Popular movements*, 151).

[19] Bailey, *¡Viva Cristo Rey!*, 37.

[20] See Torre, *En torno al Guadalupanismo*, 147–48, and Brading, *Mexican phoenix*, 317.

[21] Purnell, *Popular movements*, 64.

[22] Thompson, "On Mexico's mean streets."

of her cult are beyond doubt. A particular tribute to her role is the loyalty she has retained among the Chicanos, the formerly Mexican population of the southwestern United States: she appears, as one of them remarks, "on our banners, flags, posters, political buttons, bumper stickers, and in our rhetoric."[23] Significantly, even Chicano Protestants make much of her—one describes her as the glue that holds Chicano society together.[24]

3. High expectations

We can also find some more abstract reasons to expect a lively relationship between Catholicism and identity in Latin America. For a start, in the Islamic and Hindu cases the main factor working against a religiously based political identity was diversity—primarily ethnic in the Islamic case and primarily social in the Hindu case. Yet when we turn to Catholicism in Latin American, such obstacles more or less disappear.

The extent of the ethnic diversity of what we now know as Latin America has changed drastically over time. Prior to the arrival of the Iberians at the end of the fifteenth century, the region had a very varied population: innumerable peoples and languages, with no overarching civilization outside two limited areas that were not in mutual contact. The result was a higher level of diversity than has characterized the Islamic world. But history has been far less kind to the indigenous populations of the Americas than to those of the Old World. This is partly because the material culture of the native peoples was much less advanced than that of the European invaders but mainly a consequence of the extreme susceptibility of the Amerindian population to Old-World germs.[25] There was thus a widespread collapse of the indigenous populations of the Americas and a large-scale if imperfect cultural assimilation of those that remained. For example, despite the imposing pre-Columbian ruins to be found in Mexico, the proportion of the popu-

[23] Guerrero, *Chicano theology*, 113, and more generally 104–17.

[24] Ibid., 108; see also 109–10, 117.

[25] At the cost of occasional awkwardness, I use the term "Amerindian" in place of "Indian" when referring to the native populations of the Americas; in the context of a study that compares Latin America with India, to call them "Indians" would invite confusion. I naturally make exceptions when quoting, and I occasionally use the term "Indo-America."

lation of the country speaking an Amerindian language today is less than a tenth. Only in the Andes do really large Amerindian populations survive, and only in Bolivia are they a majority (some 60 percent).[26] Even there, we are unlikely to see the emergence of an Amerindian nation state in which high politics are transacted by Amerindians in a language of their own, if only because the Amerindians of Bolivia are not a single people with a single language.

This means that the ethnic character of the Latin American population today is largely a product of trends set in motion in the colonial period. Here the history of the region is unusual. The initial European conquest and settlement were the work of two—and only two—neighboring peoples who shared a religion and spoke closely related languages: the Spanish and the Portuguese. Just as remarkable was their success in holding on to most of their gains in subsequent centuries, despite the decline of both Spain and Portugal relative to the countries of northwestern Europe. The result was to establish and maintain the Iberian character of almost the entire South American continent, together with the southern cone of the North American mainland. The point is not that the region became Iberian in the way that Australia, for example, became British; the assimilation of the native population was as massive a process in parts of Latin America as it was marginal throughout Australia. But the culture brought by the Spanish and Portuguese faced no serious European competitors. Moreover, the history of the region after it became independent of European rule in the early nineteenth century was in general benign enough to leave this situation unchanged. The major exception to all this was in the far north, where Mexico lost half her territory to the expanding power of the United States. There were also minor exceptions in the Caribbean coastlands, where British and other intrusions have left their mark on the ethnic makeup of the Guyanas, Panama, and Belize; but for the most part the mainland was spared the kaleidoscopic colonial history of the Caribbean, where the vulnerability of island populations and the primacy of sea power meant that by the end of the nineteenth century the indigenous inhabitants had virtually disappeared and the Spanish had lost all the islands they had once possessed. The

[26] For Mexico, see Womack, *Rebellion in Chiapas*, 3; for the Andes, see the table in Albó, "Andean people," vol. 3, part 2: 767. The Guaraní speakers who constitute the core population of Paraguay are not an exception: they are a mestizo population with a Hispanic culture.

ethnic history of Latin America was thus an unusually homogenizing one.[27]

With regard to social diversity, the contrast with the Hindu case consists in the fact that there was no inherent linkage between Catholicism and the social hierarchy of Latin America. This was not for lack of hierarchy and the frictions that go with it. The "War of the Castes," a long-drawn-out and sanguinary event of mid-nineteenth-century history, took place not in India but in Yucatán, where, as in Latin America at large, the word "caste" (*casta*) had been inherited from the colonial period.[28] In fact, we can think of colonial society as made up of three castes. At the top were the whites (*blancos*, in Spanish-speaking America), the descendants of European settlers; they were, so to speak, the twice-born of Latin America, except that their distinctive status was not articulated in terms of generally accepted religious beliefs and rituals or conceived in terms of differential religious purity. At the bottom were the Amerindians (*indios*) or Africans (*negros*). We could think of them as the Untouchables of Latin America, but again their status was not tied to ideas of religious impurity, and in the Amerindian case their claim to be the indigenous population of the land was too obviously true to be in need of any discovery or invention in modern times. In between were those of mixed blood (*mestizos* or *mulatos*), comparable in their intermediate situation, if not much else, to the Śūdras of the Indian case. This crude schema was, of course, subject to variation over space and time. Geographically, it is helpful to distinguish three broad regions: an Afro-America centered on Brazil; an Indo-America centered on the Andean highlands of Bolivia, Peru, and Ecuador; and a Euro-America (where neither Amerindian nor African populations were significant) in the southern cone of South America. The most noticeable trend over time was for the Amerindian population to decline as the mixed population increased, whether by interbreeding or cultural assimilation; in Peru, for example, the Amerindian component was some 70 percent at independence, but it is only about half that today.[29]

From our point of view, what matters is the relationship between this lingering colonial caste system and the formal values of Latin American society. In the colonial period the link was a solid one: caste was a legal

[27] It thus contrasts strongly with that of Africa, a continent marked by the continuing demographic dominance of a diverse indigenous population and by the variety of European powers involved in the partition.

[28] Compare also the "caste wars" of Bolivia (Klein, *Bolivia*, 154).

[29] Skidmore and Smith, *Modern Latin America*, 177, 180.

category and subject to regulation by the state. With independence, and the advent of modern values, this sooner or later ceased to be so; to the extent that caste is still a Latin American reality, it is now only a social, not a legal phenomenon. But the key point is that the caste system was a product of the conquest situation, not of Catholicism. One could easily imagine a Catholic doctrine that on some theological ground or other categorically excluded the native populations of the Americas from participation in a sacrament such as the eucharist, much as Hindu doctrine denied Vedic mantras to their Indian counterparts. Yet despite the fact that Amerindians were indeed often excluded from the eucharist, no such doctrine seems to have emerged.[30] In short, while the formal religious heritage of the society was able to cohabit with the caste system without signs of undue strain, its role in it was not a constitutive one.

It might seem, then, that Catholicism in Latin America was in a position to serve as the basis of a modern political identity without encountering the problems that afflicted Muslim identity on the ethnic front and Hindu identity on the social front. To this we can add the religious coherence of the region. The great majority—though significantly not the entirety—of the Latin American population still retains its allegiance to the Catholicism brought by the Spanish and Portuguese. Thus, in contrast to the Hindu case, Latin America largely belongs to a single religious community that is demographically dominant in the region and committed to a uniform set of beliefs and rituals. And in contrast to the Islamic case, this community possesses a centralized ecclesiastical hierarchy. Of course, like any religion that spreads over a vast territory and adjusts to local environments over the centuries, Catholicism comprehends a measure of diversity. Above all, there is variation at the level of folk Catholicism. But the heterogeneity is not greater than in the Islamic case and far less than in the Hindu case. Whatever might be the problems of devising an effective form of Catholic identity politics, the cacophony of diversity was unlikely to be one of them.

[30] See Ricard, *Spiritual conquest of Mexico*, 122–26; Tibesar, *Franciscan beginnings*, 87–89; Acosta, *De procuranda Indorum salute*, 2: 412 §2.17, 414 §3.1 (a Jesuit work with a focus on Peru first published in 1588, in which the author champions a relative openness towards extending the eucharist to Indians); Álvarez, *De las costumbres*, 210 §363, and cf. 213 §369 (a work written by a priest in 1587–1588 arguing that the Jesuits are far too lax and that in practice no Indians should receive the eucharist). I am indebted to Kenneth Mills for referring me to the works of Acosta and Álvarez.

Let us now turn to another obvious asset for identity politics: the availability of a suitable antagonist. How well was Latin American Catholicism served in this respect?

Since the first half of the sixteenth century, the prime enemy of Catholicism has been Protestantism. Once the initial native rebellions had been overcome in the Americas, virtually all serious threats to the territory occupied by Latin American Catholicism came from Protestants. It was the Protestant Dutch who from 1630 to 1654 held the rich northeastern province of Brazil and the Protestant British who later helped themselves to what is now Belize; the same Protestant nations were likewise responsible for two of the three Guyanas. At the same time it was the British who in the nineteenth century shaped much of the global environment in which the independent countries of Latin America had to make their way. But with limited exceptions (the Falklands for Argentina, Belize for Guatemala), that history no longer matters much. Since the end of the nineteenth century, it is the United States that has figured as the key Protestant power in Latin America in both real and symbolic terms. The United States had already traumatized Mexico in the mid-nineteenth century by conquering much of its territory, at one point occupying Mexico City in the course of a war that was described by Ulysses S. Grant as "one of the most unjust ever waged by a stronger against a weaker nation."[31] Since then the United States has not formally annexed further Latin American territory. But it has a history of direct or indirect military interventions in the parts of Latin America within easy reach, and its political, economic, and cultural influence extends all the way to the southern cone.

Latin America has responded to this unwelcome presence with an anti-Americanism that is deep, widespread, and persistent.[32] It has naturally been most acute in regions directly exposed to raw American power. This applies most obviously to Mexico, the only Latin American country that has the misfortune to share a land frontier with the United States; as one Mexican president remarked, "Poor Mexico! So far from God, and so close to the United States."[33] To the Mexicans proper we can add the Chicanos. Then come the small countries of Central America and the Caribbean, where armed American interventions have been most frequent (thirty odd landings between 1898 and 1933, in other words about one a year).[34] Thus in Nicaragua the nationalist rebel San-

[31] Quoted in J. M. McPherson, *Battle cry of freedom*, 4.
[32] A. McPherson, *Yankee No!*
[33] Quoted in Skidmore and Smith, *Modern Latin America*, 217.
[34] A. McPherson, *Yankee No!*, 16.

dino was not content to denounce the American Marines as barbarians and blond beasts; his army went so far as to mint a gold coin that appears to show a Marine about to be decapitated.[35]

But if the urge to hit back has been strongest in the north, there has been no lack of anti-Americanism further south. Thus when the United States landed troops in the Dominican Republic in 1965, there were violent protests in almost all Latin American capitals.[36] In part this hostility arises from direct resentment of American power, even when it is only soft power. But it also reflects the continuing cultural conductivity of Latin America.[37] An earlier example of this conductivity was the wide dissemination of *Ariel*. This short work, published in 1900 by José Enrique Rodó (d. 1917), contained a classic articulation of Latin American anti-Americanism.[38] It reflected a period in which the Americans had made themselves thoroughly disliked by turning Cuban independence from Spain into dependence on the United States. Naturally the book had strong resonance in the parts of Latin America directly exposed to American power; thus it was reprinted in Santo Domingo in 1901, in Havana in 1905, and in Mexico in 1908;[39] in that year the governor of Nuevo León—the border state adjoining Texas—prepared a special gift edition for distribution among his friends.[40] The author of this tract was nevertheless a Uruguayan writing in Uruguay, where the book was first published, and his work received wide attention in parts of Latin America far from the direct reach of American military power. Prior to publication Rodó had written about the book in a journal published in Caracas,[41] and the work was later to be reprinted in such cities as Buenos Aires, Santiago, and Lima.[42] And indeed the threat he spoke of was subtler than that experienced by the Mexicans and Cubans, a "kind of moral conquest" in which susceptibility to the lure of

[35] Ibid., 16–17.

[36] Ibid., 138. By contrast, the Latin American response to the war between Britain and Argentina over the Falklands in 1982 seems to have been rather restrained (Freedman, "Impact of the Falklands," 18–20).

[37] Compare the literary activity of the Cuban José Martí (d. 1895) in New York in 1880–1895: his essays were published in newspapers in Mexico City, Caracas, Montevideo, and Buenos Aires (B. L. Lewis, "Sarmiento, Martí, and Rodó," 32).

[38] Rodó, *Ariel*, trans. Sayers Peden, especially 70–90. All references are to the Sayers Peden translation unless otherwise noted.

[39] See the list of printings of the work ibid., 115–21.

[40] Stabb, *In quest of identity*, 39.

[41] Ibid., 38.

[42] There was also a Portuguese translation published in Rio de Janeiro in 1933 (Rodó, *Ariel*, 117). The late date of this translation may reflect only the readiness of educated Brazilians to read Spanish (I owe this point to Jussara Quadros).

the north ("our *nordomanía*") would result in "an America de-Latinized of its own will," with the loss of its "irreplaceable uniqueness."[43] Just as far flung as the literary success of *Ariel* was the anti-Americanism of the university reform movement of 1919, which aspired to purge universities of professors who were agents of cultural imperialism.[44] As might be expected, this continuing Latin American sentiment has been articulated in a number of different registers. Rodó, looking down on the North Americans from a great height, observed that they "lack the supreme gift of *amiability*."[45] The Peruvian Víctor Raúl Haya de la Torre (d. 1979), who was more of an ideologue, often ended his letters with a formula beginning "Against Yankee imperialism."[46] The diction of an Ecuadorian graffito I copied in 1991 is more graphic: "Gringos hijos de putas." It was in that spirit that the crowds along the route by which Vice President Nixon was driven into Caracas in 1958 spat at him to such effect that his driver had to make use of the windshield wipers.[47]

At this level of sentiment, the outside world is a simpler place for Latin Americans than it is for Islamists or Hindu nationalists. Anti-Americanism is, of course, a stock-in-trade of Islamists, and it has also played a part in the rhetoric of the Hindu nationalists.[48] From their point of view, the United States is indeed the most powerful country on earth, but it is neither a neighbor nor a regional power. For Islamists, hostile neighbors on the borders of their world are legion, and there are several distinct regional powers to contend with. For the Hindu nationalists, Pakistan is the intimate enemy immediately across the border, the separatist state that shattered the unity of undivided India, and the neighbor that takes every opportunity to make trouble in Kashmir and elsewhere; China, despite a shared border, is a less intimate enemy, more of a regional strategic threat (who lost Tibet?). For Latin America, by contrast, all three relationships are collapsed into one. There is, of course, something that mitigates this effect: the fact that Latin America, like the Islamic world but unlike India, is made up of many countries. More precisely, whereas for largely fortuitous reasons

[43] Ibid., 71–72; *nordomanía* is the term used in the original Spanish (Rodó, *Ariel*, ed. G. Brotherston, 70).

[44] Pike, *Politics of the miraculous*, 39–41.

[45] Rodó, *Ariel*, 87.

[46] A. McPherson, *Yankee No!*, 20.

[47] Ibid., 29.

[48] For an example of RSS anti-Americanism, see Embree, "Rashtriya Swayamsevak Sangh," 634, but note his comment that "there is not as much criticism as one might expect."

Portuguese America held together to give us the southern colossus of Brazil, Spanish America broke up into over a dozen independent states. This inevitably works to blur the focus of anti-Americanism in the region: hostility between neighboring states is predictably greater where these states are sovereign, as is the case within Latin America as opposed to federal India. Thus Ecuadorians feel about Peruvians the way Peruvians feel about Chileans, and these feelings are nourished both by the wounds of past wars and by the possibility of future ones. But this effect is not to be exaggerated. Nationalism came easily to Latin America, since culturally it was an extension of Europe, and yet over the region as a whole antagonisms between nations remain surprisingly shallow;[49] in the present epoch it seems that only the relationship between Ecuador and Peru approaches the levels of hatred familiar from the modern history of Europe.[50]

What Latin America lacked until the last century was a significant internal Protestant presence to match the external enemy. In colonial times there was no Protestant challenge from within, and even in the nineteenth century the primary domestic enemy of Catholicism was anticlericalism, not Protestantism. But anticlericalism led to the deregulation of the religious market, thus providing an opening for the penetration of Latin America by Protestant missionaries in the early twentieth century. As a result, Latin America today has a significant Protestant minority. Pentecostals of one kind or another are the main component of this minority; and Pentecostalism, be it noted, is a movement that originated precisely in the United States. By the early 1990s Protestants were estimated to make up some 11 percent of the population of the region as a whole,[51] which is about the same as the proportion of Muslims in the population of independent India. Chile, for example, saw an early indigenization of Pentecostalism thanks to a schism in 1910, and the movement grew rapidly among the poor from the 1930s.[52] By 1955 evangelical Protestants were already estimated at 11 percent of the Chilean population;[53] since then the Protestant vote is estimated to have risen to over 20 percent—a high figure for Latin America but matched in parts of Central America and above all in

[49] Centeno, *Blood and debt*, 84–90.

[50] Ibid., 85, 89–90.

[51] I take this figure from B. H. Smith, *Religious politics*, 2.

[52] Gill, *Rendering unto Caesar*, 131. This book was drawn to my attention by Julie Taylor.

[53] Ibid.

Brazil.[54] How long this upward trend will continue is anybody's guess, but it does not augur well for the future of Latin American Catholicism that Pentecostal pastors already outnumber Catholic priests; in Brazil the ratio stands at about two to one.[55] Moreover most of the new Protestants are toward the bottom of Latin American society,[56] so their conversion could invite comparison to that of Untouchables in India. There is, of course, a significant difference:[57] the Muslim presence in India is the residue of a millennial history of Muslim invasion and conquest, whereas the Protestant presence in Latin America is new, and outside the lost Mexican territory it carries no comparable burden of historical memory. Nevertheless, the external Protestant power embodied in the looming presence of the United States has come to be matched by an internal hemorrhage to a Protestantism that largely derives from the same country. This could surely be expected to do something to rally the region's Catholics.

4. Low realizations

Let us now turn to the actual track record of Catholic identity politics in Latin America and see what it adds up to.

We can best begin by going back to anti-Americanism. Here the key point is that hostility to Protestantism has been surprisingly unimportant in the history of this powerful sentiment. If we go to Rodó's classic critique of the North Americans, we encounter a perspective that at first sight seems promising. He makes it clear that North Americans, in implicit contrast to Latin Americans, lack spirituality.[58] Their society is the embodiment of utilitarianism—"a utilitarianism void of any idealism"—and the result is that their civilization gives "a singular impression of insufficiency and emptiness."[59] Thus, they have failed to inherit the "ancestral poetic instinct" of the British.[60] The religious life of the Americans forms part of the same syndrome. Though their religion has a "firm grip on the reins of morality," it does not reach the

[54] Ibid., 185.

[55] Chesnut, *Competitive spirits*, 57, 62.

[56] See ibid., 41; also Deiros, "Protestant fundamentalism," 182.

[57] I owe this point to Jacob Mikanowski.

[58] This perception was already in the air in the middle of the nineteenth century (see Reid, "Ariel-Caliban antithesis," 349–50, 351).

[59] Rodó, *Ariel*, 71, 79, 85.

[60] Ibid., 80.

level of a "delicate and profound spiritualism."[61] He categorizes it as an "exaggeration of English religion," a connection in which he takes a dim view of the Puritans, a "doleful sect" that "persecuted beauty."[62] Such contrasts between spirituality and materialism, usually characterized as respectively "Eastern" and "Western," were, of course, a leitmotif of what we might call early Third-Worldism, a way of being subtly superior to those who were all too crudely on top of the world.[63] But when we look to see where Rodó proceeds to locate the sacred place of Latin Americans in the pages of history,[64] it is not in their Catholicism. For him, "the two highest ideals in history" are the "Greek miracle" and early Christianity—he was at some level an admirer of the teachings of Jesus.[65] But he shows no interest in later Catholicism, least of all in its Latin American form. Matters are different, of course, if we turn to Mexico and listen to such Catholic activists as the Cristeros, who rebelled against the godlessness of the Mexican revolution in the later 1920s: these pietists were happy to see their anticlerical enemy as part of a plot that was not just American but also Protestant.[66] A more interesting Mexican case is that of the failed politician but distinguished intellectual José Vasconcelos (d. 1959). Like Rodó he set great store by spirituality, but unlike him he eventually found what he was looking for in an orthodox and traditionalist Catholicism.[67] He did not quite share his mother's simpleminded horror of Protestant heresy,[68] but he regarded Protestantism as a significant part of the threat posed by the United States to his Hispanic and Catholic heritage.[69] He had, of

[61] Ibid., 76.

[62] Ibid., 52, 83.

[63] Compare Vivekānanda: "Up, India, and conquer the world with your spirituality! . . . Materialism and all its miseries can never be conquered by materialism. . . . Spirituality must conquer the West" (*Complete works*, 3: 277). Likewise Liang Ch'i-ch'ao (d. 1929), declaring his preference for Eastern methods of relieving spiritual famine: "Eastern learning has spirit as its point of departure; Western learning has matter as its point of departure" (quoted in Levenson, *Liang Ch'i-ch'ao*, 201). Sayyid Quṭb has a similar view of Islam: "Islam is the real force that resists the force of the materialistic thought worshipped equally in Europe, America, and Russia. It is Islam that . . . gives life a spiritual idea that links it to its Creator in heaven and controls its worldly tendencies so that it does not realize purely material goals" (Quṭb, *ʿAdāla*, 264.17 = 350, with notes 6 and 8).

[64] Rodó, *Ariel*, 73.

[65] Ibid., 44, 51–52, 52–53.

[66] J. A. Meyer, *Cristero rebellion*, 186; see also Bailey, *¡Viva Cristo Rey!*, 268.

[67] Marentes, *José Vasconcelos*, 2–3, 53, 55, 173, 176–77.

[68] Ibid., 42, 47.

[69] Ibid., 3, 22, 48, 65, 182. His paranoia about Protestant conspiracies was not, however, single-minded: Protestants had to share the limelight with Freemasons, Jews, Bolsheviks, and bankers (3, 18, 48).

course, many other anti-American gripes: racism, mechanization, anti-intellectualism, liberated women, bad food.[70] But Catholicism was a salient aspect of his identity as a Mexican and a Latin American.[71] The surprise is that such views were not much more widespread. This was no indication of any dearth of anti-Americanism among the population at large: American representatives in Mexico during the revolution reported that "anti-American sentiment is almost universal among rich and poor alike."[72] But just as for most of the Latin American public, hostility to Americans had little to do with their Protestantism. This may say something about the United States, with its refusal to establish an official religion and its acceptance of an increasing Catholic minority (now around 25 percent). But it says more about Latin America.

Just as notable is the fact that Latin American public opinion has not shown much concern about the growing Protestant minority in its midst, nor has it tended to see it as part of an international Protestant conspiracy. "Yankee go home" is not addressed to indigenous Protestants in Latin America, whereas the slogan about Pakistan or the cemetery is aimed directly at indigenous Muslims in India.[73] The Catholic church in Latin America has, of course, been deeply worried about the Protestant threat; as early as 1941 a Chilean Jesuit, Alberto Hurtado (d. 1952), was questioning whether Chile could still count as a Catholic country.[74] Yet the politicians, it seems, have not shared this concern, except when disposed to do political favors for the church.[75] Thus a Brazilian churchman in the 1940s portrayed the Protestant missionary threat as part of a North American plot to dominate Latin America and destroy Catholicism,[76] but such rhetoric failed to ignite public indignation outside ecclesiastical circles. One scholar offers two rather telling reasons for the indifference of the politicians. The first is that the new Protestants of Latin America were no threat to the security of the state: "Pentecostals, because of their apolitical nature, were simply no danger to politicians."[77] This is beyond question—but consider the case of India. There one could perhaps argue with a certain plausibility that conversion to Islam was a threat to the security of the state;

[70] A. McPherson, *Yankee No!*, 15.
[71] Marentes, *José Vasconcelos*, 3, 15, 29, 173–74.
[72] A. McPherson, *Yankee No!*, 16.
[73] See 93.
[74] His book bore the title *¿Es Chile un país católico?* (Gill, *Rendering unto Caesar*, 132–35).
[75] Ibid., 94, 111, 132, 168–69.
[76] Mainwaring, *Catholic Church and politics*, 38 and 265n50.
[77] Gill, *Rendering unto Caesar*, 132, and see 94.

but in the decades since independence, this allegation has had no plausibility whatever in the case of conversion to Christianity[78]—and yet in India such conversion can readily be seized on by Hindu nationalist politicians as a national scandal.[79] The second reason suggested that is relevant to our concerns is that as the Protestant movement became more indigenous, it became harder for the church to stir up nationalist sentiment against it.[80] Again the Indian contrast leaps to the eye: the Muslims of India are an overwhelmingly indigenous population. Like their Indian counterparts, political elites in Latin America have to burnish their nationalist credentials, if only for public-relations purposes, and yet they missed the opportunity to capitalize on the Protestant issue—or rather, their inactivity suggests that there was no issue there for them to exploit. Brazilians who convert to Pentecostalism are still seen as good Brazilians; they do not thereby open themselves to the charge of seceding from the national community.

In the same way communal violence between Catholics and Protestants is rare in Latin America, and there is no reason to attribute this to the presence of a more responsible political elite. Such violence just isn't on the cards. There is one revealing exception, namely the state of Chiapas in southern Mexico. There we encounter extreme bitterness between Catholics and Protestants, with Catholics expelling Protestants from their homes and Protestants dreaming of revenge against their Catholic enemies. But the conditions are peculiar. Chiapas is not just the poorest,[81] but also the most Protestant of Mexican states—and one of the most Amerindian: in 1990 Amerindians made up 26 percent of the population,[82] while Protestants of various denominations stood at 16 percent—rising to 22 percent in 2000.[83] Moreover the events that concern us took place among a set of small but rapidly growing Mayan peoples of the state. Nowhere were matters worse than in the town of San Juan Chamula.[84] This purely indigenous Tzotzil settlement of some

[78] For an implausible Hindu nationalist claim to the contrary, see Jaffrelot, "Vishva Hindu Parishad," 319.

[79] "Raking up the Christian conversion issue appeared efficacious in consolidating the Hindutva base among the middle classes" (Katju, *Vishva Hindu Parishad*, 135). There is no sign of such an effect in Latin America.

[80] Gill, *Rendering unto Caesar*, 95.

[81] Womack, *Rebellion in Chiapas*, 11.

[82] Bastian, "Religion," 101.

[83] Farfán, "Erscheinungsformen," 188, and see 206. In 1905 Chiapas had had one of the smallest Protestant populations of any state in Mexico (Baldwin, *Protestants*, 60).

[84] Of the incidents involving religious conflict in Chiapas in the decades from 1960 to 2001, 43 percent took place in San Juan Chamula (see the table in Farfán et al., *Diversi-*

50,000 people had jealously preserved a deviant folk Catholicism closely tied to the distribution of power, office, and alcohol within the community.[85] In this context Protestantism in the second half of the twentieth century offered the young and landless a devastating critique of the existing order—religious, political, social, and moral.[86] Those in charge of the community responded by expelling large numbers of Protestants (it is said some 30,000 in the 1970s and 1980s).[87] Thus when the Zapatista rebellion was launched in 1994, one Tzotzil Protestant construed the worried reaction of the Catholics of Chamula in terms of fear that the rebels would avenge the wrongs done to the Protestants.[88] In short, it was in small indigenous enclaves seeking to live a life apart from Latin America at large that this rare parallel to Indian communalism emerged. Even in Chiapas, it is untypical of Catholic-Protestant relations.[89]

If those in the business of identity politics in Latin America more or less ignore Catholicism, we should ask what they seize on instead. For an answer we can take the most clearcut example of identity politics in modern Latin American history, namely Aprismo. This is the only large-scale political movement that has attempted to remake the identity of Latin America, and it initially set about it with an organization and a passion reminiscent of the RSS. The movement was founded and inspired by Haya de la Torre, a Peruvian who had visited Argentina, Uruguay, and Chile before establishing his party in Mexico in 1924.[90] But he did not locate the identity of Latin America in Catholicism. Instead he opted for indigenism, a cultural stance with a long history in the region, above all in Mexico where it was already well established

dad religiosa, 144, and compare the map, 145). By far the most common type of incident involved expulsion (see the table and chart, 146–47).

[85] For the size and ethnicity of the population see Womack, *Rebellion in Chiapas*, 257. For a graphic account of the traditional system dating from the middle of the twentieth century, see Pozas, *Juan the Chamula*; see, for example, the account of the Day of the Dead (48–52), the comments on the role of alcohol in the governance of the community (53), and the survey of saints (92–96). In this account there are as yet no Protestants in sight.

[86] Islam could perform the same service, and a Tzotzil Muslim community of some three hundred souls has in fact emerged (Glüsing, "Allahs Indianer," 130, drawn to my attention by Teresa Bernheimer).

[87] Bastian, "Religion," 107; cf. Farfán, "Erscheinungsformen," 212. For the role of one troubled convert to Protestantism in these events, see Gossen, "Life, death, and apotheosis."

[88] See the Protestant "Tzotzil chronicle" in Womack, *Rebellion in Chiapas*, 260–63; for the rebellion and its background, see 3–59.

[89] Farfán, "Erscheinungsformen," 211–12, 213; and cf. Womack, *Rebellion in Chiapas*, 17.

[90] Pike, *Politics of the miraculous*, 45, 50.

in the colonial period.[91] The Apristas accordingly claimed that Latin America was dying and that Indo-America represented the future.[92] The claim was implausible, but as an ideological move it was not entirely foolish. The large mestizo populations of Latin America occupied an ambiguous position between those of clear European and Amerindian descent, and in the absence of Amerindian nations, the native heritage was up for grabs. Moreover, in the South American context Haya de la Torre was well placed to grab it: as a Peruvian he could lay claim to the heritage of the Incas, and as a product of the coastal city of Trujillo, near the impressive ruins of the Chimú capital, he had no need to complicate his indigenism by developing ties to the real Amerindians of the highlands.[93] The problem, of course, was that indigenism appealed mainly to the elite; as far as the mestizos were concerned, it meant that they were being asked to identify with their social inferiors, not their social superiors.

Finally we should return to the Virgin of Guadalupe. One thing that reduces her significance for us is the fact that she is unique in Latin America. Cults of the Virgin are, of course, widespread. A Bolivian example would be the Virgin of Copacabana on Lake Titicaca, another dark Virgin combining ecclesiastical approval with a strong and even subversive appeal to the Amerindian population.[94] In Colombia there is the Virgin of Chiquinquirá, whom the pope declared the patron of the new republic in 1829.[95] A later pope, responding to an entreaty from Cuba, conferred a similar role in 1916 on a Virgin long revered on the island.[96] In Brazil the strongly nationalistic dictator Getúlio Vargas (in power 1930–1945) supported an effort to have a local Virgin elevated

[91] For the development of Creole indigenism see Brading, *Origins of Mexican nationalism*, 3–23. This was a historical persuasion, and did not entail sympathy for the contemporary Amerindian population (see 16, 53, 58, 62).

[92] Pike, *Politics of the miraculous*, 50.

[93] Compare the romantic Amerindianism of mid-nineteenth century Brazil (Skidmore, *Brazil*, 48) and the effort invested by the emperor Dom Pedro II in studying Tupí alongside Arabic, Provençal, Hebrew, and Sanskrit (Lyra, *História*, 2: 103, 105, 329–30n139c). One wonders whether the emperor was sentimental enough to learn Tupinambá, already extinct but well documented from the sixteenth century, or preferred to invest his energies in the more prosaic Língua Geral, a creolized version of Tupinambá still widely spoken in his day (cf. Dixon and Aikhenvald, *Amazonian languages*, 7, 125, 127, 387).

[94] See Klein, *Bolivia*, 48–49, 61, 62, 133.

[95] Ramírez Uribe, *Nuestra Señora del Rosario*, 47. This little book is a work of piety.

[96] Portuondo Zúñiga, *La Virgen*, 245; see also Gonzalez, *Afro-Cuban theology*, 81–82, 84, 86–87.

to the status of patron saint of the nation.[97] She did achieve a modest national standing, enough to render her a target of Protestant iconoclasm: in 1995 her image was kicked and punched on national television by a Pentecostal bishop.[98] The incident gave offense to millions; but for the Virgin of Guadalupe to have been subjected to such treatment would have been almost unimaginable. In short, none of these other Virgins of Latin America seems to have achieved a comparable prominence as a national symbol, and certainly none of them has generated a comparable literature.[99]

Moreover, even the Virgin of Guadalupe plays only a limited role in the politics of her country. She is always there in the background, an uncontentious symbol of national identity that everyone accepts. But this has no implications for the nature of the Mexican polity. Her religious role poses no challenge to the secular character of the Mexican state, just as her queenship in no way undermines its republican character. No one has ever set out to create a movement of "Guadalupanismo" that would transform what it is to be Mexican. Thus the impression that her cult points to a deep involvement of religion in identity politics in Latin America is something of a mirage.

5. Explaining the Gap

Why, then, has Latin American Catholicism made so little contribution to identity politics in the region, despite what might look like objectively favorable conditions? Or, to put it the other way round, why have the politicians and intellectuals of Latin America, whether humdrum realists or extravagant visionaries, found so little invitation to identity politics in this religious tradition? To answer these questions we need to tackle issues that we have so far left out of sight. The first is whether Latin American populations have faced a real identity problem, and the second is whether Catholicism could have provided a real solution to such a problem.

With regard to the first question, our sustained attention to Muslim and Hindu identity puts us at risk of overlooking a very simple point. Most people most of the time do not think much about identity. They

[97] D. D. Brown, *Umbanda*, 206.

[98] Chesnut, *Competitive spirits*, 91–92.

[99] I have not come across a comparative study of these cults.

know perfectly well who they are; their problems in life lie elsewhere, in the difficulty of getting what they want. Movements that seek to change the way large numbers of people identify themselves and, still more, movements that succeed in such enterprises, are accordingly rare. We should therefore ask whether there is any particular reason to expect a region like Latin America to be a hotbed of identity politics. One obvious reason might be the shallowness of its national identities. It is not just that the population of a Latin American country tends not to differ very much from those of its neighbors, in either ethnic or religious terms, though that in itself is significant. There is also, for many of the Spanish-speaking countries, a question of historical legitimacy: they are the product not of the liberation itself but rather of the subsequent political disintegration—a process in which the provincial identities of late colonial times reasserted themselves against the grander notions of unity espoused by Bolívar.[100] Yet, despite the iconic status of Bolívar, this development does not seem to have led to a continuing problem of legitimacy for the nations that now make up Latin America.[101] That leaves us to reckon with the possibility that a few countries might suffer from identity problems for reasons of their own. Two merit brief discussion: Brazil and Bolivia.

Brazil has a potential ethnic problem of serious dimensions thanks to its racial composition. The country houses the largest population of African descent found anywhere outside Africa, with blacks and mulattoes making up some 45 percent of the population.[102] One might thus have expected to see the investment of considerable political energy in attempts to mobilize this population and countervailing efforts to articulate a Brazilian identity that would not fall apart in the face of racial tensions. One could even imagine Catholicism playing a central role here. In fact, there has been virtually nothing of such a kind,[103] and at some level this is not hard to explain. It is a fundamental feature of

[100] For Bolívar's somewhat protean thinking on this question, see Collier, "Nationality, nationalism." Collier stresses the absence from Bolivarian nationalism of "a genuine ethnic or cultural dimension" (43), features that became more pronounced in the nationalisms that displaced it (see M. Brown, *Adventuring through Spanish colonies*, 123; this study shows how the shift affected in very practical ways the lives of the European adventurers who had fought for the cause of liberation, see especially 110–13, 122–24).

[101] The contrast with the countries making up the Arab world is noteworthy.

[102] Andrews, *Afro-Latin America*, 156. The proportion is about the same in Venezuela.

[103] For the racially inclusive conception of Brazilian identity put forward from the 1930s by Gilberto Freyre, see Skidmore, *Black into white*, 190–92. His ideas were not a response to any fear of separatism among the colored population.

the political history of twentieth-century Brazil that the racial makeup of the population scarcely figures in it.[104] It is not that Brazil has been free of racial problems; the key point is rather that, since the tardy abolition of slavery in 1888,[105] these problems have not been projected onto the political stage. There have been black activists in Brazil since the 1920s—and still more since the 1970s;[106] by the late 1980s this ferment had spawned well over three hundred organizations.[107] But their impact on national politics has been marginal[108] since the activists have been unable to mobilize their mass constituency; one scholar stresses the preference of poor blacks for vertical ties with strong, established patrons rather than horizontal ties under the aegis of weak counterhegemonic movements.[109] Hence the potential threat of race to national unity has never been realized. In this sense Brazilian identity has not been a real problem, and there was thus no need for a solution. What is true for Brazilian politics at large is true also for Catholic politics in the country. As we will see, there have been Catholic or Catholicizing movements active in politics, on both the right and the left, but like Brazilian political actors in general, they have not engaged with race.

In the case of Bolivia, by contrast, the Amerindian problem is real—and more pressing than in any other Andean country. Here alone the indigenous population is still a majority, though divided ethnically and geographically into two major groups. One of them speaks Aymará and the other Quechua, and both languages are also spoken by significant populations in southern Peru.[110] In recent years it has been the Aymará speakers of the high plateau who have been most active in subverting the traditional ethnic order and most reluctant to see themselves as

[104] Note particularly the absence of reference to race from the *political* narrative of the twentieth century given in Skidmore, *Brazil* (for a minor exception, see 212). This author is well aware of the *social* importance of race in Brazil (see, for example, 89, 208–10, and his monograph *Black into white*).

[105] Skidmore, *Brazil*, 70.

[106] For some examples, see Degler, *Neither black nor white*, xv, 177, 179–80. The year 1931 saw the establishment of the Frente Negra Brasileira, 1978 that of the Movimento Negro Unificado Contra Discriminação Racial.

[107] Andrews, *Afro-Latin America*, 183–84.

[108] For a rare reference to the racial problem by a major political figure, see Degler, *Neither black nor white*, 270–71.

[109] Andrews, *Afro-Latin America*, 188–90.

[110] For the linguistic situation, see Klein, *Bolivia*, 265, 281–82; also Stark, "Quechua language in Bolivia," 516–17, and Briggs, "Dialectical variation in Aymara," 595. Quechua in southern Bolivia is unusual in not being confined to the native population (Stark, "Quechua language in Bolivia," 538).

belonging within a Bolivian nation. They have an extended history of confrontation with the white rulers of their territories. In 1781 they were involved in a major rebellion under Túpac Catari, after whom the militant Katarista movement that took shape around 1970 was named.[111] In the meantime they had participated in numerous risings, most notably in 1860 and again in 1921 and 1927.[112] Despite a rare episode in 1899 they were usually excluded from national politics,[113] but this began to change in the aftermath of the national trauma of the Chaco War of 1932–1935. The elite now started to address the native problem,[114] and the natives themselves began to organize and make claims on the national stage.[115] The revolution of 1952 accelerated this process, extending the franchise to the Amerindian masses[116]—though their satisfaction at the ensuing land reform tended to make them rather conservative.[117] But militancy returned with the formation of the Katarista movement and continues to this day. Here, then, was a problem of identity that posed a real threat to national unity. But those Bolivians who have been involved in Catholic politics have shown no signs of engaging with it, whether on the left or the right. They have not, for example, sought to take the cult of the Virgin of Copacabana—located as it is in the core of the Aymará territory and associated with ethnic rebellion[118]—and promote it as a symbol of national unity crossing the ethnic divide. In Peru and Ecuador, where the problem of national identity represented by the Amerindian population is less troublesome, we would be just as unsuccessful were we to go in search of attempts to use Catholicism to solve it.

That leaves us with the hypothetical question whether, if more Latin American countries had had real identity problems, Catholicism could have provided a real solution—as it manifestly did not in the Andean countries. Here again, our exposure to the Islamic and Hindu cases threatens to skew our expectations. Despite their differences a core feature of Islam and Hinduism is that both are heavily invested in identity;

[111] For the Kataristas, see Albó, "Andean people," 840–44, 848–49; Klein, *Bolivia*, 273, 284. For the rebellion of Túpac Catari, see ibid., 76.

[112] Klein, *Bolivia*, 133, 172, 177–78. For the role of the expansion of haciendas in generating some of these revolts, see 171.

[113] Ibid., 154, 163, 167.

[114] Ibid., 197, 213, 219.

[115] Ibid., 198, 235.

[116] Ibid., 232.

[117] Ibid., 234–35, 248.

[118] Ibid., 49, 133.

but the Catholic Christianity of Latin America may not be a religion of the same kind. To see whether it is or not, we need to look into two things. One is the basic character of the religion—those features of Catholicism that had taken shape long before its arrival in the New World and were unlikely to undergo drastic change there. The other is the contingencies of its history in Latin America.

Let us start with the character of Catholicism. It shares with Christianity at large a basic feature that concerns us. Christianity, to make an obvious but fundamental point, has no intrinsic ethnic identity. The only ethnic property that Christians as such have in common is not being Jewish—and even this was not a given during the earliest centuries of the religion. Historically, we might say, Christianity achieved its success as a de-ethnicized offshoot of Judaism, and this has gone well with its role as a world religion. In the more limited context of Europe, it facilitated the coexistence of religion with ethnic identity that was crucial to the emergence of the nationalist paradigm. But, by the same token, this overall indifference to ethnic identity puts limits to the ethnic appropriation of the religion. While Hinduism is explicitly about India, Christianity is not about Latin America or anywhere else. The religion has nevertheless shown a considerable ability over the course of its history to adapt to local contours through the development of national churches. Obvious examples are those of the Armenians, the Ethiopians, and eventually the English. Such churches typically combine organizational independence, the adoption of doctrinal allegiances that set them off from large parts of the Christian world, and the translation of scriptural and liturgical texts into their own distinctive languages.

But in the Catholic case, the development of national churches of this kind was precluded by a second basic feature of the religion: the Catholic church is a world religion governed from a single center. It has taken great care to maintain its organizational unity and doctrinal uniformity across the globe, and it was only in the second half of the last century that it made the concession of translating its scriptures and liturgy into the vernacular languages of its adherents. Its centralization also implied that, seen from the New World, the Catholic church was an institution with its heart far away in Europe. Thus, it was not just that Catholicism was not about Latin America; in the grand Catholic scheme of things, the status of the region was in some sense provincial.

These points about the character of Catholicism do not mean that there was no way in which the religion could warm to a particular ethnic environment. One practice that helped here was the cult of saints; we have seen how this provided Mexico with a national symbol in the person of the Virgin of Guadalupe. A strong partnership with an ethnic identity could also emerge when a Catholic people found itself in sustained confrontation with aggressively anti-Catholic antagonists; a good example would be the role of Catholicism among the Irish in their conflict with the Protestant English. But what we see here are indirect effects operating in particular cases, not the direct consecration of an ethnic identity by a religion. In other words, Catholicism is not like Hinduism in respect of identity.

Neither is it like Islam. That is to say, there has been no such thing as a sense of Catholic political identity that transcends ethnic loyalties and can be pitted against them.[119] Perhaps such a sense was emerging in Europe in the high Middle Ages, at least in the papal view of things,[120] but if so it did not survive the age of the Reformation. Even the Cristeros, with a cause that was more Catholic than that of any other mass movement in Latin America, took an unqualified pride in being Mexican. Nothing comparable to the political dimension of Muslim brotherhood is present in the foundations of the religion, and nothing of the kind has emerged in its subsequent history. Perhaps it might have done if the medieval popes had been able to establish themselves as the rulers of Europe, and not just of its church, but the speculation is idle. The upshot is that pan-Islamism is a feature of world politics that cannot be ignored, whereas pan-Catholicism as a political persuasion is no more in evidence than pan-Buddhism.

That leaves us to consider the contingencies of the history of Catholicism in Latin America. A significant point here is that Catholicism has not enjoyed much prestige in the eyes of forward-looking political and cultural elites, and it has therefore played little part in the political movements they have initiated. They have tended to see the church as having placed itself firmly on the wrong side of every morally important conflict in the history of the region: with the conquistadors against the natives, with the Spanish against the heroes of the independence movement, with the ruling oligarchies of the independent countries against the downtrodden masses. Such a perspective is, of course, simplistic. Early missionaries often sided with the natives against the conquistadors,

[119] If such a sense exists anywhere, it is among Catholic minorities in unfriendly environments such as the eastern Arab world.

[120] See Bartlett, *Making of Europe*, 250–52.

Creole priests played a considerable role in the struggle for independence, and Catholics in early twentieth-century Mexico had a serious record of concern about social problems. But there was enough truth to the stereotype of the reactionary church to render Catholicism politically unfashionable in progressive circles, and at the same time it had no intellectual cachet for them.

This lack of respect for Catholicism finds wry expression in a contemporary caricature showing Bolívar attending a religious ceremony: he kneels, but his attention is conspicuously focused on the newspaper he is reading.[121] Likewise for Rodó, as for Haya de la Torre, mainstream Catholicism held no attraction. Rodó subscribed to "our modern ideal of liberty," and one thing he admired about the churches of the North Americans was that they offered up "the prayers of many millions of free consciences."[122] This was not a respect in which Latin American Catholicism could compete. For Haya de la Torre it was tainted as a product of European invasion and so lacked authenticity; to be backward without being authentic was the worst of both worlds. Unsurprisingly, he claimed to have played a star role in opposing the plan of Augusto Leguía, the Peruvian dictator of the 1920s, to dedicate Peru to the Sacred Heart of Jesus.[123] Of course, there was always folk Catholicism, but here again neither Rodó nor Haya de la Torre rose to the bait. Rodó was too much of an elitist to want to find the soul of Latin America in so humble a setting. He believed in "the elevated life of the mind," deplored "the diminution of high culture," and had a low opinion of the "spirit of vulgarity" that was sweeping all before it in the ambience of North American democracy (good taste, he said, has eluded the North American).[124] For him the scruffiness of ordinary people in Latin America meant provinciality rather than authenticity. Haya de la Torre for his part was too much of an indigenist to give more than passing attention to folk Catholicism, for all that it would not have been hard for him to discern in its folk character some elements of an authentically Amerindian heritage.[125] The situation changed somewhat thanks to the advent of Liberation Theology, with its blend of Catholi-

[121] M. Brown, *Adventuring through Spanish colonies*, 69. Brown goes on to quote a contemporary, who describes the Liberator as "a complete atheist" who nevertheless "thought religion necessary for government."

[122] Rodó, *Ariel*, 74, 76.

[123] Pike, *Politics of the miraculous*, 48–49; cf. Skidmore and Smith, *Modern Latin America*, 195–96.

[124] Rodó, *Ariel*, 61, 80, 81, 82.

[125] For his flirtation with popular Catholicism, see Pike, *Politics of the miraculous*, 130–31.

cism and Marxism, in the second half of the twentieth century. But until then the fact that Catholicism enjoyed little prestige in progressive circles rendered it unenticing to a significant part of the elite. And in any case Liberation Theology, though susceptible to Latin American pride,[126] is not about identity.

This low esteem, taken in conjunction with the widespread reluctance of Latin American males to enter a celibate priesthood, had a further implication. In recent decades a large proportion of the Catholic clergy of the region—more than half in several Latin American countries—has been foreign;[127] in Brazil in 1970 the figure was 40 percent.[128] This did have its advantages. For the Liberationists—unlike the Cristeros—it meant good connections with Catholics outside Latin America, especially those of Europe and the United States.[129] In fact, several of the theologians active in the movement were of European origin, and many more had studied in Europe as young men.[130] The consequent moral recognition of Liberation Theology in the First World gave it an edge over the other movements considered in this study: unlike Gustavo Gutiérrez, no Hindu nationalist ideologue was frequently invited to lecture to elite American audiences in the United States.[131] Such connections were particularly valuable for the Liberationists of Central America, since they made it possible to bring domestic political pressure to bear on Washington. American Catholic martyrs, like the Maryknoll nuns killed in El Salvador in 1980, were among other things

[126] "Here, for the first time in the history of our subcontinent, a theology is appearing that belongs to us," as one Liberationist writes (Oliveros, "Theology of liberation," 3). Gustavo Gutiérrez, the leading light of Latin American Liberation Theology, wanted to do "theology in a Latin American perspective" but with the aim of contributing to "the life and reflection of the universal Christian community" (Gutiérrez, *Theology of liberation*, 11, and see xxiii (all references are to the 2002 edition unless otherwise noted)). He considered the situation in Latin America "particularly interesting" because it was "the only continent of underdeveloped and oppressed peoples who are in a majority Christians" (Gutiérrez, "Notes," 199; Gutiérrez, *Theology of liberation*, xiv).

[127] Chesnut, *Competitive spirits*, 27, 57.

[128] Mariz, *Coping with poverty*, 12–13.

[129] See, for example, Sigmund, *Liberation theology*, 134–35.

[130] This can be seen from the section on contributors at the end of a large and well-produced collection of articles by Liberationist theologians (Ellacuría and Sobrino, *Mysterium liberationis*, 735–37). Of the twenty-seven contributors listed there, we can set aside three who did not come from or live in Latin America. Of the remaining twenty-four, six were Europeans now living in Latin America; thirteen were Latin Americans who studied in Europe; and only five would seem to have lived their lives in purely Latin American contexts.

[131] For Gutiérrez, see Sigmund, *Liberation theology*, 158.

a significant asset in this context.[132] But the foreign-ness of much of the Church could also alienate. This effect was doubtless strongest among the Chicanos, where American conquest was a further factor. In a very concrete way it meant that the Catholic church in the part of the United States where they lived was not *their* church.[133] A sometime Chicano politician complained that the personnel of the church consisted of Irish, Germans, Spanish, and Italians and spoke unkindly of the "gringo priest";[134] there were no Chicano bishops till the early 1970s.[135] But the foreign-ness of so many of the clergy could also attract hostile notice elsewhere in Latin America. At one point in the violent history of El Salvador, a right-wing group was circulating handbills with the injunction "Be a Patriot, Kill a Priest."[136]

There was still room for recourse to Catholicism in the political activities of conservative circles. Thus, in Mexico in the first half of the nineteenth century, Lucas Alamán regarded the Church as the indispensable cement of national unity, "the only common bond which unites all Mexicans when all other ties have been broken."[137] Likewise some use was made of Catholicism in the early twentieth century by the Hispanists, a rather white and conservative group who were championing a Hispanic identity around which Latin America could be united against the United States;[138] like Rodó, they stood for spirituality against materialism. But such attempts never got very far.

That leaves us to review the role of Catholicism in a set of political movements that cannot comfortably be categorized as either progressive or conservative. Particularly in the 1930s there were rightist political movements in several Latin American countries that were fascistic and at the same time strongly committed to Catholicism. How apt it would be to call them fascist tout court is not a question we need agonize over; that they were under the influence of European fascism is unquestionable. But, unlike their more successful European counterparts, these Latin American movements played relatively minor or transitory roles in the politics of their countries and so have not attracted the same degree of attention from historians. It seems clear, nonetheless,

[132] Ibid., 115.

[133] For some early examples of the ways in which this tension played out, see Mora, *Border dilemmas*, 117, 120, 121–22.

[134] Guerrero, *Chicano theology*, 74.

[135] Ibid., 25.

[136] Sigmund, *Liberation theology*, 112.

[137] Brading, *Origins of Mexican nationalism*, 78; also Bailey, *¡Viva Cristo Rey!*, 11.

[138] Pike, *Politics of the miraculous*, 37–39.

that on the whole they are better described as rightist movements that latched on to religion, rather than as religious movements that latched on to the right. "Up with Catholicism," proclaimed one Peruvian conservative who shared their thinking, "up with the corporate state and fascism, with order, hierarchy, and authoritarianism."[139] However, the line between the two kinds of movement may be thin, and as we will see at least one of these movements could arguably be placed on the other side of it.

An obvious instance of such movements, though apparently little studied, is the Falange in Bolivia.[140] Its name is a transparent reference to Franco's Spain, where the Falange was an insignificant party that owed its success, such as it was, to its adoption by the Generalissimo together with the Catholic church in the course of the civil war of 1936–1939. Like its Spanish namesake, the Bolivian Falange had a Catholic orientation—in fact more so than the original Spanish Falange of 1933.[141] Another movement with a telltale name is the National Socialist Movement in Chile; it is no surprise that its leader was of German extraction.[142] Nevertheless "Nacismo" differed from its near namesake in its rejection of Nazi paganism: for the Nacis, Christianity was the foundation of Western culture and the church was a positive force for social and national solidarity.[143]

The corresponding movement in Brazil, and in its day a more significant one, was Integralism.[144] The name perhaps harks back to Integralismo Lusitano, a monarchist organization of the Portuguese radical right that was itself in the line of the monarchist and pro-Catholic Action Française.[145] However, the founder of the Integralist movement,

[139] Skidmore and Smith, *Modern Latin America*, 199.

[140] For the emergence of the Falange Socialista Boliviana in the late 1930s, see Klein, *Parties and political change*, 301–2. Thereafter it figures episodically in the narrative of Bolivian politics (see, for example, 342, and Klein, *Bolivia*, 224, 237, 242, 245, 249, 254, 258, 270).

[141] Klein, *Parties and political change*, 301n3. The Spanish Falange in its first years already had a marked pro-Catholic orientation (see Payne, *Fascism in Spain*, 93, 130–31).

[142] Sznajder, "Fascism in Chile," 562.

[143] Ibid., 573–74.

[144] For a convenient survey, see R. M. Levine, *Vargas regime*, chap. 4.

[145] For the origins and ideology of Integralismo Lusitano, see Pinto, *Blue Shirts*, 2–15. Neither Integralismo Lusitano nor the fascist Movimento Nacional-Sindicalista to which it gave rise in 1932 were particularly close to Catholicism (for relations between the latter and the church, see 161–64). Action Française was closer: its Positivist agnostic ideologue, Charles Maurras, considered Catholicism an essential part of the French heritage and a very good thing (Arnal, *Ambivalent alliance*, 14–25).

Plínio Salgado, drew political inspiration from the incontrovertible fascism of Mussolini[146]—an origin that would not lead one to expect a particularly intimate embrace of Catholicism. And indeed a sample of Integralist documents and propaganda points to a movement whose nationalism was much more pronounced than its Catholicism.[147] If we take, for example, the October Manifesto with which the movement was launched in 1932, there is an opening reference to God as directing the destinies of peoples, but the leitmotif is nationalism ("a Pátria," "a Nação Brasileira," "o nosso Nacionalismo," and so forth, with generous use of capital letters).[148] In other texts we encounter references to God, religion, Christian principles, the Christian ideal of society, and the like,[149] but no explicit mention of Catholicism; indeed there are several calls for freedom of religion,[150] and it is firmly stated that Integralism is not a religious or clerical movement.[151] In fact, occasional aspects of the movement seem positively irreligious, such as the Integralist calendar (with 1932 as its epoch) that was used in intergroup correspondence[152]—surely an infringement of the calendrical role of Christianity. And yet there is another side to the question. The Integralists and the Church cooperated extensively in the 1930s, for reasons both political and ideological.[153] Moreover, Catholic intellectuals and clergy joined the movement,[154] and Integralism "borrowed freely from the language and liturgy of Catholicism."[155] It promised to "orient and lead the Nation in conformity with the laws of Jesus Christ,"[156] and the Integralist leader averred that "my nationalism is full of God."[157] All told, it seems that what we have here is a nationalist movement that developed close ties with religion and the church.

[146] See the quotations in Trindade, "Fascism and authoritarianism," 493–94.

[147] Barroso, *O que o integralista deve saber.*

[148] Ibid., 18–34.

[149] Ibid., 43, 47, 61, 80.

[150] Ibid., 61 ("liberdade religiosa absoluta"), 80 ("liberdade de cultos"), 115 ("liberdade de confissão religiosa"). In the last passage we are reminded that the pope of the day, Pius XI, had called for a united front of Christians of all denominations, and Catholics cannot aspire to be more Catholic than the pope (117). The movement had a nonconfessional membership policy (Todaro Williams, "Integralism," 441).

[151] Barroso, *O que o integralista deve saber*, 67.

[152] R. M. Levine, *Vargas regime*, 86.

[153] Todaro Williams, "Integralism," 434–35.

[154] Ibid., 433, 443–45.

[155] Ibid., 435, 445–46.

[156] Ibid., 435, and cf. 436, 440.

[157] Ibid., 436.

That leaves Sinarquism in Mexico as the only major movement still to be discussed, and it is a significantly different case. There are strong reasons for thinking of it as primarily a Catholic movement directed against the anticlerical and antireligious character of the Mexican revolution. Despite its tactical nonviolence,[158] Sinarquism emerged from the persistent Catholic resistance that had climaxed in the Cristiada, the Cristero rebellion of 1926–1929. In that sense Sinarquism was the continuation of the Cristiada by other means. Moreover, its emergence was not a spontaneous political development but rather the result of a decision taken by a secret Catholic organization in close touch with the hierarchy;[159] indeed, the movement continued to take orders from this source—even orders that eventually put an end to its political success.[160] At the same time its most prominent leader, Salvador Abascal, was a man of great personal piety,[161] and he had made his name leading a movement to restore Catholic freedom of worship in the state of Tabasco, where the antireligious Red Shirts held sway.[162] Why, then, should we consider Sinarquism as anything but a Catholic movement?

The problem is the strength of the features linking Sinarquism to rightist nationalism. One is the name the movement chose for itself. "Sinarquism" (or to Anglicize it, "synarchism") is not a religious concept. The term "Sinarquía" had first appeared in Mexico in 1915 as the antonym of "Anarquía," in the context of an apparently secular project for restoring order amid the chaos of revolution.[163] Order, of course, is a value dear to conservative Catholics, but they have no monopoly on it. A more substantial point is the character of the movement as it appears in Sinarquist texts: they are full of nationalism of a rightist

[158] Hernández, *Sinarquista movement*, 506.

[159] Ibid., 161. For the secret organization, see 54–57, 75–77, 161–65.

[160] See ibid., 249–50, on the installation of Salvador Abascal as leader in 1940 (which was good for the movement), and 280–82, on the decision to ease him out (which was disastrous for it).

[161] Ibid., 253–54. Hernández draws a comparison between the Sinarquists and the Iron Guard in Romania (396–97). The founder of the Iron Guard, Corneliu Codreanu, is the standard example of personal piety among European fascist leaders, and his movement has been described as "arguably the best example of an overtly Christian fascism" (Eatwell, "Reflections on fascism," 145–46, 147, 153–54). Franco, by contrast, is said to have found religious ceremonial and visits by religious delegations excruciatingly boring (Preston, *Franco*, 188 in the footnote).

[162] Hernández, *Sinarquista movement*, 174–80; for the Red Shirts in Tabasco, see 123–24.

[163] Serrano Álvarez, *Batalla del espíritu*, 1: 43–45.

coloring but make very little explicit reference to Catholicism.[164] In addition, the movement felt some kinship with European fascism, in particular the Franco regime.[165] A prominent figure in it reminisced in 1948 about the admiration that had been excited by Hitler and Mussolini and their consequent influence on Sinarquism; Abascal himself had little use for either of these leaders, but a lot for Franco.[166] We thus have reason to classify Sinarquism with the other movements we have been looking at. Yet if we wish to draw a line separating primarily Catholic movements from primarily nationalist ones, then Sinarquism—unlike Integralism and its relatives—might fall on the Catholic side.

But what do these fascistic movements have to tell us about identity politics in Latin America, apart from their lack of any interest in a pan-Catholic political identity that would compare with Muslim solidarity? Nothing new, perhaps, but taken in conjunction with the Hindu nationalists, they may help to underline something we already know. These Latin American movements have several features in common with Hindu nationalism. They all belong to the same cohort, in that they emerged from the troubled aftermath of the First World War. They fit comfortably inside a big-tent conception of fascism—or if we want to be more restrictive, they are fascistic in the sense that they are unmistakably downwind of European fascism.[167] They display the strong, not to say virulent, nationalism that is part and parcel of fascism. And they share a warm relationship with the local religious heritage, be it Catholic

[164] See, for example, Hernández, *Sinarquista movement*, 197–98 (the Manifesto of 1937); Serrano Álvarez, *Batalla del espíritu*, 1: 195–97 (the Sinarquist Pentalogue of 1938), 198–200 ("Sixteen basic points of Sinarquism"), 202–3 ("Ten norms of conduct for Sinarquists"), 204 (the same for women). This last text is typical in saying more about the fatherland than God but unusual in addressing the question of the relative standing of the two; God wins ("Encima de la Patria sólo hay un amor superior: Dios"). We encounter occasional mention of a Christian social order: "el orden sinarcocristiano" (214), "un orden social cristiano" (294). Such phrases can be construed as references to the social teaching of the Catholic church (cf. 197), but the identification is not explicit. The same or similar material can be found in J. A. Meyer, *Le Sinarquisme*, chap. 4; note the claim in one text that, despite the presence of ex-Cristeros, Sinarquism is not a religious movement (126), and the existence of a Sinarquist calendar (146).

[165] The corollary of this was the hostility of the Mexican revolutionary government toward the Franco regime: Mexico stood apart from Latin America at large in never recognizing the rule of the Generalissimo (Rein, "Francoist Spain," 125).

[166] Hernández, *Sinarquista movement*, 394–96.

[167] For the appeal of Nazism to early Hindu nationalism, see especially Golwalkar, *We or our nationhood*, 35, quoted in Jaffrelot, *Hindu nationalist movement*, 55.

or Hindu—a feature that sets them apart from the Nazism of Hitler or the Fascism of Mussolini, while uniting them with the Egyptian fascistic movement of 1933–1941.[168] Indeed, the embrace of religion in the case of the Sinarquists is much closer than in the case of the Hindu nationalists.

Yet alongside these similarities two major differences stand out. The first is a matter of identity politics: the only one of these movements to confront a substantive problem of national self-definition and offer a solution was Hindu nationalism. Let us return to the Brazilian Integralists by way of contrast. Their leader, Plínio Salgado, did not see Brazil in narrowly European terms, but neither did he give serious attention to the racial composition of the nation he was bent on renewing. He did take a sentimental interest in the Amerindian heritage of a country whose native population was statistically insignificant. In the manner of the emperor Dom Pedro II, he learnt Tupinambá.[169] Indeed the greeting "Anauê" that was used between Integralists was concocted from elements of that language.[170] And on the African front the movement was sufficiently inclusive to boast of the membership of the mulatto João Cândido, the hero of the naval mutiny of 1910.[171] But Integralism offered no grand solution to the racial problem in Brazil. And as we have seen, it had no reason to: the African component of the population was itself disinclined to make a political issue of it. The other major difference between the fascistic movements of Latin America and Hindu nationalism is straightforwardly historical. None of the Latin American movements survived the vicissitudes of the mid-twentieth century—the Allied victory in the Second World War and the ensuing Cold War winter—long enough to become a political contender under the conditions of the late twentieth century. Hindu nationalism, by contrast, did survive, even if at times in hibernation, and it is by now fully

[168] For the philo-Islamic character of this movement—readily distinguishable from the Islamism of the Muslim Brothers—see Gershoni and Jankowski, *Confronting fascism in Egypt*, 235–36, 241, 260–61, 263, 265; this warmth extended to a certain pan-Islamism, see 254–55. But for the dismissive reaction of the Muslim Brothers, see 222.

[169] R. M. Levine, *Vargas regime*, 87, referring to the language as Tupí; cf. Dixon and Aikhenvald, *Amazonian languages*, 127n4.

[170] Barroso, *O que o integralista deve saber*, 149–52.

[171] R. M. Levine, *Vargas regime*, 91; for this mutiny, see Skidmore, *Brazil*, 89. Compare the racial openness of the conception of Hispanidad articulated by the rightist Spanish nationalist Ramiro de Maeztu (d. 1936): "La Hispanidad está compuesta de hombres de las razas blanca, negra, india y malaya, y sus combinaciones" (Maeztu, *Defensa de la Hispanidad*, 84). This conception was in other respects closed enough to be adopted by Franco (Rein, "Francoist Spain," 122).

accustomed to enjoying the fruits of power through electoral politics.[172] Was it perhaps the solution offered by Hindu nationalism to a substantive problem of national identity that spared it the fate of its Latin American coevals?

6. Conclusion

It seems clear that Catholicism plays no significant role in constituting political identity in Latin America.[173] Its contribution to articulating the shallow, post-Bolivarian national identities of the region is limited,[174] and it does nothing to generate a larger political identity that would subsume them. The anti-Americanism that is so widespread in Latin America is only weakly linked to the historically Protestant character of the United States and does not spill over into hostility toward the increasingly numerous indigenous Protestants; it takes persistence to find instances of communal violence pitting Protestants and Catholics against each other. The best that Catholicism has provided for Latin America is the cult of the Virgin of Guadalupe, the Mexican "national idolatry." But even in Mexico, political identity was just not at the center of such rightist Catholic movements as the Cristiada and Sinarquism; still less has it been so for the movement that will be our particular concern, Liberation Theology.

This negative outcome has two things to tell us. The first point is that political identity problems are not an invariable accompaniment of the human condition; some people have them, some don't. In Latin America most people don't, despite the legacy of the colonial caste system. The potentially vast problem of this legacy in Afro-America has not come home to roost, and the analogous problem in Indo-America has had a major political impact only in Bolivia. At the same time Aprismo, the one significant Latin American political movement with

[172] Another member of the same cohort that has survived and come to power in the same way is Revisionism in Israel—though like Hindu nationalism, it is by now much revised.

[173] Unfortunately the Pew Global Attitudes surveys cited earlier for the Islamic world and India (see 46, 120) do not cover any Latin American country.

[174] Note the ease with which Umbanda, a parvenu form of spiritualism concocted from African and European elements in the neighbourhood of Rio de Janeiro in the 1920s, could come to present itself as being about Brazil, claiming to be "a genuinely Brazilian religion" and even "the national religion of Brazil" (D. D. Brown, *Umbanda*, 39, 48–49, 159).

a focus on identity, had little success in acquiring broad support for its Indo-American vision. Overall, the relatively high degree of ethnic homogeneity across Latin America has tended to limit any appeal that identity politics might have had. The second point is that not all religions are apt vehicles for the articulation of political identity. Some are, as we have seen in the preceding chapters, but others help out only under specific circumstances. Catholicism in particular combines the intrinsic lack of a Christian ethnic identity with an ecclesiastical organization that is international in scope, but does not generate a wider political identity.

Conclusion to Part One

In September 1948 Indian troops put an end to the rule of the Niẓām of Hyderabad, defeating a militia that had pledged to "fight to the last to maintain the supremacy of Muslim power in the Deccan." Earlier that year the leader of the militia had stated, "Wherever Muslim interests are affected, our interest and sympathy will go out." The context was Pakistan, but he went on to include Palestine. He then extended the scope of his concern yet further: "Even if Muslim interests are affected in hell, our heart will go out in sympathy."[1] This may not be quite orthodox, but it says something very significant.

To make the militia leader's point in a more academic fashion, we need to distinguish between two aspects of religious commitment. One is commitment to the values of a religion—its beliefs, rituals, and rules of conduct. The other is commitment to the set of people who affirm those values, in other words to one's co-religionists.[2] The first is a form of piety, the second a form of solidarity. Thus, at one extreme we have people like the late Ottoman Shaykh al-Islām Muṣṭafā Ṣabrī (d. 1954), who fled Turkey in 1922, settled under Greek rule in Western Thrace in 1927, and suggested that a European colonialist occupation of Anatolia would have been better than Kemalist rule.[3] At the other extreme we are familiar in modern times with people like Jinnah—incidentally the hero of our militia leader—who combine a marked lack of commitment to Islamic values with a total commitment to Muslim solidarity; and yet if all Muslims were like Jinnah, we might hesitate to call what they had in common a religion. Perhaps all religions worth the name—though not their individual adherents—must combine piety and solidarity in some measure. They do not, however, have to combine them in the *same* measure. Our concern here is only with the extent of their commitment to solidarity.

When a member of such-and-such a religious community shows solidarity without piety, we can conveniently refer to him as a "political

[1] R. Guha, *India after Gandhi*, 68–70.

[2] I take this distinction from Manor, "Language, religion," 175–76.

[3] Bein, *Ottoman ulema*, 111–12. Another example of a well-known religious figure putting Islam ahead of Muslims is the *fatwā* in which Nāṣir al-Dīn al-Albānī (d. 1999) called on Palestinians to leave the occupied territories of Gaza and the West Bank since they could no longer practice Islam correctly there; protecting the faith, he held, was more important than protecting the land (Lacroix, "Between revolution and apoliticism," 70).

such-and-such." For example, a Zionist who was ready to die for the sake of a Jewish state—a state in which Jews would be a nation like any other—but who had no use for God, the rabbis, or their law, and made a point of eating pork on Yom Kippur, would be a clear example of a political Jew. In the same way there is no sense of strain about the notion of a political Hindu; indeed, as we have seen, many members of the RSS would qualify here. In each case we have a national identity associated with a religious heritage, and once one has described the situation in these terms, there is no logical problem about separating loyalty to the identity from belief in the religion. But in this context of political identity, the idea of a political Muslim, like that of a political Catholic, is more problematic.

In the case of the political Muslim, the reality of the phenomenon is not in doubt: Jinnah was one, and Jamāl al-Dīn al-Afghānī could have been another.[4] What is hard is to get a sense of the extent of the phenomenon since public professions of unbelief have not generally been welcomed in the Muslim community.[5] Nor is this illogical: if to be a Muslim is to believe and do certain things, then to call a person who neither believes nor does them a Muslim of any kind is self-contradictory. Yet the very fact that against all logic the phenomenon exists—and that we know what we mean by the phrase—is a testimony to the political solidarity associated with membership of the Muslim community.

In the case of the political Catholic, the notion could certainly mean something for political identity if one picks the right context.[6] Despite the same violation of the laws of logic, even an atheist in Northern Ireland is either a Catholic atheist or a Protestant atheist. But if the idea of

[4] For his irreligious views, see Kedourie, *Afghani and ʿAbduh*, 14, 16–17, 17, 20, 42, 45.

[5] This raises the tantalizing question of the extent of unbelief and scepticism in traditional Muslim populations. Thus, at an elite level we have fragmentary but persuasive evidence of irreligion in the early centuries of Islam (for examples of such thinking, see Stroumsa, *Freethinkers of medieval Islam*, chap. 4, and Crone, "Dahrīs," 64–68, 74). At a popular level a remarkable ethnographic study of the worldviews of the inhabitants of a village in southwestern Iran in the 1970s shows the existence of considerable scepticism (Loeffler, *Islam in practice*, especially chaps. 16–19, 21; I owe my knowledge of this book to Cyrus Schayegh). "It is all here in this world," as one of the villagers says. "Well, has anybody ever been taken to that world and then come back?" (192, and see 193, 195, 197–99, 206–7, 209–10, 221–22). Irrespective of their beliefs, many of the peasants did not pray (14).

[6] One could, of course, use the phrase "political Catholic" to refer to someone like Charles Maurras who deems Catholicism a good thing for society without himself believing in it, but that is not our concern here.

a political Catholic makes perfect if illogical sense in Northern Ireland, it fails to achieve that distinction in Latin America—just as it is hard to imagine what could be meant there by a political Pentecostalist.

These remarks may help to frame the larger conclusion of this part of the book. Despite the exotic problems faced by Hindu identity in the context of the Indian caste system, Hindu nationalism is an example of a very familiar phenomenon: religion in the service of nationalism. However, neither of the other cases falls under this rubric. In the Latin American case religion does not play a sufficiently prominent role in political identity to make a serious difference to nationalism. In the Islamic case, by contrast, religious identity bids fair to trump nationalism—though in less radical visions it can also work with it.

Part Two

Values

Introduction to Part Two

As the founder of a world religion, the figures with whom Muḥammad invites comparison are the Buddha and Jesus—in the nature of things he has no Hindu counterpart. Neither the Buddha nor Jesus could be reckoned a political innocent. When Ajātaśatru, the king of Magadha, planned to destroy the Vṛjjis, a thriving republican people of the day, he dispatched his chief minister to announce his intention to the Buddha and observe his reaction. The Buddha gave the minister an answer that endorsed the political traditions of the Vṛjjis while pointedly omitting to comment on the king's plan to destroy them.[1] Jesus acted in a similar way when confronted with the question whether it was lawful to give tribute unto Caesar, asking whose image and superscription appeared on the coinage and inferring that one should render unto Caesar the things which were Caesar's—but unto God the things that were God's.[2] In each case a religious leader was faced with a politically dangerous question and responded with an indirection that was at once principled and prudent. Both of these founding figures have been regarded by their followers as in some sense kings: the Buddha is a "king of the Law" (*dharmarājā*),[3] and Jesus is a "king of kings."[4] But neither acted as a ruler in the course of his earthly mission.

Muḥammad, by contrast, was the founder of a state as well as a religion. He therefore faced political choices on a daily basis—and not just

[1] Nakamura, *Gotama Buddha*, 2: 34–38. For the background, see J. P. Sharma, *Republics in ancient India*, 125–26.

[2] Matt. 22:15–22; Mark 12:13–17; Luke 20:20–26.

[3] Aśvaghoṣa, *Buddhacarita*, canto 1, verse 75 (Part 1, 9.2 = Part 2, 16).

[4] Rev. 17:14 (referring to Jesus as the Lamb).

on the rare occasion when he was put on the spot by an awkward question. Moreover the sources have no inhibitions about presenting him as an astute politician, a fact that is likely to reflect the character of their earliest audience: the Arab political and military elite, themselves fully active in politics. Muḥammad is thus portrayed very differently from his predecessor Moses. Like Muḥammad, Moses was the founder of a polity, but in the Pentateuchal narrative divine micromanagement leaves him only limited scope for independent decision making in his relations with his people, and the decisions he does make are not depicted as political judgment calls.[5] God does, of course, intervene in Muḥammad's political and military affairs, but He does so far less persistently, often leaving him to rely on his wits.

By way of example, let us take an incident that occurred on one of the many military expeditions that Muḥammad led out from Medina, this one mounted around 627 against a group of desert nomads who were quickly defeated and play no further part in our story.[6] Following the victory trouble flared up between Muḥammad's Meccan and Medinan supporters as a result of friction between two individuals at a watering place.[7] ʿAbdallāh ibn Ubayy ibn Salūl, a powerful but disaffected Medinese tribal chief and the leading "hypocrite" (*munāfiq*), as such covert Medinese enemies of Muḥammad were called, then worked behind the scenes to exacerbate the tensions. A boy came and reported this, and Muḥammad had to decide what to do about it. The standard narrative of the Prophet's life, though not composed by a political philosopher, implicitly separates two distinct issues that arose here. The first was whether it would be ethical to kill Ibn Ubayy; after all, the only witness against him was a boy whose testimony could hardly be relied on in such a matter. This question was resolved in an incontrovertible fashion when God sent down a revelation confirming

[5] Moses is quite capable of making decisions on prudential grounds, as when he satisfies himself that no one is looking before he kills the Egyptian who was beating a Hebrew and buries the body in the sand (Ex. 2:12). On at least two occasions he shows considerable astuteness in his handling of a difficult deity, arguing against God's intended course of action on the ground that it would lead to a public relations disaster for Him (Ex. 32:11–14, Num. 14:13–16). But he does not manifest these qualities in his frequently problematic relations with his people. Even his remark that a certain plan put to him by them "seemed good to me" (Deut. 1:23) is exceptional. Immediately after the exodus, the route to be taken by the Israelites is chosen on the ground that "if the people face war, they may change their minds and return to Egypt" (Ex. 13:17), but it is God, not Moses, who thinks in this prudential fashion.

[6] For the raid on the Banū ʾl-Muṣṭaliq, see Ibn Hishām, *Sīra*, 3–4: 289–96 = 490–93.

[7] Ibid., 3–4: 290.15 = 490–92.

the truthfulness of the boy's account (Q63:8).[8] The other question was whether, assuming it was ethical to kill Ibn Ubayy, it would also be prudent to do so. ʿUmar, one of Muḥammad's closest Meccan followers and the future second caliph, urged him to have the man killed; to this Muḥammad objected that people would say he was killing his own Companions.[9] By contrast, a Medinese supporter advised him to be gentle with the man. Muḥammad did this, and the decision worked out very well. Ibn Ubayy's position among his Medinese fellow tribesmen subsequently crumbled, and at that point Muḥammad remarked to ʿUmar how right he had been to ignore his advice and let the man live.[10] What the course of events had vindicated was not Muḥammad's rectitude, which was not in question, but his political astuteness.[11]

Muḥammad's remark that people would say he was killing his own Companions is widely attested in pre-modern Islamic texts,[12] often, though not always, in connection with the story of Ibn Ubayy's misbehavior.[13] The story itself, and hence the saying, appear in numerous collections of traditions, including the best,[14] which in turn guarantees that they get wide attention from the commentators on these collections.[15] At the same time the fact that the story is linked to a Koranic verse assures the saying a place in the vast literature of Koranic exegesis.[16] It likewise recurs in works on the life of Muḥammad,[17] in general histories,[18] and in biographical dictionaries.[19] The scholars explain that Muḥammad's concern was to avoid the appearance that he was killing

[8] Ibid., 3–4: 292.20 = 491–92.

[9] Ibid., 3–4: 291.7 = 491.

[10] Ibid., 3–4: 293.8 = 492.

[11] Cf. Ibn al-Jawzī, *Kashf al-mushkil*, 5: 12.21, speaking of *siyāsa ʿaẓīma wa-ḥazm wāfir*; Nawawī, *Sharḥ*, 15–16: 354.23, speaking of *ḥilm*.

[12] I found 134 instances of the phrase *yaqtulu aṣḥābahu* in the texts included in the electronic database al-Jāmiʿ al-Kabīr.

[13] Of the other contexts in which it appears, the most common is a tradition regarding a man who protests against Muḥammad's division of the spoils after the battle of Ḥunayn in 630 (see, for example, Muslim, *Ṣaḥīḥ*, 740 no. 1063 (*zakāt* 47)).

[14] Bukhārī, *al-Jāmiʿ al-ṣaḥīḥ*, 2: 386.3 (*manāqib* 8), 3: 355.14 (*tafsir* to Q63:6), and 3: 356.13 (*tafsir* to Q63:8); Muslim, *Ṣaḥīḥ*, 1998–99 no. 2584 (*al-birr waʾl-ṣila* 16).

[15] See, for example, Ibn Ḥajar al-ʿAsqalānī, *Fatḥ al-bārī*, 8: 527.15; Nawawī, *Sharḥ*, 15–16: 354.23.

[16] See, for example, Ṭabarī, *Tafsīr*, 12: 105–9, nos. 34,169, 34,174–75, 34,177–78 (to Q63:8); Ibn Kathīr, *Tafsīr*, 4: 390.24.

[17] See, for example, Wāqidī, *Maghāzī*, 417.18, 418.19.

[18] See, for example, Ṭabarī, *Taʾrīkh*, Series 1, 1512.12 = *History of al-Ṭabarī*, 8: 52; Ibn Kathīr, *al-Bidāya waʾl-nihāya*, 4: 157.16. Both have it from Ibn Isḥāq.

[19] See, for example, Ibn ʿAbd al-Barr, *al-Istīʿāb fī maʿrifat al-aṣḥāb*, 941.6.

his own Companions because of the damage this would have done to his image and the aversion to Islam that would have resulted among potential converts.[20] But they do not normally point to the incident as a lesson for their own times. They tend rather to stress circumstances that box the saying into the specific conditions of the early community. Thus they say that Muḥammad made a point of being nice to the hypocrites during his early years in Medina,[21] at a time when Islam was still weak, but that this indulgence was already abrogated before his death.[22] Or they observe that he had a personal right to be forbearing toward those who offended against him, an option that is no longer available to subsequent generations when injury is done to the Prophet.[23] At the same time they limit any application that the saying might have by stating that it applied only to those who had not manifested their unbelief,[24] as was the case with the hypocritical Ibn Ubayy. Thus, in general the discussion is devoid of clearcut practical implications.

Occasionally, however, the question of contemporary relevance is brought out into the open. One commentator remarks that there is disagreement among the scholars as to whether the practice of such restraint is still permitted or whether it came to an end when Islam waxed strong and the instruction to fight the hypocrites was revealed (Q9:73).[25] Ibn Taymiyya in one passage is more definite: he says that adverse consequences—such as driving away potential converts and causing Muslims to apostatize—remain to this day a valid ground for not imposing a punishment that would otherwise be incumbent.[26] Elsewhere,

[20] See, for example, ʿIyāḍ, *Sharḥ*, 8: 55.10; ʿAynī, *ʿUmdat al-qārī*, 16: 89.15; Ibn Taymiyya, *Ṣārim*, 355.2, 441.5, 680.6 (the text is in volumes 2 and 3, which have continuous pagination). This last work is a treatise proving that a *dhimmī* who insults the Prophet must be executed (for the occasion and date of composition, see 1: 167–68), and in the course of his argument Ibn Taymiyya has incidental occasion to make numerous further references to the saying (340.5, 340.8, 342.2, 355.6, 425.17, 666.6, 668.13, 669.9, 671.3, 672.15, 681.6, 683.3, 829.1).

[21] See, for example, Nawawī, *Sharḥ*, 15–16: 108.13.

[22] Ibn Taymiyya, *Ṣārim*, 441.9, 682.6; Ibn Qayyim al-Jawziyya, *Zād al-maʿād*, 3: 568.3, 5: 61.5.

[23] See, for example, Nawawī, *Sharḥ*, 15–16: 354.23 (where the point is implicit in the reference to *tark baʿḍ al-umūr al-mukhtāra*); Ibn Taymiyya, *Ṣārim*, 425.14 (contrasting what is normative today with the right of the Prophet to forgive such an offense), 828.1, 829.15 (emphasizing that the Prophet had a right to forgive that the Muslim community since his death does not possess).

[24] See, for example, Nawawī, *Sharḥ*, 15–16: 355.17, and cf. 355.21.

[25] Iyāḍ, *Sharḥ*, 8: 55.12.

[26] Ibn Taymiyya, *Ṣārim*, 681.1.

in a discussion of the permissibility of killing individual Shīʿites,[27] he says that it is indeed permitted to kill one who is a propagandist for his beliefs or otherwise engaged in vicious activities (*fasād*); if eliminating such heretics is the only way to ward off their mischief, they are undoubtedly to be killed. We do not, however, have to kill a Shīʿite if he does not manifest his doctrine or if killing him would do more harm than good; this, he observes, is why Muḥammad once spared a heretic to avoid its being said that he was killing his own Companions.[28] In a less formal vein a nineteenth-century Moroccan historian invokes Muḥammad's relations with the hypocrites and quotes the saying in criticizing the conduct of an impolitic ruler of his country who in 1729 had imprudently alienated the people of Fez in reaction to an incident that he should have overlooked.[29]

What all this established was that in public affairs it was not enough just to act out one's values. Values are, of course, fundamental; for those who are not simply selfish or cynical, they provide the purposes without which political activity is pointless. But to focus all one's attention on one's values without keeping a wary eye on public relations is to court disaster. We see here a certain political sophistication that must have appealed to the Arab elite of early Islamic times and that would also be available to modern Muslims who base their politics on their religion. But before we go on to ask what use they have in fact made of this source, we need to look at some length at the values themselves and their relevance in the modern context. We begin with social values.

[27] Ibn Taymiyya, *Majmūʿ*, 28: 499.15, in response to a question about whether Shīʿites are to be fought and declared unbelievers (468.2).

[28] Ibid., 28: 500.6 (the heretic in question is the man who protested against Muḥammad's division of the spoils after the battle of Ḥunayn).

[29] Nāṣirī, *Istiqṣāʾ*, 7: 129.13. The incident had occurred during the ruler's recent visit to Fez (126.2).

CHAPTER 4

Society

1. Introduction

When we sought to identify the assets and liabilities of our three religious heritages with regard to political identity, the only Western counterpart that required prior attention was nationalism. Once we turn to social values, however, things are more complicated. We have to reckon with two major axes along which social values may vary. On one axis the alternatives are egalitarianism and commitment to a hierarchic social order; on the other axis the contrast is between a high valuation of solidarity and a preference for a more loosely bound society, for example, one that leaves space for individualism. Combinations of these alternatives give us distinct ideological packages. These packages have played a prominent role in modern Western history, and have influenced the non-Western world to a greater or lesser extent. They form a trio:[1] conservatism, leftism, and liberalism.[2] Seen from the liberal center, conservatives are those who put too much faith in the past, while leftists are those who put too much in the future.

Conservatism represents the combination of hierarchy and solidarity. Because it has not been a particularly successful export, it is the option that will concern us least. There are two reasons for this limited marketability outside the West. One is intrinsic: conservatism is not a comfortably cosmopolitan value since by its nature it seeks to conserve a particular heritage. The other is a consequence of its role in modern European history. The point of conservatism may once have been to restore the social order of the ancien régime, but no conservative party seeking power in a democracy could win an election on such a program. The result is that European conservatism has been more a matter of ad hoc resistance to the futuristic excesses of the left than a grand vision of a return to the pre-modern past. Even a conservative as determined

[1]The unutilized combination here is a conception of society as hierarchic and loosely bound—a gap that will be relevant when we come to the Hindu case (see 194–95).

[2]Note that I leave aside fascism here because of its lack of staying power and use the words "liberal" and "liberalism" in a European, not an American sense.

and doctrinaire as Mrs. Thatcher could hardly be seen as aiming to turn the clock back any further than the nineteenth century. This is not to deny that there have been plenty of people in the non-European world of modern times who could broadly be described as conservative or that conservatives across the world share some significant values and can offer each other sympathy and inspiration. But European conservatism did not offer non-European societies a ready-made ideology that could easily be imported as a package, and even if it had done so, that ideology would have been unlikely to fit the particular past with which any given set of non-Western conservatives sought to keep faith.

Leftism represents the combination of equality and solidarity—or as French republicanism came to call it, fraternity. Unlike conservatism, leftism was a wildly successful export while the going was good, with wide appeal in the non-European world. Here the attraction of solidarity rested on two bases: it was a better fit with the values of the prevailing traditional cultures of the non-European world and sticking together seemed a better bet in a confrontation with European power. Moreover leftism did something that nationalism can also do, but did it more consistently and coherently: it provided a vantage point from which one could be both extremely hostile to European hegemony and extremely iconoclastic toward one's ancestral traditions. What adds to the interest of the phenomenon is its sudden collapse with the demise of the Soviet Union; we can thus observe with some clarity what happens in each of our three cases when leftism loses its plausibility.

Liberalism represents the combination of equality and and loose binding, specifically individualism. Its compelling quality owes a lot to the fact that, of the three European ideologies treated here, it has hitherto proved by far the most successful in sustaining the innovation that generates wealth and power. But its reception in non-European societies has been ambivalent: while its egalitarianism has often been straightforwardly attractive, its loosely bound quality has not—for the same reasons that made the leftist commitment to solidarity appealing. In its libertarian form it has accordingly been a notably unsuccessful export. In addition, there are features of recent Western egalitarianism that may not transpose easily onto non-Western societies: the extension of equality to women and to believers in all religions or none. The first can easily fall foul of non-European traditions of family values—a problem also for leftism; the second may collide with non-European conceptions of the proper relationship between religion and politics. But as we will see in a later chapter, some of the specifically political values of liberalism may prove considerably more palatable.[3]

There is also the more general question of the way in which our three European ideologies relate to religion. Conservatism is the most sympathetic: from the point of view of conservatives, the religious traditions of their own societies are typically a good thing and an aspect of the past with which they wish to keep some kind of faith. Leftism is the most hostile: for leftists the religious traditions of their own and other societies are typically a bad thing and an aspect of the past with which they seek to break. Liberalism is indifferent: unlike leftism, it is not in the business of persecuting religion, but unlike conservatism it has no particular sympathy for it. It accordingly declines to make any distinction between true and false believers and practices an indiscriminate toleration of diversity of religious belief—and of religious behavior too provided it is not seen as markedly antisocial.

This account of European ideological resources is highly schematic. It does not attempt to do justice to the range of European thinking, nor does it take into account the fact that ideologies need not be imported as packages. But these simple thoughts may nevertheless help to set the scene for the discussion of the social values of each of our three religious heritages that follows.

2. Islam

One might suppose that a major religious tradition would have something identifiable as its vision of the ideal society and that Islam would be no exception. Indeed, as we will see in a later chapter, the Islamic heritage unquestionably possesses an image of the ideal polity.[4] But does it provide a comparable image of the ideal society? It certainly has an idea of what a *virtuous* society would be: one in which everyone observed Islamic norms. But does the heritage give us a sense of what would be distinctive about the ideal society other than its virtue—what it would look like? The answer would seem to be that it does not, and this for two reasons.

[3]See chap. 7, especially 319–21, 327–30.
[4]See 309–11.

The first is that while Muḥammad created a state, he did not create a society. On the political front he found no state in existence when he arrived in Medina, and he brought none with him from Mecca; instead, he synthesized one in a previously stateless society. But no such blank slate confronted him on the social front. There was thus a large measure of social continuity among both his Meccan and his Medinese followers. The confluence of the two did lead to one interesting social innovation: soon after he came to Medina, Muḥammad paired off his followers as brothers in God, with each pair typically consisting of a Meccan and a Medinese.[5] But in retrospect this was a fleeting response to a transient situation, not an institutional building-block of future Islamic societies.

The second reason why the Islamic heritage does not possess a vision of the ideal Muslim society arises from the conditions created by the conquests in the generation after Muḥammad. The broad shape of society in this formative period was that the Muslims held military and political power, while economic activity was in the hands of the subject non-Muslims. Traditions that doubtless arose at a time when this structural feature of the conquest society was decaying reveal a strong sentiment in favor of this division of labor. Thus an eschatological tradition ascribed to an eighth-century Syrian scholar describes a land reform to be implemented by the Mahdī, the redeemer who will come toward the end of time: he will return all land in Syria to the subject Jews and Christians (*ahl al-dhimma*) and redirect all Muslims to jihad.[6] In another tradition the Prophet warns his followers that when they give themselves up to agricultural pursuits and abandon jihad, God will impose humiliation upon them until such time as they return to their religion.[7] Yet other accounts relate that when the Caliph ʿUmar (ruled 634–44) heard that the Muslims in Syria had planted a crop, he ordered it to be burnt; in the same spirit he wrote to them that he would impose the poll tax due from subject non-Muslims (*jizya*) on any Muslim who took up agriculture and was content to live by it.[8]

[5] For the *muʾākhāt*, see Ibn Hishām, *Sīra*, 1–2: 504.20 = 234–35.

[6] Nuʿaym ibn Ḥammād, *Fitan*, 218.19 (the traditionist is the Ḥimṣī Arṭāh ibn al-Mundhir (d. 779–780)); see Kister, "Land property and *jihād*," 284–85, and D. Cook, *Studies in Muslim apocalyptic*, 165, 166.

[7] Abū Dāwūd, *Sunan*, 3: 274–75 no. 3462 (*ijāra* 20); Bayhaqī, *Sunan*, 5: 316.19; Ṭabarānī, *Musnad al-Shāmiyyīn*, 3: 328–29 no. 2417; and see Kister, "Land property and *jihād*," 276–77, with numerous other references.

[8] Ibn Ḥazm, *Muḥallā*, 8: 211.5, 211.8; and see Kister, "Land property and *jihād*," 282.

In other words, the ideal behind these and other such traditions[9] was not a complete Muslim society in which all roles were assumed by Muslims but rather a composite society in which the Muslims formed a minority dedicated to warfare against the unbelievers beyond the frontiers. Such a division of labor was, of course, historically unsustainable, and to insist on it struck later generations as absurd; as an eleventh-century scholar put it, God preserve the Commander of the Faithful from having burnt the crops of the Muslims, destroyed their property, and made them pay poll tax.[10] Nor was this just the view of scholars centuries later: countertraditions in favor of agriculture are ascribed to the Prophet himself.[11]

Despite the absence of a distinctive vision of the ideal society, we do find embedded in the Islamic heritage two social values that have immediate relevance for us: equality and solidarity. Let us start with equality.[12]

In a celebrated verse the Koran declares that "the noblest among you in the sight of God is the most godfearing of you" (Q49:13). More straightforwardly, the Prophet is quoted as saying that "people are equals like the teeth of a comb," though this tradition is not included in authoritative collections. A much better attested tradition relates that the Prophet once came out to his Companions, whereupon they demonstrated their respect for him by rising to their feet; in response he instructed them not to stand up to honor people, as was the Persian practice.[13] But the most vivid illustration of the egalitarian values of early Islam is a story already alluded to, the one that recounts the visits of the Arab envoys to the Persian general Rustam on the eve of the battle of Qādisiyya around 636.[14] One of them was an unkempt bedouin. To receive him Rustam sat on a throne surrounded by a magnificent display of carpets and cushions. But the bedouin envoy did not dismount when he reached the edge of the carpeted area, and when he did dismount, he walked toward Rustam using his spear to jab holes in

[9] For a rich collection of such material, see Kister, "Land property and *jihād*," especially 276–85.

[10] Ibn Ḥazm, *Muḥallā*, 8: 211.10; compare the comment of the eleventh-century Central Asian jurist Sarakhsī that there is nothing wrong if one section of the community cultivates the land and another section wages jihad (Kister, "Land property and *jihād*," 280).

[11] Kister, "Land property and *jihād*," 290–94, 300–303.

[12] For this heritage and what became of it, see generally Marlow, *Hierarchy and egalitarianism*, and Crone, *Medieval Islamic political thought*, 334–37, 340–46.

[13] For references see M. Cook, "Political freedom," 292.

[14] See 22. For references and more detail see ibid., 289–90.

the carpets and cushions as he went. Another envoy showed how little he was in awe of the Persian general by sitting down beside him on his throne. When the Persians reacted with anger, he told them, "We Arabs are equals," only enslaving each other in warfare. He added with a pretense of naïveté that he had taken it for granted that the Persians behaved in the same way to each other; he was not to know that some of them were the owners of others. This incident elicited a divided response from the Persians present: while the common people approved of what the Arab had said, the nobles complained that this was what their slaves had always liked to hear. But there is more: When asked by Rustam why the Arabs had come to Iraq, one envoy answered that God had sent them to deliver those who so wished from being servants of men to being servants of God.[15] Another similarly included among the basic principles of Islam a commitment to "delivering men from being servants of men to being servants of God"; he added a belief in the full brotherhood of men, all alike descended from Adam and Eve.

This egalitarian view of society underlies many of the stipulations of Islamic law. Thus, in setting out the rules of retaliation (*qiṣāṣ*) for killing, the Koran specifies "freeman for freeman, slave for slave, female for female" (Q2:178); within the set of free males, no distinction is made here between high and low. Likewise a tradition from the Prophet says that the blood of the believers is of equal value (*al-muʾminūn tatakāfaʾu dimāʾuhum*); again social hierarchy makes no appearance here.[16] Conversely, another tradition has Muḥammad condemn earlier communities in which lowly offenders were punished while noble ones were let off.[17] The condemnation is in place: Roman law in imperial times prescribed very different treatment for criminals depending on their social status.[18] In fact, the same old pattern of lenience toward members of the elite was to reappear in Muslim society and even find a measure of formal recognition there,[19] but by the standards of the age, Islamic law seems to have been unusual in the extent of its egalitarian character.[20]

[15] The wording echoes a letter from the Prophet to the people of Najrān in southwestern Arabia.

[16] Abū Dāwūd, *Sunan*, 4: 181 no. 4530 (*diyāt* 11). One scholar notes that this entails equivalence between the blood of noble and commoner (*al-sharīf waʾl-waḍīʿ*)—as also of freeman and slave (Jaṣṣāṣ, *Aḥkām al-Qurʾān*, 1: 176.1).

[17] Friedmann, *Tolerance and coercion*, 50 (the tradition contrasts the treatment of the *sharīf* and the *ḍaʿīf*).

[18] For this discrimination between *honestiores* and *humiliores*, see A.H.M. Jones, *Later Roman Empire*, 519.

[19] See Fierro, "Idraʾū l-ḥudūd bi-l-shubuhāt," 229–37, especially 233–35.

[20] Like late Roman law, the criminal code of the T'ang dynasty discriminated systematically, but as might be expected the system was more complex and more state centered

Though real, this egalitarianism was not congruent with that of the present-day West. Most obviously, it did not extend to women, unbelievers, and slaves.[21] That a pre-modern society should affirm such inequalities and give legal force to them is in comparative terms unsurprising, but we should nevertheless pay some attention to the particular forms they took in the Islamic case. They constituted part of the bedrock of traditional Muslim society.

The Koran is clear about the fact that women are not the equals of men. Men are a step (*daraja*) above them (Q2:228). They are also in authority (*qawwāmūn*) over them, and reasons are given for this (Q4:34). Significant asymmetries appear in the law of marriage: polygyny is permitted (Q4:3), but polyandry would seem to be unthinkable; divorce (*ṭalāq*) is something men do to women (Q2:230–32, 236; Q33:49; Q65:1), not the other way around. In other connections women may not be left out altogether, but men get preference. Thus in the matter of inheritance, women are entitled to a share just as men are (Q4:7), but their shares are typically half those of men (Q4:11, 176); and when it comes to witnessing a loan, where two male witnesses are normally required, there is a provision that if two men are not available, then *two* women can take the place of *one* of the men (Q2:282). There are nevertheless other contexts in which men and women are referred to in ways that put them on the same footing. Thus male and female believers alike perform the prayers, pay the alms tax, and obey God and his messenger; and God has promised both alike that they will dwell eternally in Paradise (Q9:71–72, and compare Q33:35). At the other end of the scale of virtue, men and women who commit adultery incur the same hundred lashes (Q24:2), just as men and women who steal have their hands cut off irrespective of their sex (Q5:38). The Koran is concerned that women be treated decently (e.g., Q2:229, 240–41); but all told, it does not regard them as equal. The development of these themes in the larger Islamic tradition is not out of line with these scriptural foundations.

With regard to unbelievers, the Koran provides a basis for allowing them to continue to practice their false religions within certain limits, on condition that they humbly submit and pay tribute to the Muslim state: "Fight those who believe not in God and the Last Day and do

---

(see W. Johnson, *T'ang Code*, 1: 23–25). Hindu law tends to treat Brahmins more leniently (Kane, *History of Dharmaśāstra*, 3: 395–99).

[21] "The rank of a full member of society was restricted to free male Muslims. Those who lacked any of these three essential qualifications—that is, the slave, the woman, or the unbeliever—were not equal" (B. Lewis, *Jews of Islam*, 8).

not forbid what God and His Messenger have forbidden—such men as practise not the religion of truth, being of those who have been given the Book—until they pay the tribute (*jizya*) out of hand and have been humbled" (Q9:29). By common consent the "people of the Book" include at least the Jews and Christians, the tribute they are to pay is an annual poll tax, and the puzzling limitation of toleration to the atheists among them is ignored. We hear of Muḥammad imposing such a tax on the edges of his domains,[22] and it was to become the classical fiscal accompaniment of the Muslim ascendancy over subject non-Muslim populations. By contrast, Christian scripture provides no comparable basis for tolerating the practice of false religions. How things worked out in practice for non-Muslims under Muslim rule naturally brought in a range of other factors. Thus, in the later fifteenth century a Moroccan scholar made waves by fulminating against the Jews of North Africa and the Sahara. Their insolence and wrongdoing were in his view such that the terms of their submission to the Muslim community were now void, with the result that they could legally be killed, their property seized, and their women enslaved.[23] But there were different opinions on such questions among the scholars,[24] as was also the case in a later dispute. In 1612 a local ruler established a new city in southwestern Morocco, and the Jews who settled there proceeded to build themselves a synagogue.[25] Some scholars took the view that, as a synagogue newly built in the lands of Islam, it had to be demolished. Others, however, held that there was no need for this since at the time of the Muslim conquest the Jews had submitted and been allowed to continue to practice their religion on terms that entitled them to do just what they had now done; thereafter they had paid their poll tax and been humbled precisely as the law required. Opinions could also differ as to whether the presence of non-Muslims was useful to Muslims. Not everyone thought so: one seventeenth-century Ottoman writer deplored the fact that so many of those who worked in the bakeries were unbelievers who kneaded the dough with their unwashed hands while their sweat and lice poured into the tubs; he wanted the Grand Vizier to take action, either by ensuring the employment of Muslims in the bakeries or, failing that, by imposing sanitary standards so that the

[22] See, for example, Ibn Hishām, *Sīra*, 3–4: 525.16 = 607 (Ayla); 526.21 = 608 (Dūma); Bukhārī, *al-Jāmiʿ al-ṣaḥīḥ*, 2: 291.15 (*jizya* 1)(Hajar).

[23] Ḥajjī, *Ḥaraka*, 269.5; Hunwick, *Jews of a Saharan oasis*, 28.

[24] See Hunwick, *Jews of a Saharan oasis*, 33–35, 71–73.

[25] Ḥajjī, *Ḥaraka*, 272.4.

Muslims would have pure bread to eat.[26] What was axiomatic within the mainstream of Muslim thought was the ascendancy of Islam and the Muslims over such unbelievers.

The third inequality was that between free people and slaves. The Koran accepts the existence of the institution of slavery without offering a justification for it.[27] Within this framework it enjoins kindness to slaves (Q4:36) and regards manumission as a virtuous act (Q90:12f), sometimes prescribing it as a form of expiation (Q5:89). Slavegirls are available to their masters as concubines (Q70:29–30) but should not be compelled to become prostitutes if they wish to remain chaste (Q24:33). That slaves are not the equals of the free is taken for granted.

Islamic egalitarianism was thus limited to free Muslim males. Even then it did not, of course, mean that Muslim societies down the ages had no sense of hierarchy. When Jabartī (d. 1824–1825) remarked of the French who invaded Egypt in 1798 that they followed the rule (*qānūn*) that "great and small, high and low, male and female are all equal (*mutasāwiyān*)," it was not just the equality of men and women that he would seem to have found jarring.[28] In the same way the Ottoman proclamation issued in response to the invasion included in its account of the outrageous beliefs of the French their view that "all men are equal in humanity and alike in being men."[29] These negative reactions had a lot of social history behind them: those Muslim societies that had the resources to support a steeply hierarchic social structure over the centuries seem to have been perfectly comfortable doing so.[30] They regularly articulated this comfort by distinguishing between the elite (*khāṣṣa*) and the masses (*ʿāmma*), with a clear sense that the elite were better; by the time of Jabartī they had been doing this for over a millennium.[31] Indeed, Baranī, as often a bit of an extremist, considers that talent and virtue are inherited among the high-born, and vice among the low-born; hence promoting the low-born can never be a good idea.[32]

What the Islamic tradition had not done in the course of the millennium was to give formal recognition to sharp social cleavages of the kind

[26] *Kitâbu mesâlihi'l-Müslimîn ve menâfi'i'l-mü'minîn*, 106–8 = 74f (ch. 43).

[27] For what the Koran has to say about slaves, see Hunwick and Trout Powell, *African diaspora*, 2–5; for selections from Prophetic tradition on the subject, see 5–7.

[28] Moreh, *Al-Jabartī's chronicle*, 12.1 = 43; "high and low" is *al-jalīl waʾl-ḥaqīr*, which strongly suggests membership of different social strata.

[29] B. Lewis, *Muslim discovery*, 183.

[30] Marlow, *Hierarchy and egalitarianism*, 6–8.

[31] Ibid., 9.

[32] Baranī, *Fatāwā*, 296.16; Habib and Khan, *Political theory*, 97–98.

that characterize aristocratic or caste societies.[33] There were minor exceptions. One example concerns the law of marriage: because nobody wants their womenfolk to marry down, there was considerable discussion of what constitutes equality of status between marriage partners,[34] and the opinions held by the jurists varied; yet a sharp binary opposition appears only in the minority view that Arab women should not marry non-Arabs. Another example is the widespread recognition of the prestige of descent from Muḥammad, but there were few Muslim societies in which his descendants constituted anything like an aristocracy. This absence of caste or aristocracy in Islamic societies was real enough to strike observers with comparative experience in pre-modern times. Thus a Korean Buddhist pilgrim who visited Iran in the 720s found it noteworthy that among the Arabs the king and the common people wore the same kind of clothing, and he was struck by the fact that when eating they made no distinction between noble and commoner, helping themselves from the same plate.[35] A European who spent some years in the Ottoman Empire in the mid-sixteenth century was deeply impressed by Turkish meritocracy: "No distinction is attached to birth among the Turks," he wrote privately to an old friend, whereas "with us there is no opening left for merit" since "birth is the standard for everything."[36] He may have exaggerated, the Ottoman case may have been untypical, and as we will see at least one Ottoman memorialist of the next century seems to have thought that a hereditary aristocracy would be a good idea;[37] but *some* of what appeared in Europe only with the French Revolution was a given in the Islamic case. In the same way Bīrūnī had a valid point when he described the Muslim belief that everyone is equal except in piety as the greatest barrier between the Hindus and Islam.[38] Muslims are brothers in a way that Hindus are not.

What did this brotherhood mean for specifically economic inequality? As we might expect, the Islamic heritage lays great emphasis on

[33] As Lewis says of Islam: "In principle and in law, it recognizes neither caste nor aristocracy" (B. Lewis, *Jews of Islam*, 8).

[34] Marlow, *Hierarchy and egalitarianism*, 30–34, and see 63 on the case of weavers and cuppers.

[35] Yang et al., *Hye Ch'o diary*, 53 (for the Chinese original, see 103, 105); he also noted correctly that the law of the country did not prescribe prostration (sc. to fellow humans). For the dating of his travels, see 14–15. I owe my knowledge of this source to Kevin van Bladel.

[36] Forster and Blackburne Daniell, *Ogier Ghiselin de Busbecq*, 1: 154–55.

[37] See 263.

[38] Bīrūnī, *Taḥqīq*, 48.20 = *Alberuni's India*, 1: 100.

bringing about a measure of redistribution from the rich to the poor through charity. God prescribes that alms (*ṣadaqāt*) are for eight categories of people, the first two being the poor (*fuqarāʾ*) and the needy (*masākīn*); this is incumbent as a divinely imposed obligation (*farīḍatan min Allāh*) (Q9:60). The verse indicates that such obligatory almsgiving had already been institutionalized, since the third of the eight categories consists of those who collect the alms (*al-ʿāmilīna ʿalayhā*). This institution (usually known as *zakāt*) is one of the five "pillars" (*arkān*) of Islam, and in accounts of it in Ḥadīth and law, it is the poor and needy who get the lion's share of the attention.[39] In addition, the foundational texts provide extensive commendation of voluntary almsgiving (*ṣadaqa*); here again gifts are not confined to the poor, but those that go to them earn a far higher reward.[40] There is much evidence that in Muslim societies the rich did indeed convey some of their wealth to the poor.[41]

At the same time one form of poverty enjoyed a certain social prestige in Islamic societies, namely the elective poverty of the Ṣūfī saints. Such holy poverty is not written into the foundations of the religion, as it is in Christianity. No doctrine of the absolute poverty of the Prophet and his Companions could have even begun to look plausible; they may have chosen to lead simple lives, but they did not seek to be poor.[42] Of course, some of Muḥammad's followers were indeed poor, as in the case of those homeless, ill-clad, hungry Companions of his who slept in the mosque in Medina.[43] But they were poor because of their immediate circumstances, not by choice.[44] We learn that they were fed by Muḥammad and others until God brought the Muslims wealth;[45] its arrival would seem to have provided a prosaic but effective solution to their problem. A high valuation of elective poverty was nevertheless to

[39] *EI*², art. "Zakāt" (A. Zysow), 415b.

[40] Ibid., art. "Ṣadaḳa" (T. H. Weir and A. Zysow), 713.

[41] Thus for late medieval Egypt, see Sabra, *Poverty and charity*, 50–58, 85–94; for this record in a comparative perspective, see 169–77, also Lev, *Charity, endowments*, 156–59.

[42] There is a tradition in which Muḥammad says, "Let me live as a pauper (*miskīn*), and let me die as a pauper," but then again there is another in which he says that "poverty is almost infidelity" (Sabra, *Poverty and charity*, 21).

[43] For these *ahl al-ṣuffa*, so called because they lived in the portico (*ṣuffa*) of the mosque, see *EI*², art. "Ahl al-ṣuffa" (W. M. Watt); for our purposes the key account is the set of traditions from Wāqidī (d. 823) quoted by Ibn Saʿd (*Ṭabaqāt*, vol. 1, part 2:13–14), since these are not yet affected by Ṣūfism.

[44] As pointed out by one medieval critic of Ṣūfī poverty, see Sabra, *Poverty and charity*, 23.

[45] Ibn Saʿd, *Ṭabaqāt*, 1:2:13.12.

emerge among the Ṣūfīs. One Ṣūfī authority describes those who stand close to God as owning nothing, asking for nothing, expecting nothing, and accepting nothing.[46]

What is not conspicuous in the Islamic case is the preference for the poor that is so marked in the New Testament. Occasional suggestions of such reverse discrimination can indeed be found in the foundational texts. In the context of the division of the spoils of war, the Koran refers to the poor among Muḥammad's Meccan followers in ennobling terms: expelled from their homes and despoiled of their wealth, they were giving their support to God and His messenger.[47] But the tone of Muslim scripture is generally matter-of-fact and confers no apocalyptic shimmer on the poor.[48] Traditions from the Prophet are somewhat more promising. There is, for example, one in which Muḥammad avers that poor Muslims will enter Paradise five hundred years before the rich.[49] But in the foundational texts as a whole such traditions do not bulk large, and they are obliged to coexist with Muḥammad's reproof to a wealthy but poorly dressed follower: "When God gives you wealth, the mark of His beneficence and generosity should be seen on you."[50]

Finally there is solidarity, a value less at home with liberalism than equality but attractive in many contexts in the world today. It need not detain us here since we have already discussed it at length in the context of identity, noting such typical Islamic expressions of it as the Koranic affirmation that the believers are brothers (Q49:10) and the insistence of one of the envoys to Rustam that "the Muslims are like a body, parts of a whole."[51]

If this, in outline, is the character of the heritage, how would it be to invoke its resources under modern conditions? For convenience let us order the issues under the rubric of the three European ideologies distinguished above.

As already noted, conservatism is not a cosmopolitan doctrine, and is thus the least exportable of the three ideologies.[52] But if we think

[46] Sabra, *Poverty and charity*, 18, emphasizing that this view is typical among the Ṣūfīs.

[47] Q59:8 (*lil-fuqarāʾi ʾl-muhājirīn*).

[48] See, for example, Q2:177, 215, 271, 273; Q9:60; Q76:8.

[49] For references, see Wensinck, *Early Muhammadan tradition*, 181b (like many traditions, this one occurs in slightly varying forms, but the message is the same). For other traditions relating to the poor, see 188a–b.

[50] Abū Dāwūd, *Sunan*, 4: 51 no. 4063 (*libās* 15); and see Goitein, "Near-Eastern bourgeoisie," 589–90.

[51] See especially 20–22.

[52] See 165–66.

in terms of a local conservatism within Muslim societies, the heritage would clearly be supportive with regard to the inequalities affecting women, unbelievers, and slaves. All three of these inequalities mattered to conservatives in the Muslim world as it fell under Western hegemony.[53] Of conservative sentiment with regard to female equality, there is no end. Saʿīd Ḥawwā, for example, explains why men are in authority (*qawwāmūn*) over women (Q4:34) by listing some twenty respects in which God has preferred men to them,[54] and he proceeds to complain about the activities of the "merchants of politics" who go around leading people astray in the name of the freedom and equality of women.[55] Turning to the status of unbelievers, it is recorded that, after the Ottoman proclamation of 1856 declaring all subjects of the empire to be equal irrespective of religion, many Muslims complained that "the Islamic community, which was the ruling community (*millet-i ḥākime*), has now been deprived of this sacred right," and saw the occasion as one for weeping and mourning.[56] In a similar spirit the Shāfiʿite Muftī of Egypt at the time of the British invasion of 1882 remarked that things had come to such a pass that "unbelievers would ride horses or carriages with Moslems running in front of them" and that they would "extend their feet with those black shoes to Moslems in order to have them polished by them."[57] With regard to slaves, the British ambassador to Istanbul reported that, when in 1840 he raised the question of action against slavery and the slave trade, the response was "extreme astonishment"; he added that the Turks were "far from thinking our wisdom or our morality greater than their own."[58] Likewise a letter of 1842 from the British consul in Tangier to the Sultan of Morocco received a response couched in a tone of uncompromising religious righteousness: "As to what regards the making of Slaves and Trading therewith," the Sultan wrote, "it is confirmed by our Book as also by the *Sunna* [practice] of Our Prophet." He went on to say that

[53] Slavery, of course, is only marginally relevant at the present day, though the treatment of imported servants in some Muslim societies and reports of the revival of enslavement on the part of jihadis constitute exceptions.

[54] Ḥawwā, *al-Asās fī ʾl-tafsīr*, 1053.10.

[55] Ibid., 1055.18.

[56] Cevdet Paşa, *Tezâkir 1–12*, 1: 68, cited in Mardin, *Young Ottoman thought*, 18. The passage in the reform decree that provoked this response reads as follows: "Every distinction or designation tending to make any class whatever of the subjects of my empire inferior to another class, on account of their religion, language, or race, shall be forever effaced from administrative protocol" (Hurewitz, *Middle East*, 1: 316b).

[57] Peters, *Islam and colonialism*, 81; for the source, see 185n113.

[58] Toledano, *Slavery and abolition*, 116–17.

there was no disagreement among the Muslim scholars on the matter and that no one may "prohibit that which is made lawful" by God. He added that "our sacred religion is not regulated by men's counsel or deliberation" but rather inspired by God "through the tongue of our Faithful Prophet."[59] Where the foundational heritage does leave the conservative high and dry is with regard to the hierarchic relationship between elite and masses among the free, male, and Muslim population. We have already met the case of the descendants of the Prophet in Ḥaḍramawt;[60] another example would be the "feudal" landlords of Pakistan.

Unlike conservatism, leftism is—or was—very much an ideology for export.[61] It had a strong potential resonance with the Islamic heritage in the sense that both combined commitments to equality and solidarity. But Islam, or more precisely Sunnī Islam, lacked a counterpart to the Marxist proletariat—a downtrodden segment of society conspicuously marked out for future glory; the Sunnīs were traditionally the victors of history, not its victims. The Christian heritage assigns such a role to the poor, but as we have seen, the echoes of this in the Islamic tradition are rather faint; they are strongest in Ṣūfism, but this side of the Islamic heritage has been largely ignored in modern times as a resource for Islamist politics. Shīʿism, by contrast, does have a counterpart to the proletariat, and it has not been ignored.[62] But looming behind all this is the fact that leftism does not sit well with religion. Leftism could be expected to be dismissive of Islam and Islam to be correspondingly allergic to leftism. These expectations are borne out by the historical outcome of the interaction between the two, and this in a number of ways.

One is that, even before the rise of Islamism, there were indications that leftism did not in general fare as well in the Islamic world as it did in other Third World regions. There was a sense at the time that the presence of Islam displaced the political spectrum to the right. One effect of this was a certain opportunistic reticence on the part of leftists in the Islamic world when it came to the manifestation of antireligious

[59] B. Lewis, *Race and slavery*, 156 (reproducing a contemporary translation). In another letter of the same year, the sultan told the consul that the legitimacy of the slave trade required "no more demonstration than the light of day" (3, 151).

[60] See 89–90.

[61] For a brief survey of the history of Communist activity in the Middle East, see *EI*^{2}, art "Shuyūʿiyya" (J. Couland et al.).

[62] See 182–84.

sentiments. To engage in uninhibited displays of godless zealotry was to ask for trouble of the kind that arose in Syria in 1967 when an army magazine published an article denouncing God as "an embalmed toy in the museum of history."[63] "Our socialism believes in God," as one Egyptian journalist wisely put it in 1962.[64] Likewise, the Sudanese Communist Party was careful to keep on the right side of Islam and to stress that Communism and Islam had the same goals.[65] Another effect was geopolitical: almost the only fully fledged Marxist regime to emerge endogenously in the Islamic world was the People's Democratic Republic of Yemen, alias South Yemen. Moreover, this idiosyncratic state never served as a leftist beacon in the Muslim world in the way that Cuba did in Latin America. No one sees Bin Laden as a Western stooge for his vendetta against the Yemeni Marxists,[66] whereas any Latin American who had played such a role with regard to Cuba would have harvested a very mixed reputation.

Just as significant was the relative immunity of Sunnī Islamism to leftism. Arab socialism might believe in God, but as far as the Islamists were concerned, God did not deign to return the compliment. The Communist world and the socialism it came to encourage beyond its borders were, of course, realities that Islamist thinkers had to confront. They had to show that, whatever the Communist system could do, the Islamic system could do better, and they were under pressure to demonstrate this superiority in the field of social policy. But one gets no sense that Communism, or for that matter socialism, served as a stimulus to the religious imagination. One observer of the Islamists describes them as "hostile to even the slightest tinge of Marxism."[67] Why this should have been so is a good question. Part of the explanation may be that any attraction leftism might have had for Islamists had been preempted by its adoption on the part of the very regimes they sought to overthrow, be it in Iraq, Syria, Egypt, or Algeria—though we should note that Sunnī Islamists seem to have been no more open to leftism in countries whose rulers did not adopt some variety of socialism. Another part of the explanation is no doubt the general hostility of leftism

[63] Seale, *Asad of Syria*, 115.

[64] Abdel-Malek, *Égypte*, 281.

[65] Warburg, *Islam, nationalism*, 148–52. There was a significant antireligious group in the Party, but it was expelled in 1956 (150).

[66] L. Wright, *Looming tower*, 153–54.

[67] Sivan, *Radical Islam*, 10, and cf. 57–58, 59, 76. When Sivan speaks of the doctrines of Sayyid Quṭb as a "liberation theology," he means simply that they are both religious and revolutionary (108).

toward religion. To that we should add the capacity of Sunnī Islamists to buck global consensus in other areas: many of them rejected nationalism and democracy. But the point I would like to develop here is the absence from the Sunnī heritage of a counterpart to the proletariat.

Thus, if we turn to the attitude of Mawdūdī and Quṭb to the poor, we find no hint of liberation theology.[68] Mawdūdī is not unsympathetic to them: "The life of the poor man is difficult."[69] He notes, however, that the individual members of a society vary in their abilities and talents, with the result that some come to be wealthier than others. Since this situation is natural (*fiṭrī*), Islam acknowledges and regulates it;[70] the means of regulation are the alms tax (*zakāt*) and the public treasury (*bayt al-māl*).[71] The poor do indeed have rights, and it is a serious matter when the rich deny these.[72] "The rich should come to the help of the poor."[73] But it does not seem that any particular virtue attaches to the poor or that they will have a disproportionate role to play in the achievement of a better future. Quṭb has considerably more to say about the poor than Mawdūdī and is undoubtedly concerned for their welfare; he was, after all, the author of a work on social justice. He too is seriously concerned with almsgiving.[74] Yet, for the most part his tone lacks emotional exuberance. He tells us that the poor have rights vis-à-vis the rich in accordance with their needs and the interests of a well-balanced society.[75] But it is labor that is sacred,[76] not poverty; the way to solve the problem of the misery of poverty is to provide employment

[68] In fact, the social concerns of Quṭb in particular have more in common with mainstream social Catholicism (see 203) than with liberation theology (I owe this comparison to Andrew March).

[69] Maududi, *Fundamentals of Islam*, 245 (for this work, see Ahmad and Ansari, *Mawlānā Mawdūdī*, 37 no. 72).

[70] Mawdūdī, *Muʿḍilāt al-iqtiṣād*, 54.8 = Maududi, *Economic problem of man*, 31 (for this work, dating from 1941, see Ahmad and Ansari, *Mawlānā Mawdūdī*, 35 no. 34). See also Maudūdī, "Political concepts," 207 (this work gives a translation of extracts from Mawdūdī's *Tafhīm*, compiled and translated by the editor, see 163), and Nasr, *Mawdudi*, 105, 132.

[71] Mawdūdī, *Muʿḍilāt al-iqtiṣād*, 64.7 = Maududi, *Economic problem of man*, 37; see also Maududi, *Fundamentals of Islam*, 191 (chap. 5 of this work is an extensive discussion of *zakāt*). For the wider modern discussion of *zakāt*, see *EI*², art. "Zakāt," section 8.

[72] Mawdūdī, *Muʿḍilāt al-iqtiṣād*, 25.11 = Maududi, *Economic problem of man*, 14.

[73] Maudūdī, "Political concepts," 205.

[74] Quṭb, *ʿAdāla*, 83–85 = 97–100, 131–35 = 162–68.

[75] Ibid., 32.17 = 38; similarly 68.17 = 78–79.

[76] Ibid., 113.9 = 179 (*qadāsat al-ʿamal*); similarly Quṭb, *Maʿraka*, 57.6. This work was first published in 1950.

for all able-bodied men and social security for the rest.[77] The effects of poverty on those who suffer from it are merely ugly: they either hate the rich or lose their self-respect and fawn on them.[78] This is not at all a rich man's perspective, for Quṭb also tells us that the poor in every age are the victims of the rich.[79] But despite the fact that he is clearly to Mawdūdī's left, it is in the end equality of opportunity, not equality of outcomes, to which he is committed.[80] Just as with Mawdūdī, there is no hint of a preference for the poor, no sense that God regards them with particular tenderness.[81] In this respect, despite occasional exceptions,[82] Mawdūdī and Quṭb seem broadly representative of Sunnī Islamism at large.[83] Thus the founder of Sipāh-i Ṣaḥāba in Pakistan "had a reputation for being much concerned with the welfare of the poor and the helpless,"[84] and a later leader of the movement emphasizes the place of social justice in the early caliphate,[85] but neither begins to sound like a Latin American Liberationist—a point that applies more generally to the social work undertaken by Islamist movements among the poor.

[77] Quṭb, *ʿAdāla*, 257.2 = 343.

[78] Ibid., 109.19 = 133. Poverty also leads to crime and moral degradation (256.20 = 342–43).

[79] Ibid., 208.16 = 259.

[80] Quṭb, *Maʿraka*, 60.3, and cf. 20.16; Quṭb, *ʿAdāla*, 31.19 = 37. For Quṭb's views on these matters, see also Sivan, *Radical Islam*, 76.

[81] One student of Quṭb's thought writes: "Like a true liberation theologian, Quṭb exhorts the weak . . . to rise against the oppressive status quo" (Abu-Rabiʿ, *Intellectual origins*, 181, citing Quṭb, *Ẓilāl al-Qurʾān*, 2096.2; I was unable to locate the statements about the poor that Abu-Rabiʿ goes on to cite from the *Ẓilāl*). However, the Koranic verse in question (Q14:21) is set in an eschatological context in which the time for exhortation has long passed; in the face of impending doom, the weak (*ḍuʿafāʾ*) among the unbelievers protest that they had been followers of the strong, but this avails them nothing. Quṭb's commentary is appropriately unsympathetic to the weak, stressing that their weakness is no excuse for their supine conduct (2096.5, and cf. 2096.15); like the Koranic verse, it contains no exhortation.

[82] For two Morrocan Islamists with a focus on the poor, see Munson, *Religion and power*, 155–57, 164–66, 170; particularly evocative is the statement of ʿAbd al-Salām Yāsīn (d. 2012) that the hearts of the oppressed masses are full of real faith (166).

[83] Thus the view of Ḥasan al-Bannā is similar in tone (Bannā, *Majmūʿat rasāʾil*, 395.3). The only trace I have noted of an interest in the poor among the jihadis is an anonymous verse quoted by Bin Laden: "I am not on the side of the wealthy, if exaltedness is on the side of the poor" (Lawrence, *Messages*, 271; I have not seen the original). Though this might sound sound promising, it is the second line of a pair, and the context makes it clear that it is in fact for the first line that Bin Laden quotes these verses.

[84] Zaman, *Ulama*, 125.

[85] Zaman, "South Asian Islam," 78.

If Islamists were largely immune to leftism, we would not expect the professional scholars to be susceptible. There have nevertheless been occasional Sunnī scholars who were genuinely attracted to modern social radicalism. In the Indian context in particular, as has recently been shown, such scholars had a tendency to focus on a small number of long-forgotten passages in the works of their medieval forebears; these stimulating finds could be seen as supporting a leftist orientation from within the tradition.[86] One thing dependence on such passages highlights is the lack of an Islamic counterpart to the scriptural basis of the Liberationist identification with the poor.[87]

This is not to deny that Sunnī Islamism can be socially subversive, whether by supplying social services that the state is unable to deliver, as in Egypt, or by fomenting class divisions that happen to coincide with sectarian fissures, as in Pakistan. But unlike Shīʿite Islamism, it is not an articulate program of social revolution; here again, liberation theology has been conspicuously absent from Sunnī Islamism.[88] Moreover, the widespread delegitimation of Ṣūfism in modern times has precluded any contemporary relevance for Ṣūfī ideas of elective poverty. In short, for those who imported leftism into the Sunnī world, the fit with the commitment of the heritage to equality and solidarity was largely wasted.

The one success story in the interaction between Islam and leftism relates to Shīʿism in Iran—though in crude political terms the success was entirely on the Islamist, not the leftist side. There were two key figures in the development of Shīʿite opposition to the rule of the Shāh. The first was Sharīʿatī (d. 1977), who read Frantz Fanon and other leftist thinkers and translated their secular ideas into the language of his own religious tradition.[89] He writes that he was able to convince Fanon that "in some societies where religion plays an important role in the culture, religion can, through its resources and psychological ef-

[86] See Zaman, *Modern Islamic thought*, 224–25, 228, 236, 238–39, 241–42, 243. The three passages in question are from the works of Jaṣṣāṣ (d. 981), Ibn Ḥazm (d. 1064), and Shāh Walī Allāh.

[87] Cf. 201.

[88] The only Liberationist movement that I have encountered within the geographical limits of the Sunnī world is the Sabeel Ecumenical Liberation Theology Center, which describes itself as "an ecumenical grassroots liberation theology movement among Palestinian Christians" (http://www.sabeel.org, and see also Ateek, *Justice*; I owe my knowledge of this movement and these sources to Rochelle Davis).

[89] See Kepel, *Jihad*, 39, 107–8. I am indebted to Negin Nabavi for help with the literature on Sharīʿatī.

fects, help the enlightened person to lead his society toward the same destination to which Fanon was taking his own through non-religious means."[90] So where Christian Liberationists could focus on the sacralization of the poor, Sharīʿatī could play on the Shīʿite cult of the oppressed.[91] The verbal key to this alchemy was a Koranic term meaning "deemed weak," "oppressed" (*mustaḍʿafūn*); in a few contexts this was a group whose very wretchedness in the present marked them out for future deliverance (Q7:137, 8:26, 28:5).[92] Sharīʿatī accordingly used the term to translate Fanon's "wretched of the earth."[93] He further described the Prophet as assuring his poor and weak followers that they would come to rule the world,[94] and he saw the history of Shīʿism as "the history of the spirit of Islam, the soul which has been the victim of its own body."[95] Sharīʿatī was not alone in developing such ideas,[96] but politically the new doctrine fared no better in the short run than Liberation Theology in Latin America. What changed everything was the adoption—indeed the hijacking—of this Shīʿite liberationist idiom by Khumaynī (d. 1989), the second key figure, in the 1970s.[97] His appropriation of it may have been shallow, but it was stunningly effective and did much to enable him and his supporters to emerge as the victors of the Iranian revolution of 1979. This event could well be seen as the greatest political triumph of liberation theology in the entire history of the phenomenon. It is as if the Sandinista revolution had transferred power into the hands of Nicaragua's bishops, and the plausible

[90] Shariʿati, *What is to be done*, 19; and see Nabavi, *Intellectuals*, 101. For Sharīʿatī's relations with Fanon, see Rahnema, *Islamic utopian*, 126–27.

[91] It does not seem to be clear whether Sharīʿatī himself was aware of the Latin American parallel (contrast the editor's note in Shariʿati, *What is to be done*, 28n15, with the somewhat polemical remarks of Boroujerdi, *Iranian intellectuals*, 109). For interest in Fanon among the Catholic Liberationists, see Gutiérrez, *Theology of liberation*, 186n36, and cf. Boff and Boff, *Introducing liberation theology*, 39.

[92] I borrow the phrasing from M. Cook, *Muhammad*, 51–52.

[93] Abrahamian, *Khomeinism*, 47. The translation is felicitous, since in Q28:5 God speaks of "those that were oppressed *in the land*" (*alladhīna ʾstuḍʿifū fī ʾl-arḍ*). Cf. also Shariati, *Hajj*, 77–78.

[94] Shariʿati, *What is to be done*, 81–82, and cf. 54, 88, 98 (the latter speaking of the "poor and oppressed people" of the day as "humiliated by the two superpowers").

[95] Ibid., 38. In effect the Sunnīs get the blame for the victimization.

[96] Thus, for the thought of the well-known Arab Shīʿite scholar Muḥammad Ḥusayn Faḍlallāh, an Iraqi living in Lebanon, see Abu-Rabiʿ, *Intellectual origins*, chap. 7; Abu-Rabiʿ speaks of Faḍlallāh's ideas as his "liberation theology" (see, for example, 221), and the term seems to be apt (see especially 228–37). In India the dissident Bohra Asghar Ali Engineer expresses rather similar ideas, see his "Aspects of liberation theology," especially 1–3, 5–6.

[97] Kepel, *Jihad*, 40–41, 111–12; Abrahamian, *Khomeinism*, 26–27, 31–32, 47–49.

suspicion that something like this could only have happened in the Islamic world could be seen as an indication of the terms on which Islam and leftism interact there. But there was no Sunnī Sharīʿatī,[98] any more than there was a Sunnī Khumaynī, and the reasons go deeper than personality or the circumstance that leftism looked good in Iran because the Shāh was against it.

That leaves liberalism broadly conceived as the prime locus of interaction with European ideologies. Unlike conservatism, this was an ideology for export, and unlike leftism, it was not actively hostile to religion. The egalitarianism of the liberal tradition could thus be expected to resonate with that of the Islamic heritage, despite reservations with regard to its more recent commitment to female equality and its long-established practice of unlimited religious toleration. But the lack of a strong liberal commitment to solidarity was less likely to play well.

The writings of the Islamists on these issues do much to bear out these expectations. Mawdūdī lays strong emphasis on egalitarianism. For him, the social organization that the prophets sought to establish was founded on human equality. It was a basic principle of the early Islamic state that all were equal in the eyes of the law, a connection in which he cites Muḥammad's condemnation of earlier communities in which lowly offenders were punished while aristocratic offenders went free.[99] Appealing to his unusual doctrine of what we might call the caliphate of all believers,[100] Mawdūdī states: "A society in which everyone is a caliph of God and an equal participant in this caliphate, cannot tolerate any class divisions based on distinctions of birth and social position. All men enjoy equal status and position in such a society." He also expresses the same point with a touch of local color: "In the divine *darbar*, in the presence of God, all belong to one class." He quotes sayings of the Prophet, such as the simile "people are equals like the teeth of a comb" and another in which is embedded the Koranic statement that "the noblest among you in the sight of God is the most godfearing of you" (Q49:13). It is this equality that uproots the tree of that most vicious of evils, human—as opposed to divine—sovereignty (*ḥākimiyya*).[101]

Quṭb likewise articulates an Islamic egalitarianism that resonates strongly with modern values. For him, too, the underlying principle is

98 As noted by Kepel (*Jihad*, 108).

99 See 170.

100 See 332.

101 For these views of Mawdūdī's, see M. Cook, "Political freedom," 303–4.

that dominion over men belongs only to God. He tells us that Islam was born in an age when inequality was rampant, a fact he illustrates with reference to Iran, India, Rome, and even the Arabs; in the Indian case he shows his awareness of the Vedic account of the origin of the Hindu classes.[102] By contrast, the message of the new religion was absolute equality among all humans. In support he quotes the same Koranic verse, and he too repeats the saying of the Prophet that "people are equals like the teeth of a comb." But in rhetorical terms by far his most effective proof-text is the story of the Arab emissaries to Rustam. In one of the passages in which he quotes their statement that the mission of the invaders is to deliver those who so wish from being servants of men to being servants of God, he comments that in these few words are concentrated "the fundamental principle of this creed (*qāʿidat hādhihi ʾl-ʿaqīda*)," and that in them is manifested "the nature of the Islamic movement that arose from it." Admittedly this original Islamic equality did not last: massive economic and social distinctions soon emerged within Islamic society, and a class of idle aristocrats appeared. But Quṭb could still claim that Islam had anticipated the French Revolution.[103]

Other Islamists hold similar views. Thus Ḥawwā's treatment of the equality that obtains among Muslims is not as vibrant as Quṭb's,[104] but he too can give an account of the history of the Indian caste system, complete with a quotation from Manu.[105] The invocation of the French Revolution apart, the jihadis seem comfortable with Quṭb's style of thinking. Speaking of the early conquests, Bin Laden boasts: "We were the pioneers of the world. We rescued people from the worship of human beings, for the worship of the God of people."[106] He describes Islam as the religion of "total equality between all people,"[107] and he too quotes the tradition about discrimination between lowly and aristocratic offenders, observing that such is the Muslim predicament today.[108] Another jihadi articulates the theme more concretely. The preparations for the battle of the Khandaq in 627 centered on the digging

[102] On this point see Quṭb, *ʿAdāla*, 50.5 = 57. This is the account given in the *Puruṣasūkta* (see below, 191–92).

[103] For these views of Quṭb's, see M. Cook, "Political freedom," 304–5.

[104] Ḥawwā, *Islām*, 2: 73.22.

[105] Ḥawwā, *Rasūl*, 2: 168.7, 168.21.

[106] See Lawrence, *Messages*, 217 (*nunqidhuhum min ʿibādat al-ʿibād ilā ʿibādat rabb al-ʿibād*, see ʿAlī, *Tanẓīm al-Qāʿida*, 384.3).

[107] Lawrence, *Messages*, 166.

[108] Ibid., 196.

of a trench, heavy labor in which Muḥammad worked side by side with his followers. Our jihadi recognizes here a spectacle of humility and equality—an equality that is unheard of today.[109] He quotes with approval a passage in which another author notes what Muḥammad did *not* do on this occasion: he did not stage a pompous groundbreaking ceremony, holding a pickax with the tips of his fingers to convey the illusion of participation.[110]

Predictably, the attitude of Islamists toward the extension of equality to women is more conflicted; on this front Western mores—which have tended to become increasingly egalitarian over time—were a peculiarly intimate challenge to traditional Muslim values and touched matters closely related to notions of male honor. Mawdūdī was in principle an egalitarian. As he declares in his book on purdah: "None can deny the fact that as human beings man and woman are equal."[111] Women are thus fully entitled to express their opinions since they too are repositories of the caliphate (another echo of his doctrine of the caliphate of all believers).[112] But he has no liking for the incessant "propaganda of the equality of the sexes" of modern times.[113] There are distinctions to be made. Men and women may indeed be "equal in moral status and human rights," but this should not mislead us into adopting the "wrong concept of equality," a concept according to which women are "free to undertake the same sort of jobs" as men and "moral restrictions" on the sexes should be equally loose.[114] More specifically, it is for the man to earn a living and for the woman to bring up the children; authority within the family can only be vested in the man.[115] The same is true of the polity: in an Islamic state "the posts of responsibility . . .

[109] Shinqīṭī, *Numūdhaj*, 3.11; see also 2.9. I owe my copy of this text to Nelly Lahoud.

[110] Ibid., 4.3. The passage is from Būṭī, *Fiqh al-sīra*, 339.18, though the fingertips and the illusion have dropped out in Shinqīṭī's quotation. Given the close relations maintained by Būṭī (d. 2013) with the Syrian regime, his reluctance to condemn rulers as unbelievers, and his espousal of nonviolence, he is a somewhat surprising authority for a jihadi to cite (see Christmann, "Islamic scholar," 63, 73, 74, 75).

[111] Maududi, *Purdah*, 112–13; thus "the claim for equality is absolutely justified" (113; for this work, first published in 1939, see Ahmad and Ansari, *Mawlānā Mawdūdī*, 39 no. 103).

[112] Maududi, *Political theory of Islam*, 41 = Mawdūdī, *Naẓariyya*, 46.5 (for this work, first published in 1939, see Ahmad and Ansari, *Mawlānā Mawdūdī*, 35 no. 44; an abbreviated version of it appears as Maudūdī, "Political theory of Islam," see 161n32). The context is political.

[113] Maududi, *Purdah*, 21.

[114] Ibid., 12; see also 113 on the idea that "the man and the woman should have the same field of activity."

[115] Ibid., 121–22.

cannot be entrusted to a woman"[116]—though Mawdūdī was prepared to waive this principle when he found it expedient to do so.[117] In addition, there must be "safeguards" to prevent this virtuous domestic pattern from being disrupted by "foolish and senseless people."[118] These salutary safeguards are, of course, synonymous with purdah, "the set of injunctions which constitute the most important part of the Islamic system of community life."[119] These injunctions are not to be weakened; indeed current conditions in India (Mawdūdī was writing in the 1930s) require that they should be "strictly enforced rather than relaxed."[120] Thus, despite his acceptance of female equality in principle, in practice Mawdūdī appears as a social conservative.

Like Mawdūdī, Quṭb asserts a qualified egalitarianism. Women do indeed enjoy "full equality" (*musāwāt tāmma*) in most matters, but with qualifications relating to "some specific situations connected with natural and recognized capacities, skills or responsibilities, which do not affect the essential nature of the human situation of the two sexes."[121] While this sounds like Mawdūdī, there is a significant difference. Quṭb presents the harem not as something instituted by Islam but rather as the product of later injustice; he conveniently assigns particular blame to the Turks.[122] This is exactly the move that Mawdūdī does not make in his discussion of purdah, and the result is that Quṭb's thinking has a more modern tone. Women must indeed dress and behave decently; Quṭb's distaste for Western licentiousness is painfully evident in his reminiscences of his time in America.[123] But they are otherwise free

[116] Maudūdī, "Fundamentals of Islamic constitution," 282 (for this work, first published in 1952, see 271, and Ahmad and Ansari, *Mawlānā Mawdūdī*, 36 no. 47). Nor can women be elected to the legislature, though they could have a separate assembly of their own elected by female voters; this institution would mainly concern itself with "the special affairs of the women," but it would also have the right to offer criticism relating to "the general welfare of the country" (Maudūdī, "Some constitutional proposals," 345–46; for this work, which dates from 1952, see 335, and, perhaps, Ahmad and Ansari, *Mawlānā Mawdūdī*, 34 no. 8).

[117] For this embarrassing episode, see Nasr, *Vanguard of Islamic revolution*, 41–42.

[118] See the summary at Maududi, *Purdah*, 121–22.

[119] Ibid., 18.

[120] Ibid., 218.

[121] Quṭb, *ʿAdāla*, 53.19 = 61; cf. Carré, *Mysticism and politics*, 131–32.

[122] Quṭb, *Maʿraka*, 111.9, 113.4.

[123] Quṭb, *al-Islām wa-mushkilāt al-ḥaḍāra*, 73–84 (I owe my knowledge of this account to Mike Doran; the work was first published in 1962); note particularly his disapproving reference to "freedom of the mixing of the sexes" (*ḥurriyyat al-ikhtilāṭ al-jinsī*, 73.11). This Western licentiousness was an old theme (see B. Lewis, *Muslim discovery*, 287–90); to go no further back than 1798, in that year the French invaders brought their shameless

to come and go, as they were in the time of the Prophet.[124] In short, Quṭb is a puritan, and he is not a feminist, but neither is he a conservative. In this respect his thinking perhaps reflects the attitudes of an age that was socially more liberal than the present;[125] contrast the tone of Ayman al-Ẓawāhirī's incidental observation that one of the unacceptable implications of the democratic principle of equality is that it abolishes "man's dominion over woman."[126]

Islamist attitudes to the relationship between Muslims and unbelievers in the Muslim polity tend to be similarly conflicted; any challenge to the subordination of conquered unbelievers to Muslims is an attack on the Muslim ascendancy, and yet to affirm that such subordination is right and proper is to court the disparagement of Islam as discriminatory. The response of the early Islamist thinkers was to concentrate on defending the justice of Islam. This religion, Mawdūdī states in a work first published in 1939, is good to its minorities: "Islam does not want to eliminate its minorities, it wants to protect them and gives them the freedom to live according to their own culture."[127] A work he published in Pakistan in 1948 has similar provisions.[128] Of course, the Islamic state must by its very nature discriminate between Muslims and non-Muslims.[129] But the concern of the work is nevertheless to show the moral superiority of the Islamic system over others; thus, the opening pages systematically contrast the treatment of minorities by Islamic and national-democratic states,[130] and the conclusion affirms that the

---

womenfolk to Egypt, and the chronicler Jabartī was duly disgusted by their lewd behaviour (Moreh, *Al-Jabartī's chronicle*, 12.4 = 43).

[124] Quṭb, *Maʿraka*, 112.7, 112.18; but contrast Carré, *Mysticism and politics*, 129.

[125] Compare his insistence that there is no such thing as Islamic dress (Quṭb, *Maʿraka*, 89.1).

[126] Ibrahim, *Al Qaeda reader*, 135; he quotes Q4:34.

[127] Maududi, *Political theory of Islam*, 35; cf. Mawdūdī, *Naẓariyya*, 39.16 (the Arabic differs from the English, speaking not of minorities but of *ahl al-dhimma* and making no reference to cultural freedom). Likewise "the Islamic State confers all basic human rights on its non-Muslim citizens" (Maudūdī, "Political concepts," 201), and in comparison to other systems of government Islam enjoins "the most just, the most tolerant and the most generous treatment" of its minorities (Maudūdī, "First principles," 265; for this work, first published in 1952, see Ahmad and Ansari, *Mawlānā Mawdūdī*, 36 no. 48).

[128] Mawdūdī, *Ḥuqūq ahl al-dhimma*, 13.6, 19.8 = Maudūdī, "Rights of non-Muslims," 304, 308; for this work, first published in 1948, see Ahmad and Ansari, *Mawlānā Mawdūdī*, 36 no. 50.

[129] Mawdūdī, *Ḥuqūq ahl al-dhimma*, 4.12 = Maudūdī, "Rights of non-Muslims," 296. Non-Muslims can always join the ruling community (*al-jamāʿa al-ḥākima*) if they choose to convert (5.7 = 297).

[130] See especially the summary at Mawdūdī, *Ḥuqūq ahl al-dhimma*, 6.12 = Maudūdī, "Rights of non-Muslims," 299.

only guarantee of the security of non-Muslims resident in Pakistan is the establishment of an Islamic government there, not of a secular (*lā dīniyya*) democratic state on the Indian model.[131] Likewise, his account of the collection of the poll tax from non-Muslims makes no mention of the humiliation prescribed in scripture (Q9:29),[132] a strong sign that his purpose is to vindicate the justice and fairness of Islam, not to put non-Muslim minorities in their place.[133] In the same way, Quṭb's primary concern is to vindicate the exemplary fairness and sensitivity of the Islamic system,[134] rather than to call for the reimposition on the minorities of their former subordinate status. It is not that he has forgotten the idea of the Muslim ascendancy: Islam is indeed a creed of ascendancy (*istiʿlāʾ*) and pride (*iʿtizāz, kibriyāʾ*), and once the spirit of Islam awakens in a Muslim, he will not stand for anyone overtopping him (*an yaʿluwa ʿalayhi aḥad*).[135] But Quṭb's purpose in this passage is to explain why Islam is a danger to colonialism; the local non-Muslim population is not in sight. Today, as he says in a discussion of the Koranic verse about the poll tax, this issue is "purely historical, not current."[136] Thus, we should not expect him to say, as Saʿīd Ḥawwā does, that equality between Muslim and non-Muslim is a disgusting idea (*fikra khabītha*).[137] Nor does he display the virulent hatred of the Copts that was later to characterize the activities of the Jamāʿa Islāmiyya in Egypt.[138] The leaders of al-Qāʿida do not concern themselves much with the status of non-Muslims in the Muslim state, but a passing remark shows how they too have moved away from the apologetics of Mawdūdī and Quṭb. We encountered above one reason why Ẓawāhirī finds the democratic

[131] Mawdūdī, *Ḥuqūq ahl al-dhimma*, 36.17, 37.9 = Maudūdī, "Rights of non-Muslims," 320.

[132] Mawdūdī, *Ḥuqūq ahl al-dhimma*, 21–25 = Maudūdī, "Rights of non-Muslims," 310–12.

[133] By contrast, his hostility to the Aḥmadīs was intense (cf. Nasr, *Mawdudi*, 43).

[134] Quṭb, *ʿAdāla*, 93.9 = 110–11, 132.5 = 162; Quṭb, *Maʿraka*, 114.7; Quṭb, *Dirāsāt Islāmiyya*, 250.15; Quṭb, *Naḥw mujtamaʿ Islāmī*, 115.6, 118.19. In the last passage cited he specifies that his polemic is directed against those who call in question the justice of Islam (*ʿadālat al-Islām*). On his treatment of these matters in his Koran commentary, see Carré, *Mysticism and politics*, 112–15, 181–82.

[135] Quṭb, *Dirāsāt Islāmiyya*, 174.1; cf. below, 313.

[136] Carré, *Mysticism and politics*, 306.

[137] Ḥawwā, *Islām*, 2:74.2. True and false believers cannot be equal in an Islamic society (73.20). Ḥawwā nevertheless continues the apologetic concern: he remarks that Islam's superior treatment of other religions (except Arab paganism) is shown by the fact that you won't find a single Muslim in Spain, whereas you will find Christians and Jews in Syria even now (*Rasūl*, 2:220.7).

[138] See Kepel, *Jihad*, 276, 282, 283, 285–86, 290–91, 294.

principle of equality unacceptable;[139] another is that it means the abolition of the poll tax.[140] But by implication this reminds us that the jihadis can at least tolerate Jews and Christians in good conscience—something that is by no means clear in the case of their relations with Shīᶜites.

There is also the question of the status of slaves, but for the most part this is an issue only in relation to the past. Mawdūdī takes up the challenge in a pamphlet on human rights in Islam, and argues that Westerners, in view of their own past misdeeds, have no standing to criticize Muslims on this score. He does not deny the persistence of slavery under the Islamic dispensation but explains it as a humane solution to the problem of disposing of those prisoners of war who were not exchanged or ransomed.[141] In contrast to his views on women, what he has to say about slavery suggests no substantive continuity with the conservative Muslim attitudes that were still, as we have seen, very much alive in the nineteenth century. Instead, his concern is purely apologetic. Likewise for Quṭb, the fact that Islam did not abolish so inegalitarian an institution outright is a significant embarrassment, and he explains it as best he can.[142] The arguments of both Mawdūdī and Quṭb reflect the fact that Muslim societies, however resistant to European abolitionism in the middle of the nineteenth century, had gradually adapted to the dismantling of the slave trades that traditionally supplied their slave markets. Since then, some jihadis have reportedly revived the enslavement of captives deemed not to be Muslim, but as might be expected the leaders of al-Qāᶜida are not in the business of defending this practice.

It hardly needs to be added that Islamists set great store by Muslim solidarity. We have already seen the pan-Islamic aspect of this as represented by the Islamist disparagement of nationalism: Mawdūdī was strongly committed to that "precious mantle of international brotherhood," and Quṭb insisted that a Muslim has no nationality other than his creed, by virtue of which he is a member of the Muslim community.[143] But the high valuation of solidarity also finds expression in the

[139] See 188.

[140] Ibrahim, *Al Qaeda reader*, 135.

[141] Mawdūdī, *Human rights in Islam*, 19–21 (in a talk of 1975, see 7).

[142] Quṭb, *Dirāsāt Islāmiyya*, 11.2; see also Quṭb, *Naḥw mujtamaᶜ Islāmī*, 78.10; Carré, *Mysticism and politics*, 169–71, 172–73; and Quṭb, *Ẓilāl*, 229.32.

[143] See 42–43.

rejection of Western individualism,[144] a rejection for which support is found in a Prophetic tradition about some people in a boat: one of them starts making a hole in the keel, and the fate of the rest of them depends on how they react to this.[145] Islam, as Mawdūdī puts it, does not approve of "unreined individualism."[146]

The most salient feature on the social front is thus the resonance between modern European and Islamic notions of equality. At the same time, the Islamic valuation of solidarity remains attractive in the modern world, despite the fact that it finds less resonance in mainstream European values, particularly as Sunnī Islamists have on the whole displayed little patience for the European tradition of radical democracy—a disdain that bears some relation to the fact that the Sunnī (as opposed to the Shīʿite) heritage provides only limited encouragement for a liberation theology. Overall, the fact that the heritage has a much less determinate social than political vision has shaped its use in modern times: the general notions of equality and solidarity apart, those who have invoked it most strongly have usually done so in a conservative vein, to defend at least some of the inequalities inscribed in the heritage.

3. Hinduism

The law book ascribed to Manu opens with a scene in which the sages ask him to "tell us, properly and in order, the duties of all classes and also of the people who are born between."[147] The book is his response to this request, and it naturally has much to tell us about social hierarchy. The overall vision is aptly encapsulated in the account—already enshrined in the Ṛg Veda—of the origins of the four classes in the body parts of a primeval god.[148] Of the three twice-born classes, the Brahmin was made from his mouth, the Kṣatriya from his arms, and the Vaiśya from his thighs; for our purposes there is no need to elaborate further

[144] Tripp, *Islam*, 48, 52–54. See also Maududi, *Political theory of Islam*, 42 = Mawdūdī, *Naẓariyya*, 46.13; Quṭb, *ʿAdāla*, 60.2 = 68 (note the final sentence of the paragraph in the translation).

[145] M. Cook, *Commanding right*, 514–15.

[146] Mawdudi, *Let us be Muslims*, 238.

[147] Manu, *Laws*, 3 (1.1–2).

[148] Ibid., 6–7 (1.31). For a translation of the account given in the *Puruṣasūkta* (Ṛg Veda 10.90.12), see Basham, *Wonder that was India*, 240–41.

on their elevated or at least respected place in society. But that, of course, left the feet of the primeval god, and from them was made the Śūdra, whose duties and liabilities are correspondingly humble, not to say humiliating. Thus he should be stigmatized by bearing a name that breeds disgust—whereas the names of members of the twice-born classes should evoke auspiciousness, strength, and property respectively.[149] He should not have attitude: a Śūdra who is obedient to his superiors, gentle in his speech, and without egotism is rewarded by being reborn into a better class in his next life,[150] whereas one who has the temerity to shout abuse at a Brahmin suffers physical punishment in this life.[151] The Brahmins whom a Śūdra serves "should give him the leftovers of their food, their old clothes, the spoiled parts of their grain, and their worn-out household utensils."[152] He should not amass wealth, as Brahmins find this annoying.[153] Other sources contribute in the same vein. The Śūdra, we read, "is at the beck and call of others, he can be made to rise at will, he can be beaten at will."[154] Some hold that any Brahmin who touches a Śūdra must purify himself by sipping water or taking a bath.[155] Such matters remained a favorite topic of later works of Hindu law.[156]

The jurists do not deal so systematically with the forerunners of today's Untouchables. They did not think of them—as people do today—as a kind of fifth class of society (the *pañcamas*) below the Śūdras;[157] indeed, in the eyes of the ancient grammarian Pāṇini, it is clear that even the Cāṇḍāla was a kind of Śūdra.[158] What the jurists did possess was a well-developed notion of people who for one reason or another were not to be touched (*aspṛśya*). They ranged from one's wife while she was menstruating through such occupational groups as fishermen and butchers to Cāṇḍālas; thus on touching a Cāṇḍāla one should plunge into water.[159] Punishment is accordingly prescribed when an untouchable person deliberately touches one of the twice-

[149] Manu, *Laws*, 20 (2.31).
[150] Ibid., 232–33 (9.335).
[151] Ibid., 181 (8.267). The twice-born are merely fined.
[152] Ibid., 249 (10.125).
[153] Ibid., 250 (10.129).
[154] Kane, *History of Dharmaśāstra*, 2: 35 (citing the Aitareya Brāhmaṇa).
[155] Ibid., 2: 162.
[156] Derrett, *Dharmaśāstra and juridical literature*, 56–57.
[157] For the prehistory of this notion, see J. Leslie, *Authority and meaning*, 27–29.
[158] Kane, *History of Dharmaśāstra*, 2: 167–68.
[159] Ibid., 2: 168–73.

born.[160] The social implications of all this are mitigated by the fact that on certain occasions characterized by the presence of crowds touch is not polluting; cases in point are a religious procession, a marriage, a festival, or a battle.[161] But for Untouchables—not to mention Śūdras—who have developed attitude, as so many have today, the tone of the jurists is less than diplomatic.

How far do ideas about charity soften the contours of this highly inegalitarian social vision? Charity is indeed meritorious, just as one would expect. Thus Manu states: "By giving almsfood, a twice-born householder obtains as much merit as he does by giving a cow to a poor man."[162] As this suggests, what is distributed is primarily food. The recipients do indeed include the indigent;[163] they are among those who are to be fed after guests and pregnant women have been attended to.[164] Moreover, food should be given not just to a Śūdra, but also to dogs, Cāṇḍālas, outcastes, and crows (though for the last four it should be thrown on the ground).[165] Yet it appears that charity to the involuntary poor is considerably less salient in the Hindu than in the Islamic or Christian cases. Most of the juristic discussion of almsgiving in fact relates to recipients whose poverty is elective. Thus it would seem that the twice-born householder gives alms food mainly to fellow members of the higher castes who are at a different stage (*āśrama*) of the four-phase life cycle. These may be students engaged in their Vedic studies;[166] as one text says of the student, "making himself poor and feeling no shame, he begs for almsfood."[167] Or the recipients of alms food may be mendicants living a life of wandering asceticism.[168] This flow of charity within the twice-born classes is nicely caught in the prescription that when the householder finally wearies of giving alms and making offerings, he becomes a mendicant himself, and as such is

160 Ibid., 2: 176.

161 Ibid., 2: 175–76.

162 Manu, *Laws*, 53 (3.95). In this instance, however, I quote the translation in Olivelle, *Manu's code of law*, 113 (3.95); for the reading adopted by Olivelle, see the text at 464.11 and his discussion at 261, 925–26.

163 Olivelle, *Dharmasūtras*, 86–87 (5.21), 180 (2.5.19).

164 Ibid., 198 (2.13.5).

165 Ibid., 274–75 (11.9–10).

166 For students begging, see ibid., 10 (1.3.25), 136 (1.3.16), 270 (7.9), 279 (11.68). The student may in fact seek alms food from people of all classes, though not from outcastes (82 (2.35), and cf. 136 (1.3.17)).

167 Ibid., 138 (1.4.7).

168 Ibid., 83 (3.14–15), 193 (2.11.22), 207 (2.18.4), 273 (10.7). It is likewise said that the mendicant may obtain alms food from all classes (208 (2.18.14)).

fit for the eternal state.[169] The involuntary poor, by contrast, seem to take a back seat.

As this indicates, Hinduism has a high regard for elective poverty and enshrines it in the classical schema of the four-phase life cycle of the twice-born adult male: student, then householder, then forest hermit, then wandering ascetic.[170] All but the householder are marked by some measure of religious poverty, but the effect is strongest in the case of the wandering ascetic: he should "wander forth . . . abandoning his relatives and free of possessions."[171] More precisely, he carries only a bowl, a staff, and a water pot.[172] The major differences between this schema and actual practice are that in reality many householders did not become mendicants, and many of those who did become mendicants started young.[173] But there is nothing in the mainstream Hindu tradition that would extend this glow to the involuntary poor. Rather than a preference for the poor, we have a preference for the twice-born.

All in all, we could say that if any major religion can lay claim to a distinctive vision of the ideal society, it would be Hinduism. This social paradigm is the very incarnation of hierarchism: it is built around the system of classes (*varṇas*), realized on the ground in terms of castes (*jātis*). One key feature of this system was thus its inherently inegalitarian character: while there might be a considerable degree of equality among the members of a given class or caste, the inequalities between groups—both as prescribed in the normative texts and as observed in practice—were often very salient. The other key feature was that these groups were only loosely bound together into a larger unity: Hindu society as whole was more like a scattered archipelago than a solid continent. At the same time, each of these features worked against a focus on the involuntary poor as a locus of need or virtue.

Both features could be problematic under modern conditions. But it was the hierarchism that proved a public relations disaster, and this for two reasons. In the first place, the Indian social model had no counterpart in Europe, past or present. From a modern European perspective, aristocratic societies—hierarchic and tightly bound—are familiar if thoroughly old-fashioned, whereas caste societies—hierarchic and

[169] Ibid., 204 (2.17.16–17).

[170] For a summary of the schema, see Basham, *Wonder that was India*, 158–59.

[171] Olivelle, *Dharmasūtras*, 193 (2.11.16); for the absence of possessions, see also 272–73 (10.6).

[172] Manu, *Laws*, 122 (6.52).

[173] Basham, *Wonder that was India*, 159.

loosely bound—are outlandishly iniquitous. There was accordingly nothing in the European tradition that could be invoked to mitigate the incompatibility of the traditional Hindu social ideal with modern egalitarianism.[174] In addition, we should not forget the standard inequalities relating to women, false believers, and slaves. Admittedly the last two were not of great consequence. With regard to false believers, the Hindu heritage was more broadly tolerant than that of Islam, let alone Christianity;[175] and as in the Islamic case, the worldwide abolition of slavery meant that this traditional institution came to be more or less irrelevant. But the situation with regard to women looked far worse from a European perspective: child brides were married off even younger, and widows belonging to respectable castes were not permitted to remarry—indeed they might even be expected to immolate themselves on the funeral pyres of their husbands. Altogether, the flagrantly exotic inegalitarianism of the Hindu heritage did not fit well with the liberal view of things, and it did even worse with the leftist perspective, consecrating a social order that any leftist worth his salt would itch to demolish. There was thus little in the Hindu tradition that could be expected to resonate positively with European social values of any stripe, and this under conditions of prolonged European rule over the subcontinent.

The other, and ultimately more potent, reason for the public relations problem was a change affecting the mass of the Indian population. The British slowly set about introducing the institutions of electoral democracy to their Indian empire, and these institutions have been maintained and developed in independent India far more successfully than in most non-Western societies. In such a setting an unbending hierarchism is not a viable basis for mass politics, for the same reason

[174] One could, of course, respond that the absence of caste in Europe was Europe's problem, not India's. In 1898 a conservative Konkaṇastha Brahmin explained that Indian society, being older than that of Europe, had evolved further, and that Europe too would in due course advance to the level of a caste society (Lederle, *Philosophical trends*, 203–7). But in British India this ingenious argument was unlikely to cut much ice.

[175] An interesting Hindu discussion of toleration and its limits is found in the *Āgamaḍambara*, a play by the tenth-century Kashmiri scholar Jayanta Bhaṭṭa (Bhaṭṭa Jayanta, *Much ado about religion*). In a nutshell, religions whose beliefs one considers false, like Buddhism and Jainism, may be tolerated if they are old-established; religions that should be persecuted by the political authorities are those subversive of the social order (see, for example, 120–21, 130–31, 134–37, 250–53). Whether a newly formed but nonsubversive religion can be tolerated is left unclear. The limits of traditional Hindu toleration perhaps deserve more attention than they get in the secondary literature.

that a return to the ancien régime would not fly in Europe: emancipated majorities will not vote for it.

The result was that only conservatives with no stake in mass politics had much reason to invoke the Hindu heritage as a social vision, and even in their case its attractiveness in the end was limited. Some conservatives, of course, were robust enough to persevere. Śraddhā Rām in the nineteenth-century Punjab was unflinching: "If we are Hindus . . . then we should accept the commands of the Dharma Shastras without the why and the how of it, and if we accept the Dharma Shastras then we must also certainly accept the prohibition against touching low castes and eating things from their hands. . . . Meeting, touching, eating, drinking with them is forbidden in our Shastras."[176] Likewise a twentieth-century professor of Hindu law in Benares has no truck with Western notions of equality, whether between members of different castes or between the sexes (the latter a topic on which his observations are calculated to give even the mildest feminist apoplexy).[177] He emphasizes that the Hindu social system "has, at no place and for no purpose, admitted the truth of the principle of equality,"[178] and he contrasts "the unnatural doctrines of equality and freedom" with "the fundamental principles behind the Hindu Social Order."[179] Naturally "the hereditary caste" forms an integral part of this social order, alongside "the patrilineal family."[180] Another twentieth-century Hindu traditionalist is equally inflexible: "The alteration or abrogation of the *varṇa* plan by the State or mass action is not permissible, in the view of Dharmaśāstra, and it will also be futile, as it rests on Divine sanction and births are regulated by an inflexible law of Karma."[181]

But such intransigence presented too inviting a target to an increasingly vocal enemy. Phule called on the "cunning Aryan Brahmins" to "totally destroy their wicked books" that enjoined them to treat Śūdras and Untouchables as "serfs and helots,"[182] while Āmbeḍkar urged his

[176] K. W. Jones, "Two *sanātan dharma* leaders," 230, 231. Compare the Varṇāśrama Dharma movement established by Tamil Brahmins in 1915, and denounced by a fellow Brahmin as an "obscurantist body" (Irschick, *Politics and social conflict*, 299–301).

[177] For example, he says of the wife: "As her personality is to merge in that of her husband, naturally, she is to be . . . continuously under his complete domination" (Deshpande, *Dharma-shastra*, 49).

[178] Ibid., 139.

[179] Ibid., 145.

[180] Ibid., 47, 154. Caste is "the main social unit of this order" (145).

[181] Rangaswami Aiyangar, *Hindu view of life*, 99. Compare the remarks made by the Śankarācārya of Purī in Poona, above, 104.

[182] Phule, *Collected works*, 2: 11, quoted in A. Sharma, *Modern Hindu thought*, 146.

people to convert to another religion because Hindu law (*dharma*) "cannot change as it is eternal."[183] In the face of such attacks, a different tone was in order. Thus Ṭiḷak, himself a Citpāvan Brahmin, is said to have taken the bull by the horns in addressing a low-caste audience in 1918: "If God were to tolerate untouchability I would not recognize Him as God at all."[184] Others backed away from the old forms of caste discrimination with less rhetorical panache. The early Hindu nationalist who complained about "water-tight compartments" argued for cross-caste marriages to bind society together.[185] In 1981 a large number of Tamil religious figures assembled at a Hindu Solidarity Conference in the very village where so many Untouchables had recently caused public outrage by converting to Islam; they solemnly declared "that our Vedas and Shastras have not mentioned untouchability in any form, anywhere but have propounded only complete brotherhood."[186] Brotherhood aside, they may have had a point regarding the Vedas, but what they said about the traditional legal literature was at best a saffron lie.[187]

The irreconcilable tensions at work in all this are dramatized in the iconic—and anti-iconic—role of Manu. In the nineteenth century Dayānand clung to the book even as he moved away from its conception of social hierarchy,[188] whereas Phule roundly denounced it[189]—he would doubtless have placed it at the head of the "wicked books" he urged the Brahmins to destroy. In the twentieth century Manu became a favorite target of low-caste intellectuals and politicians, who sometimes destroyed the book themselves. Achūtānand strongly criticized it.[190] Āmbeḍkar burnt it in 1927 on the suggestion of a Citpāvan Brahmin associate, thereby causing shock in the higher reaches of Hindu society and awe among the Untouchables.[191] The same use was made of

[183] Gokhale, *From concessions to confrontation*, 164.

[184] Keer, *Lokamanya Tilak*, 395. To this, however, he added a less encouraging statement: "Many ask me what I am prepared to do personally in this behalf. I answer it is not my work." For his caste background, see Lederle, *Philosophical trends*, 244.

[185] Jaffrelot, *Hindu nationalist movement*, 20–21. See above, 95.

[186] Ibid., 349. See above, 78.

[187] See the discussion in Kane, *History of Dharmaśāstra*, 2: 164–79.

[188] Jordens, *Dayānanda Sarasvatī*, 44, 62, 231–32, 249, 283–84.

[189] O'Hanlon, *Caste, conflict*, 125, 146, and cf. 147–48; Phule, *Collected works*, 2: 31, 51, 84.

[190] Jaffrelot, *India's silent revolution*, 203. For an Ādi-dharm view of Manu, see Juergensmeyer, *Religion as social vision*, 45–46.

[191] Gokhale, *From concessions to confrontation*, 94; Jaffrelot, *India's silent revolution*, 203.

the book in the Tamil country, for example in 1928.[192] Nearly fifty years after Āmbeḍkar's burning, the Dalit Panthers repeated the outrage.[193] In the debate on the Maṇḍal report in the legislature in 1982, one Untouchable speaker—a member of a pig-herding caste—denounced caste hierarchy as inherent in Hinduism and cited Manu to prove his point.[194] Kānśī Rām stigmatized the twice-born as "Manuists" (Manuvādīs) and in 1998 demanded that a statue of Manu be removed from the premises of the Jaipur High Court;[195] in the same year a member of his party explained in an interview that "humans have a birth right to live in dignity and honour but this Manuwadi social structure . . . took away from me this basic human right."[196] When the RSS organized a Hindu unity procession directed against the Muslims in Poona in 1982, they still had the cheek to carry with them a copy of Manu; but they deftly neutralized it by bearing giant portraits of Phule and Āmbeḍkar (not to mention Gandhi), together with bells intended to "symbolically toll for the death of Untouchability."[197] The same sensibility can be discerned in the call of a VHP leader in 1993 for the incorporation of Āmbeḍkar's "preachings" into "a new *Manusmriti* for a modern Hindu society."[198] Manu may still be something of a conservative icon, but if left unreconstructed he is also a serious liability.

So it is not surprising that the Hindu nationalists, despite the origins of their movement among the higher castes and its continuing affinity for them, do not campaign on the basis of the preservation or restoration of the class system. In this respect they are a long way out from their heritage and in a situation very different from that of the Islamists. Moreover, their distance from their heritage lies not just in their sometimes halfhearted rejection of the inequality of the traditional social vision but also in their wholehearted call for solidarity—something the Islamists can find in their heritage with no trouble at all. Hence the best the Hindu nationalists can do in their quest for

[192] Irschick, *Politics and social conflict*, 339 and n68; Jaffrelot, *India's silent revolution*, 171. See also Richman, "Ramasami's reading," 177, 182, 199n26.

[193] Gokhale, *From concessions to confrontation*, 95.

[194] Jaffrelot, *India's silent revolution*, 329.

[195] Ibid., 391 and n12.

[196] Ibid., 406.

[197] Jaffrelot, "Politics of processions," 76. For another example of Hindu nationalist deference to "Mahatma Phule" and Āmbeḍkar, see Jaffrelot, *Hindu nationalism*, 277 (and see 264, 266 for Āmbeḍkar).

[198] Hansen, *Saffron wave*, 227. He goes on to say that "the beauty of Hindu society is its infinite capacity for change," an aesthetic that would not be shared by the Salafīs.

solidarity is to emulate the Muslims.[199] At the same time their heritage gives them few resources with which to cultivate a relationship with the poor—it took Gandhi's fertile imagination to synthesize a liberation theology in the Hindu context.[200] The tradition of religious poverty does do something for them but only by conferring authority on Hindu nationalist saints like Ritambarā.

4. Latin American Catholicism

The shape of the ideal Christian society is, if anything, even less determinate than that of its Islamic counterpart. The message of the Gospels presupposed the imminent coming of the Kingdom of God; in the meantime what Christians had to do was not to try to reform the society in which they found themselves but rather to drop out of it—even to the extent of hating their own parents and parting with all their possessions in order to become disciples of Jesus.[201] In the event, of course, the Kingdom did not come, and Christians gradually adapted to this. Yet a figure as late and influential as Augustine (d. 430)—a century after the conversion of Constantine (ruled 306–337)—still saw Christians as strangers to the surrounding society, relating to it in a manner that was at once transient and pragmatic; in effect they were a celestial diaspora.[202] Hence it is not surprising that Christianity has proved comfortable with societies of a variety of shapes—including, for example, the caste society of colonial Latin America—and that it has readily accommodated the standard inequalities affecting women, false believers, and slaves. This does not mean, however, that there is no distinctive social message to attend to in the foundational texts of the religion. In particular, the New Testament has a lot to say about the poor—a feature of the religion that had precedent in ancient Israel and was to an extent inherited by Islam. We can arrange the material under three heads.

The first is charity. Here we find the familiar idea that it is virtuous for the rich to contribute some of their wealth for the welfare of the poor and that they will be rewarded for doing so in the next world. Thus Jesus takes it for granted that giving alms is in itself meritorious

[199] See 95, and cf. 237.

[200] See 434–35.

[201] See, for example, Luke 14:26–27, 33, and cf. below, 440.

[202] As a sixteenth-century English preacher put it, "Paradise is our native country" (Walzer, *Revolution of the saints*, 130). For Augustine's views see also below, 297–98.

when he teaches that in order to be rewarded one must do it inconspicuously (Matt. 6:1–4). The implication is that the rich may continue to be rich provided they are generous to the poor. Thus Jesus tells his Pharisee host, "When thou makest a feast, call the poor, the maimed, the lame, the blind," in reward for which he would be recompensed at the Resurrection (Luke 14:13–14), and Paul writes to Timothy that he should instruct those who are "rich in this world" to be "rich in good works, ready to distribute" (1Tim. 6:17–18). A more drastic case concerns a wealthy but repentant tax collector who has much to atone for; he finds grace when he declares that he will give half his goods to the poor (Luke 19:8). All this encourages the rich to take measures to alleviate the poverty of those less fortunate than themselves. It does not aspire to abolish either wealth or poverty; as Jesus memorably points out to his disciples, "Ye have the poor with you always, and whensoever ye will ye may do them good" (Mark 14:7; cf. Matt. 26:11 and John 12:8). Overall, there is nothing distinctive about this emphasis on charity: as we have seen, it is also conspicuous in Islam and present in Hinduism.

Alongside this emphasis on charity we have the voluntary poverty of Jesus and his followers. When he sends out the twelve disciples to preach to "the lost sheep of the house of Israel," he instructs them: "Provide neither gold, nor silver, nor brass in your purses, nor scrip for your journey, neither two coats, neither shoes, nor yet staves" (Matt. 10:9–10; similarly Mark 6:8–9; Luke 9:3). Likewise when he sends the seventy ahead of him, he tells them, "Carry neither purse, nor scrip, nor shoes" (Luke 10:4). On one occasion he was accosted by a rich young man anxious to secure eternal life. When the young man pressed him with the question what he should do over and above keeping the commandments, Jesus replied: "If thou wilt be perfect, go and sell that thou hast, and give to the poor, and thou shalt have treasure in heaven: and come and follow me" (Matt. 19:21, Mark 10:21, Luke 18:22; and cf. Luke 12:33, 14:33). Jesus himself shared in this holy poverty: as Paul wrote about him to the Corinthians, "though he was rich, yet for your sakes he became poor, that ye through his poverty might be rich" (2 Corinthians 8:9). This is not to say that the New Testament supports the later Franciscan idea of the *absolute* poverty of Jesus and his apostles: on one occasion Jesus was alone at a well because "his disciples were gone away unto the city to buy meat" (John 4:8).[203] But

[203] For other verses that presuppose that the disciples had money to buy provisions, see John 6:5, 13:29. These were key proof-texts for the anti-Franciscan argument (see Lambert, *Franciscan poverty*, 140).

their *relative* poverty is not in question. Like charity, holy poverty is a familiar theme; it is more deeply rooted in Hinduism than in Islam, but it is present in both.

The third head brings us to something much more distinctive: the sense that the very poverty of the poor confers on them a special status in the present and marks them out for a glorious future from which the rich are pretty much excluded. Thus, in Nazareth Jesus gave it to be understood that the Lord had anointed him "to preach the gospel to the poor" (Luke 4:18, quoting Isaiah 61:1). To return to the rich young man in quest of eternal life, at first Jesus had told him that he had only to keep the commandments (Matt. 19:17, Mark 10:19, Luke 18:20), but after the young man had departed sorrowfully, Jesus made the comment: "It is easier for a camel to go through the eye of a needle, than for a rich man to enter into the kingdom of God" (Matt. 19:24, Mark 10:25, Luke 18:25). The parable of Dives and Lazarus carries the same message: after their deaths the rich man who dines sumptuously goes to hell, while the poor man who had desired to be fed from the crumbs falling from the rich man's table is carried by the angels into Abraham's bosom (Luke 16:19–31). Another striking formulation comes in the Sermon on the Plain: "Blessed be ye poor: for yours is the kingdom of God. . . . But woe unto you that are rich! for ye have received your consolation" (Luke 6:20, 24; cf. Matt. 5:3). As we read in the epistle of James: "Hath not God chosen the poor of this world rich in faith, and heirs of the kingdom which he hath promised to them that love him?" (James 2:5). The echoes of this preference for the poor are only faintly audible in the Islamic heritage and entirely absent from that of Hinduism.

How early Christian attitudes to the poor played out in Christian societies down the ages is a story we must leave aside, but by way of illustration a recent study conveys a vivid sense of what these values meant for the newly Christianized high society of late antiquity. There was a major contrast between pagan and Christian values with regard to charitable giving.[204] Traditional Roman aristocrats were generous, but their generosity was directed to those who had particular claims on them—their relatives, clients, dependents, and above all fellow citizens. Many of these might happen to be poor, but their poverty was not of the essence; for a rich aristocrat the most imaginatively gripping act of generosity was to display his love of his home city (*amor civicus*) by

[204] See P. Brown, *Eye of a needle*, chaps. 3–4.

spending vast sums on splendid edifices and spectacular games, in return for which he would receive the loud acclamation of the assembled citizens.[205] By contrast, what gripped the Christian imagination was the disbursement of charity to the poor irrespective of worldly ties and in expectation not of any immediate acclamation on earth but rather of the eventual enjoyment of treasure accumulated in heaven.[206] This was a far-reaching reshaping of the emotional economy of giving, and with all due qualification it is also likely to have had a palpable impact at a more material level.[207] The respect of the elite for voluntary poverty was less of a novelty; in place of the Cynics there were now monks practicing absolute poverty,[208] not to mention occasional aristocrats inspired by the Gospels to sell all they had and give the proceeds to the poor.[209] But one aspect of the Christian focus on the poor still remained latent in this period and long after: the sense of the poor as the beneficiaries of a coming redemption.[210]

What, then, has this heritage meant under modern conditions? Catholicism in Latin America has interacted with conservatism, with leftism, and with liberalism. But we can best leave the interaction with liberalism to a later chapter.[211]

On the conservative side traditional Catholicism has shown a predictable elective affinity for the right: progressive secular ideologies are the common enemy of conservatives and believers. We see this affinity at work in a diffuse form in the tendency for political and religious conservatism to overlap in Latin America at large, with a small number of organizations representing the Catholic right playing a limited role in the background.[212] The interaction had a sharper focus in the intense confrontation of the Cristero rebels with the Mexican state. But the sharpness of focus in this case was primarily a reaction to the flagrantly anticlerical—indeed antireligious—policies of the revolutionary regime. In the social domain it would be hard to identify anything

[205] See, for example, ibid., 53, 59, 62, 64–65, 68, 73, 87.

[206] See, for example, ibid., 53–54, 72, 75, 83–84.

[207] For the qualifications, see ibid., 53, 59–60, 75, 80–81.

[208] Cf. ibid., 265–66, 319.

[209] For a wry account of a young couple who made a career of this, see ibid., 291–300. As a hard-line Pelagian statement of 414 put it: "A rich man who remains in his riches will not enter the Kingdom of God unless he sells all that he has" (320).

[210] Perhaps the closest we get to it is the idea that Christ might be hiding among the poor (ibid., 319, 509–10).

[211] See 352–53.

[212] See, for example, Peña, *Theologies and liberation*, 21–25 on the indigenous Sodalitium Vitae, and 26–32 on the international Opus Dei.

we could call a Cristero vision of the ideal society, over and above the fact that it would not be godless. For one thing the Cristeros came from two very different social milieux: the insurrection drew its leadership from educated urban Catholics but found much of its rank and file among a peasantry that practiced an Amerindian folk Catholicism.[213] For another thing the peasantry itself was riven by quarrels over land, and the massive intervention of the revolutionary state in these festering disputes through land reform produced as much entropy as polarization in the countryside.[214] Thus neither the heritage of the Cristeros nor their situation favored the articulation of a coherent social vision.

On the leftist side our main concern is with Liberation Theology.[215] But the social concern that we see in Liberationism was not, of course, new to the Church. Social Catholicism was already a significant strain in nineteenth-century Europe, where it received a real if qualified endorsement from Leo XIII (in office 1878–1903) in his encyclical *Rerum novarum* of 1891.[216] As might be expected, this European development influenced Latin American Catholics. Thus in the first decade of the twentieth century, Catholic congresses were meeting in Mexico to consider what landlords should do for rural laborers, the plight of the Amerindian population, and the problems of urban workers.[217] In 1899 a Brazilian priest had written that the mission of the Brazilian clergy should be "to show the weak, the poor, the proletarians, that they are the preferred people of the Divine Master."[218] Indeed already in the middle of the nineteenth century, Bolivia was ruled for a few years by a populist with radical ideas who "expressed himself in terms of Christian socialism."[219] But such Catholic social concern had never before been so widespread or so prominent as it became in the second half of

[213] See Purnell's account of the folk Catholicism of the village of San Juan Parangaricutiro, centered on the dancing cult of the Lord of the Miracles (Purnell, *Popular movements*, 139–41).

[214] For an intriguing study of the local dynamics of the rural Cristiada, see Purnell's account of the rivalry between the two neighbouring Purépecha villages of San Juan Parangaricutiro and Paricutín in Michoacán (ibid., chap. 6); the first joined the Cristero rebels, the second fought for the regime.

[215] I am indebted to Paul Hooper for valuable research assistance with the bibliography of Liberation Theology.

[216] For the nuances of *Rerum novarum*, see Misner, *Social Catholicism in Europe*, 214–22. For the later development of such thinking, see Curran, *Catholic social teaching*, 198–209.

[217] For this record, see Bailey, *¡Viva Cristo Rey!*, 15–17.

[218] Mainwaring, *Catholic Church and politics*, 37.

[219] For the presidency of Manuel Isidoro Belzú (1848–1855) see Klein, *Bolivia*, 128–30.

the twentieth century, when the Liberationists gave it expression in a new and radical idiom.

As we will see in a later chapter, Liberation Theology can be thought of as a Catholic reception or emulation of Marxist revolutionary thought.[220] Crucial to the facilitation of this interaction was the New Testament attitude to the poor. It did not, however, extend to every aspect of this attitude. The Biblical endorsement of charity did not really suit the purposes of the Liberationists. Being modern and progressive, their ambition was not to alleviate poverty but to abolish it. As Gutiérrez tells us: "Poverty is an evil, a scandalous condition. . . . To eliminate it is to bring closer the moment of seeing God face to face."[221] He reads this radical rejection of poverty into scripture: "In the Bible poverty is a scandalous condition inimical to human dignity and therefore contrary to the will of God."[222] Moreover, the Liberationists sought to eliminate poverty not by persuading the rich to be more generous with their almsgiving but by enabling the poor to liberate themselves. The idea of holy poverty was considerably more appealing for the Liberationists than that of charity since it encouraged them to go about their work in a style that resonated with the poverty around them. "Christian poverty, an expression of love, . . . is solidarity *with the poor* and is a protest *against poverty*. . . . It is a poverty lived . . . as an authentic imitation of Christ."[223] The church itself was accordingly to be a poor church.[224] But the key thing the New Testament had to offer the Liberationists was its preferential view of the poor. It provided the basis of their "solidarity with the poor," identified as "those privileged members of the reign of God."[225] The Liberationists could thus share "God's predilection for those on the lowest rung of the ladder of history," for "the weak and abused of human history."[226] At one point Gutiérrez quotes the Magnificat: "He hath filled the hungry with good things; and the rich he hath sent empty away" (Luke 1:53). He then transposes the exultation

[220] See 353–56.

[221] Gutiérrez, *Theology of liberation*, 168, and cf. xxi, 163, 171.

[222] Ibid., 165, and cf. xxii, xxv, 40, 164. In support he cites extensively from the Old Testament (166–68); the passages he quotes denounce the maltreatment of the poor but do not in fact condemn the existence of poverty as such.

[223] Ibid., 172. For the poverty of Jesus see also 162–63. We need not concern ourselves with the way in which Gutiérrez understands "spiritual poverty" (xxv, 169–71).

[224] Ibid., xli, xlv.

[225] Ibid., xviii. For this solidarity with the poor, see also xxv, 68, 172; for the poor as the privileged members of the reign of God, see also xxxiii. Here as elsewhere, "kingdom" would fit better than the translator's "reign."

[226] Ibid., xxvi, xxvii.

of scripture into a modern Liberationist idiom: "The future of history belongs to the poor and exploited. True liberation will be the work of the oppressed themselves; in them, the Lord saves history."[227] Here we have the heart of what we can fairly call the Liberationist cult of the poor.

The devotion of the Liberationists to social work in this spirit undoubtedly had a real impact on the lives of some ordinary Latin Americans. The extent of this impact can be hard to assess because it has often been studied by researchers who have more or less bought into the Liberationist self-image.[228] But one has the impression that at its most effective the appeal of Catholic activists to local populations was somewhat analogous to that of saints moving into rural communities in earlier epochs.[229] The activists possessed manifest sincerity and conviction, they could open the eyes of the uneducated to wider horizons,[230] they were outsiders to the petty feuds of the local society in which they went to work (often outsiders to Latin America altogether), and they benefited from the brand image of the church;[231] the result was that they could create a degree of trust among local actors who had previously mistrusted each other and thereby get them to cooperate in some measure.[232] All in all, the Liberationists did much to articulate and implement a socially concerned Catholicism.

And yet there seems to have been a profound mismatch between what the Liberationists wanted from the poor and what many of the poor wanted from the church. One does not have to be a cynical outsider to see that there must be a real question whether lay people who heard the liberationist message from their priestly mentors actually

[227] Ibid., 120.

[228] For one example among many, see Berryman, *Stubborn hope*, 11–13 (on a district in Guatemala in the 1970s). It would not be unfair to say that there is a dearth of properly academic writing on Liberation Theology; most studies are strongly colored by commitment, whether for or against. Hindu nationalism is significantly better served in this respect.

[229] I base this impression on D. H. Levine, *Popular voices*, especially chap. 8.

[230] "So I joined in all that and *boom*, my eyes were opened," as one layman put it (ibid., 275).

[231] This brand image is the payoff for the high overheads of the Catholic church (which are noted in Gill, *Rendering unto Caesar*, 179–80). By contrast, if a jumped-up Pentecostal pastor runs off with your wife and your money, you may have no institution to call to account.

[232] Levine, *Popular voices*, 285, 290, 298, 313. Compare the role of the Liberationist bishop Samuel Ruiz (d. 2011) of San Cristóbal (in office 1959–2000) as mediator in the stalemate following the military but not political failure of the Zapatista rebellion in Chiapas in 1994 (Womack, *Rebellion in Chiapas*, 44, 47; for a sketch of Ruiz, see 23–33).

internalized it; the issue was already raised by a sympathetic but realistic Jesuit writing in the early 1980s.[233] Part of the trouble was the initial tendency of the Liberationists to reject popular Catholicism[234]—a form of religion that struck them as superstitious and reactionary. But of more concern to us is the point that many, if not most, Catholics were not interested in having their religion packaged with social activism.[235] Two ethnographic works about localities in Brazil provide clear evidence of this allergy.

One is a study of São Jorge in the urban periphery of Rio de Janeiro based on fieldwork done in 1987–1988.[236] The author regards his work as "partly an effort to assist Catholic pastoral agents and clergy by identifying the external and internal obstacles to their project";[237] thus his attitude, though critical, is far from sour. He describes the negative views of Catholics who do not participate in Liberationist activities. "The Church is for praying," says one such woman, "not for talking about potholes."[238] A man comments: "That's the problem with these new priests. They're mixing religion and politics."[239] "In the Assembly, they don't mix things," affirms a young Pentecostalist, drawing an unfavorable contrast between the Catholic church and the Pentecostalist Assembly of God.[240] All this, of course, is predictable.

Less so is the extent to which these attitudes are shared by members of the laity who do participate in services, though without getting involved in social activism. In a common move one such woman tones down the Liberationist message by understanding it in traditional terms: "The Church is reminding us to help our brother, to practice charity." Going on to confront the Liberationist project a bit more directly, though hardly head-on, she adds, "Some do those other things, but I don't like them."[241] She, too, echoes the mixing theme: "Sometimes the priests, they mix things together, they get agitated."[242] A woman who had dutifully learnt the Liberationist discourse acknowledged that, as far as the social practice was concerned, she was "pretty disconnected

[233] Carvalho Azevedo, *Basic ecclesial communities*, 94–95; for the dating, see 251.
[234] Mainwaring, *Catholic Church and politics*, 174–75, 176–77.
[235] Ibid., 175.
[236] Burdick, *Looking for God* (for the location, see 10–12).
[237] Ibid., viii.
[238] Ibid., 204.
[239] Ibid., 205.
[240] Ibid., 206. The Assembly of God is Brazil's largest Pentecostal church (4).
[241] Ibid., 186, and see 185.
[242] Ibid., 187.

from that stuff" and went on to say that politics "shouldn't be mixed with religion."[243] During a service she was asked to read out a letter from the bishop calling for a march against violence. She did so, keeping to herself her view that this was "mixing politics and religion." A man in the congregation was less discreet, commenting: "This is absurd! That's not something to do in church!"[244]

More telling still are the attitudes of people who not only attend the services but also join in the social politics. One woman cuts this activism down to size: "Movements are fine. But they will get you nowhere; they are to improve a little, not to transform anything. The world will only be transformed when Jesus comes."[245] Another woman, who knew the discourse and participated in activist causes, simply fails to connect the two. Asked by the ethnographer why she attended a certain demonstration, she explains that Carmen had asked her to: "Well, I go to these things. I mean, when someone asks me, I go." Heavy prompting from the ethnographer about the relevance of Jesus' message eventually elicits a religiously correct response: "Yes, right, that's what Jesus wants us to do." But asked if she was thinking of that when she went on the march, she responds unhesitatingly, as if to a silly question: "No, of course not. I went because Carmen told me about it, said we should go."[246]

Not everyone is like this: there are people for whom it all comes together, but they are very much a minority. They speak the Liberationist discourse fluently, are involved in social movements, and consistently explain this involvement in Liberationist terms. "It was very exciting," says one such activist of her involvement in the scene that developed around the Liberationist Father Orlando, priest of her parish. "It all made sense to me, that the people had to organize and fight for its rights."[247] When the struggle did not go well, "it was the faith that Jesus had come for us, the poor and oppressed, that gave me courage."[248] But this woman, like others in the same category, was by no means representative of the Brazilian poor: she was well educated, and had she been born into a more meritocratic society she would

[243] Ibid., 188–89.

[244] Ibid., 189.

[245] Ibid., 191.

[246] Ibid., 192.

[247] Ibid., 199. Perhaps it was a little too exciting: the scene folded when Father Orlando had an affair with a married woman and had to leave the church (211).

[248] Ibid., 197.

easily have made the transition to the middle class.[249] If we leave aside this activist niche, it seems clear from this study of São Jorge that what the Liberationists were eager to supply was not what the market demanded; and the author adduces evidence that the problem was not just a local one.[250]

The other ethnographic study is about the Morro da Conceição—a poor neighborhood in the northeastern city of Recife—and is based on fieldwork done in 1990–1991.[251] The ethnographer tells a dramatic story with a background in the high politics of the church. From 1964 to 1985, Dom Hélder Câmara was archbishop of Olinda and Recife. A man of ebullient enthusiasm, in his youth he had combined the priesthood with a prominent role in the Integralist movement—"a simple green-shirted priest from Ceará," as he then liked to call himself.[252] But times had changed, and by now he had a new love, Liberation Theology. Under his benevolent episcopal aegis, the church on the Morro was entrusted in 1978 to Reginaldo Veloso and in his hands became a Liberationist hotbed.[253] However, on the archbishop's retirement in 1985 the Vatican appointed a conservative to replace him, an expert on canon law who lacked the social grace and personal charm of his predecessor.[254] A confrontation gradually built up between the new archbishop and Reginaldo, climaxing in 1990 with the eviction of Reginaldo from his church (that is to say, the community's church, or the Church's church, depending on one's point of view). Perhaps a little tactlessly, the eviction was effected by five truckloads of armed riot police.[255] Yet Reginaldo, though he lost his church, would not leave the community, which was now riven by schism between his Liberationist supporters and the traditional Catholics who rallied to the newly installed priest.[256] The schism would not go away, though

[249] Ibid., 197–98.

[250] Ibid., 5–6.

[251] Nagle, *Claiming the Virgin: the broken promise of liberation theology in Brazil.* The subtitle is misleading in suggesting a polemic against Liberation Theology. The author has not in fact bought into the worldviews of either side, even as a friendly critic, and has a fine eye for the human—not to say comical—dimensions of the story. The narrative core of the book stands out in the literature on Liberation Theology as immensely readable and illuminating.

[252] Todaro Williams, "Integralism," 444–45. Ceará is on the northeast coast of Brazil.

[253] Nagle, *Claiming the Virgin*, 51–52.

[254] Ibid., 58–59.

[255] Ibid., 82–83.

[256] Ibid., 55.

Reginaldo's support tended to dwindle—particularly when he married a woman half his age and thereby forfeited his claim to the priesthood.[257]

Against the background of this grand narrative of schism we get to see the attitudes of the lesser folk involved in the conflict. We encounter a familiar theme: "I saw that it wasn't religion, it was politics."[258] What is new is that we get a better sense of just what it is about this mixing of religion and politics that the traditionalists dislike so much. Two significant points emerge here. One is that the poor may value the very disconnection of the church from the heartless world of everyday life; as the author of the study puts it, "Reginaldo had removed their one sure solace and replaced it with reminders of the very problems from which they needed relief."[259] The other is that the poor may regard Liberationism as politically foolish. Does it really pay to prefer weak community organization to strong links with powerful patrons? One exasperated parishioner responded in this way to Reginaldo's extravagant denunciations of the rich: "We always need the rich. They do favors for us. Why should we alienate them? They have been our friends for years."[260] Another complained about the way Reginaldo had driven away the rich people who used to help out with the annual religious festival that brought numerous pilgrims to the Morro. He told the rich that "there was something wrong with them because they were better off than we are." And so indeed they were. "But we need help from people like that. It's just another way Reginaldo hurt the community."[261] A similar accusation was that the Liberationists with their unending protests—such as banging pots and pans in a demand for piped water on the Morro—"embarrassed us at city hall."[262] Angering those in power seemed a sure recipe for jeopardizing the potential

[257] Ibid., 94, 156–57.

[258] Ibid., 72.

[259] Ibid., 76. Compare Nagle's account of the attitude of the conservative archbishop: "For him, the church is a sanctuary of hope, calm, and forgiveness, an oasis of peace in a chaotic world" (57–58). A similar sentiment was expressed by Edmund Burke in response to a politically radical sermon preached by a nonconformist inspired by the French revolution: "No sound ought to be heard in the church but the healing voice of Christian charity." He likewise goes on to say, "Surely the church is a place where one day's truce ought to be allowed to the dissensions and animosities of mankind" (Burke, *Reflections*, 157).

[260] Nagle, *Claiming the Virgin*, 16–17.

[261] Ibid., 68.

[262] Ibid., 151, and more generally 149–51.

gains of the community in the future.[263] In actual fact the Liberationists appear to have been rather successful with their pots and pans: in place of the old well, there was now piped water three or four days a week.[264] But the traditionalists were not about to see it that way.

Studies such as these are no substitute for the comprehensive information that we do not have, and doubtless never will. But they are enough to suggest a fundamental dissonance between Liberation Theology and the attitudes of the masses it sought to mobilize. This helps to explain the fact that the Church's option for the poor was not reciprocated: as the witticism has it, the Church chose the poor, but the poor chose the Pentecostalists. That is to say, they chose a form of religion characterized, among other things, by the absence of social radicalism,[265] one more attuned to individual success in a market economy. This does not mean that Pentecostalists are inherently apolitical;[266] but political commitment is not central to their religious

[263] Ibid., 76.

[264] Ibid., 151, and cf. 153.

[265] This indifference to social activism was not inherently Protestant. A strain of Protestant Liberation Theology did exist in Latin America (see Deiros, "Protestant fundamentalism," 165–66, 188n76; Sigmund, *Liberation theology*, 53–55), and it could draw on the same scriptural resources as its Catholic counterpart. A Presbyterian missionary who at one time lived in Peru and was close to Haya de la Torre writes that the latter "made the discovery that in the writings of the Old Testament prophets and in the teachings of Jesus were more incandescent denunciations of oppression and wrong than he or his companions had ever made" (Mackay, *Other Spanish Christ*, 194; for Mackay's relationship with Haya de la Torre, see Pike, *Politics of the miraculous*, 47). Indeed one does not even have to be a Christian to be vouchsafed this insight: in a book published in 1873, Phule mentioned Christ and the Buddha as examples of popular heroes who protected the weak from oppressive authority (O'Hanlon, *Caste, conflict*, 137). But for whatever reasons, Liberationism was a predominantly Catholic persuasion, and Pentecostalism was not socially activist. One relevant point may be that most Pentecostalist pastors did not come from elite backgrounds and had not been students—Marxists, we should remember, are people who look *down* on the petty bourgeoisie, whereas Pentecostalist pastors have been known to dress *up* to make themselves look like executives (see Birman, "Future in the mirror," 67, in an account of the Universal Church of the Kingdom of God, a Pentecostalist movement in Brazil).

[266] The findings of the recent Pew Forum survey of Pentecostals and Charismatics in ten countries suggest that "the widespread perception of pentecostals as basically apolitical in outlook might need rethinking" (Pew Forum, *Spirit and power*, 2). More specifically, though focused on spiritual matters, many Pentecostals and Charismatics "also say there is a role for religion in politics and public life" (7), and they tend to the view that "religious groups should express their views on day-to-day social and political questions" (61, and see table, 62). On the other hand, "relatively few spend much time actually discussing political issues"; indeed, "in every country surveyed majorities of pentecostals say they never discuss politics with their friends and family or that they do so only once or twice a month" (66).

convictions, and the political activity they do engage in is not radical. Theirs is a milieu for which faith healing is of great importance and "liberation" (*liberación*) means exorcism.[267] It fits with this that by far the most effective Catholic response to the Pentecostal threat came not from Liberation Theology but from Charismatic Catholicism, which has been a serious competitor in the Latin American religious marketplace since the 1970s.[268] It was Catholicized Pentecostalism, not Catholicized Marxism, that was in demand.

5. Religious elites

Before we end this chapter, there is one further topic that needs a brief treatment, namely the role of religious elites. We can best address this by taking our three heritages together. In each case there was a readily identifiable, though not sharply delimited group in which the society's religious expertise was disproportionately vested. In the Muslim case, a saying of Muḥammad had it that the scholars (*ʿulamāʾ*) were the heirs of the prophets;[269] and in historical fact they had undoubtedly found recognition as Muḥammad's heirs within a century or two of his death. As a learned religious elite their role matched that of the Jewish rabbis, though it had taken the rabbis far longer to establish themselves as the heirs of Moses.[270] In the Hindu case, unlike the Muslim one, the basic qualification for a role of religious expertise, at least in mainstream settings, was lineage: when the four classes were assigned their tasks,

[267] For faith healing see Chesnut, *Competitive spirits*, 7, 45, 81, 152; for exorcism see 5.

[268] For the rise of the Catholic Charismatic renewal in Latin America, see ibid., chap. 4. Significantly, these Charismatics initially referred to themselves as "Pentecostal Catholics" (65); like Pentecostalism, the movement originated in the United States (66). In Latin America it expanded very rapidly in the 1980s (79). By the early 1990s, even in Brazil, Charismatics outnumbered members of base communities by a ratio of two to one (92). A rare writer on Liberation Theology to acknowledge the phenomenon is Nagle (*Claiming the Virgin*, 56, 179n3); researchers with Liberationist sympathies tend to have little empathy for the concern with spirit possession and faith healing that is central to Charismatic Catholicism, as it is to Pentecostalism.

[269] Wensinck, *Early Muhammadan tradition*, 234a.

[270] Moses was the greatest of the prophets but not the last (Deut. 18:15–19, 34:10–12), and the Jews began to claim that the age of the prophets was over only after the rise of Christianity; by contrast, the Muslim consensus rejecting the idea that there could be prophets after Muḥammad took shape very early (for this contrast see Friedmann, *Prophecy continuous*, 68–69). At the same time, the establishment of the Israelite temple cult was associated both with a strong assertion of the religious authority of the king (1 Kings 5–8) and with a hereditary priesthood.

teaching and learning went to the Brahmins[271]—though by no means all of them would in fact be active members of the religious elite. The Catholic case was different again: lineage came to be formally excluded though the development of a celibate clergy, but this exclusion was more than compensated for by a powerful ecclesiastical organization. And yet the Muslims scholars, who in general lacked either lineage or organization, proved remarkably resilient.

In the modern world these religious elites have suffered from the rise of a religious egalitarianism that emboldens lay believers to think for themselves about religious issues that concern them.[272] As Ḥasan al-Bannā puts it, "All Muslims from the least to the most outstanding of them, are 'religious authorities.' "[273] This is one factor tending to limit the role of all three religious elites in modern politics. Of the men in saffron we need say only that their role in the Hindu nationalist movement has been rather marginal.[274] Something similar could be said of the largely clerical exponents of Liberation Theology in Latin America with respect to leftist politics. Likewise the Muslim scholars have not been immune to the diminution of their religious authority; Ḥasan al-Bannā is typical of the antipathy of Islamists, who are mostly laymen, to anything resembling a monopoly of religious authority on the part of the scholars.[275] The Shīʿite experience, in which the clerics were able to establish a political hegemony through the Iranian revolution of 1979, is, of course, quite exceptional in the way it has swum against the

[271] Manu, *Laws*, 12–13 (1.88).

[272] I owe this point to Patricia Crone.

[273] Euben and Zaman, *Readings in Islamist thought*, 73.

[274] See 103–5.

[275] In this respect the Islamists are in tune (if a musical metaphor may be permitted) with an adventitiously modern feature of eighteenth-century Wahhābism. Muḥammad ibn ʿAbd al-Wahhāb wrote a short epistle clearly intended for the laity in which he set out the basics of monotheism in the form of four simple principles (*qawāʿid*). The epistle exists in many different texts; one version is distinguished, among other things, by the fact that it does not just instruct ordinary believers, it shows them how they themselves can use the simple arguments of the epistle to confound the polytheists around them (see, for example, the text in Ibn Qāsim, *al-Durar al-saniyya*, 2: 19–21). Another text of the epistle, drawn to my attention by Samer Traboulsi, is to be found in the chronicle of the Yemeni historian Luṭf Allāh Jaḥḥāf (d. 1827–1828) under the events of the year 1797–1798 (*Durar nuḥūr al-ḥūr al-ʿīn*, 653–56); he records it in connection with the reception of Wahhābism in ʿAsīr. The point of interest is that he describes how the text was used in instructing people in their religion: it was memorized by all and sundry (old and young, male and female, free and slave), and they in turn would teach it to their families and anyone else they could spread it to (653.6, 656.15).

tide of lay modernity.[276] But the decline in the authority of the Sunnī scholars, though real, has not been catastrophic,[277] and they retain a significant amount of soft power in the political arena. One jihadi writing confidentially to another about the struggle in occupied Iraq lays great emphasis on the importance of not alienating the scholars under present conditions; he writes that it is simply a fact, whether we like it or not, that the scholars are the keys to the Muslim community (*mafātīḥ al-umma*) and its leadership.[278]

6. Conclusion

If we are looking for a heritage with a clear and distinctive vision of what society should look like, then the only one of the three that can offer this is Hinduism. Under contemporary conditions, however, this vision is a public relations disaster. There is no way to square its ostentatious hierarchism with modern European—now global—values and no way to market it to those at the bottom of society once they have other options. Even such euphemisms as telling the Untouchables that they are eligible for high-level positions in sanitation departments are likely to prove counterproductive.[279] Not surprisingly the Hindu nationalists, who despite the fact that they often come from high-caste backgrounds are in the business of mass politics, do not base their ideology on this aspect of the Hindu heritage; quite the contrary, their aspiration is to create out of the medley of the Hindu castes "one single homogenous family."[280] By contrast, neither the Islamic nor the Catholic heritage offers a comprehensive social vision to match that of Hinduism. Where the Islamic heritage stands apart is in providing a compelling parallel to European egalitarianism. Without question this has been one of the most attractive features of this heritage under modern conditions, a source of almost lyrical inspiration to leading Islamists. The parallel is, of course, an imperfect one. First, Muslim egalitarianism

[276] For an Indian Sunnī scholar who favored such an arrangement in the mid-twentieth century, see Zaman, "South Asian Islam," 65–67.

[277] For a balanced assessment of this effect, see Zaman, *Ulama*, 1–2, 83–86.

[278] Letter to Abū Muṣʿab al-Zarqāwī (d. 2006), the leader of al-Qāʿida in Mesopotamia, from a certain ʿAṭiyya, 2005 (dated 10 Dhū ʾl-Qaʿda 1426), 3.38 = 9 of the English translation on the same website).

[279] See 420.

[280] See 80–81.

does not apply to all and sundry—leaving Mawdūdī to underline the point that the wrong concept of equality is not to be applied to women. Secondly, this egalitarianism goes with a higher valuation of solidarity than is to be found within the liberal mainstream of European values. But the resonance is real. Meanwhile the Catholic heritage stands out by virtue of the scriptural foundation it provides for the Liberationist cult of the poor, an asset that in the Latin American context made possible a Catholic appropriation of some of the central ideas of Marxism. This syncretism may have had only a limited appeal among the Latin American poor, but it tapped a resource in the Catholic heritage to which Hinduism offered no parallel and that had a serious Islamic counterpart only among the Shīʿites.

CHAPTER 5

Warfare

1. Introduction

Religious heritages differ widely in the stances they take toward warfare. We can easily illustrate the point with two contrasting Indian religions, Buddhism and Sikhism. On the Buddhist side one canonical text warns us that "a man or woman who kills living beings, who is murderous, who has blood on his or her hands, who is given to blows and violence, who is without pity for living beings" will earn a rebirth "in a state of misfortune, an unhappy place, a state of affliction, hell."[1] In case anyone should think that soldiers might be professionally exempt from this fate, another canonical text describes how various members of this occupational category came to the Buddha, telling him they had heard it said that a soldier killed in battle would be reborn among the gods; the Buddha condemned this belief and told them that they would in fact be reborn in hell.[2] On the Sikh side things could hardly be more different. According to one Sikh rule book, "The Sikh who ventures out unarmed shall be doomed to continued transmigration," whereas a Sikh who fights "will win salvation."[3] Another such text states: "The command of the Gurus is 'Fight the barbarians, destroy them all!'"—the barbarians, as the context makes clear, being the Muslims.[4] The same text quotes the wish of the tenth Guru to die in battle,[5] avers that the Sikh who bears arms will always worship his weapon, and informs us that the Guru "approves of warfare."[6] Buddhist pacifism and Sikh militancy could thus be seen as marking the opposite ends of the doctrinal spectrum.

[1] Gethin, "Buddhist monks," 62. See also Schmithausen, "Buddhist attitude towards war," 45.

[2] Gethin, "Buddhist monks," 62, and see also 72; also Schmithausen, "Buddhist attitude towards war," 48.

[3] McLeod, *Textual sources*, 77–78; and see McLeod, *Chaupa Singh Rahit-nama*, 171 §190, 173 §250.

[4] McLeod, *Chaupa Singh Rahit-nama*, 150 §10, and see 213n32.

[5] Ibid., 160 §121.

[6] Ibid., 171 §196, §200. Such rule books are likely to date from the eighteenth or early nineteenth centuries.

On a more mundane level things are inevitably more blurred. No religion that enjoys the loyalty of a significant number of people over an extended period can consistently place itself at either end of this spectrum. Both war and peace are inescapable realities of human life, and a doctrine that categorically rejects one or the other is in the long run unsustainable. In the Buddhist case, at least in the Theravada tradition, the moment of truth came in Ceylon when the Buddhist king Duṭṭhagāmaṇī triumphed over the non-Buddhist Tamil invaders in the second century BC, or whenever it was that the story took shape between then and the redaction of our source toward 500. When this king became distraught at the carnage, we read, eight Buddhist saints arrived by air to reassure him that he would still get to heaven since almost all of those slain were "unbelievers and men of evil life" who were "not more to be esteemed than beasts"[7]—as if Tamils and beasts were not among the "living beings" of the canonical text. Unsurprisingly we encounter this story in the preaching of Buddhist monks in Sri Lanka during the recent civil war with the Tamil Tigers.[8] Other ideas developed to justify the violence of, for example, Buddhist monks in medieval Japan.[9] In the Sikh case the moment of truth came much earlier in relative terms. In one of the sources quoted above, we read

[7] Gethin, "Buddhist monks," 62–63; Schmithausen, "Buddhist attitude towards war," 56–57 (for similar sentiments in Mahāyāna Buddist texts, see 57–58). Contrast the remorse felt by the north Indian emperor Aśoka a century earlier following his conquest of Kalinga, which led him to adopt a notion of peaceful victory (*dhammavijaya*, "victory by *dharma*"), in which nobody gets hurt (see the translation of the relevant rock edict in Thapar, *Aśoka*, 255–57; for the relevant passages in the original texts, see U. Schneider, *Grossen Felsen-Edikte Aśokas*, 76 P, 78 U, 80 X, and Schneider's commentary, 174). Unfortunately this well-meaning idea does not seem to have had much of a future.

[8] See Kent, "Onward Buddhist soldiers," 166–67, and cf. 169.

[9] For the strategies used to legitimate their use of armed force, see Taira, "La légitimation de la violence," 100–103; and cf. also Adolphson, *Teeth and claws*, 55 (I owe my knowledge of both these studies to Kazuo Morimoto). Taira's analysis shows that, as might be expected, these strategies do not call in question the basic principle of nonviolence but rather seek to sideline or override it; thus a document of 1173 presents a refusal to soil one's hands with violence for the sake of the well-being of all creatures as a Hinayana trait associated with an exclusive concern for individual salvation (Taira, "La légitimation de la violence," 101–2). Perhaps the most notorious development of Buddhist militancy in Japan took place in the chaotic conditions of the sixteenth century. At least in the case of the leading Pure Land sect, the Honganji, the leadership seems not to have confronted the problem of finding a Buddhist justification for warfare (Tsang, *War and faith*, 228), though Pure Land priests of the Jishū sect had special battlefield rituals to help warriors attain rebirth in the Pure Land despite dying in a state of sin (288n88). There was a popular but unorthodox belief among Honganji members that fighting in defense of the sect would guarantee rebirth in the Pure Land, and the patriarch of the sect seems to have done nothing to discourage this idea (231). It fits with this that we hear

that members of the community "who are employed by a Muslim administration" should be forgiven their inability to observe the rules in return for a money offering; other Sikhs are not to place obstacles in their way.[10] What we see here is not just a failure to destroy the barbarians, it is active collaboration with them. In sum, neither Buddhists nor Sikhs can be relied on to speak—let alone act—as their highest principles require.

One could accordingly ask whether the contrast between Buddhist and Sikh principles makes any difference in the real world.[11] Other things being equal, do Sikhs have a greater propensity to engage in warfare than Buddhists?[12] And when they do engage in warfare, is it more likely to acquire a strong religious coloring among Sikhs than among Buddhists? The second seems more likely to me than the first, particularly in insurrectionary contexts where military force must be generated by mass mobilization. But this last point aside, I shall make little attempt to engage with these questions. Instead I shall set out from a more modest assumption: that those who want to be militant are more likely to invoke their religious heritages if they can find in them strong support for their militancy.

How then do the Islamic, Hindu, and Catholic heritages regard warfare—and in particular, warfare directed against members of other religious communities?[13]

---

of a banner borne into battle with the injunction: "Advance and be reborn in paradise. Retreat and fall immediately into hell" (229).

[10] McLeod, *Chaupa Singh Rahit-nama*, 156 §80, 183 §444–45, and see 219n106. There are three rules the violation of which cannot be forgiven, one of them being the shaving of the head or beard.

[11] For an interesting account of the difference it made in the context of the war against the Tamil Tigers in Sri Lanka, see Frydenlund, "Canonical ambiguity." Monks do not fight (108–9), and it is not appropriate for them to make outright demands for war (102), though they can call for the protection of the country (97, 102–3); when consoling soldiers they do not readily provide outright justification for the use of violence (109). Soldiers need to be consoled because they are concerned about the effects of their violence on their future rebirths (106, 109), and they may not pray to the Buddha for military success (104). For all this, see also Kent, "Onward Buddhist soldiers." None of these problems would arise in an Islamic context. Monks nevertheless played a significant role in preventing the resolution of the conflict through political compromise, and some of the military violence was atrocious. The volumes containing the papers of Frydenlund and Kent offer several further studies of Buddhist accommodations of military violence.

[12] Other things are not, of course, equal: there have been many Buddhist states in history, some of them long lasting, but only one relatively short-lived Sikh state.

[13] Note that this chapter does not attempt to cover the regulation of the conduct of warfare, nor does it discuss rebellion against rulers deemed to have apostatized.

2. Islam

Muḥammad ruled in Medina for ten years, starting with his arrival from Mecca in 622 and ending with his death in 632. During this decade, according to one of the major sources for his life, he mounted sixty-five military expeditions against unbelievers (another source makes the total seventy-four).[14] Some were offensive, as with the battle of Badr, the conquest of Mecca, and the battle of Ḥunayn; others were defensive, as with the battles of Uḥud and the Khandaq. But the net effect of these expeditions was to establish Muḥammad's power on a reasonably firm basis in the Ḥijāz and to extend it more loosely over much, if not all, of Arabia. Warfare, then, was a prominent aspect of the Prophet's career in Medina.

Just as significant for our purposes is the character of this warfare. In terms of scale, the range was considerable. Many of Muḥammad's expeditions are described as involving rather small numbers of men; for example, the figures given for four of the earliest expeditions are sixty (or eighty), thirty, eight, and eight.[15] Some were just groups of commandos dispatched to assassinate one or another of Muḥammad's opponents.[16] Other expeditions, however, were larger, and these show the increasing scale of his military activity. Thus the same source tells us that he commanded 314 men at the battle of Badr in 624, 700 at the battle of Uḥud in 625, 3000 at the battle of the Khandaq in 627, 700 or 1400 on the way to Ḥudaybiya in 628, 10,000 at the conquest of Mecca in 630, and 12,000 at the battle of Ḥunayn in the same year.[17] Yet even these larger figures, assuming they are reliable, need to be put in perspective. First, as might be expected, they are rather small by the standards of imperial warfare outside Arabia.[18] Second, they do not reflect the emergence of a standing army. Despite the fact that Muḥammad was sending out an average of six or seven expeditions a year, he assembled each one sepa-

[14] Ibn Hisham, *Sīra*, 3–4: 608.13 = 659 (27 *ghazawāt*), 609.6 = 660 (38 *buʿūth* and *sarāyā*); Wāqidī, *Maghāzī*, 7.14 (27 *maghāzī*), 7.16 (47 *sarāyā*).

[15] Ibn Hishām, *Sīra*, 1–2: 591.14 = 281, 595.13 = 283, 600.13 = 286, 601.15 = 286.

[16] An example is the group of five men who used deceit to kill Kaʿb ibn al-Ashraf (ibid., 3–4: 54.10 = 367–68).

[17] Ibid., 1–2: 706.15 = 336 (Badr), 3–4: 65.19 = 373 (Uḥud), 220.2 = 452 (the Khandaq), 309.1 = 500 (Ḥudaybiya, and see 349.15, 350.4 = 521–22, supporting the larger figure), 400.4 = 545, 421.8 = 557 (the conquest of Mecca), and 440.17 = 567–68 (Ḥunayn).

[18] A.H.M. Jones, *Later Roman Empire*, 684–85.

rately; there was no body of regular troops, no permanent command, no continuing military structure of any kind.

Another noteworthy feature of Muḥammad's warfare was his own close involvement in it. He did not delegate military activity to a handful of generals. According to our source, he personally commanded twenty-seven of the sixty-five expeditions, including most of the larger ones;[19] for the other expeditions he appointed commanders, who typically never served more than once or twice in the role.[20] On nine occasions he was engaged in the actual fighting;[21] he was in the thick of it at Uḥud, where he was badly injured.[22] Nor was it only the fighting in which he participated: in the digging of the trench (*khandaq*) that gave the battle of the Khandaq its name, he joined in the work alongside his followers.[23] He made military judgment calls, and in this he was receptive to intelligent suggestions from his followers. Shortly before the battle of Badr, one of them came up to him and told him that he had chosen the wrong place to station his troops; Muḥammad heeded this advice[24] and won the battle. He might even be too receptive: in the discussion before the defeat at Uḥud, when the Meccans and their allies were attacking Medina, it was his more impetuous followers who persuaded him against his better judgment to go out and give battle, instead of waiting to fight the enemy when they entered the oasis.[25] He had also to decide when not to fight at all, but rather to settle for a truce—as he did in 628, when he agreed to a ten-year truce (*hudna*) with the pagan Meccans.[26] Altogether, he appears as a military leader of a very practical kind.

The background to all this is the Arabian environment that set the scene for the creation of Muḥammad's state. He was engaged in building military power from scratch in an arid land populated by a fiercely independent tribal society. Among the tribesmen there were no professional soldiers, just as there were no civilians; every self-respecting tribesman bore arms and knew how to use them. This was well known to outsiders: the fourth-century historian Ammianus Marcellinus says

[19] Ibn Hisham, *Sīra*, 3–4: 608.13 = 659.
[20] There is a convenient listing of expeditions in Wāqidī, *Maghāzī*, 2–7.
[21] Ibn Hisham, *Sīra*, 3–4: 609.2 = 660.
[22] Ibid., 3–4: 79.12 = 380.
[23] Ibid., 3–4: 216.3 = 450; see above, 185–86.
[24] Ibid., 1–2: 620.7 = 296–97.
[25] Ibid., 3–4: 63.5 = 371–72.
[26] Ibid., 3–4: 316.11, 317.17 = 504. In fact the truce lasted less than two years.

of the Saracens that "all alike are warriors (*bellatores*) of equal rank."[27] At the same time the warlike values of the Arabian tribesmen are richly attested in their pre-Islamic poetry.[28] It was an environment in which making war came naturally to the bulk of the adult male population.

As we might expect from this, the theme of warfare against unbelievers—"jihad in the way of God"—is prominent in the foundational texts of Islam, the Koran and the sayings of the Prophet.[29] Thus a much-quoted verse tells the believers that when the time comes they should slay the idolaters wherever they find them unless they repent and convert (Q9:5). In another verse the believers are instructed to do their best to gather forces to "terrify thereby the enemy of God and your enemy" (Q8:60).[30] They will be amply rewarded for their efforts: "God has bought from the believers their selves and their possessions against the gift of Paradise; they fight in the way of God; they kill and are killed" (Q9:111). In short, the faithful should fight the unbelievers until "the religion is God's entirely" (Q8:39). Likewise, a famous tradition has the Prophet state: "I have been commanded to fight people till they testify that there is no god but God and Muḥammad is the messenger of God, and perform the prayer and pay the alms tax."[31] In another he says: "I have been sent with the sword so that God may be worshipped without any companion, warfare has been made my livelihood,[32] and humiliation and abasement are the lot of whoever opposes my cause."[33] Yet another tradition affirms that the most excellent man is a believer who strives in the way of God with his life and his property.[34] Further traditions identify those who are killed as martyrs (*shahīds*);[35] of the

[27] Ammianus Marcellinus, *Res gestae*, 26.16 = 27.

[28] See, for example, Nicholson, *Literary history*, 79–82.

[29] The term *jihād* literally means "effort" and can be used in this sense in nonmilitary contexts, but the default sense of the word in most Arabic texts is "religious war"—religious in the sense that it is waged for God against his enemies. As a seventeenth-century author puts it, the legal sense of the term is fighting the unbelievers, as by smiting them, plundering them, destroying their places of worship, and smashing their idols (Shaykhzāda, *Majmaʿ al-anhur*, 395.6, in a passage translated in Wendell, *Five tracts*, 147–48).

[30] The word rendered "terrify" is *turhibūna*.

[31] Bukhārī, *al-Jāmiʿ al-ṣaḥīḥ*, 1: 14.10 (*īmān* 17).

[32] Literally "my livelihood has been placed in the shadow of my lance."

[33] Ibn Ḥanbal, *Musnad*, 2: 50.21, and similarly 92.18, drawn to my attention by Bernard Haykel. These versions add the statement, "He who imitates a people is one of them."

[34] Bukhārī, *al-Jāmiʿ al-ṣaḥīḥ*, 2: 199.6 (*jihād* 2).

[35] Wensinck, *Early Muhammadan tradition*, 146–48; and see *EI*², art. "Shahīd" (E. Kohlberg), 204.

inhabitants of Paradise only the martyr wishes to return to earth, to be killed again ten times over.[36] The Prophet himself expresses a wish to be killed "in the way of God" and then resurrected to be killed again repeatedly.[37] The historical salience of warfare against unbelievers in the career of the founder was thus written into the foundational texts.

This heritage did not fall into oblivion with the passing of the centuries. The scholastic tradition treated war against unbelievers as a standard topic of Islamic law; every comprehensive Sunnī law book included a "book of jihad." This guaranteed that, unlike the theory of the caliphate, the subject would be treated repeatedly in the vast legal literature that the scholars produced generation after generation. Much of the detail would have been unknown to most Muslims, but there was nothing arcane about the concept of jihad itself. The story of Muḥammad's conflicts with unbelievers was not a monopoly of the scholars; it caught the imagination of the laity, though not always in forms of which the scholars approved.[38]

At the same time, armed conflict with unbelievers was a real-life experience that recurred often enough in Islamic history to give the heritage a continuing relevance that the scholars could easily invoke. Such conflict might be a consequence of Muslim aggression, as in the case of the Ottoman expansion in the Balkans in the fourteenth to sixteenth centuries. Thus, one early Ottoman chronicler saw the role of the struggle as "to clear the earth of the filth of polytheism,"[39] while another described the Ottoman sultans as "the pre-eminent ghazis . . . after the Apostle of God and the Four Rightly Guided Caliphs"[40]—a *ghāzī* being someone engaged in jihad.[41] Or the aggressors might be the unbelievers, as in the case of the Reconquista in Spain from the eleventh to the fifteenth centuries and the subsequent Christian attacks on North Africa. In this latter context a seventeenth-century Moroccan scholar, urging jihad on his fellow countrymen, started from the obvious point that Muslims have the duty of resisting infidel conquest of a Muslim territory (*waṭan*), and dismissed as absurd the idea that this duty could lapse once the unbelievers were in firm possession of the

[36] Bukhārī, *al-Jāmiʿ al-ṣaḥīḥ*, 2: 206.11 (*jihād* 21).

[37] Ibid., 2: 201.13 (*jihād* 7).

[38] See Shoshan, *Popular culture*, chap. 2, and Paret, *Die legendäre Maghāzi-Literatur*, 1–58.

[39] Imber, "What does *ghazi* actually mean?," 174.

[40] Imber, *Ottoman Empire*, 120.

[41] A "holy warrior," as Imber puts it ("What does *ghazi* actually mean?,"167).

territory in question; he went on to demonstrate that jihad remains obligatory even in the absence of a Muslim ruler, an argument requiring fancier footwork.[42] Meanwhile an Indian scholar writing in the late seventeenth century poured scorn on the notion put about by the Mughal emperor Akbar (ruled 1556–1605) that one should have irenic relations with everyone (*ṣulḥ al-kull*),[43] remarking that if leaving people alone were pleasing to God, He would not have imposed on them the duty of religious war, which means suffering and death for Muslims and unbelievers alike.[44]

The question who was the aggressor in these conflicts was not in fact a matter of doctrinal indifference to the scholars: they made a distinction between offensive and defensive jihad. Either way the Muslims were in the right, but of the two duties one was by far the more exigent. Offensive jihad—attacking unbelievers beyond the frontiers who were not engaged in hostilities against Muslims—was a collective duty: provided some Muslims were engaged in it, others were dispensed from it.[45] Thus a typical juristic view was that the ruler of the Muslim community had to send an expedition out into the lands of the infidel once or twice a year.[46] Defensive jihad, by contrast, was an individual duty: when unbelievers invaded Muslim territory, each and every Muslim in the region affected was obligated to participate in jihad against them; it was even held that slaves should join the struggle without the permission of their masters and women without the consent of their husbands[47]—a remarkable instance of the overriding of basic features of the structure of Muslim society. The relative downgrading of offensive jihad by the jurists is in a way the Muslim moment of truth: however glorious it might be, it is impractical to try to pursue expansive warfare in all directions all the time. This opened the door to

[42] Ḥajjī, *Ḥaraka*, 215.16. As usual, scholars complained that enthusiasm for jihad was not what it had been. One lambasted the feebleness of jihad in his day, attributing this backsliding to love of this world and reluctance to sacrifice one's life in God's cause, and contrasting the attitude of Muḥammad's Companions and the success that God bestowed on them in reward; today, he complained, the Muslims are numerous, but the damage they inflict on the unbelievers is negligible (206.10).

[43] For this idea, see *EI*², art. "Ṣulḥ-i kull" (M. Athar Ali).

[44] M. Cook, *Commanding right*, 468.

[45] See, for example, Marghīnānī, *Hidāya*, 1–2: 426.4. For a useful set of extracts from legal works of the various Sunnī law schools setting out the distinction between offensive and defensive jihad, see Bannā, *Majmūʿat rasāʾil*, 50–3 = Wendell, *Five tracts*, 147–50.

[46] Shaykhzāda, *Majmaʿ al-anhur*, 395.11, in a passage translated in Wendell, *Five tracts*, 147–48.

[47] Marghīnānī, *Hidāya*, 1–2: 426.17.

peaceful relations with non-Muslim states; non-Muslims might reside in Muslim territory, and Muslims in non-Muslim territory, with their security guaranteed by the relevant political authorities.[48] But this did not necessarily mean that the glory had departed. The role played by volunteers in jihad on the frontiers in later centuries is evidence of the continuing allure of aggressive jihad and of its appeal to people who today would be described as non-state actors.[49]

What, then, was the net effect of these attitudes in the pre-modern Muslim world? In principle a full commitment to Islamic ideals would have generated a single Muslim state at peace within itself and at war with the infidel states on its frontiers. In practice, of course, the Muslim world has not looked at all like that for most of its history. Instead there was a plurality of Muslim states making war both on infidel states and on each other. How far, if at all, geopolitical calculations were skewed by religious affiliations would be an interesting question to pursue.[50] What we can say for sure is that some sense of the gap between principle and practice remained. One testimony to this is the fact that the Islamic law of war simply failed to address directly the reality that Muslim states made war on each other.[51] Whereas wars against infidel states needed no specific justification, wars against Muslim states required special pleading.[52] Worse yet, as we have seen, was for a Muslim ruler to ally with an infidel state against a Muslim rival;[53] if nothing else, such behavior carried costs at the level of public relations.

We have, then, a heritage that remained vivid and retained its authority into modern times. It went on to play a significant part in the Muslim resistance to the imposition of Western imperial rule, with jihads led by such leaders as ʿAbd al-Qādir al-Jazāʾirī (d. 1883) against the French in Algeria, Sayyid Aḥmad al-Sharīf (d. 1933) against the Italians in Libya, the Khalīfa ʿAbdallāh (d. 1899) against the British in the Sudan, the "Mad Mullah" Muḥammad ibn ʿAbdallāh Ḥassān (d.

[48] For the legal position of Muslims residing in the territory of a non-Muslim state, see Abou El Fadl, "Islamic law," 172–81.

[49] For a presentation of a rich body of evidence of this phenomenon, see Tor, *Violent order*, 68–77, 81.

[50] Cf. 26.

[51] For the argument that such warfare was subsumed under the law of rebellion, see B. Lewis, *Political language of Islam*, 80–83.

[52] For the way the Ottomans went about this, see Imber, *Ottoman Empire*, 121–22.

[53] To the example from Muslim India cited above (26n111) we can add one from Muslim Spain (Fierro, *ʿAbd al-Rahman III*, 63).

1920) against the British in Somaliland, ʿIzz al-Dīn al-Qassām (d. 1935) against the Jews and the British in Palestine, Shāmil (d. 1871) against the Russians in the Caucasus, and Sayyid Aḥmad Barēlwī (d. 1831) against the Sikhs and the British in northwestern India.[54] A significant feature of such cases was the fact that these movements were largely dependent not on preexisting regular armies but rather on recruitment from wider populations.[55] Here again, the appeal of jihad reached deep into Muslim societies. And yet at the same time the law did not preclude peaceful relations with non-Muslim states and made some provision for the existence of a Muslim diaspora in infidel lands. A century later what did this long-lived heritage mean for Islamists?

The concept of jihad has provoked two sharply conflicting reactions in the modern world. One sees it as a piece of medieval fanaticism incompatible with the standards of the civilized world and the principles of international law. This view is naturally widespread among non-Muslims, particularly those who for one reason or another find themselves on the receiving end of jihad. Their perception, and the evidence that supports it, has caused considerable embarrassment to modern-educated Muslims attuned to current global—historically Western—values. The reaction of many Muslims has accordingly been to reinterpret jihad in such a way as to tone down or remove altogether its more objectionable features. One way to do this is to emphasize the etymology of the term—that the root sense of jihad is "striving"—and to latch onto a strain in the pre-modern Muslim tradition that declares the highest form of jihad to be a spiritual rather than a martial mode of strife.[56] Another way out is to ignore or deny the existence of offensive jihad and to affirm only the defensive form.[57] In essence this reduces jihad to self-defense, which almost all humans recognize as a right.[58] Muslim writers may go further to include in what has to be defended

[54] For surveys of such movements see Peters, *Islam and colonialism*, chap. 3, and D. Cook, *Understanding jihad*, 78–90.

[55] See, for example, Peters, *Islam and colonialism*, 48, 49, 65, 85, 97–98. In the two cases discussed by Peters involving states with regular armies, the point of the invocation of jihad was to rally wider support, as in the Egyptian resistance to the British occupation of 1882 (79), and the Ottoman declaration of jihad in 1914 that sought to foment Muslim unrest against the British and French (90–91).

[56] For this strain, see D. Cook, *Understanding jihad*, 35–39, 46–48, and for its modern apologetic use, cf. 165–66.

[57] For the pull of this view, see Peters, *Islam and colonialism*, 124–27; Schleifer, "Jihad," 27–37; D. Cook, *Understanding jihad*, 95–96, 122, and cf. 125.

[58] As Roman law has it, "vim enim vi defendere omnes leges omniaque iura permittunt" (Justinian, *Digest*, 1: 291.2, quoted in Russell, *Just war*, 41).

the freedom of Muslims to proselytize in non-Muslim countries, with the implication that in principle it would be justifiable to make war against a state that sought to obstruct Muslim missionary activities within its borders;[59] but when this is accompanied by the denial that such wars are needed under current conditions, the net effect is the same.[60] In other words, jihad as it has been understood in their pre-modern heritage is something modern Muslims of an irenic bent could do without.

Our concern, however, is with Islamists, who should presumably be made of sterner stuff. What is remarkable is that even they can be forced into an apologetic mode by the negative reaction to jihad.[61] Thus the impulse behind Mawdūdī's discussion of jihad has more to do with apologetics than with activism. It is significant here that his early interest in the subject was a reaction to Hindu accusations that Islam was spread by the sword.[62] In a similar vein he begins a pamphlet on jihad by remarking that Europeans translate the term as "Holy War" and that among them it has become synonymous with viciousness, barbarity, and bloodshed.[63] Instead, he sets out to associate it with a far more prestigious term in the Western political lexicon of his day: revolution. The truth, he explains, is that Islam is a revolutionary idea (*fikra inqilābiyya*), that the Muslims are a worldwide revolutionary party (*al-ḥizb al-inqilābī al-ʿālamī*), and that jihad is the revolutionary struggle (*al-kifāḥ al-inqilābī*) of this movement.[64] This is not, of course, an irenic version of jihad: the object of the activity is to demolish un-Islamic systems and establish in their place a government based on the principles of Islam.[65] Nor is Mawdūdī seeking to present jihad as purely defensive: the distinction between defensive and offensive warfare, he observes, has no application to Islamic jihad.[66] But the whole thrust of

[59] See Peters, *Islam and colonialism*, 122–23, 124, 127; March, *Islam and liberal citizenship*, 201–4.

[60] This is the case with Qaraḍāwī's discussion of the question (see Qaraḍāwī, *Fiqh al-jihād*, 1194.22, and for his identification of his position as defensive (*difāʿī*), 256.12; cf. also 240.22, 241.2, 256.1, 433.8, 1193.12). I owe my knowledge of Qaraḍāwī's discussion of this point to Andrew March.

[61] Compare the case of the distinguished Pakistani scholar Muḥammad Taqī ʿUthmānī (Zaman, *Modern Islamic thought*, 284–87).

[62] *EI*², art. "Mawdūdī" (F.C.R. Robinson), 872b.

[63] Mawdūdī, *Jihād*, 3.3; for this work, first published in 1962, see Ahmad and Ansari, *Mawlānā Mawdūdī*, 37 no. 68.

[64] Mawdūdī, *Jihād*, 10.11.

[65] Ibid., 35.9.

[66] Ibid., 41.7. For the phrase *al-jihād al-Islāmī*, see also 18.13.

his presentation in this pamphlet is to emphasize the elevated moral purpose of the activity. He pretty much ignores the more pedestrian legal issues it raises, shows no obvious interest in fanning its flames, and makes no appeal to Muslim youth to enlist. In the same way, a sustained discussion of jihad in another of his works is notable for the paucity of its references to military activity directed at infidel enemies.[67]

Quṭb's approach to jihad is, I think, broadly similar to Mawdūdī's. His apologetic impulse shows in his anxiety to rescue the authentic concept of jihad from its twin enemies: the Orientalists who deliberately misrepresent it as aimed at forced conversion and the defeatist Muslim apologists who respond by reducing it to purely defensive warfare.[68] Like Mawdūdī, he presents jihad as a selfless mission to destroy all the corrupt structures of power in the world; he adds the point that it is these structures that prevent people from freely choosing their religion.[69] His concern to demonstrate the righteousness of offensive jihad thus looks more like a middle-aged effort to shore up the moral self-image of Islam than a youthful call to arms. It is rare for Quṭb to match the lyrical jihadism of ʿAbdallāh ʿAzzām (d. 1989): "Love of jihad has taken over my life, my soul, my sensation, my heart and my emotions."[70] In the course of a long discussion of the causes of European hostility to Islam, Quṭb remarks that Islam, unlike Christianity, urges resistance and combat (*al-muqāwama waʾl-kifāḥ*), and he quotes some appropriate Koranic verses to demonstrate this; but the point is only to explain why European imperialism necessarily regards Islam as an enemy.[71] He did approve of violent operations in some contempo-

[67] Maududi, *Fundamentals of Islam*, 243–63.

[68] Quṭb, *Maʿālim*, 81.7 = 75–76; see also 58.1 = 56, 59.10 = 57, 64.15 = 61–62, and Carré, *Mysticism and politics*, 299–305. By way of comparison, we may note that Saʿīd Ḥawwā has a similarly apologetic tone (see Ḥawwā, *Rasūl*, 2: 225.13), whereas Ḥasan al-Bannā's discussion of jihad is far less apologetic (Bannā, *Majmūʿat rasāʾil*, 54.8 = Wendell, *Five tracts*, 151; and see Mitchell, *Society of Muslim Brothers*, 207–8).

[69] Quṭb, *Maʿālim*, 63.21 = 61, 74.25 = 70; see also Quṭb, *Hādhā ʾl-dīn*, 87.17 = 88–89; Quṭb, *ʿAdāla*, 163.10 = 213; and Carré, *Mysticism and politics*, 299–305. Compare the observation of Aquinas that "Christ's faithful often wage war on infidels, not indeed for the purpose of forcing them to believe, because even were they to conquer them and take them captive, they should still leave them free to believe or not, but for the purpose of stopping them obstructing the faith of Christ" (Aquinas, *Summa theologiae*, 32: 62.5 = 63 (2a2ae. 10, 8)).

[70] For this celebrated affirmation of ʿAzzām's, see Musallam, *From secularism to jihad*, 191.

[71] Quṭb, *ʿAdāla*, 227.1 = 286. Likewise a discussion of the nature of Islamic conquest (*ṭabīʿat al-fatḥ al-Islāmī*) is directed to establishing the righteousness of the activity, not

rary contexts, and occasional flashes of a more emotional jihadism appear.[72] But in general his attitude to jihad is not marked by enthusiasm. Despite his assertion that the tide has turned in favor of Islam,[73] he is well aware of Muslim weakness in a world dominated by non-Muslim powers, remarking that "this Western world with which our interests are interwoven is stronger than we are at present," and that we "have no control over it and no strength equal to its strength, as we did in the early days of Islam."[74] There is, however, a more fundamental and even more dispiriting reason why the Muslims do not engage in jihad today: in Quṭb's view, they no longer exist.[75] In respect of jihad at least, Quṭb is not an activist.[76]

Against the negative view of jihad to which Mawdūdī and Quṭb were reacting, there is a positive one with its origins inside the Muslim community. We live in a world in which mass mobilization and armed resistance are recurrent features of confrontations between native populations and rulers seen as foreigners or in league with foreigners. Where the native population is Muslim and the rulers, or those they are felt to be in league with, are not, jihad fits the situation like a glove; whatever costs it may carry in terms of relations with the world at large, it has strong domestic resonance. So for anyone prepared to write off the costs, the benefits can be considerable. This is where the jihadis have their role to play, and their uninhibited glorification of their violent way of life is an essential part of their image.[77] These are people who refer to themselves as lions,[78] relish their role in rubbing

---

to encouraging it (Quṭb, *Dirāsāt Islāmiyya*, 28–39, and see especially 36.12). On his treatment of jihad in his Koran commentary, see Carré, *Mysticism and politics*, chap. 10.

[72] See Shepard, *Sayyid Quṭb*, lxi n1 (translating the suppressed dedication of the first edition of Quṭb's *ʿAdāla* with its reference to future Muslim youth killing and being killed, cf. Q9:111), and Musallam, *From secularism to jihad*, 133–34 (on the jihad of the Muslim Brothers against the British in the Canal Zone in 1951); for a list of such contexts, see Carré, *Mysticism and politics*, 250.

[73] Quṭb, *ʿAdāla*, 228.20 = 288.

[74] Ibid., 229.23 = 290.

[75] Carré, *Mysticism and politics*, 306.

[76] One could, of course, interpret Quṭb not just as defending the moral standing of jihad but also as itching to engage in it as soon as conditions made it possible to do so. But the way he writes does not strike me this way.

[77] For a graphic description of the jihadi film *Badr al-Riyāḍ*, celebrating a terrorist attack mounted in Riyadh in May 2003, see Al-Rasheed, *Contesting the Saudi state*, 158–63.

[78] See, for example, Lawrence, *Messages*, 74, 158, 192. Bin Laden's training camp in Afghanistan was a *maʾsada*, a "place that abounds in lions" (32). Compare the Sikh use of the title *singh*, "lion."

America's nose in the dirt,[79] and quote defiant verses of the pre-Islamic poet ʿAmr ibn Kulthūm to the American Secretary of Defense.[80] And on a more prosaic level one of their leaders is careful to give them detailed instructions for the avoidance of obesity.[81]

A striking change between Mawdūdī and Quṭb on the one hand and Ẓawāhirī and Bin Laden on the other is accordingly the disappearance of apologetics.[82] A key text in this connection is a refutation, attributable to Bin Laden and dating from 2002, of the Saudi contribution to an exchange of views between some American and Saudi intellectuals.[83] Bin Laden foists on the Saudi intellectuals the classic apologetic belief that jihad is purely defensive. He then has a field day putting them right on this. The problem, he points out, is that offensive jihad is "an established and basic tenet of this religion."[84] He quotes the saying of the Prophet: "I have been commanded to fight people till they testify that there is no god but God and Muḥammad is the messenger of God, and perform the prayer and pay the alms tax."[85] He presses on ruthlessly: "Does Islam, or does it not, force people by the power of the sword to submit to its authority corporeally if not spiritually?" The answer, of course, is that it does. Defeated unbelievers have three choices: conversion, payment of the poll tax, or the sword.[86] The West may indeed see fighting, enmity, and hatred for the sake of religion as evil, but so what? Whose notions of justice and righteousness are correct, ours or theirs?[87] Islam is spread with the sword, just as the

[79] Ibid., 194, and cf. 192. One needs to remember that the target population for recruitment purposes is identified by Bin Laden as the cohort aged fifteen to twenty-five (see ibid., 91).

[80] See the passage by Bin Laden quoted in Shepard, "Sayyid Qutb's doctrine," 537.

[81] Al-Rasheed, *Contesting the Saudi state*, 156–57.

[82] As might be expected, Mawdūdī and Quṭb have a prominent place in the religious genealogy of the leaders of al-Qāʿida. Ẓawāhirī describes Sayyid Quṭb as "the most prominent theoretician" of radical Islamism (Mansfield, *His own words*, 137) and says that his call for the acknowledgment of God's unity and sovereignty was the spark that ignited the Islamic revolution against the enemies of Islam at home and abroad (48, and see 49–50); he quotes both Mawdūdī and Quṭb (for Mawdūdī, see Ibrahim, *Al Qaeda reader*, 123, 130; for Quṭb, see 128, 131–33). Bin Laden in his student days read books by Sayyid Quṭb and heard lectures by his brother Muḥammad Quṭb (L. Wright, *Looming tower*, 79, on the authority of a fellow student and close friend of Bin Laden).

[83] For the authorship, see Ibrahim, *Al Qaeda reader*, 285n2, and for the date, see 27.

[84] Ibrahim, *Al Qaeda reader*, 32. For the similar view of Faraj, see Jansen, *Neglected duty*, 193 §71.

[85] Ibrahim, *Al Qaeda reader*, 41; see above, 220.

[86] Ibid., 42.

[87] Ibid., 43.

Prophet was sent forth with the sword.[88] This is God's religion; why should anyone want to apologize for it?

Such affirmation of the principle of offensive jihad, and the textual evidence accompanying it, was well calculated to embarrass the Saudi intellectuals and at the same time to highlight the proud intransigence of the jihadis.[89] But we should be clear that offensive jihad does not represent the day-to-day agenda of the jihadis, either now or in the foreseeable future. Their immediate concern is with the altogether more pressing demands of defensive jihad. Unsurprisingly, they insist on the well-established doctrine that this form of jihad is an individual duty of Muslims.[90] As we have seen, this makes it a far more exigent duty than the offensive jihad with which Bin Laden tormented the Saudi intellectuals.[91] It also allows the movement to argue in propaganda directed at the West that its attacks are solely in response to prior attacks on Muslims: "We only killed Russians after they invaded Afghanistan and Chechnya, we only killed Europeans after they invaded Afghanistan and Iraq," and so forth.[92] Why else had they omitted to attack Sweden?[93] In short, the vindication of offensive jihad was not an attempt to justify the current activities of al-Qāʿida; the point was rather to dramatize the refusal of the jihadis to pander to Western values.[94]

The same refusal is in evidence in the attitude of the jihadis to being called terrorists. Bin Laden does not categorically reject the use of the term terrorism to describe what the jihadis do. Instead, he distinguishes between good and bad terrorism; that of the jihadis is, of course, the good kind.[95] We owe a more systematic discussion of the distinction between good and bad terrorism to the prolific jihadi strategist Abū

[88] Ibid., 46–47; similarly Faraj in Jansen, *Neglected duty*, 193 §71.

[89] Compare the championing of offensive jihad in a jihadi text translated in D. Cook, *Understanding jihad*, 184–85, 188.

[90] Ibrahim, *Al Qaeda reader*, 102; Lawrence, *Messages*, 60; and cf. Ibrahim, *Al Qaeda reader*, 114, and Lawrence, *Messages*, 61, 202.

[91] See 222.

[92] Lawrence, *Messages*, 236.

[93] Ibid., 238.

[94] Another likely example is the emphasis on the place of booty in jihad, which may reach the point of being purely symbolic. Thus a document instructing the hijackers of the planes that destroyed the World Trade Center in 2001—men with little prospective use for booty—counsels as follows: "Do not forget to take some of the spoils, even if only a cup of water, to drink from it and offer it to your brothers to drink, if possible" (Euben and Zaman, *Readings in Islamist thought*, 471).

[95] Lawrence, *Messages*, 120. This is not just an extremist view—Qaraḍāwī too makes such a distinction (Zaman, *Modern Islamic thought*, 274n33).

Muṣʿab al-Sūrī.[96] His main proof-text is the Koranic instruction to "terrify . . . the enemy of God and your enemy" (Q8:60);[97] with regard to assassination, he naturally refers to the small groups that Muḥammad would send out to kill individual enemies.[98] This does not mean a lack of moral scruple on the part of the jihadis. Thus Bin Laden can be put on the spot by a question about killing women and children. He admits that the Prophet forbade it but invokes various scholars as saying that if the enemy does it to us, then we can do it back to deter them.[99] He counsels Muslim youth not to take matters into their own hands in applying the law with regard to human shields; better leave such questions to the judgment of honest scholars.[100] Likewise, Ẓawāhirī strains to legitimize martyrdom operations by eliding the difference between killing onself and getting oneself killed,[101] and he states that those who unintentionally kill Muslims in the course of operations must pay blood money to their relatives.[102] But these scruples are internal to the Muslim community; they make no concession to Western values, and the apologetic mood has evaporated entirely.

As the reference to assassination suggests, the military side of Muḥammad's life plays a conspicuous part in the jihadi outlook. He is quoted as longing to be killed in jihad only to be resurrected and killed yet again[103]—part of a widespread cult of martyrdom in the contemporary Muslim world.[104] One jihadi author laments the ignorance of the military life of the Prophet that prevails in our time and the

[96] See the text translated in Lia, *Architect of global jihad*, 382–90.

[97] Ibid., 385, and see 42; and see Hegghammer, *Jihad in Saudi Arabia*, 148, for the view of the radical cleric Ḥamūd al-Shuʿaybī in November 2001, and Lahoud, "Jihadi recantations," 148, for the view of Sayyid Imām that to deny the legality of terrorism in Islam is unbelief. The verb translated "terrify" is *turhibūna*, of which *irhāb*, the modern Arabic term for terrorism, is the verbal noun. However, the verse would seem to refer to regular, rather than irregular warfare.

[98] Lia, *Architect of global jihad*, 389–90.

[99] Lawrence, *Messages*, 118–19.

[100] Ibid., 231. For the key role of authoritative scholars in granting or withholding legitimation for jihadi activities in the Saudi context, see Hegghammer, *Jihad in Saudi Arabia*, 83–84, 125, 148, 153, 202, 222.

[101] Ibrahim, *Al Qaeda reader*, 156–57; and cf. Ibrahim's comment (138). By contrast, Ẓawāhirī's tactical justification is straightforward: such operations are the most effective in inflicting damage on the opponent and the least costly in terms of casualties among the jihadis (Mansfield, *His own words*, 200, 223; the translator uses the phrase "suicide operations" in the first passage and "martyrdom operations" in the second). On the casuistry of martyrdom operations see D. Cook, *Martyrdom in Islam*, 149–53.

[102] Mansfield, *His own words*, 104.

[103] Lawrence, *Messages*, 56. Cf. L.Wright, *Looming tower*, 108, and above, 221.

[104] D. Cook, *Martyrdom in Islam*, especially 144–45, 147–48, 154–61.

tendency to play it down; a Muslim grows up hearing nothing about his Prophet except how nice he was to Jews and Christians.[105] This jihadi evokes Muḥammad's personal courage in battle[106] and is proud to describe how he would kill one man, order the assassination of a second, behead a third, and declare licit the blood of a fourth; he would raid this tribe or that, destroy their castles, burn their date palms, kill their men, and take captive their women and children.[107] Such was the life of the Prophet and his Companions: fighting, jihad, conquest, boldness, killing, capturing, slaughtering, terrorizing the enemies of God.[108] The moral is that the Muslim community can attain glory (*ʿizza*) only through jihad.[109] Another jihadi author remarks that the Prophetic model makes every individual a private soldier at the level of obedience and a commander at the level of responsibility.[110] Yet another rejoices in the number of expeditions the Prophet led in person,[111] his presence in the thick of the fighting,[112] and once more his wish to be resurrected only to be killed again.[113] He emphasizes the shameful disparity between the militancy of Muḥammad and the passivity of his community today: how could a community whose Prophet lived like *that* conduct itself like *this*?[114] Of course, the example of the Prophet also gives jihadis the pragmatic option of making a truce with the enemy for a limited time when it is opportune to do so; Bin Laden offered such an arrangement to "our neighbors north of the Mediterranean" in a letter of 2004.[115] All told, it is no mystery that the figure 314—the number of men who fought for Muḥammad at his first battle—should have a way of resurfacing in contemporary jihadi contexts.[116]

[105] Ḥusayn ibn Maḥmūd, *Muḥammad*, 4.10, 4.17; I owe my copy to Nelly Lahoud.

[106] Ibid., 5.5, 6.2, 6.11.

[107] Ibid., 6.13.

[108] Ibid., 7.2. The word I render as "terrorizing" is *irhāb*.

[109] Ibid., 7.9.

[110] Shinqīṭī, *Numūdhaj*, 13.8.

[111] Abū Baṣīr, *Hākadhā*, 6.14 (*yaqūdu . . . bi-nafsihi*; the phrase is repeated many times in the next five pages). I owe my copy of this electronic pamphlet to Nelly Lahoud.

[112] Ibid., 7.1, 10.18.

[113] Ibid., 11.6, 12.7.

[114] Ibid., 11.19, and see 11.8, 11.16. Compare the view of Faraj: "Neglecting *jihād* is the cause of the lowness, humiliation, division and fragmentation in which the Muslims live today" (Jansen, *Neglected duty*, 205 §100, and cf. 160f §3).

[115] Lawrence, *Messages*, 235. Having the option of making such a truce with the Israelis has been politically helpful for Ḥamās (see Mishal and Sela, *Palestinian Hamas*, 3, 71, 86, 108).

[116] L. Wright, *Looming tower*, 132–33, quoting from notes on a meeting in Peshawar in 1988. Cf. also Al-Rasheed, *Contesting the Saudi state*, 159 (on the film *Badr al-Riyāḍ*);

Alongside this shift from apologetic defense of jihad to enthusiastic participation there has been a second reorientation that separates the jihadis from the patriarchs of Islamism. To the extent that they thought about the need for Muslims to have military power, earlier Islamists seem to have had regular armies in mind, as when Ḥawwā looked forward to a time when the Muslim community would be the greatest political, economic, and military power on earth.[117] By contrast, the pattern of warfare that has emerged among the jihadis is a highly irregular one: they engage in insurrection, guerrilla warfare, and terrorism. There is, moreover, a significant geographical aspect to this pattern. With the exception of some dramatic terrorist excursions, they have had no success in the parts of the world endowed with the resources needed for political, economic, and military power. Instead they show a marked affinity for what Abū Muṣʿab al-Sūrī described as "areas of chaos without governmental control," "semi-autonomous tribal areas and remote areas lying far away from weak governments"; as examples of such environments he offered "the tribes in Yemen, Somalia, and the Horn of Africa, the tribes in the border areas of Pakistan, and the long arch of the Great Sahara countries in Africa, which stretches from Sudan to the shores of the Atlantic Ocean."[118] In sum, the jihadi way of life is the practice of irregular warfare, preferably in areas of chaos.

This is not to say that the jihadis are committed to maintaining this practice indefinitely. Abū Muṣʿab himself was pessimistic about its prospects since he expected the Americans to bring these areas under control and close them to jihadis—something that despite increased American activity seems unlikely to happen. He accordingly developed a new and even more anarchic model for Islamic resistance suitable for current conditions: "individual terrorism jihad" together with the

---

Rougier, *Everyday jihad*, 209–10; Hegghammer, *Jihad in Saudi Arabia*, 42, 204 (with the figure as 313, as in Wāqidī, *Maghāzī*, 152.15). See above, 218.

[117] See 49. Setting out the need to plan the development of Muslim military power in a book written in 1987, he starts with the point that modern warfare requires regular armies (*juyūsh niẓāmiyya*) with the requisite manpower and equipment (Ḥawwā, *Jund Allāh takhṭīṭan*, 117.6, and see 119.12; the armies in question seem to be those of the existing Muslim states). Later in the passage he also allows for guerrilla warfare (*ḥarb al-ʿiṣābāt*) and even finds references to it in the Koran (117.21, citing Q9:41 and Q4:71; in the latter verse he glosses *thubāt* as *ʿiṣābāt*); but he seems to see it as in the first instance something to be undertaken by states (118.1), though later he adds an endorsement of people's war (*al-jihād al-shaʿbī*, 118.26). Despite the date, the charm of the jihadi lifestyle is not yet in evidence here (for the date of writing, see 144.22).

[118] See the passage from Abū Muṣʿab al-Sūrī's treatise "The global Islamic resistance call" translated in Lia, *Architect of global jihad*, 461.

[illegible] totally separated from each [illegible]

[illegible] practice in a broader—but [illegible] As he remarks with unvar-[illegible]es achieve victory only when [illegible] Of course, in the present epoch the [illegible] regular armies against infi-[illegible] strength as the Muslim world [illegible]borationist regimes. The only [illegible]ordingly the kind of irregular [illegible] terrorists. But Ẓawāhirī makes [illegible] warfare has no value in itself. [illegible]es of peripheral disturbances unless it [illegible] of establishing an Islamic state—a restored caliphate—in the [illegible] Muslim world;[121] thus the reason he gives for forming his connection with Afghanistan is that he saw the country as a possible base for jihad in the Arab heartlands.[122] It was the [illegible] with all its weight in the heart of the Islamic world," that would then go on to lead the Muslim world in a jihad against the West[123]—a jihad that would at last be a real war. But without such a state in the heart of the Arab region, there would be no prospect of defeating the world alliance, and jihad would go nowhere.[124] The problem, of course, is how to get from the periphery to the core: as he says, the establishment of the projected state is neither easy nor close.[125]

In these larger perspectives, irregular warfare is a choice dictated by circumstances, but it is nevertheless a choice that resonates strongly with the military career of Muḥammad. He too went to work in the

[119] Ibid., 371 item 1.

[120] Mansfield, *His own words*, 214, and likewise 201; for the similar view of Abū Muṣʿab al-Sūrī see Lia, *Architect of global jihad*, 371. Compare Mearsheimer, *Great power politics*, 86: "Armies are of paramount importance in warfare because they are the main military instrument for conquering and controlling land."

[121] Mansfield, *His own words*, 201-2, 213–15, 225; and cf. V. Brown, *Cracks*, 9. Compare Ẓawāhirī's remark in his letter to Zarqāwī of 2005 that the battles fought in the far-flung regions of the Islamic world—such as Chechnya, Afghanistan, Kashmir, and Bosnia—are just a foundation for the major battles that have begun to be fought in the heart of the Islamic world (Mansfield, *His own words*, 252–53).

[122] Mansfield, *His own words*, 28.

[123] Ibid., 113.

[124] Ibid., 201; similarly 214, speaking of the heart of the Islamic world.

[125] Ibid., 201.

periphery, in an area of tribal chaos outside the control of any government. He too fought in a style that was often closer to irregular warfare than to the clashing of big battalions.[126] He too appealed to religious loyalty and the martial values of a warlike society to recruit his forces. And in the fullness of time did not his followers go on to defeat the empires of the day with something more like regular armies? This fits with the lively jihadi interest in the military aspect of Muḥammad's career that we noted above. A specific example is provided by Abū Muṣʿab al-Sūrī: he finds a useful precedent for "individual jihad and small cells" in a certain Abū Baṣīr, who "formed the first guerrilla group in Islam";[127] this man became the leader of a group of nearly seventy Muslims who harried the pagans of Mecca despite the truce that was in operation at the time.[128] Bin Laden reaches even further back in his defiant address to the Secretary of Defense: "These youths love death as you love life. They inherit dignity, pride, courage, generosity, truthfulness and sacrifice from father to father. They are most delivering and steadfast at war. They inherit these values from their ancestors (even from the time of the *Jāhiliyya*, before Islam). These values were approved and completed by the arriving Islam as stated by the Messenger of God (God's Blessings and Salutations be upon him): 'I have been sent to perfect the good values.'"[129] This seems a passable illustration of much of the argument of this section.

3. Hinduism

Hinduism, like Buddhism, has a norm of nonviolence (*ahiṃsā*), in other words not harming or giving pain to any living being.[130] Within Hinduism it goes back to the Upaniṣads and is a prime virtue and a moral duty. "Manu has said that non-violence, truth, not stealing, purification, and the suppression of the sensory powers is the duty of the four classes, in a nutshell."[131]

[126] See the discussion of "types of warfare" in Landau-Tasseron, "Pre-conquest Muslim army," 303–16, especially the summing-up (316).

[127] Lia, *Architect of global jihad*, 363.

[128] Ibn Hishām, *Sīra*, 3—4: 324.4 = 508.

[129] As quoted in Shepard, "Sayyid Qutb's doctrine," 537 (the awkward translation is not his). For the Prophetic tradition, see, for example, Bayhaqī, *Sunan*, 10:192.2 (*innamā buʿithtu li-utammima makārim al-akhlāq*).

[130] See Kane, *History of Dharmaśāstra*, 5: 944–7; also Bodewitz, "Hindu *ahiṁsā*," 19–20.

[131] Manu, *Laws*, 243 (10.63); and cf. 124 (6.75), 273 (11.223), 286 (12.83).

But Hinduism differed from Buddhism in two relevant respects. First, its canonical texts were full of martial violence: many hymns of the Ṛg Veda refer to battles,[132] and a leading figure in its pantheon is the war god Indra.[133] Second, the Hindu legal tradition laid out the law of war without blinking—what else were Kṣatriyas for? Thus, an early source informs us that, despite a long list of exceptions, a king in principle "commits no sin if he kills someone in battle."[134] Manu states without hesitation that conquest is a king's duty.[135] "By means of his army he should seek what he has not got," just as he should "guard what he has got."[136] And when he has retired from his kingship, he should go to his death in battle.[137] There are indeed serious moral standards to be upheld on the battlefield, but the legitimacy of war as such is not in question.[138] In fact, legal texts make liberal reference to the heavenly rewards awaiting those who die in battle.[139] One source dating from the early centuries of our era promises that the valiant soldier who fights on though surrounded by enemies will find divine damsels running after him in heaven to choose him as their lord.[140] Dayānand would have done well to consider this passage before asking of the Muslim paradise: "Is this a paradise or a grove of prostitutes?"[141] In short, war has an accredited place in the Hindu tradition.

But who are the Hindus fighting against in these statements of the law of war? The answer, by and large, would seem to be each other. Often the provisions in the law books take it for granted that the enemy is Hindu; thus we read that the sins of soldiers killed in battle are wiped out whichever side they are on, that the customs of a conquered country should be respected, and that care should be taken not to kill Brahmins.[142] No doubt the same assumption of a shared religious culture is behind the emphasis on decent behavior in warfare. It is rare indeed

[132] Basham, *Wonder that was India*, 32.

[133] Ibid., 233–34.

[134] So the *Dharmasūtra* of Gautama in Olivelle, *Dharmasūtras*, 94 (10.17).

[135] Manu, *Laws*, 249 (10.119).

[136] Ibid., 138 (7.101, and similarly 7.99); cf. also 139 (7.107, 109).

[137] Ibid., 232 (9.323).

[138] Kane, *History of Dharmaśāstra*, 3: 209–212. Outside the legal tradition there was indeed a view that all this was evil (see Zaehner, *Hinduism*, 155, quoting the *Mahābhārata*), but the law takes no account of this moral agonizing.

[139] Kane, *History of Dharmaśāstra*, 3: 57–58, 211–12.

[140] Ibid., 3: 211, and cf. 58 (quoting Parāśara, for whose date see 1: 464).

[141] K. W. Jones, *Arya Dharm*, 146; cf. also K. W. Jones, "Two *sanātan dharma* leaders," 239 (quoting Vivekānanda).

[142] Kane, *History of Dharmaśāstra*, 3: 57–58, 71, 209–10.

to find the jurists discussing war against non-Hindus, and when it happens the spirit is very different: one commentator on Manu, writing around the ninth century, allows for a conquest of the barbarians (*mlecchas*) in which they are reduced to a status like that of the Cāṇḍālas, the most despised stratum of Hindu society.[143] But even in eschatology the concern with the barbarians seems very leisurely: if we are willing to wait some 427,000 years for the end of the present degenerate Kali age, we can expect the advent of Kalkin, an incarnation of Viṣṇu who will destroy all the barbarians or in some accounts conquer them to become a universal emperor (*cakravartin*).[144] For the most part non-Hindus are simply ignored.

A more recent chapter in the history of warfare in India allows us to take the point a little further. Bīrūnī, the eleventh-century Muslim scholar who was by far the most serious foreign student of India before modern times, mentions that the Hindus rarely quarreled among themselves over religious disagreements with anything more than words.[145] However, in the last centuries before the establishment of the *pax Britannica*, we find that the Śaiva and Vaiṣṇava ascetics of India each had their troops of naked warriors. There are references to them fighting Muslims, but they seem above all to have gloried in slaughtering each other.[146] Thus, we are told of a major battle they fought at Hardvār in 1760 over their relative positions in the procession of pilgrims at the Kumbh Melā; it is reported that the carnage left 18,000 dead (or was it only 1800?), and that it resulted in the exclusion of the defeated Vaiṣṇavas from the ritual until the British imposed their sense of fair play several decades later.[147] On a more individual level we hear of two champions, a Śaiva and a Vaiṣṇava, neither of whom would eat his daily meals unless he had killed at least one ascetic of the other kind.[148] Here, then, is religious warfare in a Hindu context, and it is war between Hindus.

[143] Ibid., 2: 16, quoting Medhātithi (for whose date see 1: 583); and see Jha, *Manusmṛti*, 3: 238–39 (to Manu 2:23). Medhātithi here entertains the possibility of a Hindu conquest of land outside Āryāvarta.

[144] Kane, *History of Dharmaśāstra*, 3: 923, citing various Purāṇas with the comment that this is "very small consolation." In typically Hindu style this eschatological catharsis will also eliminate Śūdra kings. A late seventeenth-century source is less patient, offering the suggestion that Śivājī (ruled 1674–1680) might be "the first harbinger of that Kalkin" whose role is to "destroy the hordes of Yavanas" (926), in other words the Muslims.

[145] Bīrūnī, *Taḥqīq*, 10.5 = trans. Sachau, 1: 19.

[146] Ghurye, *Indian Sadhus*, 110–27, 201–11. More recent discussions can be found in Lorenzen, "Warrior ascetics," and Pinch, "Soldier monks," especially 148–56. If the phenomenon had a doctrinal basis, these studies do not mention it.

[147] Ghurye, *Indian Sadhus*, 124–26.

[148] Ibid., 201.

To sum up our discussion of Hinduism before modern times, this is a tradition that is comfortable with warfare—and in that respect on the same footing as the Islamic heritage. But the Hindu heritage differs from that of Islam in two significant ways. First, it shows no embarrassment when Hindus fight Hindus. Second, it shows little interest when Hindus fight non-Hindus. The very different distribution of the attention of the Hindu and Muslim jurists underlines this contrast. On the Hindu side the law of war is about conflict between Hindus, with almost no consideration given to conflict with non-Hindus. On the Muslim side the law of war is centered on conflict with non-Muslims, and the realities of conflict between Muslims are ignored or swept under the carpet.

So far in this section we have been concerned with the mainstream of the Hindu tradition. But there are also many sidestreams, and one in particular is worth a closer look than we have given it so far in this chapter: Sikhism. When this movement began in the early sixteenth century, the Sikhs did not stand out from the general run of Hindu sects.[149] But in 1699 Gobind Singh (d. 1708), the tenth and last Guru of the sect, wrought a remarkable transformation.[150] He established the Khālsā, a religious order that gradually marginalized other elements in the Sikh community. The new dispensation was characterized by new norms very different from those of earlier times. Strict rules, particularly one forbidding the cutting of the hair,[151] set Sikhs apart from the surrounding society and made their distinctiveness immediately visible.[152] There was strong emphasis on solidarity within the community: there should be "unity and friendship" among Sikhs,[153] and they should have business dealings only with each other.[154] "He who becomes a Sikh of the Guru should never strike another Sikh; and he who actually kills a Sikh will go to hell."[155] At the same time there was an intense militancy directed against outsiders, with the ultimate goal of achieving political power: "The Khalsa shall rule (*rāj karegā*), no enemy shall remain."[156] This militant Sikhism that took shape as Mughal power was declining did much to shape the subsequent history of the community. What made such a transformation possible?

[149] See McLeod, *Who is a Sikh?*, 7–8, on the place of Nānak (d. 1539), the first Sikh Guru, in the Sant tradition of northern India.

[150] McLeod, *Sikh community*, 14–15.

[151] See McLeod, *Who is a Sikh?*, 32; McLeod, *Chaupa Singh Rahit-nama*, 170 §183.

[152] McLeod, *Chaupa Singh Rahit-nama*, 168 §166.

[153] Ibid., 157 §94.

[154] Ibid., 151 §17.

[155] Ibid., 156 §79.

[156] McLeod, *Who is a Sikh?*, 50; McLeod, *Textual sources*, 78; and see McLeod, *Chaupa Singh Rahit-nama*, 171 §200, 175 §279.

First, the Sikhs were a relatively small population concentrated in a single region, the Punjab, and subject to the religious authority of a single leader, the Guru.[157] It would have been much harder to bring about a comparable change among the members of a large, sprawling, and decentralized religious community. Moreover, the fact that the tenth Guru was also the last tended to lock in the transformation; his death in 1708 did not freeze Sikhism, but he had no successors who could easily have reversed what he had done.

Second, the Sikhs had a clear enemy to mobilize against: the Muslims.[158] Sikh texts of the period are strongly, sometimes virulently, hostile to them: "The true Khalsa is one who carries arms and slays Muslims."[159] A Sikh should not befriend a Muslim, trust his word or oath, drink water from his hands, sleep in his company, be influenced by his opinions, or eat his food at a gathering.[160] Moreover, we can reasonably suspect that this hostility was tinged with emulation: the stress on communal solidarity, communal militancy, and the aspiration to rule look very much like a Hindu appropriation of Islam, an attempt—by no means unsuccessful—to beat the Muslims at their own game.

Third, the Sikhs, and in particular the Khālsā, had their demographic base in a particular part of the Punjabi population, the Jāṭs. This warlike peasant caste had a reputation for violence going back to the first Muslim invasions of India.[161] The association of Sikhism with the Jāṭs seems to have intensified over time; the Gurus themselves were not Jāṭs but Khatrīs, members of a mercantile caste.[162] The establishment of the Khālsā thus seems to have represented a powerful fusion of Sikh religiosity with the martial values of the Jāṭs.[163] In this respect it provides a striking parallel to Muḥammad's fusion of monotheist religiosity with the martial values of the pre-Islamic Arab tribesmen.

157 According to the British census of 1881, the Sikhs then numbered 1.7 million (McLeod, *Sikh community*, 93).

158 McLeod, *Who is a Sikh?*, 49–50.

159 McLeod, *Textual sources*, 79; and see McLeod, *Chaupa Singh Rahit-nama*, 171 §201, 194 §595, 195 §606.

160 McLeod, *Chaupa Singh Rahit-nama*, 150 §10.

161 For a convenient survey of their history over several centuries, see *EI*^{2}, art. "Djāṭ" (A. S. Bazmi Ansari). Some of them moved—or were moved—to Iraq and other core regions of the Islamic world and were already making trouble there in early Islamic times; for this, see the survey in *EI*^{2}, art. "Zuṭṭ" (C. E. Bosworth).

162 McLeod, *Sikh community*, 87–88. For the forms Jāṭ and Jaṭ, see McLeod, *Who is a Sikh?*, 111; for simplicity I use the first throughout.

163 McLeod, *Sikh community*, 9–14, 51–52, 92–93.

The Sikhism of the Khālsā thus represented a reversal of the pattern we saw in mainstream Hinduism: like Muslims, but on a manageably smaller scale, the Sikhs were now committed to being at peace with each other and fighting zealously against outsiders. Like Muslims, they have not always observed these norms. Sikhs have been known to fight Sikhs, and there have been long periods in which they have not engaged in religious warfare against non-Sikhs—under the British Raj, for example, when the martial energies of the Jāṭs were diverted into the Indian Army or in the period since the suppression of the Sikh separatism of the 1980s. But the Sikh transformation is a notable example of militarily significant religious change and worth bearing in mind as we come to the Hindu nationalists.

For Hindus in modern times, being heirs to a heritage that does not glorify warfare against non-Hindus is in one respect advantageous: it puts them in a strong position to make jihad a focus of polemic against Islam. They are not vulnerable to counterarguments in the way that Christians are, thanks to their medieval record as crusaders. Islam, Dayānand charged repeatedly, sanctifies war, plunder, and the slaughter of nonbelievers.[164] "Who is not a Moslem, kill him wherever you get him, but do not kill a Muslim!"[165] Lekh Rām (d. 1897), a member of the Ārya Samāj and its leading critic of Islam, published his "Tract on jihad, or the foundation of the Muḥammadan religion" in 1892. Islam, he argued, was born of violence and would always remain tied to religious warfare; he may have felt some grudging satisfaction when an outraged Muslim obliged by assassinating him five years later.[166]

Yet by the same token modern Hindus miss out on the mobilizing potential of jihad, and in this context it makes sense to look for signs of emulation.[167] The Hindi lexicon includes the term *dharmayuddh*, with the translations "a religious war" or "crusade"[168] (here *dharma* is "religion" and *yuddh* is "war"). This is a perfectly good Sanskrit compound but not to be found in such a sense in the Sanskrit lexicon;[169] it

[164] Jordens, *Dayānanda Sarasvatī*, 268–69.

[165] K. W. Jones, *Arya Dharm*, 145.

[166] Ibid., 149–50, 193–94, 334.

[167] The incidents of Hindu nationalist terrorism against Muslims in recent years are a practical example of this phenomenon.

[168] McGregor, *Oxford Hindi-English dictionary*, 525b.

[169] Macdonell, *Practical Sanskrit dictionary*, 130c, gives the term only in the sense of "fair contest," i.e., a contest conducted in accordance with *dharma*. The other dictionaries I consulted do not have the word.

presumably represents a modern rendering of "crusade" or "jihad."[170] As such it has achieved a certain currency. In the context of state elections in Maharashtra in 1990, a pamphlet issued by the BJP declared that the current election was a *dharmayuddh* and named some Hindu gods to whose assistance the party would owe its prospective victory.[171] In Gujarat at the time of the destruction of the Bābrī Masjid in 1992, the organizations linked to the party called for a *dharmayuddh*; so did slogans painted on walls.[172] As might be expected, the term is also used by the Shiv Sena; thus, an editorial in the organization's daily paper spoke of *dharmayuddh* in the context of the massive communal riots that broke out in Bombay in the winter of 1992–1993.[173] It is no accident that the contexts in which the word is used typically pit Hindus against Muslims. One accordingly suspects that those who use it are thinking more of the Muslim idea of jihad than of the Christian notion of the crusade. But even so, the term does not seem to be a central one for the Hindu nationalists. The bottom line is perhaps that the leading historian of Hindu nationalism, in a monograph of some 550 pages, never has occasion to mention it.[174]

There is also an overt borrowing that is suggestive of emulation—the term for "martyr." Lekh Rām after his assassination was eulogized as one; the term used, *shahīd*, was ironically an Islamic one.[175] In itself this might reflect only the currency of Urdu as the literary language of the Punjab at the time. But the situation was no different for Hindi speakers a century later. Even before 1990 a common slogan of the VHP summoned Hindus not to forget the *śahīds* that had fallen in the seventy-seven battles fought against Muslims at Ayodhyā, the birthplace of Rām. In that year, in the course of the agitation there, the police added some real martyrs to these legendary ones, and the slogan became "Long life to

[170] The earliest such use of the term that I have come upon dates from 1919 (Jordens, *Swāmī Shraddhānanda*, 110, in a context of nationalist agitation against the British). Hansen states that the term is taken from the writings of V. D. Sāvarkar (d. 1966) (Hansen, *Saffron wave*, 164). See also R. Guha, *India after Gandhi*, 238, 299.

[171] Hansen, "BJP," 132.

[172] Shah, "BJP's riddle," 248-49; cf. also Shakir, "Analytical view," 93 (Ahmedabad in 1969).

[173] Katzenstein et al., "Rebirth of Shiv Sena," 385, citing an editorial of January 14, 1993; and cf. 374, 386, 387.

[174] Jaffrelot, *Hindu nationalist movement*.

[175] K. W. Jones, *Arya Dharm*, 195. I do not know when this term first appears in Hindu sources.

the *śahīds* of Ayodhyā!"[176] That a movement so noisily concerned about Indian cultural authenticity should have used so transparently Islamic a term at such an emotional moment is telling.[177]

This is not to say that the Hindu nationalists have no indigenous resources to appeal to. As noted above, the *Rāmāyaṇa*, one of the two great Indian epics, has the advantage of demonizing the enemy—whereas the setting of the other, the *Mahābhārata*, is more like an agonizing civil war within the religious community.[178] Hence the verse in which Rām vows "to rid the earth of demons" is a favorite of the VHP.[179] But the Hindu nationalists get scant satisfaction from the old Hindu law of war.

In conclusion, we can say that the Hindu nationalists, like the eighteenth-century Sikhs, have chosen the Muslims as their enemy. But their situation is unlike that of the Sikhs in two respects. First, Hinduism is a religion with a large following spread over a vast territory and devoid of institutions for centralized decision making. For all the pressures of modernity, and the efforts of the VHP to introduce some degree of coordination, Hinduism does not lend itself to the kind of radical religious innovation effected by the tenth Guru. Second, the Hindu population at large is not made up of Jāṭs; unemployed urban youth can make a lot of trouble, but they are not a substitute for the peasant warriors of the Punjab.

4. Latin American Catholicism

In the respect that concerns us here, the Jesus of the Gospels was closer to the Buddha than to Muḥammad. In the Sermon on the Mount, he says "Whosoever shall smite thee on thy right cheek, turn to him the other also" (Matt. 5:39, cf. Luke 6:29) and admonishes: "Love your

[176] Jaffrelot, *Hindu nationalist movement*, 421–23 (*Ayodhyā ke śahīdoṁ ko zindābād*; the form *śahīd* transliterates the Hindi orthography). For the seventy-seven battles, see also 402 and above, 92.

[177] The idea of martyrdom is not entirely absent from traditional Hindu sources: heaven is the reward of those who die in a number of ways, including death in the course of protecting a cow or a Brahmin or in an attempt to prevent miscegenation between the four classes (Kane, *History of Dharmaśāstra*, 3:58; cf. Manu, *Laws,* 109–10 (5.95), 243 (10.62)).

[178] See 66.

[179] Lutgendorf, "Interpreting Rāmrāj," 285n30.

enemies, bless them that curse you, do good to them that hate you, and pray for them which despitefully use you, and persecute you" (Matt. 5:44, cf. Luke 6:27–28, 35). He warns his disciples: "Behold, I send you forth as sheep in the midst of wolves" (Matt. 10:16). And yet Jesus does not quite speak with a single voice, for he also tells his disciples: "Think not that I am come to send peace on earth: I came not to send peace, but a sword" (Matt. 10:34). The role of the sword in his career is nonetheless marginal: at one point he instructs his followers to buy swords, but he then pronounces two to be enough; and later he intervenes when a sword is used to defend him (Luke 22:36, 38, 49–51). There is not much foundation for Christian violence here. As Erasmus (d. 1536) was to put it, "To fight the Turks we get no instructions from Christ and no encouragement from the apostles."[180]

But there is more to Christian scripture than the Gospels. Behind them lay the Old Testament, never repudiated by mainstream Christianity and hardly a text that appeals to pacifist sensibilities. God's instructions to the Israelites regarding the conquest of the territory he is giving them are the ultimate in ethnic cleansing: "Thou shalt save alive nothing that breatheth" (Deut. 20:16).[181] And through the mouth of the prophet Jeremiah he declares, "Cursed be he that keepeth back his sword from blood" (Jeremiah 48:10).[182] There is also the violent New Testament eschatology laid out in Revelation. Here the heavens open and Christ appears on a white horse to judge and make war, followed by the heavenly hosts; he has a sharp sword coming out of his mouth with which to "smite the nations," and with it he slaughters the kings of the earth and their armies (Rev. 19:11, 14–15, 19, 21). It is thus far clearer than in the case of the Buddhist canon that pacifism is not the only doctrinal option.

Early Christianity nevertheless left a gap that needed to be filled if this religion was to meet the needs of the martial races that lived in and around the Mediterranean world. A thirteenth-century French expert on the liturgy explains that knights (*milites*) show respect for St. Paul by standing during the reading of his epistles since he was himself a knight (*miles*).[183] This seems to reflect a very generous interpreta-

[180] Housley, "Necessary evil?," 271.

[181] For the historically problematic background to this doctrine, see Walzer, *In God's shadow*, chap. 3.

[182] This was to be a favorite Biblical quotation of Pope Gregory VII (in office 1073–1085), see Bartlett, *Making of Europe*, 260.

[183] Bloch, *Feudal society*, 316.

tion of scriptural metaphor;[184] without resorting to metaphor Muslim knights of the same period would have had a choice of any number of Muḥammad's Companions as role models. As this suggests, Christianity did gradually contrive to fill the gap, but the process was slow and somewhat awkward. It was not until the fifth century that a Christian doctrine of just war emerged, not until the ninth that the notion appeared that just wars could in some sense be holy, and not until the eleventh that this tradition was fused with that of pilgrimage to form the idea of the crusade.[185]

Once the idea was there, it proved fairly robust, despite the embarrassment that reference to the pacifism of the Gospels could give rise to.[186] Criticism of the very idea of the crusade does not seem to have been widespread in medieval Europe.[187] It did nevertheless exist, the two main arguments against the crusade being that for reasons of his own God might not wish to end Muslim rule in the Holy Land[188] and that the impact of crusading on unbelievers was such as to diminish rather than increase the chances of their conversion.[189] Moreover those preaching crusades would seem to have confronted considerable scepticism from their audiences, and it is significant that a thirteenth-century manual for such preachers stresses the importance of presenting the crusade as a form of just war and accordingly as defensive rather than aggressive.[190] At the same time canon lawyers and theologians responded without enthusiasm to the appearance of the idea of the crusade;[191] their reticence regarding warfare against infidels invites comparison with that of the Muslim jurists regarding warfare against fellow believers. If we ask whether the mere fact of belief in Islam is

[184] Paul tells Timothy to endure hardship "as a good soldier of Jesus Christ" (*bonus miles Christi Iesu*, 2 Tim. 2:3) and twice describes a coworker as a "fellowsoldier" (*commilito*, Philippians 2:25 and Philemon 2). I am indebted to John Gager for putting me on the right track here.

[185] Brundage, *Medieval canon law*, 19–20, 22–23, 27.

[186] For examples see Kedar, *Crusade and mission*, 97–98, 193.

[187] As the author of a monograph on the subject puts it, "Fundamental criticism of the concept itself was rare" (Siberry, *Criticism of crusading*, 220).

[188] Ibid., 12, 84.

[189] Ibid., 207–8.

[190] Brundage, "Humbert of Romans," 306, 309–10.

[191] Russell, *Just war*, 294–96; Mastnak, *Crusading peace*, 74–78. Aquinas holds the legitimacy of all wars to depend on the same three conditions, namely the authority of the sovereign (*auctoritas principis*), just cause (*causa justa*), and right intention (*intentio . . . recta*), without making any fundamental distinction between wars against believers and those against unbelievers (*Summa theologiae*, 35: 80.27 = 81–83 (2a2ae. 40, 1)).

an offense against God sufficient to justify attacking otherwise inoffensive Muslim societies, the answer we are given by the jurists and theologians is sometimes positive, sometimes negative, and often simply unclear,[192] with the negative answer tending to prevail over time.[193] Assuming that to merit attack the Muslims did have to commit an offense against Christians over and above their adherence to a false religion, what did that offense have to be? Saracen attacks on Christian lands obviously had to be met with force. Almost as straightforward was Saracen occupation of the Holy Land since it was the rightful property of Christians.[194] But if we ask whether this irredentism should be limited to the Holy Land or extend to all territory once possessed by Christians, the answer again tends to be unclear.[195] In other words, there was no well-established, more or less homogeneous doctrine equivalent to that of offensive jihad in Islam. Altogether, the crusade was a secondary development, without direct endorsement in the foundational texts of Christianity, and this rendered it less compelling than jihad and in the long run easier to disown.

In real life the single thing that did most to undermine the plausibility of the crusade was military failure on the Muslim front. This failure is easy to explain: Spain and the Mediterranean islands apart, the target region was as difficult of access for Christian armies from Western Europe as it was easy of access for Muslim armies based in the Islamic lands. But medieval Christians responded to failure in less secular terms. Their main reaction—or at least the respectable reaction—was to blame themselves, or the crusaders in question, for their sinfulness.[196] But there was another, more revealing reaction that is sometimes recorded among the laity: blaming God for dereliction of duty.[197] One of our sources describes how, in the course of the First Crusade, the cru-

[192] For more or less positive answers, see Russell, *Just war*, 198, 201; for more or less negative answers, see 122–23, 197, 198, 199, 255, 294; for cases where the answer is unclear, see 112, 114–15, 252, 257. For an early fifteenth-century controversy on the question whether peaceful infidels (not in this case Muslims) may be attacked, as the Teutonic Knights maintained they could be, see Belch, *Paulus Vladimiri*, 418–19, 459, 709–10 (especially the second principle), 713; I owe my knowledge of this controversy to Patricia Crone.

[193] See Russell, *Just war*, 294.

[194] Ibid., 122, 199, 201, 253.

[195] Occasionally the answer limits irredentism to the Holy Land (ibid., 122, 201); but for cases where the answer is left unclear, see 198-99, 255, 257.

[196] For some early examples, see Siberry, *Criticism of crusading*, 75–77, and in general her summary, 217–18.

[197] As Siberry puts it, "At a popular level there was a tendency to accuse God of deserting his people" (ibid., 69).

saders hear a false report of a military disaster at Antioch; in an impassioned response they tell God that if the account is true, then "we and the other Christians will abandon you and remember you no more."[198] A thirteenth-century troubadour reacted even more outrageously to Christian defeat: "It is with good reason that we cease to believe in God and worship Muhammad . . . because God and the blessed Mary desire that we be conquered against all justice."[199] What this lay reaction shows is that, despite the pacifism of the Gospels, ordinary Christians did not care to think of themselves as sheep in the midst of wolves; instead they now thought of their deity as, among other things, a war god whose task it was to deliver victory to his followers. But their religious heritage overall was ambivalent in its attitude to warfare.

This background suggests that Latin American Catholics in modern times would have more than one option with regard to warfare, and history bears this out.

The Cristero rebels of western Mexico in the later 1920s represent the militant strain of Christianity. In practice they were no match for the professional armies of the regime, but they were a significant threat to its authority in the countryside, especially at times when its military attention was focused elsewhere. They sang, "Let us go, valiant crusaders; let us go, let us go to fight; let us go with Christ the King, to conquer his kingdom."[200] A particularly striking feature of their rebellion was their vivid and emotive cult of martyrdom.[201] "We must win Heaven now that it is cheap" was a typical Cristero remark. "How easy Heaven is now, mother!," a young man about to be executed told her by way of consolation. A youth who was spared while twenty-seven of his companions were shot lamented that "God did not want me as a martyr." Women too savored martyrdom: one who stepped out of a doorway to see the rifles of the enemy pointing at her recalls how "I remembered that this moment was for me, I imagined the crown and I almost touched the palm." Another woman felt abandoned by God because her family had been spared; when her only son fell fighting, her reaction was joy amidst her tears. With more of a rhetorical flourish, the Cristeros of Jalisco prayed to the Virgin of Guadalupe that

198 Hagenmeyer, *Anonymi Gesta Francorum*, 359 (XXVII, 4).

199 Siberry, *Criticism of crusading*, 194. For other examples see 193–94.

200 "Vamos, valientes cruzados / Vamos, vamos a luchar / Vámonos con Cristo Rey / Su Reinado a conquistar" (J. A. Meyer, *Cristiada*, 3: 280n22); cf. also Bailey, *¡Viva Cristo Rey!*, 33.

201 J. A. Meyer, *Cristero rebellion*, 190–93. The cult was continued by the Sinarquists (Serrano Álvarez, *Batalla del espíritu*, 1:291–5); they had sixty-four martyrs by the end of 1940 (293).

"¡Viva Cristo Rey!" should be their last cry on earth and their first song in heaven.[202] But the Cristiada was a minor and untypical event in the modern history of Mexico, let alone of Latin America as a whole.

The Liberationists were closer to the irenic strand of the Christian heritage and accordingly displayed a rather inhibited attitude to violence. Thus, in El Salvador Archbishop Romero gave only conditional legitimacy to revolutionary violence in 1979,[203] while the Basque Jesuit Ellacuría (d. 1989) endorsed "violence performed on behalf of the oppressed" as "good violence," albeit to be ended as soon as possible; even he was ambivalent about Camilo Torres, the Colombian priest who had turned guerrilla and been killed in 1966.[204] The Brazilian Leonardo Boff was considerably more circumspect. He tells us that Jesus "was not prepared to seize political power" and kept his distance from the Zealots;[205] he "preferred death to the imposition of the Reign of God by violence."[206] On the other hand, following Jesus is never just a matter of "slavish imitation,"[207] and we have to filter his example though the sieve of the relativity of historical circumstances.[208]

The difference in attitudes between the Cristeros and the Liberationists is not surprising. The Cristeros were unreconstructed conservatives in a remote area of Mexico for whom the militant strand of medieval Catholicism was still a living force. The Liberationists, by contrast, were progressives in close touch with European modernity who found their religious inspiration in the unfiltered message of the Gospels; to the extent that they espoused violence, its source was more Marxist than Christian.[209]

5. Conclusion

Of the three founders of the world religions—Buddhism, Christianity, and Islam—Muḥammad was the only one to use warfare to advance his cause. In this respect he resembles Moses more than the Buddha

[202] J. A. Meyer, *Cristiada*, 3: 280.

[203] Sigmund, *Liberation theology*, 113.

[204] Ibid., 110–11; for Torres, see 25.

[205] Boff, *Faith on the edge*, 137; he clearly sees the Zealots as the Marxist guerrillas of the day.

[206] Ibid., 139.

[207] Ibid., 142.

[208] Ibid., 143.

[209] A quite different Christian milieu is that of Protestant fundamentalism in the United States. Given the strong tradition of gun ownership and the abundant supply of weapons in the country, the relative marginality of armed violence among its religious fundamentalists is striking.

or Jesus. Our narrative record of his military activities is a vivid one, with many of his sixty-five expeditions involving small numbers of men engaged in a style of irregular warfare appropriate to the Arabian environment. At the same time the canonical sources fully reflect the values behind Muḥammad's role as a military man: warfare against unbelievers was enshrined as a central theme in the foundational texts of the new religion. The later history of Islam rendered this theme less salient because of the embarrassing frequency of war between rival Muslim states, but it was by no means forgotten. By contrast, neither Hinduism nor Christianity is like this. The Hindu tradition, despite sharing the Buddhist concept of nonviolence, was in general quite comfortable with the fact that Hindus went to war; what makes the Hindu case so different from the Islamic case is the fact that Hindus are almost always thought of as making war on each other. The Christian tradition is more seriously conflicted. There is a clear message of pacifism in the Gospels, but it is offset by a strong vein of bellicosity elsewhere in Christian scripture—and one that lent itself to the later development of the idea of the crusade. But in neither Hinduism nor Christianity do we find an unambiguous endorsement of warfare against outsiders built into the foundations of the tradition.

One illustration of this contrast is the divergent conceptions of martyrdom in war. The slain warriors of ancient India—the ones who went to heaven to be chased by divine damsels—were fighting fellow Hindus. The Christians did develop the idea that those who fell in battle in a holy war against false believers were martyrs. As we have seen, this was a prominent theme in the Cristero understanding of their struggle against the impious Mexican regime; it had already made a striking appearance in the context of papal warfare in the mid-eleventh century[210]—though in Western Europe, perhaps significantly, the idea seems not to antedate the rise of Islam. But such thinking is not just older in Islam than it appears to be in Western Christianity, it also bulks larger.[211]

Under modern conditions all this has tended to put the Islamic heritage in the limelight. On the one hand Muslims who find jihad in

[210] See Erdmann, *Idea of crusade*, 122–23, describing it as a novelty. Two Byzantine emperors had already favored the idea, the first being Heraclius (ruled 610–641) in the context of war against the Persian empire (see Howard-Johnson, "Heraclius' Persian campaigns," 85), and the second Nicephorus Phocas (ruled 963–969), whose attempt to introduce it was frustrated by the church (see Canard, "La guerre sainte," 617–18; Viscuso, "Christian participation," 37–38). I owe these references to Patricia Crone.

[211] D. Cook, *Martyrdom in Islam*, 30, 166.

one way or another embarrassing have generated a large amount of apologetic—and this includes such pioneers of Islamism as Mawdūdī and Quṭb. And on the other hand Muslims disposed to engage in military violence against others have found in it a perfect charter for jihadism, a justification of their struggle and an inspiration for their practice of irregular warfare in areas of chaos. The Hindu heritage, by contrast, does little for modern Hindus beyond providing a basis for polemic against Islam. The Hindu nationalists' concept of religious war looks like a modern calque, and their idea of the martyr who falls in combat against non-Hindus is transparently a borrowing from Islam. Meanwhile, the Christian heritage, as might be expected, has been used in antithetical ways insofar as it has been used at all: on the one hand we have the Cristeros with their cult of martyrdom, and on the other hand the reluctance of the Liberationists to do more than flirt with Marxist violence. In sum, no heritage is a reliable predictor of the behavior of those who inherit it, but just as surely heritages are not interchangeable.

CHAPTER 6

Divine jealousy

1. Introduction

Several passages of the Pentateuch speak of the deity as "a jealous God."[1] The point is always to warn the Israelites not to succumb to the temptations of idolatry or the worship of other gods; one passage makes particular mention of "the gods of the people which are round about you."[2] In a monotheistic—or perhaps we should say monolatrist—religion this is naturally the primary domain of divine jealousy. But we could easily imagine such a god seeking to monopolize far more than just the cultic loyalties of his followers: in one way or another his jealousy might extend to all knowledge or at least to all values. A religion of such a kind could aptly be called all-embracing. In practice none of the religious heritages we are concerned with fits this model exactly, but they differ significantly from one another in how close they come to it. The domains of knowledge or value worth considering here include identity, politics, philosophy, and science. But the domain that will concern us most in this chapter is law, and it generates some particularly striking contrasts between our three cases.

Our interest in these contrasts between heritages is as usual linked to differences in their adherents' responses to the pressures of modern times. In principle those in possession of an all-embracing religious heritage might be expected to insist on maintaining or restoring it in full, leaving no room for the adoption of any aspects of the cultures of the peoples round about them—an outcome that would almost certainly prove severely debilitating in the modern world. In explaining actual outcomes one thing we would thus want to ask is how far the heritage in question really was all-embracing. Did it traditionally seek to monopolize *all* domains of knowledge or value? And for those domains it did aspire to monopolize, was it in practice successful, or had it long ago resigned itself to accommodation with elements of other

[1] Ex. 20:5, 34:14; Deut. 4:24, 5:9, 6:15 (*ēl qannā*). In Ex. 20:5 and Deut. 5:9 this is a self-description.

[2] Deut. 6:14.

cultures? Here it would also be illuminating to consider the record of pre-modern encounters with other civilizations; the more jealous the god, the less encouragement he could be expected to provide for reaching accommodations with such civilizations, let alone taking them as role models.

Real-world outcomes would also obviously be influenced by other factors, of which two are worth highlighting here. The first is the degree of the pressure to adopt a given element of an alien culture. There are, for example, two domains in which this pressure can be particularly high. One is the medical domain, where the survival of the individual is at stake; the other is the military domain, where the survival of the community as such may be in question. In these fields what works can be very hard to ignore.

The other factor is the extent to which the heirs of the pre-modern heritage are actually committed to maintaining or restoring it. They will, of course, differ among themselves. But at least among the elites of non-Western societies, the default persuasion in modern times has been nationalism, and the level of substantive nationalist commitment to ancient heritages has typically been low. This is not just because a commitment to the whole heritage is usually unrealistic, though this is a crucial part of the background. It also has to do with the basic logic of nationalism. As mentioned earlier, the key element in the differentiation of the European nations among themselves was ethnicity, whereas the civilization of Christian Europe was something they shared.[3] The fact that the idea of the nation vests identity in ethnicity, not civilization, thus helped the non-Western elites who adopted it to disinvest from their own traditional civilizations. Perhaps nobody put the point as bluntly as the Turkish nationalist Ziya Gökalp (d. 1924) in the year before he died: "Civilization is the clothes of nations." The inference was clear: "Just as individuals change their clothes so nations may do."[4] Gökalp was not in fact suggesting that Islam itself should be dropped in the laundry basket: "The Turkists are those who aim at Western civilization while remaining Turks and Muslims."[5] But as this implies, Islam in his vision was to be cut down to size.[6] If such is the

[3] See 1–2.

[4] Gökalp, *Turkish nationalism*, 266.

[5] Ibid., 290.

[6] In fact he projected this retrenchment back onto the Ottoman past, seeing Islam as only one element among many that made up Ottoman civilization. This civilization was "a mixture of institutions borrowed from the Turkish, Persian, and Arab cultures, from

logic of nationalism, we cannot expect to find nationalists championing the all-embracingness of a heritage; their use of it is likely to be at most eclectic and opportunistic. But nationalists are not our sole concern in this book—or even our primary one. What, then, of people who do not regard their civilization as clothing to be discarded at will—people who take divine jealousy seriously even today and accordingly face tougher choices?

With this perspective in mind, let us now proceed to look at each of our three cases.

2. Islam

The Koran at one point describes itself as a book sent down "to make everything clear" (*tibyānan li-kulli shayʾin*, Q16:89). A leading Companion of the Prophet is said to have cited this verse to show that "every kind of knowledge (*kull ʿilm*) has been revealed in this Koran, and everything has been made clear for us in the Koran."[7] This interpretation may seem to take the phrase too literally, but it is by no means isolated. Thus a fourteenth-century commentator cites it with approval and goes on to say that the Koran includes all useful knowledge about the past and the future, everything that is permitted and forbidden, and whatever people are in need of with regard to both this world and the next.[8] Other exegetes take a more limited view of the scope of the verse. One way of thinking takes it to refer to the religious sciences alone,[9] while another restricts it to questions of what is permitted and forbidden[10]—and even there, there is the obvious point that the Koranic treatment of a question may be no more than summary, with the rest left to inference.[11] This range of views sets the scene for us. On the one hand it is clear that the idea of an all-embracing religious heritage has a certain appeal. But on the other hand we see a readiness to draw lines that leave some domains inside the heritage and others outside it.

---

the religion of Islam, and from the Eastern and, more recently, Western civilizations" (ibid., 108).

[7] Ṭabarī, *Tafsīr*, 7: 634 no. 21,861 (to Q16:89).

[8] Ibn Kathīr, *Tafsīr*, 2: 641.20 (to Q16:89).

[9] Fakhr al-Dīn al-Rāzī, *al-Tafsīr al-kabīr*, 20: 99.14 (to Q16:89). See also the tart comments of Shāṭibī, *Muwāfaqāt*, 2: 127.4.

[10] Ṭabarī himself takes such a view (7: 633.16), and all but one of the early exegetical traditions he cites support this position (633–34, nos. 21,857–60).

[11] Abū ʾl-Layth al-Samarqandī, *Tafsīr*, 2: 246.27 (to Q16:89).

The celebrated North African historian Ibn Khaldūn (d. 1406) provides us with a fine example of such line drawing: "Muḥammad was sent to teach us the religious law (*al-sharāʾiʿ*). He was not sent to teach us medicine or any other ordinary matter (*min al-ʿādiyyāt*)."[12] This was not just Ibn Khaldūn's personal opinion, for he went on to support it by referring to a variant of a well-known tradition according to which Muḥammad, on recognizing that he had given bad advice about the cultivation of palm trees, told those concerned that they knew more about their worldly affairs than he did.[13] This tradition firmly and authoritatively places the domain of agronomy outside the religious heritage. Ibn Khaldūn, however, was primarily interested in medicine, and here the situation was less clear-cut. We are told that on visiting a sick Companion, Muḥammad diagnosed a heart problem. He did not treat it and instead referred the patient to a doctor who had been trained at a major center of medical learning in the Persian Empire, where he presumably studied the Greek medical tradition associated with the names of Hippocrates (fifth century BC) and Galen (d. 199).[14] Such a referral would suggest the same deference to experts on worldly matters as in the case of the palm trees, except that Muḥammad then proceeded to complicate things by prescribing an oral medicine and instructing the patient to have the doctor administer it to him.[15] This anecdote is one of a number of traditions with medical content ascribed to Muḥammad. Several of the ninth-century collectors accordingly included such traditions in their compilations, bringing them together in sections on medicine. This phenomenon is known as "Prophetic medicine" (*al-ṭibb al-nabawī*). The pious fourteenth-century author of a book on the subject praised Muḥammad's medicine to the skies: it was as much superior to standard medicine as the latter was to the medicine of old women.[16] Ibn Khaldūn, however, dismissed it as mere folk medicine, "in no way part of the divine revelation."[17] In this he seems to have been in line with mainstream Muslim opinion: in the culture at large prestige attached to the Greek medical tradition, while Prophetic medicine remained a pietistic niche product.

[12] Ibn Khaldūn, *Muqaddima*, 3: 119.9 = Rosenthal, *Muqaddimah*, 3: 150. Shāṭibī (d. 1388) regularly uses the term *ʿādiyyāt* to refer to those domains of the law that are not *ʿibādiyyāt* (see, for example, *Muwāfaqāt*, 1: 319.2).

[13] Muslim, *Ṣaḥīḥ*, 1836 no. 2363 (*faḍāʾil* 38).

[14] For the medical education of al-Ḥārith ibn Kalada, see *EI*², *Supplement*, s.n. (C. Pellat).

[15] Abū Dāwūd, *Sunan*, 4: 7–8 no. 3875 (*ṭibb* 12).

[16] Ibn Qayyim al-Jawziyya, *al-Ṭibb al-nabawī*, 5.2.

[17] Ibn Khaldūn, *Muqaddima*, 3: 119.5 = 3: 150.

This was in accord with the prevalent attitude to science at large in the traditional Islamic world. An eleventh-century Spanish scholar, himself an expert on Islamic law who served as judge in the city of Toledo, wrote a book about the cultivation of the sciences among the nations of the world.[18] He enumerated eight nations that belonged to the scientific club and thus constituted "God's elite among the human race": the Indians, Persians, Chaldaeans, ancient Greeks, Byzantines, Egyptians, Arabs, and Hebrews.[19] Overwhelmingly, the nations he listed were non-Muslim. In other words his idea of science was a cosmopolitan one to which local religious persuasions, whether monotheistic or pagan, were irrelevant. Of course, not everyone was comfortable with this. There was, for example, an interesting discussion of the shape of the earth—was it spherical or flat?—among the Imāmī Shīʿite scholars. A fourteenth-century scholar provided a succinct and elegant demonstration that the earth is round, based on the fact that lunar eclipses are observed at times that vary with longitude.[20] An eighteenth-century scholar refuted this view on the ground that a spherical earth was manifestly incompatible with the revealed texts.[21] But a scholar who died in 1829 dismissed the arguments against a spherical earth, pouring particular scorn on the idea that we cannot trust the astronomical experts because their Islam is questionable.[22] One rhetorical question he posed comes back to medicine in a very practical way: how can one rely on the opinion of some Jewish doctor and yet disregard the views of Muslim astronomers?[23] In short, there was a clear conception of the autonomy of the sciences, and this conception, though it could be challenged, seems to have been prevalent. This did not mean that sciences of non-Islamic origin were thereby excluded from being considered in any sense Islamic. As a seventeenth-century Moroccan scholar explained, the general category of the Islamic sciences included certain sciences of the ancients (*ʿulūm al-awāʾil*). They counted as Islamic in the sense that they were practiced in the Islamic community (*fī millat*

[18] *EI*[2], art. "Ṣāʿid al-Andalusī" (G. Martinez-Gros).

[19] Ṣāʿid al-Andalusī, *Ṭabaqāt al-umam*, 39.12. For the listing of the eight, see 40.2; for these nations as God's elite (*ṣafwat Allāh min khalqihi wa-nukhbatuhu min ʿibādihi*), see 44.3.

[20] Fakhr al-Muḥaqqiqīn, *Īḍāḥ al-fawāʾid*, 1: 252.14.

[21] Baḥrānī, *Ḥadāʾiq*, 13: 266.15, 267.9.

[22] Narāqī, *Mustanad al-Shīʿa*, 4: 169.19. It was a sixteenth-century scholar who had called in question the Islam of the astronomers (ʿĀmilī, *Madārik al-aḥkām*, 3: 121.11).

[23] Narāqī, *Mustanad al-Shīʿa*, 4: 171.3. Compare the controversy over the orientation of the mosques of Fez (Dallal, *Islam, science*, 7–8).

al-Islām) and provided benefit to the religion (*fī dīn al-Islām*); they too could be described as pertaining to the Sharīʿa (*sharʿiyya*), for all that this was not common usage.[24] But even in this way of seeing things the external provenance of these sciences remains clearcut.

If the religious heritage did not comprehend all knowledge, did it nevertheless embrace all values? Here we encounter the phenomenon of domains over which the religious heritage claimed sovereignty but within which historically it reached more or less de facto accommodations with rival normative traditions. The single most important domain of this kind is law. But just because it is so central, let us postpone the discussion of the Sharīʿa to the end of this section[25] and in the meantime bring together some other instances of the phenomenon.

We have already met one relevant case: we have seen how Muslim identity coexisted with a variety of ethnic identities across the Islamic world,[26] and there is no need to return to this here. As we will see later at some length, a similar pattern obtained in the field of political values.[27] In brief, the early Islamic community was a polity, ruled first by its founder and then by his successors, the caliphs, and the caliphate retained a certain relevance down the centuries in both theory and practice. Yet when the center of gravity of the Islamic world shifted out of Arabia, there was no choice but to accommodate to the style of government that had long characterized the adjoining lands of ancient civilization.[28] Unlike the tribal values of Arabia in the time of Muḥammad, these traditions were alien to the Islamic religious heritage; this and the residual claims of Islam to be a polity meant that while it had to live with them, it could not accord them full normative status. A related development involved the steep social hierarchies that Islam learnt to tolerate without ever fully legitimating them.[29]

We can discern analogous effects on a more intellectual level. Thus the religious sciences, despite their sovereignty, continued to coexist with the Greek philosophical tradition. In an earlier chapter we encountered an argument turning on a contrast between Kurdish and Arab scholars around the beginning of the nineteenth century, but we did not stop to see what the argument was about.[30] According to the

[24] Yūsī, *Qānūn*, 177.13, and cf. 176.12; see Stearns, "Legal status of science," 276–77.
[25] See 270–82.
[26] See 8–18.
[27] See 309–19.
[28] As pointed out in Al-Azm, *Islam und säkularer Humanismus*, 28.
[29] See 173–74.
[30] See 12–13.

anecdote, the Arab scholar was deploring the fact that most Kurdish scholars of his day occupied themselves with philosophy (*falsafa*) and avoided the religious sciences, whereas Arab scholars commendably did the opposite. The Kurdish Ṣūfī won the argument by responding that regrettably the goals of both groups were worldly and that to pursue such goals by invoking the authority of God and the Prophet was in fact worse than doing so by invoking Plato and Aristotle.[31] What he conspicuously did not do was to echo the view of a scholar like Averroes (d. 1198) that cultivating philosophy was a good thing[32] and to infer from this that the Kurdish scholars had nothing to be ashamed of. The anecdote is telling because it dramatizes both of the key features of the situation. On the one hand there was the prolonged record of coexistence—which is why philosophy was still there for the Kurdish scholars to cultivate on the eve of modern times. And on the other hand there was the continuing religious hostility to it[33]—which is why both parties to the argument could still regard it with disapproval.

What this cursory survey of domains of knowledge and values shows is that there was both coexistence and tension—but that the tension was understandably greater in domains of value than in domains of knowledge.

Another approach to the workings of divine jealousy suggested above is to look at Islamic encounters with alien civilizations prior to modern times. Here, rather than go to the historical antecedents of Muslim relations with Christian Europe, it may prove more illuminating to look at the interactions with two other major civilizations of pre-modern times, those of India and China.[34]

[31] Ālūsī, *Gharāʾib*, 91.8, cited in El-Rouayheb, "Myth," 215–16.

[32] In a short work on the legal status of studying philosophy, he argued that we have an obligation to accept the truths established by the ancients and to do so with gratitude (Ibn Rushd, *Faṣl al-maqāl*, 10.13, and cf. 5.7 = Averroes, *Harmony of religion*, 48, and cf. 44). The passage was drawn to my attention by Qasim Zaman.

[33] For a classic account of this hostility, see Goldziher, "Attitude of orthodox Islam" (originally published in German in 1916). Goldziher deals with the Greek philosophical and scientific heritage at large but remarks that it was primarily Aristotelian metaphysics that was rejected by Islamic orthodoxy (192). He was well aware of the continuing coexistence (186, 209). Gutas has argued that Goldziher's account is fundamentally misconceived (Gutas, *Greek thought*, 166–75); while he himself quotes several examples of hostility to Greek learning (156–57, 160, 162, 163–64, 165), he is at pains to explain them in other ways or to minimize their significance as special cases (see generally 191).

[34] Intellectually the most impressive record of any encounter of a pre-modern Muslim with another civilization is the eleventh-century polymath Bīrūnī's account of the high culture of India, but it is barely relevant to our present concerns. For my own understanding of this encounter, see M. Cook, *Brief history*, 287–90.

In India the Muslims achieved a large measure of political and military dominance, just as they had done in the heartlands of the Islamic world. Where the Indian case differed crucially was in the failure of the Muslims to achieve demographic dominance, despite significant Indian conversion to Islam; over the subcontinent as a whole they never ceased to be dwarfed by the massive non-Muslim population. Thus Baranī quotes a thirteenth-century Muslim vizier comparing the Muslims of the country to a mere sprinkling of salt.[35] In this respect the predicament of Muslim rulers in India was quite different from that of, say, the Mamlūk rulers of Egypt and Syria (1250–1517), or even the Ottomans, whose extensive subjugation of Christian populations in the Balkans was balanced by their possession of lands that had long been predominantly Muslim. It was accordingly not hard for Muslims in India to think of themselves as foreigners in a strange land. As we have seen, Shāh Walī Allāh, who claimed Arab descent, spoke of his ancestors falling into exile (*ghurbat*) in India.[36] Indian Muslims certainly did not have to feel this way; one poet of the early fourteenth century wrote about India with eloquent patriotism.[37] But a sense of living in an alien environment remained an option even a thousand years after the Muslims had first appeared in the Indus valley. In this situation one might look for either of two reactions on the Muslim side: an even more uncompromising assertion of the Muslim ascendancy as already established in the heartlands or a willingness to accommodate the culture of the majority of the population. In fact both responses are historically well attested.

Baranī illustrates the uncompromising attitude with his usual excess.[38] It is the duty of kings, he says, to overthrow unbelief and idolatry; but should the total uprooting of idolatry not be feasible, then they should at least do their best to insult, disgrace, dishonor, and defame the Hindus, who are the worst enemies of God and the Prophet. The sign of a king who protects Islam is that when he sees a Hindu, his eyes grow red and he wishes to bury him alive. The passage is excessive because Baranī held a view that was rare among the Muslims of India, namely that Hindus were not eligible for toleration on the terms open to Jews and Christians.[39] But whether or not Muslims had to tol-

[35] Nurul Hasan, "Sahifa-i-Naʿt-i-Muhammadi," 105.10 = 102.

[36] See 14–15.

[37] Ali, "Perception of India," 217–18.

[38] Rizvi, *Muslim revivalist movements*, 9n3, passage (a); and see also Baranī, *Fatāwā*, 165.18; Habib and Khan, *Political theory*, 46.

[39] Cf. Friedmann, *Tolerance and coercion*, 84–85.

erate unbelievers, they certainly did not have to respect them. Thus Sirhindī, who believed in accepting the poll tax from the Hindus, is not far behind Baranī in the general tone of his remarks.[40] As we have seen, he held the coexistence of Islam and unbelief to be unthinkable; he believed that if one of them did well, it could only be at the expense of its rival and that "to honour the one amounts to insulting the other." The honor of Islam thus lay in insulting unbelievers, and anyone who respected them dishonored Muslims.[41] They were to be kept at arm's length like dogs, and contact with them should be minimal. Such views are not, of course, to be taken as a reliable guide to Muslim practice: Baranī complained bitterly that the Hindus were openly worshipping their idols and celebrating their festivals even in the capital city,[42] and Sirhindī was no happier with the way things were in his own day.[43] But in championing the ascendancy of Islam and the Muslims, they articulated a well-established principle and appealed to a deep-rooted loyalty, one that finds poignant expression in the faith of Shāh Walī Allāh that, were the Hindus to attain lasting dominion over the region of Hindūstān, God would inspire their leaders to adopt Islam, just as he had done with the Turks.[44]

The alternative for the Muslim elite was to seek a reconcilation with the Hindus and their culture. Such ideas were associated with the Mughal emperor Akbar (ruled 1556–1605). This ruler's dominions, as we are told by his son Jahāngīr (ruled 1605–1627), had ample room for the adherents of opposed religions—whereas in Iran there was room only for Shīʿites and in Central Asia and the Ottoman Empire only for Sunnīs.[45] One practical outcome of this irenic attitude was Akbar's translation program. He apparently held a belief of a kind that is widespread among well-meaning people in the world today, namely that hatred between Muslims and Hindus was a result of mutual ignorance. To dispel this ignorance each side had to be given access to the authoritative texts of the other.[46] Thus the *Mahābhārata* was translated from Sanskrit into Persian under Akbar, and the *Rāmāyaṇa* under Jahāngīr.[47]

[40] Rizvi, *Muslim revivalist movements*, 248. For his view of the poll tax, see 249.

[41] See 92.

[42] Schimmel, *Islam*, 20-21; and see Habib and Khan, *Political theory*, 48.

[43] See the text translated in Friedmann, *Shaykh Aḥmad Sirhindī*, 82.

[44] Walī Allāh, *Tafhīmāt*, 1: 269.13, cited in Baljon, *Religion and thought*, 15n1.

[45] Rizvi, *Muslim revivalist movements*, 221n1.

[46] See the text quoted in Schimmel, *Islam*, 85, together with that quoted in Rizvi, *Muslim revivalist movements*, 353n1.

[47] Rizvi, *Muslim revivalist movements*, 353, 447.

In the mid-1650s the Mughal prince—later emperor—Dārā Shukōh (ruled 1657–1659) translated the *Upaniṣads*—not, of course, without assistance.[48] In another work he described how, being already familiar with "the true religion of the Sufis," he now "thirsted to know the tenets of the religion of the Indian monists"; after conferring repeatedly with knowledgeable Hindus, he "did not find any difference, except verbal, in the way in which they sought and comprehended Truth."[49] It is not hard to find further examples of such thinking.[50]

But there were, of course, others who took the view that this kind of irenicism was exactly the temptation that the Muslim elite in the Indian environment had to avoid. Sirhindī responded to Akbar's initiatives by denouncing him (though not by name) as a tyrant whose misdeeds included demolishing mosques, honoring pagan temples, and translating the laws of the unbelievers into Persian with the aim of obliterating Islam.[51] Reconciliation with the Hindus was clearly not one of Sirhindī's priorities. He complained that the tyrant had forbidden the sacrifice of the cow,[52] which, as we have seen, he considered to be one of the most important rites of Islam in India thanks to the grief it gave to the Hindus.[53] He made mincemeat of a Hindu who wrote to him saying that Rāma, Kṛṣṇa, and Allāh were just different names of God.[54] Likewise Dārā Shukōh's "inclination towards the religion of the Hindus" proved useful in the context of Mughal power politics when it came to justifying his execution in 1659: were he to establish his rule, it was urged, the precepts of Islam would give way to "the rant of infidelity and Judaism."[55] We have already encountered a scholar who in the late seventeenth century poured scorn on Akbar's idea of being at peace with everyone (*ṣulḥ al-kull*).[56] And when Shāh Walī Allāh spoke of being in exile in Hindūstān, the moral was not that Muslims needed to be reconciled with Hindus but rather that they had to avoid being influenced by their abominable customs—such as not allowing a widow to remarry.[57] In short, the irenic ideas of Akbar spoke to the realities of Muslim life in

[48] Ibid., 359–60.
[49] Ibid., 356.
[50] See, for example, Alam, *Languages of political Islam*, 89–90, 93, 109, 150, 170, 173–75.
[51] Friedmann, *Shaykh Aḥmad Sirhindī*, 33–34.
[52] Ibid., 33.
[53] See 63–64.
[54] Rizvi, *Muslim revivalist movements*, 254.
[55] Ibid., 362–63. The relevance of Judaism in this context is a little obscure.
[56] See 222.
[57] Walī Allāh, *Tafhīmāt*, 2: 297.5 (he does not seem optimistic about the prospects for resisting the pull of this Hindu custom). The Koran strongly implies that widows are free to remarry (Q2:234).

India, but they had no foothold in the mainsteam of the Islamic tradition, and those who held them could always be reminded of this.

The situation of the Muslims of China was very different. They were geographically remote from the Muslim heartlands—in contrast to the Muslims of India, whose contacts were so close that to a large extent they transacted their affairs in Persian.[58] Like the Muslims of India, those of China were a minority, but a much smaller one; and unlike them they never had a chance of achieving political and military dominance. They did indeed owe their presence in China to conquest, but the conquerors in this instance were the Mongols—pagans who later turned Buddhist. Thus it was thanks to the extensive patronage extended to foreigners by the Mongol Yuan dynasty (1260–1368) that a significant Muslim community came to reside in the cities of China. But the dynasty fell, the Mongols left, and patronage on the same scale was no longer available to Muslims under the ethnically Chinese Ming dynasty (1368–1644), nor was it restored under the Manchu Ch'ing dynasty (1644–1912). This meant that Muslims left behind after the departure of the Mongols had no choice but to come to terms with the Chinese environment, becoming in effect Chinese Muslims and not just Muslims in China. More specifically, the way for elite members of the community to get ahead was now to demonstrate proficiency in Chinese literary culture by taking the official examinations that controlled entry into the bureaucracy.

The result was the appearance of a Muslim literature in Chinese that pressed the argument that Confucian and Muslim values were fully compatible, if not identical. Thus an inscription purportedly dating from 742, but likely to have been forged by Chinese Muslims in the Ming period, says of Confucius and Muḥammad that "their language differed, yet their principles agreed."[59] A seventeenth-century Muslim scholar told some officials who were inspecting a mosque: "The ethics of our teaching and those of the Confucian teaching are the same. Whoever follows our precepts and laws takes loyalty to rulers and obedience to parents as a duty."[60] Deftly exploiting internal Chinese religious

[58] In the preface to his Persian translation of the Koran, Shāh Walī Allāh explains that he intends this version for the sons of craftsmen and soldiers, who should read it as soon as they come of age (Baljon, *Religion and thought*, 149). See further Alam, *Languages of political Islam*, 132–33. Indeed one of the remarkable features of the Mughal state was the extent to which its bureaucracy was staffed by Hindus who had mastered Persian literary culture and even come to see intrinsic value in it (129–32).

[59] Mason, *Arabian prophet*, 278; somewhat differently Broomhall, *Islam in China*, 84. For the dating, see D. D. Leslie et al., *Islam in traditional China*, 54.

[60] Ben-Dor Benite, *Dao of Muhammad*, 101.

tensions, he smugly contrasted Muslim ethics with those of the "fatherless and rulerless" Buddhists and Taoists. An early eighteenth-century biographer of Muḥammad preserves an account of a consignment of books that the Arabian prophet allegedly sent to China; it states that these books "teach about loyalty to rulers and filial piety to parents" and that they "do not differ from our Confucianism."[61] Elsewhere this author explains why he had read deeply in the Chinese literary tradition: "I am indeed a scholar of Islamic learning. However, it is my opinion that if one does not read the classics, the histories, and the doctrines of the hundred schools, then Islamic scholarship will be confined to one corner and will not become the common learning of the world."[62] In a more autobiographical vein he goes on to say that after spending ten years living in seclusion in a mountain forest, he "suddenly came to understand that the Islamic classics have by and large the same purport as Confucius and Mencius."[63]

From the point of view of the wider culture of Islam, this syncretic literature of the Chinese Muslim elite was very much confined to one corner. Even on its home ground in the cities of eastern China, we should probably see it as under a degree of threat on two fronts. On the one hand there were the hardline Muslims within the community. In the eighteenth century one of them wrote a pamphlet that included the warning: "Anyone who says that the study of the means of assuring one's livelihood is more important than that of the sacred scripture will be excluded from Islam—for that is to ascribe importance to this world and to lack respect for the sacred scripture and religious doctrine."[64] He also required Muslims to practice what by Chinese standards was arrogant incivility in their relations with adherents of other religions: "If, while talking to someone, you refer to the true religion with the phrase 'my humble religion', and to another religion with the phrase 'your noble religion', you will be excluded from Islam—for that is to do honor to other religions and to disparage that of Purity and Truth."[65] And on the other hand Confucianism could be very seductive for successful members of the Muslim elite: we learn from Matteo Ricci in the early seventeenth century that "Saracens" tended to apostatize once they had passed the official examinations and lost their fear of the Muslim

[61] Ibid., 189–90.
[62] Ibid., 148–49; for another translation, see Murata et al., *Sage learning*, 93.
[63] Murata et al., *Sage learning*, 94.
[64] Mission d'Ollone, *Recherches*, 401.
[65] Ibid., 401–2.

clergy.[66] Nor is Islamic-Confucian syncretism likely to have cut much ice with the Chinese elite. One prominent Chinese Muslim author was able to persuade some Confucian scholars to write laudatory prefaces for his books,[67] and the title of his heavily Confucianized work on Muslim ritual found a place in an imperial compendium of 1773–1782. But the work was placed in the company of books that "contained little that was praiseworthy and much that was contemptible," and an editorial comment, while conceding that the author's literary style "is actually rather elegant," maintained that "the clever literary ornamentation does him no good" for the simple reason that "Islam is fundamentally far-fetched and absurd."[68] Nevertheless, what happened in this corner of the world provides a suggestive precedent for the Muslim interaction with the West as it developed in the nineteenth century: it shows that there are situations in which, confronted with the unquestionable dominance of a non-Muslim culture, Muslims could and would accommodate to its values. With this in mind let us leave China and return to the heartlands of the Islamic world.

How did divine jealousy play out there in contexts in which it seemed advantageous for Muslims to adopt elements of infidel culture? In a very basic sense Muḥammad's religion could hardly be anything but allergic to such borrowings—his message was the truth, and anything else was false. Hence his saying, "He who imitates a people is one of them":[69] ape an unbeliever and you are one.[70] But such a counsel, if applied inflexibly, could end up undermining the Muslim ascendancy. What if the unbelievers had developed a useful practice that Muslims needed to adopt to their own advantage? This was manifestly a question that would arise with particular acuteness in the field of warfare: for anyone who plays to win, the only feasible course is to adopt up-to-date military methods whatever their source. This much is common sense. But it so happens that Muḥammad had provided his followers with a fine precedent for just such adaptiveness. In a consultation before the battle of the Khandaq, a Persian follower of the Prophet described how in his country—at the time still a land of infidels—people

[66] D. D. Leslie, *Chinese Jews*, 32n2.

[67] Frankel, *Rectifying God's name*, 43–47.

[68] Ibid., 51–53.

[69] Abū Dāwūd, *Sunan*, 4: 44 no. 4031 (*libās* 4): *man tashabbaha bi-qawm fa-huwa minhum*.

[70] Cf. the lament of the Shāfiʿite Muftī of Egypt in 1882 that the collaboration of Egyptian Muslims with unbelievers had gone so far that "they have affected their manners in language and conduct" (Peters, *Islam and colonialism*, 81).

would dig a defensive trench to block the advance of enemy cavalry, and he recommended using the same tactic against the imminent attack of the pagan Meccans and their allies.[71] Muḥammad adopted this recommendation, with excellent results. There was thus precedent in the very foundations of Islam for appropriating at least the military methods of the infidel. That opened the door to a pragmatic attitude toward the useful features of infidel cultures in general.

The willingness to borrow in the military domain did not disappear. A Bosnian scholar writing in the 1590s describes the experience of the Muslims on the Croatian border over the preceding half century: every time their infidel enemies on the other side of the frontier invented some new weapon, they had the better of the Muslims; but once the Muslims adopted the invention, they would prevail again, thanks to the help of God and the strength of Islam.[72] He laments, however, that in his own day the unbelievers were forging ahead with new weapons, while the Muslim army was showing itself negligent in adopting them.[73] A little later, in 1638, a Morisco translated from Spanish into Arabic a work showing the usefulness of cannons for those engaged in jihad.[74] The original author was an Andalusian Muslim who had served as a cannoneer in the Spanish army and was familiar with new developments in cannonry in Europe and the Americas; the work survives in many manuscripts. Though not to be taken for granted, this much openness in a culture is unsurprising—its absence would be suicidal.

Muslim societies were in fact willing to go well beyond the military domain in borrowing what they deemed useful from infidel cultures. Translations provide good examples of this. Thus, in Morocco we also find works on astronomy and medicine translated from Spanish or Portuguese into Arabic;[75] in India a Sanskrit text on astronomy was rendered into Persian in the fourteenth century and one on music in the seventeenth;[76] Ottoman translations of European works made in the sixteenth to eighteenth centuries covered astronomy, geography,

[71] Wāqidī, *Maghāzī*, 445.4. Ibn Hishām does not have the story.

[72] Ḥasan Kāfī Āqḥiṣārī, *Uṣūl al-ḥikam*, 32.12 (Arabic version); İpşirli, "Hasan Kâfî el-Akhisarî," 268.28 (Turkish version).

[73] Note, incidentally, that he does not suggest that it is time for the Muslims themselves to get into the business of technological invention; he seems satisfied to leave that to the Christians.

[74] Ḥajjī, *Ḥaraka*, 163.1.

[75] Ibid., 163.11.

[76] Rizvi, *Muslim revivalist movements*, 365, 447.

and even European history.[77] We know something of the background to the first translation of a European geographical work in the mid-seventeenth century: the Ottoman polymath who was behind the project considered the state of Muslim geographical literature a disgrace in comparison to that of the Christians, wretched unbelievers whose proficiency in this science had enabled them to discover the New World and seize the ports of India.[78] On the other hand the Ottomans did not waste time on technologies they deemed useless: an Ottoman ambassador to Vienna in 1748 was given a dramatic demonstration of the phenomenon of electrical conduction but did not think it worth pursuing.[79]

What about borrowing whole institutions from the wretched unbelievers? Here we seem to encounter a certain reticence. An Ottoman reformist of the first half of the seventeenth century was persuaded that a major reason for the sad state of the empire was the fact that its officials were hired and fired at will. Instead, he wanted them to have security of tenure; more than that, he thought that they should inherit their offices.[80] This looks suspiciously like a proposal to Europeanize the empire by establishing a hereditary aristocracy. But if it was, our reformist does not make this explicit beyond a vague reference to non-Muslim nations. His main tactic is to present his prescription as something the heretical Persians had learnt from the Ottomans themselves and which the Ottomans, perhaps inspired by the Persian example, should now revive in their own empire. In a different part of the Islamic world, a Moroccan ambassador visiting Madrid in 1690–1691 gives careful descriptions of the postal system and the gazettes he encountered there, and it is hard to avoid the impression that he thought them in principle good ideas; but if he believed that the Moroccans would do well to adopt them, he does not say so.[81] On the other hand an eighteenth-century Ottoman chronicler, explaining the Grand Vizier's decision to send an ambassador to France in 1720, refers quite

[77] B. Lewis, *Muslim discovery*, 156, 169, 169–70; Adnan-Adıvar, *Osmanlı Türklerinde ilim*, 122–23, 150–51, 153, 167.

[78] Gökyay, "Kâtip Çelebi," 22n1, 23n1.

[79] B. Lewis, *Muslim discovery*, 231–32.

[80] Qochı Beg, *Risāle*, 84.6, 86.13, 114.3. By contrast, Busbecq, the mid-sixteenth century Austrian ambassador in Istanbul, was impressed precisely by the lack of a hereditary aristocracy in the Ottoman Empire and saw in this meritocracy the secret of Ottoman success (Forster and Blackburne Daniell, *Ogier Ghiselin de Busbecq*, 154–55; and see above, 174).

[81] Ghassānī, *Riḥla*, 92.19, 94.2; and see B. Lewis, *Muslim discovery*, 117–18, 303.

explicitly to the value of the intelligence that Christian states derived from sending ambassadors to the courts of other rulers.[82]

This decision, and most other instances of borrowing from a non-Muslim culture that we have looked at so far, could be understood as a variant of Muḥammad's pragmatic adoption of a Persian military tactic. One notices something useful in an alien culture, one recognizes that one could use it to realize one's own purposes, and one proceeds to appropriate it. This fits well with the cosmopolitan conception of science that we noted above.[83] But adopting the *techniques* of another culture stops a long way short of recognizing its distinctive *values*, let alone adopting them. Not that the adoption of values is historically uncommon: it happened every time a society threw itself open to what it saw as a higher religion—be it Buddhism, Christianity, or Islam—or a higher culture—be it Greek, Latin, or Chinese. But societies already in possession of such a religion and culture are unlikely to adopt the values of others under normal circumstances, and those of the traditional Islamic world were particularly unlikely to do so; the case of the Muslim community in China is an intriguing but rare exception.

Here, then, is a clear and simple distinction. On the one hand there are the techniques of other cultures, which may be borrowed when apt to serve native purposes; and on the other hand there are the values of those cultures, which are to be sedulously avoided. A distinction of this kind has proved very robust in the Islamic world under modern conditions, partly because it fits well with the pre-modern heritage and partly no doubt because it is such an obvious distinction to make.[84] It facilitated the large-scale adoption of useful Western technologies and institutions in the later nineteenth century with little or no religious friction—railways and the telegraph, for example.[85] Moreover both Mawdūdī and Quṭb were given to thinking along these lines.

Two disciples of Mawdūdī describe his attitude toward the adoption of elements of Western culture in such terms. They stress that in his view there was nothing to prevent Muslims from "abstracting the healthy achievements of the modern West—its sciences, its tech-

[82] Göçek, *East encounters West*, 7. By contrast, Ḥajarī, the seventeeth-century Morisco, saw the fact that Christian rulers maintained permanent embassies in the Ottoman capital without the Ottomans reciprocating as a reflection of superior Ottoman power (Ḥajarī, *Nāṣir al-dīn*, 126.20 = 183).

[83] See 253.

[84] For the same distinction in another culture, see Levenson, *Confucian China*, 1: 59–60.

[85] See B. Lewis, *Emergence of modern Turkey*, 180–83. More surprisingly, even banks were widely accepted (see Kuran, *Long divergence*, 161–64).

nology, its techniques of efficient organisation and administration"—provided always that these elements were "value-free" and could be assimilated into "the Islamic scheme of life." Indeed he held that such things are not intrinsically Western; they "are in fact part of the common heritage of all mankind to which all nations, including Muslims, have contributed."[86] This approach could be applied quite liberally, as in Mawdūdī's observation that there is nothing in Islamic law to prevent the consultative council (*majlis al-shūrā*) of the Islamic state from being "elected by Muslim votes," for all that there is no precedent for such a procedure from the time of the early caliphs.[87] Just as arresting is Mawdūdī's criticism of two Indian Muslim leaders of the early nineteenth century for failing to think of sending a deputation of worthy scholars to Europe "with a view to investigating and inquiring into the causes of the material superiority of her people."[88] It is thus fitting that the Mahdī, when he comes, will prove to be "the most modern of all the moderns."[89] But Mawdūdī's disciples also emphasize

[86] Ahmad and Ansari, *Mawlānā Mawdūdī*, 17. The invocation of the Muslim contribution to Western science is an old one; an Algerian author writing in 1836–1837 noted that the Franks themselves admitted to having initially derived their knowledge of the sciences from Islamic books (*kutub al-Islām*, see Ḥamdān Khwāja, *Itḥāf*, 73.1). He wrote to defend the adoption of quarantine measures by Muslim states in order to prevent the spread of plague; he mentions a recent work arguing that anyone adopting such measures is an unbeliever (149.4)—a claim that is not without a basis in revelation since Muḥammad was often understood to have denied the existence of contagion (see M. Ullmann, *Islamic medicine*, 87; Stearns, *Infectious ideas*, 25–26, 32–36). Ḥamdān Khwāja's general view is not unlike Mawdūdī's: Frankish skill in the sciences has greatly increased (*Itḥāf*, 72.9), and we should adopt their science as long as it is not in contradiction with our religion (78.2). In other respects, too, he is an interesting figure in the early interaction of educated Muslims with the West (see Pitts, "Liberalism and empire," drawn to my attention by Alexander Bevilacqua). Jeremy Bentham (d. 1832) says of him that he "wears a turban, but ridicules Mahommedanism" (298–99).

[87] Maududi, *Political theory of Islam*, 44 = Mawdūdī, *Naẓariyya*, 49.3; similarly Maudūdī, "First principles," 253, 257. Compare his references to voting under the early caliphs in the context of the election of the head of state (250, 251). The only reference to majority voting I know of in a medieval Muslim source comes in the procedure laid down by Māwardī (d. 1058) for the appointment of prayer leaders in private mosques. The choice is up to the people of the street or tribe whose mosque it is, but if they disagree, "one proceeds according to the view of the majority (*qawl al-aktharīn*)," with the ruler intervening as tiebreaker in the event that the opposed parties are equal in number (Māwardī, *al-Aḥkām al-sulṭāniyya*, 176.5).

[88] Maududi, *Short history*, 113 (for this work, first published in 1952, see Ahmad and Ansari, *Mawlānā Mawdūdī*, 40 no. 131). The passage forms part of a politically incorrect discussion in which Mawdūdī contrasts the massive progress of Europe in the eighteenth and nineteenth centuries with the fitfulness of comparable efforts on the part of the Muslims in India (109–14).

[89] Maududi, *Short history*, 41.

the aspects of Western culture that should be rejected: the Western philosophy of life, "the Western standard of evaluation," and the pervasive ills of Western social life.[90] For Mawdūdī such rejection of alien cultural influences had been a characteristic feature of Islamic revival down the centuries. A renovator (*mujaddid*), he tells us, is "a most uncompromising person with regard to un-Islam, and one least tolerant as to the presence of even a tinge of un-Islam in the Islamic system."[91] He describes how the corruption of the early Islamic polity had led to the inundation of the Muslim world by Greek, Iranian, and Indian philosophy, literature, and science.[92] Successive revivals meant renewed struggles against these poisons, particularly Greek philosophy,[93] and a similar struggle is clearly in place in our own time. Mawdūdī's hostility to Greek philosophy is a sharp reminder that he is an Islamist; he does not see the ninth-century translation movement as a demonstration of the commendable cultural openness of the Muslim elite of the day.[94] Obviously—and correctly—he did not regard the Greek philosophical tradition as "value-free." Unlike the Mahdī, Mawdūdī was by no means "the most modern of all the moderns."[95]

Quṭb too has a significant amount to say about borrowing from infidel culture. Like Mawdūdī, he is far from rejecting such borrowing categorically, for all that the basic principle of Islam is to accept God's law (*sharʿ*) alone, whatever it may be.[96] But he is keen to draw as firm a line as he can between those aspects of infidel culture that can be adopted without reservation and those that must be avoided, or at least treated with great caution. Much as Mawdūdī does, he makes a basic distinction between pure science and its practical applications on the one hand,[97] and those aspects of culture that involve values on the

[90] Ahmad and Ansari, *Mawlānā Mawdūdī*, 17.

[91] Maududi, *Short history*, 34.

[92] Ibid., 28–29, and see 52.

[93] Ibid., 57 (Ghazzālī), 65 (Ibn Taymiyya), 87 (Shāh Walī Allāh).

[94] Contrast the late-Ottoman positivist Shemseddīn Sāmī Frashëri (d. 1904), who in 1883–1884 found in the translation movement a precedent for the adoption of European civilization, writing that the descendants of the Companions of the Prophet borrowed Greek civilization "in its entirety" (see his article "Transferring the new civilization," 151a).

[95] See the tart comments of Riexinger, *Sanāʾullāh Amritsarī*, 549–53, 559.

[96] Quṭb, *Maʿālim*, 37.7 = 36. Compare the attitude of Ḥasan al-Bannā to such borrowing in the early Islamic period: there was nothing to prevent the adoption of useful features of foreign civilizations, provided this did not affect Muslim social and political unity (Bannā, *Majmūʿat rasāʾil*, 208.13 = Wendell, *Five tracts*, 18).

[97] Quṭb, *Maʿālim*, 126.11 = 109.

other.[98] He aptly quotes Muḥammad's remark to the cultivators tending the palm trees that they knew their worldly affairs better than he did, since this establishes the existence of a category of matters indifferent.[99] In this way he follows good medieval precedent in accepting the existence of a utilitarian domain of the secular, while firmly refusing to open it to non-Islamic values. But his attitude on this point does not seem entirely consistent. In his book on social justice in Islam, his statement of the general rule is that anything may be adopted that conforms to the basic conception and general spirit of Islam,[100] and he stresses that the objective is not isolation from the "caravan of mankind" (*rakb al-bashariyya*)[101]—though he dislikes the idea of joining the march at the tail of the Western caravan (*al-qāfila al-gharbiyya*).[102] This perspective does not seem to exclude some degree of appropriation of Western values.

The same kind of thinking can also be found among the jihadis. Even the Ṭālibān, when in power in Kābul, did not object to modern medicine as such—it was their puritanism with regard to the mixing of the sexes that led them to impose constraints on the functioning of hospitals.[103] One jihadi author invokes the Persian origin of the idea of digging a trench to establish the principle that we may import the latest military ideas—though this must not, of course, become a mechanism whereby irreligious concepts (*al-mafāhīm al-haddāma*) are smuggled in.[104]

But, of course, smuggling goes on all the time, as actively as in the tunnels of the Gaza Strip. A lurid example that gets less attention than it deserves is the recent explosion of popular works on eschatology

[98] I abstract this from the list given ibid., 126.3 = 108.

[99] Ibid., 126.24 = 109; also Quṭb, *Maʿraka*, 104.13; cf. above, 252. His brother Muḥammad Quṭb has a very clear exposition of this dispensation and its limits in his *Qabasāt min al-Rasūl*, 184–87; he explains that it refers only to purely technical questions, condemning those who seek to extend it to all worldly affairs (186.1).

[100] Quṭb, *ʿAdāla*, 236.8 = 328.

[101] Ibid., 238.1 = 329; and see Quṭb, *Maʿraka*, 35.16.

[102] Quṭb, *ʿAdāla*, 266.17 = 354; and cf. Quṭb, *Maʿraka*, 68.15, 69.5.

[103] Rashid, *Taliban*, 218, decree 2. The Ṭālibān are also said to have burnt medical texts, but the reason given is their objection to the depiction of the human body, not to modern medicine as such (Wielawski, "Doctors heed call"). For a sect in Upper Egypt that did reject modern medicine, see Sivan, *Radical Islam*, 86; for a Salafi-oriented community in the Gaza Strip that does not go to hospitals and clinics, see Hroub, "Salafi formations," 230.

[104] Shinqīṭī, *Numūdhaj*, 2.18. The trench is similarly invoked by Faraj (Jansen, *Neglected duty*, 210–11 §108).

in which traditional Muslim prophecies are creatively blended with contemporary Christian apocalyptic and other Western fantasies.[105] At a more elite level the Ḥamās Charter is instructive. It stresses the positive role in the Palestinian struggle of Islamic art, including songs and plays, and calls on writers, intellectuals, media people, educators, and the like to apply their skills in the service of the cause.[106] Likewise in Egypt an Islamist play was performed in 1991 for an audience of some 300 people, and at the end of the play the audience joined the actors in a song about the Islamic awakening.[107] None of this would have gone down well with the Ṭālibān,[108] and it is not reducible to mere technique. Altogether, to seek to exclude Western values from modern Muslim societies is to champion a lost cause, and it is not surprising that even Islamists fail to practice what they preach. As we will see, Quṭb espoused the Western value of freedom (*ḥurriyya*),[109] and indeed his writing shows extensive Western influence—as when he speaks of the "spirit of Islam" (*rūḥ al-Islām*).[110] In this respect he might well have come across to a conservative as too much of a Westernizer, and the same could be said of Mawdūdī.

Where does all this leave modern Islamic attitudes toward the familiar domains of secular knowledge as cultivated in the West? At one extreme we may encounter outright rejection. Such was the stance of the radical fundamentalist Shukrī Muṣṭafā (d. 1978): for him only religious knowledge was permitted, so that even arithmetic that does not

[105] See D. Cook, *Contemporary Muslim apocalyptic literature*, 77–83, 92, 188, and the summary at 214–16.

[106] See Articles 19 and 30, translated in Mishal and Sela, *Palestinian Hamas*, 187–88, 194–95.

[107] Wickham, *Mobilizing Islam*, 172–73.

[108] Cf. Rashid, *Taliban*, 218–19, decree 3. Likewise the Salafīs consider television, representative art, theatre, and sculpture to be forbidden (Bonnefoy, *Salafism in Yemen*, 50).

[109] See 334–35.

[110] Quṭb, *ʿAdāla*, 19.15 = 22, 236.8 = 328. The earliest modern Arabic attestation of this phrase that I have seen is in a work published by Muḥammad ʿAbduh (d. 1905) in 1898 (*Risālat al-tawḥīd*, 120.16; I take the date of printing from the note at the end of the text (134.9), rather than from the title page, which gives it as 1315). As pointed out to me by Qasim Zaman, the phrase had already appeared in English in the title of the second edition, published in 1891, of a work by a well-known Indian Muslim (Ameer Ali, *The Life and teachings of Mohammed or the spirit of Islâm*; note also vii, ix, xiii–xv, and the titles of chaps. 16, 18, and 19). The only medieval occurrence of the phrase known to me is in Ibn Qayyim al-Jawziyya, *al-Wābil al-ṣayyib*, 94.11, whence Saffārīnī, *Ghidhāʾ al-albāb*, 2: 383.20. For Quṭb's Western terminology, see also Shepard, "Islam as 'system,' " 44.

help us to worship God is idolatry.[111] But this attitude is rare.[112] At the other extreme, there is unqualified adoption—the secularist position. In between we find qualified adoption. One might expect the qualification to be fairly specific, as in the thinking of the religious right in the United States: there should be biology but with intelligent design in place of evolution, cosmology but with the insertion of creationism.[113] In fact, however, it tends to take a more general form, articulated in the call for the "Islamization of knowledge." This term dates only from 1977,[114] but the objective had already been formulated by Mawdūdī in 1962: "to rearrange and reconstruct the different sciences from an Islamic point of view."[115] Or as Ismāʿīl al-Fārūqī, the leading theorist of Islamization, expressed it in 1982 at the Second Conference on Islamization of Knowledge: "As disciplines, the humanities, the social sciences, and the natural sciences must be re-conceived and rebuilt, given a new Islāmic base and assigned new purposes consistent

[111]See Al-Azm, "Islamic fundamentalism reconsidered, Part I," 105, 109, 119. I am indebted to Abraham Udovitch for drawing this article and its continuation to my attention.

[112]One might perhaps expect to find such attitudes among the Salafīs. But a lively account of the differences between Salafī and non-Salafī students and teachers at a college located in a village of southern Yemen revolves around dress, chewing *qāt*, watching television, and eating French chicken (Bonnefoy, *Salafism in Yemen*, 191–99); the only indication of disagreement over the curriculum—which included English and the natural sciences—relates to the presence of pre-Islamic poetry (196).

[113]My sense would be that a paper presented at the First International Conference of Islamic Education, held in Mecca in 1977, is of this kind (Ata-ur-Rahman, "Scientific education"). The author, a chemist at the University of Karachi, has a lot to say about the need to re-Islamize the culture of the Islamic world and exclude the corrupting influence of the West, and this extends to preventing "the poison of materialistic dogma from seeping into our educational institutions" (168); presumably this would exclude evolutionism and nontheistic cosmogony from the curriculum. At one point he speaks of basing scientific education in Muslim countries on "principles and guidelines laid down in the Quran and Hadith" (174), but there is no sign that in practice he would seek to reconstruct the natural sciences, though he would impose some ethical limits on them (172–73). Indeed, he recommends the recruitment of leading Western scientists through the offer of lucrative salaries, though they would be replaced after five to seven years by Muslim scientists (176). In the end this probably reflects his greater concern with the military imbalance of power between the West and the Islamic world than with the cognitive imbalance. One of the editors of the volume is more explicit about the limits to be placed on science: after condemning the concoction of "new philosophies about the origin of the universe or the evolution of the species which blatantly contradict Allah's injunctions," he counsels that a scientist whose findings and analysis are in conflict with "fundamental assumptions stated in the Quran" should "realize that he has not as yet found complete data" (Nasseef, "Introduction," 145).

[114]See Abaza, *Debates on Islam*, 23.

[115]See Ahmad, "Islamization of knowledge," 123n1.

with Islām."[116] This latter strategy reflects a sense that modern Western learning has to be reshaped in a drastic fashion because it is alien—its methodologies are tied, as Fārūqī put it, "to the value system of an alien world."[117] How far that is true may be arguable, but there is a more basic point to be made about the alien character of modern science: however cosmopolitan in principle, it has in practice been owned and operated by the West, whereas the equally cosmopolitan science of medieval times was to a large extent owned and operated by Muslims.

Against the background of the general ideas developed in this section, we come now to the domain of law. Here we should start by attending to the implications of two grand observations of principle about the Sharīʿa in pre-modern times. The first is that it is God's law, and the second is that it does not change.

One of the central commitments of Islam is to a divine monopoly of the making of law. The Sharīʿa is the law of God, revealed through his Prophet; it is comprehensive, covering both religious and worldly affairs; it is central to his religion; and its study is the queen of sciences, the core of a scholar's education. Moreover, God's law is the only valid law; as for those who fail to judge according to what God has sent down, "they are the unbelievers" (Q5:44). In a related verse God asks disapprovingly: "Is it the judgment of pagandom (*al-Jāhiliyya*) then that they are seeking?" (Q5:50). A fourteenth-century Koranic exegete comments on this verse that God "is expressing disapproval of anyone who departs from the firmly-established law of God, which comprehends all good and forbids all evil, and instead has recourse to anything else—opinions, fancies, and terms originated by mere men without a basis in God's Sharīʿa."[118] The idea of a divine monopoly in the domain of law is thus a core component of Islam.[119] In this field, then, the aspiration of the religion to sovereignty is a strong one.

[116] Fārūqī, "Islamization of knowledge," 16. The conference was held in Islamabad. For a study of Fārūqī's thought see Stenberg, *Islamization of science*, chap. 4, especially 208–15; compare also the views of Ziauddin Sardar (81–83).

[117] Fārūqī, "Islamization of knowledge," 16. He uses the word "alien" repeatedly on this page.

[118] Ibn Kathīr, *Tafsīr*, 2: 77.4 (to Q5:50).

[119] It is not, of course, unique to Islam. In contrast to the general run of ancient Near Eastern rulers, the Israelite monarchs would seem to have had no power to make law, and the Deuteronomic prescriptions for limited monarchy emphasize the king's subjection to Mosaic law (Deut. 17:18–20, and cf. Deut. 4:44–45). See further Walzer, *In God's shadow*, 16–17, 22–25.

This characterization of Islamic law needs nevertheless to be qualified in three significant ways.

In the first place the assertion of divine monopoly did not imply a denial of continuities with pre-Islamic law, in particular that of the pagan Arabs. The jurists had no problem with the idea that many elements of Islamic law had such an origin,[120] and the antiquarians loved to describe them.[121] That even the jurists were comfortable with this is in large measure a reflection of the streak of indulgence, not to say pride, with which many Muslims regarded the heritage of pre-Islamic Arabia, the Jāhiliyya. This indulgence is nicely captured in a tradition according to which Muḥammad would sit with his Companions while they quoted poetry and conversed about matters of the Jāhiliyya; he himself would be silent during such exchanges, but would occasionally smile.[122] The jurists will accordingly affirm without hesitation that a certain compurgation procedure (*qasāma*), or a certain form of commercial partnership (*qirāḍ*), was practiced in the Jāhiliyya. What they will not do, however, is to attribute the continuing *validity* of such institutions to their pre-Islamic origin: in each case these have a place in the Sharīʿa only because they were specifically endorsed by Islam—in both these instances by the Prophet.[123] In other cases we have what looks like tacit appropriation of an element of pre-Islamic Arabian law. Thus, there is a saying to the effect that a condition agreed upon by the parties to a contract prevails in any subsequent litigation (*al-sharṭ amlak*). We are told in one antiquarian account that the first to say this was a certain judge in pre-Islamic times,[124] but when jurists use the maxim, as they occasionally do, they make no mention of the judge and usually attribute it, if at all, to the Prophet.[125] A much more widely cited saying has it that in cases of disputed paternity the child is to be assigned to the marriage bed, in other words to the mother's husband (*al-walad lil-firāsh*); again we are told that the first to say this was a judge in pre-Islamic times,[126] but again the jurists who quote the maxim ignore

[120] For lists of examples, see Shāṭibī, *Muwāfaqāt*, 2: 125.1, 524.7.

[121] See, for example, Askarī, *Awāʾil*, 1: 112.1, 113.1.

[122] See, for example, Ibn Ḥanbal, *Musnad*, 5: 105.22.

[123] For *qasāma*, see, for example, Ibn ʿAbd al-Barr, *Istidhkār*, 25: 328 no. 38,437; for *qirāḍ*, see, for example, 21: 119–20 no. 30,709.

[124] Balādhurī, *Ansāb al-ashrāf*, 9.13.

[125] As in Sarakhsī, *Mabsūṭ*, 15: 20.12, 16: 20.14, 20: 70.7. Such a tradition seems to be unknown to the traditionists.

[126] See, for example, ʿAskarī, *Awāʾil*, 1: 117.1.

this, treating the dictum as authoritative because the Prophet said it.[127] In sum, without either explicit endorsement or tacit appropriation by Islam, the law of the Jāhiliyya is of interest only to the antiquarians. If pagan law continues to be valid in Islam, it is because God and his Prophet have made it so.

In the second place establishing just what God's law might be on the basis of the Koran and Sunna was a process fraught with scholastic indeterminacy. The Sharīʿa was the subject of extensive and continuing disagreement among the jurists of the four Sunnī law schools, so much so that one thirteenth-century scholar had a dream in which God met the founders of the schools with the accusation: "I sent you a single prophet with a single law, and you've made it into four!"[128] The dream had a happy ending—but not because the charge could be refuted; the day was saved by the ingenuity with which one of the founders tied up the divine prosecution with procedural objections. What God left unmentioned here was that on many points the views of any given school might vary from scholar to scholar and be subject to change over time. All this would suggest that there must have been considerable flexibility in the process by which the jurists supposedly derived the details of the law from the foundational texts. And indeed a recent study of Ḥanafī law from the eighth to the eighteenth century shows that the flexibility was not just considerable, it was absolute, ensuring that "any conceivable candidate for the law could be reconciled with the binding texts"—though in practice, as might be expected, legal inertia meant that the law normally stayed the same.[129] But however much Sharīʿa was in practice a scholars' law, in principle it was still God's law.

In the third place declaring a monopoly and enforcing it are different things. The Sharīʿa in fact faced two serious competitors in the pre-modern Islamic world.

The first, and more limited in time and space, was a legal tradition associated with the steppe nomads who overran the northeastern Islamic world from the eleventh century onward, and in particular with the thirteenth-century Mongol conqueror Chingiz Khān. This pagan ruler promulgated, or was believed to have promulgated, a law

[127] See, for example, Māwardī, *al-Ḥāwī al-kabīr*, 14: 247.22; for the saying as a tradition of the Prophet in a canonical collection, see, for example, Muslim, *Ṣaḥīḥ*, 1080–81 nos. 1457–58 (*al-riḍāʿ* 10).

[128] Khazrajī, *al-ʿUqūd al-luʾluʾiyya*, 4: 206.2 = 1: 190–91; see Goldziher, "Catholic tendencies," 135.

[129] Sadeghi, *Logic of law making*, xiii, 14, and see also xii, 30, 172.

code known as the "Great Yāsā" (the word also appears in forms like "Yāsāq").[130] To quote the same Koranic exegete on those who fail to judge by what God has sent down (Q5:44), God in this verse condemns "the way the Tatars judge through royal rulings derived from their king Chingiz Khān, who laid down for them the Yāsaq, which consists of a book collecting together laws which he borrowed from various legal systems—Judaism, Christianity, Islam, and others—together with many laws that he derived from nothing but his own speculations and fancies. This became a law that was observed among his descendants, and which they preferred to giving judgment according to the Book of God and the practice (Sunna) of God's Messenger." The passage is not to be relied on for the history of Mongol law, but it clearly reveals a principled Islamic hostility toward those who live by man-made law: "Whoever of them does this is an unbeliever who must be fought until he returns to the law of God and His Messenger, so that he does not judge by anything else in matters great or small."[131]

Whatever our exegete might say, in practice Muslim populations in the northeastern regions of the Islamic world lived under rulers who maintained this un-Islamic legal tradition for centuries, despite their conversion to Islam. A fourteenth-century Persian historian and geographer commented that for Mongols to reside in a city was not the rule and "contrary to the Yāsāq of Chingiz Khān."[132] To the east a fifteenth-century Tīmūrid ruler in Samarqand is tendentiously remembered as having asked about the code of Chingiz Khān, only to be told that this infamous institution had been completely discarded in favor of the Sharīʿa.[133] Meanwhile Bābur (d. 1530), the Tīmūrid founder of the Mughal Empire in India, remarks that while in former times "our fathers and forefathers meticulously observed the Genghisid Code," he himself does not consider it absolutely binding.[134] But tension between Yāsā and Sharīʿa was still in evidence in sixteenth-century Central Asia under Özbeg rule[135] and was receiving attention as late as the 1630s.[136]

[130] For a brief account of this by a scholar who is sceptical of the historicity of the code, see Morgan, *Mongols*, 83–87.

[131] Ibn Kathīr, *Tafsīr*, 2: 77.7 (to Q5:50); cf. above, 270.

[132] Barthold, *Turkestan*, 461n5, where the original Persian is quoted.

[133] McChesney, "Zamzam water," 72.

[134] Thackston, *Baburnama*, 232; I owe my knowledge of the passage to Alam, *Languages of political Islam*, 81. The word translated by Thackston as "Code" is *töre*, the Turkish for *yāsā*.

[135] See Isogai, "*Yasa* and *sharīʿa*," especially 93–94.

[136] McChesney, "Zamzam water," 72.

Meanwhile to the west the Ottomans continued the steppe tradition by developing their own system of state-made law. They preferred to call it by the innocuous Arabic (originally Greek) term Qānūn, rather than perpetuate the use of the flagrantly un-Islamic Mongol term Yāsā (though in one document of 1518 confirming the existing law code of a recently conquered province in southeastern Anatolia, the two terms are used as synonyms).[137] Thus a sixteenth-century author used the term Qānūn when he stated: "The Conqueror of Istanbul, Sultan Mehmed, together with his wise vezir Mahmud Paşa, planned well for the future by establishing a venerable law."[138] At the same time the Ottomans seem to have been at some pains to reduce the substantive differences between Qānūn and Sharīʿa.[139] Ottoman Qānūn was thus by no means as flagrantly un-Islamic as Mongol Yāsā.

Yet the very existence of this brand of man-made law alongside God's law could cause the Ottomans discomfort. In Egypt in 1521, a scholar denounced an Ottoman regulation as "the Yasaq of unbelief" (*yasaq al-kufr*) and went to prison for it.[140] In 1669 the Ottomans virtually completed the conquest of Crete from the Venetians, after which they had to decide who owned the land and on what fiscal terms. They broke entirely with Ottoman tradition and proceeded "in accordance with the exalted practice (*sünnet*) of the Prophet that was followed in the realms conquered in the time of the Rightly-guided Caliphs," as set out in "the books of jurisprudence"—that is to say, the books of Islamic jurisprudence.[141] This might sound like empty rhetoric, but it was not: they went on to ban a whole list of taxes typical of the Ottoman fiscal system and

[137] Barkan, *Kanunlar,* 155. Here the title "Register of the laws (Yāsās) of the province of Urfa" is followed by the heading "Itemization of the law-code (Qānūnnāme) of the province of Urfa in accordance with the law (Qānūn) of Ḥasan Pādishāh." The latter is the Aq Qoyunlu ruler Uzun Ḥasan (ruled 1457–1478). Likewise a late sixteenth-century source defines "Yāsā" as the name of the Qānūnāme of Chingiz Khān (see *Tarama sözlüğü,* 4361). For an approving reference to *yasāgh-i pādishāhī* by a fifteenth-century Ottoman chronicler, see Heyd, *Old Ottoman criminal law,* 169–70. For the use of the term *yasaq* to refer to Ottoman law in Egypt in 1521, see Rafeq, "Syrian *ʿulamā*," 12. The word *yasak* in its modern Turkish sense of "forbidden" (sc. by the law of the state) is not a neologism (for Ottoman usage, see *Tarama sözlüğü,* 4362; Sāmī, *Qāmūs-i Turkī,* 1528–29).

[138] Fleischer, *Bureaucrat and intellectual,* 178. Compare an inscription of 1557 describing the reigning sultan, Süleymān the Magnificent (ruled 1520–1566), as *nāshir al-qawānīn al-sulṭāniyya* (Inalcık, "Suleiman the Lawgiver," 106).

[139] Cf. Imber, "*Zinā* in Ottoman law," especially the conclusion, 189.

[140] Rafeq, "Syrian *ʿulamā*," 12.

[141] Barkan, *Kanunlar,* 351.4; and see Heyd, *Old Ottoman criminal law,* 153–54; Greene, "Islamic experiment?," 61–66; Greene, *Shared world,* 22–29; Veinstein, "Les règlements fiscaux," 6–9, 11–12.

regularly set out in provincial law codes, specifying that "household tax, title-deed tax, beehive tax, scarecrow tax, pasturage tax, winter-quarters tax, summer-pasture tax, offence tax, crime tax, windfall tax, bride tax, salt tax, and other miscellaneous innovations (*bida'*) known as customary taxes (*rüsûm-ı 'örfiye*) are forbidden and abolished."[142] Instead, "only the legal taxes (*rüsûm-ı şer'iye*) derived from the books of jurisprudence . . . are to be levied on the afore-mentioned island"; the curse of God, the angels, and all mankind was invoked upon the head of anyone altering these provisions.[143] In making these unusual arrangements, the Ottoman authorities were ignoring an elaborate Islamic justification of the standard Ottoman fiscal system devised by the leading religious authority of the previous century.[144] Nor was this all: in 1696 the sultan issued a decree commanding that the Sharīʿa be the sole basis of future orders and forbidding the use of the offending term "Qānūn" in tandem with "the noble Sharīʿa."[145] This was not typical of the Ottoman situation, but it brings out a characteristic asymmetry: nobody—or nobody until the twentieth century—declared as a matter of high principle that future orders should be based solely on Qānūn and that Sharīʿa should not be mentioned alongside it. At most we find delinquent individuals invoking Qānūn to the exclusion of Sharīʿa: one tells his legal adversary that as a member of the military class he does not recognize the Sharīʿa (*ben ʿaskerī ṭāʾifesinden olmaghla sherʿ bilmem*), a second that since there is Qānūn, Sharīʿa has no role to play in their dispute (*sherʿ bizim aramıza girmez*).[146] Another such asymmetry

[142] The list is missing owing to a lacuna in the text of the regulations of 1670–1671 from which I am quoting, but it can be supplied with fair confidence from those of 1704–1705 (Barkan, *Kanunlar*, 354, §3).

[143] Ibid., 352, §7.

[144] See Inalcık, "Islamization of Ottoman laws," with a translation of a key text (103–6); note the perfunctory justification of the unlawful Ottoman tax on pigs (115).

[145] Heyd, *Old Ottoman criminal law*, 154–55; ʿOthmān Nūrī [Ergin], *Mejelle-i umūr-u belediyye*, 1: 568, in the last paragraph of the footnote. Contrast a seventeenth-century Ottoman scholar who declares Ottoman law superior to that of Chingiz Khān, giving as one reason that it is joined to the Sharīʿa of the Prophet (Heyd, *Old Ottoman criminal law*, 170). The issue recurs briefly in the story about identity politics in Istanbul in the 1730s, where the non-Arab scholars tell their Arab counterparts that "our use of these secular laws (*qawānīn*) in religious judgments" has "a valid basis (*aṣl muʿtabar*) in the great Sharī'a which is known to anyone with an advanced understanding of Koran and Sunna" (Zayyānī, *al-Turjumāna al-kubrā*, 362.15, and see above, 18–19).

[146] Menteşzāde ʿAbdürraḥīm Efendi, *Fetāvā*, 1: 91.36, 92.32, also 92.12; see Gerber, *State, society*, 111. ʿAbdürraḥīm Efendi served as Shaykh al-Islām and died in office in 1716; in each case he responds that the man in question has to renew his faith and his marriage—in other words, what he has said has made him an unbeliever.

was the lack of any tradition of scholastic commentary on the texts of Qānūn; it generated texts, but no jurisprudence. Yet overall we could well describe the Ottoman state over much of its history as effectively, if uneasily, bi-legal.[147] Something similar could be said of, for example, the Muslim states of precolonial Malaya. Here, too, we find the term *kanun* employed to refer to a kind of administrative law, and such law was regarded as the possession of the ruler.[148] This law was manifestly different from "the law of God,"[149] and there could be marked tension between them.[150]

The other major competitor of the Sharīʿa in the pre-modern world was customary law.[151] Unfortunately we hear far less about it. The mutual relations of Qānūn and Sharīʿa have left us a record going back for centuries, thanks to the fact that they played out in the cities of the Islamic world, in an arena that held the attention of both the religious and political elites. But customary law flourished outside the cities, in towns, villages, and deserts away from the limelight, especially in tribal regions where the authority of the state was weak or nonexistent. Hence, by and large it is only with the advent of the modern state and modern ethnography that a documentation of customary law has emerged comparable to what we have for Qānūn.[152] Yet working back from this documentation suggests that customary law is likely to have been a much more extensive phenomenon in the pre-modern Islamic world than state law, or even Islamic law.[153] The Sharīʿa, particularly as developed by the Ḥanafī school, had ways of accommodating numerous elements of custom,[154] but these did not extend to the

[147] In a similar way most Islamic societies were bi-calendrical: alongside the Islamic lunar calendar, which is not in phase with the seasons, they made use of some kind of solar calendar that respected the regularities of the agricultural year.

[148] Milner, "Islam and Malay kingship," 47, 49.

[149] Ibid., 48. Note that here, as in the Ottoman case, an un-Islamic feature of this administrative law is its prescription of fines as punishments.

[150] See ibid., 59, on the early decades of the nineteenth century.

[151] For surveys of customary law in the Islamic world, see *EI*^{2}, arts. "ʿĀda" (G.-H. Bousquet et al.) and "ʿUrf" (G. Libson and F. H. Stewart); the first ranges widely over the Islamic world but is dated, while the second (in its second part, that by Stewart) gives an authoritative survey of customary law in the Arab world.

[152] For Yemen as a partial exception, see *EI*^{2}, art. "Ṭāghūt," second part (F. H. Stewart). Yemen may have been unusual in the number of scholars resident in the tribal countryside.

[153] *EI*^{2}, art. "ʿUrf," 891b (F. H. Stewart).

[154] For a convenient summary, see *EI*^{2}, art. "ʿUrf," first part (G. Libson).

principled recognition of fully independent systems of customary law, such as are attested for the Bedouin of the central region of the Arab world.[155]

The second grand observation of principle about the Sharīʿa in pre-modern times is that it is unchanging. It is a matter of fundamental dogma in Islam that the process of revelation was completed in the lifetime of the Prophet. As God declares in a Koranic verse said to have been revealed during Muḥammad's last pilgrimage to Mecca a few months before he died: "Today I have perfected your religion for you" (Q5:3).[156] Up to that point the Muslim sources describe a process of continuing divine legislation in which the law might be altered in response to changing circumstances. But with this declaration the process of legislation ceased; from then on God's law was complete. This is perhaps one of the more distinctive features of Islamic law, though, as we will see, it is not quite unique. Most pre-modern legal systems included overt procedures for abolishing or amending old laws and making new ones. The law of imperial Rome could be changed at will as long as there were emperors to change it. Thus Justinian (ruled 527–565) made it very clear that his codification of Roman law owed its authority to his own imperial fiat, not to its venerable sources;[157] and he anticipated that he himself would make new law in the future.[158] In the same way the emperor of China had the power to change the law. Here, too, we find anticipation of future change: under the T'ang dynasty the question was considered what should be done in the event that, between the time when a crime was committed and the time of

[155] "Among many Bedouin tribes of the Central Region, the law does not appear to have been influenced by the *sharīʿa*; even marriage and divorce are, both in form and in substance, quite different from the corresponding institutions in Islamic law" (*EI*^{2}, art. "ʿUrf," 891b (F. H. Stewart)).

[156] Ṭabarī, *Tafsīr*, 4: 418.24 (to Q5:3). One can reach the same result through the Koranic description of Muḥammad as the "seal of the prophets" (*khātam al-nabiyyīn*, Q33:40), understood to mean the last of them (see Friedmann, *Prophecy continuous*, 53–64). Anyone foolish enough to take Muḥammad as a role model in *this* capacity was likely to receive short shrift from his fellow-Muslims (for some cases in the early centuries of Islam, see 65–67).

[157] He writes that "we ascribe everything to ourselves, since it is from us that all their authority is derived" (Justinian, *Digest*, 1: xlvii); he points out that in the process of codification "many very important changes have been made for reasons of practical utility" (lix); and he insists that "whatsoever is set down here, we resolve this and this alone be observed" (lxii). No one is to dare "to compare any ancient text with that which our authority has introduced" (lix, and see lxii).

[158] For his projected "Novels," see Nicholas, *Roman law*, 42.

sentencing, a regulation were to be issued amending the criminal code with regard to the punishment for the offense in question.[159] Nor was the presence of a state necessary for the process of legislation. Among the bedouin a tribe could alter its customary law, usually through a consensus reached at a gathering of leading men;[160] likewise in the mountains of Albania a general assembly of the tribe or village could change the law.[161] All this rests on the commonplace that the law has to change with the times. Aristotle (d. 322 BC) was already well aware that ancient laws could be barbaric, not to say silly; "even written codes of law may with advantage not be left unaltered," he advised, for "it is proper for some laws sometimes to be altered"—though only with the utmost caution.[162] Justinian observed that "the character of human law is always to hasten onward, and there is nothing in it which can abide forever, since nature is eager to produce new forms."[163] A memorial accompanying a ten-volume legal text submitted to the Japanese emperor in 834 took a similar view: "New times require new laws, which are in the spirit of those of ancient times, but suited to the present."[164] And as mentioned, during the lifetime of the Prophet the law did indeed change in response to changing circumstances. But if circumstances kept changing while he was alive, why should they cease to do so after his death? As indicated, there is nothing specifically modern about raising this question—the Muslim jurists themselves were aware that different times require different norms.[165] Yet the lack of a formal process of legislation makes the Sharīʿa look uncommonly rigid.

In practice there have always been ways around this, two in particular. One solution is internal to the Sharīʿa: the games jurists play. As we have seen, they had no problem taking God's law and turning it

[159] W. Johnson, *T'ang Code*, 37. The answer was that the lighter punishment should be imposed.

[160] *EI*², art. "ʿUrf," 891a (F. H. Stewart).

[161] Hasluck, *Unwritten law*, 11; in a letter of 1907, one tribe informs another of the enactment of new laws (271–72, and cf. 263).

[162] Aristotle, *Politics*, 128–31.

[163] Justinian, *Digest*, 1: lxi.

[164] Tsunoda et al., *Japanese tradition*, 82. In the same passage the redactors of this text describe their role as follows: "We have attempted to revise and correct the legal writings, now adding and now deleting."

[165] For the legal maxim to this effect, see Bā Ḥusayn, *al-Mufaṣṣal fī ʾl-qawāʿid al-fiqhiyya*, 459, citing Khādimī, *Majāmiʿ al-ḥaqāʾiq*, 46.26 (*lā yunkaru taghayyur al-aḥkām bi-taghayyur al-azmān*); and see Heyd, *Old Ottoman criminal law*, 200; Goldziher, *Islamic theology and law*, 234; M. Cook, *Commanding right*, 421. I am indebted to Hossein Modarressi and Intisar Rabb for assistance with this maxim.

into four, and by the same token they could change it over time—not, of course, by arrogating to themselves God's exclusive right to legislate but by suitably reinterpreting the closed canon of his legislation. The flexibility of the methods of the jurists meant that almost anything could be done in this way, and much was done. But as one historian remarks of the scholar who held the highest judicial office in the mid-sixteenth-century Ottoman Empire: "What the Islamic juristic tradition did not allow him to do was openly to espouse completely new legal principles."[166] There was no earthly locus of authority qualified to engage in such juristic innovation. The other way to circumvent the problem is for the Sharīʿa to coexist, however uneasily, with a legal system in which the power to legislate is in human hands. This is the bi-legal solution that we have already encountered. To take the prohibition of interest as an example of both solutions, the Ḥanafī school of law was particularly adept at devising legal fictions (*ḥiyal*) that accommodated the practice of charging interest,[167] while Ottoman Qānūn allowed interest up to a limit of ten percent.[168]

When we turn to the modern world, the absence of continuing legislation in Islamic law after the time of the Prophet has two significant consequences. One, which does not concern us at this point, is that it reinforces the attraction of the Sharīʿa as a legal order independent of the political system.[169] The other is that it makes it harder to adapt to modern conditions, which have a way of changing with unusual rapidity. The result of this is that some features of the Sharīʿa now appear disconcertingly archaic, just as Aristotle would lead us to expect.[170] They may be embarrassing to modern sensitivities, as with stoning adulterers or cutting off the hands of thieves (Q5:38).[171] Or they may be disruptive of modern ways of life, as with the prohibition of interest.[172] It was very likely such archaisms that Nigerian Christians had

[166] Imber, *Ebuʾs-suʿud*, 271.

[167] Schacht, *Introduction to Islamic law*, 78–82, especially 79.

[168] Heyd, *Old Ottoman criminal law*, 84 = 122 §103; and see Rafeq, "Syrian *ʿulamā*," 13–22.

[169] See 282, 329–30.

[170] Many, of course, do not; no one has a problem with rules to the effect that a debt with a specified term is to be recorded in writing (Q2:282) or that contracts are to be kept (Q5:1).

[171] The absence of discrimination between men and women could, however, be seen as a redeeming feature of both penalties from a modern perspective.

[172] Such archaisms may nevertheless be of benefit to someone: what strike Westerners as cruel and unusual punishments lend themselves to the dramatization of Islamist intransigence, and the delicate art of circumventing the prohibition of interest under

in mind when they protested against the adoption of the Sharīʿa in the northern region of their country with the slogan "Shariah is not Y2K compliant."[173] In most legal systems, if there was sufficient support for doing so, such laws could simply be abolished once and for all and new laws made in their place, but in the Islamic case any attempt to do this would be a violation of divine sovereignty.[174] This is why Mawdūdī, who is clearly uncomfortable with the more brutal punishments imposed by God's law, is unable to reject them categorically; the best he can do is to distance himself from them by insisting that they can only be put into practice in the fully Islamic society of the future, that is to say, in a society in which the destitute are properly provided for and the sexes are properly separated.[175]

But why should the solutions that worked in the past not continue to work just as well today? Both antidotes have in fact played prominent parts in the adaption of the Muslim world to legal modernity. On the one hand the market has been flooded with devices of all kinds for harmonizing the Sharīʿa with modern conditions, like that of Mawdūdī just cited. Some are of no great intellectual profundity: one can say that necessity (*ḍarūra*) renders permissible what would otherwise be forbidden, that the letter of the law must be sacrificed to higher Islamic purposes, that we should adhere to the principles of Islam and not the details, that an inconvenient rule may turn out not to be Islamic if we go back to the truly authoritative sources, that otherwise permissible acts that damage the reputation of Islam are forbidden,[176] and so forth. But others take advantage of the unusual strategic depth of Islamic jurisprudence. The clearest case of this is the invocation of the medieval theory of the purposes (*maqāṣid*) of the law, according to which the substantive provisions of the Sharīʿa are there to realize certain fundamental goods; in modern times we find this theory being applied no longer to celebrate the wisdom of the substantive law but

modern financial conditions enables large numbers of experts on "Islamic finance" to make a living.

[173] Onishi, "New strife," reporting in 2000 from the northern city of Kaduna, where hundreds were killed in communal riots sparked by the issue.

[174] This is not to say that, if the laws imposing stoning and amputation could in fact be abolished lock, stock, and barrel, there would be strong support in the Muslim world for doing so. Polls show these punishments to be supported by majorities in both Egypt and Pakistan (Kull, *Feeling betrayed*, 159 and 242n4); to use a Hindu term, they are not *lokavidviṣṭa* (see below, 284), however much they may embarrass someone like Mawdūdī.

[175] Maudūdī, "Islamic law," 55–57 (for this work, which dates from 1948, see 39, and Ahmad and Ansari, *Mawlānā Mawdūdī*, 36 no. 57).

[176] For this latter, see 367n56.

rather to reshape it.[177] And on the other hand alternative legal systems have been widely adopted[178]—occasionally even replacing the Sharīʿa, as in Turkey.

But as long as the Islamists have wind in their sails, a serious problem remains. Modern conditions generate intense pressure for legal change in Muslim societies, and the changes in question will often be unusually rapid and extensive. At the same time they tend to be manifestly exogenous. Such conditions force the issue in a way that pre-modern conditions did not. As long as the jurists could play their games discreetly, without trying to change the law too much or too fast, they could go about their work without being seen to challenge the legal sovereignty of God; but this did not mean that they could set about reinventing the law with abandon. And as long as the changes were endogenous, they did not raise the specter of God's law being recast to meet the standards of unbelievers. But that is not how things are today. At the same time the bi-legal solution has become more offensive. Under modern conditions the alternative legal systems are transplanted from the West; in 1882 the Shāfiʿite Muftī of Egypt was already complaining that the unbelievers had prevailed on the rulers of the country "to compose laws that are in conflict with the *sharīʿah* and with our rules," discarding the Book of God.[179] In that sense such imported laws resemble the pagan Yāsā of the Mongols rather than the domesticated Qānūn of the Ottomans.[180] And because of the enormous increase in the capacity of states to intervene in the societies they rule, the reach of the imported legal systems is wider and deeper than that of the Yāsā and its likes. In the face of this provocation, affirmations of divine legislative monopoly are commonplace in Islamist circles.[181] Thus al-Qāʿida declares as an article of faith that all legislation belongs to

[177] For an illuminating account of this theory and how it can be used, see March, "Theocrats," 34–40.

[178] See Coulson, *Islamic law*, 151–52.

[179] Peters, *Islam and colonialism*, 81–82; cf. Q2:101.

[180] Note how it is taken for granted that Mongol law is a negative precedent. The Islamists use it to condemn the importation of Western law, but the modernists do not cite it (as they do the ninth-century translation movement) to legitimate borrowing from the West. One could imagine someone saying something to the effect that "we did this once before, in the time of the Mongols, and it did us no harm, so we can do it again"; but I have not encountered a modernist who has the nerve to say this.

[181] See, for example, Quṭb, *Maʿālim*, 85.13 = 78. But Quṭb himself accepted the need for some kind of legislative activity (see Mitchell, *Society of Muslim Brothers*, 239), and in 1969 the then leader of the Muslim Brothers, Ḥasan al-Ḥudaybī, argued that God had transferred a part of his monopoly to humans (Ashour, "Post-jihadism," 136).

God alone and that those who adhere to "arbitrary legislation" are unbelievers; this applies particularly to rulers and their supporters.[182] The well known Salafī and jihadi ideologue Abū Muḥammad al-Maqdisī mocks compromises such as that of the Kuwaiti constitution, according to which Sharīʿa is merely a *principal* source of legislation (*maṣdar raʾīsī lil-tashrīʿ*); such a provision, he observes with fine irony, is like professing that God is merely one of the *principal* gods.[183]

This is part of the background to one of the most characteristic features of the Muslim world today: the enormous appeal of calls for the restoration of the Sharīʿa. It is not just card-carrying Islamists and professional religious scholars who would like to see this happen—the groups that have a claim to know best what God's law actually entails. The project also has wide popular appeal.[184] And in several Muslim countries—notably the Sudan, Pakistan, and Iran—there has been some real movement in this direction. The phenomenon is such an obvious feature of the Muslim world today that there is no need for us to enter into detail. But much of what will concern us in the rest of this chapter will be the absence of a comparable project in the Hindu or Catholic contexts.

3. Hinduism

In turning to the Hindu case let us begin where we just ended, with law. As a phenomenon, Hindu law resembles Islamic law in some basic ways, and yet for reasons that we will come to, the idea of restoring its hegemony has played virtually no part in the politics of modern India, even among the Hindu nationalists. Once we have considered the question of law, it will not take long to generalize our findings to the Hindu religious tradition at large.

[182] See the creed of al-Qāʿida translated in Haykel, "Salafi thought and action," 52–53, articles 5 and 19.

[183] Wagemakers, "Radical concept," 93.

[184] It is, for example, reported that the proportion of the population that would like the Sharīʿa to be the only source of legislation is a majority in Jordan, Egypt, Pakistan, Afghanistan, and Bangladesh (Esposito and Mogahed, *Who speaks for Islam?*, 48). The Arab Barometer Surveys results for 2006 add Palestine, Algeria, Morocco, and Kuwait; in each case majorities of respondents (55 percent for Palestine and around 80 percent for the other three countries) either agree or strongly agree that the government should implement only the laws of the Sharīʿa. See also Kull, *Feeling betrayed*, 118, 156–58, 163–64.

Hindu law, like the Sharīʿa, is a religious law. It grounds its claim to authority in revelation—not ongoing revelation, but again a process that was accomplished long ago.[185] In the meantime the law has come to be embodied in a dense scholastic tradition; here the counterparts of the Muslim jurists (*faqīhs*) are the *śāstrīs*. Again, like the Sharīʿa Hindu law covers both worldly matters and many aspects of specifically religious life.[186] Thus, one modern scholar describes it as "a system of thought containing a body of detailed rules, tackling every facet of life,"[187] while another remarks of Manu that only a small part of the text deals with "what we would call law";[188] this is just the kind of thing that is said about the Sharīʿa. Moreover Hindu law is arguably central to Hinduism in something of the way the Sharīʿa is to Islam. It is known as *dharma*, which is also the word for religion in general; thus law is religion par excellence. These points have a couple of closely related implications that feel familiar to any student of Islamic law. One is that whatever the superficial diversity of opinions among the jurists, it is axiomatic that the law is so far as possible to be construed as one: "all authoritative texts spoke with one voice" and "all contradictions were only apparent."[189] The other implication is that in some sense the law is immutable; it is the "eternal law" (*sanātana dharma*).[190] In the light of our discussion of this point in the Islamic context, this latter implication is worth taking a little further.

Just as in the Islamic case, the idea of an unchanging law has as much to do with rhetoric as reality. There are in fact significant mechanisms of adjustment at the interface between the prescriptions of eternity and the instability of human affairs. For example, Manu confronts the question what is to be done where no law is laid down; the answer is that a committee (*pariṣad*) of ten or more qualified persons, or three, or even a single Brahmin, can decide the law (whereas thousands of unlearned people cannot constitute such a committee);[191] this

185 For the authority of the Vedas, see especially 400–401.

186 One gets a good sense of this by scanning the "synopsis of contents" of Kane, *History of Dharmaśāstra*, vol. 2.

187 Derrett, *History of Indian law*, 29.

188 Manu, *Laws*, translator's introduction, lxi.

189 The quotations are from Derrett, *Dharmaśāstra and juridical literature*, 12. Kane is less categorical (*History of Dharmaśāstra*, 3: 443), hence my "so far as possible."

190 Derrett, *History of Indian law*, 27; for the phrase *sanātana dharma*, see Derrett, *Dharmaśāstra and juridical literature*, 12. Derrett cites Kane, *History of Dharmaśāstra*, 5: 1629, where a number of early uses of the phrase are noted. See also below, 286.

191 Manu, *Laws*, 288–89 (12.108–14).

is a more institutional approach than we would find in Islamic law. At the same time an old doctrine says that the substance of the law may vary from one age (*yuga*) to another. In particular, practices that were lawful in earlier ages may be prohibited in the present degenerate Kali age (*kaliyuga*); juristic sources provide lists of such now forbidden practices (*kalivarjyas*).[192] More boldly, a law that is "intolerable to the public" (*lokavidviṣṭa*) can be set aside.[193] Moreover, kings can issue edicts such as "today all should observe a festival in the capital," and much else[194]—though despite a certain murkiness in the texts, it seems clear that the Hindu jurists (like their Muslim counterparts) do not accord to rulers the broad power to legislate that characterizes the Roman or Chinese emperor,[195] and they give no space to such legislation in their works. In short, this is a legal tradition that has left itself with very little power to legislate; and yet, for all its eternity, it can make limited adjustments to changing times. For example, there was an inconvenient stipulation (itself a *kalivarjya* ruling) according to which a Brahmin who went overseas could not be readmitted to his caste even after performing the relevant penance.[196] When this became a pressing issue in the nineteenth century, many jurists found ways to get around the ruling through "very interesting and hairsplitting arguments."[197] But just as in the Islamic case, the existence of such mechanisms does not mean that Hindu law can reinvent itself without inhibition. A nineteenth-century reformer quotes a wise and prudent jurist to this effect: "We *Shastris* know the tide is against us and it is no use opposing. You people should not consult us, but go your own way, and do the thing you think right; and we shall not come in your way. But if you ask us and want us to twist the *shastras* to your purpose and go with you, we must speak plainly and we will oppose."[198]

[192] Kane, *History of Dharmaśāstra*, 3: 885, 891–92; for a full list of *kalivarjyas*, see 930–66. Similar thinking may be found among the Muslim scholars. Thus the Prophet ordered that women be allowed out to attend public prayers on festival days, which reflects the virtuous times in which he lived; our own time, by contrast, is so degenerate (*ʿamma ʾl-fasād fīhi*) that women have to be kept at home (ʿAynī, *ʿUmdat al-qārī*, 6:296.24; see Sadeghi, *Logic of law making*, 115–18, and for another example, 139, 149).

[193] Derrett, *Religion, law*, 89–90, quoting Yājñavalkya and other sources. For an Islamic parallel, see *EI*², art. "ʿUrf," 887–88 (G. Libson).

[194] Kane, *History of Dharmaśāstra*, 3: 98–100, citing Medhātithi and other sources.

[195] See the passage quoted and translated in Derrett, "Bhāruci," 394b; also the somewhat different translation of the same passage in Derrett, *Bhāruci's commentary*, 1: 51.5 = 2: 36.

[196] Kane, *History of Dharmaśāstra*, 3: 933, no. 10.

[197] Ibid., 3:935–57. The characterization of the arguments is Kane's.

[198] Kaikini, *Narayen G. Chandavarkar*, 35.

Hindu and Islamic law thus entered the modern world as broadly similar institutions. Anyone familiar with the recent history of the Islamic world could accordingly be forgiven for expecting to find in India a strong and persistent movement for the restoration of Hindu law.

Yet there is no such movement in sight. This absence does not reflect any lack of public attention to legal issues. In the last decades of British rule, there was considerable discussion among the Indian elite on the question of legal reform. Then, when India achieved independence in 1947, the future of law in the country became something that Indians—most of them in some sense Hindus—were in a position to decide for themselves. This led to several further years of controversy, ending in the passing of a set of statutes in 1955–1956 that codified key aspects of personal law for Hindus, together with Buddhists, Jains, and Sikhs.[199] In cultural terms this outcome can be seen as a compromise. There was no repudiation of traditional Hindu personal law in favor of an imported Western code, but neither was there any attempt to restore Hindu law as it had been before the British began to meddle with it.[200] Instead, the inherited substance was retained, but it was purged of many elements deemed incompatible with modern values and reshaped in the manner of a Western-style code. Thus, rules prescribing unequal relations between the classes (*varṇas*) of Hindu society, or denying to women the rights accorded to men, were felt to have no place in the new and progressive India.[201] The spirit behind this legislative activity is caught in a recommendation of a committee that had urged the preparation of a Hindu code in 1941: the law of marriage should be based on "the best parts of the Code of Manu rather than those which fall short of the best."[202] In other words, the project was broadly similar in style to legal reforms taking place in the Islamic world at approximately the same time, reforms that can aptly be characterized as attempts to modernize the Sharīʿa.[203]

199 Derrett, *History of Indian law*, 5 (very brief). For the inclusion of Buddhists, Jains, and Sikhs, see Derrett, *Hindu law*, 78.

200 In the discussion of the Hindu Code Bill in the Constituent Assembly in 1949–1950, one speaker noted that "the Hindu law now is the law as interpreted and as laid down by the British judges in this country," but the inference he drew from this was that "we are at least as competent to change that law as the British Judges who have changed the ancient law into the present Hindu law" (Ambedkar, *Writings and speeches*, 590; part 1 of this volume includes over 550 pages of general discussion of the Hindu Code Bill by numerous different speakers in the Constituent Assembly in 1949–1950, 229–786).

201 Derrett, *History of Indian law*, 31–32.

202 Derrett, *Hindu law*, 58.

203 See Schacht, *Introduction to Islamic law*, chap. 15. In substance, however, the Indian reforms were considerably bolder than those implemented in the Islamic world, with the exception of Tunisia (for which see 108–9).

The difference was the absence in India of a serious call for an integral restoration of Hindu law. It is not that there was any lack of conservative opposition to the new legislation. The Hindu nationalists vehemently opposed it. They attacked it as a threat to Hindu family values, and expressed exasperation at the fact that the reforms did not extend to Muslims; but they failed to mobilize widespread support.[204] Svāmī Karpātrī (d. 1982), a respected if sometimes eccentric ascetic who had gone into politics and established the Rām Rājya Pariṣad, was more successful in this respect, organizing numerous demonstrations.[205] But the opponents of the codification do not seem to have pushed for a radical alternative. This applies not just to the politicians at the center[206] but also in considerable measure to the wider society. One contemporary observer sketches an orthodox trend of thought that he describes as calling for a return to the old legal literature (*dharmaśāstra*), using reinterpretation of the authoritative texts to devise a new Hindu law.[207] Yet there does not seem to have been any substance to this, as a survey of the literature he cites will show.

In 1941 a legal journal in Madras published three articles in connection with the proposals of the committee then at work; one of them, by the Śankarācārya of Kāñcī, was of a strongly conservative character.[208] His message was that "Hindu law should have been left as it was." He deplored the innovations already made by the legislation of 1929, 1937, and 1938, together with the "similar legislation now proposed,"[209] remarking disconsolately that there can be "no end to this kind of legislation."[210] Socially, his views were rooted in his high valuation of the "strength and stability which caste-life has given to Hindu society."[211] Doctrinally, they rested on a contrast between "Vedic law" and "man-made laws": "the law whose source is the Veda, cannot be changed to suit man's changing standards or whims," for its applicability "stands valid for all time and for all men."[212] But he put forward no program beyond an end to "tampering," as he called it.[213]

[204] Jaffrelot, *Hindu nationalist movement*, 103–4.

[205] Ibid., 103.

[206] Galanter, "Aborted restoration," 55.

[207] Derrett, *Hindu law*, 29–30 and 281–82n21.

[208] Śankarācārya of Kāñcī, "Answers," second part, 127–37. For this Śankarācārya, see Cenkner, *Tradition of teachers*, 123–24.

[209] Śankarācārya of Kāñcī, "Answers," 129.

[210] Ibid., 137.

[211] Ibid., 134.

[212] Ibid., 132.

[213] Ibid., 128, 129.

The pretensions of the same committee were demolished at much greater length by a professor of Hindu law in Benares in a book of 1943.[214] His highly conservative views are not unlike those of the Śankarācārya, but he has a distinctive insistence that Hindu law, however authentically Vedic, could not in principle "be reduced to simple and uniform rules."[215] The reason for this irreducibility is the differentation of Hindu society, in which each caste has its own norms[216]—an aspect of the "organic fabric" of the "Hindu Social Order."[217] Though to a large extent the product of immemorial antiquity, such differentiation is not entirely static. New castes, our author points out, come into existence from time to time through the division of old ones: "through the ever-increasing specialization of social functions in the growing complexity of social life, further fresh subdivisions of castes naturally take place."[218] These new castes in turn could be expected to develop their own distinctive norms in conformity with the fundamental principles of the social order. Thus, it is only to be expected that, like other critics of legal reform, this author does not call for a radical restoration; and in any case the tone of his book, though caustic, is never seditious.

A less sophisticated Bengali writer contributed a pamphlet to the discussion in 1944.[219] Alarmed by the menace of feminism—"hysteric, restive women"[220]—he counseled that "forced monogamy will result in

[214]Deshpande, *Dharma-shastra*. According to a handwritten insertion on the title page of the copy in the University of Chicago Library, the author was a professor of Hindu law at Benares Hindu University. A xerox of this copy was kindly obtained for me by Asad Ahmed.

[215]Ibid., 6, 9. A somewhat similar view was expressed by a member of the Constituent Assembly. Hindu law, he argued, is not "an imposition from above" but rather "a spontaneous development from centuries past"; the principles of this law "as readable from the texts have never been the governing force of the Hindu society," which instead has been guided by "a consistently developing usage and custom governing the different sections of the society." The proposed legislation would thus take away from Hindu law its "vitality, elasticity, mobility, spontaneity and adaptability." The moral was to "be very careful before you tamper with it" (Ambedkar, *Writings and speeches*, 14: 583). This speaker was a vehemently conservative pandit from Rajasthan who saw the Hindu Code Bill as aimed at "the utter demolition of the entire structure and fabric of Hindu society" (ibid., 569, and cf. 547; for the provenance of the speaker, see 568).

[216]He writes that "these differing usages help the different groups in maintaining their distinct characteristics" (Deshpande, *Dharma-shastra*, 8) and leaves it to the imagination "how many distinct and dissimilar usages and customs must be in vogue in the large class of the Sudras" (9).

[217]Ibid., 8–9; for the phrases quoted, see 25. His conceptions are informed by genetics and evolutionary biology (117, 119, 142).

[218]Ibid., 116; also 145–46. Even those who dissent from some particular Hindu doctrine can come to form a caste within the system (150).

[219]Set, *Third Hindu code* (preface dated 1944).

[220]Ibid., 32.

increased adultery here as all over the world."[221] He saw the proposed code as "an attempt to dislodge the Hindus from their status of eternal values vouchsafed by their Shastras."[222] What he wanted was that "the Hindus should be left alone with their Smritis."[223]

Several years later another strongly orthodox scholar—like the Śankarācārya a Tamil Brahmin—adopted a more minatory stance, suggesting that the subjects of a state that makes law "in defiance of Dharma" are dispensed from the duty of obedience: "Loyalty is to Dharma, and not to any human person."[224] Yet even here, the point of his threat seems to have been no more than to persuade the state to leave things alone.

It is in subsequent decades that the extent of the divergence between the Hindu and Islamic trajectories has become fully apparent. Whereas the full restoration of Islamic law has become a major issue in the Islamic world, no such project has developed in the Hindu context. Most of the evidence for this is simply silence. But there is one abiding issue in the politics of independent India that dramatizes its absence.

As a progressive and secular nation, newly independent India aspired to have a unitary civil code covering its entire population—just as any modern Western country has. This objective was accordingly written into the Indian constitution, of which the relevant article reads as follows: "The State shall endeavour to secure for the citizens a uniform civil code throughout the territory of India."[225] So far, however, nothing has been done to create such a code, and it is not hard to see why. The legal system inherited by independent India from the British was a plural system in which Hindus had their personal law and Muslims had theirs; to impose a unitary civil code would be to abolish Islamic law for the substantial Muslim minority, a project bound to encounter enormous resistance from Muslims. The Shāh Bāno affair made this very clear. The trouble arose from a Supreme Court decision of 1985 in a case in which a Muslim ex-husband sought to stop paying alimony to his ex-wife, invoking Muslim personal law. The Supreme Court held that a section of the Indian criminal code took precedence, and at the same time it felt entitled to take the view that Muslim per-

[221] Ibid., 24.

[222] Ibid., 32.

[223] Ibid., 10. Compare a speaker from Bihar in the Constituent Assembly discussion: "I belong to that class of people which considers the *Smriti* and the school of interpretation, he follows, as sacrosanct" (Ambedkar, *Writings and speeches*, 14: 665, and cf. 297; for the provenance of the speaker, see 664).

[224] Rangaswami Aiyangar, *Hindu view of life*, 178–79.

[225] Derrett, *Hindu law*, 31.

sonal law was in this instance out of line with the Koran. The storm of protest that greeted this limited intrusion conveys a vivid sense of Indian Muslim commitment to Islamic law in matters of personal status: "Shariat is our religious right, we will die to protect it."[226]

It is thus unsurprising that the Hindu nationalists are the one part of the political spectrum in which there is strong ideological support for the project of a uniform civil code.[227] "Why should there be two sets of laws in this country?," Ritambarā demands, immediately after comparing Muslims to mosquitoes.[228] From her point of view, the role of Islamic law in the Indian legal system is just another example of the way in which the Indian state panders to its minorities; conversely, imposing a unitary civil code would be an excellent way to teach the Muslims a lesson. Accordingly, this legal reform is one of a number of items on the wish list of the BJP. These items are measures to which the Hindu nationalists are ideologically committed but which in the present epoch they cannot hope to implement; this is because, as we have noted, they can form a national government only by doing deals with coalition partners who have very different political orientations.[229] Thus, in the coalition-building of 1998, the uniform civil code disappeared from the agenda of the BJP along with the rebuilding of the temple of Rām at Ayodhyā.[230] What is interesting about the projected code in the present context is that, despite a rhetoric in which *dharma* is the essence of India,[231] even the Hindu nationalists do not appear to be interested in the substantive restoration of Hindu law.[232]

Why then does the idea of such a restoration have no leverage in Indian politics and no place in the imagination of the Hindu society at large, in stark contrast to the current situation in the Islamic world? There are perhaps three factors worth considering here.

The first is already familiar and relates to the content of the tradition. Hindu law is deeply inegalitarian.[233] A legal heritage committed

[226] Jaffrelot, *Hindu nationalist movement*, 334–35; and see Zaman, *Ulama*, 167–69.

[227] Jaffrelot, *Hindu nationalist movement*, 344, 376, and cf. 365.

[228] Kakar, *Colors of violence*, 162.

[229] See 99, 119.

[230] Jaffrelot, *Hindu nationalist movement*, 551–52.

[231] Ibid., 486, and cf. 487.

[232] As noted in Varshney, *Ethnic conflict*, 70. The same is doubtless true of the Shiv Sena. Thus the leaders of the local Shiv Sena branches provide cheap and informal conflict resolution (Eckert, *Charisma of direct action*, 22–25). But it would not occur to them to consult the *dharmaśāstras* when carrying out these quasi-judicial functions; as Eckert puts it, "judgments follow common sense" (24).

[233] See 58–59, 73–74, 191–93, 194.

to the view that the bulk of the Hindu population is servile or Untouchable may have been viable under pre-modern conditions, but it is no longer sustainable in a context in which these sectors of the population have ceased to accept their traditional roles and have taken to voting their resentments. Whatever nativist charm the idea of an integral restoration of Hindu law might possess for the twice-born is thus dissipated by the crude facts of demography.[234] For anyone aiming to generate populist solidarity—a sense of community bringing a people together with a common purpose—Hindu law is best used as a target to mobilize against.

The second factor concerns the standing of law in traditional Hindu culture, and this needs to be treated at more length. As already indicated, this standing was in no way marginal.[235] We possess over two thousand works on Hindu law, some of them very large indeed.[236] One of them, Manu, is particularly prominent—it has nine medieval commentaries, whereas the runner-up (the *Yājñavalkyasmṛti*) has only four.[237] Manu also enjoyed an iconic status in the wider culture, despite the fact that other works seem to have played a much larger role in the actual administration of justice.[238] It formed part of the select package of Indian culture exported to Southeast Asia.[239] Likewise nineteenth-century Indians made much of it: in 1850 Debendranath Tagore (d. 1905) drew heavily on it in a religious work;[240] in 1877 a conservative Maharashtrian Brahmin saw Manu as one of the glories of ancient India;[241] and the book remained a favorite of Dayānand's to the end of his life.[242] Even today parts of the text are widely known by heart in India.[243]

And yet the discipline of legal study may not have been as central in Hinduism as it was in Islam. For example, medieval South Indian

[234] Cf. Galanter, "Aborted restoration," 61.

[235] See 283.

[236] Derrett, *Dharmaśāstra and juridical literature*, 6, 19–20; Derrett, *History of Indian law*, 14–15.

[237] Derrett, *Dharmaśāstra and juridical literature*, 34 and n166; also Manu, *Laws*, translator's introduction, xviii.

[238] This at least is suggested by the adoption of such texts by the British (Derrett, *History of Indian law*, 16).

[239] Rangaswami Aiyangar, *Hindu view of life*, 5 and n4.

[240] Jordens, *Dayānanda Sarasvatī*, 79.

[241] O'Hanlon, *Caste, conflict*, 182.

[242] Jordens, *Dayānanda Sarasvatī*, 39, 44, 54, 58, 62, 66, 96, 102, 122–25, 231–32, 235, 239, 249, 250, 254, 263–64.

[243] Manu, *Laws*, translator's introduction, lvii.

inscriptions that list the subjects taught in educational institutions do not usually mention it.[244] Likewise the author of a twelfth-century encyclopedia did not regard law (*dharmaśāstra*) as a suitable topic for courtly debate or intellectual exercise,[245] and the intrusion of the "New Logic" (*navyanyāya*) in the seventeenth century does not seem to have changed matters.[246] In this connection it is noteworthy that traditional India possessed no rival schools of legal thought[247]—in contrast to those that were so prominent a feature of other aspects of the Hindu tradition, as also of Islamic law. There is indeed a tendency for particular texts to become current in particular regions, such as those in which they originated;[248] and the jurists of Mithilā were known for their disagreements with the "easterners," the jurists of Bengal.[249] But this is as far as it goes. For all these reasons we may be inclined to suspect that law did not play the same role in the education of the traditional Hindu scholar as it did in that of the traditional Muslim scholar. The typical Muslim scholar is a jurist, but the typical Hindu scholar is not. Altogether, one has the sense that Hinduism did not turn out jurists on a scale comparable to Islam. If this was so in the past, then a fortiori we can expect it to hold true in modern times. As one scholar puts it in explaining the absence of a restoration of Hindu law in the mid-twentieth century, "There was no organized body of carriers of the proposed alternative, no educational institutions to produce them and no existing group whose occupational prospects might be advanced"[250]—which is very different from the Islamic case. To this we can perhaps add a point about the role of customary law. Like Islamic law, Hindu law floated on a sea of custom. One Hindu jurist is quoted for the view that family usages should be preferred to the prescriptions of the law books;[251] another states that the customs (*dharmas*) of countries, castes, and families are binding when not opposed to the Vedas.[252] The difference between the Hindu and Islamic cases may

[244] For exceptions, see Gurumurthy, *Education in South India*, 14, 40, 50, and cf. 99.

[245] Derrett, *Dharmaśāstra and juridical literature*, 59.

[246] Ibid., 61.

[247] Ibid., 62.

[248] See, for example, ibid., 54, 57.

[249] Derrett, *History of Indian law*, 16.

[250] Galanter, "Aborted restoration," 61, contrasting Āyurvedic medicine. "Competent *shastris* are so few" (Derrett, *Hindu law*, 30).

[251] Kane, *History of Dharmaśāstra*, 3: 875 (for Sumantu see 1:296–99); Derrett, *Dharmaśāstra and juridical literature*, 36 ("ancestral customs").

[252] Kane, *History of Dharmaśāstra*, 3: 857.

be the extent to which the Hindu jurists were themselves enmeshed in a web of authoritative custom through their family and caste memberships. Dayānand, for example, tells us in his autobiography that at the age of five "my parents and elders commenced training me in the ways and practices of my family, making me learn by rote the long series of religious hymns, stanzas, and commentaries."[253] An upper-class Muslim Indian counterpart would likewise have been socialized into the ways of his family, but without this amount of home schooling in what sounds like a distinctive familial curriculum.[254] In all these ways the study of law among Hindu scholars may have been significantly less central than it was among Muslim scholars.

All this is rather vague, but there is one solid fact that suggests that it may be on the right track. This is the rapid collapse of literary production in the field of Hindu law in the middle of the nineteenth century.[255] One specialist explains this as follows: "The posts of Hindu Law Officers of the High Courts of Bombay, Calcutta, and Madras were abolished in 1864 and the incentive to write original works ceased."[256] This explanation is striking inasmuch as the reform of 1864 applied as much to Muslim as to Hindu law,[257] and yet there was no cessation of Muslim legal writing in India at this point, any more than there was in Egypt when Muftīs lost their role in the court system.[258] Clearly we are not dealing with a queen of sciences in the Hindu case—in marked contrast to the standing of law among the Islamic scholarly disciplines, which ensures it literary attention for as long as these disciplines are studied.

The third factor brings us back to the question of divine jealousy. In the Islamic case the relevance of the phenomenon is rather straightforward. There is no god but God, the maker and owner of the universe and all its contents, ourselves included. Moreover, he has revealed his will to us through the last of his prophets; the Koran in particular is literally his speech, and in it he speaks repeatedly about himself and what he wants from us.[259] And what he wants is that we should worship him alone, and side with him against his enemies. "Rectitude has become clear from error" (Q2:256); we are either for him and destined for paradise or against him and destined for hellfire. This is monotheism with

[253] Yadav, *Swami Dayanand Saraswati*, 12.

[254] See Lelyveld, *Aligarh's first generation*, 49–53, in a section entitled "Growing up sharīf," which was drawn to my attention by Qasim Zaman.

[255] Derrett, *History of Indian law*, 15.

[256] Derrett, *Dharmaśāstra and juridical literature*, 8.

[257] Zaman, *Ulama*, 25.

[258] For the reforms of 1897 and 1931, see Skovgaard-Petersen, *Defining Islam*, 104–5.

[259] The word "Allāh" occurs some 2700 times in the book.

its full polarizing force, and one senses immediately that Hinduism is not like this. The Vedas are certainly texts with an authority that transcends that of their human transmitters. But there is no single doctrine about what it is that endows them with that authority. In one view they are eternal and authorless; in another view they have a divine author who reveals them.[260] The role of this divine author (Īśvara) in the second view brings us considerably closer to the Islamic conception. But he does not have a pervasive presence within the text of the Vedas in the way that God has in the Koran. Instead, as we will see in a later chapter, we encounter a profusion of lesser deities;[261] the pantheons of polytheists are indeed subject to petty jealousies—but not in the grand manner of the monotheist God. There is the same contrast downstream of the revealed texts; here again, no single god has a presence in Hindu legal literature comparable to that of God in its Islamic equivalent. What is perhaps the oldest text of Hindu law we possess tells us that gods do not declare "this is righteous and that is unrighteous"; rather, an activity that Aryans praise is righteous and what they deplore is unrighteous.[262] Of course, Hinduism is not paganism of the kind familiar to us from the ancient Greeks and Romans, who had no counterpart to the Vedas or to the later scholastic edifice of religious law. But we could reasonably expect the effects of divine—or supernatural—jealousy to be significantly weaker in the case of Hindu law than in that of the Sharīʿa. The Hindu jurist who told the modernists to go their own way can have few counterparts in the Islamic world.[263]

These three factors do something to explain why "the symbolic gratifications to be had from the restoration of indigenous law"[264] have not prevailed in India—in sharp contrast to the experience of several

[260] For a scholar writing in the late tenth century who champions the second view and polemicizes against the first, see Chemparathy, *Indian rational theology*, 24, 51, 130, 149–50. The first view is that of the Mīmāṃsakas, the second that of the Nyāya-Vaiśeṣikas. There are yet other views, for example, one involving the colonization of the newly created earth by Brahmins from another universe (151).

[261] See 416–17.

[262] So the *Dharmasūtra* of Āpastamba, 1.20.6–7, in Olivelle, *Dharmasūtras*, 31. For the dating, see xxviii–xxxiv of Olivelle's introduction. The case of Manu is different: the code is named for the god Manu, who is responding to a request from the great sages for an account of the duties of the members of the four classes (*Laws*, 3 (1.1–4)). Though he soon hands over the task of reciting the text to a subordinate (10 (1.59)), he is mentioned from time to time thereafter, mainly as an authority on law (see the index s.n.). But he is a divine jurist, not a divine legislator.

[263] Cf. 284.

[264] The phrase is Galanter's ("Aborted restoration," 62–63). Much of Galanter's explanation is sound, but the problem is that he wrote too soon, before the Islamic contrast was sufficiently apparent.

regions of the Islamic world in the last few decades. The question of the compatibility of Hindu law with modern conditions thus barely arises. That God instructs Muslim husbands to beat their recalcitrant wives (Q4:34) is a cause célèbre among the global citizenry, but Manu's provisions on the same topic have failed to achieve a comparable notoriety.[265]

What is true for Hindu law is broadly true for the Hindu heritage at large. Much as in the Islamic case, domains that in a modern culture would lie outside the purview of religion are here traditionally part of it. As we have seen, this applies to ethnic identity—who is an Aryan?[266] It applies especially strongly to social stratification.[267] Less conspicuously, it applies to warfare.[268] It likewise applies to the polity: as we will see, the heritage has much to say about Hindu monarchy.[269] Indeed there is good reason to think of the Hindu heritage as considerably more comprehensive than that of Islam—as extending its sovereignty over the entire domain of knowledge and not just that of values.[270] The Veda, Manu tells us, "contains all knowledge."[271] There is no Hindu equivalent of the existence of the Greek philosophical tradition alongside the religious disciplines: in the Hindu context philosophy *is* a religious discipline. Even more striking is the case of the sciences, and here medicine provides a particularly illuminating example. First, the similarities. In each case there is a rather primitive form of medicine closely associated with revelation: Prophetic medicine in the Islamic case, Vedic medicine in the Hindu case. And in each case there is a more sophisticated mainstream medicine based on the theory of the humors: Galenic medicine in the Greek case, Āyurveda in the Hindu case. The difference is in the packaging of mainstream medical science: in the Islamic case it presents itself as an older tradition coming from outside the religion and fully independent of it, whereas in the Hindu case it wraps itself in the Vedic mantle.[272] So if one is looking

[265] Manu, *Laws*, 184 (8.299–300). In the same way, the global citizenry is widely aware that the Sharīʿa forbids the taking of interest but not that Hindu law has a much more accommodating attitude to the question (Kane, *History of Dharmaśāstra*, 3: 419–22).

[266] See 58–59.

[267] See 191–93.

[268] See 235.

[269] See 336–37.

[270] For the view that Hinduism contains the fullness of human knowledge as expressed in a lecture on the superiority of Hinduism in 1872, see Jordens, *Dayānanda Sarasvatī*, 78.

[271] Manu, *Laws*, 17 (2.7).

[272] See Zysk, *Medicine*, xiv–xv, 1, 10–11.

for a heritage that is genuinely all-embracing, Hinduism is a stronger candidate than Islam.

It follows that if Hindus were to adhere to their heritage to the extent that Muslims do to theirs, the results would be considerably more adverse for Hindu accommodation with the modern world. Here and there we do indeed see examples of such adherence. In the first half of the nineteenth century, the resistance of Hindus to vaccination against smallpox led British observers to describe them as "naturally averse to all innovation" and unwilling to accept "the slightest deviation from ancient usage."[273] In our own time Āyurveda survives alongside modern medicine, and traditional Indian astrology still has wide appeal. But in general the all-embracing heritage no longer matters. Aryan ethnic identity, the rights and duties of the four classes, the old Hindu law of war, the atomist theories of the Indian philosophers, Hindu rites of coronation—none of this retains its authority in India today. Perhaps nothing would disrupt India's relations with the outside world more seriously than the implementation of the old norm that one should not speak to barbarians (*mlecchas*) or study their language;[274] but in the context of the rush to master English in modern India, this norm is of no more than antiquarian interest. Why then have Hindus been more ready than Muslims to treat their religious heritage as in so many respects a back number? Of the three factors we attended to in the case of law, the second—the lower standing of the study of the subject in the traditional culture—does not have much bearing on the wider question. But the first, the inexpungeably elitist character of the heritage, certainly does, and so does the third, the lack of a monotheistic focus for divine jealousy.

This does not, of course, mean that there is nothing the Hindu nationalists can do with the Hindu heritage. But, as with law, they have no interest in the project of an integral restoration; instead, their use of the heritage is marked by eclecticism, not to say opportunism. By far the greatest example of this is the agitation they mounted over the birthplace of Rām in Ayodhyā.[275] But in the present context a couple of lesser examples should suffice to make the point.

[273] Arnold, *Colonizing the body*, 137 (the quotations date from 1804 and 1844 respectively).

[274] Kane, *History of Dharmaśāstra*, 2: 383. Compare Bīrūnī's account of how the Hindus separate themselves from foreigners for fear of pollution (Bīrūnī, *Taḥqīq*, 10.5 = trans. Sachau, 1: 19–20).

[275] See especially 422–24.

Down to the early 1980s the only religious symbol the Hindu nationalists sought to manipulate on a large scale in their political activities was the cow.[276] They were active in cow-protection campaigns in 1952 and 1966–1967; the second involved prolonged agitation, though neither achieved more than limited success.[277] In 1986 Advani was still calling for a ban on cow slaughter,[278] and in 1991 Ritambarā was still raising consciousness by telling her fellow Hindus that "if you do not awaken, cows will be slaughtered everywhere"[279]—though by then the Hindu nationalists had other and bigger fish to fry. As might be expected, the Shiv Sena has also played its part in what has been called "the defence of cow and country."[280] Here, then, was an element of the heritage that could be used to rally Hindus, especially against Muslims.

Another element that had at least a regional appeal, though no anti-Muslim potential, was suttee—what Rām Mohan Roy called "the practice of burning Hindu widows alive."[281] This had been outlawed by the British rulers of India in 1829, and it remains illegal today. But it does still happen, mainly in rural areas, above all among the Rājpūts of Rajasthan. In 1987 a young Rājpūt woman burned herself (or in another account, was burnt) on the funeral pyre of her husband, thereby becoming a "suttee mother" (*satīmātā*).[282] The incident gave rise to heated controversy, locally and nationally. It is clear that within Rajasthan feeling ran particularly high and was overwhelmingly in favor of the practice; politicians across the spectrum reacted accordingly, either jumping on the bandwagon or studiously avoiding anything that would alienate devotees.[283] This strength of feeling was rooted in the history and culture of the region. When Rājpūt rulers died in the seventeenth and eighteenth centuries, whole harems perished with them—eighty-four women in one instance.[284] Numerous temples are devoted to thriving—and profitable—suttee cults.[285] Outside Rajasthan senti-

[276] Jaffrelot, *Hindu nationalist movement*, 361.

[277] Ibid., 113, 204–13.

[278] Ibid., 376.

[279] Kakar, *Colors of violence*, 164.

[280] Spear, *History of India*, 59–60, quoted in Eckert, *Charisma of direct action*, 100 (the reference is to Śivājī); cf. 241, and Banerjee, *Warriors in politics*, 49–50.

[281] See 403. For widows to accompany their husbands in death is not a peculiarly Indian practice (see the summary survey in Fisch, *Burning women*, 458–62).

[282] See Hawley, "Hinduism," for the event and its repercussions.

[283] Ibid., 89–91.

[284] Noble and Sankhyan, "Signs of the divine," 351, 352, 354, 356, 356–57, 375n23; see also R. Sreenivasan, "Drudges, dancing girls," 150–51.

[285] Hawley, "Hinduism," 84, 86, 91–92. For a survey of suttee memorials of all kinds in the region, see Noble and Sankhyan, "Signs of the divine," 349–64.

ments for and against the practice were more evenly balanced, and the issue does not seem to have been an attractive one for politicians; the VHP in particular remained officially silent.[286]

One could easily find further examples. In 1951 the Rām Rājya Pariṣad wanted to see Āyurveda "declared as the national system of medicine,"[287] and some years ago a Hindu nationalist politician moved to start government funding for courses on Hindu astrology in Indian universities.[288] But not even the VHP, the specifically religious component of the Hindu nationalist movement, showed concern to effect any kind of restoration of the tradition across the board. They were more interested in bringing a degree of coherence to the chaotic Hindu scene. Partly this was a matter of institutions: religious organization, as a leading figure in the VHP cheerfully admitted, is "against the very principle of Hinduism," yet we live in an "age of organisation," so religion "has to get organised."[289] And partly the idea was to find some minimum version of Hinduism that everyone could come together on—an endeavor that we will return to in a later chapter.[290] In other words, like the Hindu nationalists at large, they were more concerned with boosting solidarity around a Hindu identity than with restoring a Hindu heritage. The bottom line in all this may be a remark about the BJP made by the owner of a tea shop in Ayodhyā in 2005: "They only remember Lord Ram when they are out of power."[291]

4. Latin American Catholicism

St. Augustine famously analyzed the predicament of Christians in the late Roman world in terms of a contrast between two "cities": the heavenly city (*caelestis civitas*) and the earthly city (*terrena civitas*). The Christians were part of the heavenly city, implying a profound alienation from the earthly city around them. And yet for the duration of

[286] So Hawley, "Hinduism," 88; he does not tell us what, if anything, the VHP said unofficially. One national organization sided with the practice, namely the Hindu Mahāsabhā (88); so did one national religious figure, the Śankarācārya of Purī, but he came from Rajasthan (89).

[287] Rām Rājya Pariṣad, *Election manifesto*, 35 (cf. the derogatory reference to Western medicine, 34).

[288] See Sondhi, "Black holes."

[289] Jaffrelot, *Hindu nationalist movement*, 202. For the institutions through which the VHP sought to organize Hinduism, see 351–52, 353–55.

[290] See 428.

[291] Sengupta, "Thousands are arrested."

this mortal life, these two cities, however different their purposes, had a common interest: both were in need of earthly peace (*terrena pax*). There was thus a basis for accommodation (*concordia*) between them. Augustine proceeded to describe this accommodation in the following terms: "While this heavenly city, therefore, goes its way as a stranger on earth, it summons citizens from all peoples (*ex omnibus gentibus*), and gathers an alien society of all languages (*in omnibus linguis*), caring naught what difference there may be in manners, laws and institutions (*quidquid in moribus legibus institutisque diversum est*) by which earthly peace is gained or maintained, abolishing and destroying nothing of the sort, nay rather preserving and following them, for however different they may be among different nations (*diversum in diversis nationibus*), they aim at one and the same end, earthly peace." To this formulation he added a vital qualification: "provided that there is no hindrance to the religion that teaches the obligation to worship one most high and true God (*unus summus et verus Deus*)."[292] So Christianity, unlike Hinduism, is a monotheistic religion, and on that there can be no compromise; the heavenly city cannot, as Augustine puts it, share "laws of religion" (*religionis leges*) with the earthly city.[293] On that score divine jealousy remains as potent as ever. But once the religious mission of the heavenly city is assured, there are many other things that the two cities can share while they are here on earth together. This, then, is a very clear statement that Christianity is not all-embracing. We could add that it is in fact far less embracing than either Islam or Hinduism.

Augustine's view, though it perhaps understates the potential friction,[294] was not just an idiosyncrasy. It goes back to the conditions in which Christianity first emerged, within an ethnic, social, military, cultural, and political order that in many ways it could only take as given; short of eschatology, it had no prospect of conquering or overthrowing the powers that be.[295] At the same time this Augustinian perspective articulates features of the religion that recur in many different times and places. We have already encountered aspects of this in particular domains, but it may be useful to bring them together.

[292] Augustine, *De civitate Dei*, book 19, ch. 17, 6: 192–99; for the quotation, see 196–99 (translation slightly adapted). I owe my knowledge of this passage to Gilson, *Saint Augustine*, 182 and 334n69.

[293] Augustine, *De civitate Dei*, 6: 196–97.

[294] Thus there was significant resistance to the Greek cosmological model of a spherical universe, though in the end it was generally accepted (see Inglebert, *Interpretatio Christiana*, 104–8 (summary)). I owe my knowledge of this work to Guy Stroumsa.

[295] This is why Augustine's view has more affinity with Muslim accommodation to life in the diaspora than with Islamic doctrine regarding lands under Muslim rule.

First, Christianity has historically been much more at ease with the diverse ethnic identities of the earthly city than Islam has been.[296] A few fresh examples taken somewhat at random may be in place here. A well-known Latin account of the First Crusade—by any standards a moment of high religious enthusiasm for Latin Christendom—is known as the *Gesta Francorum*, "The Deeds of the Franks";[297] and in the body of the text the author refers to the heroes of his story far more often as Franks than as Christians.[298] In a slightly later reworking of the same material, Guibert of Nogent felt the need for a theologically more correct title and accordingly called his work the *Dei gesta per Francos*, "The deeds of God through the Franks."[299] He thereby reassigned the credit to God, yet continued to identify God's agents in ethnic, not religious terms. He too regularly does the same in the course of his narrative.[300] It takes an Islamicist to be struck by this pattern of usage: Muslim sources describing the Arab conquests refer to their heroes as "Muslims" far more often than as "Arabs." To pick another example, this time involving a linguistic bond, in 1300 Polish emissaries offered the Polish throne to the king of Bohemia; they urged that "it is fitting that those who do not differ much in speaking the Slavic language enjoy the rule of a single prince."[301] This sense of the intimate relationship between language and identity could surface in a context that was no less religious than the First Crusade: at the Council of Constance (1414–1418) the English delegates claimed equality for their nation against the French on a variety of conceptions of nationhood, one of which was that a nation be understood in terms of "peculiarities of language, the most sure and positive sign and essence of a nation in divine and human law."[302] It is hard to imagine such a case being made in an Islamic context.

Second, whereas the early Islamic community was a polity, the early Christian community was not, and it lacked a conception of an intrinsically

[296] See 2, 144.

[297] See Hagenmeyer, *Anonymi Gesta Francorum*, 95, description of Codex E. The title may not go back to the original author, but it appears in a twelfth-century manuscript.

[298] See the index under "Christiani" and "Franci," and see further Bartlett, *Making of Europe*, 104, and Gabriele, *Empire of memory*, 154–57. For a succinct survey of the terms used in medieval sources to refer to crusaders, see Constable, *Crusaders and crusading*, 350–52.

[299] Guibert de Nogent, *Dei Gesta per Francos*, 84 line 122. His intention is that his title should be free of arrogance but honor the people (*gens*). On the relationship of Guibert's work to the *Gesta Francorum*, see the editor's introduction, 9.

[300] See the index under "Christiani" and "Franci, Francigenae."

[301] Bartlett, *Making of Europe*, 202.

[302] Loomis, "Nationality at the Council of Constance," 291. Note also how a French participant described the division of the Council into nations as "secular" (286–87).

Christian state—a point we will come back to.[303] The result was that as Christianity spread, it had no problem coming to terms with the imperial tradition of the Romans or the royal traditions of their Germanic heirs. All such traditions had, of course, to renounce the patronage of other gods and commit themselves to the worship of one most high and true God, but once they had done so, Christianity could comfortably relate to them as autonomous sources of political values. In the Christian world there was thus no need to justify the emulation of the Roman imperial tradition by comparing it to eating carrion in desperate circumstances, and Caesarism was not a dirty word.[304]

Third, Christianity did not aspire to monopolize the domain of law in the way that Islam did. It did indeed originate in a religion that was law-centered in the manner of Islam, but it made an early decision to jettison Jewish law, and it did not go on to replace it with a comparable law of its own.[305] The result was to leave room for other legal systems, and to ensure that the relationship was one of recognition and not just coexistence. In the first instance this meant recognition of the standing of Roman law. In his account of the composition of the *Digest*, Justinian begins by announcing that he governs "under the authority of God" and rests all his hopes "in the providence of the Supreme Trinity alone." He then goes on to explain that "nothing in any sphere is found so worthy of study as the authority of law, which sets in good order affairs both divine and human and casts out all injustice";[306] in another document he goes so far as to express his pious desire "that God should become the author and patron of the whole work."[307] Anyone more familiar with Islamic than Christian conceptions might infer at this point that the law Justinian was codifying was God's. But the account of the composition of the *Digest* immediately makes it clear that this is not the case: "We have found the whole extent of our laws which has come down from the foundation of the city of Rome and the days of Romulus to be so confused that it extends to an inordinate length and is beyond the comprehension of any human nature."[308] Confronted with this legal mess of almost 1400 years standing,[309] Justinian proceeds to put things

[303] See 351.

[304] For carrion, see 17–18, and for Caesarism 313–14.

[305] An isolated exception is Jesus' prohibition of divorce (Matt. 5:32, 19:6, 19:19, Mark 10:9, 11–12, Luke 16:18). I will touch on medieval canon law below (303).

[306] Justinian, *Digest*, 1: xlvi.

[307] Ibid., 1: lv.

[308] Ibid., 1: xlvi.

[309] For this chronology of Roman legal history, see ibid., 1: xlvii, lv.

to rights—not by sweeping away the detritus and replacing it with a Christian law authored by God but rather by tidying up the legal tradition of pagan Rome and promulgating the result as his own.[310] What is more, he was able to do this without stirring up the opposition of the bishops and monks who so energetically and successfully frustrated all his efforts to bring order to the chaos of Christian doctrine.

This Christian recognition of Roman law was subsequently extended without serious strain to the law of the Germanic successor states.[311] It is true that Archbishop Hincmar of Rheims (d. 882) warned Christians that "they are to be judged in the Day of Judgment not by Roman nor by Salic nor by Burgundian, but by divine and apostolic laws."[312] But that was the next world, whereas in this one, as he put it, "Kings and ministers of a republic have laws, by which they ought to rule the inhabitants of each territory."[313] Such laws could indeed be overridden if they were in conflict with divine justice; in such cases the king should take counsel with "those who know both laws" and issue an appropriate decree, if necessary suppressing "the law of the world" (*lex saeculi*) in favor of "the justice of God"—though it is better for both laws to be observed where they can be.[314] Equally, kings might draw on Mosaic law within the framework of their own law codes; the English king Alfred (ruled 871–899) did so on a considerable scale.[315] But as all this suggests, there was no religious hostility to the legal systems of the Germanic kingdoms as such. The preface to the Bavarian law code opens by quoting a list of law givers and the peoples they served, starting with Moses; it then concludes that "each people chooses its own law out of its custom."[316] Such legal pluralism did not sit well with Bishop Agobard of Lyons (d. 840), who wrote a polemical tract against Burgundian law, but his purpose was to persuade Louis the

[310] See 277.

[311] I am much indebted to Helmut Reimitz for his generous assistance on this point. I owe to him most of the references given in this paragraph.

[312] Wormald, *Making of English law*, 423.

[313] Ibid., 424. The legislative role of Christian kings seems clear in the continuation of the passage: he speaks of the *capitula*, "which they promulgated to be held lawfully with the general consent of their faithful men."

[314] Ibid., 425; Siems, "Entwicklung von Rechtsquellen," 266, and cf. 261, 265–66.

[315] Wormald, *Making of English law*, 421–23; for Alfred's account of his own legislative activity, see 277.

[316] Wormald, *Legal culture*, 33; *Lex Baiwariorum*, 198–200 (*unaquaque gens propriam sibi ex consuetudine elegit legem*, 200.6, and cf. 202.1). Here too, pagan custom may be overridden by Christian law (202.3). This code has been dated to the eighth century (180–81).

Pious (ruled 813–840) to subject the Burgundians to Frankish law, not to replace Burgundian law with God's law.[317] We thus find ecclesiastics playing a prominent role in the process by which kings made law[318] and speaking of royal legislative activity with approval; the Venerable Bede (d. 735) considered the code of laws devised by king Ethelbert of Kent in the early seventh century—written in Anglo-Saxon, but on the Roman model—to have been one of the good things (*bona*) he did for his people.[319] As might be expected, the compatibility of Christianity with the legal traditions of the non-Roman peoples also finds vivid illustration in Celtic Ireland.[320] We are told of an Irish poet who converted to Christianity and showed the traditional law to St. Patrick; whatever "did not conflict with the word of God" was then "fastened in the canon of the judges" by the ecclesiastics and the seers.[321] We also encounter an ingenious invocation of Moses to justify such retention of pagan law: the fact that the structure he adopted to streamline the administration of justice among the Israelites was suggested to him by his Midianite father-in-law Jethro (Ex. 18:21–22) shows that "if we find judgments of the heathen (*iudicia gentium*) good" and not displeasing to God, "we shall keep them."[322] The whole relationship between the Christian church and such legal systems is nicely dramatized in Shakespeare's *Henry the Fifth.* Here it is no less an ecclesiastic than the Archbishop of Canterbury who enables the action to proceed by providing a tedious but necessary exposition of the reason why the exclusion of women from succession in Salic law is no bar to Henry's claim to the French throne. The archbishop's argument is not that Salic law is ungodly or without authority but simply that it does not apply to France.[323] In all this the contrast with the Islamic case stands out

[317] Agobard of Lyons, "Adversus legem Gundobadi," 23 (*ut eos transferret ad legem Francorum*). Gundobad (ruled 473–516) was the Burgundian king credited with the code.

[318] For the Visigothic case, see Wormald, "Leges Barbarorum," 38. For English examples, see Attenborough, *Earliest English kings*, 36 = 37, where a king of Wessex legislating in the late seventh century mentions consultation with two of his bishops; Oliver, *Beginnings of English law*, 152 = 153, where an account of the laws of a contemporary king of Kent notes the presence of an archbishop and bishop in the assembly that made the laws.

[319] Siems, "Entwicklung von Rechtsquellen," 254–55; Bede, *Ecclesiastical history*, 78.

[320] I owe several of my Irish references to Angela Gleason.

[321] Ó Corráin et al., "Laws of the Irish," 385–86; Kelly, *Early Irish law*, 48; Charles-Edwards, *Early Christian Ireland*, 196–97.

[322] Bieler, *Irish penitentials*, 168 = 169; Ó Corráin et al., "Laws of the Irish," 392. Contrast the use of Jethro's recommendations by a Puritan author in seventeenth-century Massachusetts to design a "Christian commonwealth" (Walzer, *Revolution of the saints*, 232).

[323] Shakespeare, *Henry V*, 100–104 (act 1, scene 2). Salic (or Salian) law is Frankish law. The archbishop also cites Num. 27:8, which allows a daughter to succeed in the

very clearly. Whereas the pagan legal heritages of the Germans and the Irish were to be accepted except in cases of specific conflict with Christianity, that of the Arabs was to be rejected except in cases of specific endorsement by Islam.[324] There could be no question of the Arabs being at liberty to choose their own law out of their custom.

There is one major phenomenon in the legal history of Europe that these remarks do not take account of: the rise of canon law, particularly from the eleventh century. Like Islamic law, the canon law of Western Christendom was a religious law applicable to all believers, and thanks to its promotion by a highly organized church, its impact on the life of the average believer may well have been greater. But canon law lacked the Islamic commitment to divine legislative monopoly in two major respects. First, it did not claim to be the only legitimate form of law. It developed and flourished in elaborate and overt symbiosis with Roman law,[325] and despite boundary disputes it fully accepted the existence of competing legal systems alongside that of the church[326]—and even the role of a king in shaping canon law itself.[327] Second, while it included a core of unchanging divine law,[328] it was entirely comfortable with the idea that a large part of canon law was man-made.[329] Thus compilers of canonical collections freely edited and updated their materials,[330] and institutions made and unmade canon law through their legislative activity;[331] indeed popes would shamelessly advertise their legal innovations by gathering them together in collections of "new laws" (*novellae*) and even "newest laws" (*novissimae*).[332] A papal bull of 1322 affirms that "one cannot blame a legislator (*canonum conditor*) for revoking, modifying, or suspending canons, if he should see that they do more harm than good."[333] In these two very basic respects canon law was a different phenomenon from Islamic law. At the same time it was more the property of the church than of the wider community of believers, and its fortunes faded with those of the institution.

---

absence of a son, but he does so only as an afterthought. In the respects that concern us, Shakespeare's account is close to that of his main source (see 306–7).

[324] See 271–72.

[325] Brundage, *Medieval canon law*, 59–60, 96–97, 108, 111, 169–70, 176–77.

[326] Ibid., 71–72, 74–75, 177.

[327] Ibid., 28.

[328] Ibid., 154, 173.

[329] Ibid., 154.

[330] Ibid., 33.

[331] Ibid., 41, 53, 157, 172, and cf. 182.

[332] Ibid., 55, and cf. 165 on the *ius novum* of the thirteenth century.

[333] Nold, *Pope John XXII*, 144.

At this point it is worth recalling Ibn Khaldūn's remark that Muḥammad was sent to teach us the religious law, not medicine or any other "ordinary matter."[334] In terms of medicine, there was little difference between the Islamic and Christian dispensations. Both have some medical notions associated with the figure of the founder—Prophetic medicine in the Islamic case, faith healing and exorcism in the Christian case; and in both cases the mainstream tradition of medicine was nevertheless that inherited from the pagan Greeks. But in terms of law there is a glaring contrast: for Christians, law can be as much an "ordinary matter" as medicine. Another such case is philosophy. In the early history of Christianity there were some who, like Ephraem the Syrian (d. 373), rejected "the poison of the wisdom of the Greeks" in favor of "the simplicity of the Apostles";[335] but sooner or later they lost out, and despite occasional later echoes of such rhetoric,[336] there is no Muslim equivalent of Thomas Aquinas as an Aristotelian philosopher who was central to medieval Christian thought. All this is enough to show a very real difference between the Christian heritage on the one hand, and that of Islam—not to mention Hinduism—on the other.

This background does much to explain why we have so little to attend to in this chapter in the modern Latin American context. Divine jealousy outside the narrow confines of religious beliefs and rituals is just not a relevant category. That said, two points are perhaps worth making here. The first puts canon law in its place. It will be recalled that the conservative, uncharismatic archbishop appointed to Olinda and Recife in 1985 was an expert on canon law.[337] He had wanted to study theology, but his superior told him not to be stupid: "We have enough theologians. We need more canonical lawyers." He did as he was told and suffered ridicule in Recife as a result.[338] It would indeed be hard to imagine mass mobilization in Brazil under the slogan "Canon law is our religious right, we will die to protect it."[339] The second point

[334] See 252.

[335] For a succinct account of such rejectionism, see Drobner, "Christian philosophy," 677–80. For Ephraem's contrast between Greek wisdom and Apostolic simplicity, see Beck, *Des Heiligen Ephraem*, 7, verse 24 of both the text and translation.

[336] Note, for example, the complaint of the Protestant reformer William Tyndale (d. 1536) that the universities do not let any man look at scripture until he has been "nuzzled in heathen learning eight or nine years" (quoted in MacCulloch, *Thomas Cranmer*, 19n10). See also Walzer, *Revolution of the saints*, 101, on John Knox (d. 1572).

[337] See 208.

[338] Nagle, *Claiming the Virgin*, 58.

[339] See 289.

is the permeability of Latin American Catholicism to the seductions of Marxism. The existence of God is hardly an "ordinary matter": if Marxist atheism was not enough to trigger divine jealousy in Latin America, what would have done? In this respect the appeal of Marxism in Catholic circles is far more telling than the earlier appeal of fascism, an ideological brew in which godlessness is not of the essence. Of course, many in Latin America detested Marxism—but more because it was subversive than because it was irreligious.

There is, however, another factor at work here: the relative weakness of nativist resistance to the importation of alien culture in Latin America. Economically, Latin America is part of the Third World, but that is not a cultural category. Unlike the peoples of the Islamic world or India, most Latin Americans are not the heirs of a non-Western civilization; and for those limited populations that are, the cultural continuity was broken beyond repair by the end of the eighteenth century. For Latin America the West has been an enviable and in some respects threatening center of wealth and power, but it has not been culturally alien in the way it has for the peoples of Asia. Conservative Catholics are indeed likely to be allergic to certain kinds of change emanating from Europe and North America, but it would be hard to make sense of the conflict as one of civilizations. Secularization may seem no more culturally alien than foreign priests.

So far in this section we have proceeded as if all Christians were Catholics, which even in Latin America is far from being the case. Would matters appear significantly different if we were to look at Protestants rather than Catholics? One relevant detail is that faithful adherents of the medical tradition of the Gospels are more numerous among Protestants than among Catholics—an effect that appears particularly strong if we compare Pentecostals and Liberationists.[340] A larger point emerges if we extend the net to the evangelical Christians of North America. Here the political activities of the Christian Right bring home the fact that even zealous Christians do not have a religious law to restore; their goal is merely to incorporate Christian values into the existing fabric of American law.[341] The only exception to this is Christian Reconstructionism, a fringe movement to which we will return

[340] Cf. 211.

[341] By comparison, the traditionalist Catholic Marcel Lefebvre (d. 1991) would like to see the Ten Commandments inspire all legislation and the law of the Gospel permeate all the civil laws (Lefebvre, *They have uncrowned him*, 55, 210), but he has no problem with the existence of civil law as such.

in a later chapter.[342] In this milieu we do find an attempt to create a Christian counterpart of the Sharīʿa through a Biblical fundamentalism that reaches back to include the legal provisions of the Pentateuch.[343] It is a long shot: even the Puritans of seventeenth-century Massachusetts held back from adopting the laws of Moses as the law of the land,[344] though those of New Haven came closer to it.[345] In so holding back, the Puritans of Massachusetts had the support of no less an authority than Calvin (d. 1564). He held that subject to conformity with the higher purpose of law, we have no reason to censure such laws as nations may make, however they may differ from Jewish law or from each other; the Mosaic law, he observed, was not intended to be promulgated to all

[342] See 436–38.

[343] Rushdoony, *Institutes of Biblical law*. The backbone of the book is a survey of Biblical law organized as a series of chapters, each devoted to one of the Ten Commandments. With regard to adultery, for example, Rushdoony concludes from a discussion of Biblical texts that the death penalty is clearly God's law, and he goes on to say that a "godly law-order will restore the death penalty"—though he prudently adds that the church "must live realistically with its absence" (399). See also Al-Azm, "Islamic fundamentalism reconsidered, Part II," 96–97.

[344] In 1636 John Cotton submitted to the General Court of Massachusetts a draft code entitled "a modell of the Iudiciall lawes of Moses"; one feature of the draft that elicited criticism was the profusion of death sentences for offenses like profaning the Sabbath. The code was not accepted (see Massachusetts, *Laws and liberties*, vi, drawn to my attention by James Bell). The "Body of Liberties" of 1641 included a selection of twelve laws taken from the Bible that imposed the death penalty (Powers, *Crime and punishment*, 254–64), but other such Biblical laws were left aside, and where the Biblical penalty was specified as stoning, this seems to have been ignored (256, 257, and cf. 269; for methods of execution, usually hanging, see 303). In sum, the Puritans of Massachusetts took Biblical law seriously—but not as seriously as one might have expected. Thus, in 1638 the General Court sought proposals for "such necessary & fundamentall lawes as may bee sutable to the times & places whear God by his providence hath cast vs" (Haskins, *Law and authority*, 126–27).

[345] The title page of a publication of 1656 announces that its contents include "some Lawes for Government" published for use in the colony of New Haven but warns that some orders may be altered and "as need requireth other Lawes added" (Hoadly, *Records from May, 1653 to the union*, 560). Nevertheless in the "Articles of Confederation," negotiated with Massachusetts, Plymouth, and Connecticut and reproduced in this publication, it is acknowledged that "the Supreame power of making Lawes, and of repealing them, belongs to God onely," and that "the Lawes for holinesse, and Righteousnesse, are already made, and given us in the Scriptures, which in matters morall, or of morall equity, may not be altered by humane power, or authority"; they accordingly claim for the "Civill Rulers," beyond the power to "declare, publish and establish" the laws already made by God, only the power "to make, and repeale Orders for smaller matters, not particularly determined in Scripture, according to the more Generall Rules of Righteousnesse" (569). In a case decided in New Haven in 1641, a man convicted of bestiality was condemned to death in accordance with Lev. 20:15; the court noted that under the "fundamentall agreement" made when the colony was founded, "the judiciall

nations, and God as the legislator of the Israelites displayed a special regard for their peculiar circumstances in devising it.[346]

5. Conclusion

One respect in which religious heritages differ is how near they approach to being all-embracing. Of our trio, the Hindu case comes closest: here law is unambiguously part of the heritage, and even the mainstream medical tradition probably deriving from western Asia pretends to be. The Christian case is the most distant: not just mainstream medicine but even law falls largely outside the heritage—both are the kind of thing that in Augustine's view the heavenly city has no problem accommodating during its pilgrimage on earth, provided always that there is no hindrance to the requirements of Christianity. As Ibn Khaldūn would put it, they are "ordinary matters." The Islamic case falls in between: mainstream medicine, like science in general, is an "ordinary matter," but law is emphatically not one, however much administrative and customary law may in practice have encroached on divine territory. On this basis we would have reason to expect that acculturation to the modern world would have been easiest in the Christian case, hardest in the Hindu case, and somewhere in between in the Muslim case. This expectation would be reinforced by an obvious historical point: of our trio, the Christian heritage is the most intimately linked to the modern West, the Hindu heritage the most distant from it, and the Islamic heritage again somewhere in between.

Things look rather different, however, when we bring into play another respect in which the three cases differ, the intensity—as opposed to extent—of divine jealousy, that is to say the degree to which there is a continuing commitment to maintaining the hegemony of the religion.

---

law of God given by Moses and expounded in other parts of scripture, so far as itt is a hedg and a fence to the morrall law, and neither ceremoniall nor tipicall, nor had any reference to Canaan, hath an everlasting equity in itt, and should be the rule of their proceedings" (Hoadly, *Records from 1638 to 1649*, 69). An order of 1644 uses similar wording to enjoin that "the judiciall lawes of God, as they were delivered by Moses" should be "a rule to all the courts in this jurisdiction" but adds the proviso "till they be branched out into perticulars hereafter" (130).

[346] Calvin, *Institutes of the Christian religion*, 2: 789–91; Calvin, *Institution de la religion chrestienne*, 4: 522–23 (= book 4, ch. 20, sections 15–16). Calvin variously identifies what I have termed the higher purpose of law with the law of God, the moral law, natural law, equity, and charity.

Here the all-embracing character of the Hindu heritage has counted for rather little in the face of the willingness of its modern followers to write off or simply ignore so much of it as obsolete—partly because by modern standards some of it really is painfully obsolete and partly because the absence of a strong monotheist focus tends to weaken the force of the jealousy. The Hindu nationalists are no exception, their attitude toward their heritage being marked by an opportunistic eclecticism. Meanwhile Christians have often displayed a rather similar attitude toward aspects of their own heritage, and in any case, they have not in general had reason to feel themselves culturally foreign to the West in the way Muslims and Hindus have done. What is true for Christians in general is true for the Catholics of Latin America in particular.

Greater commitment to maintaining the hegemony of the religion is thus the factor that explains why the Islamic response has not been the mean between the other two cases but rather the outlier. This was prefigured in the pre-modern Muslim interactions with other civilizations: despite the demographic weakness of the Muslim presence in India, the tendency to seek reconciliation with Hindu culture lost out to a harder line among the ruling Muslim elite, and only in the remote and unusual case of the politically subject Muslim minority in China did the higher stratum of a Muslim population go out of its way to come to terms with the values of an alien culture. In the modern world the pressure to reach accommodation has come to affect the entire Muslim community, but on balance Muslims have put up a stronger resistance to secularization—the establishment and extension of God-free zones in areas previously subject to religious hegemony—than either Hindus or Christians.

The single most significant example of this is the lure of the idea of a restoration of Islamic law, an Islamist project that garners extensive popular support. No analogous project exercises a comparable sway over the imaginations of Hindus or Christians: Christians have no law to restore, while Hindus do have one but show little interest in restoring it. It is only in the Islamic case that there is both the will and the way—the way because the tradition claimed sovereignty over the domain of law where Christianity did not and the will because for Muslims, in contrast to Hindus, the desire to maintain this claim has not evaporated. Not surprisingly, cultural interaction with the West has been far more conflicted in the Muslim case than in either of the other two.

CHAPTER 7

Polity

1. Introduction

After treating society, warfare, and the implications of divine jealousy, we now come to the polity. Here modern values have some very definite implications for the state and its citizens. They prescribe that the form of the state should be republican, democratic, and constitutional; if monarchy is to survive at all in this context, it should be a vestigial arrangement with no real impact on the way the political system functions, a monarchical republic.[1] At the same time modern values require that the citizens of the state enjoy liberty, equality, and some measure of fraternity—to go no further than the familiar trio associated with revolutionary France.[2] These six terms may not add up to a sophisticated analysis of modern political values, but apart from nationalism they are pretty much all we need for our purposes. How, then, do they relate to the three pre-modern religious traditions with which we are concerned?

2. Islam

A key feature of the Islamic heritage is that its idea of a legitimate polity is very much its own. One obvious aspect of this is terminological. Whereas the title "king" in European usage was applied to rulers—and used by them—irrespective of their religious affiliations, the title "caliph" (*khalīfa*) could not be employed in this indiscriminate way. Taken on its own the word was indeed generic, meaning either "deputy" or "successor," and in these senses the word could, of course, be used freely in non-Muslim contexts. But in the context that concerns

[1] This term has been applied in the context of early modern England in the sense of "a form of government that, although monarchical in form, is nevertheless republican in character" (the wording is that of Skinner, "Monarchical republic enthroned," 237).

[2] Fraternity is the poor relation in this trio: for its absence from key revolutionary documents before 1848, see Antoine, *Liberté égalité fraternité*, 134.

us, the application of the term was not generic: if it meant "deputy," then it identified the ruler of the Islamic polity as the deputy of God (*khalīfat Allāh*), and if it meant "successor," then he was the successor of the Prophet (*khalīfat rasūl Allāh*). This latter view was the one that prevailed among the scholars.[3] Either way, the concept of the caliphate was unique: there could be no question of seeing rulers across the globe as deputies of God, let alone as successors of the Muslim prophet.[4] Similar points can be made about two further terms that are often interchangeable with "caliph," namely "imam" and "Commander of the Faithful." Thus, already at the level of terminology, there is a tight relationship between the conception of rulership and the religious community. This is, of course, an aspect of the fusion of religion and politics that characterized Muḥammad's venture in prophetic state formation.

A second unusual feature of the caliphate is that the caliph is conceived as the single ruler of the entire Muslim community, not to mention the numerous unbelievers who have submitted to Muslim rule and been permitted to persist in their unbelief. This is how it was in the decades following the death of the Prophet, and it was also how the religious tradition liked to see things down the centuries. In historical fact, of course, the initial political unity of the Muslim community came to be unsustainable, and by the tenth century the caliphate had definitively given way to the coexistence of a plurality of Muslim states that were frequently at war with each other.[5] These states could hardly be seen as embodiments of the Islamic polity, but they were Islamic in the rather minimal sense that Muslims ruled them.[6] The religious tradition was able to come to terms with this situation by adopting a variety of shifts, thereby accommodating the plurality of Muslim states, rather than either rejecting it outright or endorsing it as inherently right and proper.[7] What the scholars remained reluctant to do was to abandon the original unitary conception altogether.

[3] Crone, *Medieval Islamic political thought*, 18, 128–29.

[4] Muslim authors may nevertheless see the papacy as a Christian *analogue* of the caliphate. For example, one thirteenth-century author explains that the pope is considered to be the *khalīfa* of Christ (B. Lewis, *Muslim discovery*, 178, and cf. 209); another source states that the Franks consider the pope to be the deputy (*nāʾib*) of the Messiah and compares him to the Commander of the Faithful among the Muslims (Yāqūt, *Muʿjam al-buldān*, 1: 323a.29, in the entry "Bāshghird").

[5] See 26.

[6] Cf. 22–23.

[7] Crone, *Medieval Islamic political thought*, 273–75.

A third feature of the caliphate, and again one inherited from the state established by the Prophet, was that it combined political and religious authority. It was not that Muslims had any trouble imagining an alternative arrangement in which these two forms of authority were legitimately decoupled. Thus Māturīdī (d. ca. 944), after noting that the imamate includes both religious and political authority (*al-imāma maʿa amr al-dīn fīhā amr al-mulk waʾl-siyāsa*), contrasts this to a situation in which political and prophetic authority are vested in different people, as was at one stage the case among the ancient Israelites: "political authority was in the hands of kings, and religious authority in the hands of prophets" (*kāna amr al-siyāsa fī aydī ʾl-mulūk, waʾl-diyāna fī aydī ʾl-anbiyāʾ*).[8] He quotes Q2:246, from a passage on the institution of the Israelite monarchy. But the polity in which the Muslims themselves lived was not, in their view, supposed to be of this dual kind—for all that, in historical fact, it soon came to be so, with the scholars standing in for the prophets.

The religious tradition saw the historical changes affecting the early caliphate as part of a process of deep moral decay. As the Moroccan scholar Yūsī (d. 1691) put it, after the first four model caliphs were no more, men came to rule through greed and violence, the caliphate came to an end, and in its place came "biting kingship," as the Prophet had foretold.[9] In the same vein the Prophet had predicted that the caliphate would last a mere thirty years, after which its place would be taken by kingship (*mulk*)[10]—mere kingship, we might say. Baranī contrasts the one generation of righteous rule in the time of the Prophet and his immediate successors with the subsequent period in which rulership had ceased to be possible without "the majesty and pomp of monarchs" and the other iniquitous Persian practices that go with them.[11] Only in the backlands of the Islamic world, in the mountains and deserts, did the political style of the early caliphate occasionally survive in sectarian environments.[12]

All this made for a temporally very asymmetric image of the political history of the Islamic world. On the one hand there was the

[8] Nasafī, *Tabṣirat al-adilla*, 829.14 (I owe my knowledge of this passage to Sönmez Kutlu).

[9] Mdaghrī, *al-Faqīh Abū ʿAlī al-Yūsī*, 328.20 (read *al-mulk al-ʿaḍūḍ*); for an example of a tradition in which the Prophet foretells such kingship, see Bayhaqī, *Shuʿab al-īmān*, 5: 16–17 no. 5616.

[10] Tirmidhī, *al-Jāmiʿ al-ṣaḥīḥ*, 4: 503 no. 2226 (*fitan* 48).

[11] M. Cook, "Political freedom," 294. See also above, 17–18.

[12] Ibid., 298–99.

initial period when a single Islamic polity was ruled by a single legitimate caliph following in the footsteps of the Prophet. And on the other hand there were the long centuries in which, whatever the pretenses adopted to save the appearances, the polity had fragmented and the actual rulers were something very different. Just when the transition was thought to have taken place was in fact by no means clear-cut. What the religious tradition rejoiced in, as opposed to merely accommodating, was limited to the first decades of Islamic history, and yet an event as late as the Mongol destruction of the residual ʿAbbāsid Caliphate in 1258 was widely experienced as traumatic.[13] In any case, as we have just seen, the transition meant that caliphs gave way to kings; and though the word "king" (*malik*) is just one of a number of terms applied to these latter-day Muslim rulers, we can aptly call the long interval between early Islamic and modern times the age of Muslim kingship (republics barely existed and were ignored by the normative tradition).[14] Two sayings, one a commonplace and the other a paradox, may serve to set the scene for this period. The commonplace affirms that "kingship and religion are twins."[15] In other words they are very close, but they are not identical: with political power in the hands of kings and religious authority in the hands of scholars, the fusion of religion and politics central to Muḥammad's original polity has come apart, producing a duality that is in fact much more typical of complex societies in pre-modern times and more compatible with their needs.[16] The paradox goes further still: "Kingship endures with unbelief, but not with oppression."[17] That is to say, even a ruler who does not adhere to

[13] Hassan, "Loss of caliphate," chap. 1.

[14] For fleeting instances of nonmonarchic rule on a small scale, see Stern, "Constitution," 33–36. For an illuminating study of the North African Tripoli—a place that could easily have been a city state if it had had a mind to—see Brett, "City-state," especially 93. For a more stable case, located in a strongly sectarian environment in northeast Arabia, see *EI*², art. "Ḳarmaṭī" (W. Madelung), 664; a key eleventh-century account of this polity (translated in B. Lewis, *Islam from Muhammad*, 2: 65–68) describes the collective rule of six kings and six viziers (66). The ancient heritage of the early medieval Muslims did not include the concept of a republic (Crone, *Medieval Islamic political thought*, 279).

[15] Ṣaghānī, *Mawḍūʿāt*, 36 no. 29 (*al-mulk wa'l-dīn taw'amān*, as a tradition falsely ascribed to the Prophet); Miskawayh, *Tajārib al-umam*, 102.7 (*al-mulk wa'l-dīn akhawān taw'amān*, ascribed to the Persian king Ardashīr (ruled 224–240)); and cf. Lambton, *State and government*, 45; Gutas, *Greek thought*, 80–81.

[16] Crone, *Medieval Islamic political thought*, 10–16, especially 15.

[17] See, for example, Niẓām al-Mulk, *Siyar al-mulūk*, 15.8 = Nizam al-Mulk, *Book of government*, 12 (as a saying of the religious authorities, *buzurgān-i dīn*); Fakhr al-Dīn al-Rāzī, *al-Tafsīr al-kabīr*, 18: 76.13 (to Q11:117). For many more references, see Sadan, "Community," 108–11, and for the same idea expressed in other words, see Alam, *Languages of political Islam*, 72–73 (both drawn to my attention by Luke Yarbrough).

the true religion may deliver the security without which society cannot survive, while even one who believes in it may fail to deliver.

Yet it was unusual in pre-modern times for things to come to this pass. The rulers, after all, were still in general Muslims, even if not particularly good ones, and as Muslim rulers they tended to accomplish two desirable things. One was to maintain the ascendancy of Islam over domestic and—where possible—foreign unbelievers, thereby implementing the principle that "Islam is exalted, and nothing is exalted above it."[18] The other was to show some respect for the division of labor between rulers and scholars that came to mark the twinship of kingship and religion in medieval Muslim societies. As the scholars saw it, it was for them to act as exponents of the Sharīʿa and for rulers to defer to their learning and integrity; we even encounter the distinctly self-seeking view that "the kings have authority over the people whereas scholars have authority over the kings."[19] To the extent that things worked like this, we can see the scholars as a bridle restraining the tendency of rulers to the arbitrary exercise of power.[20] In exchange the ruler could expect them to use their religious resources to confer on him a measure of political legitimacy[21]—though never, of course, to take this to the lengths of deifying him.

The actual political culture of Muslim states in this period was not, however, by any means limited to the mainstream religious tradition.[22] There were a number of other idioms in which political conflicts, matters of state, and issues of legitimacy could be articulated. Thus under the Umayyads factional loyalties grounded in Arabian tribalism were a remarkably salient feature of the political scene.[23] More lasting at the level of high politics were idioms deriving from pre-Islamic Iran and the pagan nomads of the Eurasian steppes. The more outspoken scholars might deplore such influences; thus Yūsī lamented that after the caliphate had given way to kingship, Muḥammad's way of ruling (*sīra*) was displaced by Chosroism (*kisrawiyya*) and Caesarism (*qayṣariyya*)—

[18] Friedmann, *Tolerance and coercion*, 34–38. I follow Friedmann's translation of the tradition; a less elegant but more literal rendering might be "Islam is on top, and nothing overtops it."

[19] Landau-Tasseron, *Religious foundations*, 11a.

[20] For the view that this amounts to a constitution, see Feldman, *Fall and rise*, 6.

[21] Usually but not always. For an eighteenth-century Egyptian scholar who places the predatory rulers of Egypt in the same category as those who make war on God and his Prophet, see Peters, *Islam and colonialism*, 183n80. More generally, there was a sense that the best scholars were those who had least to do with rulers.

[22] Much relevant material may be found in Al-Azmeh, *Muslim kingship*.

[23] See Crone, "Qays and Yemen," especially 42–43. For the long survival of this factional opposition in Syrian society, see Goldziher, *Muslim studies*, 1: 78–79.

Chosroes and Caesar being the generic rulers of the pre-Islamic Persian and Byzantine empires respectively.[24] But despite such pietist disapproval, idioms of this kind still counted with contemporaries and left a literary deposit in such genres as historiography and mirrors for princes.

One aspect of this is the legitimation that rulers sought to derive from symbols and ceremonies. Here the mainstream Islamic tradition is remarkably restrained. It provides a rather austere set of ritual occasions on which the ruler or his representative officiates: "the Friday prayer, the two Festivals, and the Pilgrimage are with the ruler (*sulṭān*)," as one succinct formulation has it.[25] The key moment is the sermon (*khuṭba*) of the Friday prayer, in which the general practice is to mention the name of the ruler; but even this was more than the jurists prescribed.[26] In practice, as might be expected, Muslim rulers built up much more elaborate symbolic and ceremonial repertoires.[27] Some of the themes they drew on were manifestly Islamic, like the rich collections of relics amassed by major Muslim dynasties such as the ʿAbbāsids and Ottomans.[28] Some were not Islamic but not necessarily offensive to Islamic values; cases in point might be the archers deployed at the ʿAbbāsid palace to shoot down overflying crows[29] or the West African practice of throwing dust on oneself when spoken to by the ruler.[30] Some elements were downright un-Islamic: there was a widespread practice of reinforcing the authority of the ruler with music,[31] a clear though commonplace violation of Islamic norms. This does not, of course, mean that all such norms could be disregarded for the greater glory of kingship. Thus, there was no question of allowing the public display of statues and other images of the ruler that was so salient a feature of the political culture of the pagan Roman Empire

[24] M. Cook, "Political freedom," 295. It was the traditions of the pre-Islamic Persian kings that Baranī urged rulers to adopt in the same way as a starving man eats carrion (294, and above, 17–18).

[25] Ibn Abī Yaʿlā, *Ṭabaqāt al-Ḥanābila*, 1: 26.17.

[26] *EI*², art. "Khuṭba" (A. J. Wensinck); Calder, "Friday prayer," 36 (citing a view that the practice is not recommended). Historically the mention of the ruler's name in the *khuṭba* came to be paired with its inscription on the coinage.

[27] *EI*², arts. "Marāsim" (P. Sanders et al.) and "Mawākib" (P. Sanders et al.).

[28] Hilāl al-Ṣābiʾ, *Rusūm Dār al-Khilāfah*, 65, 73; Necipoğlu, *Architecture, ceremonial, and power*, 150–52.

[29] Hilāl al-Ṣābiʾ, *Rusūm Dār al-Khilāfah*, 74, and cf. 66.

[30] Ibn Battúta, *Travels in Asia and Africa*, 327.

[31] *EI*², arts. "Mehter" (W. Feldman), "Naḳḳāra-Khāna" (A.K.S. Lambton), and "Ṭabl-Khāna" (H. G. Farmer).

and lasted far into Byzantine times;[32] indeed after the monetary reform of the late seventh century, Muslim rulers could not even follow the standard practice of Eurasian monarchs west of China by putting their images on their coins. But despite these limitations the symbolic and ceremonial resources of Muslim kingship were considerable.

A regional example may help to reinforce the point. Conceptions of legitimacy in Central Asia in later centuries had a way of harking back to the Mongols, even when blended with Islamic and other elements.[33] Thus, in 1756 the powerful tribal chieftain who effectively ruled the Khānate of Bukhara decided to claim the throne for himself, and an elaborate ceremony was staged to legitimize his accession.[34] A chronicler's account of the proceedings combines elements of striking heterogeneity.[35] There are references to the descendants of Chingiz Khān (ruled 1206–1227) and their traditions, one of which provided the central moment of the ceremony: the notables gathered round the new ruler, took hold of the edges of the felt carpet on which he was sitting, and elevated him.[36] There is mention of such famous rulers of pre-Islamic Iran as the legendary Jamshīd, Darius I (ruled 522–486 BC), and Khusraw I (ruled 531–579).[37] The astrologers likewise appear, their indispensable role being to select an auspicious time for the event.[38] Last but not least there are several Islamic themes: references to the Koran, the Sharīʿa, the mention of the ruler's name in the Friday prayer, the caliphate, and a treatise on the imamate written specially for the occasion.[39] It is characteristic of the melange that seven reli-

[32] Hopkins, *Conquerors and slaves*, 220–26; Dvornik, *Christian and Byzantine political philosophy*, 648, 653–56, 686–87.

[33] See Sela, *Tamerlane*, 15–16 (a chronicle of 1525), 92–98 (an eighteenth-century account of how Tīmūr came to reign; note the ancillary roles played by a prominent Ṣūfī and the Prophet himself, 93–94, 97).

[34] Sela, *Ritual and authority*, 2–4.

[35] See the translation ibid., 5–19, followed by his commentary, especially 20–25; for the original Persian text, see 59–68.

[36] Ibid., 12; for the elevation, see 13–14. One of the new ruler's problems was that he was not of Chingizid descent (22, 24), the Chingizids being, as one fifteenth-century chronicler put it, the Quraysh of the Turks (34; cf. below, 317–18).

[37] Ibid., 9, 12, 19 (for further mentions of Khusraw, see 64.13, 66.1 of the original Persian); and note the reference to the royal *farr* or glory, an Iranian conception of venerable antiquity (16). Alexander the Great (ruled 336–323 BC) also figures (18), as do Solomon (18) and—directly or by allusion—some rulers of Islamic times (8, 12, 17).

[38] Ibid., 11.

[39] See ibid., 5, 7, 8, 10, 14 (Koranic quotations); 6, 10 (the Sharīʿa); 6, 10, 19 (the *khuṭba*); 5, 12 (the caliphate; see also 63.18); 15 (the treatise on the imamate). It is implied but not stated that the new ruler is a caliph.

gious dignitaries were among those who elevated the ruler on his felt carpet.[40]

Another such aspect of Muslim kingship is the range of idioms in which matters of state were discussed. Here an Ottoman illustration without flagrantly un-Islamic overtones should give some idea of what was involved. In the seventeenth-century Ottoman Empire there was a reformist idiom that sought a remedy for the ills of imperial decline through a return to the golden age of Süleymān "the Lawgiver (Qānūnī)" (ruled 1520–1566).[41] Despite perfunctory acknowledgment of Islamic law, the central feature of this persuasion was an appeal for adherence to "the laws (*qavānīn*) of the sultans of the past," which are "the guide to action (*destūr ül-ʿamel*) in every matter."[42] In other words, what we have here is a way of thinking about the Ottoman state that invokes specifically Ottoman norms as enshrined in a specifically Ottoman past. This particularistic trend, however, had its critics, who outflanked it by arguing in much more general terms.[43] A state, according to this view, has its life cycle just as an individual has; like individuals, states may vary as to just when decline sets in, and it may be possible to treat it symptomatically when it does. But it is futile to attempt to restore things as they were before the decline began; that would be like a graybeard dyeing his beard black and trying to prevent its going gray again. Here we see a very different way of thinking, and indeed it derived from a source outside the Ottoman Empire: the theory of the dynastic life cycle propounded by Ibn Khaldūn (d. 1406).[44] In contrast to the reformist way of thinking, this approach reduced the Ottoman Empire to a particular instance of a general rule. But however different in approach these diagnosticians of Ottoman distemper might be, they had one thing in common: the polity ruled long ago by Muḥammad and his successors was effectively irrelevant to their concerns.

In the face of the proliferation of Muslim kingship, the scholars did not simply let go of the caliphate. Instead, they continued to transmit their centuries-old theory of the institution. Admittedly they did not set out the theory very often,[45] and when they did so it tended to be

[40] Ibid., 13. Compare an accession of 1583 in which the felt carpet is supplied by a leading religious dignitary, having previously been washed in holy water in Mecca (42; McChesney, "Zamzam water," 66–67).

[41] B. Lewis, "Ottoman observers," 213–16.

[42] Qochı Beg, *Risāle*, 9.5.

[43] Kātib Chelebī, *Destūr ül-ʿamel li-iṣlāḥ il-khalel*, 122.8, 130.12, 136.8.

[44] B. Lewis, "Ibn Khaldūn," 234.

[45] It is noteworthy that the subject is not given a place within the standard compass of the Sunnī law book.

somewhat threadbare, but it nonetheless retained its place in the religious tradition.

Thus, according to Yūsī, writing in Morocco, the Muslims have the duty of appointing an imam who would possess a general authority in religious and worldly matters in succession to the prophethood of Muḥammad (*khilāfatan ʿani ʾl-nubuwwa*).[46] It would be his task to revive religion, secure the conditions under which people can make a living, command right and forbid wrong, render justice to the oppressed against the oppressor, and the like. To be eligible for the office, a person had to satisfy various conditions, as for example to be adult, sane, male, free, Muslim, respectable, courageous, and possessed of sound judgment. A further condition was genealogical: he had to belong to the tribe of Quraysh, that is to say, the tribe into which Muḥammad had been born. But even this was perhaps negotiable: it is said, Yūsī tells us, that if there is no member of Quraysh who combines all the requisite qualities, then a member of Kināna will do—Kināna being a wider genealogical unit of which Quraysh was a part. Or failing that one might appoint a descendant of Ishmael—the ancestor of the northern Arabs as a whole—or even a non-Arab. The thread connecting us to the early polity has plainly worn very thin here. There is a similar looseness about the procedure of appointment. The imamate takes effect either through designation by the previous imam or through the conclusion of an agreement (*bayʿa*) with those among the Muslims who have the rather elusive power of "loosing and binding." However, if someone who satisfies all the conditions simply goes ahead, forcing people to obey him, then the imamate comes into effect for him too. If he does not satisfy the conditions, he is an oppressor but is nevertheless to be obeyed if resisting him would lead to a greater evil. All this is scholasticism, not a call to action, but such diluted formulations did at least ensure that the caliphate retained its place on the normative map.

From the other end of the Muslim world, we could quote a similarly scholastic account by Shāh Walī Allāh. For numerous reasons, he explains, there has to be a caliph in the Muslim community.[47] Some of these reasons are matters of governance, like repelling invading armies and resolving lawsuits; others relate to religion and involve the maintenance of the Muslim ascendancy. He gives a list of the conditions to be satisfied that is similar to Yūsī's, but divided into two categories: conditions that

[46] Yūsī, *Qānūn*, 191.6.
[47] Walī Allāh, *Ḥujja*, 2: 735.8.

any human population would require of its ruler and conditions specific to the Muslim community.[48] As might be expected, one of the latter is to belong to Quraysh. Here Shāh Walī Allāh provides no escape clauses and adds a rationale that is likely to be his own contribution to the tradition: Muḥammad's revelation was in the language of Quraysh and in conformity with their customs (*fī ʿādātihim*), and it was these customs that prepared the way for many of the laws of Islam.[49] So his scholasticism is by no means as dry as dust. His account of how a caliph is appointed, or emerges, is similar to Yūsī's, though fuller in its discussion of the circumstances under which one should resist a caliph who has seized power without satisfying all the conditions.[50]

What neither Yūsī nor Shāh Walī Allāh stopped to explain was how this scholastic ghost of the early polity related to the realities of their own day, and they might not have welcomed the question. Was there no caliph in their time? Was one particular Muslim ruler the caliph? Were all Muslim rulers in some sense caliphs?[51] A sixteenth-century Ottoman composed a brief treatise arguing that the Ottoman sultan Süleymān was the caliph of the day, firmly sidelining the awkward fact that he did not belong to the tribe of Quraysh, but this author was a retired statesman, not a professional scholar.[52] At one point he quoted an anonymous scholar of the fifteenth or sixteenth century who took the view that it is not appropriate to call latter-day sultans imams or caliphs.[53] The claim of the Ottoman sultans to the caliphate nevertheless achieved a measure of recognition, enough for the abolition of the institution by the Kemalists in 1924 to cause widespread distress in the Muslim world.[54] Even more awkward might have been the question how a single caliph could ever come to rule the entire Muslim world from North Africa to Southeast Asia. The view that the facts of geography might require the existence of more than one caliph had

[48] Ibid., 2: 737.2. In a manner reminiscent of Ibn Khaldūn, Shāh Walī Allāh put considerable intellectual effort into elaborating a general understanding of human social, economic, and political development; he distinguished four cultural levels (*irtifāqs*) (Baljon, *Religion and thought*, 193–96).

[49] There is a hint of relativism here: how, we might ask, would the laws of Islam have been affected had the revelation taken place in Ireland or Japan? For modern use of this opening to relativism, see Zaman, "South Asian Islam," 60.

[50] Walī Allāh, *Ḥujja*, 2: 738.19.

[51] Cf., for example, the claims of the petty rulers of Malaya to the caliphate (Milner, "Islam and Malay kingship," 52).

[52] Gibb, "Luṭfī Paşa."

[53] Ibid., 292.

[54] Hassan, "Loss of caliphate," chap. 2.

been proposed but did not prevail.[55] One fifteenth-century Moroccan scholar could be read as taking tacit account of the problem of distance when he set out a framework for what one might call Muslim interstate relations in response to questions from a ruler on the other side of the Sahara.[56] He proceeded by distinguishing lands of three kinds. First, there is the ungoverned land whose people have no ruler (*amīr*); he told his questioner that he should, if necessary, compel such people to accept him as their ruler since it is not lawful for any group of Muslims to remain without one. Second, there is the land with a ruler who looks after the wordly and religious interests of his subjects as far as can be done in this age; no one may seek to displace such a ruler since he has a better right to his subjects than anyone else. Third, there is the land with an evil ruler. Here military intervention—jihad—to set up a good ruler in his place is appropriate if the prospective benefits outweigh the prospective costs; indeed, such intervention may take precedence over jihad against actual infidels who pose no threat to Muslims. This is a prescription for a Muslim commonwealth from which the caliphate is conspicuously absent.

There is, however, much more to the early caliphate than we have yet touched on. While the institution itself was neither republican, nor democratic, nor constitutional, it was embedded in a political culture that had some significant affinities with these values. Three features of this political culture call for our attention.

First, the ethos of the early caliphate is strongly antithetical to patrimonialism—to the kind of political culture in which the king regards his kingdom as his property and lives off the fat of the land. One respect in which this is manifest is the initial absence of hereditary succession, the standard dynastic practice whereby kings pass on their kingdoms to members of their own families. This practice did, of course, appear in the Islamic world and indeed prevailed for most of its history, but it did not take root for several decades after the death of the Prophet. Another way in which antipatrimonial attitudes are articulated is by emphasizing scrupulousness with regard to the use of public resources. An anecdote describing how the first caliph, Abū Bakr (ruled 632–634), came by his allowance is a nice example of this. The day after he became caliph, Abū Bakr, being a merchant, set out to market with a pile of clothes which he planned to sell in order to feed his family; it

[55] Crone, *Medieval Islamic political thought*, 273–74.
[56] Hunwick, *Sharīʿa in Songhay*, 27.9 = 81–82, and see 25.15 = 79.

was suggested to him that he could better attend to his public duties if, instead of going to market, he applied to the treasurer for an allowance. He did so, and the treasurer duly awarded him the allowance appropriate for one of the Prophet's Meccan Companions—not that of the best of them, nor that of the least of them—together with clothes for winter and summer. "If you wear something out," the treasurer added, "you bring it back and you get another instead."[57] Here as elsewhere the accuracy of the details of these accounts is not our concern; it is the pride with which the early sources remember them in this way that matters.[58] What we see in such anecdotes is not republicanism, but there is an analogous insistence on political power as something to be used exclusively for the public good.

The second feature is the rejection of despotism. One manifestation of this is a conspicuously reciprocal conception of the act that gives rise to political allegiance (*bayʿa*).[59] An agreement is made between the future caliph and the future subject whereby each party is to have specified rights and duties; the transaction has to be uncoerced, and it is concluded with a simple handshake. The model, significantly, is transparently commercial—the deal between two parties to buy and sell something. Another relevant theme is consultation (*shūrā*)—the duty of the caliph to consult with others before making his decision.[60] But what if he nevertheless acts wrongfully? Here again Abū Bakr supplies the answer, this time in the form of his accession speech. He announces to his subjects that he is now in authority over them, though he is not the best of them, and that they should help him if he does right but correct him if he does wrong; to this he adds that they have no duty to obey him should he disobey God and his Prophet.[61] The point here is not just that the ruler ought not to act despotically; it is that his subjects are to judge for themselves whether he has done so and to react accordingly. In another such anecdote ʿUmar, the second caliph (ruled 634–644), asks that anyone who sees any crookedness in him should tell him; a distinguished Companion of the Prophet responds that in that event "we will straighten you out with our swords," a sentiment to which ʿUmar responds with strong approval.[62] This anecdote depicts a politi-

[57] Suyūṭī, *Taʾrīkh al-khulafāʾ*, 59.22, and see M. Cook, "Political freedom," 292.
[58] Cf. the comments in Kennedy, *Great Arab conquests*, 111, 114.
[59] See Landau-Tasseron, *Religious foundations*, 1, 24, 27.
[60] See *EI*², art. "Mashwara" (B. Lewis).
[61] Ibn Hishām, *Sīra*, 3–4: 661.6 = 687; M. Cook, "Political freedom," 292.
[62] Tatāʾī, *Tanwīr al-maqāla*, 1: 370.4; Manūfī, *Kifāyat al-ṭālib*, 1: 99.24.

cal culture in which it is not just conceded that subjects are entitled, and perhaps obligated, to act in such ways; they are portrayed as ready to do so at the drop of a hat. It fits with this that we are assured that there were no prisons in the time of the Prophet or his immediate successors, the first to establish them being Muʿāwiya (ruled 661–680).[63] None of this is democracy, but it articulates attitudes that make for some kind of limited rule and gives to subjects a significant participatory role.

The third feature is a strong commitment to the rule of law, typically identified with the Book of God and the practice (Sunna) of his Prophet—in other words, the Sharīʿa. It is their knowledge of this law that enables the believers at large to judge the rectitude of the caliph and take action where necessary. Again, the ethos of the early caliphate is one in which subjects will not hesitate to do this. What we see here is not constitutionalism, but as described it delivers one of the chief goods that a modern society expects from a constitution.

If there are values associated with the early caliphate that resonate with republicanism, democracy, and constitutionalism, what of liberty, equality, and fraternity?

Liberty in the sense of political freedom is not a value enshrined in the Islamic religious tradition, though the other half of the metaphor—the equation of subjection to despotic or tyrannical rule with political slavery—is occasionally found in Muslim sources.[64] Thus two of the Arab envoys to Rustam speak of delivering people "from being servants of men to being servants of God"—or, as we could just as well render it, "from being slaves of men to being slaves of God."[65] Likewise the sectarian rebel Abū Ḥamza, denouncing the Umayyads in the later 740s, puts into their mouths the claim: "The land is our land, the property is our property, and the people are our slaves."[66] But this metaphor, however eloquent, is by no means widespread, and in particular it is not taken up in formal works of Islamic political thought.

Egalitarianism bulks much larger in the Islamic tradition. We have already discussed it in the social context,[67] and what was said there applies equally to the political domain. A further example is worth adding for its specifically political relevance. One of the clauses of the

[63] Ibn Ḥabīb, *Kitāb al-Taʾrīkh,* 119 no. 343 (but cf. 111.3 no. 317).
[64] M. Cook, "Political freedom," 284–85.
[65] Ibid., 289–90; see above, 170.
[66] Ibid., 293.
[67] See 169–70.

early document known as the "Constitution of Medina" states that the lowliest member of the community may grant (to an outsider) a protection that is binding on all members (*yujīru ʿalayhim adnāhum*).[68] This formulation does not deny the existence of social stratification, but it accords to all, high and low, the same politically potent right.

Finally, fraternity is unambiguously a central Islamic value, as we saw in our discussion of identity.[69] Like equality, this solidarity goes well with the quasi-republican character of the early polity,[70] though uneasily with the individualism of the liberal mainstream of Western thought.

There are, then, some significant affinities between the values of the early Islamic polity and those of modern times. But the relevant features of the early polity as they appear in our sources are not to be taken as signs of a precocious modernity. There is a very different historical context that makes sense of them.

One part of this context is the polity established by Muḥammad, of which the early caliphate was a continuation. Like Moses, but unlike the Buddha or Jesus, he brought a state into existence. According to our sources, this led contemporaries to ask whether he was a prophet or a king.[71] Thus, there is a story that the Christian ʿAdī ibn Ḥātim, a north Arabian tribal chief, came to visit Muḥammad in Medina with this issue in mind.[72] The Muslims had captured a female relative of his, and Muḥammad had later released her and sent her home. Since she was a woman of good judgment, ʿAdī asked her advice on how best to deal with Muḥammad. She replied that irrespective of whether he was a prophet or a king, it was in ʿAdī's interest to join him forthwith.[73] ʿAdī therefore went to Medina, where Muḥammad invited him to his home for a private conversation. In the course of this visit, ʿAdī noticed three things about Muḥammad that convinced him that he must in fact be a prophet rather than a king; two of them concern us

[68] Ibn Hishām, *Sīra*, 1–2: 502.20 = 232; Lecker, *Constitution of Medina*, 114–17. For an episode in which Muḥammad's daughter Zaynab grants such protection and announces it in the mosque in Medina, see Ibn Hishām, *Sīra*, 1–2: 657.19 = 316–17. It is, incidentally, worth noting that the fact that a woman exercised this right, and then announced in public that she had done so, does not seem to have been in any way problematic.

[69] See 20–21.

[70] As a historian of the United States remarks in explaining American attitudes in 1776: "Republicanism put a premium on the homogeneity and cohesiveness of its society" (Wood, "Monarchism and republicanism," 233).

[71] The Jewish rabbis of Medina devised a test to determine the answer (Ibn Hishām, *Sīra*, 1–2: 564.10 = 266–67).

[72] Ibid., 3–4: 578-81 = 637–9.

[73] Ibid., 3–4: 580.6 = 638.

here.[74] First, on the way to Muḥammad's home they were delayed by a frail old woman who accosted Muḥammad about some problem of hers. He spent a long time talking to her, and from this behavior ʿAdī drew the inference that he could not be a king. Second, when they finally reached Muḥammad's home, he threw ʿAdī a cushion—apparently the only one in sight—and told him to sit on it; after polite protestations ʿAdī sat on the cushion while Muḥammad sat on the ground. ʿAdī again remarked to himself that this was not the conduct of a king. In other words, what struck him was the absence of what Baranī called "the majesty and pomp of monarchs."[75] We see here the same ambience that characterizes the early caliphate. It can just as easily be illustrated by the openness of access to Muḥammad.[76] Under normal circumstances the place to find him was the mosque he constructed soon after arriving in Medina. There was no guard at the gate, and once inside the mosque a visitor who did not know Muḥammad by sight had no way to pick him out from among his followers. Once he had successfully identified him, he would sit down in front of him and transact his business with minimal formalities. In short, the early caliphs were continuing a political tradition established by Muḥammad himself.

The other part of the context—and the background to both Muḥammad's polity and its continuation by his successors—is pre-Islamic Arab society.[77] It is this background that suggests that we should not dismiss the accounts of the early polity found in our sources as purely hagiographic. Thanks to its aridity, Arabia was mostly a wilderness. This meant that its population was thin, dispersed, and poor in resources; it accordingly tended to be rather flat in its social structure, strongly tribal in its organization, and generally stateless.[78] In such a society the tendency is for every adult male to be a politician in his own right; hence the level of political participation was undoubtedly higher than we are accustomed to in modern democracies, let alone in pre-modern states based on taxing peasant agriculture. Some would call this primitive democracy. The affinity it suggests between the political values of Arab society and those of modern times may be fortuitous, but it is none the less real.

[74] Ibid., 3–4: 580.11 = 638–39.

[75] See 311.

[76] M. Cook, "Did the prophet Muḥammad keep court?," 23–26.

[77] Cf. M. Cook, "Political freedom," 290–92.

[78] Cf. the strong Koranic approval of those who respond to being wronged by helping themselves (*intaṣarū*, *yantaṣirūna*, Q26:227, Q42:39, Q42:41).

We can conclude, then, that in the domain of politics the Islamic tradition should have considerable resources to offer Muslims today if they wish to construct their political ideology out of their religious tradition. However profoundly the Buddha and Jesus may have engaged the spiritual energies of their followers, only Muḥammad was well placed to seize the political imagination of posterity. Does the modern record then bear out this expectation?

The first thing to observe is that the whole complex of phenomena referred to above as Muslim kingship has largely fallen away.[79] It did not do so immediately, and the Ottoman state in its last decades showed little inhibition about enriching its repertoire by adopting European conventions for publicizing the prestige of royalty—such as the display of portraits of the ruler in public places and the commissioning of an Ottoman coat of arms.[80] But for the most part the monarchic tradition of the Muslim world is now history. In those countries where an unusual degree of political continuity has made possible the survival of monarchic regimes from the past, as in Morocco, Jordan, Saudi Arabia, and the smaller states of the Persian Gulf, they continue to matter for regional politics. But there is a presumption that, like monarchies the world over, they are unlikely to be restored if once overthrown;[81] nobody expects to see the current problems of Tunisia, Libya, Egypt, Syria, Iraq, Yemen, Turkey, or Iran addressed through a restoration of the monarchies by which these countries were still ruled at various times in the twentieth century. In other words, the political values of Muslim monarchies, whether extant or extinct, do not grip the political imaginations of Muslims today. For example, the idea that the Ottoman Empire had enjoyed a form of constitutional government prior to the centralizing reforms of the nineteenth century, though favored by the Young Ottoman intellectual Nāmıq Kemāl,[82] is of no ideological significance in the contemporary Islamic world. Except perhaps in Morocco, the disappearance of Muslim kingship would be unlikely to generate any widespread nostalgia.

[79] Cf. 312.

[80] Deringil, *Well-protected domains*, 22, 26–27, 29. With regard to portraits ʿAbdülḥamīd II (ruled 1876–1909) was an exception, no doubt in deference to Islamic sensibilities.

[81] The exception is the Kuwaiti monarchy in 1990–1991.

[82] B. Lewis, *Emergence of modern Turkey*, 141 (noting a possible European source of the idea); Mardin, *Young Ottoman thought*, 310. The question whether in historical terms there is merit in this idea is taken up in Tezcan, *Second Ottoman Empire*, making the argument that the politics of the seventeenth-century Ottoman Empire can be analyzed in terms of "the political divide between the absolutist and constitutionalist positions" (11).

By contrast, the restoration of the caliphate is a political ideal for many Islamists—and for some a political project. In the immediate aftermath of the abolition of the caliphate in 1924, the Ottoman model still held sway: if an Ottoman sultan was no longer to hold the title, the presumption was that it would be assumed by some other ruler of the day.[83] But where the idea of a caliphal restoration stirs the hopes of subsequent Islamists, their inspiration is not the Ottoman caliphate but rather that of the immediate successors of the Prophet. Thus Mawdūdī wishes above all to see the reestablishment of an Islamic state that he sometimes refers to as the "Kingdom of God";[84] but in properly Islamic terminology, he describes it as a "Caliphate after the pattern of Prophethood,"[85] in other words, a state on the model of that ruled by Muḥammad and his successors. As we saw in considering the interaction of Muslim identity with geopolitics, such a restoration is likewise the central ambition of the pan-Islamist Ḥizb al-Taḥrīr, and it was endorsed by Ḥasan al-Bannā and Saʿīd Ḥawwā.[86] More recently, as we noted in our discussion of warfare, it forms an essential part of the grand strategy of jihadism laid out by Ẓawāhirī;[87] what he has in mind is again the restoration of the caliphate on the Prophetic model.[88] Bin Laden, too, wanted to see the unification of the Muslims and the establishment of the rightly guided caliphate;[89] he went so far as to recognize the Ṭālibān leader Mullā ʿUmar as Commander of the Faithful.[90] The creed of al-Qāʿida accordingly proclaims the goal of establishing "a rightly-guided caliphate on the prophetic model."[91] The idea of restoring the caliphate, of course, fits well with the wide horizons of global jihadis, but even jihadis whose concerns lie within the borders of their

[83] Hassan, *Loss of caliphate*, chap. 4.

[84] Maududi, *Short history*, 24; Maududi, *Political theory of Islam*, 24 = Mawdūdī, *Naẓariyya*, 26.11 (*al-mamlaka al-ilāhiyya*); Maudūdī, "Political concepts," 165; and see Maududi, *Fundamentals of Islam*, 259.

[85] Maududi, *Short history*, 37; Ahmad and Ansari, *Mawlānā Mawdūdī*, 20 (giving as the Arabic equivalent the canonical phrase *Khilāfah ʿalā Minhāj al-Nubūwah*).

[86] See 48–50. For Ḥasan al-Bannā's view that the Islamic political system was most fully realized in the decades when the community was ruled by the Prophet's successors in Medina, see his *Majmūʿat rasāʾil*, 363.10. For Saʿīd Ḥawwā's views, see further Weismann, "Democratic fundamentalism," 10, 11. For some South Asian examples, see Zaman, "South Asian Islam," 57–58, 74–77.

[87] See 233.

[88] Mansfield, *His own words*, 255, 257, 266, and cf. 252 (*dawlat al-khilāfa ʿalā minhāj al-nubuwwa* and similar phrases).

[89] Lawrence, *Messages*, 194–95, and cf. 121, 202.

[90] Ibid., 98, 101.

[91] Haykel, "Salafi thought and action," 55 no. 35.

own countries may subscribe to it. Thus Muḥammad ʿAbd al-Salām Faraj (d. 1982), the assassin of President Sādāt, emphasized the duty of restoring the caliphate.[92] At the same time, polls in several Muslim countries show majorities supporting the idea of a caliphal restoration or at least of uniting all Muslim countries into a single Islamic state.[93]

The sources of the appeal of such a restoration are not far to seek. The caliphate is a uniquely Islamic conception; it provides an emotionally powerful antidote to the sense of geopolitical deprivation arising from the current distribution of global power; it furthers a sense of Muslim unity across the globe; and it invokes a component of the religious tradition that is associated with a glorious past. And if the idea of creating a giant state out of nothing seems overly ambitious, the fact is that the Prophet and his successors did just that in the seventh century.

The aspiration does, of course, have its limits. Not every Islamist supports the project—one Moroccan Islamist "would be happy if the idea of an Islamic state were to fade."[94] And not everyone who supports it does so as a matter of urgency; Ḥasan al-Bannā's approach is unhurried,[95] as is that of Sayyid Imām, who counsels that restoring the caliphate is not yet within the power of this generation of Muslims.[96] Such prudence is no doubt linked to the obvious fact that in geopolitical terms the aspiration is not realistic and that consequently there can be no tight relationship between political activism in the here and now and this distant objective. There is also the problem that if the only proper form of the eventual Islamic state is a caliphate, that leaves it unclear what shape Islamists should give to such polities as they come to control in the meantime. The jihadis' response has been to establish "emirates"; this has the merit of sounding vaguely Islamic,[97] and the fact that an emirate is ruled by a single man fits the pattern of the caliphate better than a republic would. In this context it is perhaps significant that the state that most insistently identifies itself as the Islamic Republic should be located in Iran, where the prevailing Shīʿite

[92] See Jansen, *Neglected duty*, 162 §7, 165–66 §17. For other such jihadis in Egypt, see Gerges, *Far enemy*, 33, 45; Meijer, "Commanding right," 204, 205–6.

[93] Kull, *Feeling betrayed*, 118. Turkey is an exception.

[94] Aḥmad Raysūnī quoted in Zeghal, *Islamism in Morocco*, 191–92. Raysūnī is strongly in favor of democracy (190–91).

[95] Bannā, *Majmūʿat rasāʾil*, 285.2; see also Mitchell, *Society of Muslim Brothers*, 269.

[96] Rashwan, *Spectrum of Islamist movements*, 434; Fuchs, *Proper signposts*, 125, and cf. 59n40, 126.

[97] Cf. the passage from Bin Laden quoted in Al-Rasheed, *Contesting the Saudi state*, 115.

creed, unlike that of the Sunnīs, makes the caliphate irrelevant pending the return of the twelfth imam. More fundamentally, as already noted, the fusion of religion and politics that characterized Muḥammad's polity does not fit well with the needs of any complex society,[98] let alone a modern one; and surprisingly enough, the Koran itself can be found to provide a certain legitimation for the separation of religious and political authority.[99] Yet, whatever the problems associated with it, the idea of restoring the caliphate is very much alive.

There is, however, much more to Islamist politics than the restoration of the caliphate. This is where the affinities between the values associated with the early polity and those of modern times come into their own: they make it possible to imagine an Islamic state, and more broadly Islamic politics, in a manner that does not turn on the tenuous prospect of restoring the caliphate. How, then, have Islamists exploited these affinities to construct an image of Islamic politics that is relevant under modern conditions? As in previous discussions of Islamist appeals to the religious tradition, I shall give pride of place to the views of Mawdūdī and Quṭb.

Let us begin with what modern values demand of a polity. Here we find that the antipatrimonial and antidespotic themes associated with the early caliphate are highly attractive to Islamists. Thus Mawdūdī cites Abū Bakr's accession speech to underline the limits of the authority claimed by the early caliphs. He emphasizes that the early Muslims regarded the caliphate as elective and not hereditary; he declares monarchy to be the antithesis of Islam and refers disparagingly to the systems of Chosroes and Caesar. He dwells on the scrupulousness of early Muslims with regard to public funds, using the story of Abū Bakr's allowance as a prime example.[100] He lauds the unrestricted access people had to their caliph and rejoices in the complete freedom they enjoyed in expressing their opinions. He speaks in similar terms when discussing the Islamic state in a contemporary context. The ruler is to avoid pomp, pretension, grandiosity, and luxurious living; he has the same status under the law as his subjects; he can be taken to court by any

[98] See 312.

[99] For the Koranic passage, see 311; for its use in this sense by a major Indian scholar, see Zaman, *Ashraf ʿAlī Thanawi*, 52–56.

[100] See 319–20. He also cites the modest allowance of Abū Bakr's successor ʿUmar, see Mawdūdī, *al-Ḥukūma al-Islāmiyya*, 213.11 (for this work, see perhaps Ahmad and Ansari, *Mawlānā Mawdūdī*, 36 no. 59, first published in 1962).

of them; and he is owed obedience only if he complies with the laws of God and his Prophet.[101] In the same vein Quṭb quotes the accession speech of Abū Bakr, insists on the parity of legal status of ruler and subjects, and emphasizes the conditional nature of the obedience due to him. By contrast, he condemns the Umayyad and ʿAbbāsid rulers—he calls them kings, not caliphs—for treating public funds as private property. He grounds all this in a doctrine to which we will return in the context of freedom: that sovereignty belongs only to God, so that men are not entitled to exercise lordship over each other.[102] The early caliphate, in other words, was characterized by republican virtues—a point anticipated by Nāmıq Kemāl, who considered that at its inception the Islamic state was "a kind of Republic."[103]

Mawdūdī and Quṭb are far from alone in such views. Thus Ḥasan al-Bannā quotes the accession speech of Abū Bakr as showing the right of the Islamic community to oversee the conduct of its ruler.[104] Similarly Ḥawwā points out that obedience is not absolute,[105] and says that under the Islamic dispensation ordinary people learned that they had the right to monitor the conduct of their rulers and the duty not to give in to oppression and humiliation, just as their rulers learned that they had no rights over and above those of their subjects[106]—a dramatic change from the days when the pre-Islamic Persians deified their rulers and saw them as above the law.[107] Qaraḍāwī quotes Abū Bakr's accession speech and ʿUmar's exchange with a Companion about crookedness to show that the ruler is accountable to the community.[108] Bin Laden naturally evokes the antidespotic force of the early Islamic model in a more inflammatory style. Obedience is conditional,[109] leadership is a covenant between the leader and his subjects in which both parties have rights and duties,[110] and the current rulers of Saudi Arabia

[101] For all these views of Mawdūdī's, see M. Cook, "Political freedom," 301–2. See also Zaman, "South Asian Islam," 68, 71.

[102] For these views of Quṭb's, see M. Cook, "Political freedom," 304; and see below, 334–35.

[103] Mardin, *Young Ottoman thought*, 296–97.

[104] M. Cook, "Political freedom," 304n109.

[105] Ḥawwā, *Islām*, 2: 163.1.

[106] Ḥawwā, *Rasūl*, 2: 175.7.

[107] Ibid., 2: 170.2. However, the antipatrimonial potential of the early caliphate does not really engage Ḥawwā's political imagination, though he discusses the payment of a salary to the ruler (Ḥawwā, *Islām*, 2: 163.17).

[108] Euben and Zaman, *Readings in Islamist thought*, 236; for these anecdotes, see above, 320–21.

[109] Lawrence, *Messages*, 249, and cf. 260–61.

[110] Ibid., 272.

should restore to the people their trusteeship and let them choose a Muslim ruler[111]—failing which they will suffer the fate of the Shah of Iran.[112] Some more interesting statements are to be found in a long message from Bin Laden to the Muslims of the world, part of which was broadcast early in 2004.[113] Rulers are accountable for their actions, and the lack of a proper understanding of Islam's way of holding them accountable (*muḥāsabat al-ḥukkām*) is a major problem for the Muslim world.[114] In this connection Bin Laden draws a surprising comparison: "Spain is an infidel country, but its economy is stronger than ours because the ruler there is accountable (*li-anna hunāka ḥisāban wa-ʿiqāban lil-ḥākim*). In our countries, there is no accountability or punishment, but only obedience to the rulers."[115] Despite this appeal to a Spanish rather than a caliphal model, his reference to Islam's way of holding rulers accountable suggests such texts as Abū Bakr's accession speech. More recently, Muḥammad Mursī, in a victory speech broadcast on June 24, 2012, after his election as president of Egypt, echoed Abū Bakr in telling Egyptians that he had been given authority over them although he was not the best of them and that they should help him as long as he ruled justly and obeyed God, but that if he did not do so they had no duty to obey him.[116]

At the same time, Islamists are powerfully attracted to the endorsement of the rule of law that they find in their heritage. As Mawdūdī tells us, so great was respect for the rule of law in early Islamic times that even a Christian taken to court by the caliph could win his case.[117] This is the positive side of the otherwise inconvenient divine monopoly of legislation:[118] by locating the power to legislate outside the political system, it denies to rulers the ability to make law to suit their fancies. It is thus a significant point about the Sharīʿa that, whether we like to think of it as God's law or the scholars' law, it is in principle the antithesis of the legislative autocracy of a traditional patrimonial state or a

[111] Ibid., 273, and cf. 274. This is linked to the wider view that the current rulers of the Muslim world are apostate infidels against whom jihad must be waged (Ibrahim, *Al Qaeda reader*, 122).

[112] Lawrence, *Messages*, 273.

[113] The relevant passage is ibid., 227–30. For the date of broadcasting and the addressees, see ibid., 212, 214; for the Arabic text of the passage, see ʿAlī, *Tanẓīm al-Qāʿida*, 393–97.

[114] Lawrence, *Messages*, 229; for the original, see ʿAlī, *Tanẓīm al-Qāʿida*, 396.1.

[115] Lawrence, *Messages*, 227; for the original, see ʿAlī, *Tanẓīm al-Qāʿida*, 394.3.

[116] "Mursī fī khiṭāb al-fawz"; cf. above, 320.

[117] Mawdūdī, *al-Ḥukūma al-Islāmiyya*, 215.23.

[118] Cf. 279.

modern dictatorship.[119] As Nāmıq Kemāl once put it, since the Sharīʿa is under God's protection, "even the greatest of tyrants cannot alter it."[120] The practical question, of course, is how to make this divine protection operational in the implementation of the law by mere humans; characteristically neither Mawdūdī nor Quṭb considers what concrete institutional arrangements might be needed here. There is always the idea of giving the scholars a role in some kind of legislative process, though the experience of this device in the case of the Islamic Republic of Iran may not be encouraging.[121] But whatever the practical problems, the principle of the rule of law sits well with the heritage.

There is, however, a major point of discomfort in the interaction of early Islamic and modern values: the question of democracy. On the one hand democracy is a very powerful value across the world today and for reasons that go well beyond the prestige of Western political culture; it is thus a value that no political movement seeking a mass following can simply ignore.[122] But on the other hand democracy proclaims the sovereignty of the people, whereas Islam proclaims the sovereignty of God. Since God does not exercise His sovereignty directly in the running of the polity, it follows that those who know his will must exercise a disproportionate share of the power to control or constrain the political process.[123] The key question is then who has this knowledge, and Islamists typically see themselves as possessing it in larger

[119] Cf. Feldman's point that the attraction of the idea of restoring the Sharīʿa for Muslim populations is in large part that it promises the rule of law in place of unbridled executive power (*Fall and rise*, 9–10, 21, 79, 112–13). This is not, however, entirely supported by the polling data on Turks, Iranians, and Egyptians reported by Gallup in 2008: of those who thought the Sharīʿa should be a source of legislation, majorities—overwhelming in the Egyptian case—believed it to protect human rights and promote a fair judicial system, but less than half—just under half in the Egyptian case—believed it to limit the power of rulers (Rheault and Mogahed, "Turks, Iranians," 2).

[120] Mardin, *Young Ottoman thought*, 315.

[121] Feldman, *Fall and rise*, 127, 137. For a such an idea in a Sunnī context, that of the Syrian Muslim Brothers, see Weismann, "Democratic fundamentalism," 9, 13 (reflecting the close relations between this group and the scholars, see 3). The idea finds considerable support in polls of Muslim populations (Kull, *Feeling betrayed*, 160–61).

[122] As one political theorist puts it, "It has become ever clearer that, whatever its limitations, there is something irresistibly potent about democracy as a political rallying cry, and that any hope of halting it permanently in its tracks is utterly forlorn" (Dunn, *Democracy*, 17).

[123] Compare the view of an authoritarian New Confucian: "The benevolent government is founded on the dictatorship of Confucian scholars (*Shi*) because only Confucian scholars know the will of heaven" (Chen, "Modernity and Confucian political philosophy," 127). The wording is a paraphrase, but compare this direct quotation: "When Confucianism replaces Marxist-Leninism as state ideology and Confucian scholars re-

measure than the population at large. The outcome of this tension has been a wide range of Islamist views.

At one end of the spectrum we have the outright rejection of democracy. Quṭb was against it,[124] and the jihadis, as might be expected, followed suit. Thus Ẓawāhirī rails against democracy as "a new religion that deifies the masses," a matter of "the whims and fancies of man."[125] Similarly negative views are expressed by the Egyptian Jamāʿa Islāmiyya,[126] Sayyid Imām,[127] and Abū Muḥammad al-Maqdisī; the latter considers democracy and monotheism to be incompatible.[128] The creed of al-Qāʿida denounces democracy as "the tribulation of this age" and declares anyone who believes in it or supports it to be an apostate.[129] In northern Nigeria the movement known as Boko Haram is on record as saying that it "will never accept any system of government apart from the one stipulated by Islam" and that accordingly it will "keep on fighting against democracy, capitalism, socialism and whatever."[130]

At the other end of the spectrum are Islamists who more or less endorse democracy.[131] Mawdūdī, who rejoiced in the "democratic spirit" of the early polity,[132] is a significant example of this trend. Other things being equal, he regards democracy as a good thing.[133] He is therefore happy to call the political system of Islam "as perfect a form of democracy as there can be," although he does, of course, distinguish "Islamic democracy" from "Western democracy."[134] In fact, he is not consistently

---

place communist cadres, the process of creating a benevolent government is complete" (Dallmayr, "Introduction," 7–8).

[124] Quṭb, *ʿAdāla*, 5.14 = 1, 266.17 = 354; and see Shepard, *Sayyid Qutb*, xlii, 108; Sivan, *Radical Islam*, 73.

[125] Ibrahim, *Al Qaeda reader*, 130, 133 (quoting Q45:18 with its denunciation of the "caprices (*ahwāʾ*) of those who do not know").

[126] Meijer, "Commanding right," 206–7.

[127] See Rashwan, *Spectrum of Islamist movements*, 414–15; Fuchs, *Proper signposts*, 67; Lahoud, *Jihadis' path to self-destruction*, 133.

[128] Lahoud, *Jihadis' path to self-destruction*, 138, 171–72.

[129] Haykel, "Salafi thought and action," 53 no. 21, and cf. 54 no. 28; see also D. Cook, *Understanding jihad*, 191.

[130] From a statement of 2011 quoted in Williams and Guttschuss, *Spiraling violence*, 30.

[131] For a brief survey, see Krämer, "Islamist notions of democracy," especially 75, 79.

[132] Mawdūdī, *al-Ḥukūma al-Islāmiyya*, 217.22.

[133] See, for example, Maudūdī, "Islamic law in Pakistan," 108 (a translation of a speech of 1948, see 97, and Ahmad and Ansari, *Mawlānā Mawdūdī*, 36 no. 58); Maudūdī, "Political concepts," 197; Maudūdī, "First principles," 235; Maudūdī, "Fundamentals of Islamic constitution," 278.

[134] Mawdūdī, *Human rights in Islam*, 10 (in a talk of 1948, see 9n1).

in favor of any kind of democracy: in a talk of 1940 he argued that if the masses had not fully assimilated Islamic values, democracy would mean the election of the wrong people.[135] But he did provide a theoretical underpinning for democracy in an Islamic context through his innovative doctrine of the caliphate of all believers.[136] It comes close to being a theocratic doctrine of popular sovereignty. Each believer is a "Caliph of God" (*khalīfa min Allāh*) in his own right, and it is only because all Muslims delegate their caliphate to the ruler for administrative purposes that he has authority over them; the Islamic state is thus ruled by "the whole community of Muslims including the rank and file."[137] A milieu similarly open to democracy is that of the Muslim Brothers in Syria.[138] Their arguments in its favor seem to oscillate between asserting that it is already present in Islam (so that there is no need to adopt democracy from the West) and affirming that Islam is flexible and does not ordain a specific form of government (so that there is no reason not to adopt democracy from the West).[139] Their main reservation, as might be expected, concerns the threat posed by democracy to the divine monopoly of legislation.[140] Decisions do, of course, have to be taken about how best to apply God's law to contemporary conditions; but in the hands of a depraved people, a doctrine of popular sovereignty could lead to the abrogation of the Sharīʿa in place of its application. The generally positive attitude of the Syrian branch of the Muslim Brothers to democracy is shared by the movement at large.[141]

Other views fall somewhere in between. Yūsuf al-Qaraḍāwī at one point takes a categorically negative stand: "Islam is not democracy and democracy is not Islam, and I do not approve of Islam being seen in terms of any other principle or system." But he then goes on to concede that "the tools and guarantees developed by democracy are as close as can be to the realisation of the political principles and fundamentals brought by Islam to curb the wilfulness of rulers."[142] We could also

[135] Mawdūdī, *Minhāj al-inqilāb al-Islāmī*, 39.7.

[136] Cf. 184.

[137] See M. Cook, "Political freedom," 302–3.

[138] Weismann, "Democratic fundamentalism," 4, 6, 12.

[139] Ibid., 8–12. But for statements that appear to reject democracy, see 8, 10.

[140] Ibid., 9–10. Compare Qaraḍāwī's view (Euben and Zaman, *Readings in Islamist thought*, 241).

[141] M. Lynch, "Islam divided," 170–71.

[142] Qaraḍāwī, *Awlawiyyāt al-ḥaraka al-Islāmiyya*, 155.1 = Qaradawi, *Priorities of the Islamic movement*, 209. Rather like the Syrian Muslim Brothers, he also says that what

include Ḥawwā in this group[143] and a number of contemporary Turkish Islamist intellectuals.[144] Quṭb might have belonged to it had he been more willing to talk about what an Islamic state could look like in our time—instead he insisted that such questions will only arise once we are again living in a Muslim society.[145] A case could also be made for placing some jihadis here, for despite their strong denunciations of democracy we sometimes find them leaving the back door slightly ajar for it. Thus, in a letter to Abū Muṣᶜab al-Zarqāwī written in 2005, Ẓawāhirī criticizes him for failing to bring the people of Iraq into his movement.[146] You have to work at involving the people from the start, he tells him,[147] and once the state is established, you will have to work with their elected representatives in a consultative council.[148] Here he cites the warning example of the fall of the Ṭālibān in 2001. Because they had restricted participation in governance to the students and the people of Qandahār, denying any representation to the Afghan people at large, they had no solid political base, and the mass of the population was alienated; the result was that in the face of the American attack the emirate collapsed in a matter of days—a mistake he would naturally prefer not to see repeated in Iraq.[149] In such a context,

is called democracy "has always existed in a complete sense for us in Islam" (Lahoud, *Jihadis' path to self-destruction*, 153–54), while at the same time maintaining that it is appropriate to borrow from others the standard democratic procedures (Euben and Zaman, *Readings in Islamist thought*, 237). This latter passage forms part of an extended discussion of democracy that in general strongly endorses it (230–45), but note the qualifications of the editors in their introduction to the text (228–29).

143 Weismann, "Democratic fundamentalism," 10–11; for a statement of his that is distinctly favorable to democracy, see Lahoud, *Jihadis' path to self-destruction*, 154.

144 Karasipahi, *Muslims in modern Turkey*, 72–76, and cf. 108 (for biographical details on the intellectuals in question see 53–55), and cf. 187–88 on an earlier figure.

145 Carré, *Mysticism and politics*, 180–81, and cf. 317–18. Soon after telling us that the basis of the practice of Islamic governance is that rulers should be just, subjects should obey, and consultation should take place between them (Quṭb, *ᶜAdāla*, 94.9 = 112), he remarks that Islam lays down only the general principle of consultation, leaving scope for the use of numerous different methods (97.4 = 116–17; similarly Quṭb, *Maᶜraka*, 92.6, and Quṭb, *Naḥw mujtamaᶜ Islāmī*, 141.3; and see Carré, *Mysticism and politics*, 180). This could be read as an opening to democratic practices of Western origin, but it does not seem to be intended as such (179–81).

146 For this letter, see 361.

147 Mansfield, *His own words*, 261–62, and see 263.

148 Ibid., 260. The key phrase in the Arabic original (for which see below, 361n1) is *yantakhibuhum ahl al-bilād li-tamthīlihim* (6.20). Contrast his condemnation of such institutions as contradicting Islam in his propagandistic attack on democracy (Ibrahim, *Al Qaeda reader*, 136).

149 Mansfield, *His own words*, 262. Contrast Ẓawāhirī's claim in an interview of the same year that the failure of the Americans to capture Mullā ᶜUmar was due to the fact

it seems, a consultative council of elected representatives would not amount to a new religion. Bin Laden in the public statement in which he discusses accountability expresses himself in a more Islamic fashion, but the drift is to an extent analogous. By way of response to the current ills, he proceeds to offer a practical remedy: the appropriate people—scholars, leaders who are obeyed by their followings, dignitaries, notables, merchants—should get together in a safe place away from the shadow of these oppressive regimes and form a council qualified to appoint a ruler (*majlisan li-ahl al-ḥall waʾl-ʿaqd*).[150] For it is the community (*umma*) that has the right to appoint an imam, just as it has the right to make him correct his course if he deviates and to remove him for apostasy or treason.[151] Sayyid Imām, too, combines rejection of democracy with a proposal for quasi-democratic institutions,[152] and al-Jamāʿa al-Islāmiyya is now willing to accept the parliamentary system, though without enthusiasm.[153]

Let us turn now to liberty, equality, and fraternity. With regard to political freedom, there is, as we have seen, only a very limited basis for finding this value in the heritage,[154] but Islamists have used what there is as best they can. For Mawdūdī, God is "the true Sovereign," and "*the root-cause of all evil and mischief* in the world is *the domination of man over man*." The mission of the prophets was accordingly to put an end to man's supremacy over man in order that "man should be neither the slave (*ʿabd*) nor the master (*maʿbūd*) of his fellowbeings"; instead all should be the servants or slaves (*ʿibād*) of God—language reminiscent of that employed by the Arab envoys to Rustam. After quoting several Koranic verses that affirm monotheism but make no mention of freedom, Mawdūdī goes on to supply the missing word: "This was the proclamation that released the human soul from its fetters and set man's intellectual and material powers free from the bonds of slavery (*ghulāmī*) that held them in subjection. . . . It gave them a real charter of liberty and freedom (*āzādī*)."[155] In the same way Quṭb appropriates the term

that "the Muslim masses" had opened their hearts and homes to the jihadists and given them refuge (Ibrahim, *Al Qaeda reader*, 182, and cf. 228), and Bin Laden's statement in 2003, again in a propagandistic context, that the Ṭālibān were simply effecting a tactical withdrawal in the best traditions of Afghan guerrilla warfare (Lawrence, *Messages*, 203).

150 Lawrence, *Messages*, 229; for the original, see ʿAlī, *Tanẓīm al-Qāʿida*, 396.16.

151 Lawrence, *Messages*, 229–30; for the original, see ʿAlī, *Tanẓīm al-Qāʿida*, 396.19.

152 Fuchs, *Proper signposts*, 130–31.

153 Meijer, "Commanding right," 214.

154 See 321.

155 M. Cook, "Political freedom," 303.

"freedom" and often speaks of "liberation" (*taḥrīr*) in the context of the elimination of the dominion (*sulṭān*) of men over men.[156] It is perhaps relevant that he considered Magna Carta and the French Revolution to have been deeply influenced by Islam.[157] By contrast the jihadis, to whom such details of European history do not mean much, differ from Mawdūdī and Quṭb in saying little or nothing about freedom[158]—a fact that helps to account for their political irrelevance during the Arab Spring of 2011, in the course of which freedom ranked high among the demands of the demonstrators.

With regard to equality, the Islamists are on firmer ground, and as we saw in an earlier chapter they have made full use of this fact.[159] Without question, this is one of the most powerful intersections of Islamic and Western values.

With regard to fraternity, the Islamists have in principle no problem other than the tension between their collective values and Western individualism. There may, of course, be numerous divisions among Muslims in practice, and by definition non-Muslims are excluded from the fraternity, but these points do not concern us here.

All in all, we can conclude that the Islamic heritage offers several features that are potentially attractive under modern political conditions, and the record shows that Islamists have indeed seen this potential and used it. This does not, of course, prevent other Muslims from taking other courses. On the one hand, pietists may reject political engagement altogether, as many Salafis do,[160] or insist that the purification of doctrines and practices must take priority.[161] And on the other hand, those of a more secular turn of mind may adopt the political styles that prevail outside the Islamic world: there can be Muslim democrats, as arguably in Turkey today; there can be Muslim fascists, as in Egypt in

[156] Ibid., 305. For the phrase "jihad for the sake of liberation" (*al-jihād al-taḥrīrī*), see Quṭb, *Maʿālim*, 68.23 = 65.

[157] Quṭb, *Hādhā ʾl-dīn*, 67.13 = 69.

[158] In a statement of October 2004 addressed to the people of America, Bin Laden describes the members of al-Qāʿida as "free men" (Lawrence, *Messages*, 238, and cf. 240), but characteristically this is a rhetorical response to an earlier reference by President Bush to "a war against people who hate freedom" (see 238n3). The passage was drawn to my attention by Bernard Haykel.

[159] See 184–86.

[160] Lacroix, "Between revolution and apoliticism," 74–75, 76–77, 78; Hroub, "Salafi formations," 232; Bonnefoy, "Salafism in Yemen," 324, 326, but cf. 337; Adraoui, "Salafism in France," 371.

[161] Salomon, "Salafi critique of Islamism," 150–51; and cf. N. Hasan, "Ambivalent doctrines," 172–73.

the 1930s; and there can be Muslim leftists, a phenomenon that was widespread in the twentieth century, particularly during the Cold War. But Muslim fascists and leftists have been abandoned by the march of history, and the pull of Islamism means that both Muslim democrats and apolitical pietists are currently on a slippery slope—just how slippery remains to be seen.

3. Hinduism

In terms of the values enshrined in the Hindu heritage, there is nothing problematic about the idea of a space for Hindu politics. What occupies that space is Hindu kingship. There were indeed republics in ancient (though not medieval) India, and these are referred to in Hindu sources; but they are given little attention and lie outside the normative tradition of Hindu thought.[162] Kingship, by contrast, is elaborately and positively described in ancient and medieval Hindu texts and extensively attested in the records of Indian history. There is no sense that it lies outside the core values of Hinduism, or is in deep conflict with them, or represents a secondary accretion without foundation in the oldest strata of the tradition. In short, its seamless integration into the Hindu worldview provides no basis for questioning the cultural authenticity of the institution or substituting any other for it.

The duties of kings (*rājadharma*) are accordingly seen as the root or quintessence of all duties.[163] They are regularly covered in the legal literature.[164] Here a king gets very practical consideration: "a king on his noble throne" benefits from "instant purification" since he is seated there to protect his subjects.[165] He also gets respect: a Vedic scholar should not intentionally tread on his shadow,[166] he should refrain from speaking harshly about him, even Brahmins should honor him, one should never belittle him, a man should disown his own father if he assassinates him, and Vedic recitation is suspended for a day and a night on his death.[167] More than this, elaborate rituals detailed

[162] See J. P. Sharma, *Republics in ancient India*, 239. The Buddhist tradition is more sympathetic to republics.

[163] Kane, *History of Dharmaśāstra*, 3: 3.

[164] Witness the citations of the *dharmasūtras* and the *Laws of Manu* that follow.

[165] Manu, *Laws*, 109 (5.94), and cf. 110 (5.97); also Olivelle, *Dharmasūtras*, 103 (14.44–45), 302 (19.47–48).

[166] Manu, *Laws*, 86 (4.130).

[167] Olivelle, *Dharmasūtras*, 41 (31.5), 96 (11.8), 98 (11.32), 113 (20.1), 163 (21.4).

in the religious tradition accompany the inception of the king's rule and continue to fortify him thereafter.[168] At the same time kingship is commonly—though not invariably—seen as an institution of divine origin.[169] Indeed the king himself has claims to divinity: Manu tells us that even a boy king is not to be treated disrespectfully with the thought that he is just a human being, "for this is a great deity standing there in the form of a man."[170] As all this suggests, the relationship between the king and the Brahmins is a close, not to say cosy one. The king and the learned Brahmin are the two in the world who uphold the proper way of life, and the well-being of men and animals depends on them.[171] A key figure in this relationship is the king's personal priest: "When a Brahmin has been appointed as the kings's personal priest, the kingdom prospers."[172]

There are, of course, some qualifications to this rosy picture of religious support for Hindu kingship. The tradition does contain negative comments on kings—not just bad ones, but kings in general: the king eats his people, devouring everything he can lay hands on; he is on a par with a butcher who keeps a hundred thousand slaughterhouses; he is a calamity comparable to flood and fire.[173] But the mainstream view is that kings are the solution, not the problem—the problem being anarchy, or "fish-logic" (*mātsyanyāya*), in which big fish eat up little fish in the absence of any authority to restrain them.[174] Yet the very fact that kingship is instituted in response to this predicament does have a negative implication: our current need for kingship arises from the degeneracy of the age in which we find ourselves, whereas an earlier and better age happily did without it.[175] It was also possible to read the fact that we live in evil times in a manner more directly subversive of

[168] For the royal consecration (*rājasūya*), sprinkling of water (*abhiṣeka*), rejuvenation (*vājapeya*), and horse sacrifice (*aśvamedha*), see Basham, *Wonder that was India*, 81–82; Kane, *History of Dharmaśāstra*, 2: 1206–12, 1214–23, 1228–39, 3: 72–83 (the sprinkling of water is often referred to, conveniently but loosely, as the coronation). For the significant Vedic component of such rituals, see Witzel, "Coronation rituals of Nepal," 3–4, 8–11, 20.

[169] Kane, *History of Dharmaśāstra*, 3: 33–35; Basham, *Wonder that was India*, 82–83, 86; Manu, *Laws*, 128 (7.3).

[170] Manu, *Laws*, 128 (7.8).

[171] Olivelle, *Dharmasūtras*, 90 (8.1–3).

[172] Ibid., 299 (19.4). For the role of the *purohita*, see Kane, *History of Dharmaśāstra*, 3: 117–20.

[173] See Heesterman, "Conundrum of the king's authority," 109; for the comparison with the butcher, see Manu, *Laws*, 81 (4.86).

[174] Kane, *History of Dharmaśāstra*, 3: 20–21, 30.

[175] Ibid., 3: 4.

contemporary kingship, thereby decoupling it from the support of Hindu rituals and values. There had always been at least a strong presumption that the king should be a Kṣatriya, though this was not usually taken so far as to deny the legitimacy of kings belonging to other classes, even Śūdra kings.[176] At the same time, there were prophecies in the Purāṇas denying that Kṣatriyas would exist in the present Kali age, despite the testimony of older and more authoritative texts to the contrary. This gave an opening to some medieval and later scholars to denounce the Kṣatriyas of their day as in reality mere Śūdras.[177] But this view, though of some political importance in the time of Śivājī (ruled 1674–1680),[178] was that of a minority. All in all, the relationship of the religious tradition to Hindu kingship was a robustly supportive one and continued to be so into modern times to the extent that the institution survived the Muslim and British invasions.

Hindu kingship does nevertheless suffer from some serious limitations as a resource for modern politics.

A minor point is that, despite the thoroughly autochthonous character of the resources of Hindu kingship,[179] the tradition does not consider kingship as such to be an intrinsically Hindu institution. That is to say, it applies its standard term for "king" (*rājā*) to Hindu and non-Hindu rulers alike.[180] What is distinctive about Hindu kingship is simply that the kings are Hindus who support, and are supported by, Hindu institutions and values.

A major point is that the tradition has no commitment to the idea that all Hindus should be brought under the rule of a single Hindu monarch. It takes it for granted that under normal circumstances there will be a plurality of Hindu kings competing among themselves and that war will be an inevitable and unobjectionable feature of relations among them. As Manu says: "Kings who try to kill one another in battle and fight to their utmost ability, never averting their faces, go to heaven."[181] He later sets out the classical Indian analysis of interstate

[176] See ibid., 3: 37–40 for views on this issue.

[177] Ibid., 2: 380–82, 3: 40, 873–74.

[178] S. Bayly, *Caste, society and politics*, 59.

[179] The borrowings from Islamic kingship that appear in the later practice of Hindu kingship, like the title "sultan" (see 56), have no place in the normative religious texts.

[180] For an instance, see Thapar, "Image of the barbarian," 264n60; cf. also 245, 247, 249, 254, 256, and Kane, *History of Dharmaśāstra*, 3: 86, 97; 5: 563. Aśoka uses the term *rājā* with respect to Greek kings ruling outside India (Thapar, *Aśoka*, 251, 256; for the original, see U. Schneider, *Grossen Felsen-Edikte Aśokas*, 25 A, 76 Q, and see 104–5, 118–19).

[181] Manu, *Laws*, 137 (7.89).

relations: the king should regard a neighboring king as his enemy, the immediate neighbor of his enemy as his ally, and so forth.[182] Hindu norms seek only to restrain the excesses of this violent competition, not to shape it for some higher Hindu purpose, let alone eliminate it. Thus for someone who wants to perpetuate the substantive values of traditional Hindu society, the preservation of Hindu kingship in modern times could have its appeal; but for someone seeking rather to articulate a Hindu political identity for nationalist purposes, the tolerance of the tradition for military and political conflict among Hindus is unlikely to prove attractive. All this refers to normal conditions. But the system is, of course, inherently unstable, owing to the fact that a king naturally wishes to expand his domain through conquest. This indeed is his duty: a just king "should try to take possession of countries that he has not yet possessed."[183] If successful, he becomes some kind of emperor, ruling a territory that may range from a circle of kingdoms to the whole earth;[184] an intermediate possibility is that he comes to rule the whole of Bhāratavarṣa.[185] Of course, no Hindu king has ever done this. But what is significant is the way the tradition presents this outcome: it sees in it the practical success of one among a number of competing kings, not the achievement of a pan-Hindu polity conceived as a religious ideal. We may contrast this with the communal, not individual, aspiration to establish a Sikh state: "The Khālsā will rule" (*rāj karegā Khālsā*).[186]

The other major point that needs to be made is that it would be hard to find any significant resonance between Hindu kingship and the modern political values identified at the beginning of this chapter.

In the first place, there is nothing about Hindu kingship that offers an effective precedent for republicanism. Kings do, of course, exist for the public good. As we have seen, they are the antidote to anarchy;[187]

[182] Ibid., 144 (7.158); and see Basham, *Wonder that was India*, 127, and Kane, *History of Dharmaśāstra*, 3: 217–22. This is part of the wider Indian tradition of analysis of *realpolitik* (for the tension between *dharmaśāstra*—the science of being virtuous—and *arthaśāstra*—the science of getting what you want—see Kane, *History of Dharmaśāstra*, 3: 8–13).

[183] Manu, *Laws*, 225 (9.251); cf. 138 (7.99, 101), 139 (7.109), 249 (10.119), where justice is not mentioned.

[184] Kane, *History of Dharmaśāstra*, 3: 64–8. Various terms are used in the sources for such rulers, including *sārvabhauma* and *cakravartin*.

[185] Ibid., 3: 67, and cf. 66–67, 67–68. For Bhāratavarṣa, see above, 68.

[186] See McLeod, *Who is a Sikh?*, 50; McLeod, *Textual sources*, 78 §11, and cf. 12. It was through a process of state formation that the Sikhs became more than just another politically irrelevant Hindu sect (cf. above, 107–8, 237).

[187] See 337.

and their first duty is to protect their subjects.[188] It is even said that no one in the king's realm should suffer from hunger.[189] But in general the tradition does not conceive of kingship in the leanly functional idiom that would encourage one to think in terms of a monarchical republic. With regard to democracy, the most promising feature of the tradition is the association of early rulers with assemblies.[190] But the record leaves the nature and powers of these assemblies unclear,[191] and they are not taken up in the normative tradition of political thought. Thus, Manu says that it is for the king to appoint seven or eight advisers and that after getting the opinion of each of them, he should make his own decision.[192] Even the minority account in which kingship is a human, not a divine, remedy for anarchy fails to suggest any continuing governmental role for the people who chose the first king.[193] So Hindu kingship is, unsurprisingly, neither republican nor democratic.

Could it nevertheless be seen as a form of constitutional monarchy?[194] Obviously, as in any monarchy, there were "checks and limitations" on royal power.[195] Some will have been in the domain of practical politics, others in the domain of values. What emerges most clearly from the religious tradition is the salience of the role assigned to the Brahmins in this connection. In fact, one conspicuous aspect of this role, as it is spelled out in the normative literature, is the enormous partiality displayed by the Brahmins in devising the rules to suit themselves. Examples are legion: the king rules over everyone except the Brahmins;[196] he has precedence on the road except when he meets a Brahmin;[197] a treasure trove is the king's except when found by an upright Brahmin;[198]

[188] Manu, *Laws*, 142 (7.144); cf. Olivelle, *Dharmasūtras*, 94 (10.7), 159 (18.1), 253 (2.17), and Kane, *History of Dharmaśāstra*, 3: 56–57. In this vein kings may even be described as servants of the people (3: 27, and cf. 28).

[189] Olivelle, *Dharmasūtras*, 69 (25.11).

[190] Basham, *Wonder that was India*, 33. The terms used for these assemblies are *sabhā* and *samiti*.

[191] Kane, *History of Dharmaśāstra*, 3: 92–93 (a sober account stressing how little we know about these assemblies). Kane has no use for the "frantic efforts" of some modern Indian scholars to prove that ancient India had elective assemblies.

[192] Manu, *Laws*, 134 (7.54, 57).

[193] Kane, *History of Dharmaśāstra*, 3: 21; and cf. Basham, *Wonder that was India*, 83.

[194] Kane notes that some modern Indian writers "vehemently assert" that government in ancient India "was always some form of limited monarchy" (*History of Dharmaśāstra*, 3: 15).

[195] Ibid., 3: 96.

[196] Olivelle, *Dharmasūtras*, 96 (11.1).

[197] Ibid., 54 (11.5–6); cf. 89 (6.24–25), 284 (13.59).

[198] Ibid., 95 (10.43–44); cf. 256–57 (3.13–14).

Vedic scholars are exempt from taxes[199]—indeed even a king whose very survival is at stake should not have the temerity to tax one.[200] As might be expected, great store is set by the response of kings to the advice proffered by Brahmins: obedience to them is one of the main ways in which a king secures happiness.[201] But the Brahmin role could also be seen, less cynically, as the expression of a commitment to the rule of law, even if the law is very much Brahmins' law. Thus it is for the Brahmin to proclaim the duties of the other three classes and for the king to govern them accordingly.[202] This implies that, as we have seen above, the king's authority to legislate is very limited:[203] the predominant view is that he is there to execute the law, not to make it.[204] We have, then, an explicit notion of a monarchy limited by the rule of law, though the limitations do not relate power and values within an institutional framework that could be called a constitution—not, at least, without unduly diluting the concept.[205] This is as strong a resonance with modern Western political values as we can hope to find in the Hindu case.

Turning to liberty, equality, and fraternity, we have encountered nothing in our discussion of the Hindu polity that answers to them. Political freedom is not a traditional Hindu value. At the same time the intimate connection between Hindu kingship and the traditional structure of Hindu society precludes any relationship of equality and fraternity extending to the king's subjects as a whole. He is, after all, to watch over the social classes in accordance with their respective rules, and if some of their members should stray, he is to guide them back to their respective duties.[206]

In sum, considered as a set of norms to be applied in the real world, Hindu kingship does not have much plausibility as a solution to modern problems. To this we may add the fact that the Hindu princes lacked the will or the way to make themselves a focus of nationalist

[199] Ibid., 70 (26.9–10); cf. 90 (8.12–13).

[200] Manu, *Laws*, 142 (7.133).

[201] Ibid., 137 (7.88); cf. 131 (7.37), 134–35 (7.58).

[202] Olivelle, *Dharmasūtras*, 251 (1.40–41).

[203] See 284.

[204] See the materials from Medhātithi's commentary on Manu and elsewhere cited in Kane, *History of Dharmaśāstra*, 3: 98–101. This was not, however, the only view (see Basham, *Wonder that was India*, 87).

[205] As noted by Kane (*History of Dharmaśāstra*, 3: 98).

[206] Olivelle, *Dharmasūtras*, 96 (11.9–10); cf. 299–300 (19.7–8), and Kane, *History of Dharmaśāstra*, 3: 56–57.

loyalty against the British. Sultan Muḥammad V of Morocco (ruled 1927–1961) was in a position to represent his country in the struggle against the French: he was not just a local ruler, and he became a living martyr for the cause of Moroccan independence thanks to his timely deposition by the French in 1953.[207] But in India this role was played by an ascetic politician, not by a king. All that the Hindu princes thus amounted to at independence was a threat to national unity. We would not, then, expect to find within the spectrum of modern Indian politics any significant movement calling for the restoration of Hindu kingship, and this expectation is fully borne out by the historical record.

Most obviously, Hindu kingship has played little part in the values and concerns of the Hindu nationalists. There are aspects of the Indian constitution with which they take issue, but the fact that India is a republic is not one of them. They set considerable store by some of the Hindu kings of the past, notably the legendary Rām and the historical Śivājī. They particularly revere Śivājī for his military resistance to Muslim rule and his revival of Hindu tradition.[208] But they do not infer from this that the rulers of India today should be monarchs consecrated in the manner of such heroes of the Hindu past; while an early Hindu nationalist festival celebrated the coronation of Śivājī, the European figure to whom Sāvarkar compared him was Garibaldi (d. 1882), not Victor Emmanuel (ruled 1849–1878).[209] Thus, the Hindu nationalists did little or nothing to resist the abolition of the Hindu principalities following independence. It is true that some members of former Hindu royal families threw their support to the Hindu nationalists,[210] and one in particular, the Rājmātā of Gwalior, became an energetic participant in the movement.[211] But this was not a move aimed at securing the restoration of their principalities; at most their hope was that by joining forces with the Hindu nationalists they could impede the erosion of

[207] *EI*², art. "Muḥammad b. Yūsuf (Muḥammad V)" (R. Santucci).

[208] What goes for the Hindu nationalists would also hold true of Shiv Sena's invocation of Śivājī.

[209] Jaffrelot, *Hindu nationalist movement*, 26, 39.

[210] See, for example, ibid., 215–17, 220, 246, 248. Jaffrelot notes that some princes became deeply devoted to Hindu nationalist ideology (324, 405), but that many were opportunistic in their support (249–50, 293). Princes also supported Congress (215–16, 249–50, 293, 321), the conservative but secular Swatantra Party (218, 220, 223, 246; Brass, *Politics of India*, 83–84), and, as will be seen, the Rām Rājya Pariṣad (see 343).

[211] For her remarkable political career, see Jaffrelot, *Hindu nationalist movement*, 111–12, 216, 218, 247, 293, 316, 319, 351, 372, 420, 456–57, 499. It was she who discovered Umā Bhārtī (388).

their residual privileges. The one context in which the Hindu nationalists have shown some partiality for Hindu kingship is in their attitude to the politics of a neighboring country, Nepal.[212] They were undoubtedly saddened by the fall of the Nepalese monarchy in 2008, but the sense of loss may have had as much to do with the fact that Nepal ceased at that point to be a Hindu state as it did with the demise of the last Hindu monarchy.[213] With no commitment to the traditional Hindu polity, the Hindu nationalists could assimilate whatever form of modern politics seemed best suited to the environment in which they found themselves. Initially they were arguably Hindu fascists, later they were more like Hindu leftists, and mostly they have been Hindu democrats; at heart, of course, they have always been Hindu nationalists.

If there was any part of the political spectrum where we might expect to find an aspiration to restore Hindu kingship, it would be the Rām Rājya Pariṣad—precisely the milieu in which concern to preserve traditional Hindu society was strongest. This party, too, attracted support from princes,[214] and the fact that it named itself after "the kingdom of Rām" would have made it a suitable vehicle for monarchist sentiments. From its election manifesto of 1951 we learn that the party planned to replace the existing Indian constitution, which it described as "only a patchwork of the constitutions of the Western countries," with one in keeping with Indian "ideals and political traditions";[215] it certainly saw these ideals and traditions as monarchic, since a section of the manifesto setting out the qualities of the ideal ruler makes it clear that we are talking about a single man.[216] But there is no explicit statement as to whether the new constitution was to be republican or monarchic; and the issues in which the party, in fact, invested its political energies were the integrity of Hindu law and the protection of cows.[217]

[212] One Hindu nationalist leader writes in his memoirs that it had been his party's consistent stand that "the framework of constitutional monarchy should be preserved, since it is a symbol of Nepal's identity and sovereignty" (Advani, *My country*, 739).

[213] According to a newspaper article, the BJP had decried Nepal's giving up "the Hindu kingdom tag," but a member of the party and former minister stated that the party did not shed copious tears when the monarchy came to an end (Vyas and Joshua, "Congress, BJP").

[214] Jaffrelot, *Hindu nationalist movement*, 111, 216; Baxter, *Jana Sangh*, 78.

[215] Rām Rājya Pariṣad, *Election manifesto*, 16.

[216] Ibid., 7–8. The final sentence of the section states that in these days of "universal Democracy" the same qualities "are essential for the president of a republic," but it is not made clear how far we should take this as approving republican government; elsewhere the document disparages "Western notions of democracy" (16).

[217] For its opposition to legal reform, see 286.

4. Latin American Catholicism

If Hindu kingship bulks large in the history and thought of pre-modern India, we could surely say the same of Christian kingship in Europe. And indeed, for a long time and over large areas, it was more or less taken for granted that the polity would be both Christian and monarchic and that these two features would be suitably intertwined. The result, for many who lived in Christian kingdoms, may well have appeared as seamless as Hindu kingship. But at a deeper level there were fissures, and in the right historical context they could break through to the surface.

At the time when the New Testament was being composed, all significant monarchies were pagan. At that point the notion of a Christian kingdom had meaning only in connection with the apocalyptic future, when it would be announced in heaven that "the kingdom of this world is become the kingdom of our Lord, and of his Christ; and he shall reign for ever and ever" (Rev. 11:15). There was, of course, a monotheist kingship enshrined in the Biblical record of Israelite history—and what is more, one established by divine agency. But even this was in conception originally a pagan institution, for God was responding to the demand of the Israelites for "a king to judge us like all the nations" (1 Samuel 8:5); and while God moved to accommodate this demand, he also registered his strong disapproval of it (1 Samuel 8:7–9).[218] Moreover, in both cases the Bible uses the same vocabulary to refer to kingship, irrespective of whether it is pagan or monotheist.[219]

From the fourth century onwards the political environment changed drastically for Christians, as the Roman emperor Constantine converted to Christianity, followed sooner or later by numerous non-Roman kings. Predictably, Christians quickly warmed to this, and ecclesiastics took the opportunity to stake out a role in the polity comparable to those of the Muslim scholars and the Brahmins.[220] Eusebius of Caesaria (d. ca. 340), writing in praise of Constantine, stressed the symmetry of

[218] More generally, the Hebrew Bible does not identify any one form of government as, in Walzer's words, "the authentic biblical regime" (*In God's shadow*, 205).

[219] The Greek noun used in the phrase "the kingdom of this world" in Rev. 11:15 is *basileia*, just as the verb used for "reign" is *basileuō*; likewise Christ is described in this apocalyptic context as "King of kings" (*basileus basileōn*, Rev. 17:14, 19:16). The term for "king" used in the account of the origins of the Israelite monarchy is *melekh*.

[220] There were, of course, differences: for example, Christian ecclesiastics were better organized than their Muslim and Hindu counterparts but had less basis for denying the ruler the right to make law.

monarchy and monotheism: "A monarchy is superior to all other forms of government . . . there is but one God, not two, or three, or more . . . and one king (*basileus*), one royal word and law."[221] The link was also made to the Israelite monarchy: in Byzantium emperors were hailed as new Davids and new Solomons,[222] while in Carolingian Europe the Israelite practice of anointing kings was extensively revived by the clergy—boosting their own authority in the process.[223] But in a manner somewhat reminiscent of the Israelite adoption of kingship, all this represented a Christianization of originally pagan institutions, royal or imperial. It goes with this that the idea of a single ruler over the whole of Christendom has little purchase on the Christian political imagination. Altogether, the emergence of the Christian kingdoms of this world was very much a historically contingent phenomenon: there was nothing in the fundamentals of Christianity that required it.

This fact about the past had a significant implication for the distant future. If there was Christianity before there were Christian kingdoms, there could be Christianity after they had gone. In other words, it would not require much violence to the tradition for its followers to disengage it from kingship. In commanding obedience to the imperial authorities of the day, St. Paul had said nothing about monarchy; instead he referred in a vague and general fashion to "the higher powers," stating that "the powers that be are ordained of God" and that to resist "the power" was to resist "the ordinance of God" (Romans 13:1–2).[224] This said much about obedience to government but nothing about the form government might take. We could certainly expect to find among conservative Christians in the aftermath of the French revolutionary upheaval a deep reluctance to part with Christian kingship and a disposition to restore it where the tide of republicanism ebbed sufficiently to provide an opportunity. But such attachment to monarchy was likely to be largely a product of general conservatism, combined with antipathy toward the often aggressively secular orientation of revolutionary republicanism. Despite Eusebius, there was nothing intrinsically Christian about monarchy as such, just as there

[221] Dvornik, *Christian and Byzantine political philosophy*, 616 (translation slightly adapted).

[222] Ibid., 645.

[223] W. Ullmann, *Carolingian Renaissance*, 71–101.

[224] The word rendered "power" here is *exousia*. When the next verse speaks of "rulers," the Greek term is *archontes*, a word often used more generally for governing officials and individuals in distinguished positions (see Balz and Schneider, *Exegetical dictionary*, 1: 167–68, s.v. "archōn").

was nothing intrinsically anti-Christian about republican government. Christians who now found themselves ruled by nonmonarchic governments would have to get used to them, but in doing so they would not need to ignore values deeply embedded in their tradition, as Hindus did.

To give more substance to these remarks, let us glance at some relevant aspects of the history of republican and monarchic polities in Europe. Our starting point is the fact that republican government was a major feature of the history of pre-Christian Rome. This meant that it was entrenched in a prestigious, though pagan, component of the European literary heritage. Just as important, medieval Europe saw a revival of republican government. This, too, left its mark on the European literary tradition, with defenders of the city republics of northern Italy going on record with the affirmation that a republic is the best form of government. Thus, the Florentine Brunetto Latini (d. 1294) distinguished three kinds of government, those of kings, aristocracies, and peoples, and pronounced the third to be "far better than the others."[225] Though in this there were strong echoes of ancient republicanism,[226] the result was not usually anti-Christian.[227] Likewise, those who wrote to champion the republics of their day faced various obstacles, but the idea that republican government was incompatible with Christianity was not one of them.[228] In the same way the popes of the later twelfth century and the first half of the thirteenth had no problem allying with the republics against the German emperors.[229] And only when the pope in turn became a greater threat to the independence of the republics than the emperor did the defenders of the republics respond by attacking the pretensions of the Church to political power;[230] in this they were doing pretty much what supporters of royal authority did, and they did not wax anti-Christian any more than the royalists did. That threshold

[225] Skinner, *Modern political thought*, 1: 41–42. Ptolemy of Lucca (d. 1327) is of the same opinion (54), and Bartolus of Saxoferrato (d. 1357) comes close to it (53); for later examples, see 158–59.

[226] See, for example, Skinner, *Modern political thought*, 1: 54–55. Guicciardini (d. 1540) disparages those who "cite the Romans at every turn," but in this he was untypical (169).

[227] The main exception is Machiavelli (d. 1527). However, the incompatibility he saw between Christianity and republicanism was not a matter of Christian political doctrines but rather one of Christian moral values: by glorifying "humble and contemplative men," Christianity undermines the qualities needed for a republic to thrive (Skinner, *Modern political thought*, 1: 167).

[228] Cf. ibid., 1: 182.

[229] Ibid., 1: 12–13.

[230] Ibid., 1: 15–17, and cf. 18–22 on Marsiglio of Padua (d. 1342).

was not to be crossed in medieval Italy, or even in seventeenth-century England or eighteenth-century America, but rather in revolutionary France—and even there only in 1793–1794, four years into the revolution of 1789 and a year after the monarchy had given way to a republic.[231] Nor was it a foregone conclusion that republics downwind of the French revolution would be anti-Christian. In Italy we find that Napoleon, while engaged in establishing satellite republics during the French occupation of the 1790s, was at some pains to avoid any such impression, claiming that "the French Republic protects religion and its ministers."[232] Moreover a good many local ecclesiastics responded to this overture. "Catholic democrats" appeared among the clergy. No less a personage than Cardinal Chiaramonti, the future Pope Pius VII (in office 1800–1823), explained in his Christmas sermon of 1797 that the Christian duty to obey the powers that be is not limited to one particular form of polity, and he urged his audience not to believe that "the Catholic religion is against democracy."[233] If Christian monarchies were a historically contingent phenomenon, so too were anti-Christian republics.

There was, of course, the countervailing doctrine of the divine right of kings. It had old roots, and though far from uncontested, it became prominent in early modern Europe.[234] Thus an English preacher in 1588 declared that a prince is "in earth a certain image of the divine power" and "by office representeth God"; more arrestingly, "he is a God himselfe."[235] Sir Thomas Craig (d. 1608), a Scottish jurist close to the future James I of England (ruled 1603–1625), declared monarchy to be "the Best of all Governments," instituted by God in accordance

[231] For the unsteady course of events from September 1793 to May 1794, see Aulard, *Christianity*, chap. 3.

[232] Chadwick, *Popes and European revolution*, 452, and cf. 454, 484, 491. Chadwick describes Napoleon's claim to protect religion as "from the first a necessary part of his effort to persuade Italians of French goodwill" (453).

[233] Ibid., 454–56, and see 465.

[234] Skinner, *Modern political thought*, 2: 301. For the extent of the contestation, note Skinner's observation that "all the most influential works of systematic political theory which were produced in Catholic Europe in the course of the sixteenth century were fundamentally of a constitutionalist character" (114). For example, such authors reject patrimonialism (121, and cf. 117), affirm that political authority not merely derives from the body of the people but continues to inhere in it (119–20), and maintain that the natural condition of men is freedom, equality, and independence (155–56).

[235] Quoted in McLaren, "Challenging the monarchical republic," 166–67. Such talk of the king as a god is not isolated: Charles Du Moulain (d. 1566) says that the proper way to envisage the king's majesty is to see him as "a kind of corporeal God within his kingdom" (Skinner, *Modern political thought*, 2: 265–66).

with the law of nature, and held that God "abhors and detests" the exercise of collective sovereignty, whether in the form of "Aristocracy or Democracy."[236] As an Anglican formulation of 1640 had it: "The most high and sacred order of kings is of divine right, being the ordinance of God himself, founded in the prime laws of nature, and clearly established by express texts both of the Old and New Testaments."[237] In post-revolutionary Europe this persuasion still had adherents who stood for an unreconstructed union of throne and altar. One leading theorist of this tendency was the Vicomte de Bonald (d. 1840), who believed in a combination of absolute monarchy and intolerant Catholicism (he saw the Edict of Nantes as a fundamental error).[238] But it is hard to find post-revolutionary monarchs of such ideological purity—too many of them were men of their times, and needed to be to survive. In France Louis XVIII (ruled 1814–1824) still saw his authority as derived from God, not the people, and in his Charter declared Catholicism the state religion; but his preferred alignment was with the moderate royalists, who were comfortable with limited monarchy, and he conceded freedom of worship—a concession to error that Pope Pius VII had hoped to see avoided.[239] Charles X (ruled 1824–1830) was of a different stamp: a devout Catholic who did his best to restore the power and standing of the clergy, his constituency lay among the royalist ultras. But even he, in the course of a resolutely traditional coronation at Rheims, departed from precedent by omitting to swear to extirpate heresy.[240] Perhaps only in Spain, where the French invasion had provoked strong popular support for the union of throne and altar, was there anything even approaching a full restoration under Ferdinand VII (ruled 1814–1833); this extended to the revival of the Inquisition, the traditional guarantee of the purity of the Catholic faith.[241] And perhaps only in Spain has a reactionary tradition of this kind survived into the twenty-first century, thanks to the Carlists, the supporters of the descendants of a pretender who lost out in the civil war of the 1830s—though even

[236] McLaren, "Challenging the monarchical republic," 171.

[237] Cardwell, *Synodalia*, 389, quoted in Figgis, *Divine right of kings*, 142. The quotation is the first sentence of a set of "explanations of the regal power" that was to be read out in churches four times a year.

[238] See Reardon, *Liberalism and tradition*, 45, 49–51.

[239] Price, *Perilous crown*, 53–54, 93–94. For the attitude of the pope, see O'Dwyer, *Papacy*, 164.

[240] Price, *Perilous crown*, 11–12, 116–19. For the ideology of the ultras, see 91–92.

[241] Chadwick, *Popes and European revolution*, 527–28, 532–33, 541–43; Esdaile, *Spain in the liberal age*, 42–43.

they have adapted significantly to contemporary conditions.[242] Meanwhile such monarchies as continue to exist in Europe have done so by becoming monarchic republics. All this left plenty of room for Catholic conservatism, but for the most part it was no longer tied to prerevolutionary notions of Christian kingship. In Spain in the early 1930s many conservative Catholics were monarchists,[243] but the political organization established to bring conservative Catholics together aimed at "a corporative and conservative Catholic Republic."[244] The traditionalist Catholic Marcel Lefebvre (d. 1991) was born of a French Catholic monarchist father, but while he did not repudiate his father's monarchism, neither did he endorse it.[245] He certainly believed that the state should be strongly committed to Catholicism[246] and that "all authority comes from God."[247] But he recognized without strain that states would vary in the manner in which this authority was institutionalized, for the Catholic Church "does not indicate any preference for this or that form of government."[248] Thus one possible form was democracy. This did not, of course, mean anything like French democracy—"irremediably liberal, masonic, and anti-Catholic" in its origins and constitution.[249] But a democracy that was "openly Christian and Catholic" was another

[242] The Carlists are to be distinguished from the Alfonsists, more moderate royalists whose aim was to restore the monarchy overthrown in 1931; it was mainly to humor the Alfonsists, who were prominent in the army, that Franco paid lip service to the idea of a monarchic restoration, and it was a member of the Alfonsine line who became king on his death in 1975. The Carlists, in Franco's view, had their hearts in the right place but were terribly old-fashioned (Payne, *Fascism in Spain*, 288, and cf. 263). Of the two Carlist groups active at the present day, the Comunión Tradicionalista retains its Catholic allegiance but is against absolutism (see the manifesto "¿Qué es el Carlismo?" on the group's website), while the Partido Carlista has gone so far as to take on board a range of values like socialism, self-determination, and environmentalism (see the manifesto "Quiénes somos" on the group's website); both groups are sympathetic to Basque particularism. The rejection of absolutism goes back to the nineteenth century (see MacClancy, *Decline of Carlism*, 9, 10). I am much indebted to José Ramón Urquijo Goitia for information on the later history of Carlism and to Maribel Fierro for putting me in touch with him.

[243] Payne, *Fascism in Spain*, 44.

[244] Ibid., 45, noting Portuguese and Austrian parallels.

[245] Hanu, *Vatican encounter*, 21–23.

[246] Lefebvre, *Bishop speaks*, 62, 63, 77, and cf. 227.

[247] Lefebvre, *They have uncrowned him*, 52, quoted in Al-Azm, "Islamic fundamentalism reconsidered, Part I," 110a. This applies even in a democracy.

[248] Lefebvre, *They have uncrowned him*, 53–54; and see Lefebvre, *Bishop speaks*, 56. Lefebrvre quotes Pope Leo XIII to the same effect (54, and cf. 52–53) ; for Leo's teaching that the Church is indifferent to the form of government and can thus accept a democratic polity, see Witte and Alexander, *Modern Roman Catholicism*, 63–66, 90–93.

[249] Lefebvre, *They have uncrowned him*, 51.

matter.[250] In short, while his devotion to the traditional teachings of the Church was boundless, he did not see monarchism as one of them.

So far we have spoken only of Europe, but what was true of Europe was just as true of Latin America, if not more so. In Brazil, where the arrival of the Portuguese royal family in 1808 as refugees from the French invasion gave monarchy a local continuity not found elsewhere, the empire that emerged from the break with Portugal in 1822 and lasted till 1889 soon settled down as a constitutional monarchy, rather than a union of throne and altar. Dom Pedro I (ruled 1822–1831), despite his autocratic habits, fancied himself as a liberal;[251] in his coronation oath he described himself as emperor of Brazil "by the grace of God and the unanimous vote of the people," and he promulgated a somewhat liberal constitution.[252] His son Dom Pedro II (ruled 1831–1889) was the very model of a constitutional monarch.[253] Meanwhile the Church in Brazil was full of liberals, not to mention republicans.[254] In the former Spanish possessions there was some monarchist sentiment in the immediate aftermath of the rupture with the mother country,[255] but only in Mexico did it have a significant impact. Here the break with Spain was accomplished by Agustín de Iturbide, who stood for independence without revolution and briefly reigned as Emperor of Mexico in 1822–1823.[256] His program, set out in the Plan of Iguala of 1821, proposed a monarchy tempered by a constitution but was soundly conservative on the religious front: the reli-

[250] Ibid., 55; compare Mawdūdī's distinction between Islamic and Western democracy, but note the absence of any counterpart of the caliphate in Lefebvre's thinking (above, 331–32). As an example of the right kind of democracy, Lefebvre adduced the rule of Gabriel García Moreno (d. 1875) in Ecuador (54). Not everyone would find this reassuring; thus one academic historian associates García Moreno with "theocratic authoritarianism," "extreme clericalism," and a tendency to execute his opponents (Deas, "Venezuela, Colombia and Ecuador," 515, 527–28, 535). Contrast the much more welcoming attitude of the Catholic intellectual Jacques Maritain (d. 1973) to democracy, which he saw as inspired by and dependent on the message of the Gospels (see his *Christianisme et démocratie*, 33, 43, 67, 70, 73). For his influence on the Christian democratic parties of Latin America, see Sigmund, *Liberation theology*, 21.

[251] Haring, *Empire in Brazil*, 14, 19, 43.

[252] Macaulay, *Dom Pedro*, 132, 162; for the constitution of 1824, see also Haring, *Empire in Brazil*, 28–29.

[253] His daughter and heir, Isabel, was a committed Catholic with proclerical and perhaps absolutist tendencies, but she did not come to the throne (Haring, *Empire in Brazil*, 145–46).

[254] Ibid., 113, 117.

[255] Ibid., 1–2 (mentioning Peru, Chile, and especially Argentina).

[256] For a convenient summary of the events, see M. C. Meyer et al., *Course of Mexican history*, 227–29, 231–37.

gion of the country was to be Catholicism, with no toleration of other faiths, and the clergy would retain their exemptions and privileges.[257] Appropriately he was hailed as "our Catholic Liberator, the Second Constantine," the "frightener of the impious."[258] The other monarchic episode in the modern history of Mexico came in the 1860s, when a French occupation brought the country a new emperor, the Archduke Maximilian of Austria (ruled 1864–1867).[259] There was clearly a constituency for this restoration of monarchy among Catholic conservatives, but Maximilian himself was too liberal to play the part successfully, failing to decree the immediate reversal of the anticlerical reforms of Benito Juárez.[260] Neither in Brazil nor in Mexico did monarchism survive as a political force in the twentieth century. Catholic conservatism was indeed a significant component of Mexican politics, but neither the Cristeros nor the Sinarquists were interested in monarchy.

There is a wider point here. It is not just that Christianity can be disengaged from kingship but that it lacks a conception of an intrinsically Christian state short of the second coming of Christ. The early Christian community was not a polity, and whatever abortive hopes there may have been that Jesus would "restore again the kingdom to Israel," he himself declared firmly that his kingdom was "not of this world."[261] This made a difference. For example, anyone familiar with early Islamic history who reads about the maraudings of Christian sectarians and zealots in late antiquity feels at home with the pervasive religious violence but is struck by the absence of any project of state formation.[262] Here, however, our concern is with the implications of the absence of an idea of an intrinsically Christian state in the context of Latin American politics in the twentieth century.

If twentieth-century Latin American Christians wished to engage in political activity that took inspiration from their religion—and most

[257] Anna, *Mexican empire of Iturbide*, 4–5. The Reglamento Político of 1822 more or less delivered on these undertakings (141–44).

[258] Ibid., 33–34.

[259] For an outline of the events, see M. C. Meyer et al., *Course of Mexican history*, 290–98.

[260] Ibid., 291, 292, 294.

[261] For the hopes, see Acts 1:6; for Jesus' own statement, see John 18:36 (in both verses the word rendered "kingdom" is again *basileia*).

[262] For vivid examples of the violence, see Gaddis, *No crime*, 127–28, 177, 187–88, 188–89, and cf. 258. For the case of Axido and Fasir, the "Commanders of the Saints" (*sanctorum duces*) in the Numidian hinterland in the 340s, see Shaw, *Sacred violence*, 168–69.

of them did not—they had three main options, three forms of modern politics they could seek to reflag.

One option was Christian democracy. Christian democratic parties first arose in Europe, where they were formed in reaction to the liberal attack on the Church in the later nineteenth century.[263] In principle their emergence made it possible for European Catholics to participate in electoral politics in the hope of rendering political systems more friendly to their Christian values—though in practice these parties tended to drift away from their original religious orientation,[264] thus contrasting with the zeal of the Christian Right in the United States in its attempts to use the political process to impose its religious values on its fellow citizens. The Christian democratic parties of twentieth-century Latin America followed a trajectory similar to that of their European models. Their rewards were somewhat limited by the absence from the Latin American scene of the democratic stability that could generally be expected in Western Europe: it was never axiomatic in Latin America that the only way to attain political power was to get oneself elected, for democracy, even if here today, might be gone tomorrow. Instead, the history of the region has abounded in military regimes (as in Chile in 1924–1931 and 1973–1990), prolonged civil wars (as in Colombia for the last half century and more), and armed insurrections (issuing in leftist regimes in Cuba and Nicaragua). The only large Latin American country that enjoyed (or suffered) prolonged stability in the twentieth century was Mexico under the Partido Revolucionario Institucional—an authoritarian regime that did not encourage political competition. Yet when democracy prevailed, the rewards of participation could be considerable. Thus in Chile the Christian Democrats won presidential or congressional elections in 1964, 1965, 1989, and 1993.[265] Likewise in El Salvador, despite conditions of civil war, the Christian Democrats could contest and even win parliamentary elections, as they did in 1985, the founder of the party having been elected president the previous year.[266] In fact, no fewer than seven Christian democratic parties in Latin America were electorally successful enough to win the presidency at least once.[267] These parties have nevertheless experienced a drift away from religious commitment

[263] Kalyvas, *Rise of Christian democracy*, 171–72.

[264] Ibid., 222, 232, 245, 256.

[265] Skidmore and Smith, *Modern Latin America*, 123–24, 135.

[266] Sigmund, *Liberation theology*, 116.

[267] Mainwaring and Scully, "Diversity of Christian democracy," 32–34.

similar to that of their European counterparts,[268] and of late they have not been politically prominent.[269]

Another option was to look to fascism for a suitable political project. As we have seen, there were several examples in Latin America, though this option lost its appeal with the catastrophic defeat of fascism in the Second World War.[270] Since then, no form of rightist religious politics has emerged in Latin America on any scale.[271]

The third option, which came into its own in the second half of the twentieth century, was to look to leftism, specifically Marxism, as the Liberationists did. This option is, of course, the one that most concerns us.

That Marxism should have appealed to the political imagination of Latin American Catholics with radical tendencies is no surprise. Whatever its nineteenth-century past, in the twentieth century it became an ideology offering a powerful anti-imperialist and socially radical articulation of the discontents of the Third World. The key event was, of course, the Russian revolution of 1917, and this already had some impact on Latin America in the period between the two World Wars. But it was an event closer to home that really caught the political imagination of Latin American youth: the Cuban revolution of 1959, once it had manifested its hallmark combination of Marxist radicalism and defiance of the United States.[272] Marxism was now the movement of choice in Latin America for "the palpitating and heroic idealism of strong and impatient youths."[273] An ideology with this kind of appeal to intellectuals and students was obviously likely to exercise a pull on young Latin Americans destined for careers in the Catholic church, not to mention foreign clergy.

It thus makes sense to see Liberation Theology as a Catholic emulation of Marxism. Such emulation was not entirely new: in Chile in 1940 or earlier, priests belonging to Acción Católica Chilena were engaged

[268] Mainwaring, "Transformation and decline," 364, 365–71.

[269] Ibid., 365, 373–74.

[270] See 148–54.

[271] Cf. 202.

[272] Cuba was the ideal place for such a revolutionary icon: a Caribbean island on the edge of the Latin American world. By contrast, the geopolitical tremors from a Marxist revolution in Brazil would have greatly complicated any iconic role it might have played.

[273] The phrase was used by Alceu Amoroso Lima, a leading Brazilian lay Catholic, in endorsing the appeal of Integralism in 1935 (Todaro Williams, "Integralism," 441). In later years he became a prominent spokesman for progessive Catholicism (see Mainwaring, *Catholic Church and politics*, 30–31, 267n21).

in unionizing in the countryside and justified this "defense of the poor" on the ground that if they did not do it, the Marxists would.[274] But it was the Liberationists who took this tendency farthest. "For us," as a young Uruguayan put it, "Jesus Christ is Ché Guevara."[275] There was the same talk of imperialism, neocolonialism, and dependence; on one side were those who control the world economy, on the other the world's oppressed and dominated peoples.[276] Such talk was eminently compatible with Latin American dislike of the United States. Meanwhile, on the domestic front there were the same concepts of class struggle and revolution; here the national oligarchies were the enemy.[277] In a more syncretistic vein, social revolution—alias the Kingdom—was held out as the eschatological hope.[278] "The Exodus is the long march towards the promised land."[279] There was also a qualified openness to violence in a good cause—the qualification being doubtless of Christian rather than Marxist origin.[280] The basic recipe for this Christianization of Marxism was simple enough: both belief systems link the glorious future to those currently at the bottom of the pile. All one had to do was to appropriate the Marxist dream of revolution and to substitute the Biblical cult of the poor for the Marxist identification of the agent of the coming redemption—be it the proletariat or the peasantry. Thus in commenting on Matthew's Gospel, a Mexican Jesuit priest observes that "the good news given to the poor is that God identifies with the future of those who suffer" and goes on to say that "God has identified himself with the poor, assuming as his own their cause and destiny."[281] As Cardinal Joseph Ratzinger (later Pope Benedict XVI) put it in 1984, Liberation Theology was characterized by "a disastrous confusion between the poor of Scripture and the proletariat of Marx."[282] Or as one devotee preferred to put it: "As a Marxist Christian, I believe in the socialist revolution. As a Christian Marxist, I believe in the Second Coming of

[274] Gill, *Rendering unto Caesar*, 128.

[275] Míguez Bonino, *Revolutionary theology*, 2. This author is a Protestant, and the speaker probably was too.

[276] Gutiérrez, "Notes," 203, 208; Gutiérrez, *Theology of liberation*, 17, 54, 64.

[277] Gutiérrez, "Notes," 203, 206.

[278] Ibid., 206, 208, 211; Gutiérrez, *Theology of liberation*, 54, 97.

[279] Gutiérrez, *Theology of liberation*, 89.

[280] See 246.

[281] Bravo Gallardo, "Matthew," 192.

[282] Congregation for the Doctrine of the Faith, "Instruction on certain aspects," 406 no. 10. The Congregation is the watchdog of Catholic orthodoxy and was headed from 1982 by Cardinal Ratzinger, no friend of Liberation Theology (Sigmund, *Liberation theology*, 155–56).

Jesus Christ."[283] Whether we should describe such ideas as disastrous confusion or auspicious fusion is a question we can leave to the theologians. Historically speaking, the need to emulate Marxist radicalism in the context of middle-class youth culture explains very well the character of Liberation Theology. Just how central this emulation was to the persuasion is indicated by the timing of the eventual downturn in the fortunes of Liberation Theology: it lost traction precisely in the 1990s,[284] in the aftermath of the demise of the Soviet Union and the global collapse of faith in Marxism.

There were, of course, limits to the emulation. Although Gutiérrez did not take issue with Marxist materialism and atheism and initially made no firm statement as to where the Liberationists parted company with the Marxists,[285] even he indicated that radical ideas in the Marxist tradition were not to be adopted without question.[286] Moreover, in his later writings he had second thoughts about his enthusiasm for Marxism, though he was at pains to minimize their secondary character. In an article of 1984 on theology and the social sciences, written in response to Cardinal Ratzinger's criticisms of Liberation Theology, he did much to disengage from too close an embrace of Marxism.[287] Here, for example, we do find him spelling out a parting of the ways.[288] Likewise he rewrote the section on class struggle for the revised edition of his treatise on Liberation Theology, published in 1988: in response to the complaints from Rome, the term "class struggle" disappeared from the title of the section, and although he continued to assert the fact of class struggle, he no longer urged the duty of participation in it, at least not in so many words.[289] These grudging concessions represented the price

[283] Míguez Bonino, *Revolutionary theology*, 130, quoting a friend. Compare the "unshakable faith in the power of the oppressed to transform society" espoused by a well-known Brazilian Liberationist (Boff, *Faith on the edge*, 127).

[284] For the case of Brazil, see Ottmann, *Lost for words?*, 2, 14 (this author is nevertheless concerned to recover the future for Liberation Theology). For Latin America and beyond, cf. also Nagle, *Claiming the Virgin*, 161.

[285] Regarding the embarrassments of international Communism, he has a stray reference to Poland as a problem (Gutiérrez, *Theology of liberation*, 157) and a more veiled one to Czechoslovakia (21).

[286] Ibid., 21.

[287] Gutiérrez, "Theology and the social sciences." For the background to the piece, see 156–57.

[288] Ibid., 216–17.

[289] For the revised edition, see Gutiérrez, *Theology of liberation*, 156–61 (and see the footnote to 156, and 175–76n5). For the original version, see Gutiérrez, *Theology of liberation*, 1973, 272–79 (for participation in the class stuggle, see 274, 276, and compare 159 of the revised edition). For the objections of Cardinal Ratzinger to the use of the

he had to pay to remain in communion with the Church—and hence a real constraint on his thought. This price in turn is likely to have inhibited any adoption by the Liberationists of Marxist ideas on the shape of the political future: while they echoed their scripture by speaking vaguely of the "Kingdom of God," they developed no operational concept of the dictatorship of the poor. They were not entirely silent on politics at the level of the state: the Brazilian Leonardo Boff judiciously informs us that we do not have to deny the value of political power as a legitimate way of securing more justice for the marginalized.[290] But the Liberationists had no vision of the polity.

It fits with this that in political terms they had relatively little success. Admittedly their social activity had a widespread impact in Latin America over a period of more than twenty years, an achievement that in itself puts them well ahead of the Cristeros; many educated people in the First World have heard of Liberation Theology, whereas few have heard tell of the Cristiada. Yet the Liberationists in the end played only a marginal role in the political history of late twentieth-century Latin America. In no major Latin American country did they become political actors of real consequence, though they did somewhat better in the smaller states of Central America and the Caribbean. Thus, in El Salvador they figured in the political equation during the civil war of 1980–1992. But as a Catholic political force they were not in the same league as the Christian Democrats, and as rebels they had no place in the leadership of the FMLN, a secular organization of which the largest component was Marxist[291]—though they counted for something in the background of many of the rank and file.[292] They did not even predominate within the Salvadorian church.[293] Archbishop Romero went a long way toward joining them and died a martyr for their cause; but several of his bishops felt so little sympathy for him that they did not see fit to attend his funeral.[294] In Nicaragua, where the revolution of 1979 ended the Somoza dictatorship that had ruled the country since

---

term "class struggle" by the Liberationists, see Congregation for the Doctrine of the Faith, "Instruction on certain aspects," 402 no. 8, 405 no. 7, 411 no. 11.

[290] Boff, *Faith on the edge*, 137.

[291] McClintock, *Revolutionary movements*, 56–59.

[292] Ibid., 267–71.

[293] Berryman says of the clergy of Central America that those for whom "liberation was a primary ideal" were "always a minority, albeit an important minority" (*Stubborn hope*, 14).

[294] Ibid., 73. For a passage in which Romero places his own prospective martyrdom in the context of a Liberationist faith, see Jiménez Limón, "Suffering, death, cross," 715.

1937, the Liberationists had previously been no more than an element in a broad revolutionary coalition. At one point we hear fleetingly of a separate Christian Revolutionary Movement,[295] but in practice the only way for Liberationists like the poet and priest Ernesto Cardenal to make a difference was to join the Sandinistas.[296] After the revolution they played a more conspicuous role in the Sandinista regime of 1979–1990, providing four cabinet ministers, of whom one served as foreign minister for a decade.[297] But these Liberationists were by no means the core of the regime. The only Latin American country ever ruled by a Liberationist is Haiti,[298] where in 1990 Father Jean-Bertrand Aristide was elected to the presidency with close to 70 percent of the vote on the strength of his fiery—and courageous—preaching.[299] His presidency was, of course, a signal failure, and that no doubt reflected the combined failings of the man, his organization, and his doctrine. The problems of Haiti were unlikely to be solved by the assurance that "God will descend and put down the mighty and send them away, and He will raise up the lowly and place them on high."[300] But one might also ask why, if nothing else has ever worked for Haiti, Liberation Theology should have done any better.

5. Conclusion

As we have seen in this chapter, each of our three traditions is associated with a well-developed pattern of kingship, and these patterns have much in common. Thus, in each case kingship acquires a repertoire of symbols and ceremonies to which the religious tradition contributes more or less generously. All three take for granted a plurality of rulers

[295] Sigmund, *Liberation theology*, 122.

[296] Ibid., 121.

[297] Ibid., 126; Berryman, *Stubborn hope*, 23. One wonders whether Father Miguel D'Escoto may not have owed his tenure of the foreign ministry more to his useful connections with American Catholics than to any domestic constituency: he was a prominent Maryknoll priest and had been in charge of the order's publishing house (E. A. Lynch, *Religion and politics*, 100).

[298] I owe this point, and my knowledge of the Haitian case, to Jacob Mikanowski.

[299] Fatton, *Haiti's predatory republic*, 77; for the Liberationist background, see 59, 68–69. That a Liberationist should have come to power through an election was ironic; Aristide himself believed firmly in revolutions, not elections (66, 77). Just as ironic was the fact that, alone among Liberationists, he had the backing of the government of the United States.

[300] Ibid., 79; cf. Luke 1:52–53.

within the religious community. In each case the kings are partnered with a formal or informal religious leadership that places some limit on their power: the scholars in the Muslim case, the religiously active Brahmins in the Hindu case, the ecclesiastics in the Christian case.[301] And in each case the religious tradition has at least some reservations about kingship. Of course, the three patterns also differ from each other in nontrivial ways. Thus, there is significant variation in the extent to which the religious tradition considers warfare between its kings to be problematic, the level of such concern being lowest in the Hindu case and highest in the Muslim case. Queasiness regarding kingship as such is perhaps least in the Hindu case and certainly greatest in the Muslim case. In terms of the resources on which it draws, Hindu kingship is the most indigenous of the three, whereas Muslim kingship makes considerable use of resources from outside the Islamic tradition, and Christian kingship represents the Christianization of a preexisting pagan institution. There are also major differences in the extent to which kingship is seen as being in competition with nonmonarchic forms of polity: republics are virtually unknown to the Islamic tradition, recollected but accorded no respect in the Hindu tradition, recognized and accredited in the Christian tradition.

All this is interesting enough, but what is so striking is how little any of it matters for the outcomes that concern us. Muslim, Hindu, and Christian kingship are all equally irrelevant to modern politics except insofar as they are represented by local survivals. We might, for example, have expected it to make a considerable difference that republicanism and related modern political values are historically indigenous to Europe and so by extension to Latin America, whereas they are alien to the Hindu tradition of India with its purely monarchic values. But in fact the modern politics of the two regions show a great deal of convergence: identity politics are about nationalism, forms of government are republican, and basic political styles have been fascistic, leftist, or liberal. To an extent, though only to an extent, the politics of the Muslim world have followed the same model. In place of the pattern of kingship that prevailed on the eve of modernity, we now have a predominance of republics and a political scene that includes or has included nationalists, fascists, leftists, and liberals. Altogether, the Mus-

[301] That this structure was widespread in pre-modern kingdoms should not lead us to think of it as inevitable: except perhaps in the heyday of Chinese Buddhism, imperial China was different.

lim world, like the world at large, has been strongly shaped by these modern values.

But in the Muslim world we also have another kind of politics, namely Islamism. It, too, has been strongly affected by modern political values, but it has been at pains to discover these values, or their counterparts, in its own heritage. As we have seen, the existence of this option has to do with the content of the tradition. At first sight the Islamic heritage resembles that of Hinduism in its commitment to a monarchic perspective in which republican values have no standing. But it also bears some resemblance to the tradition of Christian Europe inasmuch as it possesses an alternative model to kingship, namely the early caliphate and the values associated with it. One difference, of course, is that the caliphate comes from within the Islamic tradition, whereas republicanism (like kingship) comes from outside the Christian tradition; a republic can thus be a secular institution, whereas the caliphate cannot be. It is not a modern institution, nor does it have much geopolitical plausibility, but it gives powerful articulation to the idea of a specifically Muslim polity. Meanwhile the political culture associated with it, despite originating in a context that is again very distant from modernity, resonates powerfully with some key modern values.

One way to point up the distinctiveness of Islamist politics is to consider what the dissolution of the Soviet Union and the collapse of faith in leftism meant in each of our three cases. For the Liberationists the outcome of the Soviet collapse was disastrous, with the demise of Marxism reflected in a sharp decline in their fortunes.[302] This linkage is not surprising. The point of the doctrine, one might say, was to provide a way of being leftist within Catholicism, and once leftism had lost its allure there was little else about Liberationism that was likely to recruit a following. The most dynamic representatives of Catholicism were now not the Liberationists but the Charismatics. For the Hindu nationalists the leftist débacle posed no threat to core convictions and tended to make politics easier. Thus, it did something to weaken the leftist competition they faced on the domestic political scene, and it left them free to discard an economic orientation borrowed from the left in favor of one more appropriate to the right. Back in the late 1960s and early 1970s the Hindu nationalist mainstream had taken its cue from the socialist tendencies of Congress, with the leading champion of a

[302] As we have seen, there were also other and in a way deeper reasons for this failure (see 205–11), but its timing can hardly be a coincidence (see 355).

market economy being expelled from the party in 1973;[303] but in the 1990s it was the proponents of the free market who set the tone, and those loyal to a more leftist orientation were left to obstruct and oppose.[304] Finally, for the Sunnī Islamists the result was pure gain. Marxist regimes no longer ruled South Yemen, Albania, Bosnia, Afghanistan, or the Muslim lands of the former Soviet Union, and none of the idiosyncratic countries in which Marxists succeeded in holding onto power despite the general collapse were located in the Islamic world; at the same time Arab socialist regimes no longer enjoyed Soviet patronage. Above all, Islamism saw an ideological competitor eliminated without any cost to its own plausibility.[305] That a political radicalism of the late twentieth century should depend so little on the plausibility of Marxism is telling.

[303] Jaffrelot, *Hindu nationalist movement*, 230–31, 233–34, and cf. 177.

[304] Ibid., 491–93 (but cf. 536–39); Jaffrelot, *Hindu nationalism*, 342–44, and the samples that follow; R. Guha, *India after Gandhi*, 701.

[305] For Shīʿite Islamism, too, the result was probably a net gain: the international loss of standing of leftism helped to degrade what had been the most determined domestic rival of the revolutionary regime, though it must also have done something to undermine the plausibility of Khomeini's adoption of the trappings of Shīʿite liberation theology.

Conclusion to Part Two

In 2005 Ayman al-Ẓawāhirī wrote a letter to the Jordanian Abū Muṣʿab al-Zarqāwī (d. 2006), the leader of al-Qāʿida in Mesopotamia.[1] It seems to be authentic: there is no specific reason to think it a forgery,[2] and it fits well with Ẓawāhirī's worldview as we know it from other sources, notably the book he wrote for a potentially wide Muslim audience sometime before the time of the collapse of the Ṭālibān in 2001.[3] The letter is a valuable text inasmuch as it is a communication from one jihadi to another, not meant for public consumption. It reveals its author to be deeply worried. As we have seen, it was Ẓawāhirī's hope that the geographically peripheral successes of the jihadis could serve as stepping-stones to the restoration of the caliphate in the core of the Muslim world.[4] But there had always been a missing link: a successful jihadi insurrection

[1] Letter from Ẓawāhirī to Zarqāwī, translated in Mansfield, *His own words*, 250–79. I am much indebted to William McCants for supplying me with a copy of the Arabic original and have checked my references against it. The letter is now available on the website of the Combating Terrorism Center at West Point. Mansfield gives the date of the letter as October 11, 2005 (250), but this is in fact the date when it was released by the American authorities; the date that appears at the end of the letter itself is July 9, 2005. However, the end of the letter may not belong to it: while the letter opens by naming its addressee as Abū Muṣʿab, i.e., Zarqāwī (250), the end of the letter clearly refers to a plurality of addressees and speaks of Zarqāwī in the third person (277–78). For background to this letter, see V. Brown et al., *Cracks*, 19–21; for a brief biography of Zarqāwī, see ʿAlī, *Tanẓīm al-Qāʿida*, 310–12.

[2] Two features of the letter were adduced as reasons to judge it a forgery in the discussion following its release. One was the inclusion of the family (*āl*) of the Prophet in the initial benediction (*al-ṣalātu waʾl-salāmu ʿalā rasūli ʾllāhi wa-ālihi wa-ṣaḥbihi wa-man wālāhu*), which was taken to indicate a Shīʿite forgery. However, Ẓawāhirī uses such language elsewhere in his writings (see ʿAlī, *Ḥilf al-irhāb*, 3: 96.12, 110.21, 162.21, 190.44), and he has excellent precedent in the works of Ḥasan al-Bannā (*Majmūʿat rasāʾil*, 6.3, 34.3, 164.2, 203.2, 302.2, 414.4, 498.12) and elsewhere. The other feature was a reference to Ḥusayn ibn Alī (d. 680) with the title imam (Mansfield, *His own words*, 255). Here again, it is not hard to find parallels in Sunnī sources. Thus, an Egyptian Mālikī who died in 1815 speaks of *al-imām al-Ḥusayn* (Dasūqī, *Ḥāshiya*, 4: 298.29 of the main text), while a Damascene Ḥanafī who died in 1708 refers to him as *al-imām al-Ḥusayn al-sibṭ raḍiya ʾllāhu ʿanhu*, with a typically Sunnī blessing (Ibn Ḥamza al-Ḥusaynī al-Dimashqī, *al-Bayān waʾl-taʿrīf*, 2: 256.9). A more recent example is an anti-Shīʿite article on the website of the Saudi cleric Salmān al-ʿAwda in which Ḥusayn is referred to as *al-imām al-Ḥusayn raḍiya ʾllāhu ʿanhu* ("Sharṭ ṣidq al-Shīʿa fī ʾl-ḥuzn ʿalā ʾl-imām al-Ḥusayn raḍiya ʾllāhu ʿanhu"); other examples can easily be found by conducting an Internet search for this or similar phrases.

[3] For a translation of his *Knights under the Prophet's banner*, see Mansfield, *His own words*, 19–225; cf. above, 233.

[4] See 233n121.

in the core. In a country like Egypt, where the jihadis confronted an indigenous regime, there was just not the same polarizing clarity as in Afghanistan, where they confronted a foreign invader.[5] Unexpectedly, the American invasion of Iraq in 2003 had now provided a "rare and golden opportunity" for such resistance.[6] As a result Zarqāwī was now in the privileged position of fighting an infidel invader in the heart of the Muslim world[7]—precisely the situation in which the masses would rally to the jihadi cause. This was vitally important: when it came to the expulsion of the Americans and the establishment of the jihadi emirate, the strongest weapon in the hands of the jihadis would be the support of the Muslim masses.[8] Without it failure would be inevitable.[9] But in Ẓawāhirī's opinion Zarqāwī was courting failure and squandering the chance of a lifetime—though Ẓawāhirī was too fraternal to put it so harshly.[10]

Zarqāwī's mistake was alienating the masses, and Ẓawāhirī makes it clear that he was doing it in several different ways. He was failing to involve the people in his movement.[11] He was making an issue of minor doctrinal differences that the masses do not understand, such as those between Ashʿarites, Māturīdites, and Salafīs (here Ẓawāhirī remarks that Mollā ʿUmar, may God protect him, is a Ḥanafī and a Māturīdite, yet his heart is in the right place).[12] He was making a public display of slaughtering hostages like animals.[13] He was ignoring the resentment of the Iraqis toward the non-Iraqi leadership of the movement.[14] And, not least, he was killing Shīʿites in large numbers.[15]

[5] Cf. Ẓawāhirī's comment on the clarity of the Afghan situation in Mansfield, *His own words*, 37. Abū Muṣʿab al-Sūrī makes a similar point more generally (Lia, *Architect of global jihad*, 375).

[6] The phrase is Bin Laden's (Lawrence, *Messages*, 272).

[7] Mansfield, *His own words*, 252, 253.

[8] Ibid., 257.

[9] Ibid., 258.

[10] Contrast the less patient tone of a letter from a senior al-Qāʿida leader to Zarqāwī dating from December 2005 (V. Brown et al., *Cracks*, 20–21, and the summary at 68–69). By this time Zarqāwī's misdeeds included the Amman bombings of 2005, to which the letter refers. For the text of this letter, see above, 213n278. The critical attitude of the leaders of al-Qāʿida to the impolitic activities of other jihadis is by now a familiar theme.

[11] Mansfield, *His own words*, 261–62, and see 263.

[12] Ibid., 263–66, especially 263–64 (the overall theme of this section of the letter is that it is unwise to disparage the scholars to the general public). This problem was not confined to Iraq: some jihadis regarded the Ṭālibān as unbelievers (Lahoud, *Jihadis' path to self-destruction*, 225, and cf. 197).

[13] Mansfield, *His own words*, 271–72.

[14] Ibid., 274.

[15] For Zarqāwī's explanation of his anti-Shīʿite strategy, see Haykel, "Al-Qa'ida and Shiism," 193–94 (and see also Zarqāwī, *Hal atāka ḥadīth al-Rāfiḍa?!*; I owe my copy of

Ẓawāhirī has no quarrel with Zarqāwī's aversion to Shīʿites.[16] In his view they are indeed bad people: they cooperated with the Americans in both Afghanistan and Iraq, their beliefs are a danger to Islam, and any truly Islamic state must collide with them sooner or later.[17] But for several prudential reasons, couldn't it be later? The majority of Muslims don't know how bad the Shīʿites are and will not understand attacks on them.[18] In any case, doesn't the current sectarian conflict make things easier for the Americans?[19] Don't we also have more than a hundred prisoners in the hands of the Iranians, and isn't it important that we and the Iranians should avoid harming each other while the Americans have us both in their sights?[20] In addition to these counsels of prudence, Ẓawāhirī advances a moral objection: even if Zarqāwī has to kill the Shīʿite elite, why go after ordinary Shīʿites when they are forgiven for the error of their ways on account of their ignorance?[21] But the balance of Ẓawāhirī's argument is prudential, not moral.

As will be apparent from this summary, much of the substance of the letter could just as well have been penned by a sympathetic leftist critic of a floundering people's war in the twentieth-century Third World. There are, of course, Islamic references in the letter, though they are relatively infrequent; for example, some rebels of the early Islamic period appear,[22] and there are several mentions of the caliphate.[23] But with one exception there is a sustained absence of religious proof-texts. The exception is a familiar one: the Prophet's remark to ʿUmar about the need to avoid the perception that he was killing his own Companions.[24] We should, Ẓawāhirī says, be guided by the concern expressed here. Significantly, he does not pause to tell the story

this tract to William McCants). For more on jihadi disagreements with Zarqāwī regarding the Shīʿites, see Gerges, *Far enemy*, 256f, 261-3; Haykel, "Al-Qa'ida and Shiism," 194-6.

[16] For the background to Ẓawāhirī's attitude to Shīʿites, see Haykel, "Al-Qa'ida and Shiism," 186–90, and for his criticism of Zarqāwī, see 195–96.

[17] Mansfield, *His own words*, 267–68.

[18] Ibid., 268.

[19] Ibid., 269.

[20] Ibid., 269–70.

[21] Ibid., 269. For the question whether one can distinguish in this way between the elite and the masses among the Shīʿites, see Haykel, "Al-Qa'ida and Shiism," 195, and cf. 192, 200n16, 201n20; also Hafez, "*Takfir* and violence," 34.

[22] Mansfield, *His own words*, 255.

[23] Ibid., 255, 257, 266, and cf. 252.

[24] Ibid., 259–60. In the original the quotation is found at 6.11, a little above the heading *qaḍiyyat al-iʿdād li-mā baʿda khurūj al-Amrīkān*. The wording of the saying as given by Ẓawāhirī (*daʿhu lā yataḥaddathu ʾl-nāsu anna Muḥammadan yaqtulu aṣḥābahu*) is identical with that given in Muslim's version and two of Bukhārī's (for references see above, 161n14).

that led Muḥammad to make this remark; he can take it for granted that a fellow jihadi will know what he is talking about.

The saying is in fact well known in mainstream jihadi circles.[25] A case in point is Abū Muḥammad al-Maqdisī, the Palestinian Salafī and jihadi ideologue who for many years wrote from prison in Jordan.[26] In a massive work intended to dampen down excessive zeal in declaring people to be unbelievers, he invokes the example (*ʿibra*) of the conduct of Muḥammad: he did not declare hypocrites to be unbelievers unless he had public proof of their infidelity, lest it be said that he was killing his own Companions, which in turn would have alienated people from him.[27] In the same vein he reminisces that during his time in Pakistan it became fashionable there to declare the leading Saudi cleric Ibn Bāz (d. 1999) and his likes to be infidels; when asked about this Maqdisī invoked the saying, refusing to wade into the question and considering it enough to warn youth against the pronouncements of such scholars on political matters.[28] As a result the zealots declared Maqdisī himself to be an unbeliever; they extended this to those who were accustomed to pray behind him on the ground that they in turn had failed to declare him an unbeliever, and then to those who failed to declare this latter group to be unbelievers, and so forth.[29]

It is therefore no surprise to find Maqdisī using the saying in the same vein as Ẓawāhirī to criticize extremist jihadi groups he sees as out of control. A work of 2004 contains several relevant passages.[30] In one he quotes the saying and stresses its importance in the phases

[25] I am much indebted to William McCants for supplying me with a collection of some twenty-five texts from the jihadi website Minbar al-Tawḥīd waʾl-Jihād (http://www.tawhed.ws) that mention or discuss the saying; all references to texts on this website given in this and the following paragraphs derive from this collection. As might be expected, these materials indicate a degree of jihadi dependence on Ibn Taymiyya. For quotations or citations of relevant passages from his *Ṣārim*, see, for example, Maqdisī, *Ishrāqa*, 19 n14; Maqdisī, *Kashf shubuhāt al-mujādilīn*, 29 n8; Abū ʾl-Mundhir al-Sāʿidī, *Khuṭūṭ ʿarīḍa*, 94.6 (in the footnote); Dawsarī, *al-Radd ʿalā bayān "al-Jabha al-Dākhiliyya,"* 6.6, 27.10, 28.4, 29.1. Another relevant passage sometimes quoted is from Ibn Taymiyya's account of forbidding wrong; see Ghunaymī, *Marāḥil tashrīʿ al-jihād*, 36.20; Ghunaymī, *Ḥukm taghyīr al-munkar*, 33.20; Ghunaymī, *Muṣṭalaḥāt wa-mafāhīm*, 64.7; *Ḍawābiṭ istinbāṭ aḥkām al-daʿwa*, 4.18. The original of this latter passage may be found in Ibn Taymiyya, *al-Amr biʾl-maʿrūf*, 22.11, and Ibn Taymiyya, *Istiqāma*, 2: 219.5.

[26] McCants, *Militant ideology atlas*, 333; Hegghammer and Lacroix, "Rejectionist Islamism," 115–16; and see now Wagemakers, *Quietist jihadi*, chap. 1.

[27] Maqdisī, *al-Risāla al-thalāthīniyya*, 515.8.

[28] Maqdisī, *Ishrāqa*, 19.17.

[29] Ibid., 20.1. Cf. Abū Jandal al-Azdī, *Nuṣūṣ al-fuqahāʾ*, 30.9.

[30] Maqdisī, *Waqafāt*; and see Hafez, "*Takfir* and violence," 41.

before the movement has achieved domination; he goes on to say that jihadis must accordingly choose targets that will not bring them into disrepute. Anyone who examines some of the operations carried out by those who are deficient in their understanding—either of reality or of the law or of both—will see that they fail to attend to this.[31] As a result, alongside the edifying activities of al-Qāᶜida, the Ṭālibān, the Chechens, and the Palestinians, we have to endure nitwits who shoot up a congregation in a mosque in the Sudan, or blow up a Shīᶜite mosque in a Pakistani village, or bomb buses crammed full of ordinary people in the streets of Karachi and Lahore, or carry out bizarre operations that kill dozens of Iraqis in the streets of Baghdad.[32] In another passage he has more to say about the Shīᶜites. He has, of course, no love for them, and he expatiates on the viciousness of their treatment of the Sunnīs. But appearances matter: in public the Shīᶜites talk about the Sunnīs as their brothers, with the result that in the eyes of the naïve and gullible it is the Sunnīs who look like the troublemakers.[33] In the face of this, we must call upon our jihadis to follow the wisdom of the Prophet as expressed in the saying; for whether the jihadis like it or not, the fact is that the world sees the Shīᶜites as Muslims, just as the hypocrites were reckoned as Muslims in the time of the Prophet.[34] The jihadis should thus avoid calling for strife with the Shīᶜites, and if such conflict is necessary it should be presented as defensive, lest it appear to others as an incitement to civil war.[35] Assassinating Shīᶜite leaders is one thing, failing to distinguish between the leaders and the masses whom they lead astray is another.[36] A final passage is concerned with the conflict between the jihadis and the infidel rulers (*ṭawāghīt*) of the Muslim world. In this conflict the jihadis must not act in such a way as to alienate people and discredit themselves, appearing as the enemies of the weak and thereby giving the rulers the opportunity to pose as their champions against terrorism; whoever disregards these considerations has failed to understand the significance of the saying.[37]

Other prominent jihadis who invoke the saying are Abū Bakr Nājī and Abū Baṣīr al-Ṭarṭūsī. Nājī seems to refer to Iraq when he remarks

[31] Maqdisī, *Waqafāt*, 10.4.
[32] Ibid., 10.14, 11.16.
[33] Ibid., 86.9.
[34] Ibid., 87.4.
[35] Ibid., 87.10.
[36] Ibid., 87.18; and see Wagemakers, *Quietist jihadi*, 90.
[37] Maqdisī, *Waqafāt*, 151.11.

that the current scene is full of groups of nationalists, Baʿthists, and Islamists, the Islamist groups being small and not linked to any overall leadership; he complains that none of these are aware of the rule embodied in the saying.[38] Ṭarṭūsī has a work on jihad and its politics that carries a dedication to Mullā Muḥammad ʿUmar and the jihadis of Palestine, Iraq, Afghanistan, Chechnya, Somalia, and elsewhere.[39] In the main body of the work, he warns that in jihad it is not enough to consider whether or not an action is permitted; one must also think about its consequences, in other words, the costs and benefits likely to accrue from it.[40] As an example he describes how the Prophet spared the arch-hypocrite (*raʾs al-nifāq*) Ibn Ubayy, briefly telling the story and quoting the saying. In the same way, if the killing of a known hypocrite would lead to internal dissension and cause people to say that the Muslims are killing their own kind, then it is better not to proceed.[41] He repeats this message in an appendix devoted to jihad in Iraq, telling the story at greater length and again quoting the saying.[42] To the views of these well-known figures we may add those of an anonymous jihadi critic of the Amman bombings of November 2005—the work of Zarqāwī's group, al-Qāʿida in Mesopotamia. This critic has no quarrel with the view that Islam calls for the elimination of the current rulers of the Muslim world.[43] But he has serious reservations about such bombings. He holds that "martyrdom operations" (the quotation marks are his) should be very much the exception rather than the rule;[44] that the ordinary citizen will not be reassured by the fact that seventeen Palestinians who had no connection to the primary targets were killed in the bombings;[45] and that the "strategy of creative anarchy" is flawed—it can turn against the jihadis themselves.[46] We jihadis, he says, are not above reproach.[47] We accordingly need to practice self-criticism and

[38] Nājī, *al-Khawana*, 60.9. For more on this jihadi strategist, and the similarity of his thinking to that of Ẓawāhirī, see Brachman and McCants, "Stealing Al Qaeda's playbook," especially 310–12 and the authors' comments at 312–13.

[39] Abū Baṣīr, *Jihād*, 2.1. For this jihadi ideologue, see McCants, *Militant ideology atlas*, 295–96.

[40] Abū Baṣīr, *Jihād*, 14.1.

[41] Ibid., 14.9.

[42] Ibid., 59.3, 59.11.

[43] *Taʿqīb*, 1.14.

[44] Ibid., 2.11.

[45] Ibid., 4.12.

[46] Ibid., 6.13, 6.24.

[47] Ibid., 3.9.

think carefully about the consequences of our actions; it is here that he quotes the saying.[48]

As we would expect, the extremists are obliged to defend themselves against this line of attack. Thus, a hard-line jihadi who calls himself Abū Maryam writes to brush aside criticism of the bombing of a general security building in Riyadh that took place in April 2004.[49] It is clear from his argument that the saying had figured prominently in this criticism.[50] His concern is accordingly to show that no comparison can be made between the circumstances in which Muḥammad originally uttered the saying and those in which the jihadis of the present epoch confront the supporters of the infidel rulers.[51] Thus, the hypocrites of Muḥammad's time did at least outwardly submit to him, whereas the apostates today flaunt their unbelief.[52] Moreover, those hypocrites were merely individuals, whereas today a whole sector of society fails to implement the Sharīʿa.[53] The significance of this distinction is obvious: such collective delinquency is far more damaging to Islam than the misbehavior of a few individuals.[54] Given the magnitude of this threat, it is frivolous to argue that preserving Islam is less important than preventing a handful of unbelievers from remarking that the Muslims, or the jihadis, kill their own companions[55] (the argument to which he is responding here being that jihadi actions of this kind inhibit conversion to Islam).[56] Indeed today's massive apostasy, which includes the

[48] Ibid., 3.13.

[49] Abū Maryam, *Shubha.*

[50] See, for example, ibid., 1.12—not to mention the title of the piece, in which the tradition is quoted.

[51] Ibid., 7.9.

[52] Ibid., 1.14, 5.10, 6.8.

[53] Cf. ibid., 1.11.

[54] Ibid., 3.25.

[55] Ibid., 4.1, 4.18, 4.21. Of the consequent loss of potential converts he remarks that a bird in the hand is worth ten in the bush (5.1).

[56] For an example of this argument, see Fatḥ Allāh, *Lā yataḥaddath*, 4.1, urging the avoidance of actions that might bring about aversion from the call of Islam (*sadd dharāʾiʿ al-nufūr ʿan daʿwat al-Islām*). The principle of *sadd al-dharāʾiʿ* rests on the observation that, as vernacular English has it, one thing leads to another; hence, actions that lead to prohibited actions are themselves prohibited. There is good medieval authority for viewing our saying as an instance of this principle (see, for example, Ibn Qayyim al-Jawziyya, *Iʿlām al-muwaqqiʿīn*, 3: 138.19, in a section on *sadd al-dharāʾiʿ*; Shāṭibī, *Muwāfaqāt*, 3: 75.11, and cf. 5: 180.13). Fatḥ Allāh explains that any purported act of jihad that leads to such aversion, or alienates Muslims, goes against the purpose of jihad (*Lā yataḥaddath*, 4.2), and that the Sharīʿa forbids an action that has such an effect, even if it is legal in itself; this is why Muḥammad did not kill any of the hypocrites—and here he quotes the

majority of so-called Muslims, is precisely the result of the failure to fight such backsliding.[57] Would any sane person, then, say that in such circumstances as these we are not permitted to fight the apostates for fear that the unbelievers might say that the jihadis are killing their own companions?[58] Abū Maryam's view that most of those who pass for Muslims today are in fact apostates—and not just the current rulers and those who support them—is, of course, typically extremist.

All this should not give the impression that the saying is monopolized by contemporary jihadis, though obviously it has particular relevance to their activities. The patriarchal figures of Islamism were naturally aware of it. Mawdūdī comes to the story at the appropriate point in his Koran commentary,[59] devoting a clear-headed footnote to its significance. Here he distinguishes the question whether someone like Ibn Ubayy *deserves* to be killed from the question whether it would in fact be *wise* to kill him; in a case in which the offender has a substantial political force behind him, it would be better not to kill him but rather to attend to the underlying political problem.[60] He makes it clear that he is setting out a principle that still applies today and not simply explaining why Muḥammad acted as he did. But so far as I know he does not take up the saying elsewhere, suggesting that in the end he did not attach great importance to it—though he is well aware that such qualities as prudence, insight, and the capacity to respond creatively to different situations are important and that good leadership depends on sound judgment.[61] Quṭb likewise tells the story and quotes the saying in his commentary on the relevant passage of the Koran,[62] commenting that the Prophet showed himself a wise and inspired leader in his handling of the incident.[63] But he does not raise the question of what we can learn from it today, and to my knowledge he does not discuss the saying in his other writings. Ḥawwā does bring up the story out-

---

saying with reference to Ibn Ubayy (4.12). If people come to see the Muslims as given to slaughtering each other, what chance can there be that they will listen to the call of Islam, let alone accept it (4.21)?

[57] Abū Maryam, *Shubha*, 4.5.

[58] Ibid., 4.23, 6.16.

[59] For his Urdu translation of the saying, see Mawdūdī, *Tafhīm*, 5: 513.17, to Q63.

[60] Mawdūdī, *Tafhīm*, 5: 514–15n1. I am much indebted to Qasim Zaman for identifying and translating this footnote for me.

[61] Mawdudi, *Islamic movement*, 95–96. For this work, first published in 1945, see Ahmad and Ansari, *Mawlānā Mawdūdī*, 40 no. 129.

[62] Quṭb, *Ẓilāl*, 3575.19, 3576.1, to Q63:5–8.

[63] Ibid., 3578.16.

side the context of a Koran commentary, adducing it in an account of Muḥammad's skill in handling the unexpected difficulties (*al-mashākil al-ṭāriʾa*) that arose with such frequency among a people as fractious as the Arabs.[64] But even Ḥawwā does nothing to highlight the aspect of the story that attracts Ẓawāhirī's attention: the fact that killing people indiscriminately can carry costs because it is bad for one's image.

More recently, the saying has had an obvious attraction for those who feel that the Muslim world would be a better place without much of the current jihadi violence. It can thus figure in the pronouncements of Islamists who from a Western point of view might be described as moderates and from a jihadi vantage point as neo-Murjiʾites, in other words, quietists.[65] An example would be the Syrian Munīr Muḥammad al-Ghaḍbān, a Muslim Brother and the author of a work on the implications of the life of the Prophet for the Islamic movement today.[66] Though he is devoted to the memory of Sayyid Quṭb,[67] he is by no means a radical; thus, when impetuous and over-zealous youth denounce the wise and deliberate leadership of the movement, his sympathies are entirely with the latter.[68] With regard to the saying, he remarks how much the troops of the Islamic movement (*al-junūd fī ʾl-ṣaff*) need to understand Muḥammad's position regarding the killing of Ibn Ubayy,[69] and he stresses that Muḥammad's purpose was to deny the enemy an opportunity to pillory the Islamic movement in front of those who were neutral in the conflict.[70] In a similar vein a more recent author describes Muḥammad's restraint as a most advantageous political decision (*min*

[64] Ḥawwā, *Rasūl*, 1: 218.1, 218.13, 219.16, 220.9. Ḥawwā presents Muḥammad's treatment of the hypocrites as the second of five examples of his political skill (218–30); he offers no commentary beyond placing the story within this framework. Though it is not clear from the context, the Arabs to whose political refractoriness he refers would seem to be those of pre-Islamic Arabia rather than his own contemporaries (compare ibid., 2: 198.17, 199.1). In his Koran commentary the saying appears twice in accounts of the incident that he quotes (Ḥawwā, *al-Asās fī ʾl-tafsīr*, 5922.4, 5923.15), but he does not take it up either in his comments on Q63:8 (5933.15) or in his account of the lessons of the Sūra (5937–38).

[65] Cf. Haykel, "Salafi thought and action," 54 no. 30.

[66] Ghaḍbān, *Manhaj*.

[67] See ibid., 7.17, and the rest of the introduction.

[68] Ibid., 270.7, and cf. 271.3, 271.12.

[69] Ibid., 270.3, quoting the saying (as he has already done in quoting a long account of the story, 260.18, and does again at 268.23, 271.2).

[70] Ibid., 270.26 (quoting the saying). Ghaḍbān also has a briefer treatment of the saying in his *Fiqh al-sīra*, see 614.16, 617.3. Another author praises the political skill displayed by the Prophet in this incident as something his community should imitate (Ṣallābī, *al-Sīra al-nabawiyya*, 2: 235.16, and see 233.6, 233.9, 234.17).

anfaʿ al-siyāsāt)[71] and goes on to complain that it is not understood by "zealous Muslim youth" (*al-shabāb al-Muslim al-mutaḥammis*).[72]

Anyone who engages in political action to realize a set of values needs some measure of prudence, even if the values in question are so uncompromising as to preclude it. In this context it is a significant feature of the Islamic tradition that the heritage itself furnishes resources for the nurturing of political prudence. In the instance considered here, the decision taken by Muḥammad in the matter of Ibn Ubayy provides a vivid dramatization of the point that killing people considered to be Muslims, even when justified, can become a public relations disaster. Whether that has caused jihadis to kill fewer people than they would otherwise have done is hard to say. But it has powerfully shaped the arguments that have arisen from their activities. There is mileage for Islamists in having a prophet who regularly confronted hard political choices in a way that the Buddha and Jesus did not.

[71] Abda, *Ṭarīq*, 106.20 (the saying is quoted at 105.5).

[72] Ibid., 107.2. As might be expected, this author likewise stresses the role of Muslim youth in the disastrous decision that led to the defeat of Muḥammad's forces at the battle of Uḥud in 625 (96.3; cf. above, 219).

Part Three

Fundamentalism

Introduction to Part Three

As is well known, the term "fundamentalist" was coined in 1920 by Curtis Lee Laws (d. 1946).[1] The editor of a Northern Baptist newspaper, Laws was commenting approvingly on the "Fundamentals Conference" that had recently been held in Buffalo. As he noted, this event had brought together a doctrinally varied assortment of North American Protestants: "pre-millennialists, post-millennialists, pro-millennialists and no-millennialists"—though he was happy to add that the group included no one who had repudiated "the blessed doctrine of the second coming of our Lord." What those attending the conference represented was "in every sense a conservative movement," and at the conference they stood "solidly together in the battle for the re-enthronement of the fundamentals of our holy faith." These, then, were good people, but the question was what to call them. Though he had just used the term himself, Laws did not favor "Conservatives"—it sounded too reactionary. He likewise rejected "Premillennialists" as too narrow; it was true that "premillennialists are always sound on the fundamentals," but as we have seen, he stressed that the group was broad enough to include people of other doctrinal persuasions. "Landmarkers" fared no better; Laws considered it to have a "historical disadvantage" and to "connote a particular group of radical conservatives."[2] He then proceeded to his

[1] Laws, "Convention side lights," 834; see Marsden, *Fundamentalism and American culture*, 159, and Ammerman, "North American Protestant fundamentalism," 2. For the background to the term "fundamentals," see Marsden, *Fundamentalism and American culture*, 118–19.

[2] Landmarkism was an uncompromising Baptist movement that took shape in the 1850s (see Leonard, *Baptists in America*, 25–26, 118–20, 144–47, 151–53; for the name, cf. Proverbs 22:28: "Remove not the ancient landmark, which thy fathers have set").

historic act of coinage: "We suggest that those who still cling to the great fundamentals and who mean to do battle royal for the fundamentals shall be called 'Fundamentalists.' " He added that he was willing to be called one himself, and that when he used the word, it would be "in compliment and not in disparagement."

Laws had, of course, no intention of inventing a concept that could be applied in a wider context. But the fact is that his definition is worded in sufficiently general terms to be readily applicable to any religious tradition within which one can distinguish a set of fundamentals. The result is that since 1920 the usage has been extended by analogy, so that we now hear about Islamic and even Hindu fundamentalism, though often in disparagement. There is, of course, nothing inherently wrong with naming things by analogy. It is a key strength of human language that in using a word we are not rigidly constrained by the context in which it first appeared. Languages change and develop. So even if the analogy was initially questionable, in the long run this may be neither here nor there. But if we are to employ the term comparatively, we need to be self-conscious about our use of it. What feature or features must a form of religion possess to qualify as fundamentalist?

Because the analogy involved is a somewhat vague one and the use of the term unsettled, there is no single right answer to this question. What might be called a maximalist approach is to list a whole cluster of properties which, taken together, more or less characterize some style of religion that we encounter in the world today and to call this cluster "fundamentalist."[3] My own approach, by contrast, is a minimalist one: I will select a single feature, incidentally one linked to the original North American context but also at variance with it, and I will use the term exclusively to refer to forms of religion that display this feature. I am not thereby implying that other usages are illegitimate, but I make no contribution to debates that revolve around them.

To identify the feature in question, let us take it as given that we have to do with religious traditions of some antiquity that are not entirely at ease in the modern world. Broadly speaking, such traditions can react to their discomfort in one of two ways: flexibly or inflexibly. In the North American Protestant context those who responded flexibly were the modernists. But our interest is in the forms of religion that refuse to bend (or at least prefer not to be seen to bend). They can display

[3]This is the approach taken in Almond et al., *Strong religion* (based on the Fundamentalism Project), especially 93–98.

their unwillingness to compromise in two rather different ways, what might be called the "upstream option" and the "downstream option."

To clarify this distinction, let us say that somewhere in the distant past your religion has its source, whence it issued as a mountain stream, later becoming a river and meandering through the plains on its way to the present, accumulating and depositing a great deal of silt in the process. What part of this course do you consider normative? At one extreme you might ascribe value only to your religion as it emerged at source, in all its pristine purity; this is the upstream option. At the other extreme, you might ascribe value only to the religion as it was passed on to you by your elders and betters, whom you see as having preserved, not polluted it; this is the downstream option. Put in more familiar terms, the upstream option is religious fundamentalism, whereas the downstream option is religious conservatism. Thus the Protestant fundamentalist and the Catholic conservative may be equally devoted to their respective religious heritages, but they want to do very different things with them: the fundamentalist to restore his heritage to its original condition, the conservative to keep his heritage the way he found it. In other words, whereas Laws saw "conservative" and "fundamentalist" as alternative labels for the same people,[4] my usage makes a basic distinction between them.

The North American Protestants who have been calling themselves fundamentalists for the best part of a century do nevertheless qualify as fundamentalists in my sense of the term. An essential point is that they display an "unwavering faith in an inerrant Bible" and a willingness to live by it.[5] But it is not this faith alone that makes them fundamentalists for me: it is also crucial that they proclaim no such faith in the inerrancy of the preachers and teachers from whom they received their religion. To spell this out a little more elaborately, what I am requiring of fundamentalists worth the name is three things: that they should identify one component of their religious tradition as its foundation while the rest is superstructure; that they should locate authority in the foundation rather than the superstructure; and that they should take the authority of the foundation seriously in a substantive way.

[4] In 1921 he quietly celebrated the success of his coinage of the previous year by remarking that "aggressive conservatives—conservatives who feel that it is their duty to contend for the faith—have, by common consent, been called 'fundamentalists' " (Marsden, *Fundamentalism and American culture*, 169).

[5] Ammerman, "North American Protestant fundamentalism," 5. She describes this belief as "central to the identity of fundamentalists" (6).

People for whom foundation and superstructure are indistinguishable, or who locate authority outside the foundation, or who pay little or no substantive attention to it, are not what I call fundamentalists.

Having said what I propose to mean by fundamentalism, there are three points I should add about it before we proceed to our case studies.

The first is that religious heritages are likely to differ in the degree to which they lend themselves to fundamentalization. The differences may relate either to form or to substance. Thus, on the formal side, whereas any heritage can be conserved, a pagan folk-cult whose remembered past possesses no autonomy in relation to its present may not be easy to fundamentalize; by contrast, a religion that is heir to a stable and ramified written heritage is likely to prove more amenable. On the substantive side, heritages vary in the extent to which they preserve aspects of the past that are adaptive in the present. Dusting them off in a fundamentalist vein may or may not deliver identities and values that are attractive under modern conditions. Undesirable things can lurk in old and forgotten places, and desirable things may have entered the tradition only at a later stage. Here fundamentalists are not to be thought of as simple-minded. It is rare for a fundamentalist to be possessed by a desire to go back to his foundation so pure and innocent that he does not care what he finds when he gets there. In short, heritages are not to be thought of as interchangeable, either formally or substantively.

The second point is that the sharp conceptual distinction I have made between fundamentalism and conservatism may not work out so neatly in the real world. Being religiously uncompromising does not commit a person to one end of the spectrum or the other. Intermediate positions are also viable, and just where one positions oneself may depend on the issue or the context. In other words, my concepts of fundamentalism and conservatism are in the nature of ideal types; in practice we are more likely to be dealing with matters of degree.

The third point is that the account of fundamentalism given above does not necessarily tell us what fundamentalists are up to. There are two aspects to this. One arises from the fact that fundamentalists in non-Western contexts, unlike conservatives, have something significant in common with their bête noire, the Westernizers.[6] This shared feature is their rejection of the here and now, or large parts of it, and

[6]The equivalent of Westernization in the North American fundamentalist context was the spread of modernism, denounced by one of its enemies in 1924 as "a revolt against the God of Christianity" (Marsden, *Fundamentalism and American culture*, 3–4). But even

their determination to replace it with something else. The difference is that where Westernizers seek to do this by importing an *alien* culture from elsewhere in the contemporary world, fundamentalists seek to do it by importing an *ancient* one from within their own past. These are not, of course, equivalent courses of action. Importing an alien but contemporary culture is more likely to be adaptive but no salve to wounded pride; by contrast, restoring one's own ancient culture is good for one's sense of pride but less likely to prove adaptive. Yet the scope for what might be called unacknowledged Westernization is in one respect greater for principled fundamentalists than it is for unbending conservatives. Their loyalty to a distant past gives fundamentalists greater leeway for jettisoning what they don't want while recovering what they do want; as a result of this strategic time-depth, their convictions are not necessarily a medieval straitjacket.[7] The other aspect to bear in mind is a countervailing one: depending on the history of the religion, fundamentalism and conservatism may or may not have significant common ground on substantive issues. The more such ground they share, the more compatible, indeed overlapping, their respective followings are likely to be.

With these points in mind we can go on to look at the role played by fundamentalism as I have defined it in modern Islam, Hinduism, and Latin American Catholicism.

---

here modernism was not perceived as homegrown: the fundamentalists saw it as ethnically alien, specifically German (148–49, 159).

[7] In practice, of course, fundamentalists may be unprincipled and conservatives may bend.

CHAPTER 8

Islam and fundamentalism

1. Introduction

The general observations on fundamentalism set out above provide us with several questions to ask about the Islamic case. Some relate to the formal structure of the tradition. Here we want to ascertain how far this structure has the potential to ease the formation of an Islamic fundamentalism, and how far this potential has in fact been realized by modern Muslims, in particular Islamists. Other questions are concerned with the substantive contents of the tradition. Here we want to know how far these contents render a fundamentalist tendency attractive in the contemporary world, and how far such a persuasion differs in its substantive implications from religious conservatism. Or to put the focus on the modern Islamic thinkers we have been concerned with in this book, we want to know whether it is accurate to describe them as fundamentalists, and if it is, what their fundamentalism does for them.

2. Form

With regard to the formal structure of the tradition, we need not beat about the bush. In obvious ways the Islamic heritage lends itself so easily to fundamentalization that it could almost be said to invite it. There are two closely related aspects to this, one historical and the other textual.

On the historical side a central feature of the Islamic tradition is the salience it gives to the time of its founder, the Prophet Muḥammad. It is not just that religious authority is overwhelmingly vested in or routed through his person, it is also that the Islamic idea of antiquity—in the sense of a time when things were right with the world in a way that remains exemplary today—is concentrated in his lifetime and that of his immediate followers. One can, of course, argue about exactly when this brief and intense period began or came to an end, but this does not affect the image of transient glory centered on a single paradigmatic individual, the "seal of the prophets" (Q33:40) and "model" (*uswa*) for the believers (Q33:21). It is to the prominence of this exemplary age, and Muḥammad's role in it, that Muslim fundamentalism owes much of its religious plausibility and emotive power. All else is tawdry by comparison.

On the textual side this situation is matched by the supreme authority of the Koran and the Ḥadīth, the former the scripture revealed by God to Muḥammad through Gabriel, the latter the corpus of traditions recording his divinely inspired sayings and doings, his Sunna—with the two together constituting God's final revelation to mankind. In stark contrast to this body of revelation stands the disparaging concept of religious innovation (*bidʿa*), understood as any "belief or practice for which there is no precedent in the time of the Prophet."[1] Here again, of course, there were boundary problems, and the scholastic tradition through which the religion was transmitted down the centuries found ways to make things more complicated. Thus, it is universally agreed that many purported sayings of Muḥammad are in fact inauthentic. But is the canon of his authentic sayings to be identified with some subset of the classical collections made by the leading scholars of the ninth century, with the contents of these collections being accepted in their entirety? Or is the question to be regarded as open to decision saying-by-saying even in our own time?[2] Given their close connection to Muḥammad, how much of what was said and done by his Companions is to count as authoritative, and how far? Indeed, are the opinions of subsequent scholars, who by applying their considerable wits to the revealed texts have given us the mainstream of Islamic thought down the ages, really to be reckoned of no account? And as to religious innovations, should we not distinguish between the good ones and the bad ones? Yet the overall structure of the tradition means that if one is looking for a foundation, it is not hard to find it; the would-be fundamentalist does not have to bend his religion out of shape just to get started on his enterprise.

It fits well with this that we already encounter fundamentalist trends in Islam in contexts as yet untouched by modern thinking. An example is the grand scheme developed by Shāh Walī Allāh to remake Islamic law by going back behind the opinions of the scholars to the original

[1] *EI*², art. "Bidʿa" (J. Robson).

[2] For differing views on this question, see J. Brown, *Canonization of al-Bukhārī*, especially 245, 320, 333. Whether a modern fundamentalist agrees or disagrees with current Western scholarship regarding the authenticity of Ḥadīth is, of course, neither here nor there.

sources. The two schools of legal thought he was familiar with in the eastern Islamic world were to be amalgamated and their doctrines collated with the books recording the Ḥadīth of the Prophet; whatever was in agreement with these books was to be retained, and whatever lacked foundation in them was to be discarded.[3] Such rejection of the authority of the legal schools in favor of adherence to the Ḥadīth of the Prophet was also a prominent persuasion in eighteenth-century Yemen, culminating in the thought of Shawkānī (d. 1834).[4] Nor was this kind of legal thinking new in the eighteenth century; indeed one could say that it had been endemic in Muslim thought for a thousand years.[5] Moreover, the fundamentalist impulse was not confined to law. A plausible example of an eighteenth-century fundamentalist in the field of theology would be Muḥammad ibn ʿAbd al-Wahhāb (d. 1792), the founder of the Wahhābī movement.[6] An early Egyptian opponent writing in 1743 understood him in just this way, quoting him as saying: "We do not go by the views of the four [founders of the legal schools] who exercised independent judgment, we have recourse only to the Book of God and the practice (Sunna) of His messenger."[7]

Such pre-modern fundamentalist trends did not go unchallenged. The Egyptian opponent of Muḥammad ibn ʿAbd al-Wahhāb, after alluding to the sayings of the Prophet according to which the scholars are

[3]Baljon, *Religion and thought*, 166–67, citing Walī Allāh, *Tafhīmāt*, 1: 279.19. For this ambition, cf. also Baljon, *Religion and thought*, 18. Shāh Walī Allāh was not always so radical in his view of the legal schools, see 168.

[4]Haykel, *Revival and reform*, 10–11, 81–82, 86, 89–90, 92, 101–2.

[5]Schacht, *Origins of Muhammadan jurisprudence*, 253–57.

[6]See Peskes, "Wahhābiyya and Sufism," 151. Peskes also sees him as a fundamentalist in the domain of law (156 and n58, 158n67). Here, however, we need to take into account a passage in an early epistle in which he denies certain charges made against him by an opponent: "Some of the counts (*masāʾil*) on which he seeks to disgrace [me] are plain calumny. They are: his statement that I declare the books of the schools (*madhāhib*) to be void; his statement that I say that people have been in error for six hundred years; his statement that I claim independent judgment (*ijtihād*); his statement that I do not follow the views of the authoritative scholars (*annī khārij ʿan al-taqlīd*); his statement that I hold the disagreement of the scholars to be a disaster . . ." (Ibn Ghannām, *Rawḍat al-afkār*, 1: 146.5).

[7]Traboulsi, "Early refutation," 397.6, and similarly 392.4 (it is, of course, Ḥadīth that attests the Sunna of the Prophet). Likewise a Baṣran opponent writing in 1745 tells Ibn ʿAbd al-Wahhāb: "It has reached us that you say that no account may be taken in matters either of conduct or of doctrine of anything but the Koran and the Sunna, and that as for these books—by which you mean the law-books (*kutub al-fiqh*) [composed by the scholars]—they are no better than stumps of palm-branches (*karab*), that is to say they are good only for burning, just as the stumps of palm-branches are good only for that purpose" (Qabbānī, *Naqḍ qawāʿid al-ḍalāl*, f. 60a.3; for this work, see Traboulsi, "Early refutation," 379).

the heirs of the prophets and the Islamic community will not agree in error, posed a rhetorical question to his readers: "How can it be permissible for one of us, in this age in which ignorance is everywhere and people's minds are too weak to understand [even] the plain sense of the law, to deduce [rulings] from the Book of God and the practice (Sunna) of His messenger, and discard the views of scholars who derived from the Book of God and the practice of His messenger [rulings] regarding which everyone, elite and masses, agrees in following them?"[8] Here a conservative denounces a fundamentalist as an arrogant impostor. But significantly, his denunciation shows that fundamentalism was already an intelligible option within the wider tradition, and he insists that the views which his antagonist proposes to discard were themselves derived from Koran and Sunna.

How far, then, have Islamists realized this fundamentalist potential in modern times? As a close reading of Mawdūdī and Quṭb will show, the answer is not entirely simple.

To begin with Mawdūdī, in a brief account of his life and thought two of his disciples describe him as "emphatic that the normative and immutable part of the Muslim heritage consists of the principles of the Qurʾān and the *Sunnah*, and nothing else."[9] In the same vein they explain his idea of Islamic revival (*tajdīd*) as "an effort to re-establish Islam in its pristine purity."[10] This would present him as a strict fundamentalist in the manner of the Ahl-i Ḥadīth, a group in modern South Asia who "deny the legitimacy not just of all practices lacking a basis in scriptural texts, but even of the classical schools of law, stringently insisting on the Qur'an and hadith as the exclusive and directly accessible sources of guidance."[11] And indeed much of what Mawdūdī has to say in his numerous publications would fit with this. Thus, after stating a certain position, he remarks that he is "open to be convinced against this, but only in the light of the Book of God and the Sunnah of His Messenger."[12] This same pair of authorities must also constitute "the basic law of an Islamic state"[13]—with no mention of the doctrines of the four schools. As to Islamic revival, he explains it as "cleansing Islam of all the un-Godly elements and presenting it and making it flourish

[8] Traboulsi, "Early refutation," 395.5.
[9] Ahmad and Ansari, *Mawlānā Mawdūdī*, 16.
[10] Ibid., 20.
[11] Zaman, *Ulama*, 11.
[12] Mawdudi, *Islamic movement*, 81, and cf. 133.
[13] Maududi, *Political theory of Islam*, 31; cf. Mawdūdī, *Naẓariyya*, 35.4.

more or less in its original pure form."[14] So he can certainly sound like a fundamentalist—more or less. And in practice it is overwhelmingly Koran and Sunna that Mawdūdī invokes as authorities in his writings.[15]

Yet this does not mean that Mawdūdī dismisses the intervening tradition as worthless. One scholar describes him as "more willing than many other Islamists have been to acknowledge the value and relevance of the premodern Islamic juristic and exegetical tradition to the understanding and interpretation of Islam in the modern world."[16] Mawdūdī's reasons for this may not have been entirely principled,[17] but he was not simply inconsistent. He saw his own revivalism in the context of a long series of revivalist efforts spread over the centuries. Such figures as the pious Umayyad ʿUmar II (ruled 717–720), the eighth- and ninth-century jurists who founded the four schools, and the scholars Ghazzālī (d. 1111), Ibn Taymiyya, Sirhindī, and Shāh Walī Allāh had all sought to revive Islam long before Mawdūdī appeared on the scene.[18] In invoking them as precedent, he was in a way making use of the fundamentalist streak that is native to the Islamic tradition,[19] and he certainly felt that a revivalist movement in his own day could benefit from those earlier experiences.[20] What it could not do, however, was to "bind itself to the cult and thought-pattern" of any of them. The reason was that the rupture between their time and ours is too great, for today we face "countless new problems of life" of which they could have had no inkling. "Therefore, the only Source of guidance and inspiration for an ideological movement for the renaissance of Islam in this age" must be "the Book of Allah and the Sunnah of His Prophet."[21] In short, Mawdūdī was able to show respect for the scholastic tradition without letting it get in his way. He could compliment the jurists on their "prodigious contribution to every branch of law"[22] and give a substantial list of medieval works of Koranic exegesis, tradition, law, and legal

[14] Maududi, *Short history*, 34.

[15] See, for example, Maududi, *Purdah*, chaps. 10–12.

[16] Zaman, *Ulama*, 102–3, and cf. 9.

[17] Zaman speaks in one instance of "an unmistakably tactical gesture of friendship towards the ʿulama" (ibid., 103).

[18] Maududi, *Short history*, chaps. 3 and 4.

[19] See, for example, Maududi, *Short history*, 55, 58–59, 66–67, 87. He quotes with approval Shāh Walī Allāh's scheme for remaking Islamic law (94–95).

[20] Thus the principles of jurisprudence developed by the founders of the four schools are ones of which no independent legal thinker of the future "will ever care to lose sight" (Maududi, *Short history*, 51). See also Ahmad and Ansari, *Mawlānā Mawdūdī*, 25.

[21] Maududi, *Short history*, 114f.

[22] Maudūdī, "Islamic law in Pakistan," 111.

theory that needed to be translated into "the national language"—though suitably rearranged in the process "on the pattern of modern books of Law."[23] After all, "our best brains thought over these problems," as he remarks when including "the rulings of the great jurists" among the sources for an Islamic constitution; nevertheless, these rulings "may not be conclusive."[24] In the end, we should probably describe Mawdūdī as a fundamentalist, though a rather open-minded and well-mannered one where the scholarly tradition is concerned.

Mawdūdī's attitude to the normative status of Islamic history is less nuanced. The focus of his attention is "the paradigmatic age of the Islamic state" (*al-ʿaṣr al-numūdhajī lil-dawla al-Islāmiyya*),[25] and it is with texts and anecdotes relating to it that he documents his claims.[26] What came after that moment—the greater part of Islamic history with the exception of the brief reign of ʿUmar II—has no such normative status. The reins of government had now passed permanently into the hands of the forces of "Ignorance";[27] the "Caliphate after the pattern of prophethood" had given way to the "tyrant kingdom" and the rule of the impious,[28] and the result was the "dark periods of monarchy" that came to characterize Islamic history.[29]

The case of Sayyid Quṭb is similar, though less clear-cut. In the works I have read he says nothing that would count as a doctrinal affirmation or denial of strict fundamentalism. He certainly believes that the community has gone horribly astray, so that the perfection of its early decades is in total contrast to its current disarray: we are today in a Jāhiliyya, a condition of utter ignorance like that which preceded the coming of Islam, or worse.[30] But it is not easy to pin down just where he places the transition from Islam to this latter-day Jāhiliyya.[31]

[23] Ibid., 112–14. Compare Ḥasan al-Bannā: on the one hand he says that the Muslim Brothers call for returning Islam "to its pure source" (*ilā maʿīnihi al-ṣāfī*), namely Koran and Sunna (Bannā, *Majmūʿat rasāʾil*, 248.13); and on the other, his discussion of jihad quotes long passages from the works of the jurists (50-3 = Wendell, *Five tracts*, 147-50).

[24] Maudūdī, "First principles," 219, 221.

[25] So the chapter title in Mawdūdī, *al-Ḥukūma al-Islāmiyya*, 201.2. See also 219.5, and cf. Maududi, *Political theory of Islam*, 48 = Mawdūdī, *Naẓariyya*, 52.9.

[26] Mawdūdī, *al-Ḥukūma al-Islāmiyya*, 201–19. By contrast he makes no reference to the political thought of Māwardī (d. 1058).

[27] Maududi, *Short history*, 52.

[28] Ibid., 26.

[29] Ibid., 31; for the transition see also Mawdudi, *Islam today*, 22.

[30] Quṭb, *Maʿālim*, 17.23 = 20. For the sources and development of Quṭb's conception of a latterday Jāhiliyya, see Shepard, "Sayyid Qutb's doctrine," especially the summary at 534.

[31] See Shepard, "Sayyid Qutb's doctrine," 529–30, and the quotations at 528.

In one work he states that it came early in relation to the domain of governance (*dāʾirat al-ḥukm*), with the replacement of the caliphate by "biting kingship," but late in the legal domain, with Islamic law remaining in force until the nineteenth century;[32] indeed he goes on to say that even today the Islamic spirit lives on in fields that are not under the influence of the official orientation of the state.[33] Elsewhere in the same book he refers approvingly to the work of the medieval jurists as mostly in agreement with the spirit of Islam (*rūḥ al-Islām*).[34] But in another book he tells us that the existence of the Muslim community (*al-umma al-Muslima*) may be considered to have ended many centuries ago,[35] leaving it buried under an accumulation of generations, concepts, practices, and systems that have nothing to do with Islam.[36] He makes it clear that he has a low opinion of the Muslim scholars of his own day,[37] and in general he sees no place for professional "men of religion" (*rijāl al-dīn*) in Islam.[38] But his charge against the scholastic tradition is not that its contents are false but rather that they are more or less useless. Islamic principles (*al-uṣūl al-Islāmiyya*) are not, he tells us, to be identified with the commentaries and supercommentaries that students at the Azhar waste their time on.[39] He supports this dismissal from his own experience: he has already written two substantial books on Islamic matters without finding it necessary to have any recourse to such works, since the authentic Islamic sources were quite sufficient for him.[40] He lists these authentic sources as the Koran, the Sunna of the Prophet, the accounts of his life, and works of history. He goes on to extend his position to the four schools of legal thought; his point is not that their doctrines are invalid but that they derive entirely from the Koran and the Sunna of the Prophet, sources in any case widely

[32] Quṭb, *ʿAdāla*, 216.22, 217.5 = 322. For "biting kingship," see above, 311.

[33] Quṭb, *ʿAdāla*, 220.1 = 325. In another passage he remarks that the spirit of Islam persists to the extent that the Islamic world is not exposed to the influence of materialistic Western civilization; he adduces the example of the Touareg (167.19 = 218).

[34] Ibid., 19.15 = 22.

[35] Quṭb, *Maʿālim*, 5.22 = 9; but cf. Carré, *Mysticism and politics*, 175, 188, 320. Carré's study, in this English translation, includes a selection of texts from Quṭb's Koran commentary translated by Shepard (270–341); I cite several of them below.

[36] Quṭb, *Maʿālim*, 6.10 = 9. Compare his complaint that later generations adulterated Koranic exegesis, theology, and jurisprudence with foreign elements (14.4 = 17).

[37] Quṭb, *Maʿraka*, 17.18.

[38] Ibid., 136.1, and cf. 80.10; also Quṭb, *Naḥw mujtamaʿ Islāmī*, 151.14.

[39] Quṭb, *Maʿraka*, 109.12.

[40] Ibid., 109.14.

available.[41] In short, from this evidence he comes across as a fundamentalist, if a somewhat untidy one.

What, then, of the way he actually goes about things? His practice—the pattern of his choice of authorities—cannot be described as consistently fundamentalist. In one passage he refers with respect to the founders of the four Sunnī schools of legal thought, going on to name five scholars of the thirteenth and fourteenth centuries in the same vein;[42] and it is his view that in teaching Islamic law today, it is the duty of professors to follow the giant strides taken by the founders (*al-aʾimma*) and their pupils in developing Islamic legislation (*tashrīʿ*).[43] And yet it is only very rarely that he cites such scholars as authorities whose opinions matter.[44] They do not play much role in his arguments, either as independent thinkers or as interpreters of the revealed texts; this makes it very clear that Quṭb is not a religious conservative championing the continuity of a tradition of scholarship. Overwhelmingly the authorities he quotes are Koran, Ḥadīth, and anecdotal or historical material about the early community, especially its first caliphs. Sometimes one has the sense that only the Koran really matters for him,[45] but as mentioned he does invoke Ḥadīth,[46] and his use of anecdotal and historical material is considerable.[47] This material aside, the great bulk of his thought is grounded in his own interpretation of the revealed texts, without attention to the dense exegetic tradition that spans the centuries between them and him.[48] All in all, we could describe Quṭb as an informal fundamentalist, looser in his thinking than Mawdūdī but not essentially different.

[41] Ibid., 110.1. The tone of this view of the founders of the law schools may be contrasted with that of Saʿīd Ḥawwā. According to Ḥawwā, there is nothing for which we would turn away from the Koran and the Sunna, for that would be unbelief, but we do turn to those who know the Koran and Sunna best, as the founders of the law schools undoubtedly did (Ḥawwā, *Jund Allāh thaqāfatan*, 175.5).

[42] Quṭb, *al-Islām wa-mushkilāt al-ḥaḍāra*, 188.12.

[43] Quṭb, *ʿAdāla*, 246.11 = 336.

[44] An exception is a view of Ibn Ḥazm to the effect that the people of a town are criminally responsible if anyone dies of starvation in it (ibid., 216.6 = 321; Quṭb respectfully refers to him as *al-imām Ibn Ḥazm*). Cf. above, 182, and see Musallam, *From secularism to jihad*, 164–65, on the texts studied by reading groups associated with Quṭb in prison.

[45] Quṭb, *Maʿālim*, 12.14 = 16.

[46] See, for example, ibid., 67.26 = 64, 132.16 = 113. The former passage appeals also to the Koran and the historical record of early Islam.

[47] The long seventh chapter of his book on social justice is devoted to the Islamic historical record and contains a mass of such material, much of it about the early caliphs (Quṭb, *ʿAdāla*, 137–214 = 182–276). He does not disturb himself with questions of authenticity.

[48] For a case where he cites the view of an eighth-century Koranic exegete, see Quṭb, *Khaṣāʾiṣ al-taṣawwur al-Islāmī*, 231.15 = Qutb, *Basic principles*, 220 (this work was first published in 1962). For his attitude to earlier commentators in his commentary on the Koran, see Carré, *Mysticism and politics*, 26–28.

Just as with Mawdūdī, this finds support in Quṭb's attitude to the normative status of Islamic history. As we have noted, he thinks that Islam lost out early in the domain of governance.[49] More specifically, he believes that the Islamic political order was fully realized only under the Prophet and the first two caliphs; it then had the misfortune to be corrupted by the Umayyads, who became powerful under the third caliph and took over as rulers after the failure of the efforts of the fourth caliph to restore the original character of the polity.[50] With the exception of the brief reign of the pious ʿUmar II, the rest of Islamic political history is clearly of little value to Quṭb.[51] It is the system embodied in the polity of that initial age of virtue that the Muslims need to restore, however difficult the enterprise may be; the achievement of ʿUmar II does at least show that a return to Islamic governance (*al-ḥukūma al-Islāmiyya*) remains possible for subsequent ages.[52] The glorious age of Islam was, after all, the result of human effort, and with a similar effort it could be restored.[53] It is accordingly to the paradigmatic age that Quṭb turns for exempla.[54]

Something similar could perhaps be said of such ideologues of al-Qāʿida as Ẓawāhirī and Bin Laden. Bin Laden tell us that society "should be as the first community of God's Messenger and his Companions."[55] Appeals to the ultimate authority of the Koran and the traditions of the Prophet appear with some frequency in his pronouncements:[56] "What goes for us is whatever is found in the Book of God and the *hadith* of the Prophet."[57] But another passage speaks of a return to the original sources—Koran and Sunna—"as understood by our predecessors."[58] In fact, both Ẓawāhirī and Bin Laden show considerable respect for the worthy scholars of the community, both past and present, and cite their

[49] See 383.

[50] Quṭb, *ʿAdāla*, 172.9 = 224, 181.19 = 270–71, 185.22 = 272. Quṭb remarks several times how much better it would have been if ʿAlī had been the third caliph and not the fourth (177.11 = 270, 186.6 = 273, 217.13 = 323; this is a heterodox view later dropped from the text, cf. 225, 235, and 277 of the translation).

[51] The ʿAbbāsids were no better than the Umayyads; they too practiced "biting kingship" (ibid., 194.6 = 244). For ʿUmar II as an exception, see 190.6 = 240.

[52] Ibid., 219.20 = 325.

[53] Quṭb, *Hādhā ʾl-dīn*, 38.7 = 39, and see March, "Taking people as they are," 193–94, 202–3, 205.

[54] Like Mawdūdī, he does not engage with Māwardī. By contrast, Ḥasan al-Bannā quotes him (*Majmūʿat rasāʾil*, 368.1, 368.21), and Saʿīd Ḥawwā cites him (*Islām*, 2: 162n1).

[55] Lawrence, *Messages*, 250.

[56] As ibid., 124, 134, 216, 228, 230. The first of these passages asserts that the Clash of Civilizations is proved by these exalted authorities.

[57] Ibid., 124–25.

[58] Ibid., 49.

opinions with some deference.[59] There is no doubt a measure of public relations in this: they have a strong interest in identifying their positions with those of the mainstream of Islamic scholarship, rather than looking like sectarian outliers. As Bin Laden remarks in one place, "It is not we who say that the infidel leader has overstepped the bounds of his authority; it is the consensus of the imams who say so."[60] In formal terms, in short, their fundamentalism is more diluted than that of Quṭb or Mawdūdī, but still palpable.

In summing up this discussion of the extent to which Islamists have realized the formal potential of the tradition for fundamentalization, we could do worse than note a remark of Mawdūdī's to the effect that the Muslims "are still enamoured of Islam in its pristine purity, as it was preached and practised by the Prophet, his first four Caliphs and his Companions."[61] Mawdūdī and Quṭb are themselves no exception to this generalization: they share the same intense focus on the short-lived period of Islamic antiquity and the same disillusionment with Islam in its subsequent adulteration and decay. It is not that they have no respect for the later tradition, but they do not regard it as authoritative, and most of the time they operate outside it. In that sense both can be described as formal, though not dogmatic, fundamentalists, and my impression is that in this respect they are broadly representative of Islamists at large.[62] In short, they are fundamentalist enough to put disproportionate emphasis on the foundations. When I speak of fundamentalism in what follows, it is usually this disproportion that I have in mind.

3. SUBSTANCE: IDENTITY

If Islamists are enamored of Islam in its pristine purity, just what is it that they are enamored of? What is it about the substantive character of their tradition that makes fundamentalism an attractive option for individuals and groups that are politically active in a modern context?

[59] See, for example, Ibrahim, *Al Qaeda reader*, 34, 35, 39, 67–68, 71, 121; Lawrence, *Messages*, 80, 199, 201, 202, 204, 249–50, 260. Ẓawāhirī wonders what Ṭabarī, Ibn Ḥazm, and Ibn Taymiyya would say if they were here now (Ibrahim, *Al Qaeda reader*, 92–93).

[60] Lawrence, *Messages*, 261.

[61] Mawdudi, *Islam today*, 19–20.

[62] Shukrī Muṣṭafā was an exception; for his unqualified fundamentalism, see Al-Azm, "Islamic fundamentalism reconsidered, Part II," 76–78.

The main themes to be considered here are not new—they have already figured prominently in the earlier chapters of this book. But how are they affected by fundamentalism? What difference does it make whether one relates to them through an upstream or a downstream option? Let us begin with identity.

The ability to mobilize populations on the basis of an appeal to Muslim solidarity, whether regionally or globally, is not, of course, dependent for its existence on fundamentalism. But the logic of the upstream option works to enhance the appeal of Muslim identity and highlight its political dimension. It does this by redirecting attention away from the large, diffuse, and fragmented Muslim world of recent centuries and toward the far more compact community of early Islamic times, when religious brotherhood was also political unity. At the same time, fundamentalism helps to sap the legitimacy of rival political identities among Muslim populations. Thus, it undermines the status of the numerous ethnic identities of later Islamic history, with their potential for evolving into nationalism; again it does this by shifting the focus to an epoch in which non-Arab ethnic identities had only a limited presence in the community, and even less normative recognition.

Fundamentalism also assists with the other side of the coin, the demonization of enemies. Generally, it can work to erode the legitimacy of later accommodations between Muslim and non-Muslim populations by invoking the values of an earlier age in which Islamic dominance was clear-cut. Specifically, it highlights confrontation with Christians and Jews. The Prophet fought both, and the Koran invests great polemical energy in confuting them; by contrast, it contains only a single reference to Zoroastrians (the Magians of Q22:17) and none at all to Hindus or Buddhists. In the Christian case the historical continuity of the threat means that fundamentalism does not make an enormous difference, though the leaders of al-Qāʿida have deftly evoked the memory of the early confrontation with the Roman or Byzantine superpower of late antiquity.[63] The Jewish case is more dramatic. The Jews were intimate enemies at the beginning of Islam by virtue of their

[63] See, for example, Lawrence, *Messages*, 217–18, where Bin Laden makes the contemporary reference explicit with the remark that "we became weak and the Romans returned." Compare the striking geopolitical metaphor used by an early exegete in describing the wretched condition of the Arabs before God brought them Islam: they were "stuck on top of a rock between the two lions, Persia and the Romans," until with the coming of Islam God made them kings lording it over others (Ṭabarī, *Tafsīr*, 6: 219 no. 15,933 (to Q8:26); for the reading of the word I have translated as "stuck" and further references, see Kister, "Al-Ḥīra," 143–44).

opposition to Muḥammad in Medina,[64] and through a remarkable turn of modern history they are once again intimate enemies by virtue of their establishment of the State of Israel; but in between they were a harmless diaspora posing no threat to the Muslim ascendancy. Here fundamentalism helps to close the gap. Thus Quṭb opens an essay on "our battle against the Jews" with the remark that the Muslim community *continues* to face the same Jewish guile and plotting that the early Muslims (*aslāfuhā*) faced, thereby linking the two periods when Jews were a serious danger to Muslims and eliding the discontinuity that intervenes.[65] Among other things this is a good example of the role of historical contingency in the relevance of fundamentalism.[66]

Whatever the initial attractions of identity politics, the outcome can, of course, turn out to be more disruptive than adaptive for the populations concerned. Thus, insofar as fundamentalism increases the appeal of such politics, it is likely to carry costs as well as benefits for those who espouse it. Perhaps the clearest example of such a cost concerns the capacity of fundamentalism to aggravate sectarian conflict, as in Iraq since the American invasion of 2003. In such contexts the divisiveness of religious identities is enhanced by a way of thinking that reawakens the substantive mythic or doctrinal issues associated with the original parting of the ways.[67] One way to see this is to compare Iraq and Northern Ireland. In Northern Ireland the opposed identities of Catholics and Protestants are historically grounded in theological

[64] Note, however, that there is no geopolitical paranoia to this enmity: the evil empires to the north of Arabia are not seen in the Arabic sources as façades of Jewish power.

[65] Quṭb, "Maʿrakatunā maʿa.. ʾl-Yahūd," 41.2 = Nettler, *Past trials*, 72; for this work, see Moussalli, *Radical Islamic fundamentalism*, 54 no. 29.

[66] By contrast, what the Koran and the Ḥadīth have to say about Arab pagans and Zoroastrians has little direct relevance to modern geopolitics; the Persian lion is useful only in a nationalist context.

[67] A nice indication of the way in which sectarian divisions can doze in the absence of fundamentalism is W. C. Smith's categorization of the divergences between Sunnīs and Shīʿites in the Indian context of the 1940s as relating to "what answers are to be given to questions which to-day do not arise" (Smith, *Modern Islām in India*, 303, aptly quoted in Zaman, "Sectarianism in Pakistan," 691n4). Fundamentalism ensures that these questions do arise, a fact that might have some relevance to the way in which the mid-twentieth-century movement for Sunnī-Shīʿite rapprochement (*taqrīb*) lost steam even before the Iranian revolution. For its moribund condition in the period 1962–1979, see Brunner, *Islamic ecumenism*, chap. 10. Brunner does not discuss the role of fundamentalism but makes it clear that there were other factors working against the movement, notably the Shah's recognition of Israel in 1960 (313–16, 351, 394) and the rise of Saudi Arabia (341)—though the latter was, of course, linked to the rise of fundamentalism. He notes that even in its best days the movement had prospered only by studiously avoiding the thorny issues (395, 396)—a tactic that fundamentalism makes it harder to implement.

disagreements that arose in sixteenth-century Europe, and yet clashing theological views on transubstantiation—unlike memories of military conflicts that took place in seventeenth-century Ireland—play no role in the acrimonious politics of the region today. By contrast, the *odium theologicum* attaching to disputes that began in the seventh century is very much alive in the current conflict between Sunnīs and Shīᶜites in Iraq,[68] just as it is in Pakistan.[69] There is not very much that violent Sunnī Islamists can do today with the denunciations of the Khārijite sectarians preserved in their heritage, other than to deny the accusation that they are Khārijites themselves.[70] But anti-Shīᶜite resources developed well over a thousand years ago can still be put to highly disruptive use in the early twenty-first century. Nor is the view that sectarianism in Iraq is disruptive confined to well-intentioned Western humanitarians; as we have seen, it was a prominent theme in the criticism of Zarqāwī's sectarian bloodbath mounted by fellow jihadis who regarded it as a political disaster.[71]

In short, the highlighting of Muslim solidarity by fundamentalism is by no means without cost. But this should not obscure the fact that it boosts an appeal that has considerable political potential in the world today.

4. Substance: Values

Let us now shift from identity to values. Here I shall examine the implications of fundamentalism with regard to a set of themes familiar from earlier chapters: society, warfare, divine jealousy, and polity.

[68] For the virulent hostility toward Shīᶜites prevalent in some jihadi circles, see Steinberg, "Jihadi-Salafism," 110–11; Lahoud, *Jihadis' path to self-destruction*, 214–18.

[69] See, for example, Zaman, *Ulama*, 122 and 236n59, on the flag of the Pakistani anti-Shīᶜite movement Sipāh-i Ṣaḥāba. Compare the use of the derogatory medieval term "Rāfiḍa" for Shīᶜites favored in some Sunnī circles as part of their unreconstructed espousal of medieval religious quarrels (see, for example, Fandy, *Saudi Arabia*, 206, quoting a Saudi *fatwā* of 1991).

[70] For the categorization, see Lahoud, *Jihadis' path to self-destruction*, 35–39, and for its rejection by the jihadis, 27, 40–43. A vivid image of medieval martyrdom operations as carried out by Khārijite sectarians is given by a tenth-century heresiographer: "As for the first sect of the Khārijites, they are the Muḥakkima, who used to go out with their swords into the markets, and people would gather around not realizing what was happening; they would shout 'No judgment but God's!' and plunge their swords into whoever they could, and then go on killing until they were killed themselves. . . . Thank God, not a single one of them remains today on the face of the earth" (Malaṭī, *Tanbīh*, 38.8).

[71] See 362–63, 365.

The key social value of early Islamic society in this context is its egalitarianism.[72] The fit with modern values is, of course, imperfect: Islamic egalitarianism did not extend to women, slaves, or unbelievers—which does not play well in today's world. Yet despite these limitations there was something very appealing about the egalitarian heritage, and as we have seen, Islamists were strongly drawn to it.[73] Mawdūdī showed a pronounced liking for the tradition according to which "people are equals like the teeth of a comb." Quṭb made particularly effective use of the interactions between the Arab envoys and the Persian general in the negotiations preceding the battle of Qādisiyya. The jihadis, despite a general lack of interest in questions of social stratification, provide occasional echoes of this theme, with Bin Laden characterizing Islam as the religion of "total equality between all people." Here the effect of fundamentalism is to focus attention on the layer of the heritage in which this value is most prominent.

In the domain of warfare the key value is, of course, jihad. This is undoubtedly one of the most conflicted values of Islam in the modern world.[74] But what concerns us here is the effect of fundamentalism, and in this connection there are perhaps two points worth making. The first and more obvious is that the shift of focus reinforces Muslim solidarity. We leave an age in which a plurality of Muslim states make war on their Muslim and non-Muslim neighbors more or less indiscriminately, and we return to one in which there is a single Islamic state fighting its infidel enemies.

The second point is a subtler one about the character of warfare in the early days of Islam. The accounts of jihad that fundamentalism most privileges are naturally those set in the lifetime of the Prophet. As we have seen, jihad in the arid tribal setting of Arabia was often very different from the massive campaigns that later Muslim states with substantial agrarian revenues were able to organize around their professional armies.[75] Those who joined Muḥammad's sixty-five expeditions were ordinary Muslims; they were no more professional soldiers than the Prophet himself. They often operated in small groups and engaged in what by modern standards would be considered irregular warfare. This, then, is a style of jihad with a recognizable affinity for many of the settings in which contemporary jihadis operate, in countries like

[72] See 169–70.
[73] See 184–86.
[74] See 244–30.
[75] See 218–20.

Somalia and Afghanistan where society is tribal and government weak at best.[76] That does not mean that jihadis are wedded to doing things this way; as Ẓawāhirī's grand strategy makes clear, he sees irregular warfare as a stepping-stone to a future in which the regular armies of an Islamic state can take and hold territory.[77] But, in the meantime, there is a significant resonance between jihadi warfare and that of the Prophet, and it is nicely caught in the jihadi use of the figure of 314 men.[78]

We come now to the ramifications of divine jealousy, which can be distinctly problematic. It is possible to imagine a religion that aspires to a monopoly of all knowledge, or if not of all knowledge, then of all values; and Islam, as we saw in an earlier chapter, in principle approximates to such a model in significant respects.[79] Thus as a worldview, a legal system, and a polity, it arguably leaves no room for alternative philosophical, legal, or political traditions from outside Islam. It did, of course, come to coexist with such traditions in practice, with varying degrees of comfort or discomfort. But because the reception of these non-Islamic components was historically secondary, the overall effect of fundamentalism is to undermine the later coexistence with them and to refocus attention on the period in which their Islamic counterparts still enjoyed something like a monopoly. This in turn calls in question the legitimacy of such coexistence today, and it is not hard to see how in a rapidly changing world an attitude of this kind could prove maladaptive and in the long run debilitating.

Against this must be set the fact that fundamentalism also has the effect of highlighting some specific elements in the tradition that discourage aspirations to monopoly.[80] As we have seen, it is related that the Prophet once gave the cultivators of palm trees advice that turned out badly; he then conceded that they were better informed about their worldly affairs than he was. He diagnosed a heart condition in one of his followers and prescribed a remedy but at the same time referred him to a doctor trained in the Persian Empire. And at a critical moment in his career, he adopted a foreign military practice suggested to him by a Persian follower. None of this would support the reception of non-Muslim *values*, which would surely fall foul of the saying of the Prophet

[76] See 232.
[77] See 233.
[78] See 231.
[79] See 251–55, 270–77, 309–19.
[80] See 252, 261–62.

that he who imitates a people is one of them; and in each case we are concerned with an aspect of life in which failure threatens disaster. But these traditions do make the point that Islam is not all-embracing and provide clear precedent for the adoption of useful non-Muslim techniques and expertise.

As we have seen, the response of the Islamists is not to categorically approve or condemn borrowing from the West but to attempt to draw a line.[81] Mawdūdī was not against the adoption of the "healthy achievements" of the West so long as they were "value-free" and could be assimilated into "the Islamic scheme of life." But he approvingly describes renovators of Islam as having no tolerance for "the presence of even a tinge of un-Islam in the Islamic system," commends their earlier struggles against Greek philosophy and other such poisons foreign to Islam, and feels the same way about the Western philosophy of life today. Quṭb thinks in terms of a similar distinction between science and values and adduces the story of the Prophet and the palm trees. Drawing the line in this fashion allows the assimilation of certain aspects of Western modernity while safeguarding the native heritage in proper fundamentalist fashion; the problem with it is, of course, that Western success can be hard to disentangle from Western values.

Here it is crucial that in political terms the early Islamic heritage preserves values that were in eclipse for much of Islamic history, but have strong resonance in the modern world.[82] As we have seen, these are not dry scholastic values: the rejection of despotism and patrimonialism is embodied in vivid anecdotes about the Prophet and the early caliphs, and is combined with a pronounced egalitarianism[83] and a very practical emphasis on the importance of political judgment.[84] The effect of fundamentalism is naturally to highlight these values. It brushes aside the political culture of later centuries, so aptly characterized by Baranī,[85] and gives sustained attention only to the early polity. This carries very little cost: conspicuously lacking in the modern Islamic world is a conservative sense that there was anything of value in the political traditions of later centuries that both modernists and fundamentalists brush aside.

[81] See 264–67.
[82] See 319–22.
[83] See 169–70, 390.
[84] See 159–61.
[85] See 17–18, 311.

Of course, the fit between these values and those of modern times is far from perfect. This is to be expected, given the historical chasm that separates the societies that gave rise to them. Thus, the early Islamic values were not matched by an explicit espousal of freedom or democracy, though the latter finds a degree of atmospheric support in the high level of political participation. Equally the resource-poor conditions in which Muḥammad created his state and the correspondingly personal character of his rule meant that his state building does not provide a model for the development of complex institutions; and even what his successors did in an incipiently imperial setting pales into insignificance if placed alongside the Ottoman record. Moreover, the union of religion and politics at the heart of Muḥammad's enterprise is a singularly unmodern feature and not readily adopted by complex societies of any period.[86] This, then, is a heritage that may be better suited to inspiring the subversion of bad government than the maintenance of good government. But for all its limited and historically adventitious character, the resonance between these values and those of the modern world is a powerful one.

As we have seen, these protorepublican values of early Islam have appealed strongly to Islamists—and not just to Mawdūdī and Quṭb but also to contemporary jihadis.[87] Thus Mawdūdī exploits the anecdotal material on the first caliphs, declares monarchy the antithesis of Islam, and speaks of the "democratic spirit" of the early polity.[88] Quṭb follows suit, though without showing Mawdūdī's warmth for democracy. The same themes recur sporadically in the pronouncements of Bin Laden, linked in one case to the Western notion of accountability.

In sum, the effects of fundamentalism in the context of values are certainly mixed. But it does give salience to some values that are very attractive in the world today.

5. Fundamentalism, Conservatism, and Modernism

How do fundamentalism, conservatism, and modernism compare? Our concern here is not to define the concepts but rather to see how the phenomena relate to each other.

[86] See 312.
[87] See 327–29.
[88] For the latter, see 331.

First, there is a significant degree of affinity between fundamentalism and modernism.[89] Fundamentalists at large bear little resemblance to the Amish-like community living near the Saudi city of Burayda that does not use electricity, cars, or telephones.[90] In fact, even with regard to the foundations, Mawdūdī and Quṭb are not entirely inflexible. For Mawdūdī, as we have seen, Islamic revival only restores Islam to "more or less" its original pure form.[91] For Quṭb, it is not the concrete seventh-century form of the Islamic polity that is to be restored, with all the accompanying hardships of desert life; rather, the Islamic system (*al-niẓām al-Islāmī*) embodied in that polity can take many forms (*ṣuwar*) depending on the development of society and the needs of the age.[92] When it comes to the superstructure, the flexibility is greater still. Thus, Mawdūdī makes a distinction between "the unalterable elements" of Islamic law, based squarely on the Koran and "the authentic Traditions of the Prophet," and the rest, which is open to modification "according to the needs and requirements of the changing times," thus ensuring "the dynamism, adaptability, progressive nature and power of evolutionary growth of the legal system of Islam."[93] This does not perhaps go as far as the ninth-century Japanese view that "new times require new laws, which are in the spirit of those of ancient times, but suited to the present."[94] Yet, despite his commitment to more than just the spirit of ancient times, there is much in Mawdūdī's perspective that a modernist could agree with. We should not forget that he expects the Mahdī—the messianic figure who is to come—to create "a *new* School of Thought on the basis of pure Islam."[95] In short, both fundamentalism and modernism can be ways to emancipate oneself from the unwanted debris of the later tradition—be it steeply hierar-

[89] This linkage is already adumbrated in the evolution of the thinking of a nineteenth-century reformer like Sayyid Aḥmad Khān. On the one hand his early writings show a concern to get back to Islam in its original purity (see Troll, *Sayyid Ahmad Khan*, 51–52, 56–57, and cf. 276–77 no. (vi)). And on the other hand he became a modernist, out to spread European civilization in order to "remove the contempt with which civilized peoples regard the Muslims" and enable them to be "reckoned among the respected and civilized people in the world" (Baljon, *Reforms and religious ideas*, 25).

[90] See Hegghammer and Lacroix, "Rejectionist Islamism," 122n88; Hegghammer, *Jihad in Saudi Arabia*, 89. For a Malaysian sect for which tables, chairs, and television were anathema, see Kepel, *Jihad*, 91–92.

[91] See 380–81.

[92] Quṭb, *Maʿraka*, 84.3, and see 82.18, 84.13.

[93] Maudūdī, "Islamic law," 60–62.

[94] See 278.

[95] Maududi, *Short history*, 42 (my italics).

chic conceptions of society, stifling scholasticism, the regional residues of a polylithic Islam, or quietism in the face of despotic government.

Second, there is an equally significant affinity between fundamentalism and conservatism. In many respects, of course, the upstream and downstream options have very different effects. Fundamentalism threatens to subvert social hierarchy, undermines the authority of the scholastic tradition, calls in question the authenticity of Ṣūfism, and erodes long-standing accommodations with non-Islamic intellectual, legal, and political traditions. But there is also common ground, over and above the fact that the fundamentalist option is itself part of the heritage. When it comes to attitudes to unbelievers, for example, fundamentalism is well placed to reinforce conservative attitudes to Muslim dominance, whether the context is jihad against invaders from outside the Muslim world or the subordination of non-Muslims within it. The same applies with regard to a more intimate aspect of traditional Islamic society, namely relations between men and women. Moreover, much of the core ritual of the religion is not at issue between fundamentalists and conservatives: mosques, prayer, fasting, and the pilgrimage to Mecca are common to both. Of course, the fit may often be approximate. Thus, Muslim feminists are able to find room to manoeuvre in the differences between the earliest Muslim society and its later counterparts.[96] Or, if the subject is the caliphate, is it the caliphate of the immediate successors of the Prophet that is to be restored, or the caliphate as described by the medieval jurists, or the caliphate as claimed by the later Ottoman sultans and abolished by the Kemalists in 1924? Nevertheless, the existence of substantial common ground between fundamentalism and conservatism is a significant feature of the context in which Islamists go to work.

In fact, the existence of this affinity between fundamentalism and conservatism illuminates a confusing but crucial feature of the modern development of Islam. In practice it is not always easy to tell fundamentalists and conservatives apart, and to the extent to which one can, they often seem to get on rather well together. The two movements that have most effectively given shape to conservative sentiment have been the Salafīs—alias Wahhābīs—with their center of gravity in Saudi Arabia, and the Deobandīs with their homeland in northern India. Here the Salafīs represent an eighteenth-century fundamentalism that arose in an inner-Arabian context where Western influence was as yet nonexistent,

[96] There is a hint of this in Quṭb's thinking, see 187–88.

while the Deobandīs were more in the nature of a nineteenth-century revivalism that took shape in response to British imperial rule. In each case the movement sooner or later assumed the character of a puritanical conservatism. Yet, the record shows that, despite their considerable fractiousness, both Salafīs and Deobandīs have been able to work with fundamentalists in the tradition of Mawdūdī and Quṭb. One instance of this compatibility is the fact that the Saudi regime was ready not merely to grant Quṭbist refugees from Egypt asylum in Saudi Arabia but also to employ them in roles in which they could exert considerable influence on the more educated young men of the country, providing the context in which Bin Laden was exposed to Quṭbist ideas.[97] Another instance is the coexistence within al-Qāʿida of Quṭbist and Salafī strains. Yet another is the symbiosis between al-Qāʿida and the Ṭālibān, who were a product of the Deobandī tradition—despite the view held by some elements in al-Qāʿida that the Ṭālibān were apostates.[98] Admittedly Ẓawāhirī brought to al-Qāʿida a certain latitudinarianism with respect to what he considered minor religious differences, and in this he represented the tradition of the Muslim Brothers going back to its founder, Ḥasan al-Bannā.[99] But such principled broad-mindedness was not matched in the Salafī tradition and was often absent from that of the Deobandīs. Without the common ground between fundamentalism and conservatism, such symbioses would have been far more problematic.

Obviously these two affinities—that between fundamentalists and modernists, and that between fundamentalists and conservatives—pull in different directions. Which pull proves stronger in any given case is likely to be a matter of contingency. To give just one example, as we have seen, Mawdūdī and Quṭb are alike in affirming men and women to be equal while going on to add qualifications. Yet they emerge with significantly different stances. Mawdūdī ends up sounding very like a conservative, staking out common ground with his view that in the India of his day the rules of purdah needed to be strictly enforced rather than relaxed. Quṭb, by contrast, sounds more like a modernist, leaving women free to come and go and delegitimizing the harem as a corruption of Islam best blamed on the Turks.[100] Clearly it depends, though it might not always be easy to say just what it depends on.

[97] For this interaction, see Kepel, *War for Muslim minds*, 170–79.
[98] See V. Brown et al., *Cracks*, 13–16, and cf. Lia, *Architect of global jihad*, 238–40, 269.
[99] See Mitchell, *Society of Muslim Brothers*, 216–17.
[100] See 186–88.

6. Conclusion

Our main findings in this chapter are not hard to summarize. In formal terms, the Islamic tradition readily admits of fundamentalization. There is a clear conception of a canon—Koran and Ḥadīth—that stands apart from the rest of the tradition: it is divine revelation, it is temporally anterior, and it is tied to the compelling figure of the prophet Muḥammad. Moreover, the idea that one can appeal to this canon to subvert the claims to authority of later figures is an old one, a fundamentalist tendency that is fully indigenous to the tradition. Given all this, it is inconvenient but not of great consequence that the exact delimitation of the corpus of authoritative Ḥadīth is open to argument. Not surprisingly, then, we find Islamists displaying a marked fundamentalist bent. Their fundamentalism may be inconsistent and untidy, but there is no question that Islamists are, as Mawdūdī put it, "enamoured of Islam in its pristine purity."[101] Nor is it obscure why they should be so enamored—and not simply as a way to bypass the professional religious scholars whose knowledge of the extended tradition they cannot match. With regard to identity, fundamentalism works to enhance the political dimension of Muslim brotherhood, while at the same time assisting with the demonization of external and, more disruptively, internal enemies. With regard to values, it highlights some features of the early polity—such as the espousal of egalitarianism and the rejection of despotism—that on balance look distinctly attractive under modern conditions. It also puts the spotlight on an early epoch in the history of the community in which Muslims fought only unbelievers and not each other, and did so in ways reminiscent of the irregular warfare of contemporary jihadis; and it foregrounds the intrinsically Islamic form of polity that prevailed in that epoch. More generally, it concentrates attention on a time when the Muslim community was extraordinarily successful, thereby pointing to a future in which it could again become the greatest power on earth. The discouragement of cultural borrowing by divine jealousy is potentially maladaptive, but there are elements in the canon that can serve to counteract this. These elements and the values that resonate with modernity make possible a significant overlap between fundamentalism and modernism; this is how Mawdūdī is able to deliver a message of flexibility and adaptiveness in the face of current challenges and to promise that the Mahdī will prove to be

[101] See 386.

"the most modern of all the moderns."[102] At the same time, the fundamentalist trend has also benefited from its overlap with conservatism with regard to such bedrock matters as the Muslim ascendancy and the status of women. In short, there is no great mystery about the fact that fundamentalism has come to be a serious contender for the political allegiance of many Muslims. What remains is for us to see how the Islamic case compares in this regard with those of Hinduism in India and Catholicism in Latin America.

[102] See 265.

CHAPTER 9

Hinduism and fundamentalism

1. Introduction

How do the issues discussed with respect to Islam in the previous chapter fare in the case of Hinduism? Formally, what would a Hindu fundamentalism look like, and has there been such a thing? Substantively, what is at stake for Hindus in the choice between the upstream and downstream options? Does the choice involve the gain or loss of identities and values that could be attractive in politics today? And what role, if any, does fundamentalism play in the religious politics of contemporary India?

With regard to the last question, some writers refer to Hindu nationalism as "Hindu fundamentalism" or call its followers "Hindu fundamentalists."[1] The usage is not standard, and its aptness has been seriously questioned; as one scholar puts it, "The Hindu nationalists are religious *nationalists*, not religious *fundamentalists*."[2] For those who use such terms, analogy is obviously at work. In principle the analogy could be with Christian fundamentalism, but given the prominence of Islamists in the world today, it seems more likely that the model is Islamic. Either way, the usage does not seem to be analytically grounded, and one sometimes has the sense that it is more in the nature of an insult felt to be appropriate for people who practice a violent brand of identity politics on the basis of religious affiliation. At that level "fundamentalist" does the work today that "fascist" would have done for an older generation.[3]

[1] For a stray example, see "Minister knocked down," 442, where a caption refers to the destruction of the Bābrī Masjid by "Hindu fundamentalists." This turn of phrase is not confined to journalists; for example, it is to some degree adopted in Bose, "Swami Vivekananda," 281–83, 299. For other examples, see Fuller, *Camphor flame*, 258–61 (but with the qualification that the term "fundamentalism" is rather misleading); R. Guha, *India after Gandhi*, 641, 645, 740; Huntington, "Clash of civilizations," 99, 127, 256. For usage in the less innocent context of the Fundamentalism Project of the 1990s, see the appendix.

[2] Varshney, *Ethnic conflict*, 70. Another scholar comments, "It is a great mistake to view this ideology as Hindu 'fundamentalist' " (Brass, *Politics of India*, 265). Cf. also Keddie, "New Religious Politics," 706–7.

[3] In fact, "fascist" may once have had more descriptive aptness than "fundamentalist." But note that the mainstream Hindu nationalists (unlike the Shiv Sena) have never had a leadership cult (Jaffrelot, *Hindu nationalist movement*, 62).

But for the moment we will do better to leave the Hindu nationalists aside and start with the more basic question of what a Hindu fundamentalism would look like.

2. Form

If we go by the criteria set out earlier,[4] the first thing a fundamentalist has to do to deserve the name is to identify one component of his religious tradition as its foundation. In the Hindu case this task presents no insuperable difficulty, since the Vedas are the obvious candidate for the role. They do not have the tight historical focus of the Muslim canon; Indian antiquity is characterized by long duration, both in historical fact and still more in its own estimation.[5] In this it resembles the antiquities of the Greeks and Chinese more than that of the Muslims. But if one is looking for a body of ancient texts that by general consent have a privileged status within the wider Hindu heritage, the Vedas fit the bill.

We have already seen that in pre-modern India the Vedas were widely—though not universally—acknowledged as a major component of the tradition.[6] Indeed in two respects their status went beyond this. First, the Vedas were manifestly the oldest textual stratum of the Hindu tradition. Indeed, as a matter of historical fact, the Ṛg Veda is the oldest text in current use in any of the world's religions. And if for historical fact we substitute the Hindu doctrine that could best be described as orthodox, the Vedas are not just old, they are eternal.[7] Second, the mainstream tradition ascribed superior authority to the Vedas. They were *śruti*, revelation. Alongside *śruti* the tradition recognized a second, rather open-ended category of authoritative texts, namely *smṛti*, literally "recollection"; but in the words of the classic exposition of such matters, "Dharma is that which is indicated by the Veda as conducive to the highest good," and "where there is conflict, the Smṛti should be disregarded."[8] Likewise Manu gives the Veda pride of place in set-

[4] See 373–74.

[5] The Kṛtayuga, when *dharma* stood on all four feet, lasted four thousand years according to one reckoning (Kane, *History of Dharmaśāstra*, 5: 688), but another reckoning would increase that by a factor of 360 (3: 891).

[6] See 61–62.

[7] On this issue, see, for example, Verpoorten, *Mīmāṃsā literature*, 20; D'Sa, *Śabdaprāmāṇyam*, 34, 197–98, and cf. 39; Kane, *History of Dharmaśāstra*, 5: 1202–4.

[8] So the *Mīmāṃsā-sūtras* of Jaimini in the commentary of Śabara (*Shabara-bhāṣya*, 4, 92). Both authors are ancient but of very uncertain date (Verpoorten, *Mīmāṃsā literature*, 5, 8, 54).

ting out the "the root of religion" and goes on to say that it "contains all knowledge"; it is the revelation (*śruti*) and as such "the supreme authority" for those who wish to understand religion.[9] In the same way for Śankara the Vedas alone can give knowledge of ultimate reality (*brahman*), not to mention more mundane matters of ritual (*dharma*).[10] Such deference was not, of course, to be found in all circles. The materialist Cārvākas had the audacity to detect error, self-contradiction, and tautology in the Vedas.[11] But the very fact that they directed their destructive energies at the Vedas reflected the status of these texts in the mainstream of elite Hinduism.

The picture has been broadly similar in modern times. Thus Rām Mohan Roy speaks of the Vedas as "our most ancient writings";[12] in arguing that Hindu law does not sanction the practice of "burning Hindu widows alive" on the funeral pyres of their husbands, he remarks that "we should first refer to the Vedas whose authority is considered paramount."[13] A Bengali Brahmin, writing in Sanskrit to refute a Christian tract in 1840, likewise insists on the prime authority of the Vedas.[14] Vivekānanda affirmed that "this perhaps is certain that no man can have a right to be called a Hindu who does not admit the supreme authority" of the Vedas.[15] Such a statement was not, of course, an expression of orthodox zeal. Vivekānanda entertained a slew of modernist notions about the Vedas that would not have endeared him to Śankara: that the Vedas are true "because they consist of the evidence of competent persons" who were reporting their "spiritual discoveries," that only those parts of the Vedas that are in harmony with reason should be accepted as authoritative, that there is a progressive development of thought within the Vedic corpus,[16] and the like. He was not alone in having unorthodox ideas about the Vedas. His own teacher Rāmakṛṣṇa (d. 1886) was a mystic in a tradition that disparaged them.[17] In the same period the opinionated Hindu intelligentsia of Calcutta has been described as sharing little beyond the conviction

[9] Manu, *Laws*, 17–18 (2.6–7, 10, 13).

[10] Rambachan, *Accomplishing the accomplished*, 31, 40–41, 65; Mayeda, *Thousand teachings*, 47.

[11] Renou, *Le destin du Véda*, 41.

[12] Damen, *Crisis and religious renewal*, 23, and cf. 31.

[13] Nag and Burman, *Raja Rammohun Roy*, 3: 132, quoted in A. Sharma, *Modern Hindu thought*, 26.

[14] Young, *Resistant Hinduism*, 131. For the date, see 14–15, and for the author, 93–94.

[15] Rambachan, *Limits of scripture*, 57.

[16] Ibid., 43, 50, 53–54.

[17] Renou, *Le destin du Véda*, 4–5; Rambachan, *Limits of scripture*, 33, 35.

that the Vedas could not be the unique and definitive revelation.[18] But again, there remained something Veda-centered about these stirrings of scepticism. If one wanted to be free, it was the "thraldom" of the Vedas from which one had to be liberated.[19] Meanwhile, mainstream Hinduism continued to recognize their primacy, even when it did little or nothing to give substance to this commitment.

The only text that was at all in competition with the Vedas for the role of the Hindu scripture was the celebrated *Bhagavad Gītā*. It formed part of the three-fold Vedānta canon, though Śankara accepted its authority only when it was compatible with the Vedas.[20] It has continued to be a prominent text in modern times. The assassin Dāmodar Cāphekar, a Citpāvan Brahmin who realized his aspiration to die after shedding the blood of the enemies of his religion in 1897, asked for Ṭiḷak's copy of the *Gītā* to take with him to the gallows (he no longer had his own copy, which he had taken to the assassination).[21] At the second International Hindu Conference in 1979, the VHP proposed a "minimum code of conduct for the daily life of every Hindu" that identified the *Gītā* as "the sacred book of the Hindus" and prescribed that every Hindu should keep a copy of it in his home.[22] Reciting the text is an integral part of the Hindu nationalist education provided at a boarding school in Madhya Pradesh.[23] Muslims have even been known to pay the *Gītā* the backhanded compliment of burning it.[24] But Hindu fundamentalism, insofar as there has been such a thing, has revolved around the Vedas.

Although selecting the Vedas as the foundation is fairly straightforward, there remains an ambiguity as to just what they are to consist of. Are there three of them or four? And for any given Veda, what becomes of the penumbra of associated texts, notably the Brāhmaṇas and Upaniṣads? Here traditional Hindus tended to be rather inclusive, using the term "Veda" to refer both to the Vedas proper (the *saṃhitās*) and to the associated texts; all this was *śruti*, "revelation." Thus when Śankara appeals to the Vedas, the texts he has in mind are primarily

[18] Jordens, *Dayānanda Sarasvatī*, 88.

[19] Ibid., 81, and see Damen, *Crisis and religious renewal*, 35–36.

[20] Mayeda, *Thousand teachings*, 12, 48 and 66n9, 213–14.

[21] See Wolpert, *Tilak and Gokhale*, 88–89, and Cāphekar's autobiography in Kedourie, *Nationalism in Africa and Asia*, 457. For his aspiration, see 423; also Cashman, *Myth of the Lokamanya*, 114.

[22] Jaffrelot, *Hindu nationalist movement*, 348.

[23] Jaffrelot, "Hindu nationalism," 206.

[24] Brass, *Hindu-Muslim violence*, 77, and cf. 112.

the Upaniṣads,[25] historically later than the original Vedic core. True to this tradition, a large assembly of orthodox Hindus that convened in Calcutta in 1881 resolved that the Brāhmaṇas are as authoritative as the four Vedas.[26] Here the need for the would-be fundamentalist to make a sharp distinction inevitably complicates things, but in the end all it means is that he has to decide where to draw his line. In that respect the situation of a Hindu fundamentalist is not essentially different from that of a Christian or Muslim one: is the Christian to include the Apocrypha, and just which of the alleged sayings of the Prophet, or collections of them, is the Muslim to include as authoritative Ḥadīth? A minimal delimitation of the Hindu canon would inevitably create some tension with traditional ideas, but fundamentalists should be inured to this.

Let us therefore assume that the fundamentalist has successfully delimited his canon, confining it to the Vedas in his chosen sense of the term. The next thing he has to do is to reject the claims to authority of whatever parts of his tradition he has not included in the foundation. This is liable to create a great deal of tension. As we have noted, in addition to *śruti*, traditional Hinduism also accepted the authority of *smṛti*.[27] Thus Manu (the *Manusmṛti*) says of *śruti* and *smṛti* that "these two are indisputable in all matters, for religion arose out of the two of them."[28] Śankara likewise recognizes the authority of *smṛti*.[29] This acceptance naturally carried over into modern times. Thus Roy in his argument against the practice of burning Hindu widows alive turns from the Vedas to *smṛti* as "next in authority to the Vedas."[30] We have already encountered Śraddhā Rām's insistence that "we should accept the commands of the Dharma Shastras without the why and the how of it"[31]—the *dharmaśāstras* being prime examples of *smṛti*. The orthodox assembly in Calcutta resolved that the other *śāstras* were as authentic as Manu.[32] And yet there was an old logic from which a fundamentalist could extrapolate. Mainstream Hinduism considered the *smṛtis* to be

[25] Renou, *Le destin du Véda*, 54–55, 76; Mayeda, *Thousand teachings*, 49; and cf. Rambachan, *Accomplishing the accomplished*, 40–41, 46.

[26] Jordens, *Dayānanda Sarasvatī*, 218.

[27] See 400.

[28] Manu, *Laws*, 17–18 (2.10).

[29] Mayeda, *Thousand teachings*, 48; Rambachan, *Accomplishing the accomplished*, 50.

[30] Nag and Burman, *Raja Rammohun Roy*, 3: 133, quoted in A. Sharma, *Modern Hindu thought*, 27.

[31] See 196.

[32] Jordens, *Dayānanda Sarasvatī*, 218.

authoritative, but not as authoritative as the Vedas. More specifically, their authority was dependent on that of the Vedas. Where *smṛti* agreed with the Vedas, it was to be accepted; where it contradicted the Vedas, it was to be discarded; and where it did neither, one gave it the benefit of the doubt by assuming it to be based on a Vedic text that had gone missing.[33] As one early commentator on Manu wroṭe, "Only the Veda is independent in respect of teaching, since it exists without reference to any other authority. . . . The *dharmaśāstra* takes its root in the Veda."[34] In this set of ideas, it is only the lost-Veda assumption that a fundamentalist has to break with. Once it is established that authority resides exclusively in the Vedas that we possess today, the *smṛtis* and a fortiori all later strata of the tradition no longer count.

If there is no serious formal obstacle to a fundamentalization of Hinduism, the next question is how far the potential has in fact been realized in modern times.

Thinking along the lines sketched above appears sporadically in nineteenth-century India. In Calcutta a heterodox commentator rather tendentiously remarked of Roy that he professed himself a "Vedic Hindu" and that his religious movement was "simply the revival of primitive Hinduism."[35] In Bombay Karsandās Mūljī (d. 1873) published a pamphlet entitled "The religion of the Vedas," in which he maintained that these texts contained the genuine kernel of Aryan religion.[36] In the 1870s the Brahmin reformer Kandukūri Vīreśalingam (d. 1919) in coastal Āndhra was contrasting the purity of thought of the Vedas (including the Upaniṣads) with the gross superstitions found in the *smṛtis* and later works.[37]

But the thinker who pursued this line of thought in the most sustained and systematic way was Dayānand. He was by no means born to it. He acquired the idea in the 1860s from Virjānand (d. 1868), a teacher of grammar in Mathurā with whom he went to study at the age of thirty-

[33] Mayeda, *Thousand teachings*, 48, 66n9, 213–14 no. 8; Rambachan, *Accomplishing the accomplished*, 50 and 142n114; Verpoorten, *Mīmāṃsā literature*, 29; Kane, *History of Dharmaśāstra*, 3: 831–32. The lost-Veda assumption appears already in the *Dharmasūtra* of Āpastamba (probably third or second century BC); for the passage, see Olivelle, *Dharmasūtras*, 22 (1.12.10); for the dating, see xxxiii–xxxiv of the translator's introduction, and for the idea, see xli.

[34] Derrett, *Bhāruci's commentary*, 1:285.1 = 2:430.

[35] Damen, *Crisis and religious renewal*, 30–31.

[36] Jordens, *Dayānanda Sarasvatī*, 129. For another such figure in Bombay in this period, see Conlon, "Polemic process," 15, 19–20.

[37] Leonard and Leonard, "Viresalingam," 160.

six.[38] Virjānand had come to divide Hindu texts into two groups: those that went back to the sages (*ṛṣis*) and were thus authoritative (*ārṣa*), and those that did not and so were lacking in authority (*anārṣa*).[39] At the end of his studies, Virjānand made Dayānand promise to devote his life to the propagation of the books of the sages and the "Vedic religion"[40]—which he did. In the course of it, Dayānand progressively narrowed the canon of authoritative works.[41] Everything outside the Vedic corpus was to be stripped of its authority: the Purāṇas, the epics, even the *Gītā*.[42] He also came to restrict the canon of Vedic revelation to the Vedas proper, excluding even the Brāhmaṇas.[43] In line with this, he greatly increased the number of Vedic quotations in his major work, the *Satyārth Prakāś*, between the first edition of 1875 and the second of 1883.[44] As we have seen, he was also concerned that the Vedas should be available to all, including Śūdras, Untouchables, and women;[45] indeed, he wanted to translate them into Hindi.[46] Here, above all, it is plausible to think that Dayānand was reacting to the Protestant scripturalism of the missionaries. As he once remarked: "Look at the Christians! They are translating the Bible into all languages and they are available for two annas each!"[47] He did indeed have contacts with missionaries and was interested in what European scholars had to say on Vedic matters.[48] But one of his key moves was very much internal to the Hindu tradition: he denied the traditional belief in lost Vedas.[49]

Dayānand was thus a Hindu fundamentalist, if ever there was one. But even at the formal level he was not an entirely convincing one. He showed himself very reluctant to part company with Manu, a text that a consistent Vedic fundamentalist could only classify as noncanonical. Given the iconic status of Manu in the Hindu tradition, it is natural enough that Dayānand should have relied on it before he began to insist on the exclusive authority of the Vedas.[50] But we find him

[38] Jordens, *Dayānanda Sarasvatī*, 32.
[39] Ibid., 36–38.
[40] Ibid., 38–39.
[41] Ibid., 278.
[42] Ibid., 54–55, 70, 278; contrast 58.
[43] Ibid., 55–56, 278.
[44] Ibid., 102, 250.
[45] Ibid., 262; see above, 80.
[46] Ibid., 154.
[47] Ibid., 166, and cf. 279.
[48] See, for example, ibid., 51, 56, 72, 157, 177–78.
[49] Ibid., 56–57, 112.
[50] See ibid., 58, for an early listing of Manu among the "true *Shāstras*."

filling even the second edition of the *Satyārth Prakāś* with quotations from Manu,[51] and he was teaching or recommending the text to native princes in Rajasthan in the last years of his life.[52] He did not treat Manu as infallible,[53] but he leant on it more than seems appropriate for a fallible text. Thus after complaining that the courts of his day were too lenient toward thieves, gamblers, and adulterers, he went on to say that reinstating Manu's Draconian punishments—branding, amputation, and death—would provide an effective deterrent;[54] he does not seem to have concerned himself with the question of the Vedic standing of these punishments.

A comparable formal laxity appears in one of Dayānand's most radical (and least successful) innovations, his attempt to revive *niyoga*, an archaic practice reminiscent of levirate marriage.[55] The main purpose of this procedure in ancient India was to secure a son for a man who had died without leaving one; to this end a temporary sexual union was established between his widow and a male relative, usually a brother of the deceased. As might be expected, the practice was severely restricted: the permission of the elders was necessary, and the couple were to copulate joylessly. Later legal authorities abandoned the institution altogether, often declaring it a *kalivarjya*—a practice lawful in earlier and more virtuous epochs but prohibited in the present degenerate age.[56] Dayānand now sought to revive it as a solution to a quite different problem, that of widows—many of them child brides—who in respectable Hindu families could not remarry; under the influence of the British, this had become a highly contentious issue in nineteenth-century Hindu society. Not only did Dayānand seek to revive the ancient institution for the transparently modern purpose of making life more bearable for widows, he also changed the rules pretty much as he thought fit, even dropping the fundamental requirement that the widow's previous marriage should not have produced a son (though he retained the ancient rule that the new union had to be terminated after

[51] Ibid., 250, 263–64, and cf. 249, 254; for the first edition, see 102, and for the justification he gives there, see 311n11.

[52] Jordens, *Dayānanda Sarasvatī*, 231–32, 235, 239. Likewise, in 1884 one member of the Ārya Samāj referred to "the laws of the greatest law giver, Manu" (K. W. Jones, *Arya Dharm*, 100n15), and in 1891 another published a tract defending Manu against the calumny of the Christian priests (143n69).

[53] Jordens, *Dayānanda Sarasvatī*, 55, 283–84.

[54] Ibid., 124–25 (citing the first edition of the *Satyārth Prakāś*).

[55] Ibid., 117–19. His followers ignored the idea (117, 197).

[56] See the account of the institution in Kane, *History of Dharmaśāstra*, 2: 599–607.

the birth of two sons). Taking such liberties in bridging the gap between one's heritage and the contemporary world is nothing unusual. But to anyone with a background in the history of law in the modern Islamic world, Dayānand's solution looks more like modernism than fundamentalism.

Dayānand's attitude to another nineteenth-century issue, Hindu reconversion, was in a way more flagrant, though less idiosyncratic. Traditional Hindu society as it emerged into modern times had apparently no way of receiving back into the community a Hindu who had converted to another religion and now thought better of it.[57] Against the background of intercommunal competition for numbers in the later nineteenth century, the resulting demographic hemorrhage came to be felt acutely, and the solution that was found was to adapt an old ritual for the removal of pollution (*śuddhi*) to meet the new need. This procedure was used by Dayānand,[58] and in the face of necessity even the orthodox came to accept it.[59] The irony is that there was in fact ancient authority for an appropriate ritual, but Dayānand had failed to notice it.[60]

If Dayānand's credentials as a card-carrying fundamentalist are open to doubt, those of his heirs in the Ārya Samāj are negligible. When the movement was established in Lahore in 1877, its creed was embodied in a list of ten principles, of which the third states that the Veda is "the book of true knowledge" and that it is "the highest duty of all Aryans to study and propagate" it.[61] But the Ārya Samāj was an implausible vehicle of Vedic fundamentalism. Its primary appeal was to the budding English-educated Hindu elite of the Punjab,[62] and the single most

[57] I follow the secondary literature in assuming that there was no current ritual practice of reconversion. But note that in 1676 one of Śivājī's generals, who had converted to Islam on defecting to the Mughals, reconverted to Hinduism with an appropriate ceremony (Laine, *Shivaji*, 38, from Sarkar, *House of Shivaji*, 173).

[58] Jordens, "Reconversion to Hinduism," 216–17; Jordens, *Dayānanda Sarasvatī*, 169–71; K. W. Jones, *Arya Dharm*, 28. But note the sceptical comment of Jaffrelot, "Les (Re) conversions," 75.

[59] For orthodox attitudes, see K. W. Jones, *Arya Dharm*, 303, 309.

[60] Jordens, *Dayānanda Sarasvatī*, 169–70; Kane, *History of Dharmaśāstra*, 2: 385–87 (on the *vrātyastoma* rituals); and compare 389–91 (on a legal text likely to date from the time of the early Muslim invasions). A Muslim source of the tenth century describes a ritual used by the "Brahmins" (*Barāhima*) for the purification of apostates (Maqdisī, *al-Badʾ waʾl-taʾrīkh*, 4: 12.5 = 4: 10; I owe this reference to Patricia Crone).

[61] K. W. Jones, *Arya Dharm*, 37–38, 321; Jordens, *Dayānanda Sarasvatī*, 174–75, 340 (I quote the translation from the Hindi given on this page).

[62] K. W. Jones, *Arya Dharm*, 50.

important thing it had to offer this elite was modern education for their children in institutions where they would not be exposed to the seductions of Christian missionaries.[63] It was not for nothing that the movement named its flagship institution the Dayanand *Anglo*-Vedic College.[64] Had the members of the Ārya Samāj been Muslims, they would undoubtedly have been Islamic modernists or nationalists, not fundamentalists. Indeed a prominent figure closely associated with the Anglo-Vedic College believed that religion was just one of the "outward clothes" around the "inner feeling" of communal loyalty[65]—a view deeply at odds with religious fundamentalism.

Besides the mainstream of the Ārya Samāj, there was also a faction with a markedly different orientation. Here the leading figure was initially Paṇḍit Guru Datta (d. 1890).[66] His eccentricities included devotion to Sanskrit and Vedic studies, hostility to English education, a scheme for educational reform that would have done much to take the "Anglo" out of "Anglo-Vedic," and a belief in the infallibility of Dayānand and his writings.[67] As one scholar puts it: "His religiosity pulled Guru Datta away from the mainstream of the Samaj"[68]—a comment that would sound odd if we thought of those in the mainstream as religious fundamentalists. He also alienated the members of his caste by insisting on giving his parents a funeral conducted on "Vedic principles."[69] In other words he was a plausible heir to Dayānand's fundamentalism, but in the end he was a figure of limited importance even for his own followers. Like the main branch of the movement, they were in the business of education, and to a considerable extent they too found themselves purveying modern science and English to the new generation of the Hindu elite.[70]

The work of these two branches of the movement among the cultural elite does not exhaust its activities. There were also vernacular preachers, and about them it seems we know little.[71] But from what

[63] Ibid., 66, 235; see also Langohr, "Colonial education systems," 175–81.

[64] K. W. Jones, *Arya Dharm*, 68, and cf. 77.

[65] Ibid., 287, 333.

[66] For Guru Datta, see ibid., 50–51, 330. Jones does not really take us inside this wing of the Ārya Samāj.

[67] Ibid., 86, 90, 161, 167.

[68] Ibid., 167.

[69] Ibid., 96–97. His was a Vaiśya caste.

[70] Jordens, *Swāmī Shraddhānanda*, 56–57, 67–68, 70–71. Note also the willingness of Śraddhānand (d. 1926), their leading figure, to find room even for atheists in "the broad lap" of Hindu society (Jaffrelot, *Hindu nationalism*, 83).

[71] K. W. Jones, *Arya Dharm*, 124–25; cf. Jaffrelot, *India's silent revolution*, 189–90 and n19.

we can tell, the Ārya Samāj as a whole, though formed to propagate Dayānand's ideas, was not a fundamentalist movement. To the extent that Dayānand himself was a fundamentalist, he was ill served by his heirs.

In sum, while there was nothing about the form of the Hindu heritage that ruled out the emergence of a Hindu fundamentalism, the phenomenon proved to be stillborn. If we want to know why, we need to turn from form to substance.

3. Substance: Identity

In the Islamic case shifting from the downstream to the upstream option does not entail a change of identity; the identity remains the same, but the intensity and exclusivity of the commitment to it is enhanced. In the Hindu case, by contrast, the shift means abandoning one identity for another, so that Aryans take the place of Hindus.

This change could be regarded as advantageous in two respects. First, it replaces a foreign term with an indigenous one[72]—a problem to which there is no Muslim equivalent. "Hindu," as we have seen, is a Persian loanword; it was only in the later centuries of Muslim rule that it began to be adopted into Indian vernaculars and used by Hindus to refer to themselves. "Aryan," by contrast, is a self-designation as old as the Vedas, indeed older. Second, while neither term is just a religious label, the two differ in their further implications: religion apart, Hindus as native inhabitants of India have only culture and geography in common, whereas Aryans as a people share the more powerful bond of ethnicity, despite the absence of a focus on a single historic polity such as we find in the Islamic case. For both of these reasons, discarding a Hindu identity and adopting an Aryan one might seem like a good idea.

And yet, like much of Dayānand's fundamentalism, this idea went nowhere. It is true that the movement he founded continued to call itself the Ārya Samāj. But, as we have seen, its members soon went back to identifying themselves as Hindu,[73] and outside the movement Aryan identity had little appeal. A major reason for this lies in the peculiar relationship between identity and the caste structure of Indian society.

[72] See 56–57.
[73] See 57.

In this context a Hindu identity was problematic enough under modern political conditions since it invited the ambivalence or hostility of large sections of the population[74]—a serious problem for an identity that aspires to be that of a nation. But if a Hindu identity was socially problematic, an Aryan identity was even worse. In terms of the traditional social hierarchy, "Aryan" is a much more sharply defined term than "Hindu," and its implication would be that only the twice-born belong to the nation. This is not a marketable idea in Indian politics today. Thus, if the Hindu nationalists had been inspired by the legacy of Dayānand to reinvent themselves as Aryan nationalists, their social problem would have been exacerbated, not resolved.

It is also worth noting what fundamentalism would mean for some less salient contrasts between Hindu and Muslim identity. One regards sectarian divisions. Whereas in the Islamic context fundamentalism works to aggravate these divisions by endorsing Sunnism against Shīʿism, in the Hindu case its effect is to delegitimate the sects altogether. In principle this may be benign, but in practice it means that fundamentalism is left without a mainstream to identify with. Another contrast concerns ethnicity. Whereas Islamic solidarity is the clear antithesis of the ethnic identities that divide the Muslim world, Hindu nationalism barely figures in such a role. That is to say, its raison d'être is not to counter Tamil separatism and other ethnic loyalties associated with India's linguistic states but rather to oppose the secular pan-Indian nationalism of Congress. Here fundamentalism would only make things worse, privileging a time when the Aryan homeland was limited to north—or indeed northwestern—India, delegitimizing the larger but later conception of Bhāratavarṣa, and excluding the entire south, just as Hindi chauvinism does. Finally, in the Hindu as opposed to the Islamic context, fundamentalism does not help much with enemies. As we have seen, there is no sharp dichotomy at any stage of the tradition between Hindus and others.[75] Moreover, the enemies of the Aryans who figure in the Vedas, the Dāsas and Paṇis,[76] had long disappeared, and their names were not recycled as classicizing labels for contemporary peoples. At the same time the Vedas can have nothing to say about the two foreign enemies who have mattered most for India in the last thousand years, the Muslims and the Christians. From

[74] See 59–60.
[75] See 60.
[76] Basham, *Wonder that was India*, 32.

this point of view the epoch of the Vedas, unlike that of the Koran, was just too distant in time to be helpful.[77]

On balance, then, Hindu fundamentalism does not have much to offer with regard to identity. Let us now turn to values.

4. Substance: Values

In this section I will follow the same agenda as in the Islamic case, looking in turn at society, warfare, divine jealousy, and the polity. As it happens, this misses what from Dayānand's point of view was the single greatest merit of his fundamentalist program, its monotheism, but we will come to that in the next section.

On the social side the greatest liability of Hinduism was its richly inegalitarian tradition of social stratification. Fundamentalism could help with one aspect of this: if we go back to the Vedas, the familiar caste system disappears, including the Untouchables as a distinct social category.[78] At the same time many of the more invidious traditional rules governing relations between the classes cease to be binding. The social aspect of food pollution is an obvious example: "I can eat the food of any man however humble he may be," or so Dayānand informed a missionary.[79] In these respects an exclusive reliance on the Vedas could be helpful in coming to terms with the modern world. But that still left the hierarchic conception of the four classes intact; indeed, the myth

[77] The Sanskrit *mleccha,* a term meaning "non-Aryan" or "barbarian" that, though not strictly Vedic, appears already in the *Śatapatha Brāhmaṇa,* survives in a vernacular form in Kashmiri with the sense of "non-Hindu" and in Punjabi with the sense of "Moslem, unclean outcaste, wretch" (Turner, *Comparative dictionary,* 599–600 no. 10,389; Turner gives the Punjabi form as *milech*). But I have seen no reference to these survivals in the context of contemporary Indian politics, though curiously the Punjabi usage appears in the report of a court of inquiry into the disturbances that took place on the Pakistani side of the border in 1953. Here some religious leaders calling for an Islamic state were asked how they would regard it were India to treat its Muslims as "*malishes* or *shudras* under the law of Manu"; two had no objection, one declined to answer, and one indicated that he would "march on India and conquer her" (Punjab, *Report of the Court of Inquiry,* 227–29, cited in Nasr, *Mawdudi,* 80–81, 166n6). For an appearance of the term *malech* in a strongly anti-Muslim context in a mid-eighteenth-century Sikh text, see McLeod, *Chaupa Singh Rahit-nama,* 150 §10; McLeod comments that the use of the word to refer to Muslims is normal in traditional Sikh terminology (213n32). See also O'Connell, "Word 'Hindu,' " 342a, on Bengali usage in the sixteenth to eighteenth centuries.

[78] Kane, *History of Dharmaśāstra,* 2: 165–67.

[79] Jordens, *Dayānanda Sarasvatī,* 63, and see 61, 63–64, 121.

describing how they came into existence through a primeval sacrifice is already found in the Ṛg Veda.[80] So, as might be expected, in traditional India breaking with caste was associated with rejecting the Vedas, not returning to them.[81] The best Dayānand could do was to interpret the Vedic account of the sacrifice metaphorically and to claim that the class system was not a religious institution but rather a product of the action of the state; he could then maintain to his own satisfaction that "all men are of equal nature, of the same species, and brothers."[82] Here again, the liberties he takes remind us of the Islamic modernists. The plain fact was that in the Hindu context an honest fundamentalism could not deliver a counterpart to the egalitarianism enshrined in the Islamic tradition. Hence Mawdūdī as an Indian Muslim was happy to point out that in the society established by Islam, everyone "interdined and intermarried freely";[83] by contrast he held that Hinduism, because of its inegalitarian values, was unfit to serve as a philosophy for the integration of the human race.[84]

With regard to warfare, fundamentalism has little to offer in the Hindu context. The later Hindu tradition sees war as something that typically takes place between rival Hindu monarchs,[85] and if we go back to the Vedas matters are not very different. Despite a lingering confrontation with the indigenous inhabitants of the land, the hymns of the Ṛg Veda make frequent references to battles between Aryan tribes, for example the "Battle of the Ten Kings."[86] Nor is there any noteworthy affinity between Vedic and modern warfare. In fact, Dayānand in his discussion of military matters depended on Manu.[87] He also found occasion to denounce Christians and Muslims for their bellicosity: the Christians "have taken war as their *guru-mantra*," while Islam sanctifies war, plunder, and the slaughter of nonbelievers.[88] Fundamentalism would not have helped him here.

Turning to divine jealousy, there is clearly a sense in which we can think of the later Hindu tradition as all-embracing, and more so than Islam. As we saw, medicine belonged within the religious tradition, rather than

[80] See 191–92.
[81] See, for example, Jordens, *Dayānanda Sarasvatī*, 26, on the Lingāyats.
[82] Ibid., 62–63.
[83] Maududi, *Unity*, 20.
[84] Ibid., 9–11.
[85] See 235–36.
[86] Basham, *Wonder that was India*, 32, 34; Kane, *History of Dharmaśāstra*, 3: 63.
[87] Jordens, *Dayānanda Sarasvatī*, 264.
[88] Ibid., 268–69, and see above, 239.

outside it.[89] But if the tradition was all-embracing, its embrace was a loose one, leaving adequate room for the reception of foreign sciences; in that respect the gods of India were not notably jealous. Against this background, what would be the effect of a shift to the upstream option? Dayānand believed that wisdom and science originated in Āryāvarta, whence they spread eastwards and westwards, eventually reaching England;[90] he saw the Vedas as the repository of such scientific truths as the theory of telegraphy.[91] Among other things, this pan-Vedism could easily serve as a cover for unacknowledged Westernization.[92] But in practice Hindu fundamentalism has been too weak a force to have a significant impact here; as we saw, the movement that came out of it, the Ārya Samāj, found its niche educating the children of the Hindu elite in English and modern science, while keeping them safe from Christian missionaries.[93]

On the political side, one of the most attractive values that fundamentalism can recover from the early Islamic heritage is the rejection of despotic and patrimonial forms of state power. There is no counterpart to this in the Hindu heritage. The Vedas are already very much at home with the institution of kingship, however petty;[94] and they are happy to celebrate it—as one king boasts in a hymn preserved in the Ṛg Veda, "I am Indra and Varuṇa, I am the wide and the deep Heaven and Earth, I am the son of Aditi."[95] As we have noted, the power of a king in Vedic times does not seem to have been absolute, being tempered by the presence of assemblies of some kind.[96] But the Islamic focus on a paradigmatic polity seen in antithesis to the normal run of Near Eastern monarchies has no equivalent here. Thus, there was no conception of the Hindu state with adventitiously modern features to be recovered through fundamentalism, and Dayānand made no attempt in this direction. Instead, he based his treatment of politics, as of war, almost exclusively on Manu.[97]

The straightforward conclusion to this survey is that in substantive terms Hindu fundamentalism did not have much to offer. Dayānand's

[89] See 294.

[90] Jordens, *Dayānanda Sarasvatī*, 110.

[91] Ibid., 272. Compare the wise kings who ruled Āryāvarta in its days of glory: they knew the secrets of firearms and airships (124).

[92] See 418.

[93] See 407–8.

[94] Basham, *Wonder that was India*, 33.

[95] Kane, *History of Dharmaśāstra*, 3: 32. Varuṇa, like Indra, is a god, and Aditi is the mother of the gods.

[96] See 340.

[97] Jordens, *Dayānanda Sarasvatī*, 122, 263–64.

return to the Vedas thus tended to be seen by his fellow Hindus as an irrelevance. "What does it matter if Dayanand Saraswati says the Vedas and the Vedas alone are the revelation of God?," as M. G. Rānaḍe (d. 1901) is said to have asked, impatient to move on to more significant aspects of Dayānand's message.[98] To my knowledge only scholars have occupied themselves with attempting to answer his question.

It is in fact a noteworthy feature of the religious movements that have appeared among Hindus in modern times that they are decidedly nonfundamentalist.[99] They tend to be too ecumenical,[100] or too *guru*-centered,[101] or too conservative,[102] or too tied to the medieval Hindu devotional tradition,[103] or too frankly innovative,[104] or even explicitly antiscripturalist.[105] The one exception is Dayānand himself. By contrast, several religious movements among Indian Muslims of the same period have shown marked fundamentalist tendencies.[106] An obvious reading of this contrast would be that differences of heritage matter.

There is, however, another major aspect to the unattractiveness of fundamentalism in the Hindu context, and one that the agenda of this section has tended to obscure. We will take it up in the next section.

5. Fundamentalism, Conservatism, and Modernism

We come now to the affinities—or the lack of them—between fundamentalism, conservatism, and modernism in the Hindu context.

We do not need to look far beneath the surface to see a certain affinity between Dayānand's fundamentalism and modernism. It is not

[98] Kaikini, *Narayen G. Chandavarkar*, 543, quoted in Jordens, *Dayānanda Sarasvatī*, 136.

[99] This is easily seen from the information contained in the useful survey provided in K. W. Jones, *Socio-religious reform movements*, though Jones himself considers all the movements he describes to be fundamentalist (217).

[100] For such movements, see ibid., 30–39, 41–46, 167–79, 186–89.

[101] Ibid., 72–77, 103–6, 125–28, 189–92. One such *guru* was deified during his lifetime, and an idol representing him was worshipped by his followers (128); another instituted the worship of himself and God—but on second thoughts discarded that of God (105). Alongside such claims, those made by and on behalf of the founder of the Aḥmadī sect on the Muslim side of the fence seem modesty itself (116, 200).

[102] Ibid., 77–82, 106–9.

[103] Ibid., 128–31, and perhaps 131–35.

[104] Ibid., 179–82, 203–7.

[105] See ibid., 139–41, for a movement that as a matter of principle rejected any religion claiming to possess "the infallible record of God's revelation to man" (140), and 141–44 for one holding that no book should be revered as "the infallible word of God" (143).

[106] Again, Jones provides a convenient survey (see ibid., 18–25, 53–57, 57–62).

that he was born to be modern; his life was a long journey that began in a thoroughly traditional world. If we seek a turning point, it might be his visit to Calcutta in the early 1870s, when he was persuaded to start covering his nakedness and delivering his message in Hindi.[107] But whatever its medium, the message had some modernist potential to free Hindus of aspects of their heritage that were becoming acutely embarrassing in nineteenth-century India, especially for an elite increasingly schooled in a Western culture.

One major embarrassment was caste. We have already seen how Dayānand sought to break free of the caste system by taking refuge in the Vedas—and how, in fact, this shift could only alleviate the problem, not solve it.[108] And as we have seen at some length in an earlier chapter, caste remains a central problem for the Hindu nationalists.[109]

The other major embarrassment was the richly pagan character of Hinduism, with its polytheistic beliefs and idolatrous practices. Here again, going back to the Vedas offered at least a partial cure. The Vedas are free of idolatry; more precisely, it seems that while there are a couple of Vedic texts that suggest the existence of idols, there are none that explicitly mention them or prescribe their worship.[110] A thoroughgoing Vedic revivalism was thus an effective way to rid oneself of idolatry.[111] This strategy may not have been Dayānand's alone,[112] but it was he who deployed it most insistently. Idol worship, he declared, was absent from the Vedic texts, and the claim that it had once been present in Vedas now lost was false.[113] When he toured the Punjab in 1877–1878, attacking idolatry and insisting on Vedic infallibility, some of those

[107] Jordens, *Dayānanda Sarasvatī*, 82–83. The enthusiasm Dayānand developed for Hindi (224–25, 239–40) anticipated one of the favorite causes of the Hindu nationalists; a true fundamentalist should surely have worked for the restoration of Sanskrit.

[108] See 411–12.

[109] See, for example, 87, 88.

[110] Kane, *History of Dharmaśāstra*, 2: 706–7.

[111] The rejection of idolatry was not new in Hinduism, but earlier instances were not associated with Vedic fundamentalism. Some involved sects that in any case rejected the Brahmins, such as the Lingāyats (Jordens, *Dayānanda Sarasvatī*, 26) and the Sādhs (73); cf. also the Jain sect of the Sthānakavāsīs (13). Other instances were linked to the Vedānta tradition, as with Roy's reformed Hinduism and a movement initiated by a strict Śankarite Vedāntin in Gujarat in 1824 (10). Idols of Śankara himself nevertheless remain widespread among his devotees to this day (see Cenkner, *Tradition of teachers*, 152–53, describing "formidable" Śankara idols at Kāñcī, Purī, and Dvārkā and the practice of keeping Śankara idols in the home).

[112] Cf. Conlon, "Polemic process," 15, for what may be a parallel from the 1850s.

[113] Jordens, *Dayānanda Sarasvatī*, 112 (citing the first edition of the *Satyārth Prakāś*); and cf. 44, 46, 51, 55–56, 68, 90.

he converted to his cause threw their idols into the river or smashed them in the bazaars.[114] In 1879 a preacher belonging to the Ārya Samāj went so far as to claim that in Vedic times idolatry would have been punished.[115] There were, of course, orthodox Hindus who responded vocally and sometimes very ably to these attacks on their traditional religion,[116] but the combination of the low regard in which idols were held in the West and the absence of Vedic sanction for idolatry gave fundamentalist thinking considerable traction here.

But if Vedic fundamentalism could easily dispose of idolatry, it had a harder time eliminating polytheism. Like Dayānand, numerous modern Hindu thinkers have been at pains to show that, however polytheistic the popular beliefs of ordinary Hindus may be today, the elite tradition of their religion is essentially monotheistic. This is by no means a groundless claim, and it helps to explain why Śankara has been so attractive a figure in modern India. He is as monist as anyone could ask for, and at the same time his monism is sufficiently theistic to pass as monotheism;[117] thus he gives us to understand that it is the Lord who reveals the Vedas at the beginning of each cosmic cycle,[118] a reassuringly monotheistic idea. Hence Roy's enthusiasm for Vedānta.[119] Vedānta, of course, presupposes the Vedas, and for Roy "the doctrine of the divine unity" was "firmly maintained" by "our most ancient writings commonly called the Veds."[120] But it was no accident that the "Vedic" foundation to which both Śankara and Roy appealed was over-

[114] K. W. Jones, *Arya Dharm*, 36.

[115] Ibid., 45.

[116] See, for example, ibid., 36–37, 109–10; Jordens, *Dayānanda Sarasvatī*, 218; Dalmia, "Modernity of tradition," 85–89. Tradition has handed down to us both the Vedas and the worship of idols, so by what logic can one accept the authenticity of the one and reject that of the other (87)? For a strikingly similar argument in a Jewish context, see Fishman, "Guarding oral transmission," 46, second displayed quotation (I owe my knowledge of this article to Luke Yarbrough).

[117] For the interchangeability of *brahman* (the absolute) and *īśvara* (the Lord) in Śankara's thought, see Mayeda, *Thousand teachings*, 19. But note that for Śankara initiation into such truths is reserved to Brahmins (90, 97n18, 211, 228n6), leaving no place for the likes of the non-Brahmin Vivekānanda.

[118] Rambachan, *Accomplishing the accomplished*, 37–38. He nonetheless describes them as authorless (*apauruṣeya*).

[119] Damen, *Crisis and religious renewal*, 19, 21; Nag and Burman, *Raja Rammohun Roy*, 2: 59–61, quoted in A. Sharma, *Modern Hindu thought*, 9–11. It was also possible to champion monotheism from a narrowly Vaiṣṇavite perspective, as did one scholar of nineteenth-century Benares: in the most ancient period, he affirmed, the Aryans had just one god, and all them were Vaiṣṇavas (Dalmia, *Nationalization of Hindu traditions*, 417).

[120] Damen, *Crisis and religious renewal*, 23. Roy clearly had in mind the Islamic doctrine of *tawḥīd* (cf. 18, 19, where the title of Roy's Persian work should read *Tuḥfat al-*

whelmingly the Upaniṣads, with their refined musings on the nature of reality. By contrast, the Vedas proper are the textual heritage of an earlier, less sophisticated, and frankly polytheistic culture.[121] A consistent Vedic fundamentalist might therefore have seen it as his mission to launch a movement to replace the gods and goddesses of contemporary Hinduism with those of the Vedas. In practice, however, such a project—whatever its intrinsic charm—would have had no appeal in the modern world. It was certainly the last thing Dayānand wanted. Having proclaimed the sole authority of the Vedas, he hastened to interpret them in such a fashion as to strip out their pervasive polytheistic character. Everybody has to bend scripture, but this, it might be said, is bending it almost completely out of shape. Almost, because there is a statement in the late, speculative stratum of the Ṛg Veda that saves the day: the wise call by manifold names (Indra, Mitra, Varuṇa, Agni, and so forth) what is in reality but one.[122] It was in this vein that Dayānand could argue that the Vedas conveyed pure monotheism, for all that they used many names for God.[123] He thus opened his *Satyārth Prakāś* with the hundred names of God, instantaneously transmuting Vedic polytheism into monotheism.[124] Yet the texture of the Vedic texts remains obstinately polytheistic. Here the Islamic fundamentalist is in a much more comfortable position: for all that God may have 99 names, the Koran is an incontrovertibly monotheist text, and those who read it are not dependent on drastic exegetical intervention to see this. In fact, if monotheism is the name of the game, then Islam trumps trinitarian Christianity; Hinduism, even in the hands of a Vedic fundamentalist, is much harder to bring into line.

Unlike the issue of caste today, these questions of gods and idols no longer matter as much as they did for Dayānand and his contemporaries and thus are not a pressing concern for the Hindu nationalists. The elimination of Muslim and Christian power, combined with the secular drift of global culture, have reduced the prestige of monotheism in India and made it a more comfortable place for pagans. This is brought home by the lack of embarrassment with which a VHP pamphlet on

---

muwaḥḥidīn). Damen describes the Vedic texts recited at Roy's "Society of Friends" as "carefully chosen to further the monotheistic conception" (21–22).

[121] For a survey of the gods of the Ṛg Veda, see Basham, *Wonder that was India*, 233–38.

[122] Zaehner, *Hinduism*, 51–52, citing Ṛg Veda, 1.164.46; cf. Gonda, *Vedic literature*, 136–38, speaking of a "clearly monotheistic tendency" and "tentative monotheism." The passage is cited in Dayanand Saraswati, *Satyarth Prakash*, 11 no. 8.

[123] Jordens, *Dayānanda Sarasvatī*, 89.

[124] Ibid., 104–5, with reference to both editions; and see 271.

Ayodhyā refers to the fourteen pillars of the former temple on which, despite the presence of the mosque, "idols of Hindu gods and goddesses are still alive."[125] It is Western academics, not Hindu nationalists, who cringe at the mention of idols.

One other aspect of Dayānand's affinity with modernism is worth mentioning here: his positive attitude to science.[126] As noted, he believed that modern scientific knowledge is to be found in the Vedas—and indeed originated there.[127] This idea was obviously intended to boost indigenous pride, but it also had a significant modernist implication: if all knowledge is Aryan, what reason could there be for Aryans to reject any of it as alien?

In short, Dayānand's fundamentalism had a significant affinity with modernism, though what it promised in this vein was considerably more than it could deliver.

Things are far less ambivalent when we turn to the extent of the ground shared by fundamentalism and conservatism and the degree of rapport this could create between them.

In contrast to the Islamic case, the foundational texts of Hinduism are well over two thousand years old—and in some cases well over three thousand. Time brings change in the history of any religion, but here we are dealing with an unusually long period. Moreover, the preservation of the Vedas has not been the common enterprise of the society as a whole but rather the task of the Brahmins, who have traditionally withheld them from all but the twice-born. These circumstances have two implications. First, the greater part of Hinduism as Hindus know it disappears in the course of a return to the Vedas.[128] It is not just the devotional cults, the Hindu counterpart of Ṣūfism, that are set to vanish; so too are such widespread and long-standing practices as

[125] Jaffrelot, *Hindu nationalist movement,* 402. The pamphlet is likely to date from 1989.

[126] For Dayānand's attitude to science, see Prakash, *Another reason,* 92–96, especially the quotation, 93–94. Compare the Christian fundamentalists of North America, who, despite their antimodernism, took the idea of science rather seriously (see Marsden, *Fundamentalism and American culture,* especially 55, 57–58). Note, for example, the statement of William Jennings Bryan in the speech he prepared for the trial of John Scopes in Tennessee in 1925: "It is not scientific truth to which Christians object, for true science is classified knowledge, and nothing can therefore be scientific unless it is true" (Hankins, *Evangelicalism and fundamentalism,* 86).

[127] See 413.

[128] As with the Islam of the Muslim Chams, we have here a form of religion that is within sight of instantiating Bevir's idea of a tradition whose contents have been entirely replaced with the passage of time (see xvi).

temple worship and pilgrimage.[129] It is as if Muslim fundamentalism were to delegitimize the mosque and the Ḥajj. Second, to the extent that Vedic rituals survived, they traditionally involved only a minority of the population.[130] Thus, one of the titles that distinguishes the twice-born Hindu from the rest is "he who has the prerogative of performing *Sandhyā*"[131] (that is, the standard daily prayers—the equivalent of the five daily prayers of Islam). Indeed it was often the Brahmins alone who kept Vedic rituals alive.[132] Hence, for most Hindus most of the time, Vedic fundamentalism would mean not a reform of their familiar religious tradition but its outright replacement. So radical a program could be implemented within the sectarian environment of the Ārya Samāj but not in Hindu society at large. "Great sage" though Dayānand may be to the Hindu nationalists,[133] the impact on them of his view that pilgrimage is useless[134] and the Ganges "only water"[135] has been minimal, as it has been for Hindu society at large. The predictable outcome of fundamentalism in the Hindu case has thus been the formation of yet another minor Hindu sect.[136]

All this meant that fundamentalists and conservatives did not have much to share. Moreover, there were aspects of Vedic religion whose revival was likely to be greeted by conservatives with distaste. Thus, one orthodox Tamil Brahmin pointed out that the Atharva Veda contains "many incantations and spells," of which he remarks judiciously that to "put them into practice on the ground of Vedic sanction may not be consistent with Dharma."[137] Likewise, many Hindus are strongly committed to vegetarianism, despite its marginality in the modern world

[129] For the lack of a clear canonical basis for pilgrimage in the Vedas, or even the *dharmaśāstras*, see Bhardwaj, *Hindu places of pilgrimage*, 3–5. The Calcutta council of 1881 nevertheless resolved that pilgrimage was sanctioned by the *śāstras* (Jordens, *Dayānanda Sarasvatī*, 218). For Dayānand's break with all non-Vedic rituals, see ibid., 283.

[130] See the remarks of Renou, *Le destin du Véda*, 19–22.

[131] Stevenson, *Rites of the Twice-born*, 209. There is a view among the jurists that *śūdras* may perform rituals of the twice-born provided they do so without Vedic mantras (Kane, *History of Dharmaśāstra*, 2: 159), but this does not seem to have been a widespread practice.

[132] Jordens, *Dayānanda Sarasvatī*, 8.

[133] "Hail the great sage Dayananda!," as Ritambarā says in the preamble to her speech in Hyderabad (Kakar, *Colors of violence*, 156).

[134] Jordens, *Dayānanda Sarasvatī*, 259. He held that "no place can sanctify, only acts can do so."

[135] Ibid., 64.

[136] Compare the rejection of pilgrimages among such sects as the Lingāyats and the Sādhs (ibid., 26, 73).

[137] Rangaswami Aiyangar, *Hindu view of life*, 64.

at large; yet the Vedas do not share this attitude—the Ṛg Veda makes frequent references to the cooking of beef,[138] and one of the Brāhmaṇas affirms that "meat is the best kind of food."[139] A member of the Ārya Samāj set off a furious controversy within the movement by defending the eating of meat in 1892[140]—and this in a milieu that was supposed to take fundamentalism seriously. It was thus appropriate for a reformer who was making the point that he was not a revivalist to ask rhetorically whether we should revive "the old habits of our people" from the time when the "most sacred of our caste" indulged in the abomination of eating "animal food."[141]

At the same time, there was much in the Hinduism they knew that conservatives would be loath to sacrifice—and not just in matters of ritual and diet. The arch-conservative Karpātrī and his Rām Rājya Pariṣad, founded in 1948, stood for the perpetuation of the caste system; they generously offered Untouchables high-level posts in sanitation departments and resisted a proposed amalgamation with the Jana Sangh and the Hindu Mahāsabhā by objecting to the admission of Untouchables and demanding a party constitution based on the *śāstras*.[142] More broadly, as we have seen, the opposition to the codification of Hindu law was very much the work of conservatives, Karpātrī and others.[143] Yet a form of Hindu law derived directly and exclusively from the Vedas would probably have struck them as just as alien, and they might well have resented the meddling of fundamentalists as much as the meddling of the state. The nonfundamentalist character of the views of the conservative professor in Benares is particularly noteworthy. Though he speaks in one place of the eternal validity of Hindu law,[144] his conception of an immemorial but not unchanging social order would be incompatible with a project of fundamentalist restoration since no one state of Hindu law in the past would exactly fit the present constellation of castes. Indeed, one of his many criticisms of the committee's

[138] Kane, *History of Dharmaśāstra*, 2: 772.

[139] Ibid., 2: 773.

[140] K. W. Jones, *Arya Dharm*, 170.

[141] M. G. Rānaḍe in an address of 1897 (Chintamani, *Indian social reform*, 2d part, 90, quoted in A. Sharma, *Modern Hindu thought*, 160). Rānaḍe was a Konkaṇastha Brahmin (Lederle, *Philosophical trends*, 85).

[142] Rām Rājya Pariṣad, *Election manifesto*, 36; Baxter, *Jana Sangh*, 79, 132. See also Graham, *Hindu nationalism*, 95.

[143] See 286–88.

[144] Deshpande, *Dharma-shastra*, 143.

opportunistic attempts to invoke ancient authority could just as well serve as a critique of fundamentalism: "The Committee is continuously labouring under the misconception that at some time in the remote past there was a simple and uniform code of law for all the Hindus and this golden age was replaced by the present chaos as a result of the unwarranted interferences of incompetent commentators in this simple and uniform scheme."[145]

In sum, the lack of common ground between fundamentalism and conservatism does a lot to explain the general marginality of fundamentalism in the Hindu as opposed to the Islamic case.

The same lack of common ground helps to illuminate the religious politics of the Hindu nationalists, for all that they are neither fundamentalists nor conservatives. Were they fundamentalists, this would undermine those aspects of the Hindu tradition from which they have derived most political benefit: the cow, the Rām cult, and religious occasions (festivals, processions, pilgrimages) that can be relied on to gather large crowds. All three fit much better with a loose use of the downstream option. It is thus no mystery that the approach of the Hindu nationalists to these matters has been anything but fundamentalist, as a brief review will bring home.

With regard to the killing of cows, the Hindu tradition does not speak with one voice, but over time, as we have seen, it has become increasingly hostile to it.[146] The tradition itself is well aware of this shift, as is shown by the fact that the jurists see cow killing as a *kalivarjya*.[147] The change has thus been no secret in modern times. As we saw, an orthodox Tamil Brahmin felt no discomfort in pointing out that the "horror of cow-killing grew with time";[148] and an early Hindu nationalist, himself a meat eater, went so far as to call for the restoration of Vedic animal sacrifices as a way to instill in Hindus the physical courage displayed by Muslims.[149] A consistent fundamentalism would thus tend to weaken, rather than strengthen the prohibition. That the Hindu nationalists at large had no wish to see such a thing happen was dramatized by their reaction in 2002 to a book provocatively entitled *The myth of the holy cow*. The book was an academic study setting

[145] Ibid., 83.
[146] See 64–65.
[147] D. N. Jha, *Holy cow*, 114, 116–19.
[148] See 64.
[149] Jaffrelot, "Politics of processions," 66, and see 65n9.

out the conflict within the tradition, but as its title indicates it was hardly innocent of a desire to cause grief to the Hindu nationalists.[150] In this it succeeded, and the VHP proceeded to denounce it as "sheer blasphemy,"[151] thereby ensuring its publication and sale in the West. The reaction of the Hindu nationalists may not have been good scholarship, but politically it made sense: to admit that the ancient Indians had been cow killers would have taken the wind out of their sails, disrupting the rhetoric of the cow as "the eternal symbol of our culture," protected and worshipped since "immemorial times."[152] To put it more cynically, cow protection was too good an instrument of political mobilization to do without.

The same could be said of the Rām cult. Rām is unknown to the Vedas,[153] but the Hindu nationalists did not concern themselves with this. Instead, they were content to start from the tradition as it had come down to them. Though the Hindu nationalists had been interested in Rām from the outset,[154] the major agitation over the Bābrī Masjid at Ayodhyā began in 1984 and reached its climax with the destruction of the mosque in 1992.[155] They naturally took the view that the mosque occupied the exact site of the birth of the ancient hero and latter-day god, and they proposed to replace it with a temple that over twenty years later has yet to be built.[156] The focus of the agitation was, of course, on Ayodhyā itself, but there was also much theatrical activity elsewhere. In 1984 there was a procession from Bihar to Ayodhyā; its centerpiece was a lorry carrying idols of Rām and his consort Sītā beneath a banner with the slogan "Hail to Mother India!"[157] Then came

[150] In his preface Jha speaks of "the increasing weight of Hindu fundamentalism in our country" (*Holy cow*, xii); his choice of language clearly reflects his dislike of the phenomenon. He is sometimes tendentiously inaccurate. For example, he states that as late as 1874 the "sacrificial killing of cows and buffaloes" was practiced in one part of Rajasthan (120), but the source he cites (125n50) supports this only for buffaloes, not cows.

[151] Eakin, "Holy cow a myth?"

[152] Graham, *Hindu nationalism*, 148, quoting a Jana Sangh manifesto of 1954.

[153] Basham, *Wonder that was India*, 39–40.

[154] Frykenberg, "Hindu fundamentalism," 241. The Hindu Mahāsabhā in 1940 formed a paramilitary group called the Rām Senā (Jaffrelot, *Hindu nationalist movement*, 74). In his account of the fortunes of the major deities of India in the interaction between Hindu nationalism and popular Hinduism, Fuller has helpful comments on the relative merits of the various gods as potential "celestial nationalists" and shows why Rām has tended to outstrip his competitors (Fuller, *Camphor flame*, 263–79, 286), but among gods as among men, no one is perfect.

[155] Jaffrelot, *Hindu nationalist movement*, 363, 455.

[156] For an illustration showing the future temple with the sacred syllable *Om* floating above it, see ibid., 393.

[157] Ibid., 363–64.

1989, the year of the Rām Śilā Pūjans, some 200,000 ceremonies held all over the country to procure bricks; these bricks had their places of origin written on them, and they were transported to Ayodhyā where they were to be used to build (or rebuild) the temple.[158] The next year, 1990, was a bumper year. There was the Rath Yātrā, in which Advani toured India in a vehicle designed to resemble an ancient chariot (*rath*) until arrested in Bihar by the Yādav Chief Minister of the state.[159] There were the local Rām Jyoti Yātrās, torch processions synchronized with the festival of Dīvālī, when houses are illuminated with candles.[160] Finally there were the twenty-two Asthi Kalaś Yātrās, processions that carried the ashes of the martyrs of Ayodhyā from one part of the country to another.[161] In all this the Hindu nationalists drew on Hindu traditions but showed no inhibition about adapting them in flagrantly innovatory ways. For example, Advani's "chariot" during his Rath Yātrā of 1990 was not devised according to specifications found in ancient texts; it was modeled on the chariot of the noble Arjuna as shown in the version of the *Mahābhārata* epic serialized on Indian television in 1988–1990.[162] Another part of the background was that the *Rāmāyaṇa*, essentially in the version of Tulsīdās, had already been broadcast on national television in 1987–1988 and had proved very popular, especially in the north.[163] These films served well as Hindu nationalist propaganda, and Sevā Bhārtī used vans with video equipment to show them in the slums.[164] Likewise, the iconography of Rām changed with his political role, so that he now came to be presented as a muscular warrior; the resulting figure had much in common with the heroes of Hindi popular films.[165] Other sources of novelty would seem to have been Islam and Christianity. At the moment when the foundation stone of the new temple was being laid, all Hindus were to turn toward Ayodhyā[166]—just as Muslims turn toward Mecca in prayer; and one figure in the VHP proposed removing all Muslims from

[158] Ibid., 385–86, 403.

[159] Ibid., 416–19.

[160] Ibid., 419.

[161] Ibid., 422–23.

[162] Jaffrelot, "Politics of processions," 82.

[163] Jaffrelot, *Hindu nationalist movement*, 389–90. The production itself was not a piece of Hindu nationalist propaganda and was marked by elements of political correctness (see Veer, *Religious nationalism*, 178; van der Veer also reports reactions of Indian Muslims to the drama that would not have played well in Saudi Arabia, 177).

[164] Jaffrelot, *India's silent revolution*, 456.

[165] Jaffrelot, *Hindu nationalist movement*, 390–92, 428.

[166] Ibid., 387–88, 400 (noting the Meccan analogy), 403.

Ayodhyā to make it the Hindu Vatican.[167] Mixed in with all this we find occasional elements that relate to an older heritage. During the laying of the foundation, there is mention of a Vedic sacrifice and of a procedure prescribed in the "Hindu scriptures" involving the first five bricks of the 167,063 that had been collected at Ayodhyā.[168] But in the overall context this was eclecticism, not fundamentalism.

Outside the context of Ayodhyā, the Hindu nationalists made similarly creative use of the mass religious events characteristic of contemporary Hinduism. Here, too, they did so without worrying about the Vedic standing of such events. They showed no interest in reviving so spectacular an ancient ritual as the seventeen-day Vājapeya, with its seventeen animal sacrifices, seventeen chariots, seventeen drums, and fee of seventeen hundred cows, seventeen slave girls, seventeen elephants, and the like.[169] Here they parted company with Karpātrī, who despite his general convervatism did promote the revival of large-scale Vedic sacrifices.[170] Needless to say, Karpātrī's initiative went nowhere, whereas the Hindu nationalist adaptation of existing religious practices proved extraordinarily successful. The idea was not entirely new: such choreography was in an older but modern tradition of using public displays of traditional Hindu religiosity—festivals and associated processions—for the purposes of political mobilization. This tradition went back to the late nineteenth century; it was pioneered by Ṭiḷak, who adapted the Gaṇapati festival in Maharashtra for his nationalist purposes, at the same time using it to distance Hindus from Muslims.[171] While it is not entirely clear from the secondary literature just what it was about the Gaṇapati festival that Ṭiḷak changed,[172] the basic idea, as expressed at the time, was simple enough: "Why shouldn't we convert the large religious festivals into mass political rallies?"[173] In Maharashtra these festivals were duly inherited by the

[167] Ibid., 401.

[168] Ibid., 399–400. It is not specified what scriptures are referred to.

[169] Kane, *History of Dharmaśāstra*, 2:1206–12. Rather disappointingly, the chariots have only four horses each, not seventeen.

[170] Lutgendorf, "Interpreting Rāmrāj," 273.

[171] Cashman, *Myth of the Lokamanya*, 77–80, 92; and cf. Jaffrelot, "Politics of processions," 63n3. This anti-Muslim theme was inescapably present in a second festival that Ṭiḷak created in 1896 in commemoration of Śivājī: though he said it was not intended "to alienate or even irritate the Mahommedans," what made Śivājī memorable was precisely the lesson he had taught the Muslims of his day (Cashman, *Myth of the Lokamanya*, 105–6, 107–8).

[172] Note particularly an Italian observer's account of the festival as it was in Bombay in 1885, before Ṭiḷak had taken it up, quoted in Cashman, *Myth of the Lokamanya*, 76.

[173] Ibid., 79.

Shiv Sena.[174] The ritual form on which the Hindu nationalists of the 1980s seized was, however, a cross between the procession and the pilgrimage. The first of their pilgrimages, the Ekātmatā Yātrā, was organized by the VHP in 1983.[175] It involved three long-distance processions; one, for example, made its way from Hardvār to Cape Comorin.[176] All three converged on Nāgpūr before continuing on their assigned routes. They carried and distributed holy water, and were accompanied by a chariot (*rath*) with idols representing the Ganges and Mother India (Bhārat Mātā); what Dayānand would have thought of the holy water and the idols we need not inquire. This new form of political theatre soon became well established, as we have seen in the case of the agitation over the Bābrī Masjid.[177] Thus the Ektā Yātrā of 1991 made its way from Cape Comorin almost to Kashmir in an effort to dramatize the BJP's concern for the territorial integrity of the country; the four Janadeś Yātrās of 1993 converged on Bhopāl to protest against a bill designed to separate religion and politics;[178] and in 1995 ten processions converged on the Āmbeḍkar memorial in Nāgpūr in an unsuccessful effort to rally the Untouchables to the cause.[179] This choreographic style was not a monopoly of the Hindu nationalists,[180] but they used it to the greatest effect. Like Ṭiḷak, they were content to take the Hindu tradition as it came down to them and adapt it to their political needs. For example, they could draw inspiration from a form of pilgrimage in which ascetics would carry holy water from the source of the Ganges to the far south.[181] But in such matters the Hindu nationalists could be shamelessly creative since, unlike Islamists, they

[174] Banerjee, *Warriors in politics*, 118–19.

[175] Jaffrelot, *Hindu nationalist movement*, 360–62.

[176] For Hindu nationalist interest in Cape Comorin, see Beckerlegge, "Saffron and *seva*," 37.

[177] See 422–24.

[178] Jaffrelot, *Hindu nationalist movement*, 450, 487.

[179] Hansen, *Saffron wave*, 227–28.

[180] When the regionalist Telugu Desam was formed in Andra Pradesh in 1982, the film star leader of the new party went around in a van remodelled to look like a chariot and dressed himself in saffron (R. Guha, *India after Gandhi*, 549). At the same time the Yātrā was taken up by practitioners of the politics of caste who likewise shared none of the values of the Hindu nationalists. In 1984 a Dalit party known as the DS-4 organized processions of cyclists that left from five peripheral provinces to converge on Delhi and establish the Bahujan Samāj Party (Jaffrelot, *India's silent revolution*, 395; the DS-4 had in fact organized a smaller cyclist procession in 1983, several months *before* the Ekātmatā Yātrā). Mulāyam Singh Yādav mounted a Krānti Yātrā ("Pilgrimage for revolution") in 1987 (369), and in the winter of 1992–1993 another Yādav politician organized a Maṇḍal Rath Yātrā (366).

[181] As pointed out in Jaffrelot, *Hindu nationalist movement*, 361n97.

showed not the slightest concern for the faithful performance of ancient rituals.[182]

This discussion of the Hindu nationalist use of contemporary religious forms to stage theatric events does in fact suggest something interesting about the Islamic case. Islamism is bad for political theatre.[183] One reason for this is that the Sunnī tradition, particularly when seen through a fundamentalist lens, is poorly equipped with emotive public rituals of the kind that can serve to mobilize a crowd. There are the congregations that gather every week for Friday prayers, and these can be large; there is the annual pilgrimage to Mecca, which can be huge; and there are a handful of other festivals that are celebrated in the course of the year. But the religiosity associated with these occasions is a restrained one, far more so than is the case with comparable Hindu festivals. Of course, the mere existence of large crowds can lead to subversive activity; but in Syria in the summer of 2011, it was when people left the mosque *after* the Friday prayer that the demonstrations started, and here Islamist leaders had no monopoly. A second reason is that the Islamic tradition is a markedly conservative one in matters of ritual. Its allergy to flagrant religious innovation—the uninhibited invention of tradition—means that anyone displaying the creativity of the Hindu nationalists would risk placing themselves beyond the pale of orthodoxy. The Hindu nationalists had no qualms about asking all Hindus to turn toward Ayodhyā,[184] just as they were happy to spread the worship of Mother India, a goddess invented in modern times with no roots in the traditional Hindu pantheon. Sunnī Islamists, by contrast, are precluded from making such moves. Along with the lack of emotive mass rituals in their tradition, this bar to creativity may be one reason why they do not have an impressive record of large-scale mobilization.

[182] An interesting intermediate case is the formation of state Shintō in Meiji Japan. Much of the process has been plausibly described in terms of the invention of tradition (Hardacre, *Shintō*, 4, 8), and subsequently the authorities had no qualms about issuing a handbook entitled "The *new* ceremonies for shrines" (Holtom, *National faith of Japan*, 155n2, my italics). But they seem to have been much less inventive than the Hindu nationalists. The text of the prayers imposed by the state was taken from an early tenth-century source, with such alterations as were deemed necessary "to make them conform more exactly to modern needs" (ibid., 75–76, 159–60, and see 18).

[183] Compare the Protestant antipathy to pilgrimages and processions (in England the reformers outlawed pilgrimages in 1538 and abolished processions in 1547, see Duffy, *Stripping of the altars*, 407, 451).

[184] There are reported to be contemporary Muslim groups that adopt Jerusalem as their direction of prayer (*qiblat al-Quds*, see Almond, *Strong religion*, 52, in a chapter by E. Sivan). Given that Mecca is currently in no credible danger from infidels, whereas Jerusalem is under their control, this is potentially a highly expressive political gesture, but it far exceeds the level of tolerance of religious innovation typically found among Islamists.

In fact, we do not need to go outside Islam to the Hindus for a relevant contrast.[185] The Ṣūfism widely associated with Sunnī Islam generates massive public events. A Ṣūfī festival in Egypt can bring together a million people,[186] far more than any Islamist event has ever attracted in the Sunnī world.[187] Thus the Islamist leaders who came to power in Sarajevo had the political good sense to preside over the annual celebration of the Ajvatovica, the Ṣūfī pilgrimage that is a key symbol of Muslim Bosnia.[188] But this is a very untypical part of the Islamic world, and in general Islamists have been far too hostile to Ṣūfism to make effective use of its political potential.[189] The other form of Islam that lends itself to political theatre is Imāmī Shīʿism, and here the potential has been exploited very effectively, not least in Iran in the course of the Islamic revolution of 1978–1979.[190] The richer resources of the Shīʿite heritage in this regard are surely part of the explanation for the greater success of Shīʿite revolutionaries in mobilizing their masses.[191]

[185] A Catholic contrast worth noting is the annual Carlist event at Montejurra in Navarre in the time of the Franco regime. This gathering first took place in 1939 and was attracting at least forty thousand devotees by the mid-1960s (MacClancy, "Anthropological approach," 300–301; this article was brought to my attention by José Ramón Urquijo Goitia). As might be expected, the event combined religion and politics in large doses (for examples of each, see 300, 315). In the present context it has two significant features. One is that it is rooted in popular Catholicism: "Its basic ceremonial structure derives from the vigorous, nationwide tradition of *romerías*," which are "pilgrimages held by the people of a village, set of villages, or town" (302). The other significant feature takes us closer to much of the Islamic world than does the Hindu case: the Carlists were operating in a politically repressive environment in which Catholicism was in favor but political dissidence was not. Thus, "the only way Carlist leaders could hold mass gatherings that would be tolerated was to frame their events as religious ceremonies" (305).

[186] "The moulids are popular festivals attracting up to a million pilgrims apiece" (Hoffman, *Sufism, mystics*, 18).

[187] Very large crowds of Sunnī Muslims may also be found at the annual gatherings of the Tablīghī Jamāʿat in South Asia, but this pietistic organization has hitherto maintained a studiously apolitical stance (see *EI*^{2}, art "Tablīghī Djamāʿat" (M. Gaborieau)).

[188] Kepel, *Jihad*, 252.

[189] For an interesting exception to the general hostility, see Lauzière, "Post-Islamism." Lauzière comments that Yāsīn's partial rehabilitation of mysticism was politically rewarding since it provided him with an inclusive religious ideology that contributed to making his movement one of the most popular Islamist organizations in Morocco (249).

[190] Khumaynī later sought to extend the theatre to the Ḥajj, with the result that in the decade after the revolution it was quite common for the Iranian pilgrims to engage in noisy political demonstrations against their Saudi hosts (see Goldberg, "Saudi Arabia," 159, 164–65). It is perhaps significant that no comparable effort has been mounted by Sunnī Islamists opposed to the Saudi regime.

[191] There is, however, evidence from Pakistan that to an extent Sunnī Islamists can learn from Shīʿites: the virulently anti-Shīʿite Sipāh-i Ṣaḥāba, who want Shīʿite Muḥarram processions to be banned, themselves emulate Shīʿite devotion to the imams by venerating the Companions of the Prophet with invented rituals (Zaman, *Ulama*, 121–23). Likewise, an example from India shows that Muslims can learn from Hindus: in Hyderabad

Returning to the Hindu case, what is true of the various forms of religious politics at the national level is also true of suttee in the context of Rajasthan. Its politically inflammatory potential has to do with regional religious conservatism; though the custom is indeed ancient, there is a dearth of early support for it in the authoritative Hindu texts.[192] Once again, the effect of fundamentalism would be to undermine it, and those who champion it are not fundamentalists.

All this shows very clearly why fundamentalism would be an inept strategy for the Hindu nationalists. And if we look at even the most religious of the Hindu nationalist organizations, the VHP, it quickly becomes apparent that its concerns are not fundamentalist. One of them has been to produce a minimal version of Hinduism that all sects and creeds can agree on.[193] At the congress of 1966, a subcommittee was set up with a view to simplifying the purification rites, making five principal festivals official, and devising an appropriate ritual code. The subcommittee decided that all Hindus should adopt two rituals: the morning bath (*prātaḥsnāna*) and the ritual remembrance of God (*īśvarasmaraṇa*).[194] At the conference of 1979, the resolutions called for sun worship twice a day (sc. *sandhyā*), the regular use of the written form of the sacred syllable *Om*, and—as we have already seen—the *Gītā* as the sacred book of the Hindus.[195] Here *sandhyā*, for example, is a Vedic ritual that has survived well, while the *Gītā* is not a Vedic text; there is no sign of a fundamentalist logic at work in this quest for a lowest common denominator. Thus, for all the reverence they accord him, the Hindu nationalists are not the heirs of Dayānand. Nor would he have approved of the fact that the VHP is at ease with the idea that there are many gods and many paths to God.[196]

---

the local Muslim party, wanting to counter the processions of the Hindu nationalists, engineered a new procession for a local Ṣūfī shrine (Varshney, *Ethnic conflict*, 182; note the recourse to Ṣūfism).

[192]See Kane, *History of Dharmaśāstra*, 2: 625–35; Brick, "Dharmaśāstric debate," especially 203–4, 221–22.

[193]The attempt to standardize Hinduism goes back to the efforts of the orthodox Bhārat Dharma Mahāmaṇḍala, founded in 1887 (K. W. Jones, *Socio-religious reform movements*, 82). Compare Śraddhānand's proposal for a Catholic Hindu Mandir as opposed to a sectarian Hindu temple (Jaffrelot, *Hindu nationalist movement*, 22).

[194]Jaffrelot, *Hindu nationalist movement*, 200–201. For the morning bath, see Kane, *History of Dharmaśāstra*, 2: 658–59, 661–63 (though the VHP would probably not recommend the recital of the *Puruṣasūkta*).

[195]Jaffrelot, *Hindu nationalist movement*, 348; and see above, 402.

[196]Veer, "Hindu nationalism," 658. Likewise Vivekānanda, who called for "the recognition of one religion throughout the length and breadth of this land," went on to say that "this religion of ours admits of a marvellous variation" and insisted only on "certain common ideas" (*Complete works*, 3: 287–88, mostly quoted in Dixit, "Political and social

In sum, it is not surprising that fundamentalism in the Hindu context has proved to be a one-man show. And even then, it is telling that when Dayānand ventured into politics he should have agitated in an anti-Muslim vein for Hindi and cow protection.[197] Great sage though he may have been, as a politician he looked more like a Hindu nationalist than a Vedic fundamentalist.

6. Conclusion

Despite the occasional appearance of the term "Hindu fundamentalism," there is no such thing in India today. In one way this is surprising. In formal terms, constructing a Hindu fundamentalism is a relatively straightforward project. Though the Vedas have not been venerated by all Hindu sects, they stand out as a plausible foundation: they are widely regarded as the most authoritative texts of the heritage, and their prestige is boosted by their antiquity—not to say eternity. So it is hardly a puzzle that when Dayānand set out to rid Hinduism of its nineteenth-century embarrassments, in a context in which the voices of Protestant missionaries were particularly audible, he proceeded to develop a Vedic fundamentalism. But he himself was not a particularly consistent fundamentalist, and despite the fact that he gave birth to a movement that endures to this day, it soon became clear that his successors were not fundamentalists at all.

The explanation for the failure of Hindu fundamentalism to catch on lies not in the form of the tradition but rather in its substance. In terms of identity, the shift from Hindu to Aryan carried more cost than benefit, and in practice it was soon reversed. In terms of values, Vedic fundamentalism delegitimated only the worst excesses of the Hindu social hierarchy. It also meant a focus on a period in which Hindus fought mainly against each other, and kings ruled without setting any precedent for modern political values. At the same time it enabled Dayānand to dispose of idolatry but left him with the problem of polytheism to smooth over. His affinity with the modernists, clearest in his endorsement of modern science as a Vedic legacy, was matched by the great gulf between him and the religious conservatives: his Vedic fundamentalism

---

dimensions," 300). Unlike the Japanese state in the early Meiji period, the VHP has not made the disastrous mistake of seeking to define the membership of the upper reaches of the pantheon (for the Pantheon Dispute of the 1870s and its consequences, see Hardacre, *Shintō*, 48–51, and cf. 43).

[197] Cf. Jordens, *Dayānanda Sarasvatī*, 290.

would have meant the end of Hinduism as they knew it. It is no marvel that there has not been any other Hindu fundamentalist movement in modern times and that the Hindu nationalists in their opportunism have tended to behave more like conservatives than fundamentalists. They needed the holy cow, the Rām cult, and the mass gatherings with their potential for political theatre. It is not just that they did not stand to gain much from fundamentalism, they also had a lot to lose. One reason for this is quite simply the extreme antiquity of the Vedas: over the course of three millennia, let alone eternity, relevance has a way of dissipating.

CHAPTER 10

Latin American Catholicism and fundamentalism

1. Introduction

It was among Christians that the concept of fundamentalism was born. But the milieu in question was Protestant, not Catholic, and it could well be argued that the notion of a Catholic fundamentalism is a contradiction in terms. Even if it were not, one might reasonably hesitate to apply the term to Liberation Theology. And yet its central value is to an extent reminiscent of fundamentalism, and on the formal side it has a significant if indirect historical link to it. This is not enough to justify calling Liberation Theology fundamentalist, but it does make it worth including in the framework of our comparison.

2. Form

Christianity as such is a religion whose form invites fundamentalization. There is the Bible and there is the rest; all one has to do is to set aside the rest and go back to the Bible. Catholics can make this choice as much as any other Christians. The problem they face, however, is that they thereby cease to be Catholics. A Catholic by definition recognizes the binding character of the continuing authority of the church; a fundamentalist by definition does not. This is one reason for the schismatic outcome of the Reformation in the sixteenth century. In the twentieth century it meant that Liberationists, whatever else they might be, could hardly be both Catholics and fundamentalists.

For a Liberationist, remaining a Catholic carries a certain cost. The Catholic church is a large and powerful organization, shaped around the continuing organizational and doctrinal sovereignty of an ecclesiastical hierarchy headed by the pope.[1] This makes it a seriously constricting

[1] As Keddie points out, Catholicism is "the only major religion with a single doctrinal leader" ("New Religious Politics," 704).

environment for many of its inmates, and by breaking with it they can look to achieve greater freedom of thought and action. But with that step they also forego the manifold advantages of belonging to such an organization—its support, its resources, its networks, its wide acceptance among ordinary people, not to say its brand image (assuming it weathers the child-abuse scandals of the late twentieth and early twenty-first centuries). We do not need to attempt to weigh up these costs and benefits; what matters is that the Liberationists themselves made clear their preference for being dissidents within the church rather than schismatics outside it. As one activist put it, "The hierarchy has meaning to the people. Attacking the hierarchy means losing contact with the people."[2] A well-known Brazilian Liberationist theologian took a similar view, even in the face of an investigation of his orthodoxy mounted by the Vatican: "I prefer to walk with the Church than go it alone with my theology."[3] Or as a dissident priest said of his membership of the Catholic church, "History put me here."[4] This meant that a thoroughgoing fundamentalism would not have been an option for the Liberationists even had they been attracted by the idea.

Our comparative experience, however, is that thoroughgoing fundamentalism is rare. What we should look for is rather a shift in emphasis, and this we can readily identify among the Liberationists of Latin America. Let us take as an example the classic expositions of Liberation Theology published by the Peruvian Gustavo Gutiérrez in 1970–1971 and examine the authorities he cites.

Sure enough, the Bible is by far the most prominent. Moreover, Gutiérrez quotes it without reference to the Catholic exegetical tradition down the ages. More generally, he cites few Catholic authorities from the period between the New Testament and modern times; even such giants as Aquinas (d. 1274) are rarely mentioned.[5] However, the fact that he cites figures from this epoch at all makes it clear that we are not dealing with a doctrinaire fundamentalism, and there is a reference to "the great ecclesial tradition within which every sound theology is located."[6]

This allegiance to the church is considerably more in evidence when we turn to the modern period. Here Gutiérrez often cites recent church documents—papal encyclicals, proceedings of the Second Vatican Coun-

[2] D. H. Levine, *Popular voices*, 84–85.

[3] Sigmund, *Liberation theology*, 159.

[4] Nagle, *Claiming the Virgin*, 67.

[5] For occasional references to Aquinas, see, for example, Gutiérrez, "Notes," 200; Gutiérrez, *Theology of liberation*, 4–5.

[6] Gutiérrez, *Theology of liberation*, xxxv.

cil (1962–1965), and decisions of the council of Latin American bishops held at Medellín in 1968.[7] He does not treat these documents with the same deference as the Bible; he feels comfortable praising their strong points and occasionally lamenting their weak points[8]—the latter something he does not do with Biblical texts. He particularly likes what John XXIII (in office 1958–1963) said about the church being "especially the church of the poor."[9] Overall, it is clear that for Gutiérrez these documents are basically authoritative.

But another noteworthy feature of the way he goes about things is the number of modern authorities he cites who are not Catholic at all—Hegel, Marx, Freud, Sartre, Che Guevara, even Luther.[10] One senses that Gutiérrez regards any major figure in modern intellectual history as fair game, though there are some conspicuous omissions—Adam Smith, for example. All in all, it is evident that in formal terms his fundamentalizing tendency is a soft one.

That leaves the question of the source of this tendency. As we have seen, a major development contemporary with the rise of Liberation Theology in Latin America was the spread of Protestantism.[11] This challenge naturally foregrounded the Bible. As early as 1941 Hurtado was recommending the creation of small groups focused on the Bible to counter the Protestant threat in Chile.[12] Later the lay Catholic religious groups associated with the Liberationists—the new "ecclesial base communities"—felt the need to do the same. In other words, the Catholic church was under pressure to emulate Protestant fundamentalism at a popular level. This turn toward the Bible was not an effortless one for Catholics: people had to be disabused of the idea that the Bible had been written by Protestants and that it was therefore heretical to read it.[13] But the Protestant factor does much to account for the prominence of the Bible in Liberation Theology.

[7] Gutiérrez, "Notes," 201; *Theology of liberation*, 22–23.

[8] See, for example, Gutiérrez, *Theology of liberation*, 23, 99.

[9] Ibid., xxvi, xli, 162 (but cf. 164–65).

[10] For such references, see, for example, Gutiérrez, *Theology of liberation*, 8, 18–21, 30, 32, 52, 56, 93, 101, 112, 125, 138.

[11] See 133–34.

[12] Gill, *Rendering unto Caesar*, 134; and cf. 96 on Catholic distribution of Bibles in Argentina and Brazil in the 1930s.

[13] Ibid., 89, and cf. 93–94. Compare a remark made by a Colombian Catholic who had taken a *cursillo* (a short religious course): those who had not taken the course thought that those who had done so "were not Catholics any more, but had joined some [Protestant] sect" (D. H. Levine, *Popular voices*, 303). Charismatic Catholics making pastoral visits to Catholic homes have likewise been mistaken for Protestants (Chesnut, *Competitive spirits*, 86).

3. Substance

Since Liberation Theology is not about identity, we are concerned here only with values. In assessing what a fundamentalizing emphasis does for the Liberationists, let us follow the usual order. As in the previous section I will give some incidental attention to Protestant fundamentalism, though here more by way of comparison than historical explanation.

On the social front going back to the Bible does something dramatic for Liberation Theology. Its view of the poor is founded directly on scripture, especially the New Testament—and as usual, with no significant recourse to later Catholic exegesis.[14] As we have seen, what made this view of the poor and its scriptural foundations so seductive for the Liberationists was the prestige of Marxism[15] and not the challenge of Protestantism. But the significant point here is that Christian scripture was ready to provide them with the wherewithal to construct their leftist syncretism.

The equivalent foundational texts of Islam and Hinduism would have been much less helpful. In the Islamic case the poor may be at the head of the queue to enter Paradise, but in the meantime they are given no promise that theirs is the kingdom of God.[16] This helps to explain why figures like Mawdūdī and Quṭb displayed no interest in elaborating a theology of liberation with such a focus.[17] Likewise, the strong endorsement of social hierarchy in the Hindu case makes the mainstream tradition, even in its Vedic form, an inhospitable setting for a preference for the poor. And sure enough, movements championing those at the bottom of Hindu society have taken one of two forms: either they are religious movements that have broken with mainstream Hinduism or they are secular movements that do not relate to it.[18] One might perhaps argue that Gandhi's crusade against untouchability was an exception. Indeed, as a member of the elite who identified with the poor and downtrodden, he did have a real spiritual affinity with the Liberationists; in a religious idiom unavailable to them, he averred that if he had to be reborn, it should be as an Untouchable "so that I may share their sorrows, sufferings, and the affronts leveled at them."[19] But his idiosyncratic religiosity was far from mainstream—and in no way fun-

[14] See 199–201, 204–5.
[15] See 353–55.
[16] See 174–76.
[17] See 180–81.
[18] See 76–77, for examples of the former, and 86–87 for a case of the latter.
[19] Quoted in Jordens, *Gandhi's religion*, 104. Again: "Self-realisation I hold to be impossible without service of and identification with the poorest" (242).

damentalist. He relativized Hinduism through his belief that "there is one true and perfect religion, but it becomes many as it passes through the human medium."[20] He ascribed a higher authority to his moral convictions than to the Hindu scriptures, which he considered like all scriptures to be man-made.[21] And while he held that untouchability had no support in the Hindu scriptures,[22] he also affirmed that were he to be persuaded otherwise, he would discard his religion "as I should throw overboard a rotten apple."[23] The Hindu value he did espouse in his political life was nonviolence (*ahiṃsā*),[24] but his deployment of this value in politics was no part of the Hindu tradition.

We come now to what fundamentalism would mean for attitudes to warfare. In a Latin American context in which nonviolence cut no ice and insurrection was the order of the day, a focus on Jesus did not have much to offer the Liberationists. It might have been different if, like the Christian Reconstructionists, they had been prepared to take their inspiration from the Old Testament[25] or if, like the Cristero rebels of western Mexico in the 1920s, they had been comfortable with the later record of Catholic belligerency.[26] But the Jesus of the New Testament gave no support to insurrection. This helps to explain the ambivalence displayed by the Liberationists in this regard, caught as they were between the violence of the Marxists and the pacifism of the Gospels. No such problem confronted violent Islamists.

Our next topic, divine jealousy, need hardly detain us. More than either Islam or Hinduism, it has been the historical lot of Christianity to accommodate itself to legal, intellectual, and political traditions that took shape independently of it—the process so eloquently acknowledged by Augustine.[27] A return to the values of the founder does little to destabilize these accommodations since it was he who advised his followers to render "unto Caesar the things which are Caesar's" (Matt. 22:21; Mark 12:17; Luke 20:25). As far as the Liberationists are concerned, divine jealousy is a nonissue.

[20] Ibid., 154, and see 74, 150, 151, 156. From 1930 on he did not even assert that Hinduism was better than other religions (154). Likewise he came to know the *Gītā* thanks to his contacts with the Theosophists (10, 27) and was a disciple of Tolstoy (14, 31, 34, 62–63).

[21] Ibid., 65–66, 76, 128–29, 133, 145. He did try to read the Vedas but without much success (140).

[22] Ibid., 92, 104.

[23] Ibid., 104, and cf. 103.

[24] Ibid., 222–23, 231–32.

[25] See 305–6, 436–38.

[26] Cf. the Cristero song quoted above, 245.

[27] See 297–98.

Finally, we come to the polity. As we have noted, in their political thought the Liberationists lacked a conception of the Christian state—a gap in their thinking that reflects a gap in the foundations of Christianity.[28] We do not need to elaborate on this here, but it may be worth a digression to see how the same lacuna affects the Protestant fundamentalists of North America. Most Christian fundamentalists in the United States have no conception of what it would mean to set about establishing an intrinsically Christian state. If a Christian fundamentalist is nevertheless determined to construct such a notion, there are only two ways to go: forward into the eschatological future, or back to the pre-Christian Israelite polity of the Old Testament. I will not take up the eschatological option here, but it is worth spending a moment on the Israelite alternative.

Among North American fundamentalists, those who think seriously about the establishment of a Christian state as a political project are the Christian Reconstructionists.[29] They represent a small minority among Christian fundamentalists, "a movement within a movement,"[30] "a tiny fringe."[31] In a manner reminiscent of Sayyid Quṭb, they see "the rejection of God's government for man's government" as a form of apostasy.[32] As God tells Samuel when the Israelite elders express their desire to have a king "like all the nations," "they have not rejected thee, but they have rejected me, that I should not reign over them."[33] Yet even in this fringe milieu there is some hesitation about making a clean break with the existing American polity, and it surfaces in divergent attitudes to the American Constitution. Two of the leading Reconstructionist thinkers are Rousas John Rushdoony (d. 2001) and his estranged son-in-law Gary North.[34] One aspect of Rushdoony's thought that North

[28] See 351.

[29] For a sketch of this school of thought, see English, "Christian Reconstructionism," especially 167–73. I am indebted to Robert Wuthnow for his helpful response to my queries. For a broader comparison of Christian Reconstructionist thought with Muslim fundamentalism, see Al-Azm, "Islamic fundamentalism reconsidered, Part II," 90–97.

[30] Shupe, "Reconstructionist movement," 880.

[31] Wilcox, *Onward Christian soldiers*, 127–28. English states that the movement "experienced its greatest flourish in the late 1980s," but that "as soon as it stepped into the spotlight, its popularity began to plateau and fade" ("Christian Reconstructionism," 169). By contrast, a secularist commentator writing in an alarmist vein sees Reconstructionism as "a little-known political theology that is steadily gaining adherents" and influence (Pottenger, *Reaping the whirlwind*, 208).

[32] Rushdoony, *Institutes of Biblical law*, 34, 797–99.

[33] 1 Samuel 8:7, quoted in Rushdoony, *Institutes of Biblical law*, 797.

[34] English, "Christian Reconstructionism," 167–68. Rushdoony and North never spoke to each other after a clash in 1981.

mercilessly attacks is what he calls Rushdoony's thirty-year defense of the American Constitution as "an implicitly Christian document."[35] By contrast, North himself denounces the Constitution as "anti-Christian,"[36] "an apostate covenant,"[37] a "demonic plan" devised by James Madison;[38] the problem with the document "was and is polytheism,"[39] and its adoration is a popular form of "idol worship."[40] When the nation ratified the Constitution, it broke with its Christian past "by covenanting with a new god, the sovereign People."[41] In the premises of his thinking about a properly Christian political order, North thus stands out as a figure inviting comparison with numerous Islamists; he sounds just like Ẓawāhirī denouncing democracy.[42] By the same token, Christian fundamentalists at large fall well short of this standard. But the substance of what North is proposing would not have much appeal to Islamists. One of its characteristic features is a commitment to reducing the role of the state to a minimum, even in a fully Christian society, whereas for obvious reasons Muslim fundamentalists want their Islamic state to be strong.[43] Thus North speaks of "self-government under God,"[44] just as he looks forward to the eventual emergence of a republic that will be "decentralized, international, theocratic."[45] In other words, the Reconstructionist paradigm is the premonarchic, not to say anarchic,

[35] North, *Political polytheism*, 683. He quotes Rushdoony's claim that to read the Constitution as "the charter for a secular state" is a radical misreading of history and that the Constitution "was designed to *perpetuate* a Christian order" (701, citing Rushdoony, *American system*, 2). For more on such views of the Constitution among Reconstructionists, see Pottenger, *Reaping the whirlwind*, 228–31. For the similar view of the Catholic Jacques Maritain, see his *Man and state*, 183–84, speaking of "this great political Christian document," and cf. his *Christianisme et démocratie*, 37.

[36] North, *Political polytheism*, 681.

[37] Ibid., 691.

[38] Ibid., 696.

[39] Ibid., 701.

[40] Ibid., 655, 702.

[41] Ibid., 654–55.

[42] See 331.

[43] If we go in search of Islamic Reconstructionists championing a decentralized, bottom-up political order, perhaps the only context in which a few are to be found is ninth-century Baṣra (see Crone, "Ninth-century Muslim anarchists," 16–19).

[44] North, *Political polytheism*, 590. Another Reconstructionist writer, Gary DeMar, affirms that Reconstructionists believe in a "minimal state" (North and DeMar, *Christian Reconstruction*, 92), and advocate "a decentralized social order," not "a centralized political order" (94–95).

[45] North, *Political polytheism*, 590, and see English, "Christian Reconstructionism," 172. Likewise, North identifies "the creation of a worldwide theocratic republic" with "the creation of a bottom-up political order" (North, *Political polytheism*, 650) and speaks of "a decentralized, international theocracy" (659).

phase of the Israelite polity. As we have seen, there is good scriptural authority for this choice, but it is also aligned with the prominence of libertarian thinking in the United States and no doubt strongly influenced by it.[46] This is not a style of political thought with much appeal outside North America, either for Islamists or for Liberationists. There is, nevertheless, one significant overlap between the two visions: both Christian Reconstructionists and Islamists focus on a past in which dynastic succession, and the patrimonialism that inevitably goes with it, were conspicuously absent.[47]

What emerges from this discussion is that Liberation Theology, insofar as it can be described as fundamentalist at all, is characterized by a one-track fundamentalism that does not go beyond the preference for the poor.[48]

4. FUNDAMENTALISM, CONSERVATISM, AND MODERNISM

The relationship of Liberation Theology to modernism need hardly detain us: the Liberationists *are* modernists. Insofar as one aspect of their thought can be seen as a return to the foundations, it served the thoroughly modernist purpose of importing into Catholicism what many progressive Latin Americans saw as the leading secular ideology of the day.

The interaction between Liberationists and Catholic conservatives was more conflict prone. Most obviously, they were at different ends of the political spectrum. They also represented very different religious styles. It is true that basic elements of Catholic religious life—such as churches and masses—remained constant, much as in the Muslim, though not the Hindu case. But, as we have seen, the Liberationists had little sympathy for popular religion and no idea how to build on it:[49] so

[46] This is not to say that Christian Reconstructionism is libertarian. Once its vision is realized, the heresy of democracy will have disappeared (cf. English, "Christian Reconstructionism," 172), Christians will have dominion over the entire world, those who refuse to submit will be denied citizenship, religious liberty will be withheld from "the enemies of God" (173), and—particularly striking in an American context—the Biblical laws of slavery will be upheld (178n30).

[47] For this aspect of the Biblical heritage, see Walzer, *In God's shadow*, chap. 4, especially 50–51.

[48] As the Boffs say about the Biblical themes emphasized by Liberation Theology, they "may not be the most *important* themes in the Bible" in themselves, but they are "the most *relevant*" to the poor (Boff and Boff, *Introducing liberation theology*, 33).

[49] See 206.

where the Hindu nationalists knew just what to do with the traditional religious processions of India, those of Latin America were wasted on the Liberationists. They had no kinship with the Cristeros of an earlier epoch, whose insurrection against the irreligion of the Mexican state was a desperate attempt to preserve the kind of traditional Catholicism that the Liberationists despised. Nor did any rapport develop between Liberation Theology and the diffuse but widespread religious conservatism that continues to exist among pious Latin American Catholics.[50]

5. Conclusion

Though Christianity and fundamentalism go well together, Catholicism and fundamentalism are arguably mutually exclusive. What we see in the case of Liberation Theology is in fact no more than the presence of an isolated fundamentalist motif, the privileged role ascribed to the poor. Formally the Liberationists owed it to the Protestants, whose presence explains their focus on the Bible; substantively they derived the idea from the Marxists, with the poor substituting for the proletariat as the agent of revolutionary transformation. But their scripture did not offer the Liberationists any equivalent of the armed violence of the Marxists or their conception of a postrevolutionary political order, nor did it have anything relevant to tell them about identity. That one fundamentalist motif apart, the Liberationists can best be described as modernists—devotees of a modern rather than a jealous god and in sharp conflict with conservatives. Overall, religious fundamentalism has played no more part in politics in Latin America than it has among the Hindus.

[50] For this conservatism, see, for example, Malkin, "Many states in Mexico."

Conclusion to Part Three

It is in the nature of any enduring religion's foundational texts that they were composed a long time ago in a very different environment. Hence, much of what they have to say is likely to be irrelevant to the conditions under which the adherents of the religion currently live, and some of it will be incompatible with them. Thus, for Christian fundamentalists, who see themselves as champions of family values in a morally reprobate America, it is not helpful to have Jesus say this: "If any man come to me, and hate not his father, and mother, and wife, and children, and brethren, and sisters, . . . he cannot be my disciple" (Luke 14:26). Likewise his promise that those who believe will be able to handle snakes and drink poison with impunity (Mark 16:18) seems downright bizarre in the world we live in today. Obvious parallels are the incantations and spells of the Atharva Veda, and what the Koran has to say about beating a recalcitrant wife (Q4:34) or the metamorphosis of humans into monkeys and pigs (Q2:65, 5:60, 7:166). Times change, and as a result such dislocations are inevitable.

This means that for a society under threat from more modern competitors, fundamentalism does not look like a sensible choice. When conservatism isn't working, the obvious alternative is modernism—to become more modern by adopting those aspects of the culture of one's competitors that are reckoned to be the basis of their success. In the past two centuries, outside the Western world, this has meant Westernization. Such an option does not entail an outright rejection of one's past—or at least not of all of it; one can still retain self-esteem by looking back for inspiration to a golden age of one's own, and nationalists do this as a matter of course. But inspiration is not a blueprint; directly or indirectly, the blueprints have come from the West. If we leave aside those populations that were demographically overwhelmed, responses along the lines just sketched are typical of the ways in which non-Western populations have reacted to the Western impact. There was, of course, a great deal of variety to these responses. Societies differed as to how long they clung to conservatism—the Koreans longer than the Japanese—and whether they opted for a democratic or an authoritarian political model—the Indians as against the Chinese. What all these societies nevertheless have in common is that they abandoned conservatism for modernism. Insofar as fundamentalism played a part in their responses at all, it was marginal, as our discussion of India and Latin America has amply illustrated.[1]

For much of the modern history of the Muslim world, and for many Muslims today, as no doubt in the future, things are not very different. It is only in the last few decades that an Islamism with a marked fundamentalist emphasis has emerged as a significant political contender; before that the Muslim world did not seem to diverge very much from the rest of the non-Western world. But the phenomenon is now sufficiently salient among a variety of Muslim populations across the globe to constitute a large and conspicuous exception to the normal pattern. As such, it demands explanation, and as usual there is more than one explanatory question to ask. The issue this book has been concerned with is why the divergent pattern should have emerged in the Muslim world and not among other non-Western populations. Here, as I hope to have shown, an examination of the character of the Islamic heritage can contribute materially to an answer.

Just as religious heritages differ, so also do the effects that fundamentalist highlighting has on them. The chapters in this section have shown the implications of these two factors in combination. In the Hindu case fundamentalizing one's heritage has little to offer its modern heirs, and in the Catholic case it provides only a single asset. In the Islamic case, by contrast, it delivers several assets. Of course, fundamentalism also has its downsides, as we have seen in each case; but the most serious one in the Islamic case—the force of divine jealousy—is internally mitigated,[2] and it does not appear to outweigh the attractions of fundamentalism. The key finding of this part of the book is thus that in the context of modern politics there is more to be recovered from the foundations of Islam than from those of Hinduism or Christianity—and this in terms of both identity and values.

Another way to put this is to say that the overlap between fundamentalism and modernism is greatest in the Islamic case. But, as we have seen, this affinity is reinforced by another overlap, that between fundamentalism and conservatism. Here, too, a tendency to fundamentalism works best in the Islamic context.

[1] One might see the imperial loyalism of the Meiji Restoration as a kind of fundamentalism, but the program of the new regime was unashamedly modernist.

[2] See 391–92.

Afterword

1. Looking back

Half a century ago it was widely thought that in the modern world religion was doomed to fade away. This was a bold conjecture but by no means a silly one. With regard to Western Europe, after all, it continues to hold up rather well. Thus in Britain, historically a champion of embattled Protestantism, a book published a few years ago announced the death of Christianity[1]—an exaggeration, perhaps, but not a gross one. In Spain, historically a bastion of intransigent Catholicism, Christianity is unquestionably alive, but it is only a shadow of its former self.[2] In both countries true believers are still to be found, but it is significant that many of them belong to immigrant populations from Muslim countries. With regard to the rest of the world, the conjecture had at least a certain logic going for it: given the enormous influence that Western Europe has exerted as the pioneer of modernity, it did not seem unreasonable to expect it to serve as the world's model in relation to the future of religion.

Half a century later it is clear that, as a generalization about humanity at large, the conjecture is false. The massive Islamic revival is in itself enough to refute it. But is it Western Europe or the Islamic world that constitutes the exception to wider global trends? If our mistake then was to be overly Eurocentric, are we now being overly Islamocentric?[3] Since our central concern in this book is precisely with the Islamic side of things, we should make some effort to counteract any distortion of perspective this is likely to induce. Let us therefore

[1] C. G. Brown, *Death of Christian Britain*. The decline of traditional "church Christianity" does not, however, mean the death of religiosity (see Woodhead, "Introduction," 5–8).

[2] Loewenberg, "Spaniards lose their religion." In marked contrast to Latin America, only 2 percent of the population declare themselves adherents of non-Catholic confessions (Bedoya, "El 'tren,' " 34; this article was sent to me by Maribel Fierro).

[3] Paying too much attention to Islam may be behind a thesis of Samuel Huntington's: "In the modern world, religion is a central, perhaps *the* central, force that motivates and mobilizes people" (Huntington, *Clash of civilizations*, 66, his italics).

break up the complex phenomenon of the Islamic revival into more manageable components and look for non-Islamic parallels for each in turn.

The first of these is also the most widespread: an increase in religiosity whereby large numbers of people "get religion," for the most part without any involvement in political activism or militancy. A conspicuous example is the activity of the Tablīghī Jamāʿat, including the massive pietistic gatherings that it hosts annually in South Asia.[4] Although we have not attended directly to this phenomenon, it has always been present in the background to our discussion of modern Islam.[5] If we go in search of a parallel development outside the Muslim world, we have no trouble finding one: the rise of Pentecostalism and Charismatic Catholicism in Latin America and elsewhere.[6] But this does not mean that the increase in religiosity is as great in Latin America as it has been in the Islamic world; it is telling that the religiously indifferent are not on the defensive in Latin America as they are in Muslim countries. Nor does the parallel imply that levels of religiosity have been rising everywhere outside Western Europe.[7] There seems to be no indication

[4] See 427n187.

[5] Something that tends to call in question the reality or distinctiveness of the Islamic revival is Fish's finding that in the early twenty-first century "Muslims are not dramatically more religious than non-Muslims and are only slightly more religious—if even that—than Christians" (*Are Muslims distinctive?*, 42, and see 24–26, 45). There is, however, a crucial distinction here. In the World Values Survey used by Fish, respondents are asked to state whether they belong to a religious denomination, and if so, which one (21). We may call those who name a denomination in this way *professed* members of the religious community in question. Others, however, may declare no denomination, despite belonging to populations that were historically part of that community (22–23). For Fish respondents of the second kind do not count as members of the community though, as he remarks of the Christian case, other scholars might regard them as nominal Christians; here we may call them *historic* members of the community. Including or excluding historic members makes very little difference on the Muslim side of the fence (22, bar what looks like an error in the case of Pakistan, see 347n13). But it can make a major difference on the Christian side; in the case of Britain, for example, nearly half the population is at stake (23). Comparing professed Muslims with professed Christians is a meaningful comparison, as is one that includes historic Muslims and historic Christians; but the two comparisons do not mean the same thing, and the second would very likely show Muslims as considerably more religious than Christians.

[6] For Latin America, see 133–34, 210–11. The regions in which Pentecostalism has been most successful—Latin America and parts of sub-Saharan Africa—are also the regions outside the West where the religious market is most free; this suggests that the potential for the spread of Pentecostalism elsewhere could be considerable. For the distinctiveness of these two regions, see Fox, *World survey*, 249, 290, and cf. 287.

[7] As this paragraph makes clear, I have reservations about the idea that there has been a "worldwide resurgence of religion" (Berger, "Desecularization," 11) or a "global religion rebellion" (Juergensmeyer, *Global rebellion*, 249). Casanova, too, speaks of "the

that non-Muslims in India are more religious than they used to be, and there has been no largescale religious revival in East Asia—with the obvious caveat that we do not know what would happen in the unlikely event that the Chinese regime were to extend its market reforms to religion.[8] Moreover, two significant regions seem to be moving toward rather than away from the Western European pattern. One is Eastern Europe, where the young are markedly less religious than their elders.[9] The other, perhaps more surprising, is the United States, where the last two decades have seen a significant increase in the proportion of people declaring that they have no religious affiliation.[10]

The second component of the Islamic revival is the expansion of the role of Islam in politics. This too, as we have seen, is complex, but we can divide it into three parts: the politics of Muslim identity, the politics of Islamic social values, and the politics of the Islamic state.

We can expect to find some version of the politics of Muslim identity in almost any Islamic society. But the phenomenon assumed a particularly dramatic form a couple of decades before the onset of the Islamic revival, in the process that led to the partition of India and the formation of Pakistan under the aegis of the Muslim League. As we have seen, we do not have to look far to find a major non-Muslim parallel

---

worldwide character of the contemporary religious revival across all civilizations" but adds that "it is not religion in the abstract which is returning, nor is it returning everywhere" (Casanova, *Public religions*, 227).

[8] One analyst points out that fewer people in China belong to a religion than in any other country covered by the World Values Survey (F. Yang, *Religion in China*, 129). He estimates that there may be about 100 million people in the "red market" (the officially approved sector) and between 100 million and 200 million in the "black market" (the officially banned sector), leaving about a billion people to be accounted for. Most of these latter do not identify with a religion, but most nonetheless hold some kind of religious beliefs or engage in some degree of religious practice (118–19). From this he rightly or wrongly infers the existence of "a huge gray market with hundreds of millions of potential religious consumers" (120).

[9] See Norris and Inglehart, *Sacred and secular*, 120, reporting "a clear overall decline in all indicators of religiosity across successive birth cohorts" (with graphs for individual countries, 121–22). The data are for 1990–2001.

[10] See ibid., 93, and for a discussion incorporating the results of a survey of 2012, Pew Forum, *"Nones" on the rise*. The proportion of the unaffiliated, which was less than 10 percent from the early 1970s to the early 1990s, is now nearly 20 percent, and significantly for the future it rises to 32 percent for those aged 18 to 29; on the other hand, the proportion of Americans who say that religion is very important in their lives is still around 60 percent, about three times as high as in Western Europe. A similar but smaller rise in the percentage of the population claiming no religious affiliation—or professing outright unbelief—has also been reported in Brazil and elsewhere in Latin America (Romero, "Revitalizing Catholicism").

to this organization: its obvious counterpart is the Hindu nationalist movement.[11] But, that said, we should note that Hindu nationalism is an unusual phenomenon in the non-Muslim world.[12]

The politics of Islamic social values are also widespread in the Islamic world. This is the kind of political activity in which Islamists seek to impose their religious values on their fellow believers, whether by direct action or by gaining control of the state apparatus. Here, too, it is not hard to find a non-Muslim parallel: the Christian Right in the United States is an obvious case in point, despite a conspicuous difference in attitude toward female displays of naked hair. But again, non-Muslim parallels do not grow on trees. There is no comparable phenomenon in Latin America today,[13] just as there is none that I am aware of in the Orthodox Christian countries of Eastern Europe or the Buddhist countries of Asia.[14]

When we turn to the politics of the Islamic state, it ceases to be possible to find significant parallels outside the Islamic world. In the United States, as we have seen, only a small group on the fringes of the Christian Right aspires to replace the existing republic with an intrinsically Christian political order, one to be based on that of premonarchic Israel.[15] To my knowledge these Christian Reconstructionists have no counterpart in Latin America or elsewhere in the Christian world.[16]

The third and final component of the Islamic revival is the rise of jihadism. The point is not just that jihadi organizations engage in armed combat to advance the cause of their religion or co-religionists but that they do so in fulfilment of a duty that is part and parcel of their religious heritage. Here we do have a parallel ready to hand, namely the

[11] See 117–18.

[12] Israel is an obvious place to look for parallels on a much smaller scale. But the mainstream Zionist movement is too secular, and the National Religious Party too Orthodox, to fit the bill.

[13] For an older parallel, the attempt of the Ecuadorian president Gabriel García Moreno (d. 1875) to stamp out drunkenness and extramarital sex, see Henderson, *Gabriel García Moreno*, 171–74.

[14] The religious parties in Israel—the National Religious Party and the Ḥaredi parties—do offer parallels, albeit on a small scale. They seek to impose their social values by participating in the existing political system through coalition building (for a brief account see Arian, *Politics in Israel*, 151–53). At the same time groups sharing these values engage in acts of violence to promote their aims (Ben-Yehuda, *Theocratic democracy*, 86, 92, 93–96, 99).

[15] See 436–38.

[16] Are there Israeli parallels? Ben-Yehuda speaks of some of the groups whose violence he catalogs as intending "to seize control of the country" and "create a Jewish theocracy" (*Theocratic democracy*, 86), but he does not give any details of this project and says nothing about its relationship to the Judaic political heritage.

militancy of the Sikhs.[17] But if we seek further non-Muslim parallels in the modern world we are likely to be disappointed.[18]

What we have seen can thus be summed up in two main points. The first is that for each feature of the Islamic revival identified above we can find a non-Muslim parallel. In other words, no one feature of the revival is unique. The second point is that in assembling a full array of parallels we were obliged to enlist a number of different non-Muslim movements: Pentecostalism, Hindu nationalism, the mainstream Christian Right, its Christian Reconstructionist fringe, and Sikhism. In other words, the *combination* of features making up the Islamic revival as a whole is indeed unique.[19] A further point is worth adding. While the Christian movements in this list emerged far from any Islamic influence, this is not true of the two Indian movements. Both militant Sikhism and Hindu nationalism took shape in the shadow of Islam, and both were clearly in the business of emulating Muslims. In short, the Islamic revival may be no more representative of a global trend than the decline of Christianity in Western Europe. It too is something rather distinctive.

In the course of this study I have sought to explain this distinctiveness by exploring the relevant aspects of the Islamic tradition, looking at them one by one as potential assets or liabilities in the context of modern politics and noting the parallels or lack of them in our other two cases. At this point it may be worth returning to these findings in the light of a couple of features that our three cases have in common.

The first feature, hitherto for the most part left implicit, is that all three concern Third-World populations, which is to say populations that by definition are not doing well in the global rat race, a competition in which wealth, power, and prestige are disproportionately located in the First World.[20] This predicament is both distressing and

[17] See 237–39.

[18] It is not clear to me how far Jewish extremists who engage in terrorism against Palestinians have an equivalent of the doctrine of jihad (Ben-Yehuda, *Theocratic democracy*, 89–91, 97–98).

[19] There is another way to make what is essentially the same point. Hegghammer sets out a useful typology of Islamist activism in the form of a matrix, distinguishing five rationales on the vertical axis (state-oriented, nation-oriented, *Umma*-oriented, morality-oriented, and sectarian activisms) and two forms on the horizontal axis (nonviolent and violent activisms), making ten distinct manifestations in all (Hegghammer, "Jihadi-Salafis," 259; also in his *Jihad in Saudi Arabia*, 6). What is unusual about the Muslim world is that all these different activist manifestations should be found under a single aegis—and what is more a religious one.

[20] The term "Third World" has become somewhat anachronistic since the disappearance of most of the Second World, but this disappearance has also made the Third-World predicament more acute through the diminution of options for alliance and acculturation.

confusing for such populations, including almost all Muslim ones, whatever the variety of their local circumstances; it generates antithetical needs on two fronts. One is the external front. On one level this front calls for a posture of defiance. Irrespective of how far the predicament of the Third World is the fault of the First World, it is assured that Third-World populations will often see it that way, creating a rich vein of resentment that cries out for articulation. This can take the form of graffiti like "Gringos hijos de putas,"[21] or of altogether more sophisticated ideological constructions. Yet on another level, Third-World populations frequently have little choice but to cooperate with those of the First World if they are not to incur heavy costs; like the good citizens of the Morro da Conceição, they need the rich and powerful to be their friends and do them favors.[22] The other front is internal. Here, on the one hand there is the need to conserve an indigenous heritage against the tide of Western culture that has deluged the globe, if only because loss of heritage means loss of identity. Yet on the other hand there is a need for large-scale acculturation through the adoption of the culture and institutions of the modern West, if only because they tend to work better than their indigenous counterparts. How, then, is a Third-World population to position itself? Defiance and conservatism fit together very well; the only problem is that this combination has proved a recipe for failure in the modern world, a fact that was already painfully obvious in the nineteenth century.[23] Cooperation and acculturation likewise go well together, but success with this combination has tended to be limited to small and unusual countries like Singapore and Taiwan. By contrast, cooperation and conservatism are not a good fit; they can be compatible as in Oman before 1970—and to an extent in Saudi Arabia today—but in the long run they do not provide a sustainable option. A better bet is combining defiance with acculturation in the form of emulation, a process that involves learning from one's competitors the better to compete with them; but this is inherently tense. The bottom line is that there is no comfortable resolution between the antithetical demands of the Third-World predicament and no coherent way to give them ideological articulation as a whole.

Large Muslim populations find themselves in this predicament, and the result, a recent study suggests, is not surprisingly that they are con-

[21] See 132.
[22] Cf. 209.
[23] Cf. 440.

flicted: "Most Muslims endorse both Islamist and liberal principles."[24] On the one hand they want to defy the West, evict American troops from Muslim countries,[25] and preserve their Islamic culture by keeping Western values out of the Islamic world.[26] And on the other hand they strongly favor such Western values as democracy, freedom of religion, freedom of expression, and a world order constrained by international law;[27] in this vein they would like to see the West—more particularly the United States—live up to its values rather than simply go away.[28] Of course, Muslims who do not want to be mixed up do not have to be: some achieve ideological coherence as pro-Western secularists; rather more do so as anti-Western Islamists. But many, perhaps most, are somewhere in between, and in typical human fashion they cope by muddling through. Against this background the Islamic heritage provides resources for a considerable—and antithetical—range of stances.[29]

At one end of the spectrum, the heritage is easily invoked to justify rejectionist stances that may be deeply at odds with many features of the modern world. One can insist that there is no valid political identity other than that of the Muslim community, thereby committing oneself to geopolitical overreach, a host of quarrels with regional ethnic identities, and bad relations with numerous non-Muslim populations, not to mention heterodox Muslim ones. One can complement this by requiring the reestablishment of the caliphate, thereby compounding the geopolitical overreach, staking success on an unsustainable fusion of religion and polity, and very likely breaking with the current global consensus in favor of democracy. One can set about realizing these political goals by invoking the militancy of the heritage to unleash mayhem on non-Muslims, heterodox Muslims, and large numbers of mainstream Muslims. One can turn divine jealousy against modern

[24] Kull, *Feeling betrayed*, 148. Cf. his references to an "inner clash of civilizations" (27) and to other tensions within Muslim views (101, 103, 109, 115, 128–36, 154, 156–58, 174, 181–82). The book is based on a range of opinion polls, combined with the use of focus groups.

[25] Ibid., 117.

[26] Ibid., 34.

[27] Ibid., 148–51, 173–74, 175–76, 182–89. Opinion is divided as to whether or not democracy should take a form unique to Islam (154).

[28] Ibid., 36–41. The resulting sense of having been let down by America gives the book its title.

[29] For a rigorous assessment of these resources with regard to one particular issue, the relationship of Muslims living in liberal non-Muslim countries to their host societies, see March, *Islam and liberal citizenship*.

education and polio vaccination, with spectacular recourse to violence in both cases,[30] and one can quote God's law to justify the enthusiastic implementation of what by modern standards are rated cruel and unusual punishments. And, of course, one can seek in it sanction for the treatment of women in ways that by the same standards are liable to appear as grossly inequitable, for example by denying them the right to drive, or even to receive an education.[31] At the present day this kind of rejectionism is most dramatically manifested in parts of the Islamic world like northern Nigeria and the tribal areas of Pakistan, but it is by no means confined to them. All this is strikingly high on defiance and cultural conservation and correspondingly low on cooperation and—if we leave aside military technology—acculturation.

At the other end of the spectrum, it is possible to draw on the heritage in a way that, without being defeatist or collaborationist, does not threaten to isolate Muslims from what Quṭb called the "caravan of mankind."[32] In other words, Islamism in this vein is an Islamic way of being modern, as opposed to an Islamic way of rejecting modernity. In comparison to the rejectionist stances, this means downplaying or ignoring some elements of the religious heritage and highlighting others. Thus, such Islamism may value the transnational bonds of the Muslim community and its social inclusiveness without insisting on giving it a monopoly of political identity. It may set great store by a role for Islam in politics without committing itself to the restoration of the caliphate or the rejection of democracy. It may seek to neutralize the license accorded by the heritage to militancy and to exploit mechanisms in the heritage that make possible irenic relations with non-Muslims.[33] It may take advantage of the fact that the tradition does not claim to

[30] For the first, see Williams and Guttschuss, *Spiraling violence*, 32, 57, on the activities of Boko Haram in northern Nigeria; for the second, see, for example, Walsh and McNeil, "Gunmen in Pakistan," and McNeil, "Gunmen kill workers."

[31] The violence directed against female education by the Pakistani Ṭālibān reached a climax with their attempt to kill the schoolgirl Malāla Yūsufzai on October 9, 2012. The Afghan Ṭālibān, by contrast, have indicated a certain softening in this regard (Crews, "Taliban and nationalist militancy," 368). In both countries polls of 2009 show overwhelming majorities supporting education for girls or denying that the Sharīʿa forbids it (Kull, *Feeling betrayed*, 159–60, 180).

[32] See 267.

[33] Note, for example, the view expressed by the apparently repentant Sayyid Imām that entering a Western country with a visa, even a forged one, and then attacking it constitutes breaching a safety agreement (*amān*, see Ashour, "Post-jihadism," 140–41; also Lahoud, "Jihadi recantations," 145). In juristic terms such a view is mainstream (March, *Islam and liberal citizenship*, 183–89).

be all-embracing but instead creates a space for "ordinary matters."[34] It may distance itself from the more unpalatable features of Islamic criminal law. It may tone down the unequal status of women and their exclusion from the public sphere. Not least, it can energetically exploit the availability within the tradition of indigenous versions of some of the more attractive Western values: the affirmation of the equality of free adult males and more generally what I have called the protorepublican values of Islam. This in turn makes possible the appropriation of these values without recourse to the indignity of borrowing them from foreigners—instead of imitating infidels, Muslims have only to be true to themselves.[35] Much of this could pass for a loose description of the contemporary Muslim Brothers.[36] It is markedly higher on cooperation and acculturation and correspondingly lower on defiance and cultural conservation. It is not, however, to be mistaken for a philo-Western liberalism in the style of Sir Sayyid Aḥmad Khān; for that we would have to go beyond the Islamist spectrum altogether.

Taking both ends of the spectrum together, not to mention everything in between, it is evident that the Islamic heritage engages the predicament of Third-World populations on a broad front, providing resources that can be used for thinking, feeling, and talking about it. Moreover, we have here a case of the whole being greater than the sum of its parts: the fact that the same ancient religion can provide all these resources as a package adds to its potential political salience. But, of course, no heritage speaks to its followers with one voice—Manichaeism, which perhaps came closest to monophony, is extinct—and the ensuing polyphony, not to say cacophony, is particularly evident

[34]For Ibn Khaldūn's notion of an "ordinary matter" see 252. But note the much greater flexibility of the Japanese heritage in this respect: the fact that the Japanese could see a large, central, and accredited part of their culture as an import from China facilitated its replacement with equally large doses of Western culture in the later nineteenth century. The category of alien wisdom thus has a much larger and more secure place in Japanese than in Islamic culture, and because it included law, there is no Japanese equivalent to the project of a restoration of the Sharīʿa.

[35]Such thinking is, of course, no monopoly of Islamists. At the annual conference of the Conservative Party in Manchester on October 5, 2011, the British Prime Minister, David Cameron, admonished those who had pointed to India, China, and Brazil as economic models for Britain: "We need to become more like us. The real us. Hardworking, pioneering, independent, creative, adaptable, optimistic, can-do" (Burns, "British leader pushes"). The "real us," it happily turns out, have all the virtues of Indian, Chinese, and Brazilian entrepreneurs without the stigma of being foreign; all we have to do is be true to ourselves.

[36]Cf. M. Lynch, "Islam divided," 167. This paper provides a helpful survey of the various local manifestations of the Muslim Brothers today.

in the Islamic case. A position based on one element in the heritage can always be subverted by appeal to another. Thus, Indian Muslims who disliked the reformist ideas of Sayyid Aḥmad Khān had no problem articulating their distaste in vividly Islamic terms, with the result that, as fast as he was trying to get Islam off the hook of archaism, others were hard at work making sure it stayed there.[37] There is, indeed, a certain asymmetry here: often the rejectionists can launch immediate appeals to the more emotive elements of the heritage, while those looking for accommodation have to make do with a cerebral consequentialism.[38] But this is not always so: the protorepublican values of the heritage are a case in point.[39] They are also an example of the fact that many of the effects we have noted are enhanced by a fundamentalist recourse to the heritage in its earliest form. In addition, the plausibility of the fundamentalist option is enhanced by the fact that it can overlap significantly with both modernism and conservatism.

How does all this compare with our Hindu and Catholic cases? On the Hindu side the most obvious point is that the heritage has far less to contribute to modern political ideology. Thus, it offers only a weak political identity that is unattractive to a large part of the population. It does not back up this identity with support for militancy against outsiders. It has no interest in the idea of a single state ruling all Hindus. It comes with a social vision that is a nonstarter under all but the most repressive forms of modern politics (which is why the attempt of the Rām Rājya Pariṣad to incorporate the perpetuation of untouchability into its formal political program was merely comical, despite the fact that the social legacy of untouchability in modern India is a serious matter). It lacks values that resonate with those of the modern West, the only political model it purveys being a celebration of monarchy that under modern conditions is as irrelevant as its social vision. At the same time, the effect of fundamentalism is on balance to make things worse rather than better, not least by opening up a great gulf between fundamentalists and conservatives. None of this is to deny that India's Hindu past is

[37] Baljon, *Reforms and religious ideas*, chap. 5. Admittedly he might have done better if he had confined himself to social and educational reform and left matters of doctrine to the traditional scholars.

[38] The ways in which repentant jihadis justify their repentance provide telling examples of this (see Ashour, "Post-jihadism," 137, 139).

[39] So also is the question put to Ẓawāhirī in an online forum in 2008: "And what is it that makes legitimate the spilling of the blood of even one Muslim?" (Hafez, "*Takfir* and violence," 26; for the relevant saying of the Prophet, see 35, and for the consequentialist arguments with which jihadis are obliged to respond to such questions, see 35–38).

of consequence for what the country is today, sometimes in unexpected ways. But as far as the political invocation of the heritage is concerned, perhaps one of the great strengths of contemporary India is the ease with which the traditions inscribed in the law books, with their vast potential to disrupt acculturation, can simply be ignored—an ease that has something, though by no means everything, to do with the character of the heritage.

Meanwhile, the Catholic heritage in Latin America contributes even less. It plays little role in political identity, it is ambivalent with regard to militancy, and it lacks a vision of the proper shape of either society or polity. Nor does a return to the sources of the religion help much in these respects. What has given Catholicism its multiple roles in modern politics has been less the content of the heritage than the company it has kept, be it conservative, fascistic, liberal, or leftist. The only significant exception is the preference for the poor, a feature written into the foundational texts of Christianity that resonated powerfully with modern leftism. At the same time, the political invocation of the Catholic heritage, like that of the Hindu heritage, has not in general posed a serious obstacle to acculturation in recent decades. One reason for this is, of course, the fact that Catholicism, like Christianity in general and unlike Islam or Hinduism, spans the Third and First Worlds at the level of majority populations.

What I have just said about the Hindu and Catholic heritages in relation to acculturation stands in need of a more extensive historical commentary than I can give it. If we went back to the nineteenth century, we could readily make a case for the propensity of both heritages to get in the way of modernization and to provide their devotees with rationales for such obstruction.[40] What we would see at work is full-blooded conservatism making its last stand,[41] dramatically in the case of Catholicism, perhaps more diffusely in the case of Hinduism. They were not, of course, engaged in last stands as religions but rather as heritages that could be invoked with authority to block the inroads of modernity across a broad front. Thus, the First Vatican Council of 1870 and the decades that followed represented a desperate Catholic attempt to preserve the religious aspect of an ancien régime that had otherwise disintegrated. Thereafter the two heritages might still cause considerable drag, but increasingly their authority would be invoked

[40] Cf. 295, on Hindu resistance to smallpox vaccination, and 462, on the pope's refusal to be reconciled with modern civilization.

[41] Cf. M. C. Wright, *Last stand of Chinese conservatism.*

only to resist select features of modernity that had taken on the character of shibboleths: notably cow killing for the Hindus and contraception for the Catholics.[42] It was against this background that twentieth-century reactionaries like Svāmī Karpātrī and Marcel Lefebvre came to appear as hopeless anachronisms rather than serious menaces to modernity. Such conservative last stands were also a feature of the nineteenth-century history of the Islamic world; we have seen hints of them in the Ottoman and Moroccan responses to the European drive to end the slave trade.[43] The difference would seem to be that the Islamic heritage was not sidelined by the failure of conservatism: it either did not lose, or later recovered, its authoritative standing when invoked to block acculturation.[44]

The other feature that our three cases have in common is already advertised in the title of this book: Islam, Hinduism, and Christianity are all three of them religions—and what is more mass religions. This may be the time to contrast them briefly with two persuasions that have a lot to say about politics but are not, or not quite, religions.

The first of these is Confucianism. Like our three religions, it is a tradition of venerable antiquity, but it differs from them in being an elite philosophy rather than a mass religion: despite considerable trickle-down into the lower reaches of Chinese society, and an undeniable religious tinge, Confucianism never took on the shape of a religion reaching from the top of society to the bottom. This meant that, once abandoned as an elite persuasion in the early twentieth century, it lacked a popular constituency to fall back on in the manner of Turkish Islam during the high tide of Kemalist secularism. Thus Buddhism, despite the rather low regard in which it was often held by the Chinese elite over many centuries, has survived much better in China today than Confucianism. Indeed, it could be said that in mainland China Confucianism did not survive at all: insofar as it is found there today, it is the result of a late twentieth-century revival spurred by a surge of cultural nationalism.[45] More generally, what we see here is that non-

[42] Thus among Catholic conservatives in the United States, adherence to the Papal encyclical *Humanae vitae* of 1968 is regarded as "a shibboleth of exemplary Catholic identity" (Cuneo, *Smoke of Satan*, 27).

[43] See 177–78.

[44] The remarks in this paragraph are sketchy in the extreme; there is a book to be written on this subject.

[45] For the early history of the revival, which began outside mainland China, see Tu, "Search for roots." For a detailed study of the life and thought of the "New Confucian" thinker T'ang Chün-i (d. 1978), see Metzger, *Cloud across the Pacific*, 185–278. T'ang is

Western religions, even when heavily repressed as in the case of mainland China,[46] have survived the onslaught of modernity far better than non-Western philosophies.

The other persuasion we should say a word about is Communism, a specifically modern and resolutely secular doctrine. While it lasted, it was far more successful as a political ideology than Islamism has yet to be: it came to power in numerous countries, including two continental empires, reshaped the geopolitical order,[47] and provided many Third-World countries with non-Western allies and role models. Yet despite this remarkable success it did not last. Its impermanence clearly had to do with its failure to secure the long-term commitment of the masses over which it held sway. That failure was most obviously economic, but it may also have been in some sense spiritual. Religions, which can rely on the spiritual commitment of their followers, regularly survive devastating political failures sustained by their adherents; in the absence of such commitment, it is not so surprising that Communism did not.

All this makes China, which has survived the successive demise of both Confucianism and Communism as credible belief systems, an interesting country. This is not the place to enlarge on this thought, but there is one development that makes for a particularly instructive comparison with the Islamic world: the virtual disappearance of the seclusion of women in Chinese society. For over two thousand years this society, like that of the Islamic world, was committed to separating the sexes; already in Han times Chinese commentators looked askance at neighboring peoples who failed to do this.[48] Yet with the demise of

---

an interesting figure because his Confucianism was not a whimsical revival but rather an obstinate survival, albeit an adaptive one in which some basic features of the tradition were jettisoned—notably the traditional cosmology, the idea of antiquity as a golden age, and the authority of the Classics (270–71). For a characterization of the Confucian revival as a form of cultural nationalism largely restricted to academics, particularly those in philosophy departments, and with "a body of discourse" as its most visible expression to date, see Makeham, *Lost soul*, 15–17, 112–15, 130.

[46] From 1966 to 1979, the Chinese regime sought to eradicate religion (Yang, *Religion in China*, 121, 127–28).

[47] Note that the Islamists, unlike the Communists, have had no opportunity to take over such empires due to the early demise of the Ottoman Empire and the absence of other giant states in the modern Islamic world. To this extent the geopolitically utopian character of Islamist ideology is a consequence of historical bad luck.

[48] Hinsch, "Origins of separation," 606–7. Note also the insistence in Sung times that a woman who has to leave the inner quarters should cover her face (Ebrey, *Inner quarters*, 23–25). It would be interesting to know whether there was a disparity between the

Confucianism this practice has come to be vestigial in Chinese society today, even in those parts of the Chinese world that were not exposed to the radical reforms of Maoism.[49] The contrast with the Islamic experience suggests that the entrenchment of social values in a mass religion—as opposed to an elite philosophy—can give them a significant measure of protection against the inroads of modernity.[50]

Part of what we see in these comparisons—not all, but a significant part—is that Islamism possesses a double strength by virtue of its relationship to Islam. On the one hand, this religion, in contrast to Hinduism and Christianity, occupies the political terrain in a manner that is both deep-rooted and relevant. And on the other hand, in contrast to political philosophies like Confucianism and Communism, Islam has the survivorship of a mass religion; indeed it is the mass religion that has probably suffered the least corrosion from the spread of doubt in modern times.[51] In that sense Islamism has the best of both worlds.

2. Looking ahead

The reader may have noticed that, while I have some fairly developed notions about what makes the Islamic heritage attractive as a resource for modern politics, I have no good explanation of the timing of the

---

Islamic world and China in the extent to which upper-class norms of female seclusion reached down into the lower orders of society.

[49] For the dissolution of female seclusion in China, see Mann, *Gender and sexuality*, 28, 35–39, 48–49, 187–88. According to a New Confucian philosopher at a university in Shanghai, the true Confucian view of the proper relations between men and women holds the balance between a distorted Confucianism that sees women as inferior to men and a Western feminism that insists on absolutely equal rights and responsibilities; this could almost be Mawdūdī speaking (cf. above, 186–87), except that we hear nothing of the separation of the sexes (Wang, "Towards a proper relation," 94, 100, 104).

[50] Note the conclusion of Norris and Inglehart that with regard to "gender equality and sexual liberalization" Western societies are the most liberal, Muslim ones the most traditional, and others somewhere in between (*Sacred and secular*, 149). It is not just the West but also the Islamic world that is out on a limb here. In their figure plotting attitudes to gender equality, China appears distinctly higher (more favorable in its attitudes) than the Muslim countries shown (with the exception of Albania) but well below the Western countries (152, Figure 6.3; for what is involved, cf. 144).

[51] Charles Taylor has described a crucial component of the religious evolution of the modern West as a change "from a society in which it was virtually impossible not to believe in God, to one in which faith, even for the staunchest believer, is one human possibility among others" (Taylor, *Secular age*, 3). If such a transition has begun in the Muslim world, it is as yet barely perceptible.

emergence of Islamism. The European impact on the Islamic world became serious toward the end of the eighteenth century, but the Islamist reaction did not really get under way until the first half of the twentieth century and did not become a major factor in the politics of the region till the second half of that century.[52] By the same token I have no idea when Islamism is likely to lose its attractiveness. I tend assume that some day it will, though only on the flimsy grounds that nothing is forever and that ideologies in particular have shorter half-lives than religions. But, for what it is worth, I can see several possibilities, though the chances of the future coinciding with any one of them are minimal.

The first and simplest possibility is that things will continue pretty much as they have been since the end of the Cold War. This makes two assumptions, one about international relations and the other about domestic politics in the Muslim world. With regard to international relations, it assumes that quite some time must pass before the rise of China makes the United States look more like an ally than an enemy to Islamists. With regard to domestic politics, it takes it for granted that the "Arab Spring"—the events that began in December 2010 and are still continuing as of 2013—will not have a dramatic effect on the fortunes of Islamist movements overall. In one respect this still seems plausible: there is little reason to expect Islamist movements to be derailed by the manifest popularity among Muslims of a Western political value poorly anchored in the Islamic tradition, namely political freedom. But in another respect the Arab Spring, despite continuing uncertainties, has made it harder to assume continuity with the last two decades: it has clearly worked to the advantage of the Islamists—and not just because of their organizational edge over all other domestic political actors bar the state.

A second possibility is that the Islamists will win, taking power in many countries of the Muslim world as they have already done in Tunisia and for a while in Egypt. How this would play out would depend in considerable measure on the uncertain relationship between Islamism and democracy. One possibility is that democracy loses out, leaving the

[52] Insofar as I have an explanation to offer, it would be that prior to the achievement of independence nationalism had an edge because it provided a language in which claims could be made against imperial powers, and that prior to the demise of the Soviet Union leftism had an edge because it provided a language in which claims could be made on Communist powers, whereas today what matters most is to have a language in which claims can be made on the loyalties of the indigenous populations of Muslim countries.

Islamists to establish authoritarian regimes and entrench their power and patronage for the long haul. This would, of course, also provide them with an almost irresistible opportunity to discredit themselves by abusing their power at the expense of their subjects, thereby giving rise to widespread disillusionment. Another possibility is that Islamist parties adapt their goals and methods to a democratic environment, giving up on the sweeping restoration of the Sharīʿa and the establishment of an Islamic state and instead presenting themselves as champions of conservative social values and the public display of religious symbolism. We can see the first as the Iranian model and the second as the Turkish model; which of these approximates more closely to the future of Islamism in countries like Tunisia and Egypt remains to be seen.[53]

A third possibility is that Islam—or what Muslims want from it—will change in a way that significantly reduces its political profile. An idea that has had some appeal in the West is that Islam should undergo a reformation comparable to the one that gave us Protestant Christianity, thereby enabling liberal values to flourish. This is not a particularly sensible idea: the reformation in Europe unleashed forces of fanaticism and intolerance that issued in sustained bloodshed—hardly something that the Muslim world needs more of today.[54] The fulminations of John Knox (d. 1572) in 1554 against the "abominable idolators" who briefly triumphed in England under the rule of the Catholic Queen Mary (ruled 1553–1558) set the tone: "Their cities shall be burnt, their land shall be laid waste, and their daughters shall be defiled, their children shall fall on the edge of the sword, mercy shall they find none because they have refused the God of all mercy."[55] In the event the insular English were spared the implementation of this genocidal fantasy, so reminiscent of contemporary Iraq or Pakistan. But even in England heretics were burnt at the stake until 1612, and the inhabitants of the European continent were considerably less fortunate. Yet the basic Western idea here, however infelicitously expressed, is rather that through some process of internal change Islam should become a nicer religion—more like post-Enlightenment Christianity outside the Bible Belt or, in Islamic terms, more like Ṣūfism as seen in the West. Here the Ṣūfī reference is intriguing. Admittedly the historical track record of Ṣūfism does not

[53] This paragraph owes much to the comments of Bernard Haykel.

[54] As Sedgwick aptly remarks, "Pundits who wish for a 'reformed' Islam . . . are actually hoping for an Enlightened Islam. It was the Enlightenment, not the Reformation, that produced tolerant liberalism in the West" (Sedgwick, "Counter-reformation," 125).

[55] Walzer, *Revolution of the saints*, 100.

suggest that it is reliably apolitical, irenic, or tolerant; Shaykh Aḥmad Sirhindi was none of these, and he was very much a Ṣūfī.[56] But Ṣūfism does lend itself to the role of an apolitical spirituality, in other words a form of religion very different in character from that of the Islamists; and despite the fact that it has been on the defensive in modern times, it may well retain a greater mass appeal. What is interesting is the comparison this invites with Pentecostalism, the rather apolitical spirituality of Latin America and other parts of the Christian world. If we were to take Latin America—rather than Western Europe or the Islamic world—as the model for the global religious future, then a Ṣūfī revival would provide the natural counterpart to the rise of Pentecostalism—and what is more a fully indigenous one.[57] Thus, an observer of Ṣūfism in Egypt in the 1980s characterizes it as "a nonviolent, apolitical alternative that is culturally authentic";[58] she remarks that this nonviolent character of Ṣūfī activities can help to attract a following[59] and makes the point that devotees may be in search of a peaceful refuge from the turbulence of their lives[60]—a theme familiar to us from negative responses to Liberation Theology in Latin America.[61] And, like Pentecostalism, Ṣūfism typically offers a combination of emotive rituals, music, and faith healing.[62] But a change along such lines would mean a major

[56] To quote Sedgwick again: "In all periods and regions, there are many examples of Sufi involvement in politics. Mostly this involvement is marginal" (Sedgwick, *Sufism*, 74). As to militancy, several of the early leaders of Muslim resistance to the European expansion (see above, 223–24) were Ṣūfīs, and more recently there was a report of a Ṣūfī militia formed in Somalia to resist the Shabāb (Gettleman, "Chaos breeds new agony").

[57] There has also been some direct influence of Pentecostalism on the Muslim world, though it remains marginal. For a case from Lagos, where Muslims are exposed to the ebullient Pentecostalist scene of southern Nigeria, see Sengupta and Rohter, "Where faith grows," last column of the article; known as Nasfat, this group was established in the mid-1990s. For charismatic Muslim televangelists in Indonesia and Egypt, see Micklethwait and Wooldridge, *God is back*, 239–41.

[58] Hoffman, *Sufism, mystics*, 377, and see 362–63.

[59] Ibid., 375.

[60] Ibid., 105, 107.

[61] See 209.

[62] For Ṣūfī rituals and music, see, for example, Hoffman, *Sufism, mystics*, 7–8, 113, 171–72, 182; for healing, 154, 301, 325, 374–75. When Hoffman remarks that Ṣūfism "promises profound moral change, and carries with it the proof of power through healing and changed lives" (377), she could just as well be writing about Pentecostalists. Another point of comparison is the role of women. Their presence in Pentecostal and Charismatic movements is quite disproportionate (Chesnut, *Competitive spirits*, 16, 158). The receptiveness of Ṣūfism to women is uneven (for examples of the exclusion or absence of women, in principle and in practice, see Hoffman, *Sufism, mystics*, 14, 25, 46, 178, 226, 247). But on balance it seems clear that the role of women in public religion has traditionally been more pronounced for Ṣūfī rituals than for those of the mosque

upheaval in the standards of right religion that are currently dominant in the Islamic world. It is not that those who uphold these standards condemn Ṣūfism lock, stock, and barrel; their tendency is rather to make an exception in favor of "true and genuine" Ṣūfis, as Mawdūdī has it, and condemn the rest.[63] But, as one expert in the field has put it, Ṣūfism is "indisputably in eclipse" in the Arab world, at least among the elites.[64] Moreover, a shift of this kind would also very likely require a drastic change in the present geopolitical situation since without it adopting a more irenic Islam looks too much like telling the West what it wants to hear. There is, however, one internal process that is worth keeping in mind here: over time people tend to tire of the politicization of religion.[65] In a revolutionary situation they may be entranced by those "who under the name of religion teach little else than wild and dangerous politics."[66] But under more normal conditions a revenge effect is likely to set in; as one disillusioned American pastor who had been active in the Christian Right remarked, "When you mix politics and religion, you get politics."[67] In this context it is also worth quoting an acute observation from a study of religion and politics in Morocco: "The very fact that the fundamentalists feel compelled to stress constantly that religion and politics are inseparable in Islam illustrates that this is not how most Muslims perceive their religion."[68] There is also a

(see, for example, ibid., 110, 119, 129, 226, 227, 232–33, 244, 247–48; by contrast, "the mosque functions as something of a men's house" to which "until recently, women had little access," 227). It also appears that the participation of women in Ṣūfism may be on the increase (see the survey of the role of women in Ṣūfī orders in Hoffman, "Oral traditions," 373–79, and the remarks on their increasing role, 380).

[63] Mawdūdī concedes the existence of "quite a few of true and genuine Sufis who walked the straight path" in medieval times (Maududi, *Short history*, 64) and sees Sirhindī as a representative of "the real and pure" Ṣūfism of Islam (78). But he feels that in our time Ṣūfism, though allowable, should be shunned as soporific (106, 108). In the same vein Ḥasan al-Bannā states that the thought of the Muslim Brothers is, among other things, Ṣūfī (Bannā, *Majmūʿat rasāʾil*, 248.18), an affirmation to be read in the context of his approval of "pure" Ṣūfism (Mitchell, *Society of Muslim Brothers*, 214).

[64] Sedgwick, "Counter-reformation," 126. The article nevertheless describes a Ṣūfī order that has been exceptionally successful among the Moroccan elite (133–41). In general it is not hard to find examples of Ṣūfī revival here and there in the Islamic world (see, for example, Knysh, "*Tariqa* on a landcruiser," 406–12, on a revival in Ḥaḍramawt), but it is hard to know what they amount to for the Islamic world as a whole.

[65] A notable example is the collapse of Islamist sentiment in Imbāba, a neighbourhood of Cairo once known as a hotbed of militant Islamism (Shadid, "One slice of Egypt").

[66] Burke, *Reflections*, 223.

[67] The Reverend Gene Carlson quoted in Kirkpatrick, "Evangelical crackup," 60.

[68] Munson, *Religion and power*, 177. He points out that fundamentalists do not stress what they know Muslims take for granted—for example, that Muḥammad was the last of the prophets or the reality of the afterlife.

crudely material factor to consider here: the use of oil revenues for the purpose of religious patronage. Such patronage is by no means the only reason for the rise of Salafism, but it has certainly helped; what, then, would a future look like in which oil revenues dwindled away, or were diverted to Ṣūfī causes?

A fourth possibility is that some new secular belief system will arise to occupy the space vacated by the demise of Marxism. Muslim intellectuals need to be able to adopt the ways of the modern West without looking like shameless collaborators and at the same time to oppose the power of the West without looking hopelessly anachronistic.[69] It was in considerable measure Marxism, in however diluted a form, that enabled them to do this in the past: it gave them a vantage ground from which they could be at once iconoclastic about their own tradition and hostile to Western power.[70] The fact that there is no longer such a place to stand is one reason for the salience of Islamism in the last twenty years. If a new and inspiring secular ideology were to arise somewhere in the world—preferably somewhere outside the West—things would be different.[71] But this does not look very likely.[72]

[69] As Cemil Aydin has pointed out, the dichotomy between pro-Western secularists and anti-Western religious revivalists in the Middle East is historically false (*Politics of anti-Westernism*, 2).

[70] An example may lend color to this point. The philosopher Akeel Bilgrami, a professor at Columbia University in New York, mentions in an article on Islamic identity that he grew up, presumably in India, "in a home dominated by the views of an irreligious father" and then "for some years adopted the customary aggressive secular stance of those with communist leanings" (Bilgrami, "What is a Muslim?," 822). He gives no further details, and his use of the term "customary" suggests that he was able to appropriate this leftist stance without having to think very hard about it. But the point of the article is to argue that moderate Muslims who are opposed to "Islamic absolutists" now have to think very hard indeed. Their problem is that "their commitment to Islam today is to a large extent governed by a highly defensive function"; this is why "moderate Muslims find it particularly difficult to make a substantial and sustained criticism of Islamic doctrine" (835; he glosses "absolutists" as "fundamentalists," though he regards the latter term as misleading, 824). Bilgrami goes on to say that their defensiveness "inhibits them with the fear that such criticism would amount to a surrender to the forces of the West, which have for so long shown a domineering colonial and postcolonial contempt for their culture." Though he does not mention this, it is clearly the demise of the Soviet Union and the waning prestige of Marxism that have rendered the predicament he describes so acute: before that intellectuals could criticize aspects of their Islamic heritage without the stigma of surrender to the West, and they did so extensively, if not always freely.

[71] They would be even more different if the link between modernity and the West were to become a historical fact of no continuing relevance. This has yet to happen, but is easier to imagine than it used to be.

[72] Non-Muslim intellectuals in Third-World countries have it easier: to an extent, at least, old-fashioned nationalism still does the trick.

Finally there is what we might call the Catholic model—something along the lines of the evolution of Catholicism over the last century and a half. It is easy to forget that in the middle of the nineteenth century it seemed obvious to all concerned that Catholicism was not compatible with the modern world. One scholar nicely sums up the view of "all reasonable men" at the time: "Catholics were unenlightened, intolerant bigots whose religion was opposed to sound economic progress and liberal political developments."[73] In substance Pope Pius IX (in office 1846–1878) did not disagree: his Syllabus of Errors of 1864 famously denounced the view that the Roman pontiff "can and should reconcile himself and come to terms with progress, with liberalism, and with modern civilization."[74] Another scholar remarks that as of 1900 few believed that one could be devoted both to Catholic doctrine and to the Declaration of the Rights of Man.[75] And yet today it takes imagination for younger mainstream Catholics to understand what all the fuss was about. What has changed between then and now is not so much Catholicism as Catholics, with the exception of the conservative and traditionalist fringes.[76] In another century and a half the same might be true of Islam and Muslims.[77] In the end time heals all wounds—or causes us to forget them by inflicting new ones.

[73] Holmes, *More Roman than Rome*, 43–44.

[74] Christoffe and Minnerath, *Le "Syllabus,"* 68 no. 80, as translated in Pelikan, *Christian tradition*, 5: 175. For a sustained comparison of nineteenth-century Catholic fundamentalism (or as I would call it, conservatism) and the Muslim fundamentalism of the later twentieth century, see Al-Azm, "Islamic fundamentalism reconsidered, Part I."

[75] Arnal, *Ambivalent alliance*, 10.

[76] For a vivid account of the conservatives within the Church and the traditionalists outside it in the American context, see Cuneo, *Smoke of Satan*, chaps. 2 and 4. For a comparison of the traditionalist views of Marcel Lefebvre with those of his Muslim counterparts, see again Al-Azm, "Islamic fundamentalism reconsidered, Part I."

[77] Compare the remarks of the Egyptian political analyst Amr El Shobaki about the contemporary "Egyptian habit of shrugging off apparent contradictions between a traditionalist faith and modern lifestyles" (Kirkpatrick and El-Naggar, "Poll finds Egyptians"; the wording is that of the journalists).

Appendix

"HINDU FUNDAMENTALISM" AND THE FUNDAMENTALISM PROJECT

THE USE OF THE TERMS "fundamentalism" and "fundamentalist" in the modern Hindu context is adopted wholeheartedly by several of the relevant contributors to the five volumes of the Fundamentalism Project.[1] By contrast, Kumar prefers to speak of "revivalism," rather than "fundamentalism," "mainly because the latter seems inappropriate to Hinduism."[2] Likewise Lal, despite an opening reference to "Hindu fundamentalism," adopts the term "revivalism," though allowing it to be equated with "fundamentalism" in a weak sense; he explains his choice in terms of the absence from Hinduism of any religious fundamentals around which a fundamentalist movement could be built—indeed he endorses the view that "Hindu fundamentalism is a contradiction in terms."[3] One contributor, van der Veer, seems to ignore the usage, perhaps because, as he observes, the VHP (and a fortiori, one assumes, Hindu nationalism at large) is not a scripturalist movement.[4] Against this background the usage is adopted somewhat halfheartedly in *Strong religion*, a collective work by Almond and others that distills the wisdom of the Fundamentalism Project.[5]

The authors of *Strong religion* distinguish Hindu fundamentalism from their core cases of the phenomenon (which are Christian, Islamic, Judaic, and Sikh) by placing it in a category of "syncretic fundamentalism."[6]

[1] Gold, "Organized Hinduisms," 533, 563, 571, 575, etc; Frykenberg, "Hindu fundamentalism," 233, 244, 251, etc.; also Frykenberg, "Accounting for fundamentalisms," 600, 602; Embree, "Rashtriya Swayamsevak Sangh," 630, 635, 643; Oberoi, "Mapping Indic fundamentalisms," 97, 101, 110. The five volumes of the Fundamentalism Project are a rich source of information on religious movements of the kind we are concerned with in this book.

[2] Kumar, "Hindu revivalism," 537.

[3] Lal, "Economic impact," 410–11.

[4] Veer, "Hindu nationalism," 658, 666.

[5] Almond et al., *Strong religion*, 90, 110, 173.

[6] Ibid., 111, no. 4.

Movements in this category "are those in which ethnocultural or ethnonational features take precedence over religion or are inseparable, as in Hindu fundamentalism."[7] In another formulation these movements "are based at least as much on ethnonationalism as on religion."[8] In a third, less emphatic version, there is "also an ethnonationalist component."[9] The basic idea here is that core fundamentalisms are concerned primarily with "the erosion of religion and its proper role in society,"[10] whereas syncretic fundamentalisms mobilize against rival "ethnonational" communities and "are not directed primarily toward [sc. against] modernization and secularization."[11] Elsewhere the authors tell us that Hindu fundamentalism falls short of core status because of its "lack of clear-cut doctrinal content,"[12] but they do not take this idea much further, and it is clearly not central to their thinking.

There can be no objection to the view that the people we are concerned with are nationalists of some kind; what is open to question is the idea that they are also in some measure fundamentalists. Here, of course, it is crucial how fundamentalism is defined, and from the point of view of this work all we need ask is whether some kind of return to the fundamentals of the religion is to be a defining property of fundamentalism. On this point the authors do not seem entirely consistent. In a definition of the term offered early in the book,[13] such a criterion does not figure at all, and at one point the authors state explicitly that "Scriptural inerrancy" is not "the defining mark" of all fundamentalisms.[14] They do, however, remark that each of the "synthetic" Asian fundamentalisms "tends to select and canonize a corpus of sacred texts, transforming epics and poems and other open-ended genres into the stuff of 'fundamental', 'inerrant' Scriptures."[15] Indeed more than just a tendency seems to be involved here: they also state that "the assertion that their innovative programs are based on the authority of the sacred past" is "a *crucial* element of their rhetoric and self-understanding"[16] and that a "pronounced rootedness in Scripture and/

[7] Ibid., 110; for "inseparable" we also find "difficult to separate" (99).
[8] Ibid., 90.
[9] Ibid., 172.
[10] Ibid., 93.
[11] Ibid., 110.
[12] Ibid., 173.
[13] Ibid., 17.
[14] Ibid., 14.
[15] Ibid., 16; "synthetic" seems to be a variant of "syncretic."
[16] Ibid., 92 (my italics).

or 'purified' tradition . . . *characterizes* fundamentalism as a religious mode."[17] These statements prepare us for the subsequent inclusion of "inerrancy" among the "defining characteristics"[18] of fundamentalism;[19] this looks like an abrogation of the earlier statement to the contrary. However, this inclusion seems to be qualified in two ways. First, the authors take the view that the *degree* to which there can be a belief in inerrancy depends on whether there is a sacred code or canon in the religious tradition.[20] Thus, in the Hindu case "textual inerrancy is difficult to sustain in view of the large and complex corpus" of Hindu literature;[21] in Hinduism "texts are cited, but their normative character is more ambiguous and, in the nature of the case, less authoritative. Nevertheless . . . there is an affirmation of the absolute validity of the 'fundamentals' of the tradition."[22] Second, for all that the authors include inerrancy among the defining characteristics of fundamentalism, they do not for that reason insist that a movement *must* possess it in order to be called fundamentalist. They assign such a force to only one of their defining characteristics.[23] For the rest, movements only have to manifest a "sufficient number" of the defining characteristics of fundamentalism to qualify—they do not have to display "every single one of them in every case."[24]

In terms of the rules of their game, the authors of *Strong religion* can thus maintain the term "Hindu fundamentalism" in one of two ways: they can argue that the movement believes in the inerrancy of some canon, or they can allow that it does not but accord the movement fundamentalist status on the basis of other criteria that need not concern us. In fact, they seem to be of two minds over this. Several of the formulations quoted above do indeed suggest that the "Hindu fundamentalists" have equipped themselves with some kind of inerrant canon, although perhaps in a somewhat ad hoc fashion;[25] the authors likewise describe them as "privileging certain ancient texts"[26] and say that "the doctrine of *Hindutva*" supplied the "missing" inerrant feature normally

[17] Ibid., 92–93 (my italics).
[18] Ibid., 94.
[19] Ibid., 96.
[20] Ibid.
[21] Ibid., 172.
[22] Ibid., 96.
[23] Ibid., 93–94.
[24] Ibid., 94.
[25] See also ibid., 102.
[26] Ibid., 111.

associated with the core fundamentalisms.[27] But against all this, Table 2.2 shows "inerrancy" as "absent" in the case of the RSS.[28] In my view this latter is the better choice. Indeed, the authors adduce no evidence for the contrary view, and I know of none that would support it.

In toying with the idea that Hindu nationalism adheres to some form of scriptural inerrancy, the authors are perhaps influenced by Frykenberg. In his main paper he was able to find in Sāvarkar's *Hindutva* "the basis for fundamentalism in classic form," namely a defense of "the Truth" as found in "a literal or strict interpretation of an inerrant body of scriptural text, imprinted in genomes and cosmic sounds of Brahma (stemming from the *Rig Veda,* as conveyed from the mouths of sages or prophets)."[29] For this Frykenberg cites an earlier study of Hindu nationalism by Andersen and Damle.[30] In the relevant passage, however, these authors are not talking about the Hindu nationalists; they are describing aspects of the thought of the *Gītā* that have no apparent connection with scriptural inerrancy then or now. Frykenberg makes similar statements in a later contribution, affirming that no fundamentalism can exist without a conception of "the Truth" that is "objectified in a sacred text or sacred code."[31] To judge by the examples he gives, "sacred code" is a somewhat open-ended category, but "sacred text" is scriptural.[32] Which does he have in mind in the Hindu case? One passage speaking of "sacred texts" suggests scripture, but another states that the "textual inerrancy" of the "New Hinduism" lay in "genomes" and in "race and place."[33] I do not claim to understand this second notion of textual inerrancy, but it seems clear that it has nothing to do with texts and therefore need not concern us. To the extent that Frykenberg is speaking of scriptural inerrancy in a literal sense, his view of Hindu nationalism seems to me mistaken.

By contrast, the other contributors make no attempt to represent the Hindu nationalists as believing in scriptural inerrancy. Gold does not offer a rationale for his use of the term "fundamentalism," but it is evident that he does not see scriptural inerrancy as something to which the Hindu nationalists (as opposed to Dayānand) are committed.[34] Em-

[27] Ibid., 136.
[28] Ibid., 247.
[29] Frykenberg, "Hindu fundamentalism," 240, 254n7.
[30] Andersen and Damle, *Brotherhood in saffron,* 76.
[31] Frykenberg, "Accounting for fundamentalisms," 593.
[32] Ibid, 614nn6–7, with another reference to Andersen and Damle.
[33] Ibid., 601–2.
[34] Gold, "Organized Hinduisms," 542.

bree states explicitly that members of the RSS have little to say about religion in their publications and often emphasize in private conversations that they are not religious.[35] Oberoi makes it clear that he regards the association of fundamentalism with scriptural inerrancy as Abrahamic parochialism,[36] and develops a quite different argument to justify his use of the term in the Hindu context.[37] Van der Veer—who unlike these contributors does not use the term "fundamentalism"—considers, as we have seen, that the VHP is not scripturalist.[38]

My conclusion would be that, insofar as the participants in the Fundamentalism Project apply the term "fundamentalism" in the Hindu context, and insofar as they mean it in the sense in which I use it in this work, they are mistaken about the character of Hindu nationalism. But for the most part they either do not use the term or do not use it in this way.

[35] See 112.
[36] Oberoi, "Mapping Indic fundamentalisms," 96.
[37] For a summary statement, see ibid., 109–10.
[38] See 463.

Bibliography

NOTE: WHEN THE WORKS OF Islamists writing in Islamic languages are translated into English, their names are likely to be transcribed in a variety of ways. In the footnotes, my practice is to give the name exactly as it appears on the relevant title page. In the bibliography, however, some measure of consolidation is called for. Thus of the two works of Sharīʿatī that I cite in translation, one gives his name as "Shariati," the other as "Shari'ati"; I respect this difference in the footnotes, but place both under "Shariati" in the bibliography. Two cases call for further comment.

One is Sayyid Quṭb. In the bibliography I have consolidated his works into two groups: Arabic originals are placed under "Quṭb, Sayyid" (with diacritic), followed by English translations under "Qutb, Sayyid" (without diacritic). A deviant forms of the name—"Kutb"—is also listed, but only with a cross-reference to "Qutb."

The other problematic case is Mawdūdī. Here again, in the bibliography I consolidate his works into two groups: works in English are placed under the form of his name that they commonly, but not always, use, namely "Maududi," while works in Arabic (and Urdu) are placed under "Mawdūdī." The awkwardness here is that a few of the English translations of his works give his name as "Mawdudi": his *Islam today*, his *Islamic movement*, and his *Let us be Muslims*. As English translations they are nevertheless entered in the bibliography under "Maududi."

Where the name of an author or the like does not appear as such on the title page of a work but is inferred from the title or elsewhere, it is followed by a dash (—).

Abaza, M. *Debates on Islam and knowledge in Malaysia and Egypt: shifting worlds*. London, 2002.

ʿAbd al-Ghanī al-Nābulusī. *al-Qawl al-sadīd fī jawāz khulf al-waʿīd waʾl-radd ʿalā ʾl-Rūmī al-ʿanīd*. Ms. Istanbul: Süleymaniye, Esad Efendi 3606.

ʿAbda, Muḥammad al-. *al-Ṭarīq ilā ʾl-Madīna: muqaddamāt fī fiqh al-sīra*. Riyadh, 1424.

Abdel-Malek, A. *Égypte: société militaire*. Paris, 1962.

ʿAbduh, Muḥammad. *Risālat al-tawḥīd*. Būlāq, 1316.

Abou El Fadl, K. "Islamic law and Muslim minorities: the juristic discourse on Muslim minorities from the second/eighth to the eleventh/seventeenth centuries." *Islamic Law and Society* 1 (1994).

Abou El Fadl, K. *Rebellion and violence in Islamic law*. Cambridge, 2001.

Abrahamian, E. *Khomeinism: essays on the Islamic Republic*. Berkeley, 1993.

Abū Baṣīr al-Ṭarṭūsī, ʿAbd al-Munʿim Muṣṭafā Ḥalīma. *Hākadhā kānat ḥayāt al-nabī Muḥammad ṣallā ʾllāhu ʿalayhi wa-sallam*. http://www.tawhed.ws. 2003 (dated 1 Dhū ʾl-Qaʿda 1423).

———. *al-Jihād waʾl-siyāsa al-sharʿiyya: munāṣaḥa wa-mukāshafa lil-jamāʿāt al-jihādiyya al-muʿāṣira*. http://www.abubaseer.bizland.com. 2007 (dated February 15, 2007).

Abū Dāwūd. *Sunan*, edited by M. M. ʿAbd al-Ḥamīd. Cairo, n.d.

Abū Ḥāmid al-Qudsī. *Duwal al-Islām al-sharīfa al-bahiyya*, edited by Ṣ. Labīb and U. Haarmann. Beirut, 1997.

Abū Jandal al-Azdī, ed. *Nuṣūṣ al-fuqahāʾ ḥawl aḥkām al-ighāra waʾl-tatarrus*. http://www.tawhed.ws. 2003 (dated 17 Rabīʿ al-Awwal 1424).

Abū ʾl-Layth al-Samarqandī. *Tafsīr*, edited by ʿA. M. Muʿawwaḍ et al. Beirut, 1993.

Abū Maryam. *Shubhat "lā yataḥaddathu ʾl-nāsu anna rasūla ʾllāhi yaqtulu aṣḥābahu."* http://www.tawhed.ws. N.d.

Abū ʾl-Mundhir al-Sāʿidī. *Khuṭūṭ ʿarīḍa fī manhaj al-jamāʿa al-Islāmiyya al-muqātila*. http://www.tawhed.ws. N.d.

Abu-Rabiʿ, I. M. *Intellectual origins of Islamic resurgence in the modern Arab world*. Albany, 1996.

Abū Yūsuf. *Kitāb al-kharāj*, edited by M. I. al-Bannā. Cairo, 1981.

Acosta, José de. *De procuranda Indorum salute*, edited by L. Pereña et al. Madrid, 1984–1987.

Adnan-Adıvar, A. *Osmanlı Türklerinde ilim*. Istanbul, 1943.

Adolphson, M. S. *The teeth and claws of the Buddha: monastic warriors and sōhei in Japanese history*. Honolulu, 2007.

Adraoui, M.-A. "Salafism in France: ideology, practices and contradictions." In *Global Salafism: Islam's new religious movement*, edited by R. Meijer. New York, 2009.

Advani, L. K. *My country my life*. New Delhi, 2008.

Ageron, C.-R. *Les algériens musulmans et la France (1871–1919)*. Paris, 1968.

Agobard of Lyons. "Adversus legem Gundobadi." In *Agobardi Lugdunensis opera omnia*, edited by L. van Acker. Turnhout, 1981.

Ahmad, A. "Islamization of knowledge: a futurist perspective." In *Islam and knowledge: al Faruqi's concept of religion in Islamic thought*, edited by I. Yusuf. London, 2012.

Ahmad, Khurshid, and Zafar Ishaq Ansari. *Mawlānā Mawdūdī: an introduction to his life and thought*. Leicester, 1979.

Aḥmad Bābā. *Miʿrāj al-ṣuʿūd*, edited and translated by J. Hunwick and F. Harrak. Rabat, 2000.

Alam, M. *The languages of political Islam: India 1200-1800*. Chicago, 2004.

Al-Azm, S. J. *Islam und säkularer Humanismus*. Tübingen, 2005.

———. "Islamic fundamentalism reconsidered: a critical outline of problems, ideas and approaches, Part I." *South Asia Bulletin* 13 (1993).

———. "Islamic fundamentalism reconsidered: a critical outline of problems, ideas and approaches, Part II." *South Asia Bulletin* 14 (1994).

Al-Azmeh, A. *Muslim kingship: power and the sacred in Muslim, Christian, and pagan polities*. London, 1997.
Albó, X. "Andean people in the twentieth century." In *The Cambridge history of the native peoples of the Americas*, edited by B. G. Trigger et al., vol. 3 part 2. Cambridge, 1996–2000.
ʿAlī, ʿAbd al-Raḥīm. *Ḥilf al-irhāb: tanẓīm al-Qāʿida min ʿAbdallāh ʿAzzām ilā Ayman al-Ẓawāhirī*. Cairo, 2004.
———. *Tanẓīm al-Qāʿida: "ʿishrūn ʿāman.. waʾl-ghazw mustamirr."* Cairo, 2007.
Ali, M. Athar. "The perception of India in Akbar and Abuʾl Fazl." In *Akbar and his India*, edited by I. Habib. Delhi, 1997.
Allouche, A. *Mamluk economics: a study and translation of al-Maqrīzī's Ighāthah*. Salt Lake City, 1994. Original Maqrīzī, *Ighāthat al-umma*.
"'All we are breaking are stones': Afghan militia leader." http://www.rawa.org/statues.htm. AFP report from Kabul, February 27, 2001.
Almond, G. A., et al. *Strong religion: the rise of fundamentalisms around the world*. Chicago, 2003.
Al-Rasheed, M. *Contesting the Saudi state: Islamic voices from a new generation*. Cambridge, 2007.
Ālūsī, Maḥmūd al-. *Gharāʾib al-ightirāb*. Baghdad, 1327.
Álvarez, Bartolomé. *De las costumbres y conversión de los Indios del Perú*, edited by M. Martín Rubio et al. Madrid, 1998.
Ambedkar, Babasaheb. *Writings and speeches*. Vol. 14, edited by V. Moon. Bombay, 1995.
Ameer Ali, Syed. *The life and teachings of Mohammed or the spirit of Islâm*. London, 1891.
ʿĀmilī, Muḥammad ibn ʿAlī al-. *Madārik al-aḥkām*. Qum, 1410.
ʿĀmirī. *al-Iʿlām bi-manāqib al-Islām*, edited by A. ʿA. Ghurāb. Cairo, 1967.
Ammerman, N. T. "North American Protestant fundamentalism." In *Fundamentalisms observed*, edited by M. E. Marty and R. S. Appleby. The Fundamentalism Project, vol. 1. Chicago, 1991.
Ammianus Marcellinus. *Res gestae*. With translation by J. C. Rolfe. Cambridge, MA, 1950–1956.
Andersen, W. K., and S. D. Damle. *The brotherhood in saffron: the Rashtriya Swayamsevak Sangh and Hindu revivalism*. Boulder, 1987.
Andrews, G. R. *Afro-Latin America, 1800–2000*. Oxford, 2004.
Anna, T. E. *The Mexican empire of Iturbide*. Lincoln, 1990.
Ansari, A. M. *The politics of nationalism in modern Iran*. Cambridge, 2012.
Antoine, G. *Liberté égalité fraternité ou les fluctuations d'une devise*. Paris, 1981.
Āqḥiṣārī, Ḥasan Kāfī. *Uṣūl al-ḥikam fī niẓām al-ʿālam*, edited by N. R. al-Ḥamūd. Amman, 1986. Turkish version: İpşirli, "Hasan Kâfî el-Akhisarî."
Aquinas, Thomas. *Summa theologiae*. London, 1964–1976.
Arab Barometer Surveys. Results for 2006. http://www.arabbarometer.org/reports/countryreports/comparisonresutls06.html.
Arberry, A. J. *The Chester Beatty Library: a handlist of the Arabic manuscripts*. Dublin, 1955–1966.
Arian, A. *Politics in Israel: the second republic*. Washington, D.C., 2005.
Aristotle. *Politics*. Edited with a translation by H. Rackham. London, 1932.

Arnakis, G. G. "Gregory Palamas among the Turks and documents of his captivity as historical sources." *Speculum* 26 (1951).

Arnal, O. L. *Ambivalent alliance: the Catholic church and the Action Française, 1899–1939*. Pittsburgh, 1985.

Arnold, D. *Colonizing the body: state medicine and epidemic disease in nineteenth-century India*. Berkeley, 1993.

Ashour, O. "Post-jihadism and the ideological revisions of armed Islamists." In *Contextualising jihadi thought*, edited by J. Deol and Z. Kazmi. New York, 2011.

ʿAskarī, Abū Hilāl al-. *Awāʾil*, edited by W. Qaṣṣāb and M. al-Miṣrī. Riyadh, 1981.

Astarābādī, Aḥmad ibn Tāj al-Dīn. *Āthār-i Aḥmadī*, edited by M. Muḥaddith. Tehran, 1374 sh.

Aśvaghoṣa. — *The Buddhacarita*, edited and translated by E. H. Johnston. New Delhi, 1972.

Ata-ur-Rahman. "Scientific education in Muslim countries—principles and guidelines." In *Social and natural sciences: the Islamic perspective*, edited by Isma'il R. Al-Faruqi and Abdullah Omar Nasseef. Sevenoaks, 1981.

Ateek, Naim Stifan. *Justice, and only justice: a Palestinian theology of liberation*. Maryknoll, 1990.

ʿAṭiyya. Letter to Abū Muṣʿab al-Zarqāwī. http://www.ctc.usma.edu/posts/atiyahs-letter-to-zarqawi-original. 2005 (dated 10 Dhū ʾl-Qaʿda 1426). English translation on the same website.

Attenborough, F. L., ed. and trans. *The laws of the earliest English kings*. Cambridge, 1922.

Augustine. *De civitate Dei*. In Augustine, *The city of God against the pagans*, edited by G. E. McCracken et al., translated by W. C. Greene. Loeb Classical Library. Cambridge, MA, 1957–1972.

Aulard, A. *Christianity and the French Revolution*. Boston, 1927.

Averroes. *On the harmony of religion and philosophy*, translated by G. F. Hourani. London, 1961. Original: Ibn Rushd, *Kitāb faṣl al-maqāl*.

Aydin, C. *The politics of anti-Westernism in Asia: visions of world order in pan-Islamic and pan-Asian thought*. New York, 2007.

Aymonier, M. E. *Les Tchames et leurs religions*. Paris, 1891.

ʿAynī, Badr al-Dīn al-. *ʿUmdat al-qārī*. Beirut, n.d.

Bacchetta, P. "Hindu nationalist women as ideologues." In *Embodied violence: communalising women's sexuality in South Asia*, edited by K. Jayawardena and M. de Alwis. London, 1996.

Baer, G. *Egyptian guilds in modern times*. Jerusalem, 1964.

Baḥrānī, Yūsuf al-. *al-Ḥadāʾiq al-nāḍira*. Najaf, 1377–1409.

Bā Ḥusayn, Yaʿqūb ibn ʿAbd al-Wahhāb al-. *al-Mufaṣṣal fī ʾl-qawāʿid al-fiqhiyya*. Riyadh, 2010.

Bailey, D. C. *¡Viva Cristo Rey! The Cristero rebellion and the church-state conflict in Mexico*. Austin, 1974.

Baker, D. "Sibling rivalry in twentieth-century Korea: comparative growth rates of Catholic and Protestant communities." In *Christianity in Korea*, edited by R. E. Buswell and T. S. Lee. Honolulu, 2006.

Baker, R. W. *Islam without fear: Egypt and the New Islamists*. Cambridge, MA, 2003.

Bakker, H. *Ayodhyā*. Groningen, 1986.

Bakrī al-Ṣiddīqī, Muṣṭafā ibn Kamāl al-Dīn al-. *al-Faraq al-muʾdhin biʾl-ṭarab fī ʾl-farq bayn al-ʿAjam waʾl-ʿArab*. Ms. Dublin, Chester Beatty 4761.

Balādhurī. *Ansāb al-ashrāf*. Vol. 1, edited by M. Ḥamīd Allāh. Cairo, 1959.

Baldwin, D. J. *Protestants and the Mexican Revolution: missionaries, ministers, and social change*. Urbana, 1990.

Baljon, J.M.S. *The reforms and religious ideas of Sir Sayyid Aḥmad Khân*. Leiden, 1949.

———. *Religion and thought of Shāh Walī Allāh Dihlawī, 1703–1762*. Leiden, 1986.

Balz, H., and G. Schneider, eds. *Exegetical dictionary of the New Testament*. Grand Rapids, 1990–1993.

Banaji, D. R. *Slavery in British India*. Bombay, n.d.

Banarlı, N. S. "Ahmedî ve Dâsitan-ı tevârih-i mülûk-i Âl-i Osman." *Türkiyat Mecmuası* 6 (1939).

Banerjee, S. *Warriors in politics: Hindu nationalism, violence, and the Shiv Sena in India*. Boulder, 2000.

Bannā, Ḥasan al-. *Majmūʿat rasāʾil al-imām al-shahīd Ḥasan al-Bannā*. Beirut, 1965. Partially translated by C. Wendell as *Five tracts of Ḥasan Al-Bannā (1906–1949)*. Berkeley, 1978.

Baranī, Ḍiyāʾ al-Dīn. *Fatāwā-yi jahāndārī*, edited by A. S. Khan. Lahore, 1972.

Barkan, Ö. L. *Kanunlar (= XV ve XVI ıncı asırlarda Osmanlı imparatorluğunda ziraî ekonominin hukukî ve malî esasları*, vol. 1). Istanbul, 1943.

Barroso, Gustavo. *O que o integralista deve saber*. Rio de Janeiro, 1935.

Barthold, W. *Turkestan down to the Mongol invasion*. London, 1928.

Bartlett, R. *The making of Europe: conquest, colonization and cultural change, 950–1350*. Princeton, 1993.

Bary, W. T. de, et al., eds. *Sources of Indian tradition*. New York, 1958.

Barz, R. *The bhakti sect of Vallabhācārya*. Faridabad, 1976.

Basham, A. L. *The wonder that was India*. New York, 1959.

Bastian, J.-P. "Religion, différenciation intra-ethnique et ethnicité chez les Mayas du Chiapas au Mexique." In *Dealing with difference: religion, ethnicity, and politics: comparing cases and concepts*, edited by T. Hanf. Baden-Baden, 1999.

Baudesson, H. *Indo-China and its primitive people*. New York, n.d.

Baxter, C. *The Jana Sangh: a biography of an Indian political party*. Philadelphia, 1969.

Bayhaqī. *Shuʿab al-īmān*, edited by M. B. Zaghlūl. Beirut, 1990.

———. *al-Sunan al-kubrā*. Hyderabad, 1344–1355.

Bayly, C. A. "The pre-history of 'communalism'? Religious conflict in India, 1700–1860." *Modern Asian Studies* 19 (1985).

Bayly, S. *Caste, society and politics in India from the eighteenth century to the modern age. The New Cambridge History of India*, part 4: 3. Cambridge, 1999.
Bazzāz, M. A. al-. *Tārīkh al-awbiʾa waʾl-majāʿāt biʾl-Maghrib fī ʾl-qarnayn al-thāmin ʿashar waʾl-tāsiʿ ʿashar*. Rabat, 1992.
Beck, E., ed. *Des Heiligen Ephraem des Syrers Hymnen de Fide*. Louvain, 1955. (= Corpus Scriptorum Christianorum Orientalium, Scriptores Syri, vol. 73) = E. Beck (trans.), *Des Heiligen Ephraem des Syrers Hymnen de Fide*, Louvain 1955 (= Corpus Scriptorum Christianorum Orientalium, Scriptores Syri, vol. 74).
Beckerlegge, G. "Saffron and *seva*: the Rashtriya Swayamsevak Sangh's appropriation of Swami Vivekananda." In *Hinduism in public and private: reform, Hindutva, gender, and sampraday*, edited by A. Copley. Oxford, 2003.
Bede. *The ecclesiastical history of the English people*, edited by J. McClure and R. Collins. Oxford, 1994.
Bedoya, J. G. "El 'tren' de la mayoría católica." *El País*, August 7, 2005.
Bein, A. *Ottoman ulema, Turkish Republic: agents of change and guardians of tradition*. Stanford, 2011.
Belch, S. F. *Paulus Vladimiri and his doctrine concerning international law and politics*. The Hague, 1965.
Ben-Dor Benite, Z. *The Dao of Muhammad: a cultural history of Muslims in late imperial China*. Cambridge, MA, 2005.
Ben-Yehuda, N. *Theocratic democracy: the social construction of religious and secular extremism*. Oxford, 2010.
Berger, P. L. "The desecularization of the world: a global overview." In *The desecularization of the world: resurgent religion and world politics*, edited by P. L. Berger. Washington, D.C., 1999.
Bernstorff, D. "Region and nation: the Telengana movement's dual identity." In *Political identity in South Asia*, edited by D. Taylor and M. Yapp. London, 1979.
Berryman, P. *Stubborn hope: religion, politics, and revolution in Central America*. Maryknoll, 1994.
Bevir, M. *The logic of the history of ideas*. Cambridge, 1999.
Bhardwaj, S. M. *Hindu places of pilgrimage in India*. Berkeley, 1973.
Bhaṭṭa Jayanta. *Much ado about religion*, edited and translated by C. Desző. New York, 2005.
Bieler, L., ed. and trans., *The Irish penitentials*. Dublin, 1963.
Bilgrami, Akeel. "What is a Muslim? Fundamental commitment and cultural identity." *Critical Inquiry* 18 (1992).
Birman, P. "Future in the mirror: media, evangelicals, and politics in Rio de Janeiro." In *Religion, media, and the public sphere*, edited by B. Meyer and A. Moors. Bloomington, 2006.
Bīrūnī. — *Alberuni's India*, translated by E. C. Sachau. London, 1910. Original: Bīrūnī, *Taḥqīq*.
———. *Taḥqīq mā lil-Hind*, edited by E. Sachau. London, 1887. Translated as Bīrūnī, *Alberuni's India*.
Bloch, M. *Feudal society*, translated by L. A. Manyon. London, 1961.

Blum, J. *Lord and peasant in Russia from the ninth to the nineteenth century*. New York, 1964.
Bodewitz, H. W. "Hindu *ahiṁsā* and its roots." In *Violence denied: violence, non-violence and the rationalization of violence in South Asian cultural history*, edited by J.E.M. Houben and K. R. van Kooij. Leiden, 1999.
Boff, Leonardo. *Faith on the edge: religion and marginalized existence*, translated by R. R. Barr. Maryknoll, 1991.
Boff, Leonardo, and Clodovis Boff. *Introducing liberation theology*. Maryknoll, 1987.
Bolívar, Simón. *Obras completas*. Caracas, n.d.
Bonnefoy, L. "How transnational is Salafism in Yemen?" In *Global Salafism: Islam's new religious movement*, edited by R. Meijer. New York, 2009.
———. *Salafism in Yemen: transnationalism and religious identity*. London, 2011.
Boroujerdi, M. *Iranian intellectuals and the West: the tormented triumph of nativism*. Syracuse, 1996.
Bose, N. S. "Swami Vivekananda and the challenge to fundamentalism." In *Swami Vivekananda and the modernization of Hinduism*, edited by W. Radice. Delhi, 1998.
Bosworth, C. E. *The new Islamic dynasties: a chronological and genealogical manual*. New York, 1996.
Brachman, J. M., and W. F. McCants. "Stealing Al Qaeda's playbook." *Studies in Conflict & Terrorism* 29 (2006).
Brading, D. A. *Mexican phoenix: Our Lady of Guadalupe: image and tradition across five centuries*. Cambridge, 2001.
———. *The origins of Mexican nationalism*. Cambridge, 1985.
Brass, P. R. *The politics of India since Independence. The New Cambridge History of India*, part 4: 1. Cambridge, 1994.
———. *The production of Hindu-Muslim violence in contemporary India*. Seattle, 2003.
Bravo Gallardo, Carlos. "Matthew: good news for the persecuted poor." In *Subversive scriptures: revolutionary readings of the Christian Bible in Latin America*, edited and translated by L. E. Vaage. Valley Forge, 1997.
Brett, M. "The city-state in medieval Ifriqiya: the case of Tripoli." *Les Cahiers de Tunisie* 34 (1986).
Brick, D. "The Dharmaśāstric debate on widow-burning." *Journal of the American Oriental Society* 130 (2010).
Briggs, L. T. "Dialectical variation in Aymara." In *South American Indian languages: retrospect and prospect*, edited by H. E. Manelis Klein and L. R. Stark. Austin, 1985.
Brockington, J. L. *Righteous Rāma: the evolution of an epic*. Delhi, 1985.
Broomhall, M. *Islam in China: a neglected problem*. London, 1910.
Brown, C. G. *The death of Christian Britain: understanding secularisation, 1800–2000*. London, 2001.
Brown, D. D. *Umbanda: religion and politics in urban Brazil*. Ann Arbor, 1986.
Brown, J. *The canonization of al-Bukhārī and Muslim: the formation and function of the Sunnī ḥadīth canon*. Leiden, 2007.

Brown, M. *Adventuring through Spanish colonies: Simón Bolívar, foreign mercenaries and the birth of new nations*. Liverpool, 2006.

Brown, P. *Through the eye of a needle: wealth, the fall of Rome, and the making of Christianity in the West, 350–550 AD*. Princeton, 2012.

Brown, V., et al. *Cracks in the foundation: leadership schisms in al-Qa'ida 1989–2006*. http://ctc.usma.edu. Combating Terrorism Center at West Point, September 2007.

Brundage, J. A. "Humbert of Romans and the legitimacy of crusader conquests." In *The horns of Ḥaṭṭīn*, edited by B. Z. Kedar. Jerusalem, 1992.

———. *Medieval canon law and the crusader*. Madison, 1969.

Brunner, R. *Islamic ecumenism in the 20th century: the Azhar and Shiism between rapprochement and restraint*. Leiden, 2004.

Bujra, A. S. *The politics of stratification: a study of political change in a South Arabian town*. Oxford, 1971.

Bukhārī. *al-Jāmiʿ al-ṣaḥīḥ*, edited by L. Krehl. Leiden, 1862–1908.

Burdick, J. *Looking for God in Brazil: the progressive Catholic Church in urban Brazil's religious arena*. Berkeley, 1993.

Burke, Edmund. *Reflections on the revolution in France*, edited by J.C.D. Clark. Stanford, 2001.

Burnet, Gilbert, see: Gilbert Bishop of Sarum.

Burns, J. F. "British leader pushes for 'can-do optimism' and faith in austerity path." *New York Times*, October 6, 2011.

Būṭī, Muḥammad Saʿīd Ramaḍān al-. *Fiqh al-sīra*. N.p., 1968.

Cabaton, A. *Nouvelles recherches sur les Chams*. Paris, 1901.

Calder, N. "Friday prayer and the juristic theory of government: Sarakhsī, Shīrāzī, Māwardī." *Bulletin of the School of Oriental and African Studies* 49 (1986).

Callewaert, W. M. *The hagiographies of Anantadās: the bhakti poets of north India*. Richmond, 2000.

Calvin, John. *Institution de la religion chrestienne*, edited by J.-D. Benoit. Paris, 1957–1963. *Institutes of the Christian religion*, translated by J. Allen. Philadelphia, n.d.

Camelin, S. "Reflections on the system of social stratification in Hadhramaut." In *Hadhrami traders, scholars and statesmen in the Indian Ocean, 1750s–1960s*, edited by U. Freitag and W. G. Clarence-Smith. Leiden, 1997.

Canard, M. "La guerre sainte dans le monde islamique et dans le monde chrétien." *Revue Africaine* 79 (1936).

Cardwell, E., ed. *Synodalia*. Oxford, 1842.

Carré, O. *Mysticism and politics: a critical reading of Fī ẓilāl al-Qurʾān by Sayyid Quṭb (1906–66)*. Leiden, 2003.

Carvalho Azevedo, Marcello de. *Basic ecclesial communities in Brazil: the challenge of a new way of being church*. Washington, D.C., 1987.

Casanova, J. *Public religions in the modern world*. Chicago, 1994.

Cashman, R. I. *The myth of the Lokamanya: Tilak and mass politics in Maharashtra*. Berkeley, 1975.

Caskel, W. *Ǧamharat an-nasab: das genealogische Werk des Hišām ibn Muḥammad al-Kalbī*. Leiden, 1966.
Cenkner, W. *A tradition of teachers: Śaṅkara and the jagadgurus today*. Delhi, 1984.
Centeno, M. A. *Blood and debt: war and the nation-state in Latin America*. University Park, 2002.
Cevdet Paşa. *Tezâkir 1–12*, edited by C. Baysun. Ankara, 1953.
Chadwick, O. *The Popes and European revolution*. Oxford, 1981.
Chapoutot-Remadi, M. "Une grande crise à la fin du XIIIe siècle en Egypte." *Journal of the Economic and Social History of the Orient* 26 (1983).
Charles-Edwards, T. M. *Early Christian Ireland*. Cambridge, 2000.
Chattopadhyay, A. K. *Slavery in the Bengal Presidency, 1772–1843*. London, 1977.
Chattopadhyaya, B. *Representing the Other? Sanskrit sources and the Muslims (eighth to fourteenth century)*. New Delhi, 1998.
Chemparathy, G. *An Indian rational theology: introduction to Udayana's Nyāyakusumāñjali*. Vienna, 1972.
Chen, Ming. "Modernity and Confucian political philosophy in a globalized world." In *Contemporary Chinese political thought: debates and perspectives*, edited by F. Dallmayr and Zhao Tingyang. Lexington, 2012.
Chesnut, R. A. *Competitive spirits: Latin America's new religious economy*. Oxford, 2003.
Chintamani, C. Y., ed. *Indian social reform*. Madras, 1901.
Christmann, A. "Islamic scholar and religious leader: Shaikh Muhammad Sa'id Ramadan al-Buti." In *Islam and modernity: Muslim intellectuals respond*, edited by J. Cooper et al. London, 1998.
Christoffe, P., and R. Minnerath. *Le "Syllabus" de Pie IX*. Paris, 2000.
Church of England. *The book of common prayer*. Cambridge, n.d.
Chyet, M. L. *Kurdish-English dictionary*. New Haven, 2003.
Clarence-Smith, W. G. *Islam and the abolition of slavery*. Oxford, 2006.
Clayer, N. *Aux origines du nationalisme albanais: la naissance d'une nation majoritairement musulmane en Europe*. Paris, 2007.
Clémentin-Ojha, C. *Le trident sur le palais: une cabale anti-vishnouite dans un royaume hindou à l'époque coloniale*. Paris, 1999.
Collier, S. "Nationality, nationalism, and supranationalism in the writings of Simón Bolívar." *Hispanic American Historical Review* 63 (1983).
Comunión Tradicionalista. "¿Qué es el Carlismo?" http://www.carlismo.es.
Congregation for the Doctrine of the Faith. "Instruction on certain aspects of the 'theology of liberation.'" Reprinted in *Liberation theology: a documentary history*, edited by A. T. Hennelly. Maryknoll, 1990.
Conlon, F. F. "The polemic process in nineteenth-century Maharashtra: Vishnubawa Brahmachari and Hindu revival." In *Religious controversy in British India: dialogues in South Asian languages*, edited by K. W. Jones. Albany, 1992.
Constable, G. *Crusaders and crusading in the twelfth century*. Farnham, 2008.
Cook, D. *Contemporary Muslim apocalyptic literature*. Syracuse, 2005.
———. *Martyrdom in Islam*. Cambridge, 2007.
———. *Studies in Muslim apocalyptic*. Princeton, 2002.
———. *Understanding jihad*. Berkeley, 2005.

Cook, M. *A brief history of the human race*. New York, 2003.

———. *Commanding right and forbidding wrong in Islamic thought*. Cambridge, 2000.

———. "Did the prophet Muḥammad keep court?" In *Court cultures in the Muslim world: seventh to nineteenth centuries*, edited by A. Fuess and J.-P. Hartung. London, 2011.

———. "Is political freedom an Islamic value?" In *Freedom and the construction of Europe*, edited by Q. Skinner and M. van Gelderen. Vol. 2: *Free persons and free states*. Cambridge, 2012.

———. *Muhammad*. Oxford, 1983.

Coulson, N. J. *A history of Islamic law*. Edinburgh, 1964.

Coward, H. G. "The revival of Buddhism in modern India." In *Religion in modern India*, edited by R. D. Baird. New Delhi, 2001.

Cram, I. "The Danish cartoons, offensive expression, and democratic legitimacy." In *Extreme speech and democracy*, edited by I. Hare and J. Weinstein. Oxford, 2009.

Crews, R. D. "The Taliban and nationalist militancy in Afghanistan." In *Contextualising jihadi thought*, by J. Deol and Z. Kazmi. New York, 2011.

Crone, P. "The Dahrīs according to al-Jāḥiẓ." *Mélanges de l'Université de Saint-Joseph* 63 (2010–2011).

———. *Medieval Islamic political thought*. Edinburgh, 2004.

———. *The nativist prophets of early Islamic Iran: rural revolt and local Zoroastrianism*. Cambridge, 2012.

———. "Ninth-century Muslim anarchists." *Past and Present* 167 (2000).

———. "Were Qays and Yemen of the Umayyad period political parties?" *Der Islam* 71 (1994).

Crook, J. A. *Law and life of Rome*. London, 1967.

Cuneo, M. W. *The smoke of Satan: conservative and traditionalist dissent in contemporary American Catholicism*. New York, 1997.

Curran, C. E. *Catholic social teaching, 1891 – present: a historical, theological, and ethical analysis*. Washington, D.C., 2002.

Dallal, A. *Islam, science, and the challenge of history*. New Haven, 2010.

Dallmayr, F. "Introduction." In *Contemporary Chinese political thought: debates and perspectives*, edited by F. Dallmayr and Zhao Tingyang. Lexington, 2012.

Dalmia, V. "The modernity of tradition: Harishchandra of Banaras and the defence of Hindu *dharma*." In *Swami Vivekananda and the modernization of Hinduism*, edited by W. Radice. Delhi, 1998.

———. *The nationalization of Hindu traditions: Bhāratendu Hariśchandra and nineteenth-century Banaras*. Delhi, 1997.

Damen, F. L. *Crisis and religious renewal in the Brahmo Samaj (1860–1884)*. Louvain, 1983.

Dankoff, R. "Kāšγarī on the tribal and kinship organization of the Turks." *Archivum Ottomanicum* 4 (1972).

Dasūqī, Muḥammad ibn ʿArafa al-. *Ḥāshiya* to Aḥmad al-Dardīr, *al-Sharḥ al-kabīr* on the *Mukhtaṣar* of *Khalīl*. Cairo, n.d.

Ḍawābiṭ istinbāṭ aḥkām al-daʿwa min al-sīra al-nabawiyya. http://www.tawhed.ws. Taken from the *Majallat al-Murābiṭīn.* Peshawar, n.d.
Dawsarī, Muḥammad b. Sālim al-. *al-Radd ʿalā bayān "al-Jabha al-Dākhiliyya."* http://www.tawhed.ws. 2003 (dated Ṣafar 1424).
Dayanand Saraswati. *Satyarth Prakash,* translated by D. Prasad. New Delhi, 1972.
Deas, M. "Venezuela, Colombia and Ecuador: the first half-century of independence." In *The Cambridge History of Latin America.* Vol. 3: *From independence to c. 1870,* edited by L. Bethell. Cambridge, 2002.
Degler, C. N. *Neither black nor white: slavery and race relations in Brazil and the United States.* Madison, 1986.
Deiros, P. A. "Protestant fundamentalism in Latin America." In *Fundamentalisms observed,* edited by M. E. Marty and R. S. Appleby. The Fundamentalism Project, vol. 1. Chicago, 1991.
Deliège, R. *The Untouchables of India.* Oxford, 1999.
Deringil, S. *The well-protected domains: ideology and the legitimation of power in the Ottoman Empire, 1876–1909.* London, 1998.
Derrett, J.D.M. "Bhāruci on the royal regulative power in India." *Journal of the American Oriental Society* 84 (1964).
———. *Bhāruci's commentary on the Manusmṛti.* Wiesbaden, 1975.
———. *Dharmaśāstra and juridical literature.* In *A history of Indian literature,* edited by J. Gonda, vol. 4. Wiesbaden, 1973.
———. *Hindu law past and present.* Calcutta, 1957.
———. *History of Indian law (dharmaśāstra).* In the *Handbuch der Orientalistik.* Leiden, 1973.
———. *Religion, law and the state in India.* New York, 1968.
Desai, Mahadev. — *The diary of Mahadev Desai.* Vol. 1. Ahmedabad, 1953.
Deshpande, V. V. *Dharma-shastra and the proposed Hindu Code.* Benares, 1943.
Devahuti, D. *Harsha: a political study.* Delhi, 1983.
Dixit, P. "The political and social dimensions of Vivekananda's ideology." *Indian Economic and Social History Review* 12 (1975).
Dixon, R.M.W., and A. Y. Aikhenvald, eds. *The Amazonian languages.* Cambridge, 1999.
Drobner, H. R. "Christian philosophy." In *The Oxford handbook of early Christian studies,* edited by S. A. Harvey and D. G. Hunter. Oxford, 2010.
D'Sa, F. X. *Śabdaprāmāṇyam in Śabara and Kumārila: towards a study of the Mīmāṃsā experience of language.* Vienna, 1980.
Duffy, E. *The stripping of the altars: traditional religion in England, c. 1400 – c. 1580.* New Haven, 2005.
Duncan, R. I. "Levels, the communication of programmes, and sectional strategies in Indian politics." Ph.D. diss., University of Sussex, 1979.
Dunn, J. *Democracy: a history.* New York, 2005.
Durand, le R. P. "Les Chams Bani." *Bulletin de l'Ecole Française d'Extrême Orient* 3 (1903).
Dvornik, F. *Early Christian and Byzantine political philosophy: origins and background.* Washington, D.C., 1966.

Eakin, E. "Holy cow a myth? An Indian finds the kick is real." *New York Times*, August 17, 2002.

Eaton, R. M. "Temple desecration and Indo-Muslim states." In *Beyond Turk and Hindu: rethinking religious identities in Islamicate South Asia*, edited by D. Gilmartin and B. B. Lawrence. Gainesville, 2000.

Eatwell, R. "Reflections on fascism and religion." In *Religious fundamentalism and political extremism*, edited by L. Weinberg and A. Pedahzur. London, 2004.

Ebrey, P. B. *The inner quarters: marriage and the lives of Chinese women in the Sung period*. Berkeley, 1993.

Eckert, J. M. *The charisma of direct action: power, politics, and the Shiv Sena*. Oxford, 2003.

EI², see: *Encyclopaedia of Islam*.

Ellacuría, I., and J. Sobrino, eds. *Mysterium liberationis: fundamental concepts of liberation theology*. Maryknoll, 1993.

Ellis, H., ed. *The pylgrymage of Sir Richard Guylforde to the Holy Land, A.D. 1506*. London, 1851.

El-Rouayheb, K. *Before homosexuality in the Arab-Islamic world, 1500–1800*. Chicago, 2005.

———. "The myth of 'the triumph of fanaticism' in the seventeenth-century Ottoman Empire." *Die Welt des Islams* 48 (2008).

Embree, A. T. "The function of the Rashtriya Swayamsevak Sangh: to define the Hindu nation." In *Accounting for fundamentalisms*, edited by M. E. Marty and R. S. Appleby. The Fundamentalism Project, vol. 4. Chicago, 1994.

Encyclopaedia of Islam. 2nd ed. [abbreviated *EI²*.] Leiden, 1960–2009.

Engineer, Asghar Ali. "On some aspects of liberation theology in Islam." In *Islam and liberation theology: essays on liberative elements in Islam*, by Asghar Ali Engineer. New Delhi, 1990.

English, A. C. "Christian Reconstructionism after Y2K: Gary North, the new millennium, and religious freedom." In *New religious movements and religious liberty in America*, edited by D. H. Davis and B. Hankins. Waco, 2002.

Erdem, Y. H. *Slavery in the Ottoman Empire and its demise, 1800–1909*. Basingstoke, 1996.

Erdmann, C. *The origin of the idea of crusade*. Princeton, 1977.

Esdaile, C. J. *Spain in the liberal age: from constitution to civil war, 1808–1939*. Oxford, 2000.

Esposito, J. L., and D. Mogahed. *Who speaks for Islam? What a billion Muslims really think*. New York, 2007.

Euben, R. L., and M. Q. Zaman, eds. *Princeton readings in Islamist thought: texts and contexts from al-Banna to Bin Laden*. Princeton, 2009.

Fakhr al-Dīn al-Rāzī. *al-Tafsīr al-kabīr*. Cairo, ca. 1934–1962.

Fakhr al-Muḥaqqiqīn. *Īḍāḥ al-fawāʾid*. N.p., 1387–1389.

Fandy, M. "Egypt's Islamic Group: regional revenge?" *Middle East Journal* 48 (1994).

———. *Saudi Arabia and the politics of dissent*. New York, 2001.

Farfán, C. R. "Erscheinungsformen des religiösen Lebens in Chiapas." In *Chiapas: Aktuelle Situation und Zukunftsperspektiven für die Krisenregion im Südosten Mexikos,* edited by U. Köhler. Frankfurt am Main, 2003.

Farfán, C. R., et al. *Diversidad religiosa y conflicto en Chiapas: intereses, utopías y realidades.* Mexico City, 2005.

Fārūqī, Ismāʿīl Rājī al. "Islamization of knowledge: problems, principles and prospective." In *Islam: source and purpose of knowledge: proceedings and selected papers of Second Conference on Islamization of Knowledge 1402 AH / 1982 AC.* International Institute of Islamic Thought. Herndon, 1988.

Fatḥ Allāh, Wasīm. *Lā yataḥaddathu ʾl-nās anna Muḥammadan yaqtulu aṣḥābahu.* http://www.tawhed.ws. N.d.

Fatton, R. *Haiti's predatory republic: the unending transition to democracy.* Boulder, 2002.

Feldman, N. *The fall and rise of the Islamic state.* Princeton, 2008.

Fierro, M. *ʿAbd al-Rahman III: the first Cordoban caliph.* Oxford, 2005.

———. "Idraʾū l-ḥudūd bi-l-shubuhāt: when lawful violence meets doubt." *Hawwa* 5 (2007).

———. "*Mawālī* and *muwalladūn* in al-Andalus (second/eighth–fourth/tenth centuries)." In *Patronate and patronage in early and classical Islam,* edited by M. Bernards and J. Nawas. Leiden, 2005.

Figgis, J. N. *The divine right of kings.* New York, 1965.

Fisch, J. *Burning women: a global history of widow sacrifice from ancient times to the present.* Oxford, 2006.

Fish, M. S. *Are Muslims distinctive? A look at the evidence.* Oxford, 2011.

Fishman, T. "Guarding oral transmission: within and between cultures." *Oral Tradition* 25 (2010).

Fleischer, C. H. *Bureaucrat and intellectual in the Ottoman Empire: the historian Mustafa Âli (1541–1609).* Princeton, 1986.

Forster, C. T., and F. H. Blackburne Daniell. *The life and letters of Ogier Ghiselin de Busbecq.* London, 1881.

Fox, J. "Is Islam more conflict prone than other religions? A cross-sectional study of ethnoreligious conflict." *Nationalism & Ethnic Politics* 6, no. 2 (2000).

———. "Two civilizations and ethnic conflict: Islam and the West." *Journal of Peace Research* 38 (2001).

———. *A world survey of religion and the state.* Cambridge, 2008.

Frankel, J. D. *Rectifying God's name: Liu Zhi's Confucian translation of monotheism and Islamic law.* Honolulu, 2011.

Frashëri, Shemseddīn Sāmī. "Transferring the new civilization to the Islamic peoples." In *Modernist Islam, 1840–1940: a sourcebook,* edited by Charles Kurzman. New York, 2002.

Freedman, L. "The impact of the Falklands conflict on international affairs." In *The Falklands conflict twenty years on: lessons for the future,* edited by S. Badsey et al. London, 2005.

Freeman, E. A. "Race and language." In *Historical Essays,* by E. A. Freeman. 3rd ser. London, 1879.

Freitag, U. *Indian Ocean migrants and state formation in Hadhramaut: reforming the homeland.* Leiden, 2003.

Friedmann, Y. *Prophecy continuous: aspects of Aḥmadī religious thought and its medieval background*. New Delhi, 2003.

———. *Shaykh Aḥmad Sirhindī: an outline of his thought and a study of his image in the eyes of posterity*. Montreal, 1971.

———. *Tolerance and coercion in Islam: interfaith relations in the Muslim tradition*. Cambridge, 2003.

Frydenlund, I. "Canonical ambiguity and differential practices: Buddhism and militarism in contemporary Sri Lanka." In *Buddhism and violence: militarism and modern Asia*, edited by V. Tikhonov and T. Brekke. New York, 2013.

Frykenberg, R. E. "Accounting for fundamentalisms in South Asia: ideologies and institutions in historical perspective." In *Accounting for fundamentalisms*, edited by M. E. Marty and R. S. Appleby. The Fundamentalism Project, vol. 4. Chicago, 1994.

———. "Hindu fundamentalism and the structural stability of India." In *Fundamentalisms and the state*, edited by M. E. Marty and R. S. Appleby. The Fundamentalism Project, vol. 3. Chicago, 1993.

Fuchs, S. W. *Proper signposts for the camp: the reception of classical authorities in the ǧihādī manual al-ʿUmda fī iʿdād al-ʿudda*. Würzburg, 2011.

Fuller, C. J. *The camphor flame: popular Hinduism and society in India*. Princeton, 2004.

Gabriele, M. *An empire of memory: the legend of Charlemagne, the Franks, and Jerusalem before the First Crusade*. Oxford, 2011.

Gaddis, M. *There is no crime for those who have Christ: religious violence in the Christian Roman Empire*. Berkeley, 2005.

Galanter, M. "The aborted restoration of 'indigenous' law in India." *Comparative Studies in Society and History* 14 (1972).

———. *Competing equalities: law and the backward classes in India*. Berkeley, 1984.

García Gutiérrez, J. "La Virgen insurgente y la Virgen gachupina." *Ábside: Revista de Cultura Mexicana* 4 (1940).

Gay, J. *Le pape Clément VI et les affaires d'Orient (1342–1352)*. New York, 1972.

Gellner, D. N., et al. *Nationalism and ethnicity in a Hindu kingdom: the politics of culture in contemporary Nepal*. Amsterdam, 1997.

Gerber, H. *State, society, and law in Islam: Ottoman law in comparative perspective*. Albany, 1994.

Gerges, F. A. *The far enemy: why jihad went global*. Cambridge, 2005.

Gershoni, I., and J. Jankowski. *Confronting fascism in Egypt: dictatorship versus democracy in the 1930s*. Stanford, 2010.

Gethin, R. "Buddhist monks, Buddhist kings, Buddhist violence: on the early Buddhist attitudes to violence." In *Religion and violence in South Asia: theory and practice*, edited by J. R. Hinnells and R. King. London, 2007.

Gettleman, J. "Chaos breeds new agony for Somalia: religious war." *New York Times*, May 24, 2009.

Ghaḍbān, Munīr Muḥammad. *Fiqh al-sīra al-nabawiyya*. Mecca, 1995.

———. *al-Manhaj al-ḥarakī lil-sīra al-nabawiyya*. Zarqāʾ, 1984.

Ghassānī al-Andalusī, Muḥammad al-. *Riḥlat al-wazīr fī ʾftikāk al-asīr*. Abu Dhabi, 2002.

Ghunaymī, ʿAbd al-Ākhir Ḥammād al-. *Ḥukm taghyīr al-munkar biʾl-yad li-āḥād al-raʿiyya*. http://www.tawhed.ws. 1997–1998 (2nd printing, dated 1418).

———. *Marāḥil tashrīʿ al-jihād: naskh al-lāḥiq minhā lil-sābiq*. http://www.tawhed.ws. 1998 (dated 2 Ramaḍān 1419).

———. *Muṣṭalaḥāt wa-mafāhīm*. http://www.tawhed.ws. 1998 (dated October 1, 1998).

Ghurye, G. S. *Indian Sadhus*. Bombay, 1953.

Gibb, H.A.R. "Luṭfī Paşa on the Ottoman Caliphate." *Oriens* 15 (1962).

Gilbert Bishop of Sarum. *An exposition of the thirty-nine articles of the Church of England*. London, 1705.

Gill, A. *Rendering unto Caesar: the Catholic Church and the state in Latin America*. Chicago, 1998.

Gilson, E. *The Christian philosophy of Saint Augustine*. London, 1961.

Glasenapp, H. von. *Heilige Stätten Indiens*. Munich, 1928.

Glüsing, J. "Allahs Indianer." *Der Spiegel*, May 30, 2005.

Göçek, F. M. *East encounters West: France and the Ottoman Empire in the eighteenth century*. New York, 1987.

Goitein, S. D. "The rise of the Near-Eastern bourgeoisie in early Islamic times." *Cahiers d'Histoire Mondiale* 3 (1957).

Gökalp, Ziya. *Turkish nationalism and Western civilization*, edited and translated by N. Berkes. London, 1959.

Gokhale, J. *From concessions to confrontation: the politics of an Indian Untouchable community*. Bombay, 1993.

Gökyay, O. Ş. "Kâtip Çelebi; hayatı, şahsiyeti, eserleri." In *Kâtip Çelebi: hayatı ve eserleri hakkında incelemeler*. Ankara, 1957.

Gold, D. "Organized Hinduisms: from Vedic truth to Hindu nation." In *Fundamentalisms observed*, edited by M. E. Marty and R. S. Appleby. The Fundamentalism Project, vol. 1. Chicago, 1991.

Goldberg, J. "Saudi Arabia and the Iranian revolution: the religious dimension." In *The Iranian revolution and the Muslim world*, edited by D. Menashri. Boulder, 1990.

Goldziher, I. "The attitude of orthodox Islam toward the 'ancient sciences.'" In *Studies on Islam*, edited and translated by M. L. Swartz. New York, 1981.

———. "Catholic tendencies and particularism in Islam." In *Studies on Islam*, edited and translated by M. L. Swartz. New York, 1981.

———. *Introduction to Islamic theology and law*, translated by A. and R. Hamori. Princeton, 1981.

———. *Muslim studies*, translated by C. R. Barber and S. M. Stern. London, 1967–1971.

Golwalkar, M. S. *We or our nationhood defined*. Nagpur, 1939.

Gonda, J. *Vedic literature*. In *A history of Indian literature*, edited by J. Gonda, vol. 1. Wiesbaden, 1975.

Gonzalez, M. A. *Afro-Cuban theology: religion, race, culture, and identity*. Gainesville, 2006.

Gordon, S. "Maratha patronage of Muslim institutions in Burhanpur and Khandesh." In *Beyond Turk and Hindu: rethinking religious identities in Islamicate South Asia*, edited by D. Gilmartin and B. B. Lawrence. Gainesville, 2000.

Gossen, G. H. "Life, death, and apotheosis of a Chamula Protestant leader: biography as social history." In *Telling Maya tales: Tzotzil identities in modern Mexico*, by G. H. Gossen. New York, 1999.

Gould, W. *Hindu nationalism and the language of politics in late colonial India*. Cambridge, 2004.

Graham, B. D. *Hindu nationalism and Indian politics: the origins and development of the Bharatiya Jana Sangh*. Cambridge, 1990.

Greene, M. "An Islamic experiment? Ottoman land policy on Crete." *Mediterranean Historical Review* 11 (1996).

———. *A shared world: Christians and Muslims in the early modern Mediterranean*. Princeton, 2000.

Gross, R. L. "Hindu asceticism: a study of the sādhus of North India." Ph.D. diss., University of California, Berkeley, 1979.

Guerrero, A. G. *A chicano theology*. Maryknoll, 1987.

Guha, R. *India after Gandhi: the history of the world's largest democracy*. New York, 2007.

Guha, S. "Slavery, society, and the state in western India, 1700–1800." In *Slavery and South Asian history*, edited by I. Chatterjee and R. M. Eaton. Bloomington, 2006.

Guibert de Nogent. *Dei Gesta per Francos et cinq autres textes*, edited by R.B.C. Huygens. Turnhout, 1996.

Gurumurthy, S. *Education in South India (ancient and medieval periods)*. Madras, 1979.

Gutas, D. *Greek thought, Arabic culture*. London, 1998.

Gutiérrez, Gustavo. "Notes for a theology of liberation." Reprinted in *Liberation theology at the crossroads: democracy or revolution?* by P. E. Sigmund, appendix 1. New York, 1990.

———. "Theology and the social sciences." Partially reprinted in *Liberation theology at the crossroads: democracy or revolution?* by P. E. Sigmund, appendix 2. New York, 1990.

———. *A theology of liberation: history, politics and salvation*. Maryknoll, 1973. *A theology of liberation: history, politics, and salvation*. Maryknoll, 2002 [references are to this edition unless otherwise stated].

Haarmann, U. "Ideology and history, identity and alterity: the Arab image of the Turk from the ʿAbbasids to modern Egypt." *International Journal of Middle East Studies* 20 (1988).

———. "*Rather the injustice of the Turks than the righteousness of the Arabs*—changing *ʿulamāʾ* attitudes towards Mamluk rule in the late fifteenth century." *Studia Islamica* 68 (1988).

Habib, I. *The agrarian system of Mughal India (1556–1707)*. London, 1963.

Habib, M., and A.U.S. Khan. *The political theory of the Delhi Sultanate*. Allahabad, n.d.

Hafez, M. M. "*Takfir* and violence against Muslims." In *Fault lines in global jihad: organizational, strategic, and ideological fissures*, edited by A. Moghadam and B. Fishman. London, 2011.

Hagenmeyer, H., ed. *Anonymi Gesta Francorum et aliorum Hiersolymitanorum*. Heidelberg, 1890.

Haider, N. “A ‘Holi riot’ of 1714: versions from Ahmedabad and Delhi.” In *Living together separately: cultural India in history and politics*, edited by M. Hasan and A. Roy. New Delhi, 2005.

Ḥajarī, Aḥmad ibn Qāsim al-. *Kitāb nāṣir al-dīn ʿalā ʾl-qawm al-kāfirīn*, edited and translated by P. S. van Koningsveld et al. Madrid, 1997.

Ḥajjī, M. *al-Ḥaraka al-fikriyya biʾl-Maghrib fī ʿahd al-Saʿdiyyīn*. N.p., 1976–1978.

Ḥamdān Khwāja. *Itḥāf al-munṣifīn waʾl-udabāʾ fī ʾl-iḥtirāz ʿan al-wabāʾ*, edited by M. ʿAbd al-Karīm. Algiers, 1968.

Hanioğlu, M. Ş. *Atatürk: an intellectual biography*. Princeton, 2011.

Hankins, B., ed. *Evangelicalism and fundamentalism: a documentary reader*. New York, 2008.

Hansen, T. B. “BJP and the politics of Hindutva in Maharashtra.” In *The BJP and the compulsions of politics in India*, edited by T. B. Hansen and C. Jaffrelot. Delhi, 1998.

———. *The saffron wave: democracy and Hindu nationalism in modern India*. Princeton, 1999.

———. *Wages of violence: naming and identity in postcolonial Bombay*. Princeton, 2001.

Hanu, Jose. *Vatican encounter: conversations with Archbishop Marcel Lefebvre*. Kansas City, 1978.

Hardacre, H. *Shintō and the state, 1868–1988*. Princeton, 1989.

Haring, C. H. *Empire in Brazil: a New World experiment with monarchy*. Cambridge, MA, 1969.

Harper, K. *Slavery in the late Roman world, AD 275–425*. Cambridge, 2011.

Harvey, L. P. *Muslims in Spain, 1500–1614*. Chicago, 2005.

Hasan, N. “Ambivalent doctrines and conflicts in the Salafi movement in Indonesia.” In *Global Salafism: Islam’s new religious movement*, edited by R. Meijer. New York, 2009.

Ḥasan, Y. F. *The Arabs and the Sudan*. Edinburgh, 1967.

Haskins, G. L. *Law and authority in early Massachusetts: a study in tradition and design*. New York, 1960.

Hasluck, M. *The unwritten law in Albania*. Cambridge, 1954.

Hassan, M. F. “Loss of caliphate: the trauma and aftermath of 1258 and 1924.” Ph.D. diss., Princeton University, 2009.

Hawley, J. S. “Hinduism: *satī* and its defenders.” In *Fundamentalism and gender*, edited by J. S. Hawley. New York, 1994.

Ḥawwā, Saʿīd. *al-Asās fī ʾl-tafsīr*. Cairo, 1985.

———. *al-Islām*. Beirut, 1969–1970.

———. *Jund Allāh takhṭīṭan*. Cairo, 1988.

———. *Jund Allāh thaqāfatan wa-akhlāqan*. Beirut, 1971.

———. *al-Rasūl*. Beirut, 1969.

Haykel, B. “On the nature of Salafi thought and action.” In *Global Salafism: Islam’s new religious movement*, edited by R. Meijer. New York, 2009.

———. “Al-Qa’ida and Shiism.” In *Fault lines in global jihad: organizational, strategic, and ideological fissures*, edited by A. Moghadam and B. Fishman. London, 2011.

Haykel, B. *Revival and reform in Islam: the legacy of Muhammad al-Shawkānī.* Cambridge, 2003.

Heesterman, J. C. "The conundrum of the king's authority." In *The inner conflict of tradition: essays in Indian ritual, kingship, and society*, by J. C. Heesterman. Chicago, 1985.

Hefner, R. W. "Of faith and commitment: Christian conversion in Muslim Java." In *Conversion to Christianity: historical and anthropological perspectives on a great transformation*, edited by R. W. Hefner. Berkeley, 1993.

Hegghammer, T. *Jihad in Saudi Arabia: violence and pan-Islamism since 1979.* Cambridge, 2010.

———. "Jihadi-Salafis or revolutionaries? On religion and politics in the study of militant Islamism." In *Global Salafism: Islam's new religious movement*, edited by R. Meijer. New York, 2009.

———. "The rise of Muslim foreign fighters: Islam and the globalization of jihad." *International Security* 35, no. 3 (Winter 2010/11).

Hegghammer, T., and S. Lacroix. "Rejectionist Islamism in Saudi Arabia: the story of Juhayman al-ʿUtaybi revisited." *International Journal of Middle East Studies* 39 (2007).

Hellie, R. *Slavery in Russia, 1450–1725.* Chicago, 1982.

Henderson, P.V.N. *Gabriel García Moreno and conservative state formation in the Andes.* Austin, 2008.

Hernández, H. *The Sinarquista movement with special reference to the period 1934–1944.* London, 1999.

Herzfeld, M. *Ours once more: folklore, ideology, and the making of modern Greece.* New York, 1986.

Heyd, U. *Ottoman documents on Palestine, 1552–1615: a study of the firman according to the Mühimme Defteri.* Oxford, 1960.

———. *Studies in old Ottoman criminal law.* Oxford, 1973.

Hilāl al-Ṣābiʾ. *Rusūm Dār al-Khilāfah (The rules and regulations of the ʿAbbāsid court)*, translated by E. A. Salem. Beirut, 1977.

Hill, W.D.P. *The holy lake of the acts of Rāma: a translation of Tulasī Dās's Rāmacaritamānasa.* Calcutta, 1971.

Hinsch, B. "The origins of separation of the sexes in China." *Journal of the American Oriental Society* 123 (2003).

Hoadly, C. J. *Records of the colony and plantation of New Haven, from 1638 to 1649.* Hartford, 1857.

———. *Records of the colony or jurisdiction of New Haven, from May, 1653, to the union together with the New Haven code of 1656.* Hartford, 1858.

Hoffman, V. J. "Oral traditions as a source for the study of Muslim women: women in the Sufi orders." In *Beyond the exotic: women's histories in Islamic societies*, edited by A. E. Sonbol. Syracuse, 2005.

———. *Sufism, mystics, and saints in modern Egypt.* Columbia, 1995.

Holmes, J. D. *More Roman than Rome: English Catholicism in the nineteenth century.* London, 1978.

Holt, P. M. *The Mahdist state in the Sudan, 1881–1898.* Oxford, 1970.

Holtom, D. C. *The national faith of Japan: a study in modern Shinto.* New York, 1938.

Hopkins, K. *Conquerors and slaves.* Cambridge, 1980.
Housley, N. "A necessary evil? Erasmus, the crusade, and war against the Turks." In *Crusading and warfare in medieval and Renaissance Europe,* by N. Housley. Aldershot, 2001.
Howard-Johnson, J. "The official history of Heraclius' Persian campaigns." In *The Roman and Byzantine army in the east,* edited by E. Dąbrowa. Cracow, 1994.
Hoyland, R. G. *Arabia and the Arabs from the Bronze Age to the coming of Islam.* London, 2001.
Hroub, K. *Hamas: political thought and practice.* Washington, D.C., 2000.
———. "Salafi formations in Palestine: the limits of a de-Palestinised milieu." In *Global Salafism: Islam's new religious movement,* edited by R. Meijer. New York, 2009.
Hudson, D. D. "Arumuga Navalar and the Hindu renaissance among the Tamils." In *Religious controversy in British India: dialogues in South Asian languages,* edited by K. W. Jones. Albany, 1992.
Huntington, S. P. "The clash of civilizations?" *Foreign Affairs* 72, no. 3 (Summer 1993).
———. *The clash of civilizations and the remaking of world order.* New York, 1996.
Hunwick, J. *Jews of a Saharan oasis: elimination of the Tamantit community.* Princeton, 2006.
———. *Sharīʿa in Songhay: the replies of al-Maghīlī to the questions of Askia al-Ḥājj Muḥammad.* Oxford, 1985.
Hunwick, J., and E. Trout Powell. *The African diaspora in the Mediterranean lands of Islam.* Princeton, 2002.
Hurewitz, J. C. *The Middle East and North Africa in World Politics: a documentary record.* New Haven, 1975–1979.
Ḥusayn ibn Maḥmūd. *Muḥammad rasūl al-malḥama.* http://www.tawhed.ws. 2002 (dated 22 Shawwāl 1423).

Ibn ʿAbd al-Barr. *Istidhkār,* edited by ʿA. A. Qalʿajī. Damascus, 1993.
———. *al-Istīʿāb fī maʿrifat al-aṣḥāb,* edited by ʿA. M. al-Bajāwī. Cairo, n.d.
Ibn ʿAbd Rabbih. *al-ʿIqd al-farīd,* edited by A. Amīn et al. Cairo, 1940–1949.
Ibn Abī Shayba. *Muṣannaf,* edited by K. Y. al-Ḥūt. Beirut, 1989.
Ibn Abī Yaʿlā. *Ṭabaqāt al-Ḥanābila,* edited by M. Ḥ. al-Fiqī. Cairo, 1952.
Ibn Battúta. *Travels in Asia and Africa, 1325–1354,* translated by H.A.R. Gibb. London, 1929.
Ibn Ghannām. *Rawḍat al-afkār.* Bombay, 1337.
Ibn Ḥabīb, ʿAbd al-Malik. *Kitāb al-Taʾrīkh,* edited by J. Aguadé. Madrid, 1991.
Ibn Ḥajar al-ʿAsqalānī. *Fatḥ al-bārī.* Beirut, 1988.
Ibn Ḥamza al-Ḥusaynī al-Dimashqī. *al-Bayān waʾl-taʿrīf.* Aleppo, 1329.
Ibn Ḥanbal. *Musnad.* Būlāq, 1313.
Ibn Ḥazm. *Muḥallā.* Beirut, n.d.
Ibn Hishām. *al-Sīra al-nabawiyya,* edited by M. al-Saqqā et al. Cairo, 1955. Translated by A. Guillaume as *The life of Muhammad: a translation of Ibn Isḥāq's Sīrat Rasūl Allāh.* Karachi, 1980.

Ibn al-Jawzī. *Kashf al-mushkil*, edited by M.Ḥ.M.Ḥ. Ismāʿīl. Beirut, 2004.
Ibn Kathīr. *al-Bidāya waʾl-nihāya*. Cairo, 1351–1358.
———. *Tafsīr al-Qurʾān al-ʿaẓīm*. Beirut, 1990–1991.
Ibn Khaldūn. *ʿIbar*. Būlāq, 1284.
———. *Muqaddima*, edited by E. M. Quatremère. Paris, 1858. Translated by F. Rosenthal as *The Muqaddimah: an introduction to history*. Princeton, 1967.
Ibn Qāsim al-ʿĀṣimī, ʿAbd al-Raḥmān ibn Muḥammad. *al-Durar al-saniyya fī ʾl-ajwiba al-Najdiyya*. Beirut, 1982.
Ibn Qayyim al-Jawziyya. *Iʿlām al-muwaqqiʿīn*. Beirut, 1973.
———. *al-Ṭibb al-nabawī*, edited by S. and ʿA. al-Arnaʾūṭ. Beirut, 1981.
———. *al-Wābil al-ṣayyib*, edited by ʿA. Ḥ. Ibn Qāʾid. Mecca, 1425.
———. *Zād al-maʿād*, edited by S. and ʿA. al-Arnaʾūṭ. Beirut, 1979.
Ibn Rushd. *Kitāb faṣl al-maqāl*, edited by G. F. Hourani. Leiden, 1959. Translated by G. F. Hourani as Averroes, *On the harmony*.
Ibn Saʿd. *al-Ṭabaqāt al-kabīr*, edited by E. Sachau et al. Leiden, 1904–1921.
Ibn Taymiyya. *al-Amr biʾl-maʿrūf waʾl-nahy ʿan al-munkar*, edited by Ṣ. al-Munajjid. Beirut, 1984.
———. *Iqtiḍāʾ al-ṣirāṭ al-mustaqīm*, edited by M. Ḥ. al-Fiqī. Cairo, 1950. Partially translated by Memon as *Ibn Taymīya's struggle*.
———. *Istiqāma*, edited by M. R. Sālim. Riyadh, 1983.
———. *Majmūʿ fatāwā Shaykh al-Islām Aḥmad ibn Taymiyya*, collected and arranged by ʿA. M. Ibn Qāsim al-ʿĀṣimī. Beirut, 1997.
———. *al-Ṣārim al-maslūl ʿalā shātim al-rasūl*, edited by M.ʿA.ʿU. al-Ḥulwānī and M.K.A. Shawdarī. Beirut, 1997.
Ibrahim, R., ed. and trans. *The Al Qaeda reader*. New York, 2007.
Ifrānī. *Nuzhat al-ḥādī bi-akhbār mulūk al-qarn al-ḥādī*, edited by ʿA. al-Shādilī. Casablanca, 1998.
Imber, C. *Ebuʾs-suʿud: the Islamic legal tradition*. Edinburgh, 1997.
———. "The Ottoman dynastic myth." *Turcica* 19 (1987).
———. *The Ottoman Empire, 1300–1650: the structure of power*. Basingstoke, 2002.
———. "What does *ghazi* actually mean?" In *The balance of truth: essays in honour of Professor Geoffrey Lewis*, edited by C. Balım-Harding and C. Imber. Istanbul, 2000.
——— "*Zinā* in Ottoman law." In *Studies in Ottoman history and law*, by C. Imber. Istanbul, 1996.
Inalcık, H. "Islamization of Ottoman laws on land and land tax." In *Festgabe an Josef Matuz: Osmanistik—Turkologie—Diplomatik*, edited by C. Fragner and K. Schwarz. Berlin, 1992.
———. "Suleiman the Lawgiver and Ottoman law." *Archivum Ottomanicum* 1 (1969).
India. Census of 2001. http://censusindia.gov.in/Census_Data_2001/Census_Data_Online/Language/Statement6.htm.
Inglebert, H. *Interpretatio Christiana: les mutations des savoirs (cosmographie, géographie, ethnographie, histoire) dans l'Antiquité chrétienne (30–630 après J.-C.)*. Paris, 2001.

Inglehart, R., and C. Welzel. *Modernization, cultural change, and democracy: the human development sequence*. Cambridge, 2005.
İpşirli, M. "Hasan Kâfî el-Akhisarî ve devlet düzenine ait eseri." *Tarih Enstitüsü Dergisi* 10–11 (1979–80). Arabic version: Āqḥiṣārī, *Uṣūl al-ḥikam*.
ʿIrāqī, Zayn al-Dīn al-. *al-Qurab fī maḥabbat al-ʿArab*. Bombay, 1303.
Irschick, E. F. *Politics and social conflict in South India: the non-Brahman movement and Tamil separatism, 1916–1929*. Berkeley, 1969.
Isogai, K. "*Yasa* and *shariʿa* in early 16th century Central Asia." In *L'Héritage timouride: Iran—Asie centrale—Inde, XVe-XVIIIe siècles*, edited by M. Szuppe. Tashkent, 1997.
ʿIyāḍ. *Sharḥ Ṣaḥīḥ Muslim*, edited by Y. Ismāʿīl. Manṣūra, 1998.
Iyer, S. "Jinnah favoured a secular Pakistan: Advani." *Hindustan Times*, June 5, 2005.

Jaffrelot, C. "The 2002 pogrom in Gujarat: the post-9/11 face of Hindu nationalist anti-Muslim violence." In *Religion and violence in South Asia: theory and practice*, edited by J. R. Hinnells and R. King. London, 2007.
———. "The BJP and the 2004 general election: dimensions, causes and implications of an unexpected defeat." In *Coalition politics and Hindu nationalism*, edited by K. Adeney and L. Sáez. London, 2005.
———. "From Indian territory to Hindu *bhoomi:* the ethnicization of nation-state mapping in India." In *The politics of cultural mobilization in India*, edited by J. Zavos et al. New Delhi, 2004.
———, ed. *Hindu nationalism: a reader*. Princeton, 2007.
———. "Hindu nationalism and the social welfare strategy." In *Modern roots: studies of national identity*, edited by A. Dieckhoff and N. Gutiérrez. Aldershot, 2001.
———. *The Hindu nationalist movement and Indian politics*. New Delhi, 1999.
———, ed. *A history of Pakistan and its origins*. London, 2002.
———. *India's silent revolution: the rise of the lower castes in North India*. New York, 2003.
———. "The politics of processions and Hindu-Muslim riots." In *Community conflicts and the state in India*, edited by A. Basu and A. Kohli. Delhi, 1998.
———. "Les (Re)conversions à l'hindouisme (1885–1990): politisation et diffusion d'une 'invention de la tradition.' " *Archives de Sciences Sociales des Religions* 87 (1994).
———. "The Vishva Hindu Parishad: structures and strategies." In *The Sangh Parivar: a reader*, edited by C. Jaffrelot. New Delhi, 2005.
Jansen, J.J.G. *The neglected duty: the creed of Sadat's assassins and Islamic resurgence in the Middle East*. New York, 1986.
Jaṣṣāṣ. *Aḥkām al-Qurʾān*. Beirut, 1994.
Jevdet. *Tārīkh*. Istanbul, 1309.
Jha, D. N. *The myth of the holy cow*. London, 2002.
Jha, G., ed. and trans. *Manusmṛti with the Manubhāṣya of Medhātithi*. Delhi, 1999.

Jiménez Limón, Javier. "Suffering, death, cross, and martyrdom." In *Mysterium liberationis: fundamental concepts of liberation theology*, edited by I. Ellacuría and and J. Sobrino. Maryknoll, 1993.

Jinnah. — *Speeches and writings of Mr. Jinnah*, edited by Jamil-ud-Din Ahmad. Lahore, 1960–1964.

Johnson, H. L. "The Virgin of Guadalupe in Mexican culture." In *Religion in Latin American life and literature*, edited by L. C. Brown and W. F. Cooper. Waco, 1980.

Johnson, W., trans. *The T'ang Code*. Vol. 1: *General principles*. Princeton, 1979.

Jones, A.H.M. *The later Roman Empire, 284–602: a social economic and administrative survey*. Oxford, 1964.

Jones, A. K., "Muslim politics and the growth of the Muslim League in Sind, 1935–1941." Ph.D. diss., Duke University, 1977.

Jones, K. W. *Arya Dharm: Hindu consciousness in 19th-century Punjab*. Berkeley, 1976.

———. *Socio-religious reform movements in British India. The New Cambridge History of India*, part 3: 1. Cambridge, 1989.

———. "Two *sanātan dharma* leaders and Swami Vivekananda: a comparison." In *Swami Vivekananda and the modernization of Hinduism*, edited by W. Radice. Delhi, 1998.

Jordens, J.T.F. *Dayānanda Sarasvatī: his life and ideas*. Delhi, 1978.

———. *Gandhi's religion: a homespun shawl*. Basingstoke, 1998.

———. "Reconversion to Hinduism: the *shuddhi* of the Arya Samaj." In *Religion in South Asia: religious conversion and revival movements in South Asia in medieval and modern times*, edited by G. A. Oddie. New Delhi, 1991.

———. *Swāmī Shraddhānanda: his life and causes*. Delhi, 1981.

Juergensmeyer, M. *Global rebellion: religious challenges to the secular state, from Christian militias to al Qaeda*. Berkeley, 2008.

———. *Religion as social vision: the movement against untouchability in 20th-century Punjab*. Berkeley, 1982.

Justinian. *Digest*, edited by T. Mommsen and P. Krueger, and translated by A. Watson. Philadelphia, 1985.

Kafadar, C. "A Rome of one's own: reflections on cultural geography and identity in the lands of Rum." *Muqarnas* 24 (2007).

Kaikini, L. V., ed. *The speeches & writings of Sir Narayen G. Chandavarkar*. Bombay, 1911.

Kakar, S. *The colors of violence: cultural identities, religion, and conflict*. Chicago, 1996.

Kalyvas, S. N. *The rise of Christian democracy in Europe*. Ithaca, 1996.

Kane, P. V. *History of Dharmaśāstra*. Poona, 1930–1962.

Karasipahi, S. *Muslims in modern Turkey: Kemalism, modernism and the revolt of the Islamic intellectuals*. London, 2009.

Kāshgharī. *Dīwān lughāt al-Turk*, edited by Kilisli Rifʿat. Istanbul, 1333–1335.

Kāshī, Ḥasan. "Maʿrifatnāma." In *Tārīkh-i Muḥammadī*, by Ḥasan Kāshī, edited by R. Jaʿfarīyān. Qumm, 1377 sh.

Kātib Chelebī. *Destūr ül-ʿamel li-iṣlāḥ il-khalel*. In *Qavānīn-i āl-i Othmān der khulāṣa-i maḍāmīn-i defter-i dīvān*, by ʿAyn-i ʿAlī. Reprinted Istanbul, 1979.
Katju, M. *Vishva Hindu Parishad and Indian politics*. New Delhi, 2003.
Katzenstein, M. F., et al. "The rebirth of Shiv Sena: the symbiosis of discursive and organizational power." *Journal of Asian Studies* 56 (1997).
Kedar, B. Z. *Crusade and mission: European approaches toward the Muslims*. Princeton, 1984.
Keddie, N. R. *An Islamic response to imperialism: political and religious writings of Sayyid Jamāl ad-Dīn "al-Afghānī."* Berkeley, 1968.
———. "The New Religious Politics: where, when, and why do 'fundamentalisms' appear?" *Comparative Studies in Society and History* 40 (1998).
———. *Sayyid Jamāl ad-Dīn "al-Afghānī": a political biography*. Berkeley, 1972.
Kedourie, E. *Afghani and ʿAbduh: an essay on religious unbelief and political activism in modern Islam*. London, 1997.
———, ed. *Nationalism in Africa and Asia*. London, 1971.
———. "Religion and politics." In *The Chatham House version and other Middle-Eastern Studies*, by E. Kedourie. London, 1970.
Keer, D. *Lokamanya Tilak: father of the Indian freedom struggle*. Bombay, 1969.
Kelly, F. *A guide to early Irish law*. Dublin, 1988.
Kennedy, H. *The great Arab conquests: how the spread of Islam changed the world we live in*. London, 2007.
Kent, D. W. "Onward Buddhist soldiers: preaching to the Sri Lankan army." In *Buddhist warfare*, edited by M. Jerryson and M. Juergensmeyer. Oxford, 2010.
Kepel, G. *Jihad: the trail of political Islam*. Cambridge, MA, 2002.
———. *The war for Muslim minds: Islam and the West*. Cambridge, MA, 2006.
Khādimī, Abū Saʿīd al-. *Majāmiʿ al-ḥaqāʾiq*. Istanbul, 1292.
Khazrajī. *al-ʿUqūd al-luʾluʾiyya*, edited and translated by M. B. ʿAsal and J. W. Redhouse. Leiden, 1906–1918.
Khilnani, S. *The idea of India*. New York, 1997.
Kinsley, D. *Hindu goddesses: visions of the divine feminine in the Hindu religious tradition*. Berkeley, 1986.
Kirkpatrick, D. D. "The evangelical crackup." *New York Times Magazine*, October 28, 2007.
Kirkpatrick, D. D., and M. El-Naggar. "Poll finds Egyptians full of hope about future." *New York Times*, April 26, 2011.
Kister, M. J. "Al-Ḥīra: some notes on its relations with Arabia." *Arabica* 15 (1968).
———. "Land property and *jihād*: a discussion of some early traditions." In *Concepts and ideas at the dawn of Islam*, by M. J. Kister. Aldershot, 1997.
Kitâbu mesâlihi'l-Müslimîn ve menâfi'i'l-mü'minîn. Reproduced and transcribed by Y. Yücel. Ankara, 1980–1981.
Klein, H. S. *Bolivia: the evolution of a multi-ethnic society*. New York, 1992.
———. *Parties and political change in Bolivia, 1880–1952*. Cambridge, 1971.
Knysh, A. "The *Tariqa* on a landcruiser: the resurgence of Sufism in Yemen." *Middle East Journal* 3 (2001).
Krämer, G. "Islamist notions of democracy." In *Political Islam: essays from Middle East Report*, edited by J. Beinin and J. Stork. Berkeley, 1997.

Kramer, M. "Coming to terms: fundamentalists or Islamists?" *Middle East Quarterly* 10, no. 2 (2003).
———. *Islam assembled: the advent of the Muslim congresses*. New York, 1986.
Küçükhüseyin, Ş. *Selbst- und Fremdwahrnehmung im Prozess kultureller Transformation: anatolische Quellen über Muslime, Christen und Türken (13.–15. Jahrhundert)*. Vienna, 2011.
Kuijp, L.W.J. van der. "The earliest Indian reference to Muslims in a Buddhist philosophical text of *circa* 700." *Journal of Indian Philosophy* 34 (2006).
Kull, S. *Feeling betrayed: the roots of Muslim anger at America*. Washington, D.C., 2011.
Kumar, K. "Hindu revivalism and education in north-central India." In *Fundamentalisms and society*, edited by M. E. Marty and R. S. Appleby. The Fundamentalism Project, vol. 2. Chicago, 1993.
Kuran, T. *The long divergence: how Islamic law held back the Middle East*. Princeton, 2011.
Kurzman, C., ed. *Modernist Islam, 1840–1940: a sourcebook*. Oxford, 2002.
Kushner, D. *The rise of Turkish nationalism, 1876–1908*. London, 1977.
Kutb, Sayyid, see: Qutb, Sayyid.

Lacroix, S. "Between revolution and apoliticism: Nasir al-Din al-Albani and his impact on the shaping of contemporary Salafism." In *Global Salafism: Islam's new religious movement*, edited by R. Meijer. New York, 2009.
Lahoud, N. "Jihadi recantations and their significance: the case of Dr Fadl." In *Fault lines in global jihad: organizational, strategic, and ideological fissures*, edited by A. Moghadam and B. Fishman. London, 2011.
———. *The jihadis' path to self-destruction*. New York, 2010.
Laidlaw, J. *Riches and renunciation: religion, economy, and society among the Jains*. Oxford, 1995.
Laine, J. W. *Shivaji: Hindu king in Islamic India*. Oxford, 2003.
———. "Śivājī as epic hero." In *Folk culture, folk religion and oral traditions as a component in Maharashtrian culture*, edited by G.-D. Sontheimer. New Delhi, 1995.
Lal, D. "The economic impact of Hindu revivalism." In *Fundamentalisms and the state*, edited by M. E. Marty and R. S. Appleby. The Fundamentalism Project, vol. 3. Chicago, 1993.
Lambert, M. D. *Franciscan poverty: the doctrine of the absolute poverty of Christ and the apostles in the Franciscan order, 1210–1323*. New York, 1998.
Lambton, A.K.S. *State and government in medieval Islam*. Oxford, 1991.
Lamotte, E. *History of Indian Buddhism from the origins to the Śaka era*. Louvain-la-Neuve, 1988.
Landau, J. M. *The politics of Pan-Islam: ideology and organization*. Oxford, 1990.
Landau-Tasseron, E. "Features of the pre-conquest Muslim army in the time of Muḥammad." In *The Byzantine and early Islamic Near East*. Vol. 3: *States, resources and armies*, edited by A. Cameron. Princeton, 1995.
———. *The religious foundations of political allegiance: a study of bayʿa in premodern Islam*. Hudson Institute, Research Monographs on the Muslim World, Series 2, Paper no. 4. Washington, D.C., 2010.

Lane, E. W. *An account of the manners and customs of the modern Egyptians.* London, 1895.

———. *An Arabic-English lexicon.* London, 1863–1893.

Langohr, V. "Colonial education systems and the spread of local religious movements: the cases of British Egypt and Punjab." *Comparative Studies in Society and History* 47 (2005).

Lauzière, H. "Post-Islamism and the religious discourse of ʿAbd al-Salam Yasin." *International Journal of Middle East Studies* 37 (2005).

Lawrence, B., ed. *Messages to the world: the statements of Osama bin Laden.* London, 2005.

Laws, Curtis Lee. "Convention side lights." *Watchman-Examiner* 8, no. 27 (July 1, 1920).

Lecker, M. *The "Constitution of Medina": Muḥammad's first legal document.* Princeton, 2004.

Lederle, M. *Philosophical trends in modern Mahārāṣṭra.* Bombay, 1976.

Lee, T. S. "Beleaguered success: Korean Evangelicalism in the last decade of the twentieth century." In *Christianity in Korea*, edited by R. E. Buswell and T. S. Lee. Honolulu, 2006.

Lefebvre, Marcel. *A bishop speaks: writings and addresses, 1963–1975.* Edinburgh, n.d.

———. *They have uncrowned him: from liberalism to apostasy: the conciliar tragedy.* Kansas City, 1992.

Lelyveld, D. *Aligarh's first generation: Muslim solidarity in British India.* Princeton, 1978.

Lemercier-Quelquejay, C. "Les missions orthodoxes en pays musulmans de Moyenne- et Basse-Volga, 1552–1865." *Cahiers du Monde Russe et Soviétique* 8 (1967).

Leonard, B. J. *Baptists in America.* New York, 2005.

Leonard, J., and K. Leonard. "Viresalingam and the ideology of social change in Andhra." In *Religious controversy in British India: dialogues in South Asian languages*, edited by K. W. Jones. Albany, 1992.

Leslie, D. D. *The survival of the Chinese Jews: the Jewish community of Kaifeng.* Leiden, 1972.

Leslie, D. D., et al. *Islam in traditional China: a bibliographical guide.* Sankt Augustin, 2006.

Leslie, J. *Authority and meaning in Indian religions: Hinduism and the case of Vālmīki.* Aldershot, 2003.

Leuba, J. *Les Chams d'autrefois et d'aujourd'hui.* Hanoi, 1915.

Lev, Y. *Charity, endowments, and charitable institutions in medieval Islam.* Gainesville, 2005.

Levenson, J. R. *Confucian China and its modern fate: a trilogy.* Berkeley, 1968.

———. *Liang Ch'i-ch'ao and the mind of modern China.* Berkeley, 1970.

Levine, D. H. *Popular voices in Latin American Catholicism.* Princeton, 1992.

Levine, R. M. *The Vargas regime: the critical years, 1934–1938.* New York, 1970.

Lewis, B. *The emergence of modern Turkey.* London, 1961.

———. "Ibn Khaldūn in Turkey." In *Islam in history: ideas, people, and events in the Middle East*, by B. Lewis. Chicago, 1993.

———. *Islam from the Prophet Muhammad to the capture of Constantinople.* New York, 1987.

Lewis, B. *The Jews of Islam*. Princeton, 1984.
———. *The Muslim discovery of Europe*. New York, 1982.
———. “Ottoman observers of Ottoman decline.” In *Islam in history: ideas, people, and events in the Middle East*, by B. Lewis. Chicago, 1993.
———. *The political language of Islam*. Chicago, 1988.
———. *Race and slavery in the Middle East: an historical enquiry*. New York, 1990.
Lewis, B. L. “Sarmiento, Martí, and Rodó: three views of the United States in the Latin American essay.” In *Portrayal of America in various literatures*, edited by W. T. Zyla. Lubbock, 1978.
Lex Baiwariorum, edited by E. von Schwind. In *Monumenta Germaniae historica, Legum Sectio I, Leges nationum germanicarum*, vol. 1, part 2. Hanover, 1926.
Li, L. M. *Fighting famine in North China: state, market, and environmental decline, 1690s–1990s*. Stanford, 2007.
Lia, B. *Architect of global jihad: the life of al-Qaida strategist Abu Musʿab al-Suri*. New York, 2008.
Lindekilde, L. “Soft repression and mobilization: the case of transnational activism of Danish Muslims during the cartoons controversy.” *International Journal of Middle East Studies* 42 (2010).
Loeffler, R. *Islam in practice: religious beliefs in a Persian village*. Albany, 1988.
Loewenberg, S. “As Spaniards lose their religion, church leaders struggle to hold on.” *New York Times*, June 26, 2005.
Loomis, L. R. “Nationality at the Council of Constance: an Anglo-French dispute.” In *Change in medieval society: Europe north of the Alps, 1050-1500*, edited by S. L. Thrupp. New York, 1964.
Lorenzen, D. N. *Kabir legends and Ananta-das's Kabir Parachai*. Albany, 1991.
———. “Warrior ascetics in Indian history.” *Journal of the American Oriental Society* 98 (1977).
———. “Who invented Hinduism?” *Comparative Studies in Society and History* 41 (1999).
Luṭf Allāh Jaḥḥāf. *Durar nuḥūr al-ḥūr al-ʿīn*, edited by ʿĀ.M.ʿA.F. al-Raʿawī. Ṣanʿāʾ, 2004.
Lutgendorf, P. “Interpreting Rāmrāj: reflections on the ‘Rāmāyaṇ,’ bhakti, and Hindu nationalism.” In *Bhakti religion in North India: community identity and political action*, edited by D. N. Lorenzen. Albany, 1995.
Lütt, J. “The Śankarācārya of Puri.” In *The cult of Jagannath and the regional tradition of Orissa*, edited by A. Eschmann et al. New Delhi, 1978.
Lynch, E. A. *Religion and politics in Latin America: Liberation Theology and Christian Democracy*. New York, 1991.
Lynch, M. “Islam divided between jihad and the Muslim Brotherhood.” In *Fault lines in global jihad: organizational, strategic, and ideological fissures*, edited by A. Moghadam and B. Fishman. London, 2011.
———. *Voices of the new Arab public: Iraq, al-Jazeera, and Middle East politics today*. New York, 2006.
Lyra, H. *História de Dom Pedro II, 1825–1891*. Belo Horizonte, 1977.

Macaulay, N. *Dom Pedro: the struggle for liberty in Brazil and Portugal, 1798–1834*. Durham, 1986.

———. "First principles of the Islamic state." In *The Islamic law and constitution*, by Sayyid Abul Aʿlā Maudūdī, edited and translated by K. Ahmad. Lahore, 1960.

———. *Fundamentals of Islam*. Lahore, 1975.

———. "Fundamentals of Islamic constitution." In *The Islamic law and constitution*, by Sayyid Abul Aʿlā Maudūdī, edited and translated by K. Ahmad. Lahore, 1960.

———. "How to introduce Islamic law in Pakistan." In *The Islamic law and constitution*, by Sayyid Abul Aʿlā Maudūdī, edited and translated by K. Ahmad. Lahore, 1960.

———. *Human rights in Islam*. Delhi, n.d. (preface dated 1980).

———. *Islam today*. Delhi, 1989.

———. "The Islamic law." In *The Islamic law and constitution*, by Sayyid Abul Aʿlā Maudūdī, edited and translated by K. Ahmad. Lahore, 1960.

———. *The Islamic law and constitution*, by Sayyid Abul Aʿlā Maudūdī, edited and translated by K. Ahmad. Lahore, 1960.

———. *The Islamic movement: dynamics of values, power and change*, translated by K. Murad. Leicester, 1984.

———. *Let us be Muslims*. Leicester, 1985.

———. "Political concepts of the Qurʾan." In *The Islamic law and constitution*, by Sayyid Abul Aʿlā Maudūdī, edited and translated by K. Ahmad. Lahore, 1960.

———. *Political theory of Islam*, translated by K. Ahmad. Lahore, 1976. Arabic translation: Mawdūdī, *Naẓariyya*.

———. "Political theory of Islam." Abbreviated version. In *The Islamic law and constitution*, by Sayyid Abul Aʿlā Maudūdī, edited and translated by K. Ahmad. Lahore, 1960.

———. "The problem of electorate." In *The Islamic law and constitution*, by Sayyid Abul Aʿlā Maudūdī, edited and translated by K. Ahmad. Lahore, 1960.

———. *Purdah and the status of woman in Islam*, translated by Al-Ashʿari. Lahore, 1983.

———. "Rights of non-Muslims in Islamic state." In *The Islamic law and constitution*, by Sayyid Abul Aʿlā Maudūdī, edited and translated by K. Ahmad. Lahore, 1960. Arabic translation: Mawdūdī, *Ḥuqūq ahl al-dhimma*.

———. *A short history of the revivalist movement in Islam*, translated by Al-Ashʿari. Lahore, 1963.

———. "Some constitutional proposals." In *The Islamic law and constitution*, by Sayyid Abul Aʿlā Maudūdī, edited and translated by K. Ahmad. Lahore, 1960.

———. *Unity of the Muslim world*, edited by K. Ahmad. Lahore, 1967.

Māwardī. *al-Aḥkām al-sulṭāniyya*, edited by M. Enger. Bonn, 1853.

———. *al-Ḥāwī al-kabīr*, edited by ʿA. M. Muʿawwaḍ and ʿA. A. ʿAbd al-Mawjūd. Beirut, 1994.

Mawdūdī, Abū ʾl-Aʿlā al-. *Bayn al-daʿwa al-qawmiyya waʾl-rābiṭa al-Islāmiyya*. Cairo, n.d.

———. *al-Ḥukūma al-Islāmiyya*, translated by A. Idrīs. Cairo, 1977.

———. *Ḥuqūq ahl al-dhimma fī ʾl-dawla al-Islāmiyya*. N.p., n.d. English translation: Maudūdī, "Rights of non-Muslims."

Mawdūdī, Abū ʾl-Aʿlā al-. *al-Jihād fī sabīl Allāh*. Lebanon, n.d.
———. *Minhāj al-inqilāb al-Islāmī*. Cairo, n.d.
———. *Muʿḍilāt al-iqtiṣād wa-ḥalluhā fī ʾl-Islām*. Cairo, 1371. English translation: Maududi, *The economic problem*.
———. *Naẓariyyat al-Islām al-siyāsiyya*. Rawalpindi, n.d. English translation: Maududi, *Political theory*.
———. *Tafhīm al-Qurʾān*. Lahore, 1958–1972.
"Maya threatens to embrace Buddhism." *Times of India*, April 14, 2003.
"Mayawati justifies lighting Kanshi Ram's funeral pyre." http://news.oneindia.in/2006/10/16/mayawati-justifies-lighting-kanshi-rams-funeral-pyre-1161013354.html. *Oneindia*, October 16, 2006.
Mayeda, S. *A thousand teachings: the Upadeśasāhasrī of Śaṅkara*. Albany, 1992.
McCants, W., ed. *Militant ideology atlas: research compendium, November 2006*. Combating Terrorism Center, West Point. http://www.ctc.usma.edu/posts/militant-ideology-atlas.
McChesney, R. D. "Zamzam water on a white felt carpet: adapting Mongol ways in Muslim Central Asia, 1550–1650." In *Religion, customary law, and nomadic technology*, edited by M. Gervers and W. Schlepp. Toronto, 2000.
McClintock, C. *Revolutionary movements in Latin America: El Salvador's FMLN & Peru's Shining Path*. Washington, D.C., 1998.
McGarry, J., and B. O'Leary. *The Northern Ireland conflict: consociational engagements*. Oxford, 2004.
McGregor, R. S. *The Oxford Hindi-English dictionary*. Oxford, 1993.
McKean, L. "Bhārat Mātā: Mother India and her militant matriots." In *Devī: goddesses of India*, edited by J. S. Hawley and D. M. Wulff. Berkeley, 1996.
McLaren, A. "Challenging the monarchical republic: James I's articulation of kingship." In *The monarchical republic of early modern England: essays in response to Patrick Collinson*, edited by J. F. McDiarmid. Aldershot, 2007.
McLeod, W. H. *The Chaupa Singh Rahit-nama*. Dunedin, 1987.
———. *The evolution of the Sikh community*. In *Sikhs and Sikhism*, by W. H. McLeod. New Delhi, 1999.
———. *Textual sources for the study of Sikhism*. Chicago, 1990.
———. *Who is a Sikh? The problem of Sikh identity*. In *Sikhs and Sikhism*, by W. H. McLeod. New Delhi, 1999.
McNeil, D. G. "Gunmen kill Nigerian polio vaccine workers in echo of Pakistan attacks." *New York Times*, February 9, 2013.
McPherson, A. *Yankee No! Anti-Americanism in U.S.–Latin American relations*. Cambridge, MA, 2003.
McPherson, J. M. *Battle cry of freedom: the Civil War era*. New York, 1988.
Mdaghrī, ʿAbd al-Kabīr al-ʿAlawī al-. *al-Faqīh Abū ʿAlī al-Yūsī: numūdhaj min al-fikr al-Maghribī fī fajr al-dawla al-ʿAlawiyya*. N.p., 1989.
Mearsheimer, J. J. *The tragedy of great power politics*. New York, 2001.
Meijer, R. "Commanding right and forbidding wrong as a principle of social action: the case of the Egyptian al-Jamaʿa al-Islamiyya." In *Global Salafism: Islam's new religious movement*, edited by R. Meijer. New York, 2009.
Memon, M. U. *Ibn Taymīya's struggle against popular religion*. The Hague, 1976. Original: Ibn Taymiyya, *Iqtiḍāʾ*.

Mendelsohn, O., and M. Vicziany. *The Untouchables: subordination, poverty and the state in modern India*. Cambridge, 1998.
Menteşzāde ʿAbdürraḥīm Efendi. *Fetāvā*. Istanbul, 1243.
Meserve, M. *Empires of Islam in Renaissance historical thought*. Cambridge, MA, 2008.
Metzger, T. A. *A cloud across the Pacific: essays on the clash between Chinese and Western political theories today*. Hong Kong, 2005.
Meyer, J. A. *The Cristero rebellion: the Mexican people between church and state, 1926–1929*. Cambridge, 1976.
———. *La cristiada: los cristeros*. Mexico City, 1974.
———. *Le Sinarquisme: un fascisme mexicain? 1937-1947*, Paris 1977.
Meyer, M. C., et al. *The course of Mexican history*. New York, 2011.
Micklethwait, J., and A. Wooldridge. *God is back: how the global revival of faith is changing the world*. New York, 2009.
Míguez Bonino, José. *Revolutionary theology comes of age*. London, 1975.
Milner, A. C. "Islam and Malay kingship." *Journal of the Royal Asiatic Society*, 1981.
"Minister knocked down by court verdict on mosque demolition." *Nature*, October 2, 2003.
Mishal, S., and A. Sela, *The Palestinian Hamas: vision, violence, and coexistence*. New York, 2000.
Mishra, D. N. *RSS: myth and reality*. Sahibabad, 1980.
Miskawayh. *Tajārib al-umam*. Vol. 1, edited by L. Caetani. Leiden, 1909.
Misner, P. *Social Catholicism in Europe: from the onset of industrialization to the First World War*. New York, 1991.
Mission d'Ollone. *Recherches sur les musulmans chinois*. Paris, 1911.
Mitchell, R. P. *The Society of the Muslim Brothers*. London, 1969.
Mitteis, L. *Reichsrecht und Volksrecht in den östlichen Provinzen des römischen Kaiserreichs*. Leipzig, 1891.
Mobini-Kesheh, N. "Islamic modernism in colonial Java: the al-Irshād movement." In *Hadhrami traders, scholars and statesmen in the Indian Ocean, 1750s–1960s*, edited by U. Freitag and W. G. Clarence-Smith. Leiden, 1997.
Mora, A. *Border dilemmas: racial and national uncertainties in New Mexico, 1848–1912*. Durham, 2011.
More, J.B.P. *Muslim identity, print culture and the Dravidian factor in Tamil Nadu*. Hyderabad, 2004.
Moreh, S., ed. and trans. *Al-Jabartī's chronicle of the first seven months of the French occupation of Egypt*. Leiden, 1975.
Moreland, W. H. *From Akbar to Aurangzeb: a study in Indian economic history*. London, 1923.
———. *India at the death of Akbar: an economic study*. Delhi, 1990.
Morgan, D. *The Mongols*. Oxford, 2007.
Mottahedeh, R. "The Shuʿûbîyah controversy and the social history of early Islamic Iran." *International Journal of Middle East Studies* 7 (1976).
Moussalli, A. S. *Radical Islamic fundamentalism: the ideological and political discourse of Sayyid Quṭb*. Beirut, 1992.
Mukerji, A. B. *The Chamars of Uttar Pradesh: a study in social geography*. Delhi, 1980.

Munson, H. *Religion and power in Morocco*. New Haven, 1993.

Murata, S. et al. *The sage learning of Liu Zhi: Islamic thought in Confucian terms*. Cambridge, MA, 2009.

"Mursī fī khiṭāb al-fawz: sa-akūnu raʾīsan li-kull al-Miṣriyyīn." http://hespress.com/international/57009.html. June 24, 2012.

Musallam, A. A. *From secularism to jihad: Sayyid Qutb and the foundations of radical Islamism*. Westport, 2005.

Muslim ibn al-Ḥajjāj. *Ṣaḥīḥ*, edited by M. F. ʿAbd al-Bāqī. Cairo, 1955–1956.

"Muslim leaders condemn Taliban destruction." http://www.rawa.org/statues.htm. *Times of India*, March 2, 2001.

Mutanabbī. *Dīwān*, edited by F. Dieterici. Berlin, 1861.

Nabavi, N. *Intellectuals and the state in Iran: politics, discourse, and the dilemma of authenticity*. Gainesville, 2003.

Nadwī, Abū ʾl-Ḥasan al-. *al-ʿArab waʾl-Islām*. Beirut, n.d.

Nag, K., and D. Burman, eds. *The English works of Raja Rammohun Roy*. Calcutta, 1945–1951.

Nagle, R. *Claiming the Virgin: the broken promise of liberation theology in Brazil*. New York, 1997.

Nājī, Abū Bakr. *al-Khawana: akhass ṣafqa fī taʾrīkh al-ḥaraka al-Islāmiyya al-muʿāṣira*. http://www.tawhed.ws. N.d.

Nakamura, H. *Gotama Buddha: a biography based on the most reliable texts*, translated by G. Sekimori. Tokyo, 2002–2005.

Nakash, Y. *Reaching for power: the Shiʿa in the modern Arab world*. Princeton, 2006.

Narāqī, Aḥmad al-. *Mustanad al-Shīʿa*. Mashhad, 1415-1420.

Narayanan, V. "Religious vocabulary and regional identity: a study of the Tamil *Cirappuranam*." In *Beyond Turk and Hindu: rethinking religious identities in Islamicate South Asia*, edited by D. Gilmartin and B. B. Lawrence. Gainesville, 2000.

Nasafī, Abū ʾl-Muʿīn al-. *Tabṣirat al-adilla*, edited by K. Salāma. Damascus, 1990–1993.

Nāṣirī, Aḥmad ibn Khālid al-. *Istiqṣāʾ*, edited by J. al-Nāṣirī and M. al-Nāṣirī. Casablanca, 1954–1956.

Nasr, S.V.R. *Mawdudi and the making of Islamic revivalism*. New York, 1996.

———. *The vanguard of the Islamic revolution: the Jamaʿat-i Islami of Pakistan*. Berkeley, 1994.

Nasseef, Abdullah Omar. "Introduction." In *Social and natural sciences: the Islamic perspective*, edited by Isma'il R. Al-Faruqi and Abdullah Omar Nasseef. Sevenoaks, 1981.

Nawas, J. A. "A profile of the *mawālī ʿulamāʾ*." In *Patronate and patronage in early and classical Islam*, edited by M. Bernards and J. Nawas. Leiden, 2005.

Nawawī. *Sharḥ Ṣaḥīḥ Muslim*. Beirut, 1994.

Necipoğlu, G. *Architecture, ceremonial, and power: the Topkapı Palace in the fifteenth and sixteenth centuries*. Cambridge, MA, 1991.

Nehru, Jawaharlal. *An autobiography, with musings on recent events in India*. London, 1989.

Nettler, R. L. *Past trials and present tribulations: a Muslim fundamentalist's view of the Jews*. Oxford, 1987. Original: Quṭb, *Maʿrakatunā*.

Nicholas, B. *An introduction to Roman law*. Oxford, 1991.

Nicholson, R. A. *A literary history of the Arabs*. Cambridge, 1956.

Nilakanta Sastri, K. A. *The Pāṇḍyan kingdom from the earliest times to the sixteenth century*. London, 1929.

Niẓām al-Mulk. *Siyar al-mulūk (Siyāsat nāma)*, edited by H. Darke. Tehran, 1994. Translated by H. Darke as *The book of government or rules for kings*. London, 1978.

Noble, W. A., and A. R. Sankhyan, "Signs of the divine: *satī* memorials and *satī* worship in Rajasthan." In *The idea of Rajasthan: explorations in regional identity*, edited by K. Schomer et al., vol. 1. New Delhi, 1994.

Nold, P. *Pope John XXII and his Franciscan cardinal: Bertrand de la Tour and the apostolic poverty controversy*. Oxford, 2003.

Norris, P., and R. Inglehart. *Sacred and secular: religion and politics worldwide*. Cambridge, 2011.

North, Gary. *Political polytheism: the myth of pluralism*. Tyler, 1989.

North, Gary, and Gary DeMar. *Christian Reconstruction: what it is, what it isn't*. Tyler, 1991.

Nuʿaym ibn Ḥammād. *Fitan*, edited by S. Zakkār. Mecca, n.d. (preface dated 1991).

Nurul Hasan, S. "Sahifa-i-Naʿt-i-Muhammadi of Zia-ud-Din Barani." *Medieval India Quarterly* 1, nos. 3–4 (n.d., ca. 1951).

Oberoi, H. "Mapping Indic fundamentalisms through nationalism and modernity." In *Fundamentalisms comprehended*, edited by M. E. Marty and R. S. Appleby. The Fundamentalism Project, vol. 5. Chicago, 1995.

O'Connell, J. T. "The word 'Hindu' in Gauḍīya Vaiṣṇava texts." *Journal of the American Oriental Society* 93 (1973).

Ó Corráin, D., et al. "The laws of the Irish." *Peritia* 3 (1984).

O'Dwyer, M. M. *The papacy in the age of Napoleon and the Restoration: Pius VII, 1800–1823*. Lanham, 1985.

O'Hanlon, R. *Caste, conflict, and ideology: Mahatma Jotirao Phule and low caste protest in nineteenth-century western India*. Cambridge, 1985.

Olivelle, P., trans. *Dharmasūtras: the law codes of Āpastamba, Gautama, Baudhāyana, and Vasiṣṭha*. Oxford, 1999.

———, trans. *Manu's code of law: a critical edition and translation of the Mānava-Dharmaśāstra*. Oxford, 2005.

Oliver, L. *The beginnings of English law*. Toronto, 2002.

Oliveros, Roberto. "History of the theology of liberation." In *Mysterium liberationis: fundamental concepts of liberation theology*, edited by I. Ellacuría and J. Sobrino. Maryknoll, 1993.

Omvedt, G. *Dalits and the democratic revolution: Dr. Ambedkar and the Dalit movement in colonial India*. New Delhi, 1994.

Onishi, N. "New strife tests Nigeria's fragile democracy." *New York Times*, March 15, 2000.

ʿOthmān Nūrī [Ergin]. *Mejelle-i umūr-u belediyye*. Istanbul, 1330-8 mālī

Ottmann, G. F. *Lost for words? Brazilian liberationism in the 1990s*. Pittsburgh, 2002.

Özbaran, S. *Bir Osmanlı kimliği: 14.–17. yüzyıllarda Rûm/Rûmi aidiyet ve imgeleri*. Istanbul, 2004.

Özcan, A. *Pan-Islamism: Indian Muslims, the Ottomans and Britain (1877–1924)*. Leiden, 1997.

Pande, G. C. *Life and thought of Śaṅkarācārya*. Delhi, 1994.

Pandey, G. *The construction of communalism in colonial north India*. Delhi, 1990.

———. "Peasant revolt and Indian nationalism: the peasant movement in Awadh, 1919–22." In *Selected subaltern studies*, edited by R. Guha and G. C. Spivak. New York, 1988.

Paret, R. *Die legendäre Maghāzi-Literatur: arabische Dichtungen über die muslimischen Kriegszüge zu Mohammeds Zeit*. Tübingen, 1930.

Parthasarathy, R., trans. *The Cilappatikāram of Iḷaṅkō Aṭikaḷ: an epic of South India*. New York, 1993.

Partido Carlista. "Quiénes somos." http://partidocarlista.com.

Parvate, T. V. *Gopal Krishna Gokhale: a narrative and interpretative review of his life, career and contemporary events*. Ahmedabad, 1959.

Payne, S. G. *Fascism in Spain, 1923–1977*. Madison, 1999.

Paz, R. "Jihadists and nationalist Islamists: al-Qa'ida and Hamas." In *Fault lines in global jihad: organizational, strategic, and ideological fissures*, edited by A. Moghadam and B. Fishman. London, 2011.

Pelikan, J. *The Christian tradition: a history of the development of doctrine*. Chicago, 1975–1991.

Pelteret, D.A.E. *Slavery in early mediaeval England from the reign of Alfred until the twelfth century*. Woodbridge, 1995.

Peña, M. *Theologies and liberation in Peru: the role of ideas in social movements*. Philadelphia, 1995.

Peskes, E. "The Wahhābiyya and Sufism in the eighteenth century." In *Islamic mysticism contested: thirteen centuries of controversies and polemics*, edited by F. de Jong and B. Radtke. Leiden, 1999.

Peters, R. *Islam and colonialism: the doctrine of jihad in modern history*. The Hague, 1979.

Pettifer, P., and M. Vickers, *The Albanian question: reshaping the Balkans*. London, 2007.

Pew Forum on Religion & Public Life. *"Nones" on the rise: one-in-five adults have no religious affiliation*. http://www.pewforum.org/Unaffiliated/nones-on-the-rise.aspx. 2012.

———. *Spirit and power: a 10-country survey of pentecostals*. http://www.pewforum.org/newassets/surveys/pentecostal/pentecostals-08.pdf. 2006.

Pew Global Attitudes Project. *Islamic extremism: common concern for Muslim and Western publics*. 17-Nation Pew Global Attitudes Survey. http://www.pew

global.org/2005/07/14/islamic-extremism-common-concern-for-muslim-and-western-publics/. 2005.

———. *Muslims in Europe: economic worries top concerns about religious and cultural identity*. 13-Nation Pew Global Attitudes Survey. http://www.pewglobal.org/2006/07/06/muslims-in-europe-economic-worries-top-concerns-about-religious-and-cultural-identity/. 2006.

Phule. — *The collected works of Mahatma Jotirao Phule*, translated by P. G. Patil. Bombay, 1991–.

Pike, F. B. *The politics of the miraculous in Peru: Haya de la Torre and the spiritualist tradition*. Lincoln, 1986.

Pinch, W. R. "Soldier monks and militant sadhus." In *Contesting the nation: religion, community, and the politics of democracy in India*, edited by D. Ludden. Philadelphia, 1996.

Pinto, A. C. *The Blue Shirts: Portuguese fascists and the New State*. Boulder, 2000.

Pitts, J. "Liberalism and empire in a nineteenth-century Algerian mirror." *Modern Intellectual History* 6 (2009).

Pollock, S. *The language of the gods in the world of men: Sanskrit, culture, and power in premodern India*. Berkeley, 2006.

———. "Rāmāyaṇa and political imagination in India." *Journal of Asian Studies* 52 (1993).

Poole, S. *Our Lady of Guadalupe: the origins and sources of a Mexican national symbol, 1531–1797*. Tucson, 1995.

Portuondo Zúñiga, O. *La Virgen de la Caridad del Cobre: símbolo de cubanía*. Santiago de Cuba, 1995.

Pottenger, J. R. *Reaping the whirlwind: liberal democracy and the religious axis*. Washington, D.C., 2007.

Powell, A. A. *Muslims and missionaries in pre-Mutiny India*. Richmond, 1993.

Powers, E. *Crime and punishment in early Massachusetts, 1620–1692*. Boston, 1966.

Pozas, R. *Juan the Chamula: an ethnological re-creation of the life of a Mexican Indian*, translated by L. Kemp. Berkeley, 1962.

Prakash, G. *Another reason: science and the imagination of modern India*. Princeton, 1999.

Preston, P. *Franco: a biography*. London, 1993.

Price, M. *The perilous crown: France between revolutions, 1814–1848*. London, 2007.

Punjab. — *Report of the Court of Inquiry constituted under Punjab Act 11 of 1954 to enquire into the Punjab disturbances of 1953*. Lahore, 1954.

Purnell, J. *Popular movements and state formation in revolutionary Mexico*. Durham, 1999.

Qabbānī, Aḥmad ibn ʿAlī al-. *Naqḍ qawāʿid al-ḍalāl wa-rafḍ ʿaqāʾid al-ḍullāl*. Ms. Princeton, Yahuda 3788.

Qaraḍāwī, Yūsuf al-. *Awlawiyyāt al-ḥaraka al-Islāmiyya fī ʾl-marḥala al-qādima*. Cairo, 1991. *Priorities of the Islamic movement in the coming phase*. Cairo, 1992.

Qaraḍāwī, Yūsuf al-. *Fiqh al-jihād: dirāsa muqārana li-aḥkāmihi wa-falsafatihi fī ḍawʾ al-Qurʾān waʾl-sunna*. Cairo, 2009.

Qazwīnī, ʿAbd al-Jalīl. *Naqḍ*, edited by J. Ḥusaynī Urmawī. N.p., 1371.

Qochı Beg. *Risāle*. In Kitābkhāne-i Ebü ʾl-Ḍiyāʾ. Istanbul, 1303.

Qurṭubī. *al-Jāmiʿ li-aḥkām al-Qurʾān*. Cairo, 1967.

Quṭb, Muḥammad. *Qabasāt min al-Rasūl*. Beirut, 1973.

Quṭb, Sayyid. *al-ʿAdāla al-ijtimāʿiyya fī ʾl-Islām*. Cairo, n.d. [1949]. Translated by Shepard as *Sayyid Qutb and Islamic activism*.

———. *Dirāsāt Islāmiyya*. Damascus, 1953.

———. *Fī ẓilāl al-Qurʾān*. Beirut, 1986.

———. *Fiqh al-daʿwa: mawḍūʿāt fī ʾl-daʿwa waʾl-ḥaraka*. Beirut, 1970.

———. *Hādhā ʾl-dīn*. N.p., n.d. (translation: Qutb, *Islam—the true religion*).

———. *al-Islām wa-mushkilāt al-ḥaḍāra*. Cairo, 1962.

———. *Khaṣāʾiṣ al-taṣawwur al-Islāmī wa-muqawwimātuhu*. Part 1. Cairo, 1962 (translation: Qutb, *Basic principles*).

———. *Maʿālim fī ʾl-ṭarīq*. N.p., 1973 (translation: Qutb, *Milestones*).

———. *Maʿrakat al-Islām waʾl-raʾsimāliyya*. Cairo, 1952.

———. "Maʿrakatunā maʿa.. ʾl-Yahūd." In *Maʿrakatunā maʿa.. ʾl-Yahūd*, by Sayyid Quṭb. Jeddah, 1970. Translated by Nettler as *Past trials*.

———. *al-Mustaqbal li-hādhā ʾl-dīn*. N.p., n.d. (translation: Qutb, *Islam: the religion of the future*).

———. *Naḥw mujtamaʿ Islāmī*. Amman, 1969.

———. *al-Salām al-ʿālamī waʾl-Islām*. Cairo, 1951 (translation: Qutb, *Islam and universal peace*).

Qutb, Sayyid, *Basic principles of the Islamic worldview*, translated by R. David. North Haledon, 2006. Original: Quṭb, *Khaṣāʾiṣ*.

———. *Islam and universal peace*. Indianapolis, 1977. Original: Quṭb, *al-Salām al-ʿālamī*.

——— *Islam: the religion of the future*. Delhi, 1990. Original: Quṭb, *al-Mustaqbal li-hādhā ʾl-dīn*.

———. *Islam—the true religion*, translated by R. A. Fidai. Karachi, 1988. Original: Quṭb, *Hādhā ʾl-dīn*.

Qutb (Kutb), Sayyid. *Milestones*. New Delhi, 2005. Original: Quṭb, *Maʿālim*.

Rabīʿ, *ʿAlī-nāma*, with introductions by M. Shafīʿī Kadkanī and M. Omidsalar. Tehran, 1388 sh.

Raby, J. "Mehmed the Conqueror's Greek scriptorium." *Dumbarton Oaks Papers* 37 (1983).

Raeside, I. *The decade of Panipat (1751–61)*. Bombay, 1984.

Rafeq, A.-K. *The province of Damascus, 1723–1783*. Beirut, 1966.

———. "The Syrian *ʿulamā*, Ottoman law and Islamic *sharīʿa*." *Turcica* 26 (1994).

Rahnema, A. *An Islamic utopian: a political biography of Ali Shariʿati*. London, 1998.

Rambachan, A. *Accomplishing the accomplished: the Vedas as a source of valid knowledge in Śaṅkara*. Honolulu, 1991.

———. *The limits of scripture: Vivekananda's reinterpretation of the Vedas*. Honolulu, 1994.

Ramírez Uribe, Leonardo. *Nuestra Señora del Rosario de Chiquinquirá Patrona de Colombia*. Bogota, 1986.

Rám Náráyan. "Translation of the Ayodhyá Máhátmya, or 'Pilgrimage to Ayodhyá,'" *Journal of the Asiatic Society of Bengal* 44 (1875).

Rām Rājya Pariṣad. — *The election manifesto of the all-India Rāmarājya-Pariṣad*. Delhi, n.d.

Rangaswami Aiyangar, K. V. *Some aspects of the Hindu view of life according to Dharmaśāstra*. Baroda, 1952.

Rao, V. N. *Śiva's warriors: the Basava Purāṇa of Pālkuriki Somanātha*. Princeton, 1990.

Rashid, A. *Taliban: militant Islam, oil and fundamentalism in Central Asia*. New Haven, 2001.

Rashwan, D., ed. *The spectrum of Islamist movements*. Berlin, 2007.

Raymond, A. *Artisans et commerçants au Caire au XVIIIe siècle*. Damascus, 1973–1974.

Reardon, B. *Liberalism and tradition: aspects of Catholic thought in nineteenth-century France*. Cambridge, 1975.

Reid, J. T. "The rise and decline of the Ariel-Caliban antithesis in Spanish America." *Americas* 34 (1978).

Rein, R. "Francoist Spain and Latin America, 1936–1953." In *Fascism outside Europe: the European impulse against domestic conditions in the diffusion of global fascism*, edited by S. U. Larsen. Boulder, 2001.

Renou, L. *Le destin du Véda dans l'Inde*. Vol. 6 of *Études védiques et pāṇinéennes*, by L. Renou. Paris, 1960.

Reynolds, M. A. *Echoes of empire: Turkey's crisis of Kemalism and the search for an alternative foreign policy*. Saban Center for Middle East Policy at Brookings, Analysis Paper no. 26. Washington, D.C., 2012.

Rheault, M., and D. Mogahed, "Many Turks, Iranians, Egyptians link Sharia and justice." http://www.gallup.com/poll/109072/many-turks-iranians-egyptians-link-sharia-justice.aspx. 2008.

Ricard, R. *The spiritual conquest of Mexico: an essay on the apostolate and the evangelizing methods of the mendicant orders in New Spain: 1523–1572*, translated by L. B. Simpson. Berkeley, 1966.

Richman, P. "E. V. Ramasami's reading of the *Rāmāyaṇa*." In *Many Rāmāyaṇas: the diversity of a narrative tradition in South Asia*, edited by P. Richman. Berkeley, 1991.

Riexinger, M. *Sanāʾullāh Amritsarī (1868–1948) und die Ahl-i-Ḥadīs im Punjab unter britischer Herrschaft*. Würzburg, 2004.

Rizvi, S.A.A. *Muslim revivalist movements in northern India in the sixteenth and seventeenth centuries*. Agra, 1965.

Robinson, F. "The Congress and the Muslims." In *Islam and Muslim history in South Asia*, by F. Robinson. New Delhi, 2000.

———. "Islam and Muslim separatism." In *Islam and Muslim history in South Asia*, by F. Robinson. New Delhi, 2000.

Robinson, F. "Islam and Muslim society in South Asia." In *Islam and Muslim history in South Asia*, by F. Robinson. New Delhi, 2000.

Rodinson, M. *Mohammed*, translated by A. Carter. New York, 1971.

Rodó, José Enrique. *Ariel*, edited by G. Brotherston. Cambridge, 1967. *Ariel*, translated by M. Sayers Peden. Austin, 1988. All references are to this translation unless otherwise stated.

Romero, S. "A laboratory for revitalizing Catholicism: in Brazil, countering evangelicalism and secularism with livelier worship." *New York Times*, February 15, 2013.

Rosenthal, F., trans. *The Muqaddimah: an introduction to history*. Princeton, 1967.

Rougier, B. *Everyday jihad: the rise of militant Islam among Palestinians in Lebanon*. Cambridge, MA, 2007.

Rubin, B. R. *The fragmentation of Afghanistan: state formation and collapse in the international system*. New Haven, 2002.

Rushdoony, Rousas John. *The institutes of Biblical law*. N.p., 1973.

———. *The nature of the American system*. Fairfax, 1978.

Russell, F. H. *The just war in the Middle Ages*. Cambridge, 1975.

Śabara. — *Shabara-bhāṣya*, translated by G. Jha. Baroda, 1933–1936.

Sabeel Ecumenical Liberation Theology Center. http://www.sabeel.org.

Sabra, A. *Poverty and charity in medieval Islam: Mamluk Egypt, 1250–1517*. Cambridge, 2000.

Sadan, J. " 'Community' and 'extra-community' as a legal and literary problem." *Israel Oriental Studies* 10 (1980).

Sadeghi, B. *The logic of law making in Islam: women and prayer in the legal tradition*. Cambridge, 2013.

Saffārīnī. *Ghidhāʾ al-albāb*, edited by M. ʿA. al-Khālidī. Beirut, 1996.

Ṣaghānī. *Mawḍūʿāt*, edited by N. ʿA. Khalaf. Damascus, 1985.

Ṣāʿid al-Andalusī. *Ṭabaqāt al-umam*, edited by Ḥ. Bū ʿAlwān. Beirut, 1985.

Ṣallābī, ʿAlī Muḥammad Muḥammad al-. *al-Sīra al-nabawiyya: ʿarḍ waqāʾiʿ* wa-taḥlīl aḥdāth. Damascus, 2004.

Salomon, N. "The Salafi critique of Islamism: doctrine, difference and the problem of Islamic political action in contemporary Sudan." In *Global Salafism: Islam's new religious movement*, edited by R. Meijer. New York, 2009.

Sāmī, S. *Qāmūs-i Turkī*. Istanbul, 1317.

Śankarācārya of Kāñcī. "Answers to the questionnaire issued by the Hindu Law Committee," 2nd part. *Madras Law Journal*, June 1941.

Sarakhsī. *Mabsūṭ*. Cairo, 1324–1331.

Saray, M. *Rus işgali devrinde Osmanlı devleti ile Türkistan hanlıkları arasındaki siyasi münasebetler (1775–1875)*. Istanbul, 1984.

Sarıtoprak, Z. "Fethullah Gülen: a Sufi in his own way." In *Turkish Islam and the secular state: the Gülen movement*, edited by M. H. Yavuz and J. L. Esposito. Syracuse, 2003.

Sarkar, J. *House of Shivaji*. Calcutta, 1955.

Savarkar, V. D. *Hindutva: who is a Hindu?* Bombay, 1969.

Schacht, J. *An introduction to Islamic law*. Oxford, 1964.

———. *The origins of Muhammadan jurisprudence*. Oxford, 1950.
Schaller, J. "Sanskritization, caste uplift and social dissidence in the Sant Ravidās Panth." In *Bhakti religion in North India: community identity and political action*, edited by D. N. Lorenzen. Albany, 1995.
Schimmel, A. *Islam in the Indian subcontinent*. Leiden, 1980.
Schleifer, S. A. "Jihad: modernist apologists, modern apologetics." *Islamic Quarterly* 28 (1984).
Schmithausen, L. "Aspects of the Buddhist attitude towards war." In *Violence denied: violence, non-violence and the rationalization of violence in South Asian cultural history*, by J.E.M. Houben and K. R. van Kooij. Leiden, 1999.
Schneider, I. *Kinderverkauf und Schuldknechtschaft: Untersuchungen zur frühen Phase des islamischen Rechts*. Stuttgart, 1999.
Schneider, U. *Die Grossen Felsen-Edikte Aśokas: kritische Ausgabe, Übersetzung und Analyse der Texte*. Wiesbaden, 1978.
Seale, P. *Asad of Syria: the struggle for the Middle East*. London, 1988.
Searle-Chatterjee, M. "Caste, religion and other identities." In *Contextualising caste: post-Dumontian approaches*, edited by M. Searle-Chatterjee and U. Sharma. Oxford, 1994.
———. "Urban 'untouchables' and Hindu nationalism." *Immigrants and Minorities* 13 (1994).
Sedgwick, M. J. "In search of a counter-reformation: anti-Sufi stereotypes and the Budshishiyya's response." In *An Islamic reformation?*, edited by M. Browers and C. Kurzman. Lanham, 2004.
———. *Sufism: the essentials*. Cairo, 2000.
Sela, R. *The legendary biographies of Tamerlane: Islam and heroic apocrypha in Central Asia*. Cambridge, 2011.
———. *Ritual and authority in Central Asia: the Khan's inauguration ceremony*. Bloomington, 2003.
Sengupta, S. "Thousands are arrested in India in unrest over temple site." *New York Times*, July 7, 2005.
Sengupta, S., and L. Rohter, "Where faith grows, fired by Pentecostalism." *New York Times*, October 14, 2003.
Serrano Álvarez, P. *La batalla del espíritu: el movimiento sinarquista en el Bajío (1932–51)*. Mexico City, 1992.
Seshadri, H. V. *RSS: a vision in action*. Bangalore, 1988.
Set, Narendranath. *Third Hindu code*. Calcutta, n.d.
Shadid, A. "In one slice of Egypt, daily woes top religion." *New York Times*, February 16, 2011.
Shah, G. "The BJP's riddle in Gujarat: caste, factionalism and Hindutva." In *The BJP and the compulsions of politics in India*, edited by T. B. Hansen and C. Jaffrelot. Delhi, 1998.
Shaikh, F. "*Millat* and *mazhab*: rethinking Iqbal's political vision." In *Living together separately: cultural India in history and politics*, by M. Hasan and A. Roy. New Delhi, 2005.
Shakespeare, William. *Henry V*, edited by G. Taylor. Oxford, 1982.
Shakir, M. "An analytical view of communal violence." In *Communal riots in post-independence India*, edited by A. A. Engineer. London, 1984.

Shariati, Ali. *Hajj*, translated by A. A. Behzadnia and N. Denny. Houston, 1994.
———. *What is to be done: the enlightened thinkers and an Islamic renaissance*, edited and annotated by F. Rajaee. Houston, 1986.
Sharkey, H. J. *American evangelicals in Egypt: missionary encounters in an age of empire*. Princeton, 2008.
Sharma, A. *Modern Hindu thought: the essential texts*. New Delhi, 2002.
Sharma, J. P. *Republics in ancient India, c. 1500 B.C.–500 B.C.* Leiden, 1968.
Sharma, R. B. *Christian missions in northern India, 1813–1913*. Delhi, 1988.
Sharma, U. *Caste*. Buckingham, 1999.
"Sharṭ ṣidq al-Shīʿa fī ʾl-ḥuzn ʿalā ʾl-imām al-Ḥusayn raḍiya ʾllāhu ʿanhu." Website of Salmān al-ʿAwda, http://muntada.islamtoday.net/showthread.php?p=486268.
Shāṭibī. *Muwāfaqāt*, edited by A.M.Ḥ. Āl Salmān. Khubar, 1997.
Shaw, B. D. *Sacred violence: African Christians and sectarian hatred in the age of Augustine*. Cambridge, 2011.
Shaykhzāda, ʿAbd al-Raḥmān ibn Muḥammad. *Majmaʿ al-anhur fī sharḥ Multaqā ʾl-abḥur*. Istanbul, 1276.
Shepard, W. E. "Islam as a 'system' in the later writings of Sayyid Qutb." *Middle Eastern Studies* 25 (1989).
———. *Sayyid Qutb and Islamic activism: a translation and critical analysis of Social Justice in Islam*. Leiden, 1996. (Original: Quṭb, *al-ʿAdāla al-ijtimāʿiyya*.)
———. "Sayyid Qutb's doctrine of *jāhiliyya*." *International Journal of Middle East Studies* 35 (2003).
Shinqīṭī, Muḥammad ibn Aḥmad ibn Zārūq al-. *al-Numūdhaj al-nabawī fī ʾl-qudwa min khilāl ghazwat al-Khandaq*. Minbar al-Tawḥīd waʾl-Jihād. http://www.tawhed.ws. 2004–2005 (dated 1425).
Shoshan, B. *Popular culture in medieval Cairo*. Cambridge, 1993.
Shupe, A. "The Reconstructionist movement on the new Christian right." *Christian Century* 106 (1989).
Siberry, E. *Criticism of crusading, 1095–1274*. Oxford, 1985.
Siems, H. "Die Entwicklung von Rechtsquellen zwischen Spätantike und Mittelalter." In *Von der Spätantike zum frühen Mittelalter: Kontinuitäten und Brüche, Konzeptionen und Befunde*, edited by T. Kölzer and R. Schieffer. Ostfildern, 2009.
Sigmund, P. E. *Liberation theology at the crossroads: democracy or revolution?* New York, 1990.
Sivan, E. *Radical Islam: medieval theology and modern politics*. New Haven, 1990.
Skidmore, T. E. *Black into white: race and nationality in Brazilian thought*. Durham, 1993.
———. *Brazil: five centuries of change*. New York, 1999.
Skidmore, T. E., and P. H. Smith, *Modern Latin America*. New York, 2001.
Skinner, Q. *The foundations of modern political thought*. Cambridge, 1978.
———. *Liberty before liberalism*. Cambridge, 1998.
———. "The monarchical republic enthroned." In *The monarchical republic of early modern England: essays in response to Patrick Collinson*, edited by J. F. McDiarmid. Aldershot, 2007.

———. "The principles and practice of opposition: the case of Bolingbroke versus Walpole." In *Historical perspectives: studies in English thought and society*, edited by N. McKendrick. London, 1974.
Skovgaard-Petersen, J. *Defining Islam for the Egyptian state: muftis and fatwas of the Dār al-Iftā*. Leiden, 1997.
Smith, B. H. *Religious politics in Latin America, Pentecostal vs. Catholic*. Notre Dame, 1998.
Smith, D. E. *India as a secular state*. Princeton, 1963.
Smith, J. I. *Islam in America*. New York, 1999.
Smith, W. C. *Islam in modern history*. New York, 1959.
———. *Modern Islām in India: a social analysis*. London, 1946.
Sondhi, S. "Black holes & MM Joshi's retro chic." *Outlook*, September 3, 2001.
Sousa, L., et al., eds. and trans. *The story of Guadalupe: Luis Laso de la Vega's Huei tlamahuiçoltica of 1649*. Stanford, 1998.
Spear, P. *A history of India*. Baltimore, 1965.
Spencer, T. "Turks and Trojans in the Renaissance." *Modern Language Review* 47 (1952).
Sreenivasan, K. *Sree Narayana Guru: saint philosopher humanist*. Trivandrum, 1989.
Sreenivasan, R. "Drudges, dancing girls, concubines: female slaves in Rajput polity, 1500–1850." In *Slavery and South Asian history*, edited by I. Chatterjee and R. M. Eaton. Bloomington, 2006.
"Sri Lanka marks 2nd tsunami anniversary." http://english.peopledaily.com.cn/200612/27/eng20061227_336047.html. *People's Daily Online*, December 27, 2006.
Srinivas, M. N. "The cohesive role of Sanskritization." In *Collected essays*, by M. N. Srinivas. New Delhi, 2002.
———. "A note on Sanskritization and Westernization." In *Collected essays*, by M. N. Srinivas. New Delhi, 2002.
Stabb, M. S. *In quest of identity: patterns in the Spanish American essay of ideas, 1890–1960*. Chapel Hill, 1967.
Stansfield, G. "Governing Kurdistan: the strengths of division." In *The future of Kurdistan in Iraq*, edited by B. O'Leary et al. Philadelphia, 2005.
Stark, L. R. "The Quechua language in Bolivia." In *South American Indian languages: retrospect and prospect*, edited by H. E. Manelis Klein and L. R. Stark. Austin, 1985.
Stearns, J. K. *Infectious ideas: contagion in premodern Islamic and Christian thought in the western Mediterranean*. Baltimore, 2011.
———. "The legal status of science in the Muslim world in the early modern period: an initial consideration of *fatwās* from three Maghribī sources." In *The Islamic scholarly tradition*, edited by A. Q. Ahmed et al. Leiden, 2011.
Steinberg, G. "Jihadi-Salafism and the Shi'is: remarks about the intellectual roots of anti-Shi'ism." In *Global Salafism: Islam's new religious movement*, edited by R. Meijer. New York, 2009.
Stenberg, L. *The Islamization of science: four Muslim positions developing an Islamic modernity*. Lund, 1996.

Stern, S. M. "The constitution of the Islamic city." In *The Islamic city*, edited by A. H. Hourani and S. M. Stern. Oxford, 1970.

Stevenson, M. *The rites of the Twice-born*. London, 1920.

Stietencron, H. von. "Hinduism: on the proper use of a deceptive term." In *Hinduism reconsidered*, edited by G.-D. Sontheimer and H. Kulke. New Delhi, 1997.

Strayer, J. R., ed. *Dictionary of the Middle Ages*. New York, 1982–1989.

Stroumsa, S. *Freethinkers of medieval Islam: Ibn al-Rāwandī, Abū Bakr al-Rāzī, and their impact on Islamic thought*. Leiden, 1999.

Subramanian Swamy, "How to wipe out Islamic terror." http://bharatabharati.wordpress.com/2011/10/04/how-to-wipe-out-islamic-terror-subramanian-swamy/, posted October 4, 2011.

Sümer, F. *Kara Koyunlular*. Vol. 1. Ankara, 1967.

Suyūṭī. *Taʾrīkh al-khulafāʾ*. Beirut, 1988.

Sznajder, M. "Was there fascism in Chile? The Movimiento Nacional Socialista in the 1930's." In *Fascism outside Europe: the European impulse against domestic conditions in the diffusion of global fascism*, edited by S. U. Larsen. Boulder, 2001.

Ṭabarānī. *al-Muʿjam al-awsaṭ*. Cairo, 1995.

———. *Musnad al-Shāmiyyīn*, edited by Ḥ. ʿA. al-Salafī. Beirut, 1989–1996.

Ṭabarī. *Tafsīr*. Beirut, 1992.

———. *Taʾrīkh al-rusul waʾl-mulūk*, edited by M. J. de Goeje et al. Leiden, 1879–1901. Translation: *The History of al-Ṭabarī*. Vol. 8: *The victory of Islam*, translated by M. Fishbein. Albany, 1997. Vol. 12: *The battle of al-Qādisiyyah and the conquest of Syria and Palestine*, translated by Y. Friedmann. Albany, 1992.

Ṭabbākh, Muḥammad Rāghib al-. *Iʿlām al-nubalāʾ bi-taʾrīkh Ḥalab al-shahbāʾ*. Aleppo, 1923–1926.

Ṭabrisī. *Majmaʿ al-bayān*. Qumm, 1403.

Taira, M. "La légitimation de la violence dans le bouddhisme au Moyen Âge." In *Légitimités, légitimations: la construction de l'autorité au Japon*, edited by A. Bouchy et al. Paris, 2005.

Taji-Farouki, S. *A fundamental quest: Hizb al-Tahrir and the search for the Islamic Caliphate*. London, 1996.

Talbot, I. *Pakistan: a modern history*. London, 1998.

Taʿqīb ʿalā "Tafjīrāt ʿAmmān." http://www.tawhed.ws. 2005 (dated 7 Shawwāl 1426).

Tarama sözlüğü. Ankara, 1963–1974.

Tatāʾī. *Tanwīr al-maqāla fī ḥall alfāẓ al-Risāla*, edited by M.ʿA.ʿA. Shabīr. N.p., 1988–.

Taylor, C. *A secular age*. Cambridge, MA, 2007.

Tekin, T. *A grammar of Orkhon Turkic*. Bloomington, 1968.

Tezcan, B. *The second Ottoman Empire: political and social transformation in the early modern world*. Cambridge, 2010.

Thackston, W. M., trans. *The Baburnama: memoirs of Babur, prince and emperor*. New York, 1996.

Thapar, R. *Aśoka and the decline of the Mauryas*. Oxford, 1961.

——. "The image of the barbarian in early India." In *Cultural pasts: essays in early Indian history*, by R. Thapar. New Delhi, 2000.

Therwath, I. " 'Far and wide': the Sangh Parivar's global network." In *The Sangh Parivar: a reader*, edited by C. Jaffrelot. New Delhi, 2005.

Thompson, G. "On Mexico's mean streets, the sinners have a saint." *New York Times*, March 26, 2004.

Tibesar, A. *Franciscan beginnings in colonial Peru*, Washington, D.C., 1953.

Tietze, A. *Muṣṭafā ʿĀlī's Counsel for Sultans of 1581*. Vienna, 1979–1982.

———. *Muṣṭafā ʿĀlī's description of Cairo of 1599*. Vienna, 1975.

Tirmidhī. *al-Jāmiʿ al-ṣaḥīḥ*, edited by A. M. Shākir and others. Cairo, n.d.

Todaro Williams, M. "Integralism and the Brazilian Catholic Church." *Hispanic American Historical Review* 54 (1974).

Toledano, E. R. *The Ottoman slave trade and its suppression: 1840-1890*. Princeton, 1982.

———. *Slavery and abolition in the Ottoman Middle East*. Seattle, 1998.

Tor, D. G. *Violent order: religious warfare, chivalry, and the ʿAyyār phenomenon in the medieval Islamic world*. Würzburg, 2007.

Torre Villar, E. de la. *En torno al Guadalupanismo*. Mexico City, 1985.

Traboulsi, S. "An early refutation of Muḥammad ibn ʿAbd al-Wahhāb's reformist views." *Die Welt des Islams* 42 (2002).

Trindade, H. "Fascism and authoritarianism in Brazil under Vargas (1930–1945)." In *Fascism outside Europe: the European impulse against domestic conditions in the diffusion of global fascism*, edited by S. U. Larsen. Boulder, 2001.

Tripp, C. *Islam and the moral economy: the challenge of capitalism*. Cambridge, 2006.

Trivedy, S. "Breaking the status quo." In *Freeing the spirit: the iconic women of modern India*, edited by M. Singh. New Delhi, 2006.

Troll, C. W. *Sayyid Ahmad Khan: a reinterpretation of Muslim theology*. New Delhi, 1978.

Tsang, C. R. *War and faith: ikkō ikki in late Muromachi Japan*. Cambridge, MA, 2007.

Tsunoda, R., et al. *Sources of the Japanese tradition*. New York, 1958.

Turner, R. L. *A comparative dictionary of the Indo-Aryan languages*. London, 1966.

Tu Wei-ming. "The search for roots in industrial East Asia: the case of the Confucian revival." In *Fundamentalisms observed*, edited by M. E. Marty and R. S. Appleby. The Fundamentalism Project, vol. 1. Chicago, 1991.

Ullmann, M. *Islamic medicine*. Edinburgh, 1978.

Ullmann, W. *The Carolingian Renaissance and the idea of kingship*. London, 1969.

Vālmīki. *The Rāmāyaṇa of Vālmīki: an epic of ancient India*. Vol. 1: *Bālakāṇḍa*, translated by R. P. Goldman. Princeton, 1984.

Varshney, A. *Ethnic conflict and civic life: Hindus and Muslims in India*. New Haven, 2002.

Vaudeville, C. *A weaver named Kabir: selected verses with a detailed biographical and historical introduction*. Delhi, 1993.

Veer, P. van der. "Hindu nationalism and the discourse of modernity: the Vishva Hindu Parishad." In *Accounting for fundamentalisms*, edited by M. E. Marty and R. S. Appleby. The Fundamentalism Project, vol. 4. Chicago, 1994.

———. *Religious nationalism: Hindus and Muslims in India*. Berkeley, 1994.

Veinstein, G. "Les règlements fiscaux ottomans de Crète." In *The eastern Mediterranean under Ottoman rule: Crete, 1645–1840*, edited by A. Anastasopoulos. Rethymno, 2008.

Venkataramanayya, N., and M. Somasekhara Sarma. "Vilasa grant of Prolaya-Nayaka." In *Epigraphia Indica* 32 (1957–1958). Delhi, 1962.

Verlinden, C. *L'Esclavage dans l'Europe médiévale*, vol. 1. Bruges, 1955.

Verpoorten, J.-M. *Mīmāṃsā literature*. In *A history of Indian literarature*, edited by J. Gonda, vol. 6. Wiesbaden, 1987.

Vickers, M., and J. Pettifer. *Albania: from anarchy to a Balkan identity*. London, 1997.

Vidal Castro, F. "Sobre la compraventa de hombres libres en los dominios de Ibn Ḥafṣūn." In *Homenaje al Prof. Jacinto Bosch Vilá*. Granada, 1991.

Viscuso, P. "Christian participation in warfare: a Byzantine view." In *Peace and war in Byzantium: essays in honor of George T. Dennis, S.J.*, edited by T. S. Miller and J. Nesbitt. Washington, D.C., 1995.

Vivekānanda. — *The complete works of the Swami Vivekananda*, vol. 3. Mayavati, 1922.

Vyas, N., and A. Joshua. "Congress, BJP express concern over Nepal." http://www.thehindu.com/2009/05/05/stories/2009050559681000.htm. *Hindu*, May 5, 2009.

Wagemakers, J. "The enduring legacy of the second Saudi state: quietist and radical Wahhābī contestations of *al-walāʾ wa-l-barāʾ*." *International Journal of Middle East Studies* 44 (2012).

———. *A quietist jihadi: the ideology and influence of Abu Muhammad al-Maqdisi*. Cambridge, 2012.

———. "The transformation of a radical concept: *al-walaʾ wa-l-baraʾ* in the ideology of Abu Muhammad al-Maqdisi." In *Global Salafism: Islam's new religious movement*, edited by R. Meijer. New York, 2009.

Wagle, N. K. "Hindu-Muslim interactions in medieval Maharashtra." In *Hinduism reconsidered*, edited by G.-D. Sontheimer and H. Kulke. New Delhi, 1997.

Wagle, N., and A. R. Kulkarni, eds. and trans. *Vallabha's Paraśarāma Caritra: an eighteenth century Marāṭhā history of the Peśwās*. Bombay, 1976.

Wagoner, P. B. " 'Sultan among Hindu Kings': dress, titles, and the Islamicization of Hindu culture at Vijayanagara." *Journal of Asian Studies* 55 (1996).

Walī Allāh Dihlawī. *Ḥujjat Allāh al-bāligha*, edited by al-Sayyid Sābiq. Cairo, n.d.

———. *al-Tafhīmāt al-ilāhiyya*, edited by G. M. al-Qāsimī. Ḥaydarābād (Sindh), 1967–1970.

Walsh, D., and D. G. McNeil. "Gunmen in Pakistan kill 5 women who were giving children polio vaccines." *New York Times*, December 19, 2012.
Walzer, M. *In God's shadow: politics in the Hebrew Bible*. New Haven, 2012.
———. *The revolution of the saints: a study in the origins of radical politics*. Cambridge, MA, 1965.
Wang, Tangjia. "Towards a proper relation between men and women: beyond masculinism and feminism." In *The renaissance of Confucianism in contemporary China*, edited by Ruiping Fan. Dordrecht, 2011.
Wāqidī. *Maghāzī*, edited by M. Jones. London, 1966.
Warburg, G. *Islam, nationalism and Communism in a traditional society: the case of Sudan*. London, 1978.
Weismann, I. "Democratic fundamentalism? The practice and discourse of the Muslim Brothers movement in Syria." *Muslim World* 100 (2010).
Wendell, C., trans. *Five tracts of Ḥasan Al-Bannāʾ (1906–1949)*. Berkeley, 1978. Original: Bannā, *Majmūʿat rasāʾil*.
Wensinck, A. J. *A handbook of early Muhammadan tradition*. Leiden, 1927.
Wickham, C. R. *Mobilizing Islam: religion, activism, and political change in Egypt*. New York, 2002.
Wielawski, I. M. "Doctors heed call for books." *New York Times*, August 31, 2010.
Wikipedia. "Indian general election, 2009." http://en.wikipedia.org/wiki/Indian_general_election,_2009.
Wilbur, C. M. *Slavery in China during the former Han dynasty, 206 B.C.–A.D. 25*. New York, 1967.
Wilcox, C. *Onward Christian soldiers? The religious right in American politics*. Boulder, 2000.
Wilkinson, S. I. *Votes and violence: electoral competition and ethnic riots in India*. Cambridge, 2004.
Williams, D., and E. Guttschuss. *Spiraling violence: Boko Haram attacks and security force abuses in Nigeria*. Human Rights Watch. N.p., 2012.
Williams, R. B. *A new face of Hinduism: the Swaminarayan religion*. Cambridge, 1984.
Winter, M. *Egyptian society under Ottoman rule, 1517–1798*. London, 1992.
———. "A polemical treatise by ʿAbd al-Ġanī al-Nābulusī against a Turkish scholar on the religious status of the *ḏimmīs*." *Arabica*. 35 (1988).
Witte, J., and F. S. Alexander, eds. *The teachings of modern Roman Catholicism on law, politics, and human nature*. New York, 2007.
Witzel, M. "The coronation rituals of Nepal with special reference to the coronation of King Birendra (1975)." In *Heritage of the Kathmandu Valley*, edited by N. Gutschow and A. Michaels. Sankt Augustin, 1987.
Wolpert, S. A. *Tilak and Gokhale: revolution and reform in the making of modern India*. Berkeley, 1962.
Womack, J. *Rebellion in Chiapas: an historical reader*. New York, 1999.
Wood, G. S. "Monarchism and republicanism in early America." In *The idea of America: reflections on the birth of the United States*, by G. S. Wood. New York, 2011.

Woodhead, L. "Introduction." In *Religion and change in modern Britain*, edited by L. Woodhead and R. Catto. London, 2012.
Woods, J. E. *The Aqquyunlu: clan, confederation, empire*. Salt Lake City, 1999.
Wormald, P. *Legal culture in the early medieval West*. London, 1999.
———. "The *Leges Barbarorum*: law and ethnicity in the post-Roman West." In *Regna and gentes: the relationship between late antique and early medieval peoples and kingdoms in the transformation of the Roman world*, edited by H.-W. Goetz et al. Leiden, 2003.
———. *The making of English law: King Alfred to the twelfth century*. Vol. 1: *Legislation and its limits*. Oxford, 1999.
Wright, J. *The trans-Saharan slave trade*. London, 2007.
Wright, L. *The looming tower: al-Qaeda and the road to 9/11*. New York, 2006.
Wright, M. C. *The last stand of Chinese conservatism: the T'ung-Chih restoration, 1862–74*. Stanford, 1957.

Yadav, K. C., ed. *Autobiography of Swami Dayanand Saraswati*. New Delhi, 1976.
Yang, F. *Religion in China: survival and revival under Communist rule*. Oxford, 2012.
Yang, H.-S., et al. *The Hye Ch'o diary: memoir of the pilgrimage to the five regions of India*. Berkeley, n.d.
Yāqūt. *Muʿjam al-buldān*. Beirut, 1957.
Young, R. F. *Resistant Hinduism: Sanskrit sources on anti-Christian apologetics in early nineteenth-century India*. Vienna, 1981.
Yūsī. *al-Qānūn fī aḥkām al-ʿilm wa-aḥkām al-ʿālim wa-aḥkām al-mutaʿallim*, edited by Ḥ. Ḥimmānī. Rabat, 1998.

Zaehner, R. C. *Hinduism*. London, 1962.
Zamakhsharī. *Kashshāf*, edited by ʿA. A. ʿAbd al-Mawjūd et al. Riyadh, 1998.
Zaman, M. Q. *Ashraf 'Ali Thanawi: Islam in modern South Asia*. Oxford, 2008.
———. *Modern Islamic thought in a radical age: religious authority and internal criticism*. Cambridge, 2012.
———. "Sectarianism in Pakistan: the radicalization of Shiʿi and Sunni identities." *Modern Asian Studies* 32 (1998).
———. "South Asian Islam and the idea of the caliphate." In *Demystifying the caliphate: historical memory and contemporary contexts*, edited by M. Al-Rasheed et al. London, 2013.
———. *The ulama in contemporary Islam: custodians of change*. Princeton, 2002.
Zarqāwī, Abū Muṣʿab al-. *Hal atāka ḥadīth al-Rāfiḍa?!*, Minbar al-Tawḥīd waʾl-Jihād. http://www.tawhed.ws. 2006 (dated Jumādā al-Ūlā 1427).
Ẓawāhirī, Ayman al-. Letter to Abū Muṣʿab al-Zarqāwī. http://www.ctc.usma.edu/posts/zawahiris-letter-to-zaraqawi-original. July 9, 2005. Translated in Mansfield, *His own words*.
Zayd ibn ʿAlī. *Ṣafwa*, edited by N. Ḥasan. Baghdad, 1967.
Zayyānī, Abū ʾl-Qāsim al-. *al-Turjumāna al-kubrā fī akhbār al-maʿmūr barran wa-baḥrā*, edited by ʿA. al-Filālī. Rabat, 1991.

Zeghal, M. *Islamism in Morocco: religion, authoritarianism, and electoral politics*. Princeton, 2008.
Zilfi, M. C. *Women and slavery in the late Ottoman Empire: the design of difference*. Cambridge, 2010.
Zvelebil, K. V. *Tamil literature*. Leiden, 1975.
Zysk, K. G. *Medicine in the Veda: religious healing in the Veda*. Delhi, 1996.

Index